VALENCE AND VISION:
A Reader in
Psychology

VALENCE AND VISION: A Reader in Psychology

Edited by Rich Jones and Richard L. Roe

Rinehart Press / Holt, Rinehart and Winston

San Francisco

Library of Congress Cataloging in Publication Data

Jones, Richard T   1948–   comp.
    Valence & vision; a reader in psychology.

    Includes bibliographies.
    1. Psychology—Addresses, essays, lectures.
I. Roe, Richard L., joint comp. II. Title.
[DNLM: 1. Psychology. BF121 V152 1974]
BF149.J6   150   73-19683
ISBN 0-03-008416-4

Design: Louis Neiheisel
Photography: Stephen Harrison
Cover sculpture: William Hartwick

The works by M. C. Escher are reproduced by permission of the
Escher Foundation—Haags Gemeentemuseum, The Hague.

© 1974 by Rinehart Press
5643 Paradise Drive
Corte Madera, Calif. 94925

A division of Holt, Rinehart and Winston, Inc.

PRINTED IN THE UNITED STATES OF AMERICA

4 5 6 7   090   9 8 7 6 5 4 3 2 1

To Richard and Margaret Jones
and Bob and Helen Andreis

Contents

Contents

Contents

Preface

The theme of this anthology is simple: that the study of psychology is fascinating. The intent is also uncomplicated: to engage the interest and stimulate the curiosity of students who are beginning the study of psychology.

To accomplish this, we have approached the growing edges of psychology in a fresh, creative—and, if you will—visionary manner. We have assembled the scientific "fact" and the "fiction" of psychology in a balance that deals with the revolutionary aspects of psychology that are rooted in the contemporary trajectory of technology. As Alvin Toffler has noted in *Future Shock,* "Science fiction has immense value as a mind-stretching force for . . . an imaginative exploration of the jungle of political, social, psychological and ethical issues" that confront us today. That confrontation gains even more urgency by the fact that, as Arthur C. Clarke has suggested, scientific *fact* is increasingly more incredible than the visions of science fiction.

This anthology has thus been designed to note the revolutionary valence of contemporary psychology and to indicate the imaginative vision with which that valence must be approached.

Acknowledgments

I have had several reservations about this thing with acknowledgments. To begin with, sometimes it seems a bit pretentious to have any acknowledgments at all for a book of readings. This is related to my feeling that most of the people I would like to acknowledge have had nothing to do with the actual construction of this book. Yet at the same time, these people have had a great deal to do with my own intellectual and personal growth, and I think that is what it all boils down to. Without the influence of the following people, my own valence and vision would not have developed to the point where this book could have been envisioned and actualized.

I have appreciated George and Claudia Corning, Dema Staley, Scott and Molly Glover, Dana Dunn, Tony Dolz, George Guardiola, Pam Fritz, Dimitri Zerdavis, Jean Shinn, Roger Hastings, Larry Gray, Curt Groninga, Manny Lask, Gail Hershberger, Tom Belle, Vicki and Walt Allen, Mike Chamberlain, and Fred Swegles.

As an undergraduate I was extremely fortunate to have been incited to think by Diane Franklin, Don Lewis, Sandy Wilcox, Alan Bomser, Steve Riskin, and Logan Fox. Without the vision of Diane Henschel, I would have never been encouraged to attempt this anthology.

I owe special thanks to Steph and Tom Benner, Alex Jones, Carol Leatherwood, Steve Jama, Angela Lask, Kahler Hench, and Jane Scott.

A final note of appreciation to Emmett Dingley, editor at Rinehart Press, and Dick Roe, for encouragement and enthusiasm.

Rich Jones

I.
Valence and Vision: Introductory Notes

1. "Psychology in the Year 2000" by Gardner Murphy

1.
Psychology in the Year 2000
GARDNER MURPHY

By way of introduction, Gardner Murphy outlines the valence and vision contained within the trajectory of contemporary psychology.

Our profound ambivalence about human futures, and our hopes and fears regarding the possibility of intelligent planning for the future, appear in a charming phrase of Sir George Thomson. Regarding the role of science in planning for new potentialities within the human germ cell, he says that the likelihood of genetic improvements is about like the probability of improving a statue by spraying it with machine gun bullets. Instantly, however, he catches himself up in the remark that with the electron microscope, the localization of individual genes is already very close. One dares not be overbold for fear the critics will laugh, while actually the science fiction, and the casual predictions of scientists for the last hundred years or so, have been much too modest—in fact, much too myopic—as to what actually can be achieved. The best guide here is a systematic and reasonable extrapolation from identifiable trends and, at the same time, a cautious but systematic utilization of the principle of emergence in which new realities constantly come into being, not through the extrapolation of separate curves, but through specific interaction processes. Many of these new emergents are known in metallurgy, in embryology, and in the field of psychology. Some of them have to do with new perceptual and conceptual wholes as shown in countless studies of music and of painting; some of them have to do with dyadic or group

From Gardner Murphy, "Psychology in the Year 2000," *American Psychologist,* May 1969, pp. 523–530. Copyright 1969 by the American Psychological Association, and reproduced by permission.

1. Psychology in the Year 2000

patterns that come into existence when new relationships are achieved, for the first time, as shown in the dynamic leadership patterns of Lewin, White, and Lippitt. An ultracautious note may indeed *sound* like science, but only like the plodding science of Sir Francis Bacon's *Novum Organum,* not the creative science that indeed has remade the world, and is remaking the world through the extravagant inventiveness of a Planck and an Einstein. In this spirit, I shall attempt some predictions that, I believe, are just as likely to prove shallow and banal as to prove ultimately extravagant and exotic.

The 10 topics which I shall attempt to survey are extrapolations based upon (a) the current extraordinary development of *psychophysiology;* (b) together with such psychophysiology, the new possibilities of *internal scanning,* in the discovery of the inner human world; the renewed capacity to *observe, with full objectivity, a great deal that has long been regarded as hopelessly subjective;* (c) herewith, the direct *confrontation of the unconscious world* that merges into, and is isomorphic with, the world of physiology; (d) following these discoveries, the development of *voluntary control over the inner world,* such as scientists previously never dared to dream; (e) a new definition of a wide variety of nameless states, *psychological states for which there are no good names,* including feeling states, cognitive states, and volitional states, upon which human destiny almost literally may depend, with resulting understanding of those profound alterations in states of consciousness, well known to the East, regarding which Western man usually has expressed doubt or scorn; (f) together with these, the objective exploration of the vast sphere of *parapsychology,* at the edges of which science is nibbling, but so far has failed massively to invade; (g) a fresh *reconsideration of the relations of psychology to the biological sciences,* especially genetics; (h) a renewed *consideration of psychology in relation to the social sciences,* notably in the new science of social ecology, entailing cross-cultural collaboration of cross-cultural realities; (i) a note on the way in which changes in research *methods* alter all these basic concepts; (j) finally, a consideration, in all these terms, of the nature of the *human predicament* to which expanding science, which I am describing, may make a serious and indeed a crucial contribution.

Psychophysiology

First, then, as to psychophysiology. Partly as a result of new concepts of the wholeness, the integrity, of the living system, as voiced for example by Sir Charles Sherrington in the *Integrative Action of the Nervous System,* and partly as a result of the sheer power of the research tools that have been developed, psychophysiology has become a dramatically new science in recent decades. Problems of specialization and subspecialization of tissues, as within the mammalian cerebral cortex, have assumed astonishing forms with Penfield's discovery of specific memory localization, with various techniques for studying the electronic functional realities inside the indi-

3

vidual nerve cell, with X-ray studies of lattices, and with fine localization of sensory and motor function through implanted electrodes. Both the cruder spot localizations, earlier used in the study of the aphasias, and also the extreme equipotentiality concepts, based largely on extirpation studies, have yielded to a dialectical reconsideration of both local and general aspects of functioning, and with an extraordinary directness of application to the world of immediate experience. Donald Hebb's brilliant breakthrough in the study of sensory deprivation has helped scientists to think of the amazing possibilities of sensory enrichment. One can no longer speak of sensory deprivation or sensory enrichment without thinking, in the manner of David Krech, about the biochemistry and physiology of the mammalian cortex, as profoundly affected by very early postnatal experience. One begins to see, quite literally, the likelihood, in the next few decades, of a thoroughgoing isomorphism of physiological process and psychological process right across the board. Biochemical and neurophysiological progress has been so astonishing in the last few years that psychologists may look quite confidently for a rapidly advancing series of discoveries related specifically to the different kinds of human experience, essentially the sensory, the imaginal, the conceptual, the affective, and indeed certain types of experience that have never been analyzed finely enough to name. Psychopharmacology, long considered to be limited to the specific effects of toxins, is rapidly taking on the form of a powerful organist having at his command banks upon banks of keys, and hundreds of stops, calling into existence an incredible gamut of new experiences.

Internal Scanning

Following from, or upon, this concurrent study of psychophysiology and biochemistry on the one hand, and the phenomenal world of immediate experience and function on the other hand, psychologists will be drawn, as in a vortex, into the rich field of the study of internal scanning. By this I mean, first, the process by which delicate messages from the striped musculature can be identified more accurately as our subjects carry out reflex or skilled movements. Like a tea taster or a wine sampler, the subject, in several laboratories today, recognizes quickly the kinesthetic messages in different magnitude from different muscles. Specific muscular activities are experienced kinesthetically at the same time he sees on the panel the electronic evidence of what is occurring in specific muscle groups, so that he learns to identify and name them. He is learning, in the same way, to recognize on the panel many other messages that come from organs that are under autonomic control. One may think of the studies by the U.S.S.R. scientists, Bykov and Lisina, relating to proprioceptive and interoceptive conditioning.

But the work will soon move further along. Giving the subject feedback on a panel that shows him what specific internal activities are going on, he can be taught to make more and more refined differentiation within the inner world. His searching, his sweeping, his scanning, and his identifying of the different components from the proprioceptive world, as identical or isomorphic with the same messages from the exteroceptive world on the panel or conveyed to him through tones, give him more and more information as to the rich system of internal messages that have previously been nearly a blur, so precise that he can begin to play the instrument himself. The ancient prejudice that exteroceptive information has a kind of place in the reality world, which is lacking for the other sensory functions, has begun to collapse. A rich variety of internal messages has exactly the same possibility of cross-checking, consensual validation, as has held for sight, hearing, and touch. It is hard to set any limits. Something is known about discriminability when working with teas and wines, or even two-point thresholds on the finger tip, but these studies have never been pushed to their true physiological limits. Nor is it known how they are affected by a variety of parameters, anatomical distribution of receptors and afferent fibers, which in the past have never been sufficiently important to investigate; but today they are being seen in terms of individuality—an individuality based upon heredity, growth, and the learning process. A whole internal world is awaiting discovery.

Confrontation of the Unconscious World

Third, this internal world, as Gregory Razran has pointed out, would include the entire world of the "observable unconscious," the world of psychologically meaningful, but hitherto not directly observable, processes discovered by Freud and his followers. More and more it appears to be the same world as that which anthropologists, playwrights, poets, and prophets have often enjoined without knowing, in any scientific sense, what they were doing.

But it is one thing to observe the separate components, of course, and another thing to study creatively how they can be put together into new and emergent wholes. Both Arnheim, in *Art and Visual Perception,* and Freud, in *The Interpretation of Dreams,* have applied some of the first informative steps regarding the synthesis, the creative reorganization, of a world that offers vast possibilities. Literally there are hundreds of experiences waiting patiently to be discovered through experimentation. It will not be just the clinicians and the "encounter" groups that will discover them; such discoveries will soon yield rich new harvests to general experimental psychology. I might remind you that while Chaucer, 600 years ago, had only a few words for colors, there are today some thousands of color terms, mostly representing *new* colors that have evolved in the last century as a result of industrial chemistry—colors that do not appear in any rainbow, natural sunset, or natural color scheme. There are not only the stock experiences that human beings have by virtue of their anatomical equipment and their physiological capacity as human beings, but thousands of newly created colors. There also are many new kinds of inner experiences,

5

ranging from the effects of new foods, drugs, smogs, exercise, fatigue, strain, anxiety, and ecstasy—scores upon scores of new kinds and shades of inner experience. Of course, many of the new methods may involve risks, and many of them will come under some sort of social control. Whether it will be control by a wise and humane Federal agency, or by public opinion, no present reliable clues are extant.

Inner responses include those called affective and impulsive states, and the vast range of expressions of mood and temperament used in the aesthetic world and in the personal world generally. There are new worlds just waiting; and they will not have to wait very long. Experimental methods for the study of differentiation are developing; for example, experiments in the Soviet Union proved that two-point thresholds within the body, say from the gastric mucosa, can be measured. It is believable that as such differentiations are carried out by classical psychophysical methods, experimenters may first identify a very large range of internal messages and, second, may learn how to integrate them in thousands of new ways.

Voluntary Control

Fourth, insofar as these new messages can be differentiated, tagged, and named, they apparently can be brought under voluntary control. A wide array of new possibilities exists, for example, in Hefferline's study of rapid acquisition of operant control over slight movements that are effective in cutting out a disagreeable hum spoiling music at the time. That is, individuals who could differentiate at all, could also learn, even though unwittingly, to bring in or shut out particular messages. Other laboratories are now continuing what Hefferline started. It appears to be a very refined, delicate, and far-below-threshold type of activity that can bring in an astonishing range of experimentally prepared visual and auditory material. Soviet work on voluntary control of cardiovascular processes appears to concur with what Robert Malmo has reported in Montreal. There are studies of bladder and of capillary control, using panel feedback techniques, strongly suggesting that the autonomically controlled organs are capable of being brought rapidly into the same sphere of voluntary control as that which obtains for the striped muscle responses. Within the next decade or two certainly a very significant control of cardiovascular and gastrointestinal responses may be anticipated, not only with immediate clinical values in bringing in or shutting out various classes of bodily information, but with the deeper scientific value of giving a much wider view of what the human potentialities for such inner experience and such inner control may be. Wenger and Bagchi studied adepts in yoga in various ashrams in India, while Anand and his collaborators pushed their studies further. The keen interest of Indian investigators in putting to experimental tests the classical yoga sutras of Patanjali means not only cross-national research collaboration but, what is more important, the serious awakening of Western psychologists to the fact that experiences treasured and cultivated on the other side of the globe may be as worthy of investigation as those encountered in Detroit, Cambridge, or Topeka.

Last, but by no means least, the process of directly observing one's own electroencephalogram, notably one's own alpha, was developed by Joe Kamiya at Langley Porter and independently by Barbara Brown at the Sepulveda Veterans Administration Hospital. With Kamiya, a 400-cycle tone is activated by the individual's own alpha rhythm, so the subject given the task of increasing the amount of alpha he is exhibiting can rapidly learn, through the feedback that this tone gives him, to bring this under control. Soon he is turning on or turning off his own alpha. Apparently alpha is not the only rhythm that he can control. There are staggering possibilities for the understanding of the nature of central nervous system control by the organized central nervous system itself in the form that is called voluntary, and likewise a vast area of further implications for the understanding of the isomorphic relation between a variety of subjective states that accompany the alpha and the exteroceptive patterns that are seen when observing the visual tracing or hearing an appropriate tone. While the clinical applications are important, it is this larger vision of learning to control the brain rhythms themselves that is likely to mean most to the scientist oriented to the year 2000.

Nameless States

Fifth, while neither Kamiya nor anyone else, so far as I know, has published the implications that these new methods have for the study of whole new areas of experience only dimly describable today, it is highly probable that before the year 2000 there will be both identification of many kinds of phenomenological states that are anchored upon particular types of EEGs, and the invention of appropriate *names*, appropriate language to describe the newly identified and newly integrated components. I am thinking particularly of cognitive states, conceptualizing states, creative states that may, while retaining all their charm and all their majesty, become far more describable, controllable, and achievable.

Parapsychology

Sixth, it is characteristic of science at any given period to cultivate the belief that it has a rather well-integrated system into which new observations can fit. While it is at many points open-ended, with really fuzzy edges, there would be chaos indeed if scientists relinquished their passion for a unified field of science. Suppose science was an archipelago of little, spotty, factual details, with no possibility of an implied closed system, an ocean bed unifying all the little islands that appear at the surface level. There is very good psychological reason why science, as it grows, takes on the conservative, the resistive character that is apparent. Under these conditions it is hardly surprising that there is some restlessness, or even resistance, when talking about the discovery of kinds of experience about which nothing has been known. Of course, there are many good reasons, in polite society, why people do not know too much about their insides. These have to do with delicate and complex systems of human expression, some related very broadly to love, some related very broadly to destructiveness, but a great many others that almost every human individual encounters, but does not really want at this time to communicate on a massive basis. I do not anticipate very much actual interference with science on this count, but I do think one must be honest in admitting that this quest of the inside will entail not only triumphs but occasional acrimonious encounters.

While saying this I must add that the resistance toward types of human communication, which presently are not understood, has shown the same attributes. One can understand very clearly the natural fear of scientists that their whole tough labor would be disturbed if they should admit perceptual, memoric, affective, or volitional processes that now are not explainable in terms of the basic biochemical and biophysical realities of human conduct. Even the thought elements that the Würzburg School brought into Wundt's psychological system led to much hostility. Today more serious difficulties are being dealt with as the study of *parapsychology* moves into more systematic experimental form. Most of the data, when closely observed, are like the perceptual and affective data already known, but appear to occur under conditions in which the time and space parameters are unfamiliar. For example, in several recent studies, the telepathic phenomena occur when sender and receiver are separated by very long distances; and while the data can be described psychologically without any mystery, a physical difficulty is encountered because how to conceptualize energies that could carry over these long distances is not known. In other words, the difficulty is at the level of physics, not at the level of psychology. Psychologists may be a little bewildered when they encounter modern physicists who take these phenomena in stride; in fact, take them very much more seriously than psychologists do, saying, as physicists, that they are no longer bound by the types of Newtonian energy distribution, inverse square laws, etc., with which scientists used to regard themselves as tightly bound. In the same way, new physical conceptions regarding the nature of time seem to remove a large part of the trouble that appears in precognition experiments, in which a randomly determined target order of stimulus materials can be foreseen by certain subjects. I think that with the computer methods that are now coming into use, and with the progressive rigidity in experimental controls, psychologists probably will witness a period of slow, but definite, erosion of the blandly exclusive attitude that has offered itself as the only appropriate scientific attitude in this field. The data from parapsychology will be almost certainly in harmony with general psychological principles, and will be assimilated rather easily within the systematic framework of psychology as a science when once the imag-

8

ined appropriateness of Newtonian physics is put aside, and modern physics replaces it.

Psychology and Biology

As I turn to genetics, I would venture to predict a period of massive reorientation of psychology to the biological roots of which it used to boast. The very substance of growth, of motivation, of the learning process, and indeed of most of the basic realities with which the modern evolutionary psychology will have to cope, are provided by the DNA–RNA system; the elements of field physics as they are known in the embryology of Spemann and Weiss; the intricacies of polygenic determination of structure and function; and the broad recognition that individuality in tissue systems, as described by Roger Williams, rewrites the psychology of individual differences in astonishing terms. These genetic terms, of course, will be held by some to be fatalistic, as indicating the genetically given limitations upon all human endeavor. But in two respects these discoveries will be most encouraging: (a) It will be realized that individuality always applies to the growth *potential,* which can be utterly different when a new environmental situation is supplied. An example is the discovery of the Mendelian basis of the phenylpyruvic type of mental defect that has nevertheless yielded, to a large degree, to a carefully prepared diet. In other words, that which was genetically determined was controllable. Through respect for the genetics of human individuality, how to become better environmentalists will be understood. (b) As Sir George Thomson's statement, quoted earlier, implied, scientific insight is moving rapidly to a point such that the electron microscope can greatly aid in studies of the internal organization of individual cells. This, together with some control of mutations and a great deal of control of selective breeding and the application of the principles of population genetics, makes it likely that, within a few generations, to a considerable degree, some of the most abhorrent threats to human development may be eliminated. In anticipating the year 2100 or 2500, biologists could talk quite rationally about not only the prevention of deterioration, but plans for the actual long-range improvement of genetic potentials.

Psychology and Social Science

But the biological sciences do not have the whole exigent message. There is equal need for big gains in the social sciences, especially in the development of a social ecology. Ecology has been the most neglected aspect, I think, of the entire behavior field. The experimental psychologist may control, say a 10 X 10 X 10 foot area, and, with enormous and devoted attention to detail, think of everything that is in that space at a given time. Organisms, however, have life histories in segments of space time about which a fair amount is known if they are hatched or born in the laboratory. But if not, the higher they are in the phylogenetic tree, the more likely they

9

I. Valence and Vision: Introductory Notes

are to bring more from their past into the laboratory. Mark May used to say that the American sophomore, from whom are derived findings from humanity at large, was expected to "park his culture outside." Only the regions of time and space that are involved in the experiment are observed, ignoring the whole vast area from which the individual organism comes.

The needed studies of ecological organization are vastly more complex than anybody has imagined so far. The maps that Roger Barker has drawn of a Kansas town, and the lists of situational pressures that Saul Sells has devised as a preparation for space travel, will be only a tiny sampling of that vast conception of past and present environmental totalities that Egon Brunswik asked scientists to imagine. It will be a genetics that is oriented to a systematic and scientific science of ecology that will really give new field clues to human behavior. By field clues I hope to suggest the modalities of interaction between the edge of the organism and the edge of the environment, such that a complete and real fusion is created. I mean the kind of thing that is involved in interaction between the visual centers in the brain, the retina, the external light source, the laboratory conditions, personalities of the experimenters, the laboratory tradition, and laboratory culture, all of which must be considered when a person sees an inkblot or a social scene enacted before him. There must be whole organisms and whole environments to be studied for the sake of the modalities of reciprocity that develop between them. Psychologists began to learn from Lewin, as earlier they began to learn from Clerk-Maxwell, how to think in field terms; but they really have not done much of the sort on a scale demanded by present knowledge. The subspecialization has driven them more and more from organs to tissues, from tissues to cells, from cells to molecules, from molecules to atoms, from atoms to microparticles. All this specialization is, of course, absolutely necessary. The job of seeing psychological function, however, in combined biological and cultural terms is mostly a promissory note with as yet very little backing.

Because of its rarity, I shall mention the example of audiogenic seizures in mice, which Benson Ginzburg showed to have a not too complex Mendelian basis. But some of the mice that were expected to have convulsions and die had no convulsions, or had convulsions but did not die. He then attacked the problem from the pharmacological viewpoint and, in terms of biochemistry, found a way to buffer the lethal effects of the genes. Allow me a free analogy in the field of human ecology: What will happen when one finds a human environment of space–time–sensory enrichment, maternal warmth, generous and skillful experimental reinforcement that will allow a poorly endowed, frightened, aggressive ghetto child to develop into full humanness? This is exactly the type of experiment now being launched at several outposts of research on disadvantaged children. Before long thought in terms of biology versus the social sciences will cease; an ecological science will be developed so rich and so concrete that it will articulate closely with the new biology of individual growth.

10

1. Psychology in the Year 2000

And if psychologists mean quite seriously that man, as man, is richly intertwined with his ecology, it follows that the psychology of the next two decades will depend enormously upon the discovery of new forms of cross-cultural, cross-national communication. Indeed, it follows that unless there is very broad cross-national communication and action, there will be no human race to investigate. It will not do for American psychology, now having about 92% of the world's psychological personnel and about 92% of its published communications, to undertake a bland and supposedly disinterested study of the rest of the world in order that the wise and productive science, which they represent, can convey appropriate knowledge to those struggling along in less enlightened paths of endeavor. The study of the human predicament can come from a human race familiar with the method of science, but a human race speaking many tongues, regarding many values, and holding different convictions about the meaning of life, sooner or later will have to consult all that is human. There are a few living today who will still be alive in the year 2000, if there is a year 2000; and I hope they will still be battling the problem of developing a sufficiently coherent, human enough point of view to speak for all kinds of human beings. This will mean that the genetic and ecological progress that I am describing will have actually helped toward a psychology that is common human, that entails not only a study of all human beings, but a study by trained and devoted individuals within all human groups. Following the American habit of delivering "State of the Union" messages, the Secretary-General of the United Nations has been asked to report on the "state of the human race." I personally do not understand why governments, and indeed professional psychologists, as well, are almost wholly ignoring the challenge to study directly the possibilities of achieving an international and intercultural plan for world order. Aiming at this goal, it is conceivable that there will be worldwide human modalities of investigation like those already existing in astronomy and in medicine, but oriented to the behavioral sciences. And it is even possible that they will be oriented not only to the behaviors as such, but toward the deep inner humanness that I have tried to describe as an object of study. This, in relation to the dyadic and group problems of the behavior sciences, may give both insight and control over the more destructive tendencies, and may utilize the common human aspiration to live not only more safely and a little more comfortably, but also a little more creatively and a great deal more humanly.

The Role of Method

You have noted that new discoveries in the field of psychology, and, I believe, in all scientific fields, are largely the children of new *methods*. Consider what the compound microscope did to histology, what X-rays did for diagnostic procedure, and what the puzzle box, the maze, the Skinner box have done in the development and documentation of seminal scientific theories. I am raising these issues not simply to welcome the computer to our side, as a new brother, but to ask one final question. Psychologists can, as A. H. Maslow has pointed out, strip down the study of man to those methods common to the other sciences that do not deal with man; they can assume that the human sciences can best do their job by leaving humanness out. There is, however, another possibility. They might conceivably find that science can become big enough to develop fully human methods oriented to the complete panoply of human problems, that empathy, "tlc," rich dyadic methods of communication between subjects and experimenters, through patience, discipline, and imagination, might give them in the year 2000 a science more competent to deal with all the discoverable aspects of human nature.

But a still more basic problem of method relates to the way in which they try to hook together the data from laboratory, from clinic, from field observation, from home, from neighborhood, and from observation of human gatherings in schools, churches, juries, parliamentary bodies. On the one hand, they have neglected the use of laboratories, and today they are beginning to discover a more suitable laboratory approach to a wide variety of spontaneous human situations. They are discovering that inventive experimentalists can do even better work in free human situations than they can in the classical, highly planned, settings. But now I am referring mainly to the manner in which the experimental method does its work. Long ago, psychologists established for themselves the impossible task of creating a psychology through intensive observation of those phenomena that occur under controlled laboratory conditions, and then systematizing a psychology based solely on such findings. They tried to set up physics and chemistry, sometimes the biological sciences of genetics, embryology, and physiology, as models. Belatedly they have discovered that beautiful scientific structures, such as that of modern geology, with only slight use of experimental method, can be developed through the integration of many types of observations, short-term and long-term, outdoors and indoors, pinpointed or extravagantly blown up to cosmic proportions. The geologist uses experimental methods, but he uses them in the total context of his work. It is mother earth, not her fingernails, that interests him. Psychology, which attempted to pinpoint its existence in the nineteenth-century terms of Weber and Fechner, is now beginning a great awakening, a sort of Rip Van Winkle awakening; for we are discovering, and will discover more fully in the next few decades, the vast dimensions in which a mature psychology can be conceived. It will make even more use of experimental method than it does at present. But the experiments will be suggested, and the techniques controlled, rather largely by the broad perception of the nature of the human animal in his whole ecological setting. The observational systems that will develop cannot be categorized by any one word that is now known. The word *experimental* is a fine word, but it will have to be replaced by something much more systematic. Even

12

1. Psychology in the Year 2000

the developmental approach will mean something quite new when conceived in the kind of general systems terms, the kind of life science terms, that I am trying to suggest. Mathematical models certainly will both benefit and be benefited by the transitions that I am suggesting; and, of course, the engineering skills, already so important in psychophysiology, will become even more important.

I think psychologists will have to admit that many of this era will be unable to see the promised land that begins to be sketched out. Psychologists who will be extant in the year 2000 will have to be smarter than the psychologists today, as well as enormously better trained—I might add, enormously more *broadly* trained—than the subspecialized people turned out today. The blade of the modern mind is sharpened until it breaks, and we damn the blade instead of asking the metallurgist to develop tools from which sharp weapons can be prepared that, while still unscathed, can cut through the hard inscrutable rock of man's basic resistance to discovering his own nature.

The Human Predicament

The year 2000 can come, and the twenty-first century can offer less terror and more joy, but only if psychologists have learned both *how to look inside* and *how to look outside;* how to recognize the reciprocities of inner and outer, through methods that are as far ranging and as deeply human as is the human stuff that is being studied.

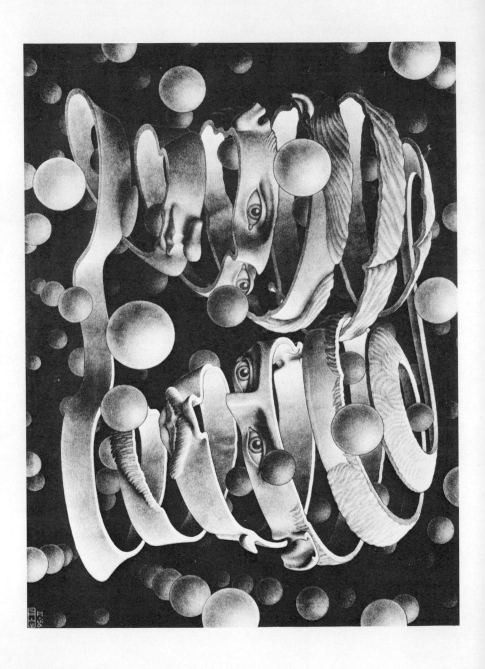

II.
The Emergence of a Biomedical Technology

2.
VALENCE:
The New Biology:
What Price Relieving Man's Estate?

LEON R. KASS

In the following article, Leon R. Kass provides a thorough discussion of the changes—and the challenges—intrinsic to the emerging biomedical technology.

Recent advances in biology and medicine suggest that we may be rapidly acquiring the power to modify and control the capacities and activities of men by direct intervention and manipulation of their bodies and minds. Certain means are already in use or at hand, others await the solution of relatively minor technical problems, while yet others, those offering perhaps the most precise kind of control, depend upon further basic research. Biologists who have considered these matters disagree on the question of how much how soon, but all agree that the power for "human engineering," to borrow from the jargon, is coming and that it will probably have profound social consequences.

These developments have been viewed both with enthusiasm and with alarm; they are only just beginning to receive serious attention. Several biologists have undertaken to inform the public about the technical possibilities, present and future. Practitioners of social science "futurology" are attempting to predict and describe the likely social consequences of and public responses to the new technologies. Lawyers and legislators are exploring institutional innovations for assessing new technologies. All of these activities are based upon the hope that we can harness the new technology of man for the betterment of mankind.

Yet this commendable aspiration points to another set of questions, which are, in my view, sorely neglected—questions that inquire into the

From *Science,* Vol. 174, pp. 779–788, 19 November 1971. Copyright 1971 by the American Association for the Advancement of Science.

2. VALENCE: The New Biology

meaning of phrases such as the "betterment of mankind." A *full* understanding of the new technology of man requires an exploration of ends, values, standards. What ends will or should the new techniques serve? What values should guide society's adjustments? By what standards should the assessment agencies assess? Behind these questions lie others: what is a good man, what is a good life for man, what is a good community? This article is an attempt to provoke discussion of these neglected and important questions.

While these questions about ends and ultimate ends are never unimportant or irrelevant, they have rarely been more important or more relevant. That this is so can be seen once we recognize that we are dealing here with a group of technologies that are in a decisive respect unique: the object upon which they operate is man himself. The technologies of energy or food production, of communication, of manufacture, and of motion greatly alter the implements available to man and the conditions in which he uses them. In contrast, the biomedical technology works to change the user himself. To be sure, the printing press, the automobile, the television, and the jet airplane have greatly altered the conditions under which and the way in which men live; but men as biological beings have remained largely unchanged. They have been, and remain, able to accept or reject, to use and abuse these technologies; they choose, whether wisely or foolishly, the ends to which these technologies are means. Biomedical technology may make it possible to change the inherent capacity for choice itself. Indeed, both those who welcome and those who fear the advent of "human engineering" ground their hopes and fears in the same prospect: *that man can for the first time re-create himself.*

Engineering the engineer seems to differ in kind from engineering his engine. Some have argued, however, that biomedical engineering does not differ qualitatively from toilet training, education, and moral teachings—all of which are forms of so-called "social engineering," which has man as its object, and is used by one generation to mold the next. In reply, it must at least be said that the techniques which have hitherto been employed are feeble and inefficient when compared to those on the horizon. This quantitative difference rests in part on a qualitative difference in the means of intervention. The traditional influences operate by speech or by symbolic deeds. They pay tribute to man as the animal who lives by speech and who understands the meanings of actions. Also, their effects are, in general, reversible, or at least subject to attempts at reversal. Each person has greater or lesser power to accept or reject or abandon them. In contrast, biomedical engineering circumvents the human context of speech and meaning, bypasses choice, and goes directly to work to modify the human material itself. Moreover, the changes wrought may be irreversible.

In addition, there is an important practical reason for considering the biomedical technology apart from other technologies. The advances we shall examine are fruits of a large, humane project dedicated to the con-

17

quest of disease and the relief of human suffering. The biologist and physician, regardless of their private motives, are seen, with justification, to be the well-wishers and benefactors of mankind. Thus, in a time in which technological advance is more carefully scrutinized and increasingly criticized, biomedical developments are still viewed by most people as benefits largely without qualification. The price we pay for these developments is thus more likely to go unrecognized. For this reason, I shall consider only the dangers and costs of biomedical advance. As the benefits are well known, there is no need to dwell upon them here. My discussion is deliberately partial.

I begin with a survey of the pertinent technologies. Next, I will consider some of the basic ethical and social problems in the use of these technologies. Then, I will briefly raise some fundamental questions to which these problems point. Finally, I shall offer some very general reflections on what is to be done.

The Biomedical Technologies

The biomedical technologies can be usefully organized into three groups, according to their major purpose: (i) control of death and life, (ii) control of human potentialities, and (iii) control of human achievement. The corresponding technologies are (i) medicine, especially the arts of prolonging life and of controlling reproduction, (ii) genetic engineering, and (iii) neurological and psychological manipulation. I shall briefly summarize each group of techniques.

1. *Control of death and life.* Previous medical triumphs have greatly increased average life expectancy. Yet other developments, such as organ transplantation or replacement and research into aging, hold forth the promise of increasing not just the average, but also the maximum life expectancy. Indeed, medicine seems to be sharpening its tools to do battle with death itself, as if death were just one more disease.

More immediately and concretely, available techniques of prolonging life—respirators, cardiac pacemakers, artificial kidneys—are already in the lists against death. Ironically, the success of these devices in forestalling death has introduced confusion in determining that death has, in fact, occurred. The traditional signs of life—heartbeat and respiration—can now be maintained entirely by machines. Some physicians are now busily trying to devise so-called "new definitions of death," while others maintain that the technical advances show that death is not a concrete event at all, but rather a gradual process, like twilight, incapable of precise temporal localization.

The real challenge to death will come from research into aging and senescence, a field just entering puberty. Recent studies suggest that aging is a genetically controlled process, distinct from disease, but one that can be manipulated and altered by diet or drugs. Extrapolating from animal studies, some scientists have suggested that a decrease in the rate of aging might also be achieved simply by effecting a very small decrease in human body temperature. According to some estimates, by the year 2000 it may be technically possible to add from 20 to 40 useful years to the period of middle life.

Medicine's success in extending life is already a major cause of excessive population growth: death control points to birth control. Although we are already technically competent, new techniques for lowering fertility and chemical agents for inducing abortion will greatly enhance our powers over conception and gestation. Problems of definition have been raised here as well. The need to determine when individuals acquire enforceable legal rights gives society an interest in the definition of human life and of the time when it begins. These matters are too familiar to need elaboration.

Technologies to conquer infertility proceed alongside those to promote it. The first successful laboratory fertilization of human egg by human sperm was reported in 1969 (1). In 1970, British scientists learned how to grow human embryos in the laboratory up to at least the blastocyst stage [that is, to the age of 1 week (2)]. We may soon hear about the next stage, the successful reimplantation of such an embryo into a woman previously infertile because of oviduct disease. The development of an artificial placenta, now under investigation, will make possible full laboratory control of fertilization and gestation. In addition, sophisticated biochemical and cytological techniques of monitoring the "quality" of the fetus have been and are being developed and used. These developments not only give us more power over the generation of human life, but make it possible to manipulate and to modify the quality of the human material.

2. *Control of human potentialities.* Genetic engineering, when fully developed, will wield two powers not shared by ordinary medical practice. Medicine treats existing individuals and seeks to correct deviations from a norm of health. Genetic engineering, in contrast, will be able to make changes that can be transmitted to succeeding generations and will be able to create new capacities, and hence to establish new norms of health and fitness.

Nevertheless, one of the major interests in genetic manipulation is strictly medical: to develop treatments for individuals with inherited diseases. Genetic disease is prevalent and increasing, thanks partly to medical advances that enable those affected to survive and perpetuate their mutant genes. The hope is that normal copies of the appropriate gene, obtained biologically or synthesized chemically, can be introduced into defective individuals to correct their deficiencies. This *therapeutic* use of genetic technology appears to be far in the future. Moreover, there is some doubt that it will ever be practical, since the same end could be more easily achieved by transplanting cells or organs that could compensate for the missing or defective gene product.

Far less remote are technologies that could serve *eugenic* ends. Their development has been endorsed by those concerned about a general dete-

19

rioration of the human gene pool and by others who believe that even an undeteriorated human gene pool needs upgrading. Artifical insemination with selected donors, the eugenic proposal of Herman Muller (3), has been possible for several years because of the perfection of methods for long-term storage of human spermatozoa. The successful maturation of human oocytes in the laboratory and their subsequent fertilization now make it possible to select donors of ova as well. But a far more suitable technique for eugenic purposes will soon be upon us—namely, nuclear transplantation, or cloning. Bypassing the lottery of sexual recombination, nuclear transplantation permits the asexual reproduction or copying of an already developed individual. The nucleus of a mature but unfertilized egg is replaced by a nucleus obtained from a specialized cell of an adult organism or embryo (for example, a cell from the intestines or the skin). The egg with its transplanted nucleus develops as if it had been fertilized and, barring complications, will give rise to a normal adult organism. Since almost all the hereditary material (DNA) of a cell is contained within its nucleus, the renucleated egg and the individual into which it develops are genetically identical to the adult organism that was the source of the donor nucleus. Cloning could be used to produce sets of unlimited numbers of genetically identical individuals, each set derived from a single parent. Cloning has been successful in amphibians and is now being tried in mice; its extension to man merely requires the solution of certain technical problems.

Production of man–animal chimeras by the introduction of selected nonhuman material into developing human embryos is also expected. Fusion of human and nonhuman cells in tissue culture has already been achieved.

Other, less direct means for influencing the gene pool are already available, thanks to our increasing ability to identify and diagnose genetic diseases. Genetic counselors can now detect biochemically and cytologically a variety of severe genetic defects (for example, Mongolism, Tay–Sachs disease) while the fetus is still in utero. Since treatments are at present largely unavailable, diagnosis is often followed by abortion of the affected fetus. In the future, more sensitive tests will also permit the detection of heterozygote carriers, the unaffected individuals who carry but a single dose of a given deleterious gene. The eradication of a given genetic disease might then be attempted by aborting all such carriers. In fact, it was recently suggested that the fairly common disease cystic fibrosis could be completely eliminated over the next 40 years by screening all pregnancies and aborting the 17,000,000 unaffected fetuses that will carry a single gene for this disease. Such zealots need to be reminded of the consequences should each geneticist be allowed an equal assault on his favorite genetic disorder, given that each human being is a carrier for some four to eight such recessive, lethal genetic diseases.

2. VALENCE: The New Biology

3. *Control of human achievement.* Although human achievement depends at least in part upon genetic endowment, heredity determines only the material upon which experience and education impose the form. The limits of many capacities and powers of an individual are indeed genetically determined, but the nurturing and perfection of these capacities depend upon other influences. Neurological and psychological manipulation hold forth the promise of controlling the development of human capacities, particularly those long considered most distinctively human: speech, thought, choice, emotion, memory, and imagination.

These techniques are now in a rather primitive state because we understand so little about the brain and mind. Nevertheless, we have already seen the use of electrical stimulation of the human brain to produce sensations of intense pleasure and to control rage, the use of brain surgery (for example, frontal lobotomy) for the relief of severe anxiety, and the use of aversive conditioning with electric shock to treat sexual perversion. Operant-conditioning techniques are widely used, apparently with success, in schools and mental hospitals. The use of so-called consciousness-expanding and hallucinogenic drugs is widespread, to say nothing of tranquilizers and stimulants. We are promised drugs to modify memory, intelligence, libido, and aggressiveness.

The following passages from a recent book by Yale neurophysiologist José Delgado—a book instructively entitled *Physical Control of the Mind: Toward a Psychocivilized Society*—should serve to make this discussion more concrete. In the early 1950's, it was discovered that, with electrodes placed in certain discrete regions of their brains, animals would repeatedly and indefatigably press levers to stimulate their own brains, with obvious resultant enjoyment. Even starving animals preferred stimulating these so-called pleasure centers to eating. Delgado comments on the electrical stimulation of a similar center in a human subject (4, p. 185).

> [T]he patient reported a pleasant tingling sensation in the left side of her body 'from my face down to the bottom of my legs.' She started giggling and making funny comments, stating that she enjoyed the sensation 'very much.' Repetition of these stimulations made the patient more communicative and flirtatious, and she ended by openly expressing her desire to marry the therapist.

And one further quotation from Delgado. (4, p. 88).

> Leaving wires inside of a thinking brain may appear unpleasant or dangerous, but actually the many patients who have undergone this experience have not been concerned about the fact of being wired, nor have they felt any discomfort due to the presence of conductors in their heads. Some women have shown their feminine adaptability to circumstances by wearing attractive hats or wigs to conceal their elec-

21

trical headgear, and many people have been able to enjoy a normal life as out-patients, returning to the clinic periodically for examination and stimulation. In a few cases in which contacts were located in pleasurable areas, patients have had the opportunity to stimulate their own brains by pressing the button of a portable instrument, and this procedure is reported to have therapeutic benefits.

It bears repeating that the sciences of neurophysiology and psychopharmacology are in their infancy. The techniques that are now available are crude, imprecise, weak, and unpredictable, compared to those that may flow from a more mature neurobiology.

Basic Ethical and Social Problems
in the Use of Biomedical Technology

After this cursory review of the powers now and soon to be at our disposal, I turn to the questions concerning the use of these powers. First, we must recognize that questions of use of science and technology are always moral and political questions, never simply technical ones. All private or public decisions to develop or to use biomedical technology— and decisions *not* to do so—inevitably contain judgments about value. This is true even if the values guiding those decisions are not articulated or made clear, as indeed they often are not. Secondly, the value judgments cannot be derived from biomedical science. This is true even if scientists themselves make the decisions.

These important points are often overlooked for at least three reasons.

1. They are obscured by those who like to speak of "the control of nature by science." It is men who control, not that abstraction "science." Science may provide the means, but men choose the ends; the choice of ends comes from beyond science.

2. Introduction of new technologies often appears to be the result of no decision whatsoever, or of the culmination of decisions too small or unconscious to be recognized as such. What can be done is done. However, someone is deciding on the basis of some notions of desirability, no matter how self-serving or altruistic.

3. Desires to gain or keep money and power no doubt influence much of what happens, but these desires can also be formulated as reasons and then discussed and debated.

Insofar as our society has tried to deliberate about questions of use, how has it done so? Pragmatists that we are, we prefer a utilitarian calculus: we weigh "benefits" against "risks," and we weigh them for both the individual and "society." We often ignore the fact that the very definitions of "a benefit" and "a risk" are themselves based upon judgments about value. In the biomedical areas just reviewed, the benefits are considered to be self-evident: prolongation of life, control of fertility and of population size, treatment and prevention of genetic disease, the reduction of anxiety and aggressiveness, and the enhancement of memory, intelligence, and pleasure. The assessment of risk is, in general, simply pragmatic—will the technique work effectively and reliably, how much will it cost, will it do detectable bodily harm, and who will complain if we proceed with development? As these questions are familiar and congenial, there is no need to belabor them.

The very pragmatism that makes us sensitive to considerations of economic cost often blinds us to the larger social costs exacted by biomedical advances. For one thing, we seem to be unaware that we may not be able to maximize all the benefits, that several of the goals we are promoting conflict with each other. On the one hand, we seek to control population growth by lowering fertility; on the other hand, we develop techniques to enable every infertile woman to bear a child. On the one hand, we try to extend the lives of individuals with genetic disease; on the other, we wish to eliminate deleterious genes from the human population. I am not urging that we resolve these conflicts in favor of one side or the other, but simply that we recognize that such conflicts exist. Once we do, we are more likely to appreciate that most "progress" is heavily paid for in terms not generally included in the simple utilitarian calculus.

To become sensitive to the larger costs of biomedical progress, we must attend to several serious ethical and social questions. I will briefly discuss three of them: (i) questions of distributive justice, (ii) questions of the use and abuse of power, and (iii) questions of self-degradation and dehumanization.

Distributive Justice

The introduction of any biomedical technology presents a new instance of an old problem—how to distribute scarce resources justly. We should assume that demand will usually exceed supply. Which people should receive a kidney transplant or an artificial heart? Who should get the benefits of genetic therapy or of brain stimulation? Is "first-come, first-served" the fairest principle? Or are certain people "more worthy," and if so, on what grounds?

It is unlikely that we will arrive at answers to these questions in the form of deliberate decisions. More likely, the problem of distribution will continue to be decided ad hoc and locally. If so, the consequence will probably be a sharp increase in the already far too great inequality of medical care. The extreme case will be longevity, which will probably be, at first, obtainable only at great expense. Who is likely to be able to buy it? Do conscience and prudence permit us to enlarge the gap between rich and poor, especially with respect to something as fundamental as life itself?

Questions of distributive justice also arise in the earlier decisions to acquire new knowledge and to develop new techniques. Personnel and facilities for medical research and treatment are scarce resources. Is the development of a new technology the best use of the limited resources, given current circumstances? How should we balance efforts aimed at prevention against those aimed at cure, or either of these against efforts to redesign the species? How should we balance the delivery of available levels of care against further basic research? More fundamentally, how should we balance efforts in biology and medicine against efforts to eliminate poverty, pollution, urban decay, discrimination, and poor education? This last question about distribution is perhaps the most profound. We should reflect upon the social consequences of seducing many of our brightest young people to spend their lives locating the biochemical defects in rare genetic diseases, while our more serious problems go begging. The current squeeze on money for research provides us with an opportunity to rethink and reorder our priorities.

Problems of distributive justice are frequently mentioned and discussed, but they are hard to resolve in a rational manner. We find them especially difficult because of the enormous range of conflicting values and interests that characterizes our pluralistic society. We cannot agree—unfortunately, we often do not even try to agree—on standards for just distribution. Rather, decisions tend to be made largely out of a clash of competing interests. Thus, regrettably, the question of how to distribute justly often gets reduced to who shall decide how to distribute. The question about justice has led us to the question about power.

Use and Abuse of Power

We have difficulty recognizing the problems of the exercise of power in the biomedical enterprise because of our delight with the wondrous fruits it has yielded. This is ironic because the notion of power is absolutely central to the modern conception of science. The ancients conceived of science as the *understanding* of nature, pursued for its own sake. We moderns view science as power, as *control* over nature; the conquest of nature "for the relief of man's estate" was the charge issued by Francis Bacon, one of the leading architects of the modern scientific project (5).

Another source of difficulty is our fondness for speaking of the abstraction "Man." I suspect that we prefer to speak figuratively about "Man's power over Nature" because it obscures an unpleasant reality about human affairs. It is in fact particular men who wield power, not Man. What we really mean by "Man's power over Nature" is a power exercised by some men over other men, with a knowledge of nature as their instrument.

While applicable to technology in general, these reflections are especially pertinent to the technologies of human engineering, with which men deliberately exercise power over future generations. An excellent discussion of this question is found in *The Abolition of Man*, by C. S. Lewis (6).

> It is, of course, a commonplace to complain that men have hitherto used badly, and against their fellows, the powers that science has given them. But that is not the point I am trying to make. I am not speaking

24

of particular corruptions and abuses which an increase of moral virtue would cure: I am considering what the thing called "Man's power over Nature" must always and essentially be. . . .

In reality, of course, if any one age really attains, by eugenics and scientific education, the power to make its descendants what it pleases, all men who live after it are the patients of that power. They are weaker, not stronger: for though we may have put wonderful machines in their hands, we have pre-ordained how they are to use them. . . . The real picture is that of one dominant age . . . which resists all previous ages most successfully and dominates all subsequent ages most irresistibly, and thus is the real master of the human species. But even within this master generation (itself an infinitesimal minority of the species) the power will be exercised by a minority smaller still. Man's conquest of Nature, if the dreams of some scientific planners are realized, means the rule of a few hundreds of men over billions upon billions of men. There neither is nor can be any simple increase of power on Man's side. Each new power won *by* man is a power *over* man as well. Each advance leaves him weaker as well as stronger. In every victory, besides being the general who triumphs, he is also the prisoner who follows the triumphal car.

Please note that I am not yet speaking about the problem of the misuse or abuse of power. The point is rather that the power which grows is unavoidably the power of only some men, and that the number of powerful men decreases as power increases.

Specific problems of abuse and misuse of specific powers must not, however, be overlooked. Some have voiced the fear that the technologies of genetic engineering and behavior control, though developed for good purposes, will be put to evil uses. These fears are perhaps somewhat exaggerated, if only because biomedical technologies would add very little to our highly developed arsenal for mischief, destruction, and stultification. Nevertheless, any proposal for large-scale human engineering should make us wary. Consider a program of positive eugenics based upon the widespread practice of asexual reproduction. Who shall decide what constitutes a superior individual worthy of replication? Who shall decide which individuals may or must reproduce, and by which method? These are questions easily answered only for a tyrannical regime.

Concern about the use of power is equally necessary in the selection of means for desirable or agreed-upon ends. Consider the desired end of limiting population growth. An effective program of fertility control is likely to be coercive. Who should decide the choice of means? Will the program penalize "conscientious objectors"?

Serious problems arise simply from obtaining and disseminating information, as in the mass screening programs now being proposed for detection of genetic disease. For what kinds of disorders is compulsory screening justified? Who shall have access to the data obtained, and for what pur-

II. The Emergence of a Biomedical Technology

poses? To whom does information about a person's genotype belong? In ordinary medical practice, the patient's privacy is protected by the doctor's adherence to the principle of confidentiality. What will protect his privacy under conditions of mass screening?

More than privacy is at stake if screening is undertaken to detect psychological or behavioral abnormalities. A recent proposal, tendered and supported high in government, called for the psychological testing of all 6-year-olds to detect future criminals and misfits. The proposal was rejected; current tests lack the requisite predictive powers. But will such a proposal be rejected if reliable tests become available? What if certain genetic disorders, diagnosable in childhood, can be shown to correlate with subsequent antisocial behavior? For what degree of correlation and for what kinds of behavior can mandatory screening be justified? What use should be made of the data? Might not the dissemination of the information itself undermine the individual's chance for a worthy life and contribute to his so-called antisocial tendencies?

Consider the seemingly harmless effort to redefine clinical death. If the need for organs for transplantation is the stimulus for redefining death, might not this concern influence the definition at the expense of the dying? One physician, in fact, refers in writing to the revised criteria for declaring a patient dead as a "new definition of heart donor eligibility" (7, p. 526).

Problems of abuse of power arise even in the acquisition of basic knowledge. The securing of a voluntary and informed consent is an abiding problem in the use of human subjects in experimentation. Gross coercion and deception are now rarely a problem; the pressures are generally subtle, often related to an intrinsic power imbalance in favor of the experimentalist.

A special problem arises in experiments on or manipulations of the unborn. Here it is impossible to obtain the consent of the human subject. If the purpose of the intervention is therapeutic—to correct a known genetic abnormality, for example—consent can reasonably be implied. But can anyone ethically consent to nontherapeutic interventions in which parents or scientists work their wills or their eugenic visions on the child-to-be? Would not such manipulation represent in itself an abuse of power, independent of consequences?

There are many clinical situations which already permit, if not invite, the manipulative or arbitrary use of powers provided by biomedical technology: obtaining organs for transplantation, refusing to let a person die with dignity, giving genetic counselling to a frightened couple, recommending eugenic sterilization for a mental retardate, ordering electric shock for a homosexual. In each situation, there is an opportunity to violate the will of the patient or subject. Such opportunities have generally existed in medical practice, but the dangers are becoming increasingly serious. With the growing complexity of the technologies, the technician gains in authority, since he alone can understand what he is doing. The patient's lack

26

2. VALENCE: The New Biology

of knowledge makes him deferential and often inhibits him from speaking up when he feels threatened. Physicians *are* sometimes troubled by their increasing power, yet they feel they cannot avoid its exercise. "Reluctantly," one commented to me, "we shall have to play God." With what guidance and to what ends I shall consider later. For the moment, I merely ask: "By whose authority?"

While these questions about power are pertinent and important, they are in one sense misleading. They imply an inherent conflict of purpose between physician and patient, between scientist and citizen. The discussion conjures up images of master and slave, of oppressor and oppressed. Yet it must be remembered that conflict of purpose is largely absent, especially with regard to general goals. To be sure, the purposes of medical scientists are not always the same as those of the subjects experimented on. Nevertheless, basic sponsors and partisans of biomedical technology are precisely those upon whom the technology will operate. The will of the scientist and physician is happily married to (rather, is the offspring of) the desire of all of us for better health, longer life, and peace of mind.

Most future biomedical technologies will probably be welcomed, as have those of the past. Their use will require little or no coercion. Some developments, such as pills to improve memory, control mood, or induce pleasure, are likely to need no promotion. Thus, even if we should escape from the dangers of coercive manipulation, we shall still face large problems posed by the voluntary use of biomedical technology, problems to which I now turn.

Voluntary Self-Degradation and Dehumanization

Modern opinion is sensitive to problems of restriction of freedom and abuse of power. Indeed, many hold that a man can be injured only by violating his will. But this view is much too narrow. It fails to recognize the great dangers we shall face in the use of biomedical technology, dangers that stem from an excess of freedom, from the uninhibited exercises of will. In my view, our greatest problem will increasingly be one of voluntary self-degradation, or willing dehumanization.

Certain desired and perfected medical technologies have already had some dehumanizing consequences. Improved methods of resuscitation have made possible heroic efforts to "save" the severely ill and injured. Yet these efforts are sometimes only partly successful; they may succeed in salvaging individuals with severe brain damage, capable of only a less-than-human, vegetating existence. Such patients, increasingly found in the intensive care units of university hospitals, have been denied a death with dignity. Families are forced to suffer seeing their loved ones so reduced, and are made to bear the burdens of a protracted death watch.

Even the ordinary methods of treating disease and prolonging life have impoverished the context in which men die. Fewer and fewer people die in the familiar surroundings of home or in the company of family and

27

II. The Emergence of a Biomedical Technology

friends. At that time of life when there is perhaps the greatest need for human warmth and comfort, the dying patient is kept company by cardiac pacemakers and defibrillators, respirators, aspirators, oxygenators, catheters, and his intravenous drip.

But the loneliness is not confined to the dying patient in the hospital bed. Consider the increasing number of old people who are still alive, thanks to medical progress. As a group, the elderly are the most alienated members of our society. Not yet ready for the world of the dead, not deemed fit for the world of the living, they are shunted aside. More and more of them spend the extra years medicine has given them in "homes for senior citizens," in chronic hospitals, in nursing homes—waiting for the end. We have learned how to increase their years, but we have not learned how to help them enjoy their days. And yet, we bravely and relentlessly push back the frontiers against death.

Paradoxically, even the young and vigorous may be suffering because of medicine's success in removing death from their personal experience. Those born since penicillin represent the first generation ever to grow up without the experience or fear of probable unexpected death at an early age. They look around and see that virtually all of their friends are alive. A thoughtful physician, Eric Cassell, has remarked on this in "Death and the physician" (8, p. 76):

> [W]hile the gift of time must surely be marked as a great blessing, the *perception* of time, as stretching out endlessly before us, is somewhat threatening. Many of us function best under deadlines, and tend to procrastinate when time limits are not set. . . . Thus, this unquestioned boon, the extension of life, and the removal of the threat of premature death, carries with it an unexpected anxiety: the anxiety of an unlimited future.
>
> In the young, the sense of limitless time has apparently imparted not a feeling of limitless opportunity, but increased stress and anxiety, in addition to the anxiety which results from other modern freedoms: personal mobility, a wide range of occupational choice, and independence from the limitations of class and familial patterns of work. . . . A certain aimlessness (often ringed around with great social consciousness) characterizes discussions about their own aspirations. The future is endless, and their inner demands seem minimal. Although it may appear uncharitable to say so, they seem to be acting in a way best described as "childish"—particularly in their lack of a time sense. They behave as though there were no tomorrow, or as though the time limits imposed by the biological facts of life had become so vague for them as to be nonexistent.

Consider next the coming power over reproduction and genotype. We endorse the project that will enable us to control numbers and to treat

28

individuals with genetic disease. But our desires outrun these defensible goals. Many would welcome the chance to become parents without the inconvenience of pregnancy; others would wish to know in advance the characteristics of their offspring (sex, height, eye color, intelligence); still others would wish to design these characteristics to suit their tastes. Some scientists have called for the use of the new technologies to assure the "quality" of all new babies (9). As one obstetrician put it: "The business of obstetrics is to produce *optimum* babies." But the price to be paid for the "optimum baby" is the transfer of procreation from the home to the laboratory and its coincident transformation into manufacture. Increasing control over the product is purchased by the increasing depersonalization of the process. The complete depersonalization of procreation (possible with the development of an artificial placenta) shall be, in itself, seriously dehumanizing, no matter how optimum the product. It should not be forgotten that human procreation not only issues new human beings, but is itself a human activity.

Procreation is not simply an activity of the rational will. It is a more complete human activity precisely because it engages us bodily and spiritually, as well as rationally. Is there perhaps some wisdom in that mystery of nature which joins the pleasure of sex, the communication of love, and the desire for children in the very activity by which we continue the chain of human existence? Is not biological parenthood a built-in "mechanism," selected because it fosters and supports in parents an adequate concern for and commitment to their children? Would not the laboratory production of human beings no longer be *human* procreation? Could it keep human parenthood human?

The dehumanizing consequences of programmed reproduction extend beyond the mere acts and processes of life-giving. Transfer of procreation to the laboratory will no doubt weaken what is presently for many people the best remaining justification and support for the existence of marriage and the family. Sex is now comfortably at home outside of marriage; child-rearing is progressively being given over to the state, the schools, the mass media, and the child-care centers. Some have argued that the family, long the nursery of humanity, has outlived its usefulness. To be sure, laboratory and governmental alternatives might be designed for procreation and child-rearing, but at what cost?

This is not the place to conduct a full evaluation of the biological family. Nevertheless, some of its important virtues are, nowadays, too often overlooked. The family is rapidly becoming the only institution in an increasingly impersonal world where each person is loved not for what he does or makes, but simply because he is. The family is also the institution where most of us, both as children and as parents, acquire a sense of continuity with the past and a sense of commitment to the future. Without the family, we would have little incentive to take an interest in anything after our own deaths. These observations suggest that the elimination of the family would weaken ties to past and future, and would throw us, even more than we are now, to the mercy of an impersonal, lonely present.

Neurobiology and psychobiology probe most directly into the distinctively human. The technological fruit of these sciences is likely to be both more tempting than Eve's apple and more "catastrophic" in its result (10). One need only consider contemporary drug use to see what people are willing to risk or sacrifice for novel experiences, heightened perceptions, or just "kicks." The possibility of drug-induced, instant, and effortless gratification will be welcomed. Recall the possibilities of voluntary self-stimulation of the brain to reduce anxiety, to heighten pleasure, or to create visual and auditory sensations unavailable through the peripheral sense organs. Once these techniques are perfected and safe, is there much doubt that they will be desired, demanded, and used?

What ends will these techniques serve? Most likely, only the most elemental, those most tied to the bodily pleasures. What will happen to thought, to love, to friendship, to art, to judgment, to public-spiritedness in a society with a perfected technology of pleasure? What kinds of creatures will we become if we obtain our pleasure by drug or electrical stimulation without the usual kind of human efforts and frustrations? What kind of society will we have?

We need only consult Aldous Huxley's prophetic novel *Brave New World* for a likely answer to these questions. There we encounter a society dedicated to homogeneity and stability, administered by means of instant gratifications and peopled by creatures of human shape but of stunted humanity. They consume, fornicate, take "soma," and operate the machinery that makes it all possible. They do not read, write, think, love, or govern themselves. Creativity and curiosity, reason and passion, exist only in a rudimentary and mutilated form. In short, they are not men at all.

True, our techniques, like theirs, may in fact enable us to treat schizophrenia, to alleviate anxiety, to curb aggressiveness. We, like they, may indeed be able to save mankind from itself, but probably only at the cost of its humanness. In the end, the price of relieving man's estate might well be the abolition of man (11).

There are, of course, many other routes leading to the abolition of man. There are many other and better known causes of dehumanization. Disease, starvation, mental retardation, slavery, and brutality—to name just a few—have long prevented many, if not most, people from living a fully human life. We should work to reduce and eventually to eliminate these evils. But the existence of these evils should not prevent us from appreciating that the use of the technology of man, uninformed by wisdom concerning proper human ends, and untempered by an appropriate humility and awe, can unwittingly render us all irreversibly less than human. For, unlike the man reduced by disease or slavery, the people dehumanized à la *Brave New World* are not miserable, do not know that they are dehumanized,

2. VALENCE: The New Biology

and, what is worse, would not care if they knew. They are, indeed, happy slaves, with a slavish happiness.

Some Fundamental Questions

The practical problems of distributing scarce resources, of curbing the abuses of power, and of preventing voluntary dehumanization point beyond themselves to some large, enduring, and most difficult questions: the nature of justice and the good community, the nature of man and the good for man. My appreciation of the profundity of these questions and my own ignorance before them makes me hesitant to say any more about them. Nevertheless, previous failures to find a shortcut around them have led me to believe that these questions must be faced if we are to have any hope of understanding where biology is taking us. Therefore, I shall try to show in outline how I think some of the larger questions arise from my discussion of dehumanization and self-degradation.

My remarks on dehumanization can hardly fail to arouse argument. It might be said, correctly, that to speak about dehumanization presupposes a concept of "the distinctively human." It might also be said, correctly, that to speak about wisdom concerning proper human ends presupposes that such ends do in fact exist and that they may be more or less accessible to human understanding, or at least to rational inquiry. It is true that neither presupposition is at home in modern thought.

The notion of the "distinctively human" has been seriously challenged by modern scientists. Darwinists hold that man is, at least in origin, tied to the subhuman; his seeming distinctiveness is an illusion or, at most, not very important. Biochemists and molecular biologists extend the challenge by blurring the distinction between the living and the nonliving. The laws of physics and chemistry are found to be valid and are held to be sufficient for explaining biological systems. Man is a collection of molecules, an accident on the stage of evolution, endowed by chance with the power to change himself, but only along determined lines.

Psychoanalysts have also debunked the "distinctively human." The essence of man is seen to be located in those drives he shares with other animals—pursuit of pleasure and avoidance of pain. The so-called "higher functions" are understood to be servants of the more elementary, the more base. Any distinctiveness or "dignity" that man has consists of his superior capacity for gratifying his animal needs.

The idea of "human good" fares no better. In the social sciences, historicists and existentialists have helped drive this question underground. The former hold all notions of human good to be culturally and historically bound, and hence mutable. The latter hold that values are subjective: each man makes his own, and ethics becomes simply the cataloging of personal tastes.

Such appear to be the prevailing opinions. Yet there is nothing novel about reductionism, hedonism, and relativism; these are doctrines with

31

II. The Emergence of a Biomedical Technology

which Socrates contended. What is new is that these doctrines seem to be vindicated by scientific advance. Not only do the scientific notions of nature and of man flower into verifiable predictions, but they yield marvelous fruit. The technological triumphs are held to validate their scientific foundations. Here, perhaps, is the most pernicious result of technological progress—more dehumanizing than any actual manipulation or technique, present or future. We are witnessing the erosion, perhaps the final erosion, of the idea of man as something splendid or divine, and its replacement with a view that sees man, no less than nature, as simply more raw material for manipulation and homogenization. Hence, our peculiar moral crisis. We are in turbulent seas without a landmark precisely because we adhere more and more to a view of nature and of man which both gives us enormous power and, at the same time, denies all possibility of standards to guide its use. Though well-equipped, we know not who we are nor where we are going. We are left to the accidents of our hasty, biased, and ephemeral judgments.

Let us not fail to note a painful irony: our conquest of nature has made us the slaves of blind chance. We triumph over nature's unpredictabilities only to subject ourselves to the still greater unpredictability of our capricious wills and our fickle opinions. That we have a method is no proof against our madness. Thus, engineering the engineer as well as the engine, we race our train we know not where (12).

While the disastrous consequences of ethical nihilism are insufficient to refute it, they invite and make urgent a reinvestigation of the ancient and enduring questions of what is a proper life for a human being, what is a good community, and how are they achieved (13). We must not be deterred from these questions simply because the best minds in human history have failed to settle them. Should we not rather be encouraged by the fact that they considered them to be the most important questions?

As I have hinted before, our ethical dilemma is caused by the victory of modern natural science with its nonteleological view of man. We ought therefore to reexamine with great care the modern notions of nature and of man, which undermine those earlier notions that provide a basis for ethics. If we consult our common experience, we are likely to discover some grounds for believing that the questions about man and human good are far from closed. Our common experience suggests many difficulties for the modern "scientific view of man." For example, this view fails to account for the concern for justice and freedom that appears to be characteristic of all human societies (14). It also fails to account for or to explain the fact that men have speech and not merely voice, that men can choose and act and not merely move or react. It fails to explain why men engage in moral discourse, or, for that matter, why they speak at all. Finally, the "scientific view of man" cannot account for scientific inquiry itself, for why men seek to know. Might there not be something the matter with a knowledge of man that does not explain or take account of his most distinctive activities, aspirations, and concerns (15)?

2. VALENCE: The New Biology

Having gone this far, let me offer one suggestion as to where the difficulty might lie: in the modern understanding of knowledge. Since Bacon, as I have mentioned earlier, technology has increasingly come to be the basic justification for scientific inquiry. The end is power, not knowledge for its own sake. But power is not only the end. It is also an important *validation* of knowledge. One definitely knows that one knows only if one can make. Synthesis is held to be the ultimate proof of understanding (16). A more radical formulation holds that one knows only what one makes: knowing *equals* making.

Yet therein lies a difficulty. If truth be the power to change or to make the object studied, then of what do we have knowledge? If there are no fixed realities, but only material upon which we may work our wills, will not "science" be merely the "knowledge" of the transient and the manipulatable? We might indeed have knowledge of the laws by which things change and the rules for their manipulation, but no knowledge of the things themselves. Can such a view of "science" yield any knowledge about the nature of man, or indeed, about the nature of anything? Our questions appear to lead back to the most basic of questions: What does it mean to know? What is it that is knowable (17)?

We have seen that the practical problems point toward and make urgent certain enduring, fundamental questions. Yet while pursuing these questions, we cannot afford to neglect the practical problems as such. Let us not forget Delgado and the "psychocivilized society." The philosophical inquiry could be rendered moot by our blind, confident efforts to dissect and redesign ourselves. While awaiting a reconstruction of theory, we must act as best we can.

What Is To Be Done?

First, we sorely need to recover some humility in the face of our awesome powers. The arguments I have presented should make apparent the folly of arrogance, of the presumption that we are wise enough to remake ourselves. Because we lack wisdom, caution is our urgent need. Or to put it another way, in the absence of that "ultimate wisdom," we can be wise enough to know that we are not wise enough. When we lack sufficient wisdom to do, wisdom consists in not doing. Caution, restraint, delay, abstention are what this second-best (and, perhaps, only) wisdom dictates with respect to the technology for human engineering.

If we can recognize that biomedical advances carry significant social costs, we may be willing to adopt a less permissive, more critical stance toward new developments. We need to reexamine our prejudice not only that all biomedical innovation is progress, but also that it is inevitable. Precedent certainly favors the view that what can be done will be done, but is this necessarily so? Ought we not to be suspicious when technologists speak of coming developments as automatic, not subject to human control? Is there not something contradictory in the notion that we have the power to control all the untoward consequences of a technology, but lack the power to determine whether it should be developed in the first place?

What will be the likely consequences of the perpetuation of our permissive and fatalistic attitude toward human engineering? How will the large decisions be made? Technocratically and self-servingly, if our experience with previous technologies is any guide. Under conditions of laissez-faire, most technologists will pursue techniques, and most private industries will pursue profits. We are fortunate that, apart from the drug manufacturers, there are at present in the biomedical area few large industries that influence public policy. Once these appear, the voice of "the public interest" will have to shout very loudly to be heard above their whisperings in the halls of Congress. These reflections point to the need for institutional controls.

Scientists understandably balk at the notion of the regulation of science and technology. Censorship is ugly and often based upon ignorant fear; bureaucratic regulation is often stupid and inefficient. Yet there is something disingenuous about a scientist who professes concern about the social consequences of science, but who responds to every suggestion of regulation with one or both of the following: "No restrictions on scientific research," and "Technological progress should not be curtailed." Surely, to suggest that *certain* technologies ought to be regulated or forestalled is not to call for the halt of *all* technological progress (and says nothing at all about basic research). Each development should be considered on its own merits. Although the dangers of regulation cannot be dismissed, who, for example, would still object to efforts to obtain an effective, complete, global prohibition on the development, testing, and use of biological and nuclear weapons?

The proponents of laissez-faire ignore two fundamental points. They ignore the fact that not to regulate is as much a policy decision as the opposite, and that it merely postpones the time of regulation. Controls will eventually be called for—as they are now being demanded to end environmental pollution. If attempts are not made early to detect and diminish the social costs of biomedical advances by intelligent institutional regulation, the society is likely to react later with more sweeping, immoderate, and throttling controls.

The proponents of laissez-faire also ignore the fact that much of technology is already regulated. The federal government is already deep in research and development (for example, space, electronics, and weapons) and is the principal sponsor of biomedical research. One may well question the wisdom of the direction given, but one would be wrong in arguing that technology cannot survive social control. Clearly, the question is not control versus no control, but rather what kind of control, when, by whom, and for what purpose.

Means for achieving international regulation and control need to be devised. Biomedical technology can be no nation's monopoly. The need for

2. VALENCE: The New Biology

international agreements and supervision can readily be understood if we consider the likely American response to the successful asexual reproduction of 10,000 Mao Tse-tungs.

To repeat, the basic short-term need is caution. Practically, this means that we should shift the burden of proof to the *proponents* of a new biomedical technology. Concepts of "risk" and "cost" need to be broadened to include some of the social and ethical consequences discussed earlier. The probable or possible harmful effects of the widespread use of a new technique should be anticipated and introduced as "costs" to be weighed in deciding about the *first* use. The regulatory institutions should be encouraged to exercise restraint and to formulate the grounds for saying "no." We must all get used to the idea that biomedical technology makes possible many things we should never do.

But caution is not enough. Nor are clever institutional arrangements. Institutions can be little better than the people who make them work. However worthy our intentions, we are deficient in understanding. In the *long* run, our hope can only lie in education: in a public educated about the meanings and limits of science and enlightened in its use of technology; in scientists better educated to understand the relationships between science and technology on the one hand, and ethics and politics on the other; in human beings who are as wise in the latter as they are clever in the former.

---

1.   R. G. Edwards, B. D. Bavister, P. C. Steptoe, *Nature* **221,** 632 (1969).

2.   R. G. Edwards, P. C. Steptoe, J. M. Purdy, *ibid.* **227,** 1307 (1970).

3.   H. J. Muller, *Science* **134,** 643 (1961).

4.   J. M. R. Delgado, *Physical Control of the Mind: Toward a Psychocivilized Society* (Harper & Row, New York, 1969).

5.   F. Bacon, *The Advancement of Learning, Book I,* H. G. Dick, Ed. (Random House, New York, 1955), p. 193.

6.   C. S. Lewis, *The Abolition of Man* (Macmillan, New York, 1965), pp. 69–71.

7.   D. D. Rutstein, *Daedalus* (Spring 1969), p. 523.

8.   E. J. Cassell, *Commentary* (June 1969), p. 73.

9.   B. Glass, *Science* **171,** 23 (1971).

10.   It is, of course, a long-debated question as to whether the fall of Adam and Eve ought to be considered "catastrophic," or more precisely, whether the Hebrew tradition considered it so. I do not mean here to be taking sides in this quarrel by my use of the term "catastrophic," and, in fact, tend to line up on the negative side of the questions, as put above. Curiously, as Aldous Huxley's *Brave New World* [(Harper & Row, New York, 1969)] suggests, the implicit goal of the biomedical technology could well be said to be the reversal of the Fall and a return of man to the hedonic and immortal existence of the Garden of Eden. Yet I can point to at least two problems. First, the new Garden of Eden will probably have no gardens; the received, splendid world of nature will be buried beneath asphalt, concrete, and

35

II. The Emergence of a Biomedical Technology

other human fabrications, a transformation that is already far along. (Recall that in *Brave New World* elaborate consumption-oriented, mechanical amusement parks—featuring, for example, centrifugal bumble-puppy—had supplanted wilderness and even ordinary gardens.) Second, the new inhabitant of the new "Garden" will have to be a creature for whom we have no precedent, a creature as difficult to imagine as to bring into existence. He will have to be simultaneously an innocent like Adam and a technological wizard who keeps the "Garden" running. (I am indebted to Dean Robert Goldwin, St. John's College, for this last insight.)

11. Some scientists naively believe that an engineered increase in human intelligence will steer us in the right direction. Surely we have learned by now that intelligence, whatever it is and however measured, is not synonymous with wisdom and that, if harnessed to the wrong ends, it can cleverly perpetrate great folly and evil. Given the activities in which many, if not most, of our best minds are now engaged, we should not simply rejoice in the prospect of enhancing IQ. On what would this increased intelligence operate? At best, the programming of further increases in IQ. It would design and operate techniques for prolonging life, for engineering reproduction, for delivering gratifications. With no gain in wisdom, our gain in intelligence can only enhance the rate of our dehumanization.

12. The philosopher Hans Jonas has made the identical point: "Thus the slow-working accidents of nature, which by the very patience of their small increments, large numbers, and gradual decisions, may well cease to be 'accident' in outcome, are to be replaced by the fast-working accidents of man's hasty and biased decisions, not exposed to the long test of the ages. His uncertain ideas are to set the goals of generations, with a certainty borrowed from the presumptive certainty of the means. The latter presumption is doubtful enough, but this doubtfulness becomes secondary to the prime question that arises when man indeed undertakes to 'make himself': in what image of his own devising shall he do so, even granted that he can be sure of the means? In fact, of course, he can be sure of neither, not of the end, nor of the means, once he enters the realm where he plays with the roots of life. Of one thing only can he be sure: of his power to move the foundations and to cause incalculable and irreversible consequences. Never was so much power coupled with so little guidance for its use." [*J. Cent. Conf. Amer. Rabbis* (January 1968), p. 27.] These remarks demonstrate that, contrary to popular belief, we are not even on the right road toward a rational understanding of and rational control over human nature and human life. It is indeed the height of irrationality triumphantly to pursue rationalized technique, while at the same time insisting that questions of ends, values, and purposes lie beyond rational discourse.

13. It is encouraging to note that these questions are seriously being raised in other quarters —for example, by persons concerned with the decay of cities or the pollution of nature. There is a growing dissatisfaction with ethical nihilism. In fact, its tenets are unwittingly abandoned, by even its staunchest adherents, in any discussion of "what to do." For example, in the biomedical area, everyone, including the most unreconstructed and technocratic reductionist finds himself speaking about the use of powers for "human betterment." He has wandered unawares onto ethical ground. One cannot speak of "human betterment" without considering what is meant by *the human* and by the related notion of *the good for man*. These questions can be avoided only by asserting that practical matters reduce to tastes and power, and by confessing that the use of the phrase "human betterment" is a deception to cloak one's own will to power. In other words, these questions can be avoided only by ceasing to discuss.

14. Consider, for example the widespread acceptance, in the legal systems of very different societies and cultures, of the principle and the practice of third-party adjudication of disputes. And consider why, although many societies have practiced slavery, no slave-holder has preferred his own enslavement to his own freedom. It would seem that some notions of justice and freedom, as well as right and truthfulness are constitutive for any society, and that a concern for these values may be a fundamental characteristic of "human nature."

2. VALENCE: The New Biology

15.   Scientists may, of course, continue to believe in righteousness or justice or truth, but these beliefs are not grounded in their "scientific knowledge" of man. They rest instead upon the receding wisdom of an earlier age.

16.   This belief, silently shared by many contemporary biologists, has recently been given the following clear expression: "One of the acid tests of understanding an object is the ability to put it together from its component parts. Ultimately, molecular biologists will attempt to subject their understanding of all structure and function to this sort of test by trying to synthesize a cell. It is of some interest to see how close we are to this goal." [P. Handler, Ed., *Biology and the Future of Man* (Oxford Univ. Press, New York, 1970), p. 55.]

17.   When an earlier version of this article was presented publicly, it was criticized by one questioner as being "antiscientific." He suggested that my remarks "were the kind that gave science a bad name." He went on to argue that, far from being the enemy of morality, the pursuit of truth was itself a highly moral activity, perhaps the highest. The relation of science and morals is a long and difficult question with an illustrious history, and it deserves a more extensive discussion than space permits. However, because some readers may share the questioner's response, I offer a brief reply. First, on the matter of reputation, we should recall that the pursuit of truth may be in tension with keeping a good name (witness Oedipus, Socrates, Galileo, Spinoza, Solzhenitsyn). For most of human history, the pursuit of truth (including "science") was not a reputable activity among the many, and was, in fact, highly suspect. Even today, it is doubtful whether more than a few appreciate knowledge as an end in itself. Science has acquired a "good name" in recent times largely because of its technological fruit; it is therefore to be expected that a disenchantment with technology will reflect badly upon science. Second, my own attack has not been directed against science, but against the use of *some* technologies and, even more, against the unexamined belief—indeed, I would say superstition—that all biomedical technology is an unmixed blessing. I share the questioner's belief that the pursuit of truth is a highly moral activity. In fact, I am inviting him and others to join in a pursuit of the truth about whether all these new technologies are really good for us. This is a question that merits and is susceptible of serious intellectual inquiry. Finally, we must ask whether what we call "science" has a monopoly on the pursuit of truth. What is "truth"? What is knowable, and what does it mean to know? Surely, these are also questions that can be examined. Unless we do so, we shall remain ignorant about what "science" is and about what it discovers. Yet "science"—that is, modern natural science—cannot begin to answer them; they are philosophical questions, the very ones I am trying to raise at this point in the text.

3.
VISION:
A Visit to Cleveland General
SYDNEY VAN SCYOC

A personality-adjustment problem not currently addressed by personality theorists is the subject of Sydney Van Scyoc's "A Visit to Cleveland General."

The credibility gap may be at its widest in hospitals. Whether they're telling you "Now, this won't hurt" or "There there, you'll be all right in just a few days," can you believe it? Here is a slightly nightmarish view of a hospital of the future—and like most nightmares, it's more believable than we'd like it to be.

His eyes carefully averted, Albin Johns swiped the depilatory off his jaws and splashed his face with water. He slapped his shirt shut. Then, forgetting, he glanced at the face in his mirror. It was a dark face, assertively intelligent, youthfully stern.

He blinked away, shuddering. His hand, lurching, cornered the jug of pink capsules, shoved one into his mouth. He gulped, as he did every morning.

He frowned at the jug's label. ONE DAILY. FOR MEMORY.

It annoyed him that he couldn't remember why he swallowed that daily capsule. It seemed a purely automatic action of hand and mouth, a muscular act beyond voluntary control. True, some mornings the reason loomed momentarily as near as that disturbing face in his mirror. But it always slipped away.

Usually right after he swallowed the memory capsule.

The timespot chimed the hour. Johns's saucer thumped softly at the parlor window, announcing its arrival from the parking tower. Briskly,

From *Galaxy*, 1968. Reprinted by permission of the author.

3. VISION: A Visit to Cleveland General

Johns strapped the speech recorder to his wrist, checking to be absolutely certain he had inserted a fresh capsule the night before.

It was a lucky break, just three months out of news school, to be sent to Cleveland General Hospital in Tac Turber's stead. Turber had done the local medical column for seventeen years, until his recent illness. No one at the *News Tribune* knew how long Turber might remain in Florida on recuperation leave—perhaps weeks; perhaps months. If Johns handled Turber's hospital feature well, he might be given other of Turber's regular assignments, until Turber returned.

Johns smoothed his hair nervously, resisting the impulse to check himself in the mirror. The saucer thumped again. Johns approached the parlor, drew a deep breath, and hoped.

In vain. "Albin, I was afraid you had overslept," his mother trilled from Washington state. She glowed upon his westerly wall, coffee cup in hand. "I was about to cast myself into the bedroom to check."

Limited though she was to a single plane, his mother nevertheless tripped the circuit that turned him defensive. "I had to order a clean shirt," he mumbled, glancing hopelessly at the window, so near, so far.

Her image sharpened. "Why didn't you order one last night? Before you slept?" Her face was much like the one he had confronted in his mirror, dark, assertively intelligent, promising myriad opinions aggressively articulated.

"I—I took care of everything else then. I refilled my recorder and ordered fresh shoes. Everything else." He edged toward the window and the waiting saucer.

She eyed him acutely. "I simply don't comprehend, Albin. Before the accident you would *never* have forgotten to order a fresh shirt. That's the sort of thing I could have expected of poor Deon. But you were always *meticulous*, Albin. I used to say, 'Albin is *my* son—Deon is his father's.' "

"I take a memory capsule every morning, Mother." Johns had reached the window. He tapped the pane. It slid. The saucer extended its entry hatch into the parlor.

"You take a memory capsule every morning, yet you're about to step out the window without even swallowing breakfast," she said bitingly. "You're more like Deon every day, Albin. Giving up your law studies for news school. Forgetting to order fresh shirts, going out without breakfast and then bolting a burger at some drop-in. Sometimes I think you're trying to *be* your brother." She leaned into the camera menacingly. "*Are* you trying to make it up to Deon for dying in that hideous crash? By taking up all his habits, his interests?" Her eyes narrowed. "Well, are you?"

"I—no, of course not." Johns backed across the room to the serving counter. Breakfast waited, seven green pills, two violet capsules, a wafer. Unfortunately his hand shook. Pills spilled across the carpet.

"No, *no!* Don't crawl around in your fresh clothes. Dial fresh pills, Albin," his mother shrieked from the state of Washington.

39

II. The Emergence of a Biomedical Technology

Abashed, Johns jumped up and dialed.

"I'm doing everything a mother can," his mother moaned. "I supervise your breakfast every morning. I see that at least you go out the window with nourishment in your stomach." Her features enlarged ominously. "Albin, do you want me to come there? Do you need your mother?"

Johns choked. "N-n-*no!*"

His mother's eyebrows crashed into her hairline. Her coffee cup clattered. "Well! Take a tranquilizer, Albin. We'll speak again this evening." With an angry flash, she ended transmission.

Albin Johns breathed again. He jabbed a tranquilizer from the serving counter and gulped. After a moment, he punched aspirin as well. For some reason, he had a headache.

Fortified, he stepped to the window.

"Albin, take care," his mother pleaded unexpectedly from the wall. "You know how I fret."

Sighing, he faced her. "Yes, Mother."

"You're all I have, Albin. Promise."

Meekly he promised. Then he scrambled into the waiting saucer.

He hung beside the building, composing himself. His mother harbored the notion that he had been injured in the saucer crash that had killed his elder brother, Deon, a year ago. It was useless explaining, repeatedly, that if he had been involved, he would have memory of the accident, however fragmentary.

Unfortunately, he couldn't remember his brother Deon either.

That, he admitted, disturbed him. He was virtually certain Deon had not been a figment of his mother's imagination. His father spoke of Deon too, insistently. They had even taken down the family album, on Albin's last visit home.

Albin had refused to examine his dead brother's photo. Now he made excuses not to visit Washington. Better to deal with his mother two-dimensionally.

Composed, he took the controls. The saucer scudded over the city. Morning smacked blue against the dome.

Today he began his career in earnest, after years of anticipation. He had edited his high school paper for three years. Made top of the class at news school. He'd played newsman from the time he'd learned to write.

He smiled, remembering. As a boy, he'd taken grim pleasure in writing up his mother's monologues, word for word. ". . . *and* you forgot to clean your nails again." ". . . just like your father. You walked right out without leaving a message with the computer. I fretted for hours." "Your brother, Albin, would never—"

He halted the sound track. Backed it. Replayed. ". . . just like your father . . ." "Your brother, Albin . . ."

3. VISION: A Visit to Cleveland General

The saucer wavered, bucked under his suddenly spastic grip. A tight band crushed his chest. Sweat popped from his forehead.

Breathing deeply, he eased his grip on the saucer's controls. Systematically, he loosened the panic-knotted muscles of his body.

He had suffered occasional moments of panic for months. Since the time he had supposedly been injured in the accident. With his brother. Deon.

He gritted his teeth, ran the sequence through again. Accident. Brother: Deon.

He relaxed, smiling, almost proud. His mother was right. His brother's —Deon's—death had been a disorganizing shock. Only time and patience could effect recovery.

He peered over the saucer rim. Cleveland General Hospital jumbled glassy black below. Johns lowered the saucer to control altitude. The autoguide beamed by the hospital's parking system locked the manual controls. The saucer sank and swooped into the parking tower.

The saucer split. Johns glanced around the tower, feeling a return of tension. The saucer snapped shut behind him. Johns set his feet to the guide arrows that glowed across the pavement.

The arrows led him to a disk shaft. The disk hovered. Johns boarded. It settled swiftly. Johns stepped onto a second arrowed pavement.

The walls converged. Johns faced a dark, misty corridor. He hesitated, frowning back at the guide arrows. They unmistakably indicated the foggy darkness as his route into the hospital.

A streamer of pastel fog wafted from the tunnel, touched Johns's nostrils. His tensed muscles relaxed. He stepped into the soft, damp darkness.

The floor shuddered, carrying him forward. The walls glowed darkly, richly. The ceiling undulated. A low growling rumble throbbed through the tunnel, the grumble of distant machinery, monstrous but benign. Rainbowed fog sank lightly and refreshingly into Johns's lungs.

When the tunnel floor deposited Johns in the lobby, he was pleasantly relaxed, light of limb. A crisp elderly guard manned the computer console. Johns fumbled for press card and visitor's permit.

The guard fed both to the console. "*News Tribune*, heh? Your first visit to Cleveland General?"

Johns nodded, glancing uneasily around the vaulted lobby. It was disturbingly familiar, as if he had seen it before, from a different angle, with the sun slanting low through the rainbow panes.

The guard chuckled. "Well, you've seen our little establishment often enough on vidi. Makes you feel almost like you've been here in person."

Johns frowned. He didn't recall ever catching a vidi on Cleveland General. But there were, after all, any number of things he didn't remember. Despite his daily capsule.

The guard launched him with a friendly thump. "The blue walkstrip will deliver you right to Dr. Jacobs's office. Write us up good!"

41

II. The Emergence of a Biomedical Technology

The blue strip slid across the lobby and trundled into another dark, mumbling tunnel. Johns inhaled hopefully. His entire body relaxed. His head dropped. His knees sagged. Consciousness faded.

Then he stood blinking in a sunlit office. The receptionist, smiling, said, "Dr. Jacobs will see you immediately."

Dr. Jacobs was an erect old whippet with piercing pale eyes. He gripped Johns's hand coldly, fixed Johns with a blue-white gaze. "We're sorry to hear of Mr. Turber's illness. I don't suppose you know the exact nature of that illness, Mr. Johns."

"No one seems to know exactly," Johns admitted.

Dr. Jacobs nodded tersely. "And I don't suppose you have ever been with us as a patient, Mr. Johns?"

Johns was oddly disturbed by the question. "I—I'm—certain I haven't."

Dr. Jacobs sighed, scowling. "Well, I suppose you've done your homework, at least. Reviewed Turber's columns of the past year."

Johns nodded. The columns were freshly in mind, rich with detail, crammed with statistic, but eminently readable.

"Then you know that through computer diagnostics and the automated nursing system, we've overcome the human factor that flawed medical care for centuries. We've achieved perfection in physical care.

"But over the years we've learned the importance of non-medical factors. Even the best in purely physical care is not enough for the anxious patient, the depressed patient, the patient harried by financial or personal worries. And so all major modern hospitals maintain teams of trained social workers to lend moral and practical support to the patient. This facilitates an optimum rate of recovery. The patient returns to the community fit to function as a fully adjusted, contributing member of society."

Dr. Jacobs's pale eyes glittered fanatically. "Our senior social worker has consented to let you accompany her on her rounds today. Miss Kling remembers vividly the day when doctors maintained private practices, saw dozens of outpatients daily and made all their diagnoses without computer aid." Dr. Jacobs speared Johns with a stern gaze. "You will be free to observe Miss Kling's working method, to draw upon her reminiscences of days past and to form your own conclusions about medical progress during the past quarter century."

"I'm very grateful," Johns faltered.

Jacobs swallowed, jabbed a desktop button. The far wall of the office slid. "Please step into the decontamination lock. Leave your garments and personal possessions on the shelf. Press the white button to release the fog. Then pull on the sterile coverall. Miss Kling will meet you in the outside corridor."

Johns hesitated. "I'd like to keep my recorder, sir."

"Mr. Johns, we cannot allow personal effects in the wards. There is constant danger of contamination." Jacobs glittered down his long, bleak nose. "Mr. Turber was well able to compose his reports from memory."

Reddening, Johns stumbled into the lock. The wall slid. Johns unstrapped his recorder with reluctant fingers, remembering the facility with which Turber had used names and dates, medical terms, statistics.

Sighing, he stepped out of his clothing.

Absentmindedly, he glanced down at his torso. His fingertips trembled unbelievingly over the sharp red scars that split his abdomen. He stared, uncomprehending. He shut his eyes, opened them again.

The scars remained.

Johns's hand jerked upward, as if reaching reflexively for the jug of pink capsules on his bathroom shelf.

Instead he encountered a white pushbutton. He jabbed it, desperately. A rainbow cloud puffed into the chamber. He inhaled heavily.

Gratefully, he felt the familiar relief of tension. He gulped the cloud. He sagged, unconscious.

Coolly the world returned. The ceiling glowed violetly, pinkly, greenly.

Gravelly laughter jarred into Johns's pastel coma. "You sucked that happy cloud so hard I had to wrestle you into your coverall myself."

Flushing, Johns sat up. "Miss Kling?"

She was anybody's tough old granny, a beefy, redfaced woman with hair of steel, a strong right arm and a ribald twinkle in her eye. "That's me. I must say you've healed up handsome, young Johns."

He stared at her blankly.

"Don't you remember me? That's how it goes—forget us the minute you leave us." She laughed raucously. "Well, let's go. I've got a workload that would kill an ox."

Disoriented, he followed her down a long, glowing corridor set at intervals with numbered steel doors.

"We'll do Ward 17 first." She keyed open a steel door.

Johns's legs carried him through the door, then turned to stone. His jaw froze, painfully. Sweat beaded over his suddenly marbleized face.

The ward was an expanse of black glass floor set with a maze of freestanding cubicles. Each cubicle was fully glassed, brilliantly lit, permitting full view of its interior. Music streamed through the ward, but beneath lay the rumble and grumble of unseen machinery. Small, gleaming robots twinkled over the glassy floor.

Johns groaned, unable to move.

Miss Kling boomed with laughter. She flourished an aerosol can that had been holstered at her belt. A minty cloud mantled them. "Gulp hard, but don't pass out again."

Blessedly, Johns's body became flesh again. The rock in his chest dissolved. He blinked away the last brittle web of panic.

"Just a touch of trauma. Happens to a lot of our patients when they come back. You start developing a tolerance for your amnesiac after a few months. We'll have to get your dosage adjusted."

Johns smiled condescendingly. He had never, of course, been hospitalized in his life. And the capsules he took were to improve his memory, not impede it. But he felt too blissfully at peace to argue.

"First stop: Maternity. Don't worry—everybody's decent." Chortling ribaldly, she piloted him across the glassy floor.

Johns surveyed the cubic maze loftily. Obviously a superior system. Each specimen housed in its own sterile environment.

Mothers napped, plucked eyebrows, stared at vidi. Strips of sensor tape, at wrists and temples, transmitted patient data to the central monitor system. Mounted on each cubicle was a manual control panel.

Miss Kling halted before a glowing cubicle, cocked her head shrewdly at the unmaternal little figure within. "Good morning, Edna," she boomed.

The girl splashed against the glass, an overripe little plum with flaming hair and feral black eyes. "You! Where's my kid? Three days you've told me you'd get him up here next day for sure. Ten days, and I haven't seen him yet. First that campaign to get me to sign adoption papers. Ha! Then you're keeping him till I'm strong enough to hold him—you say. Now for three days this yack about him being deformed."

Miss Kling chuckled blandly. "Now you know we've been waiting to see if he could survive, Edna. We wanted to spare you seeing the little thing if he couldn't live."

"Look, granny, I told you—I wasn't so dopey I didn't see the kid down in delivery. I got a good look. Nine pounds plus and everything where it belongs. Lungs like a pair of bellows. A natural born fullback. The doctor said so himself. I—"

Miss Kling rasped prevailingly, "Now, Edna, be calm. I'll have Dr. Dover explain the cause of death to you in person. I want you to consider it God's mercy—"

"Death!" the girl shrilled.

"—the little fellow didn't live to suffer. A single girl couldn't hope to care for such a terribly handicapped child all by herself. The expenses alone . . ."

Miss Kling's stubby fingers crawled over the control panel. Rainbow fog seeped into the cubicle.

The girl's face discolored with rage. "I sure don't need any *man* to pay my way! I'm nineteen years old! I make good dollars dancing the nudie circuit. I come and go as I please. It's nothing to me Gordy ran out with that freak Gandi before I got him down to Marriage Hall."

Miss Kling smiled. "Dear, I wouldn't presume to judge your morals. I'm just Kling, your old granny in your time of trouble."

The girl's tirade ended abruptly. She blinked stupidly and sank to her knees in the swirling rainbow fog. "What did you say? About my baby?"

"Now, you saw the poor little fellow yourself, Edna. Poor guy."

3. VISION: A Visit to Cleveland General

Edna sobbed thickly. "Poor little kid. And it's all Gordy's fault! He's the one made our baby deformed. He's the one ran off—"

"Now, Edna, one of our pretty little nurse machines will come," Miss Kling cooed. "You're going to have an injection. It's just a little something we give all our unwed mothers. It won't hurt at all, and you won't have to worry about babies for years and years."

"Won't have to worry?" Edna murmured.

"No more about babies. Not for five years. Why, by then you might be married. You might even *want* another baby in five years."

Edna smiled softly, curled up on the floor. Her hair piled scarlet over her face.

Johns stared at her, peacefully asleep on the glassy floor, awash in pastel fog. Then he noticed Miss Kling had trundled away. He hurried after her. "I've never heard of that particular law, Miss Kling."

"What law?"

"That you sterilize unmarried mothers for five years."

"Who said there was a law?" She pulled an aerosol from her belt. "Air's getting stale." She clouded the air generously.

Johns frowned. "I wouldn't expect any individual to have power to make that kind of decision for another individual. I mean—" He stopped, blinking through the pale cloud in confusion.

Her voice poured over him, suggestively. "My girls are here to recuperate, young Johns. I don't want them worrying over laws, or making big decisions all by themselves. If a girl has learned her lesson, why, I forget all about having her injected. But if I see she's going to land herself here again, get herself taken advantage of and then run out on, I give her the best protection we've got. That's what I'm here for, young Johns—to see my patients get what they need. Without having to fret themselves."

The cloud had slipped into Johns's lungs sweetly. Johns smiled. Then he had to wipe a tear from his eye. "That's—that's—" He couldn't express his feelings. To think that in this vast, impersonal institution, doughty Miss Kling pitched right in and fought for her patients!

"Glad you understand." Miss Kling holstered the aerosol. She halted before a cubicle containing a slight, pale girl in her twenties. "Good morning, Trenda. I'm Mabel Kling, your social caller. How do you feel?"

The girl looked up listlessly. "I'm all right, thank you." She touched a tear off her cheek.

Miss Kling beamed. "The nurse will bring your brand new son in just a moment. Don't you want to pretty up a little, for your first visit?"

"My—son?" the girl said gropingly.

Miss Kling's fingers crawled over the control panel. The cubicle began to fog. Miss Kling chuckled reassuringly. "He's a real football player. Scaled nearly ten pounds this morning—you'd swear he was a couple of weeks old already. Lungs like a pair of bellows. And he has a mop of red hair. Just like your husband."

II. The Emergence of a Biomedical Technology

The girl sat up, confused. "But the baby wasn't even due for another three months. They gave me shots, but the pains wouldn't stop and—"

Miss Kling chuckled. "Happens all the time. We get girls having babies months and months early. Sometimes Old Momma Nature's adding machine doesn't use the same math the rest of us do."

The girl struggled to believe. "You mean the baby's really all right? He wasn't born too early?"

"You can see for yourself in a couple of minutes. You feel up to hefting a ten-pounder?"

"Oh, yes!" The cubicle was densely fogged. The girl's face flushed with excitement. "Why I—I even thought I heard someone say it was a girl!"

They left her excitedly dabbing her lips with color, lost in lavender fog. Johns sobbed brokenly, overwhelmed.

"Now there's a case to make my job worthwhile," Miss Kling rumbled. "That sweet little girl lying there heartbroken, and I fixed everything up smart. By the time she gets the baby home, she won't even remember her sad hours."

Miss Kling launched herself upon another patient, but Johns was too choked with emotion to care.

Then Miss Kling checked her list and nodded with satisfaction. "That's Maternity. Time for a quick tour of Surgery." She chuckled. "Tac Turber was a real surgery fan—had to run him through butcher alley every time he came out."

Johns felt his mouth dry ominously.

"Coming?" she chuckled.

He followed her to and through the glowing corridor, each step shakier than the last. Finally he blurted, "I read someplace that they—used to take organs from one person and—transplant them in another. Kidneys and hearts and spleens. I even read they transplanted brains—sometimes."

Miss Kling keyed the door into Surgery. She eyed him narrowly. "Where did you read all that?"

"I d-don't remember. Not in Tac Turber's columns." Hopefully he ventured, "I guess they don't do much of that any more . . . ?"

Miss Kling chuckled. "Now, just think. If you had one man's heart, another man's liver, and maybe a lobe of somebody else's brain, you'd feel mighty confused, wouldn't you?"

"I—yes!" The word came with unexpected force.

"You can't go out and pull your weight if you aren't even sure who you are. Can you?"

"I—no. No."

"Now, do you think our fine doctors are going to devote themselves to turning out patchwork people? Sending people out into the world without an identity to call their own? Do you think old Granny Kling would let any patient of hers go wandering around without a name?"

46

3. VISION: A Visit to Cleveland General

"N-no. Of course not." He frowned, trying to follow her argument.

"Well, then?" Deftly she steered him into Surgery.

The floor stretched vast and white. The surgical cubicles were spacious, brilliantly lit, jammed with complex machinery. White clad figures huddled. Nurse machines scuttered. Auto-stretchers bore unconscious passengers silently.

"In the old days, the average doctor spent so much time on routine, he hardly had time for a good day's surgery. Now the mech-clinics take care of the coughs and sniffles, the nurse machines bandage the cuts and the doctors can get down to business."

"I see," Johns said, dimly, swaying. Blood crashed in his ears. His hands twitched. Unable to resist, he tilted his head to stare at the ceiling. The patterned white on white held dreadful, compelling familiarity.

"I've never been here before," he croaked. He couldn't bring his head down. "I've never been in this hospital before. I've never seen this ceiling before. I've—"

Miss Kling jammed an inhaler into his nose. He struggled, then inhaled. After a moment his head fell. He felt suddenly sluggish, torpid. "I've never been here before," he muttered.

"Of course you haven't," Miss Kling said sharply. "You don't have any scars. Do you?"

He frowned, trying to remember. "I—"

"Well, if you don't have scars, you haven't been in surgery. Have you?"

"I—no, of course not," he said with relief. Then he said, querulously, "My head hurts."

She touched the back of his head. "Here? Where they put the stainless plate in?"

He nodded. His head pounded with agony.

"Keep the inhaler in place. I'll get Little Bayer."

She returned with a spidery little machine. It gripped his arm, injected him briskly and spidered away.

The pain eased. Miss Kling removed the inhaler and puffed him thoroughly with aerosol. He inhaled, smiled foolishly, gratefully.

Miss Kling beamed upon him. "Well now, I bet you're tired with all that walking. How did you enjoy your tour of Surgery?"

"Very interesting," Johns mumbled foolishly. It seemed somewhat dim. In fact, he didn't remember touring Surgery at all.

"Ummm hmmm," she said shrewdly. "Then we'll scoot on down the hall to the party."

He followed her into the long, glowing corridor, smiling agreeably. The party. He always enjoyed parties.

Too bad he couldn't remember about this one.

He was a little surprised when she keyed the door marked TERMINAL WARD.

"All our terminal patients have a little party before they go. But it's

47

seldom they have dear ones to spend their last minutes with. Tac Turber's going to be mighty pleased."

Johns felt mildly surprised. "Mr. Turber hardly knows me."

She chortled. "You'll be carrying on his hospital column, won't you? That makes you almost a son."

He drifted through the ward in her wake. Patients beamed rosily from their glassed cases. Miss Kling waved and yoo-hooed.

Finally Johns said, disbelievingly, "These people aren't all going to die, are they?"

"That's what they're here for," she said cheerfully.

He frowned around him, at the healthy, smiling faces.

"I nursed my own mother through her last illness," Miss Kling rasped. "Seventeen months I stood by, night and day. Couldn't afford a nursing machine, and I wouldn't send her to a home."

He murmured sympathetically.

"Knew as soon as the diagnosis was made she'd never recover. But in those days there wasn't anything to do but stand by and watch her waste off.

"I always remember that when my rounds bring me here. I'm proud my patients don't have to suffer through that. They go out quick and clean, with steak and whiskey on the house. And they know if there's any little piece that can be salvaged, why, our boys in butcher alley will find it. The spirit may die, young Johns—but the tissue lives on!"

They rounded a corner and confronted Tac Turber, glassed. Miss Kling rapped the glass, slid the entry panel.

Tac Turber bounced from the bed, a big man, burly in his hospital gown. "Well, well! Hear you got a promotion, Johns!" He pumped Johns's hand heartily.

Johns stammered, "Editor Downs is letting me handle your column until —until you get back."

Turber grinned. "Then it's yours for life, kid." He whacked Johns on the back. His eyes twinkled. "I guess everyone's heard I won't be back?"

"We heard you were going to Florida to recuperate from—whatever it is."

"Ah, the stories that make the rounds," Turber laughed. He sobered. "No, Johns, I'm journeying on to another life. A different life, but one certainly as useful as the one I've already led. My only regret is that I won't be able to do one last column. I've always wanted to write up the work they do down there in Surgery." He frowned. "But somehow it always slips my mind, once I'm back outside."

Miss Kling said, "You can't crowd everything in."

Turber shook his head impatiently. "No, that's not it." He turned back to Johns. "There's so much excitement, Johns, so much to see. Sometimes when I get back to the saucer, I can hardly remember writing the report I'm holding in my hand." He frowned thoughtfully. "I guess I stop to use

48

3. VISION: A Visit to Cleveland General

one of the machines in the director's office. But afterward . . ." He shook his head, bemused.

Miss Kling stepped out to the control panel. Stepping back, she closed the entry panel. Rainbow fog drifted lazily up from the floor.

Turber sniffed. His frown faded. He grinned. "Well, it's been a good beat, Johns. You don't remember the old days, the old hospitals, the fear and uncertainty the human animal had to endure. And only the poor or the disturbed had someone like Miss Kling to help them out. Everyone else had to muddle through as well as he could."

The entry glass slid. A robotable wheeled in, bearing a feast.

Turber's eyes lit. "Looks like they catered for you too, Johns." He splashed Scotch into both glasses, then frowned. "They forgot you, Miss Kling."

Miss Kling scowled over the table. Her face sagged. "They never think to send a whiskey glass for me. I go to every party on the ward, but there's never a glass for me."

Turber lifted a panel and punched the table's controls. Utensils, napkins and whiskey glasses clattered out. Beaming, Turber poured into a dozen glasses. He lifted two. "A toast to immortality!"

"A toast to your immortal liver and lights! Haw!" Miss Kling roared, swaying. "You know something, boys? I was supposed to plug in fresh nose filters half an hour ago. And I forgot. Haw! I forgot my fresh filters —now I'm going to forget everything!"

Johns laughed to be polite. Then he laughed some more. Soon he was bellowing and snorting in the swirling pale fog, gulping the whiskey as fast as Turber poured.

Then the bottle was empty. The steaks lay congealed, untouched. There was a squeak of wheels, and an autostretcher rolled into the cubicle.

"My car!" Turber hopped aboard. He threw himself upon his back, roaring with delight. "Home, James!"

The stretcher molded itself around him. A mask fell heavily over his face. Turber flailed, then lay limp. The stretcher squeaked away.

Miss Kling regarded the congealed feast regretfully. "Young Johns, I think I've forgotten something. But I can't remember what."

Johns said solemnly, "They're going to cut old Tac up and use his parts, aren't they?"

"Haw! I'll never tell!" Miss Kling frowned, regarding him with bleary thoughtfulness. "But I do remember a boy. No, two boys. Brothers. A smart-looking dark kid. Just like you, in fact. And a big handsome redhead, a year or two older. Crashed their saucer down the skylane a piece. The dark one got the back of his skull smashed, and the redhead got it in the belly." She scratched her chin thoughtfully. "But I guess that's about all I remember."

Johns nodded owlishly. "I don't even remember that much. I forget it every morning at eight."

II. The Emergence of a Biomedical Technology

She nodded. Then light came to her eyes. "Haw!" She drew a small green can from her belt. "My remembering spray. I remember that much! If I whiff the wrong color air, I just spray myself green and everything comes back." She sprayed.

Johns sniffed. It was very fresh, very clean, the green. He inhaled deeply.

"There. Clears all the synapses. Or something like that." Miss Kling's facial contours firmed with returning character.

It was as if the green spray had penetrated forgotten chambers of his mind, clearing them of obstruction. "I remember *now*," he said, softly. "I remember—"

He was low over the countryside at the controls of his old saucer. A spring day. His brother perched nervously on the passenger's seat.

His brother—Albin. His dark, meticulous younger brother who had stopped in Ohio on his way east to law school.

He—Deon—grinned reassuringly. The saucer had developed a recurring shimmy a bit to the north. He was taking it low and slow back to the city.

The shimmy hit again. He handled the controls coolly. He was still working when the sudden, terrible shudder came. The gauges flashed peril. Alarms squalled. The controls jerked from his hands.

They were falling. He wrestled the controls, uselessly. He heard his brother's voice. "Deon, can't you—"

Impact. A few minutes of painful half-consciousness. He opened his eyes, saw his brother—Albin—sprawled nearby, a metal splinter imbedded in his abdomen, the back of his head smashed, the quick, meticulous brain destroyed.

Later he opened his eyes again, to watch the ambulance ship settle. The medic jabbed him. He drifted away.

"This one took it in the breadbasket," the medic said dimly, beside him.

"This one too. And the back of the head. Think they can combine the pieces?"

Consciousness-remembered faded, momentarily.

But the green mist had suffused the cubicle. Johns's mind remained mercilessly clear, relentlessly unfolding the film of memory. He screamed, hoarsely.

The voice beside him said, disinterestedly, "Oh, they'll patch something together."

Because next he would open shock-blurred eyes upon the ceiling—*that* ceiling, white on white. He would roll his head, see his brother—Albin—face down upon the adjacent stretcher. His own stretcher would detect consciousness, would clamp its mask to him. Then—

He fought as Miss Kling rammed the inhaler home. Then he fell heavily upon the bed Turber had vacated. Miss Kling pulled a mask from her belt and applied it to his face.

"You yourself again?" she rasped after a while.

3. VISION: A Visit to Cleveland General

"I guess so." It seemed an unfair question, since he wasn't absolutely certain just who himself was.

She removed the mask. A small mirror lay on the bedside table. Johns studied the dark, intelligent face that was his, yet wasn't.

"I have a few more calls to make," Miss Kling rumbled thoughtfully. "But I'm going to get you right down to the hypno chamber, before you blow again."

Stumbling, he followed her down the glowing corridor to the door marked by the giant, hypnotic eye.

"You step inside, young Johns. There'll be someone right with you. They'll get your memory pruned back the way it should be—cut that dead wood out and throw it away. And they'll give you something to keep it that way."

He pushed the door obediently.

At the last moment, she squeezed his arm roughly. "You're a good boy, Johns. Both of you." Her lips scraped his cheek.

Numbly, he stepped into the darkened hypno chamber.

Minutes later—or was it hours?—he sat high above the cubic jumble of Cleveland General, at the controls of his saucer. He put the saucer on auto and glanced through the papers in his hand.

Funny. He must have used a machine in the director's office to type the material, while it was still fresh in mind. But he didn't remember doing so. And the stuff wasn't even his usual style. He'd have some rewriting to do.

He glanced over the paragraph about Miss Mabel Kling, senior social worker. He smiled. She sounded like a salty old character. Too bad he hadn't met her in person. But if Tac Turber was still in Florida on recuperation leave next month, perhaps Johns would be back.

He stuffed the papers into the carry-bin, along with the big jug of violet capsules labeled TWO DAILY. FOR MEMORY. Swooping into the clouds, he slid the hatch to feel the cool breeze of altitude on his face. The sun blazed. The skylanes stretched blue and inviting. Even at this altitude he could feel spring easing warmly, greenly over the earth.

A thought flowered in his mind as if it had been planted there. He examined it, smiled, and took it for his own: A great day to be alive!

4.
VALENCE:
We Have
the Awful Knowledge
to Make Exact Copies of Human Beings

WILLARD GAYLIN, M.D.

Few science-fiction writers have approached the subject of cloning. This may be due, in part, to the subject matter being less a matter of fiction than of fact. This is demonstrated in the following article by Willard Gaylin.

In the winter of 1971, before a committee of the House of Representatives, the biologist J. D. Watson expressed dismay that the population had been insufficiently alerted to some of the profound implications of new technologies in genetic research. To the uninitiated, the fact that the statement came from a scientist whose own research is in that field may seem analogous to Dr. Frankenstein chastising the Swiss citizenry for failing to storm his laboratories. But this forceful testimony by the distinguished codiscoverer of DNA has been applauded by a growing group of scientists, social scientists and ethicists who sense that the people are shielded, by the complexity of genetic science, from an understanding of the nature and magnitude of threats it poses to their ways of life, their identities and their very existence as a species. The public attention to Watson's testimony—confirming their thesis—was minimal.

The Frankenstein myth has a viability that transcends its original intentions and a relevance beyond its original time. The image of the frightened scientist, guilt-ridden over his own creations, ceased to be theoretical with the explosion of the first atomic bomb. The revulsion of some of the young, idealistic men who were involved in the actual making of the bomb or in the theoretical work that led to it, had a demonstrable influence in the scientific community from the nineteen-fifties forward. Some biological scientists, now wary and forewarned, are trying to consider the ethical,

4. VALENCE: We Have the Awful Knowledge

social and political implications of their research before its use makes any contemplation merely an expiating exercise. They are even starting to ask whether some research ought to be done at all. With the serious introduction of questions of "ought," ethics has been introduced—and is beginning to shake some of the traditional illusions of a "science above morality," or a "value-free science."

Of course, in 1818 when Mary Shelley first created her story, the scientific domination of society was just beginning. The idea of one human being fabricating another was purely metaphorical. The process was presumed to be impossible, a grotesque exaggeration which cast in the form of a Gothic tale the author's philosophical concern about man's constant reaching for new knowledge and control over the forces of nature (the traditional Greek anxiety about *hubris*). It was, to use her words, "a ghost story," a fantasy to frame a poetic truth.

But the inconceivable has become conceivable, and in the 20th century we find ourselves, indeed, patching human beings together out of parts. We sew on detached arms, and fix shattered hips in place with metal spikes; we patch arterial tubing with plastic; we borrow corneas from the dead, and kidneys from the living or dead; automatic, rechargeable pacemakers placed under the skin regulate the heartbeat, and radio receivers placed in the brain case may shortly control behavior; there are artificial limbs, artificial lungs, artificial kidneys and artificial hearts; and respected scientific researchers—in a real-life parody of art—are publicly accused of stealing secret and mysterious devices from the laboratories of their rivals.

The issue which seemed most worrisome to Watson, and in his opinion called for a campaign to inform the world's citizens so that they might take part in planning possible control measures, was the cloning of human beings. Cloning is the production of genetically identical copies of an individual organism. Just as one can take hundreds of cuttings from a specific plant (indeed, the word *klon* is the Greek word for "twig" or "slip"), each of which can then develop into a mature plant—genetic replicas of the parent—it is now possible to clone animals. The possibility of human cloning seems to produce in nonscientists more titillation than terror or awe—perhaps because it is usually visualized as "a garden of Raquel Welches," blooming by the hundred, genetically identical from nipples to finger nails.

Peas and Carrots

To understand the complications and implications of human cloning it is necessary to review some of the "facts of life" and to approach distressingly close to those bromides, the birds and the bees.

Every species of living organism has the capacity to reproduce its own kind. Indeed, this capability is so fundamental to the concept of being "alive" that it is part of the definition distinguishing animate from inanimate. The mechanism whereby species likeness is transmitted from one

53

generation to the other was discovered by the Austrian priest Gregor Mendel in the 19th century, in some of the most amazing research of modern science. While it is not possible to do justice here to Mendel's genetic principles, it is necessary to recall a few of his conclusions. Working with common garden peas, taking such variables as the color of the flower, the size of the plant, the shape and texture of the seeds, Mendel defined the basic laws of heredity. Unlike previous vague conceptions of offspring as some loose amalgam of parental qualities (Darwin's *panmixis*) in which blood lines fused just as blue and yellow water colors blend to make green, Mendel established that the offspring inherit relatively discrete, independent traits which never mix nor modify each other, but maintain a segregated existence ready to be passed on in pure form to a future generation. He saw the instrument for transfer as a discrete body, later to be called a gene, and recognized that while one gene might dominate another, thus appearing as a particular property, they both existed and were ready to be shipped out to a next generation, again in pure and segregated form. Generally speaking, for example, if you inherit a gene for blue eyes and a gene for brown eyes, you do not usually get the muddy mixture of the two but will have the brown eyes of the dominant gene. Nonetheless, the gene for blue eyes is a part of your genetic potential ready to be handed down intact to your children.

As a corollary of this segregation principle, Mendel observed that the various traits are inherited relatively independently of each other. There may be a separate gene for the size of the pea, the color of the flower and the height of the plant, and in hybridization a variety of gene patterns is possible through chance combinations. It is obvious to even those who are not interested in gardening that this has now become a mechanism for controlling, in plants at least, the development of specialized and desired traits; for example, one could grow a large, fully double, high-centered, heavily scented, disease-resistant, thornless rose of a specific color.

Perhaps the most striking fact about Mendel's laws is that they are valid for *all* living beings. The principles of heredity discovered in the garden pea also apply to the prelate who discovered them. We have since discovered that not only is the principle the same, but that it works in all organisms by means of the identical chemical (DNA) mechanism!

Heredity, however, can be modified by the mechanisms of reproduction, which are not the same in all living beings. Humans, like most advanced life forms, reproduce sexually, which might not seem like the hottest piece of news, but the biological significance of this fact must be understood. Sexual reproduction does not always depend upon copulation. While that happens to be the means available to human beings, the variety of methods evolved in nature might overwhelm the imagination of man, whose sexual fantasy, even, is defined by the specific nature of his own rather limited sexual apparatus. Obviously, plants do not copulate, yet they have a

4.   VALENCE: We Have the Awful Knowledge

variety of mechanisms for self-pollination or, more commonly, cross-pollination (those bees again), both of which are examples of *sexual* reproduction.

Animals also have a wide range of reproductive styles. Sexual reproduction can take place within a single organism—the hermaphrodite forms— but consider the case of the earthworm: Hermaphrodite though it be, producing both sperm and egg, the earthworm, like most higher plants, generally eschews self-fertilization; instead, it seeks out a partner and, in what seems to be a model of sexual courtesy and cooperation, inseminates the other while being inseminated itself. At the other extreme are forms in which fertilization of the egg by the sperm occurs outside of the organism, without contact between the parents.

What is essential to the definition of sexual, as distinguished from asexual, reproduction is that the new generation is formed by a combination of individual genes, half contributed by one parent and half by the other —the variability of the mix in the higher species being so complex as to almost guarantee the uniqueness of each individual. By contrast, in the asexual reproduction of lower forms such as the amoeba, there is a splitting of the organism and the genetic makeup of the two creatures derived from the original is identical, carrying the same undisturbed gene pattern as the "parent" organism.

The genes in human beings are distributed among 46 chromosomes. These 46 chains of inheritance exist in the nucleus of every single body cell of the organism *except* for the sex cells. These cells, ova in women and sperm in men, contain only half the normal quantity—23—and are called haploid. When fertilization occurs, the nuclei of the sperm and the egg fuse, forming an egg cell with a full complement of chromosomes. The fertilized egg proceeds to undergo spontaneous division into two, then four, then eight, finally into the billions of cells that comprise the human body. In the meantime, the cells "differentiate," changing drastically in shape and function, thus forming the various tissues and organs of the body. The genetic code, embodied in that chance mixture of genes from parental chromosomes, guides and contributes in some as yet unknown way to the ultimate form of the adult organism. Sexual reproduction with separate male and female forms guarantees a richness and a variability to the species. This process, combined with Darwinian principles, permits the evolution of individuals with enhanced adaptability and survival values. It is sexual reproduction which mandates continued change—and, therefore, ultimately, improved adaptive capacity.

The process of differentiation represents one of the great unsolved mysteries in biology. How can these cells, which are identical in early divisions with each containing the exact same nucleus (meaning the full potential to form the entire creature) evolve so differently? Lung tissue looks different from bone, skin from blood, muscle from cartilage, because the microscopic cells that make up the tissue have evolved into entirely different forms. The individual cell—ignoring most of its potential—becomes a specialist, and takes the form most suited to its function, which also has become specialized. Some cells will become chemical manufacturing units —reproducing, for example, insulin; some will be the wirelike cells of the nervous system that conduct impulses from other cells that have become pain receptors in the skin, to still others that have become "appreciators" of pain in the brain.

However it may have occurred, once differentiation develops it would seem that there is virtually no way back, short of regeneration itself. If this is true of an animal, it seems equally true of a vegetable.

If man's heredity mechanism was first understood from common garden peas, it seems only equitable that the mechanism's undoing may be from the common garden carrot. Most of us have had the experience of growing vegetables from seeds. The seed is the equivalent of the fertilized egg ready to go, and, since the earth is its natural womb, the planter is merely a mechanical middleman. In a startling set of experiments during the early nineteen-sixties, Prof. F. C. Steward, a cellular physiologist at Cornell University, began agitating individual cells from carrot root in various nutritive media. Almost any mechanical or chemical stimulus can cause an egg or seed cell to begin dividing—heat, light, touching, shaking, or more exposure to a nutrient medium. Steward used differentiated cells, not seeds, yet amazingly these cells began to proliferate. Eventually, with patience and changing media and techniques, Steward was able to force the individual root cells to form clumps and organized masses; what is more, they began to differentiate again into other kinds of cells.

He finally succeeded in carrying one individual cell to the ultimate stage of a full-grown carrot plant—roots, stalk, leaves, flowers, seeds and all. Any cell can, conceivably, be thus forced, once the technology is understood, to grow into a full plant. And what is possible with a vegetable cell is, at least theoretically, just as possible with an animal cell. Animal cells, of course, have already been cultured in the laboratory. Tissue cultures are a basic medical research tool. But tissue cultures are not whole organisms —merely sheets of identical type cells—and the concept of growing a whole organism from one cell asexually in a laboratory would seem impossible. But that Cornell carrot confronts our incredulity. To a scientific mind, the leap from single cell to cloned carrot is greater than the leap from cloned carrot to cloned man.

Man the Creator

Is cloning a man foreseeable in any reasonable time? Years ago, J. B. S. Haldane, the brilliant British biologist and mathematician, confidently assumed the imminence of human cloning and eagerly anticipated its potential uses. Yet, to most people, such a development was inconceivable. One could imagine taking a single sloughed cell from the skin of a person's hand, or even from the hand of a mummy (since cells are neither "alive" nor "dead," but are merely intact or not intact), and seeing it perpetuate itself into a sheet of skin tissue. But could one really visualize the cell forming a finger, let alone a hand, let alone an embryo, let alone another Amenhotep?

There is an entirely different laboratory procedure, known for years, that also offers an alternative to sexual reproduction. When an egg cell is stimulated mechanically or chemically, it will start the division process which leads to the adult form even though it is unfertilized. This virgin birth, or parthenogenesis, occurs in nature, the typical example being the honey bee, whose fertilized eggs produce workers and queens and whose unfertilized eggs develop parthenogenetically into drones or males. Beginning with simple sea forms, laboratory parthenogenesis progressed up the evolutionary ladder to the point that in 1939 a whole rabbit was reported created from an unfertilized egg. However, since in most species the unfertilized sex cell, unlike all of the other cells of the body, is haploid, the individual formed is *not genetically* identical to its mother, or indeed genetically identical to anything.

It remained for Prof. John Gurdon, a biologist at Oxford, to perform the stunning experiment that bridged the technology of parthenogenesis and that of Steward's carrots. In the mid-sixties, Professor Gurdon, working with a frog's eggs, devised a technique, employing radiation, that destroyed the nucleus of an egg cell without damaging the body of the egg. Then, by equally complicated mechanisms, he managed to take the nucleus from an ordinary body cell of the frog (with its full complement of chromosomes) and intrude it into the egg cell. Until now, it was an unproved assumption that the nuclei of all cells, regardless of how different they might be, were identical in their genetic inheritance and contained the entire latent potential for reproduction of a differentiated, multicelled adult. If Gurdon's hypothesis was correct, the newly constructed egg cell was now the equivalent of a fertilized egg and should, on stimulation, be capable of producing an adult form. This is precisely what happened. Some of the cells, on division, formed perfectly normal tadpoles, some of which, indeed, became perfectly normal frogs genetically identical to the frog that donated the nucleus.

John Gurdon used an intestinal cell. He could have used any other body cell, and the cell could have been from a male or a female. The enucleated egg into which the nucleus was injected was also unimportant, genetically speaking; it was merely the environment. The means now exist to produce thousands of genetically identical offspring in the laboratory—at least in frogs.

What seemed like Haldane's immense and overvalued faith in scientific technology now sounds like a rational prediction. In 1969 Robert Sinsheimer, chairman of the division of biology at California Institute of Technology, stated that he assumed it would be possible to clone human organisms within 10 to 20 years. The way has thus been paved for the production of genetic copies of particularly prized individuals, in enormous quantities if desired—for whatever purposes.

There are still major obstacles to the cloning of human beings. Human ova and frog ova are vastly different in some respects—size, for one. Contrary to what one might guess, the frog egg is huge compared to the microscopic human ovum. This is because the frog egg, like a chicken egg, must contain all the nutrient to support the complete development of the embryo; in the human being the egg is implanted in the wall of the maternal uterus soon after fertilization, and a placenta forms which permits direct feeding of the fetus by the mother. The size of human ova, therefore, is incredibly small considering the size of the offspring. H. J. Muller, the great biologist, calculated that all the human eggs from the total population of the earth (then two and one-half billion) would occupy less than a gallon of space. Because of the minute size of human ova, further advances in microsurgery and laboratory techniques will be necessary before cloning becomes possible.

Gurdon has already supplied most of the technology for human cloning. Following the method he used on frogs, the nucleus of an egg cell from any donor would be destroyed. A nucleus (they are all alike) from any convenient cell of the person to be "replicated" would be inserted into the enucleated egg by microsurgical techniques (which have not yet been developed). On placing this new egg cell into an appropriate nutrient medium—a number of recipes have been devised—the "normal" process of division would commence. By the time it has divided into the 8- to 32-cell stage—four to six days—it would be ready for implantation.

A number of simple implantation devices have already been successfully worked out in animals. The developing egg can be injected directly into the uterine wall at the proper menstrual stage of receptivity. Or, more elegantly, it may be injected into the Fallopian tube and permitted to pass normally into the uterine cavity for self-implantation.

Many technical problems still remain, but given sufficient imperative they will be solved. Whether we will actually do human cloning involves other considerations.

Ought Man?

The types of questions that normally arise about any new and dramatic technological procedure fall into the categories of: can man, will man, and ought man. There is a tendency, particularly in antitechnology treatises, to lump the first two together and to consider the third an independent problem. This kind of reasoning usually assures us that what science can do, it will do. The facts are more complicated, as usual, than the polemics. There is much that man can do which he does not do—because he is aware that he ought not. We do not, for example, perform many behavioral

4. VALENCE: We Have the Awful Knowledge

experiments on babies, even though some research would unquestionably contribute to knowledge and the common good. Societal morality has traditionally disapproved of the use of human beings as research animals. Their humanness protects them from certain kinds of destructive research. But even this rule is being violated in some instances. In at least one recent situation, for example, human fetuses that were about to be aborted were used as part of an experiment to determine the potentially harmful effects of ultrasound.

The typical scientist is a product of the culture's ethical system and reacts intuitively to its built-in values—even if he has never thought through its philosophical premises. In general, the culture-value system is one input into the broader psychological forces that drive men toward certain goals and tacitly discourage others.

In pure research, however, a goal may be pursued with no advance knowledge of its utility. Thus may a startling technique become available before we are prepared to consider all the implications of its application. Similarly, confusion can arise when the pursuit of one problem leads, accidentally, to the solution of another which, because unanticipated, was insufficiently evaluated. In these circumstances, the experimentalist is often tempted to do what can be done—merely for the excitement of doing it. The work on DNA of J. D. Watson and Francis Crick has opened the way to all sorts of experiments in genetic surgery that may be beyond the intent of the two pioneers.

What would be the value of cloning? The most immediate answer comes from the field of animal husbandry, which would gain new breeding techniques on a par with those already available to the plant biologist. If a particular brand of rice or wheat is developed, a true line can be offered so that the genetically pure strain, and only that strain, can be propagated. With animals, we have been dependent on the chance fusion of chromosomes from a champion race horse or a prize steer with those of their respective mates. Cloning would give us the option of making 10,000 identical copies of the champion race horse. Of course, that might raise the question of why we would then bother racing horses at all!

This technique would also permit us to manipulate the massive genetic multiples involved in breeding the best cattle possible for meat. It would, however, stop the evolutionary process, for it is precisely the random combination and recombination of genes from one parent and another that produce not only lesser creatures than the parents but superior creatures, and thus permit the continuing expansion and enrichment of the gene pool itself. Cloning could also be used to augment the number of members of an endangered species to that critical level necessary for group survival.

Would there be legitimate uses for human cloning? Certainly the general speculation about multiple Mozarts, basketball teams composed of five Kareem Abdul-Jabbars (four more on the bench?) or an army of supersol-

II. The Emergence of a Biomedical Technology

diers who are identical in every respect, with replaceable parts available for convenient transplants in case of injury, are insufficient to motivate scientific research.

They are not only insufficient, they are naive—as are the horror stories about the power-hungry dictator cloning his race of *Uebermenschen.* A human being is more (or less) than his genetic potential. It is the interaction of his genetic variables with the environment that produces the "person." The idea of seeing "yourself" born—as has been suggested—is a joke. The individual can be altered by the cytoplasm of the egg; by the biochemistry of the circulating blood through the placenta; by the diet and emotions of the woman carrying the child and by the trauma of the birth process. And all these environmental influences come to bear before what is usually visualized as life experience has yet begun!

Take identical twins—nature's cloning. Even though they share "the same" prebirth environment, they will emerge as different in such simple matters as weight and size. When identical twins are separated after birth, they develop remarkable variability while growing up—not just in achievement and psychological makeup, but in body weight and height.

The artificially cloned individual would have to be raised in a culture at least one generation apart from that of its donor (parent? sponsor?); this amount of time would be necessary to evaluate the worth and success of the prototype. To get an idea what a difference one generation makes, we need only look at our own bewildering offspring. Life experience pounds, pulls and shapes the same genetic clay into wondrous and ludicrous variations. If identical twins separated from birth show disparate form and personality, identical twins separated by a generation of time—clones— might not even recognize one another. We are not only what we are genetically given, but what we eat, hear, see, smell, learn, feel, touch, do and have done to. A genetic St. Francis clone could evolve into a tyrant. Or, more optimistically, a Hitler clone has the potential for sainthood.

The technical steps necessary to do human cloning are likely to be inspired not by the quest for a super race but by the need to solve compelling problems. Once developed to a point of predictable success, cloning will first be used as an eccentric application of a standard procedure, for a humanitarian end, as illustrated by a hypothetical case: A couple which has one adored infant and is incapable of having another learns that the child has been mortally injured. What possible harm would result, it may be asked, if one of the child's cells is taken so that he could be genetically reproduced (with the clone implanted in his mother's womb, or a substitute's) and nine months later "reborn" to the delight and comfort of his mourning parents?

Cloning—that most artificial of phenomena—would in this way be exploited to serve the most fundamental of human needs, bearing and raising children. Yet, on the other hand, it would totally cleave that need from related physiological and procreative behavior (sexual passion, tenderness and romantic love) which have traditionally initiated, accompanied and complemented parenthood.

Cloning as Metaphor

Cloning commands our attention more because it dramatizes the developing issues in bioethics than because of its potential threat to our way of life. Many biologists, ethicists and social scientists see it not as a pressing problem but a metaphoric device serving to focus attention on identical problems that arise from less dramatic forms of genetic engineering and that might slip into public use, protected from public debate by the incremental nature of the changes they impose.

All the issues have certain common features. The new technology will be motivated by the most humanitarian ends (with the exception of biological war research—another story). Its purpose will be to relieve suffering, to conquer disease, to restore normal capacities (as in conceiving or bearing a child). The difficulties of assessing the worth of this work *vs.* the cost are compounded because the benefits are immediate, concrete and tend to serve the individual, while the costs, if any, are perceived in abstractions ("humanness," "relatedness" and "quality of life"), are apparent only with time and are paid for by society as a whole or future generations.

The human being is the only species capable of systematically altering its "normal" biological system by use of its equally "normal" intellectual capacity. Cloning is but one example of such an intrusion into the reproductive area. The oldest is probably birth control of one sort or another. This capacity, when institutionalized, has a greater impact on a society than merely determining family size. It is a factor in defining the social roles available to women, levels of affluence of the society, and so on and on.

Abortion is also on its way to becoming institutionalized, in the sense of becoming accepted, relatively without question, as part of the normal order of things. It, too, will produce broad social effects, particularly when combined with amniocentesis, a technique which permits diagnosis of intrauterine fetal conditions (by withdrawing a sample of the amniotic fluid with needle and syringe) and would thus give couples the choice of aborting a defective fetus in its early stages.

Artificial insemination as a solution for male sterility has been accepted, with some discussion of its psychological reverberations but little of its possible sociological impact.

A parallel problem exists when the husband produces adequate semen, but the wife either fails to produce eggs or has a blocked passageway from the ovary to the uterus. If the woman merely has the blocked passageway, it might indeed be possible to remove an egg from the ovary, fertilize it in a test tube, and replant it at the proper stage of division in her uterine wall. Each clause in that statement represents staggering technical prob-

61

lems—yet each problem has been solved, or is on the verge of solution. Drs. R. G. Edwards and P. C. Steptoe, who have been instrumental in much of the work in this area, are expected imminently to attempt the implantation in a uterus of an in-vitro fertilized egg, with a good chance that it will grow into a normal baby. They may have already tried it, but so far there has been no news about the results if they have. In-vitro fertilization offers an added advantage—or complication, depending on your moral position —over more traditional methods. In the laboratory, during the short interval of days between fertilization and implantation, the sex of the newborn baby will be determinable. There are now selective stains which when applied to a single cell can establish gender without even a chromosome smear and evaluation. Therefore, one could fertilize a number of eggs and offer the parents a choice of gender—as well as other options of genetic composition. On the other hand, it would probably be safer to allow implantation, wait a few weeks and then determine genetic composition by amniocentesis—aborting, if the fetus does not meet parental expectations or standards.

By utilizing the same technology, a woman with no ovaries but a healthy uterus can borrow an egg from a donor, just as semen may be obtained from a donor. It can then be fertilized by her husband's semen in the test tube and, when ready, implanted in her uterus. By the same token, if a woman has intact ovaries but has had her uterus removed (a not uncommon procedure), she can have a laboratory conceived baby that genetically is hers and her husband's, and ask that it be raised in the uterus of another woman for nine months. There is no technical problem here at all. It is just as simple to insert the fertilized egg into one uterus that has been prepared for it as another.

Once such procedures become accepted, need the reasons for utilizing them be limited to the biological?

A professional woman, for reasons of necessity, vanity or anxiety, might prefer not to carry her child. She might gladly pay for nine months' service from another woman. While certain liberationists might applaud the idea of freeing women from the nine-month pregnancy period, they might be appalled at the exploitation of another woman. This should provide the incentive for the development of an artificial placenta—doing away with the need for carrying the fetus in the womb—an undertaking that should not be immensely difficult.

A Greater Danger

The artificial placenta is a long way from coitus interruptus, but in a definite continuum. Each step in the continuum offers potential for satisfying legitimate needs of individuals—and potentials for creating harm. Each step will incrementally influence society for good or bad or both beyond its meaning for those who are directly served. Some of the problems raised

4. VALENCE: We Have the Awful Knowledge

by tampering with reproduction may not be so obvious. To what degree will the procedure itself—independent of utility—reduce man by altering the concept of the sanctity of life, birth and death? To what degree will it intrude on institutions and relationships traditionally deemed fundamental to human experience, perhaps to "humanness"? When might a technique that satisfies certain individual needs become a sociological or psychological problem?

We know now that simple conditioning can take place in the uterus. An embryo can be trained to move, for example, when exposed to specific sounds. The internal environment, then, is already operating on the embryo. Certainly, so is the more immediate environment of maternal emotion and physiology, in ways not yet known.

After birth, conditioning potential is increased enormously. Evidence in animals has demonstrated that when the neonate is given a "perfect" environment, but deprived only of affectual contact with the mother, monstrous psychological damage is done to the developing infant.

We must take particular care that we do not produce physiologically sound semblances of human beings who will turn out, at some later time, to contain deep psychological flaws. For this very reason, some scientists might argue, we should employ intelligent, systematic conditioning in-vitro, in-utero or neonatally—to guarantee some optimal future character or personality traits.

Who will determine what will be done and what will not? Who will determine what should be done and what should not? What controls should there be? How do we balance private rights and the general good? On what basis will we allocate decisions to either personal conscience or public policy?

Are there areas in which control of human development and behavior is bad *per se,* independent of the nature of the controlled things, the intention of the controller or the reasons for control? Are there processes which, once started, will bring irreversible changes so slight as to not be significant in one generation—but may, inexorably and incrementally, bring major changes to successive generations?

And if we do attempt human cloning, what will we do with the "debris," the discarded messes along the line? What will we do with those pieces and parts, near-successes and almost-persons? What will we call the debris? At what arbitrary point will the damaged "goods" become damaged "children," requiring nurture rather than disposal? The more successful one became at this kind of experimentation, the more horrifyingly close to human would be the failures. The whole thing seems beyond contemplation for ethical and esthetic, as well as scientific reasons.

Planned single alterations inevitably turn out to be package deals. The unpredicted complexities of environmental intervention, with the resulting ecological disasters, should serve as a warning model. Improvement is a form of substitution. The increasing capacity of man to reconstruct himself is, by definition, the capacity to destroy himself through transformation into another creature—perhaps better, but not man.

Any attempt at genetic engineering is bound to spark a public debate because it involves *physical* tampering with the substance of living things, and to most people physical tampering seems more permanent, more irreversible, and therefore more serious than mere psychological manipulation.

Scientists, however, are impressed with the similarities, rather than the differences, between the effectiveness of direct, physical control of behavior—for example, by electrical stimulation of the brain—and psychological conditioning. And it has been demonstrated in much research that one can successfully condition babies in the first days of life. For example, the neonate can be taught to switch on either a sound or light show on the basis of his sucking speed—and neonates do elect the entertainment of their choice with great consistency.

The psychologist and psychiatrist have been aware that early imprinting on the mind and emotions has as profound a hold on an organism, and is as inflexible a determinant of adult behavior, as any genetic trait or physiological endowment. Now research is confirming that beyond even this, early environmental conditioning will actually produce organic, neurological changes in the brain.

That wise and sensitive geneticist Theodosius Dobzhansky has constantly emphasized that man's culture is not only his product, but his creator:

> Culture is, however, an instrument of adaptation which is vastly more efficient than the biological processes which led to its inception and advancement. It is more efficient among other things because it is more rapid—changed genes are transmitted only to the direct descendants of the individuals in whom they first appear; to replace the old genes, the carriers of the new ones must gradually outbreed and supplant the former. Changed culture may be transmitted to anybody regardless of biological parentage, or borrowed ready-made from other peoples. . . .
> In producing the genetic basis of culture, biological evolution has transcended itself—it has produced the superorganic.

Controlled culture has become a substitute for the natural selection of lower animals, and, with the homogenizing of the world's cultures, the variability and richness that randomness and chance produce are still further diminished.

If, in a time of anxiety, when the human species is unsure of its future and frightened by developments it does not understand, it is offered a planned environment, it may accept. If man is promised security and assured survival at the cost of his personal freedom and essential dignity, he may accept, particularly if he is told that the freedom he abandons is

4. VALENCE: We Have the Awful Knowledge

an illusion and the dignity only a conceit. Modern learning theory applied early through global television (the average American 4-year-old already watches 40 to 60 hours a week) and other teaching machines can program man beyond anything yet seen. The real danger of "pure strains" may come equally from conditioning and cloning. And both, as well as a frightening array of other problems not mentioned, demonstrate the fine line between promise and perdition in the new biotechnology.

When Mary Shelley conceived Dr. Frankenstein, science was all promise. The technological age existed only in the excitement of anticipation, and there was leisure to philosophize. Man was ascending, and the only terror was that in his rise he would offend God by assuming too much and reaching too high, by coming too close. The scientist was the new Prometheus.

By the end of the 19th century, technology had surpassed even its own expectations. Man was too arrogant to recognize arrogance. Man did not have to fear God, he had replaced him. There was nothing that technology would not eventually solve. The whole of history seemed to be contrived to serve the purposes and glorify the name of Homo sapiens.

It seems grossly unfair that so short a time as the last 25 years should have produced so precipitous a fall. But then, the way down the mountain has traditionally been faster than the way up. Man has been handed the bill and he is not sure he has enough assets to pay up. We have destroyed much of our environment, exhausted much of our resources and have manufactured weapons of total destruction without sufficiently secure control mechanisms. The biological revolution may offer relief or hasten total failure. Unfortunately, things now move faster, and we are less sure of how to even recognize success or failure.

But technology has elevated man—and there is no going back. "Natural man" is the cooperative creation of nature and man. Antitechnology is self-hatred.

The tragic irony is not that Mary Shelley's "fantasy" once again has a relevance. The tragedy is that it is no longer a fantasy—and that in its realization we no longer identify with Dr. Frankenstein but with his monster.

III.
Nature or Nurture–
Once More with Feeling

5.
VALENCE:
Genetics
and the Diversity of Behavior
THEODOSIUS DOBZHANSKY

In "Genetics and the Diversity of Behavior," Theodosius Dobzhansky advances the proposition that there may be a natural basis in genetics for assigning social roles and obligations. This general idea is what catches Isaac Asimov's eye in the following excerpt from the story "Profession."

Among the founders and pioneers of behavior genetics, R. C. Tryon holds a prominent place. His work was seminal in a field apparently destined to become one of the fastest growing points of modern biology. Behavior genetics may be as important and exciting in the near future as molecular genetics has been for our present generation. The relevance of behavior genetics to man's understanding of himself is beyond doubt. "Know Thyself" are words of wisdom which more than two millennia ago were inscribed on a temple in Delphi. Self-knowledge remains a permanent challenge to man.

Tryon's classical experiments were admirably simple in conception. In several consecutive generations, he selected rats that were able to learn fastest a maze devised for this purpose. In another line the slowest learners were selected to be the parents of the next generation. The two lines diverged to become "maze bright" and "maze dull," respectively. The brightness and dullness were conditioned genetically.

These experiments were made at a time when some authorities contended that behavior could not be inherited. Behavior, it was argued, is a process, not a structure or a substance like, for example, curly hair or skin pigment. Even a modern author demands "biochemical analyses in which

From Theodosius Dobzhansky, "Genetics and the Diversity of Behavior," *American Psychologist,* June 1972, pp. 523–530. Copyright 1972 by the American Psychological Association, and reproduced by permission.

a direct link between chemistry and certain behavioral potentials is established." This reasoning is fallacious. One may as well argue that curly hair and skin pigments are not inherited either, because they are not present as such in egg and sperm cells. Biological and legal inheritance should not be confused; inherited money or real estate is transferred from one owner to another; in this sense, only genes are inherited.

Biological inheritance is realized through a process of development, the instructions for which are coded in this marvelous chemical substance—DNA—of which the genes are principally composed. Curly hair, skin pigment, maze brightness or maze dullness in rats, photopositivity and geopositivity or geonegativity in drosophila flies, all emerge as visible, or otherwise perceptible, results of networks of developmental processes. The links between the DNA of the genes and the observable, phenotypic characteristics of the organism may be far from direct. They may involve long sequences of chemical reactions and developmental processes. It may well be that the developmental complexity is particularly great for some forms of behavior.

Our task is to discover what I like to call the genetic architecture of behavior. What kinds of genetic systems underlie the individual, racial, and species differences in behavior? Are they mostly monogenic or polygenic? Do they involve additive or epistatic gene actions? Are they organized in supergenes? Do they frequently involve phenomena like heterotic interactions and genetic homeostasis? At present we know next to nothing about these things. Yet they are crucial for understanding and evaluating the alleged genetic differences between social classes and races of man, and the evolutionary future of such differences. The hot polemics about these issues can only be said to be raging in a vacuum of ignorance.

Drosophilae Selected for Responses to Light and to Gravity

Jerry Hirsch, one of Tryon's ablest students, constructed a classification maze to quantify the responses of drosophila flies to gravity. In this maze, a fly has to make 15 choices of going upward or downward through a series of funnel-shaped passages. A geotactic score for a sample of a fly population can be calculated as the mean number of downward choices. Working with *Drosophila melanogaster,* Hirsch and his students were able to select for genetically conditioned geopositivity or geonegativity. They also showed that the differences between the geopositive and geonegative strains were apparently polygenic, due to several or many genes in different chromosomes of the fly. Hadler adapted Hirsch's maze to measure the response of the fly to light. A fly makes 15 choices of going through light passages or through dark passages. Starting with an initially photoneutral population, Hadler obtained by selection photopositive and photonegative strains.

III. Nature or Nurture—Once More with Feeling

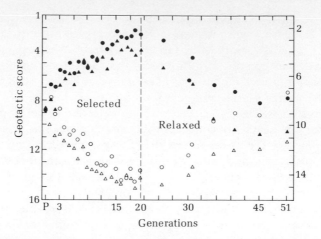

Figure 1. Response to selection, and to relaxation of selection, for phototactic behavior in *Drosophila pseudoobscura*.

My colleagues, B. Spassky and O. Pavlovsky, and myself utilized a different species, *Drosophila pseudoobscura,* to select for photopositivity, photonegativity, geopositivity, and geonegativity. The results are summarized in Figures 1 and 2. Our starting materials were populations descended from flies collected in the wild and bred in the laboratory in population cages rather than in standard culture bottles. The flies in these populations were originally photoneutral and geoneutral on the average. That is, although some flies chose light or dark passages more often than others, or made upward or downward turns more often than other individuals, the average scores for the populations were neutral. (The ideal neutrality score on our mazes is 8.5, and the scores made by unselected populations are mostly within statistically legitimate sampling errors from the ideal. The distribution of individual scores follows a normal bell-shaped curve, but the variance is greater than would be expected if the flies went up or down, in the light or in the dark, merely at random.) It is interesting to note that natural populations of a closely related species, *Drosophila persimilis,* are not neutral but photopositive on the average; they are, however, geotactically neutral. The reactions to light and to gravity are genetically independent.

The selection that we practiced was rather rigorous. In every generation, 300 females and 300 males from each of the four selected populations were run through either the phototactic or the geotactic mazes, and 25 "best" individuals of each sex were selected to be parents of the next generation. Best means simply flies that went farthest toward the positive or the negative ends of the maze, depending on the direction in which we wished to select. As shown in Figures 1 and 2, the selection was quite effective. After about 12 generations, the positively and negatively phototactic lines diverged so much that only a few flies made similar numbers of light and dark choices, in contrast with the initial population in which such flies

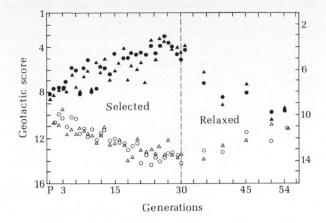

Figure 2. Response to selection, and to relaxation of selection, for geotactic behavior in *Drosophila pseudoobscura*.

were most numerous. The average phototactic scores in the positive line were between 13 and 15, and in the negative line, between 2 and 4. In the selection for geotaxis, the individual scores are more variable, but after some 20 generations the difference in behavior was quite striking; the mean scores in the positive line were between 12 and 14, and in the negative line, between 3 and 5.

Heritability

The power of selection to alter the reactions of drosophila flies to light and to gravity shows that there are genes present in natural populations which influence these reactions. It is now appropriate to inquire how great a part of the observed variance in these behavioral traits can be ascribed to heredity, and how much of it is due to chance and to environmental influences. There being no monozygotic twins in drosophila flies, the favored method of estimation of heritability of human traits is inapplicable. We have used instead a measure known as realized heritability. This is a ratio of the differences between the mean scores of the populations under selection in succeeding generations and the selective differentials in the same generations. A selective differential is the difference between the population average and the average of the individuals selected from this population to be the parents of the next generation. A heritability of 1 (or 100%) would mean that the selective differential is exactly equal to the selection gain, while a 0 heritability would mean that the selection is without effect.

Those familiar with current estimates of the heritability of IQ in certain human populations (said to be 80%) will find the heritabilities of phototactic and geotactic responses in drosophila flies remarkably small. Computed for the first 10 generations from the start of the experiments, the figure for phototaxis is only 9%, and for geotaxis, a mere 4%. As the

71

selection progresses, the heritability falls to 0. Richmond's estimates of the heritability in the first generation of selection, computed from parent–offspring correlations, is only about twice our figures for the first-10-generations interval. Yet, despite the heritabilities being so low, selection is able to change the behavior of the flies in quite striking a manner. This is, of course, due to a high intensity of the selection which we practiced, plus the avoidance of close inbreeding, which is a disturbing factor in many selection experiments. I submit, however, that variable traits in human populations with heritabilities as low as the phototactic and geotactic responses in drosophila flies would probably be believed devoid of a genetic component in their variation.

Genetic Complexity

Experiments have been made intercrossing selected photopositive with photonegative, and geopositive with geonegative, populations. The intercrosses gave F_1 hybrids mostly intermediate between the parents, that is, approximately neutral to light and to gravity. The F_2 generation remains intermediate on the average, and not perceptibly more variable than the F_1. These results are consistent with those obtained by Hirsch and Erlenmeyer-Kimling in *Drosophila melanogaster;* the behavior differences induced by selection are polygenic. A most interesting exception has been observed by Woolf in a cross between a geopositive and a geonegative population, *Drosophila pseudoobscura.* The differentiating gene or genes proved to be carried mainly in the sex-determining X chromosomes. Here the F_1 hybrid females are intermediate, but the males behave approximately like those in the maternal populations. In the F_2 generation, both females and males are intermediate.

The results obtained by Hirsch and his collaborators in *Drosophila melanogaster,* and by our group in *Drosophila pseudoobscura,* are interesting to compare with those of Benzer on the reaction to light in the former species. Benzer's experimental technique was quite different from ours. He used a so-called countercurrent apparatus instead of a maze, and instead of selecting in a series of generations, he picked up discrete mutants that change the fly's response to light. In his apparatus, "normal" flies run toward light, but he did obtain mutants that make the flies photoneutral. Professor Benzer has kindly sent us some of his mutants and control strains. Tested in our mazes, they did not differ much in their reactions either to light or to gravity.

This result may seem surprising, but only at first sight. It is quite analogous to what happened to Tryon's maze-bright and maze-dull rats when tested by Searle in mazes constructed differently from Tryon's. In these mazes, the "brights" became "dull," and vice versa. Does this contradict Tryon's conclusion that rats can be selected genetically for learning ability?

5. VALENCE: Genetics and the Diversity of Behavior

Surely not; this shows only that one can select for different perceptual abilities that facilitate learning under different circumstances. My tentative interpretation of the drosophila results is as follows.

Both *Drosophila melanogaster* and *Drosophila pseudoobscura* evince, when disturbed, an escape reaction. The flies tend to move upward and toward light. Benzer's mutants have lost this escape reaction, at least as far as the behavior with respect to light is concerned. While the flies may be said to be normally photopositive, the mutants are photoneutral. By contrast, in our experiments the flies have 24 hours or more to work their way undisturbed through the mazes. Under these conditions, the progenies of wild-collected flies are, on the average, photoneutral and geoneutral. They go through light and through dark passages, or go upward or downward, about equally often. Benzer and ourselves have studied really different kinds of responses to light and to gravity. The "photopositivity" and "photoneutrality" refer to different kinds of behavior in the two kinds of experiments, just as the success in maze learning is due to different sorts of genetically conditioned behavior in the experiments of Tryon and of Searle. It is not surprising that the behavioral variants observed by Benzer are monogenic, while in our experiments they are polygenic. It would certainly be interesting to find polygenes that modify the behavior of the flies under Benzer's experimental procedure, and to find monogenic differentials in our kind of experiments. Perhaps the above-mentioned findings of Woolf, on sex-linked genes that govern the geotaxis in *Drosophila pseudoobscura,* come close to a monogenic situation.

Genetic Homeostasis

Let us consider once more the experiments on *Drosophila pseudoobscura* depicted in Figures 1 and 2. Despite the low heritability of the phototactic and geotactic responses, selection continued for 20 or 30 generations, resulting in populations strikingly different in behavior. These behavioral differences, however, do not remain fixed when the selection is relaxed. The positive and negative populations were maintained for a series of generations in the same way as when the selection was practiced, but the individuals that served as parents of the following generations were taken at random with respect to their behavior in the mazes. The behavioral differences were eroded gradually, and eventually were lost altogether. In other words, the positive and negative populations gradually converged and became indistinguishable by their behavior. The selection gains, which added up under selection to very substantial differences between the populations, are lost without further selection about as rapidly as they were accumulated.

Loss upon relaxation of selection of what the selection had accomplished is not a new phenomenon. It has often been encountered by breeders of domestic animals. Selected and "improved" varieties do not always conserve the high levels of performance when the selection is discontinued. To maintain these varieties at desired levels, continued selection is necessary. The phenomenon has been called by Lerner genetic homeostasis, defined as "the property of the population to equilibrate its genetic composition and to resist sudden changes."

According to Lerner, there is more than a single mechanism that may bring about genetic homeostasis, but I must forbear from going into technical details here. To put it most simply, natural selection generally maintains traits and characteristics of wild species at levels as close as possible to those giving optimal adaptedness in the environment in which the population lives. The average body size, weight, body proportions, and modalities of behavior are thus controlled and adjusted by natural selection. Artificial selection works for the benefit of the breeder or experimenter, not for the benefit of the animal population selected. It drives the population toward greater or lesser development of the characteristics selected; this may result in a lower adaptedness of the population in its natural, though not necessarily in experimental, habitats or under domestication. Therefore, when the artificial selection is discontinued, natural selection will act to undo what artificial selection had wrought. Whether or not the return to the original state will actually take place will depend on the availability of genetic variance upon which natural selection can act. If such variance exists, then the relaxation of the artifical selection will leave the field open for the action of the natural one.

Professor Howard Levene of Columbia University has made a thorough statistical analysis of the data obtained in our experiments on the selection, and the relaxation of selection, for phototaxis and geotaxis in *Drosophila pseudoobscura.* Genetic homeostasis obviously involves natural selection opposite in direction to the artificial selection that preceded it. The problem was to estimate the magnitude of this natural selection, which was designated as the "homeostatic strength." This turned out to be between .05 and .07 (or between 5% and 7%). These values are remarkably similar to the estimates of the realized heritability in the first 10 generations of artificial selection referred to above. To put it in a different way, our selection, which resulted in clearly photopositive, photonegative, geopositive, and geonegative populations, had to be powerful enough not only to overcome the homeostatic strength but also to displace the behavior modalities from the points at which they were fixed in the history of the species. This conclusion has been tested by a special experiment (unpublished). For 18 generations, four populations were propagated in the following manner: 30 pairs of flies (30 females + 30 males) were taken at random from the previous generation, and to them were added 10 pairs that showed distinctly positive or negative behavior. The selection had in this case no effect whatever: the average behavior of the populations remained unchanged until the end of the experiment. Here the homeostatic strength merely balanced the strength of the artificial selection.

5. VALENCE: Genetics and the Diversity of Behavior

Genetic Architecture of the Behavior Traits Studied

It is a reasonable assumption, although we have no definitive evidence in its favor, that it is advantageous for *Drosophila pseudoobscura* in its natural habitats to be neutral to light and to gravity. Or, to state the assumption more cautiously, it is advantageous to these flies to have their reactions to light and to gravity equilibrated so that when tested in Hirsch–Hadler mazes, the average behavior is at or near the neutrality point.

There are two ways in which evolution controlled by natural selection could bring about such behavior. First, and it might seem to be the simplest way, is to have genes selected that make the flies uniformly photoneutral and geoneutral. The final outcome of this selection would eventually be a species in which all individuals are homozygous for the genes guaranteeing photoneutrality and geoneutrality. There would be, then, no genetic diversity among individuals in their reactions to light or to gravity. Neither natural nor artificial selection could change these reactions, unless new genetic variants arise by mutations. Second, an average photoneutrality and geoneutrality can be achieved by having a genetic diversity of individuals, some of them more or less positive, others negative, and still others neutral. If the frequencies of the positive deviations from neutrality balance those of the negative deviations, a population or a species as a whole will be neutral on the average. In contrast to the first kind of genetic architecture, the second would make the species genetically plastic. Natural as well as artificial selection could rapidly produce genetically positive as well as genetically negative populations. Furthermore, the genetic changes in the populations would be easily reversible; if the selection which had favored positivity changed to one favoring negativity, the populations could respond by altering the genetic conditioning of this behavior.

Which of the two above kinds of genetic architecture of a character or a function is preferable? Neither one is unqualifiedly superior. Every species, man included, has structures, functions, and behavior patterns that are advantageous or indispensable for survival and reproduction over the entire range of environments in which it lives. A drosophila fly must be able to feed, to avoid heat and desiccation, to mate, and to deposit its eggs in a place where the larvae can develop successfully. Traits of this kind will be genetically as well as physiologically buffered; they will, under ordinary circumstances, develop in every individual that does not die before completing its life cycle. On the other hand, every species, and indeed every individual, faces a variety of environments and may have a choice among a variety of habitats. How can it cope with this variety? There are again two ways. The first can be labeled phenotypic plasticity or developmental homeostasis. The range of reactions of a genotype may be such that it responds to frequently encountered environments in ways that increase the probability of survival and reproduction. The second is genetic plasticity, intrapopulational polymorphism, and interpopulational racial variation. The species includes a variety of genotypes which yield superior adaptedness in different environments, or habitats, at different times, or under different circumstances.

The evidence obtained in our experiments on *Drosophila pseudoobscura* is consistent with the view that the genetic basis of its reactions to light and to gravity is not a single genotype but a multiplicity of genotypes. Suppose that in some localities, at some seasons, or under some ecological conditions it becomes advantageous for the flies to respond positively to light or to gravity. A population exposed to these conditions can within a few generations become more or less positively phototactic or geotactic on the average. However, in undergoing such a genetic adaptation the population does not become irreversibly committed to any particular environment. An environment may change again to a state where phototactic and geotactic neutrality confer superior adaptability. Selection, acting in concert with genetic homeostasis, will readily accomplish a genetic readaptation. Nor do we need to suppose that the genetic variety confers adaptability only because the environment undergoes changes in time. A drosophila population probably always faces a variety of environments in the same locality and at the same time. There may be available different foods, hiding places, and microclimates. It is probable that a population which contains photopositive or geopositive, neutral, and negative individuals can exploit the variety of accessible resources more efficiently than could a genetically monolithic population.

In Praise of Genetic Diversity

Man is not just an overgrown drosophila. I do not intend to commit the egregious error to which so many of us biologists are prone. I shall not assume that what we have learned about the genetics of behavior of drosophila applies necessarily to man's behavior. Most certainly, man is a living being, a sexually reproducing and outbreeding species, and a product of evolutionary development. He is therefore subject to some of the same biological laws and regularities which apply also to drosophila. The genetic basis of man's behavioral adaptability is nevertheless different from drosophila, and for that matter from rats, mice, monkeys, and even anthropoid apes.

Man is the only species on earth, and almost certainly in the cosmos, that relies for its adaptability mainly, though not exclusively, on culture learned by each individual in his or her lifetime and transmitted largely by means of symbolic language. Species other than man become adapted by changing their genes to fit their environments. *Drosophila pseudoobscura* survives winters of the Sierra Nevada and the Rocky Mountains; many tropical species of drosophila are quickly killed by cold. The resistance or susceptibility to cold is genetic. Man, by means of his culture and technology, changes his environments to fit his genes. He prevails against cold weather by dressing in warmer garments and heating his dwellings. This difference is fundamental. Ignoring it leads to delusions and fallacies. But it is also a fallacy to claim that the biological evolution of mankind terminated with the appearance of culture. Cultural evolution is superimposed on the biological.

Culture has a genetic basis. Mankind is the sole possessor of culture because it is the sole possessor of a genetic basis for culture. This statement is not falsified by finding rudiments of cultural transmission of learned behavior in some animals. Culture did not suddenly fall from the heavens, complete and unalterable. Its genetic basis was compounded gradually by natural selection from genetic building blocks that existed in man's precultural ancestors. The formation of this genetic basis was due to positive feedback between biological and cultural evolutions. Neither culture nor its genetic basis is now fixed and stationary. For good as for ill, they continue evolving.

Two points must be clarified here, because their miscomprehension leads to confusion. First, the genetic basis of culture is a common attribute of mankind as a biological species. Second, this genetic basis is not invariant but is subject to individual and group diversification. The universality in the human species of the capacity to acquire culture is no more surprising than that all humans have, when in good health, nearly the same body temperature, an ability to walk erect, and a very large brain in relation to the body size. As pointed out above, the development of traits indispensable for survival is genetically and physiologically buffered. They develop in every individual that survives at all.

The capacity to acquire culture, to be enculturated, is surely indispensable to man. It does not, however, follow that this capacity must be monolithic and undiversified. Individual humans play varied roles within a culture and in different cultures. Did natural selection promote in human evolution a standardization and uniformity of the capacity for acquisition of culture? Or did it further a genetic diversity, tempered by developmental flexibility, in human capacities, like it did in drosophila's reactions to light and to gravity? I keep my promise not to mistake man for an overgrown drosophila. A parallel is warranted, however, despite this fundamental difference: much of man's behavior is molded by learning, while learning plays a very small, if any, part in the behavior of drosophila. Many breeds of domesticated animals have been selected for an at least relative fixity of the kinds of behaviors which fit these breeds for the particular employments for which man uses them. It has often been asserted without proof, or on flimsiest evidence, that the "breeds" of man have similarly been selected for fixity of behavior and abilities. This ignores the fundamental peculiarity of human evolution: man has been selected for trainability, educability, and consequent plasticity of behavior.

Culture, trainability, and educability are not devices to make everybody alike. If behavioral uniformity were adaptive in the human species, as it apparently is in some animal breeds, it would probably have been achieved by genetic fixation. Just the opposite is observed in reality. Pathological deviants aside, any individual can be trained to perform different functions and to acquire skills for a variety of occupations needed in the society of which he is a member. Free choice of occupation to be trained for is, by and large, characteristic of modern meritocratic societies. To be sure, a diversity of functions and occupations within a society can also be served by genetic specialization. There may exist within a society a genetic diversity, different individuals predestined by their genetic endowments to take up different careers and occupations. This assumption was implicit in the classical Hindu caste society, and so it was in the *Brave New World* utopia.

The above two modes of achieving adaptive diversity of behaviors in a human society are not mutually exclusive. Both of them are in fact made use of. This is not unusual in evolution; with a thoroughgoing opportunism, evolution often employs two or more means at the same time to promote adaptability of a species to its environments. Such opportunism is, however, something that many scientists find hard to accept. It seems contrary to the principle of Ockham's razor, which counsels parsimony of assumptions used to explain a phenomenon. It would please many simplifiers to have the diversity of human abilities and behaviors either all due to training or all predetermined genetically. The partisans of these two oversimplifications engage in interminable polemics which get hot and even abusive at times. Yet nature is often prodigal instead of parsimonious. In the light of evolutionary considerations, one can make sense of this prodigality.

Genetic fixity and developmental rigidity of behavior may be advantageous where the environment is uniform in space and stable in time. They are also advantageous in organisms with short life spans and with little or no opportunity for learning. A drosophila fly hatching from a pupa must "know" how to find food, a mate, perform the often quite elaborate rituals of courtship and copulation, locate a proper place to deposit its eggs, and all that with little or no opportunity to observe how other conspecific individuals do these things. Innate drives and releaser mechanisms are required to perform these tasks satisfactorily. One needs not dogmatically deny the existence of such drives and releasers also in higher animals with greater longevity and with opportunity for learning and for imitation of the behavior of conspecific individuals. The point is simply that here genetic and developmental flexibility may to a greater or lesser extent displace the rigidity. The degree of rigidity or flexibility will depend on the diversity and changeability of the environments.

Mankind is biologically the most successful species that evolution has brought into being. The key to man's evolutionary success is neither bodily strength, nor robust health, nor resistance to environmental insults. It is adaptability by cultural means. Adaptation by cultural changes is vastly more efficacious than adaptation by genetic change. Genetic "inventions," having arisen by mutation or gene recombination, can be transmitted only to direct descendants of the individuals in whom these inventions first appeared. New ideas and human inventions are under no such limitation. This is why adaptation by learned behavior is ineluctably displacing that by genetic fixation. The displacement began probably at least two million years ago, and the process is going on.

Now let us look at the other side of the coin. In many animal species, including some mammals, individuals are solitary except during the mating season. Every individual must consequently do for himself everything that is needed to remain alive. Not so in man. Apparently at all stages of cultural evolution, from its beginning to this day, prehumans and humans lived in bands, clans, communities, and organized societies with other men. An individual living strictly alone is a freak in the human species. Group living is advantageous for common defense; it also permits division of labor and specialization in the performance of socially useful functions. In monkey bands, every individual past infancy fends for himself procuring food; however, adult males defend females and young against predators, even endangering their own lives. Culture and technology have created a multiplicity of functions in every human society. How can these many functions be provided for most competently?

A theoretical ideal is an all-purpose genetic endowment. Any individual could be trained to become any kind of generalist or specialist. This ideal is approached in the human species, whose prime adaptive mode is trainability or educability for the performance of whatever functions the society is in need of. Yet educability is compatible with a multiplicity of genetic endowments. Carriers of different genotypes reach highest levels of proficiency when trained for occupations most suitable for them. I probably could have been brought up to be a peasant tilling the soil, a clerk, an engineer, or even a soldier. No training on earth could, however, have made me a concert pianist, a painter, a champion boxer or sprinter, or a mathematical prodigy. Yet there are people who take to training for these occupations with greatest ease and willingness. They are not necessarily so specialized genetically that they could not survive also in other professions. Directional natural selection in man has always and unrelentingly promoted a general educability. Diversifying (also called disruptive) natural selection promoted a genetic diversity of aptitudes, talents, skills, and tastes. Mankind is a product of both kinds of selection.

Concluding Remarks

All bodily structures and functions, without exception, are products of heredity realized in some sequence of environments. So also are all forms of behavior, also without exception. Nothing can arise in any organism unless its potentiality is within the realm of possibilities of the genetic endowment. Lest I sound to you an extreme hereditarian, I hasten to add that the potentialities that are realized in a given sequence of environments

are, especially in man, only a tiny fraction of the individual's total potentialities. If an individual with the same genotype would develop and be
brought up in some different environment, he might develop quite differently. This is demonstrated by monozygotic twins reared apart in dissimilar environments. It is idle to speculate what sort of a person I might have
become if my biography were different from what it was in fact. Surely,
almost everyone has an intuitive certainty that he or she would be a
different person in more favorable or in more adverse circumstances.

In flies, as well as in men, the genetic endowment determines the entire
range of reactions, realized and unrealized, of the developing organism in
all possible environments. A much less happy formulation, often met with
in the literature, is that the genotype determines the limits, the upper and
the lower extremes, which a character, say a geotactic response, or stature,
or IQ, can reach. This would make sense only if we were able to test the
reactions of a genotype in all possible environments. Environments are
infinitely variable, however, and new ones are constantly invented and
added. Possibly I could have grown to be a six-footer, but is this my
absolute upper limit? Is it not conceivable that a new growth hormone will
some day be discovered that would make everybody a foot taller, or a foot
shorter, than they grow in the present environments? It would require not
a scientific but something like a divine knowledge to predict how much the
stature, or IQ, or mathematical ability of any individual or population
could be raised by environmental or educational modifications or improvements. More research on the genetic conditioning and developmental realization of various kinds of behavior is needed. One can be certain that such
research will ultimately benefit mankind.

6.
VISION:
Profession

ISAAC ASIMOV

The remark made by Dobzhansky that "Carriers of different genotypes reach highest levels of proficiency when trained for occupations most suitable for them," is a remark that may be receiving emphasis in the following story by Isaac Asimov.

For most of the first eighteen years of his life, George Platen had headed firmly in one direction, that of Registered Computer Programmer. There were those in his crowd who spoke wisely of Spationautics, Refrigeration Technology, Transportation Control, and even Administration. But George held firm.

He argued relative merits as vigorously as any of them, and why not? Education Day loomed ahead of them and was the great fact of their existence. It approached steadily, as fixed and certain as the calendar—the first day of November of the year following one's eighteenth birthday.

After that day, there were other topics of conversation. One could discuss with others some detail of the profession, or the virtues of one's wife and children, or the fate of one's space-polo team, or one's experiences in the Olympics. Before Education Day, however, there was only one topic that unfailingly and unwearyingly held everyone's interest, and that was Education Day.

"What are you going for? Think you'll make it? Heck, that's no good. Look at the records; quota's been cut. Logistics now—"

Or Hypermechanics now—Or Communications now—Or Gravitics now—

Especially Gravitics at the moment. Everyone had been talking about Gravitics in the few years just before George's Education Day because of the development of the Gravitic power engine.

From *Astounding Science Fiction,* July 1957. Reprinted by permission of the author.

III. Nature or Nurture—Once More with Feeling

Any world within ten light-years of a dwarf star, everyone said, would give its eyeteeth for any kind of Registered Gravitics Engineer.

The thought of that never bothered George. Sure it would; all the eyeteeth it could scare up. But George had also heard what had happened before in a newly developed technique. Rationalization and simplification followed in a flood. New models each year; new types of gravitic engines; new principles. Then all those eyeteeth gentlemen would find themselves out of date and superseded by later models with later educations. The first group would then have to settle down to unskilled labor or ship out to some backwoods world that wasn't quite caught up yet.

Now Computer Programmers were in steady demand year after year, century after century. The demand never reached wild peaks; there was never a howling bull market for Programmers; but the demand climbed steadily as new worlds opened up and as older worlds grew more complex.

He had argued with Stubby Trevelyan about that constantly. As best friends, their arguments had to be constant and vitriolic and, of course, neither ever persuaded or was persuaded.

But then Trevelyan had had a father who was a Registered Metallurgist and had actually served on one of the Outworlds, and a grandfather who had also been a Registered Metallurgist. He himself was intent on becoming a Registered Metallurgist almost as a matter of family right and was firmly convinced that any other profession was a shade less than respectable.

"There'll always be metal," he said, "and there's an accomplishment in molding alloys to specification and watching structures grow. Now what's a Programmer going to be doing. Sitting at a coder all day long, feeding some fool mile-long machine."

Even at sixteen, George had learned to be practical. He said simply, "There'll be a million Metallurgists put out along with you."

"Because it's good. A good profession. The best."

"But you get crowded out, Stubby. You can be way back in line. Any world can tape out its own Metallurgists, and the market for advanced Earth models isn't so big. And it's mostly the small worlds that want them. You know what per cent of the turn-out of Registered Metallurgists get tabbed for worlds with a Grade A rating. I looked it up. It's just 13.3 per cent. That means you'll have seven chances in eight of being stuck in some world that just about has running water. You may even be stuck on Earth; 2.3 per cent are."

Trevelyan said belligerently, "There's no disgrace in staying on Earth. Earth needs technicians, too. Good ones." His grandfather had been an Earth-bound Metallurgist, and Trevelyan lifted his finger to his upper lip and dabbed at an as yet nonexistent mustache.

George knew about Trevelyan's grandfather and, considering the Earth-bound position of his own ancestry, was in no mood to sneer. He said diplomatically, "No intellectual disgrace. Of course not. But it's nice to get into a Grade A world, isn't it?

"Now you take Programmers. Only the Grade A worlds have the kind of computers that really need first-class Programmers so they're the only ones in the market. And Programmer tapes are complicated and hardly any one fits. They need more Programmers than their own population can supply. It's just a matter of statistics. There's one first-class Programmer per million, say. A world needs twenty and has a population of ten million, they have to come to Earth for five to fifteen Programmers. Right?

"And you know how many Registered Computer Programmers went to Grade A planets last year? I'll tell you. Every last one. If you're a Programmer, you're a picked man. Yes, sir."

Trevelyan frowned. "If only one in a million makes it, what makes you think *you'll* make it?

George said guardedly, "I'll make it."

He never dared tell anyone; not Trevelyan; not his parents; of exactly what he was doing that made him so confident. But he wasn't worried. He was simply confident (that was the worst of the memories he had in the hopeless days afterward). He was as blandly confident as the average eight-year-old kid approaching Reading Day—that childhood preview of Education Day.

Of course, Reading Day had been different. Partly, there was the simple fact of childhood. A boy of eight takes many extraordinary things in stride. One day you can't read and the next day you can. That's just the way things are. Like the sun shining.

And then not so much depended upon it. There were no recruiters just ahead, waiting and jostling for the lists and scores on the coming Olympics. A boy or girl who goes through the Reading Day is just someone who has ten more years of undifferentiated living upon Earth's crawling surface; just someone who returns to his family with one new ability.

By the time Education Day came, ten years later, George wasn't even sure of most of the details of his own Reading Day.

Most clearly of all, he remembered it to be a dismal September day with a mild rain falling. (September for Reading Day; November for Education Day: May for Olympics. They made nursery rhymes out of it.) George had dressed by the wall lights, with his parents far more excited than he himself was. His father was a Registered Pipe Fitter and had found his occupation on Earth. This fact had always been a humiliation to him, although, of course, as anyone could see plainly, most of each generation must stay on Earth in the nature of things.

There had to be farmers and miners and even technicians on Earth. It was only the late-model, high-specialty professions that were in demand on the Outworlds, and only a few millions a year out of Earth's eight billion population could be exported. Every man and woman on Earth couldn't be among that group.

But every man and woman could hope that at least one of his children could be one, and Platen, Senior, was certainly no exception. It was obvious to him (and, to be sure, to others as well) that George was notably intelligent and quick-minded. He would be bound to do well and he would have to, as he was an only child. If George didn't end on an Outworld, they would have to wait for grandchildren before a next chance would come along, and that was too far in the future to be much consolation.

Reading Day would not prove much, of course, but it would be the only indication they would have before the big day itself. Every parent on Earth would be listening to the quality of reading when his child came home with it; listening for any particularly easy flow of words and building that into certain omens of the future. There were few families that didn't have at least one hopeful who, from Reading Day on, was the great hope because of the way he handled his trisyllabics.

Dimly, George was aware of the cause of his parents' tension, and if there was any anxiety in his young heart that drizzly morning, it was only the fear that his father's hopeful expression might fade out when he returned home with his reading.

The children met in the large assembly room of the town's Education hall. All over Earth, in millions of local halls, throughout that month, similar groups of children would be meeting. George felt depressed by the grayness of the room and by the other children, strained and stiff in unaccustomed finery.

Automatically, George did as all the rest of the children did. He found the small clique that represented the children on his floor of the apartment house and joined them.

Trevelyan, who lived immediately next door, still wore his hair childishly long and was years removed from the sideburns and thin, reddish mustache that he was to grow as soon as he was physiologically capable of it.

Trevelyan (to whom George was then known as Jaw-jee) said, "Bet you're scared."

"I am not," said George. Then, confidentially, "My folks got a hunk of printing up on the dresser in my room, and when I come home, I'm going to read it for them." (George's main suffering at the moment lay in the fact that he didn't quite know where to put his hands. He had been warned not to scratch his head or rub his ears or pick his nose or put his hands into his pockets. This eliminated almost every possibility.)

Trevelyan put *his* hands in his pockets and said, "My father isn't worried."

Trevelyan, Senior, had been a Metallurgist on Diporia for nearly seven years, which gave him a superior social status in his neighborhood even though he had retired and returned to Earth.

6. VISION: Profession

Earth discouraged these re-immigrants because of population problems, but a small trickle did return. For one thing the cost of living was lower on Earth, and what was a trifling annuity on Diporia, say, was a comfortable income on Earth. Besides, there were always men who found more satisfaction in displaying their success before the friends and scenes of their childhood than before all the rest of the Universe besides.

Trevelyan, Senior, further explained that if he stayed on Diporia, so would his children, and Diporia was a one-spaceship world. Back on Earth, his kids could end anywhere, even Novia.

Stubby Trevelyan had picked up that item early. Even before Reading Day, his conversation was based on the carelessly assumed fact that his ultimate home would be in Novia.

George, oppressed by thoughts of the other's future greatness and his own small-time contrast, was driven to belligerent defense at once.

"My father isn't worried either. He just wants to hear me read because he knows I'll be good. I suppose your father would just as soon not hear you because he knows you'll be all wrong."

"I will not be all wrong. Reading is *nothing*. On Novia, I'll *hire* people to read to me."

"Because *you* won't be able to read yourself, on account of you're *dumb!*"

"Then how come I'll be on Novia?"

And George, driven, made the great denial, "Who says you'll be on Novia? Bet you don't go anywhere."

Stubby Trevelyan reddened. "I won't be a Pipe Fitter like your old man."

"Take that back, you dumbhead."

"You take *that* back."

They stood nose to nose, not wanting to fight but relieved at having something familiar to do in this strange place. Furthermore, now that George had curled his hands into fists and lifted them before his face, the problem of what to do with his hands was, at least temporarily, solved. Other children gathered round excitedly.

But then it all ended when a woman's voice sounded loudly over the public address system. There was instant silence everywhere. George dropped his fists and forgot Trevelyan.

"Children," said the voice, "we are going to call out your names. As each child is called, he or she is to go to one of the men waiting along the side walls. Do you see them? They are wearing red uniforms so they will be easy to find. The girls will go to the right. The boys will go to the left. Now look about and see which man in red is nearest to you—"

George found his man at a glance and waited for his name to be called off. He had not been introduced before this to the sophistications of the alphabet, and the length of time it took to reach his own name grew disturbing.

The crowd of children thinned; little rivulets made their way to each of the red-clad guides.

III. Nature or Nurture—Once More with Feeling

When the name "George Platen" was finally called, his sense of relief was exceeded only by the feeling of pure gladness at the fact that Stubby Trevelyan still stood in his place, uncalled.

George shouted back over his shoulder as he left, "Yay, Stubby, maybe they don't want you."

That moment of gaiety quickly left. He was herded into a line and directed down corridors in the company of strange children. They all looked at one another, large-eyed and concerned, but beyond a snuffling, "Quitcher pushing" and "Hey, watch out" there was no conversation.

They were handed little slips of paper which they were told must remain with them. George stared at his curiously. Little black marks of different shapes. He knew it to be printing but how could anyone make words out of it? He couldn't imagine.

He was told to strip; he and four other boys who were all that now remained together. All the new clothes came shucking off and four eight-year-olds stood naked and small, shivering more out of embarrassment than cold. Medical technicians came past, probing them, testing them with odd instruments, pricking them for blood. Each took the little cards and made additional marks on them with little black rods that produced the marks, all neatly lined up, with great speed. George stared at the new marks, but they were no more comprehensible than the old. The children were ordered back into their clothes.

They sat on separate little chairs then and waited again. Names were called again and "George Platen" came third.

He moved into a large room, filled with frightening instruments with knobs and glassy panels in front. There was a desk in the very center, and behind it a man sat, his eyes on the papers piled before him.

He said, "George Platen?"

"Yes, sir," said George, in a shaky whisper. All this waiting and all this going here and there was making him nervous. He wished it were over.

The man behind the desk said, "I am Dr. Lloyd, George. How are you?"

The doctor didn't look up as he spoke. It was as though he had said those words over and over again and didn't have to look up any more.

"I'm all right."

"Are you afraid, George?"

"N—no, sir," said George, sounding afraid even in his own ears.

"That's good," said the doctor, "because there's nothing to be afraid of, you know. Let's see, George. It says here on your card that your father is named Peter and that he's a Registered Pipe Fitter and your mother is named Amy and is a Registered Home Technician. Is that right?"

"Y—yes, sir."

"And your birthday is February 13, and you had an ear infection about a year ago. Right?"

"Yes, Sir."

"Do you know how I know all these things?"

"It's on the card, I think, sir."

86

6. VISION: Profession

"That's right." The doctor looked up at George for the first time and smiled. He showed even teeth and looked much younger than George's father. Some of George's nervousness vanished.

The doctor passed the card to George. "Do you know what all those things there mean, George?"

Although George knew he did not he was startled by the sudden request into looking at the card as though he might understand now through some sudden stroke of fate. But they were just marks as before and he passed the card back. "No, sir."

"Why not?"

George felt a sudden pang of suspicion concerning the sanity of this doctor. Didn't he know why not?

George said, "I can't read, sir."

"Would you like to read?"

"Yes, sir."

"Why, George?"

George stared, appalled. No one had ever asked him that. He had no answer. He said falteringly, "I don't know, sir."

"Printed information will direct you all through your life. There is so much you'll have to know even after Education Day. Cards like this one will tell you. Books will tell you. Television screens will tell you. Printing will tell you such useful things and such interesting things that not being able to read would be as bad as not being able to see. Do you understand?"

"Yes, sir."

"Are you afraid, George?"

"No, sir."

"Good. Now I'll tell you exactly what we'll do first. I'm going to put these wires on your forehead just over the corners of your eyes. They'll stick there but they won't hurt at all. Then, I'll turn on something that will make a buzz. It will sound funny and it may tickle you, but it won't hurt. Now if it does hurt, you tell me, and I'll turn it off right away, but it won't hurt. All right?"

George nodded and swallowed.

"Are you ready?"

George nodded. He closed his eyes while the doctor busied himself. His parents had explained this to him. They, too, had said it wouldn't hurt, but then there were always the older children. There were the ten- and twelve-year-olds who howled after the eight-year-olds waiting for Reading Day. "Watch out for the needle." There were the others who took you off in confidence and said, "They got to cut your head open. They use a sharp knife that big with a hook on it," and so on into horrifying details.

George had never believed them but he had had nightmares, and now he closed his eyes and felt pure terror.

He didn't feel the wires at his temple. The buzz was a distant thing, and there was the sound of his own blood in his ears, ringing hollowly as though it and he were in a large cave. Slowly he chanced opening his eyes.

III. Nature or Nurture—Once More with Feeling

The doctor had his back to him. From one of the instruments a strip of paper unwound and was covered with a thin, wavy purple line. The doctor tore off pieces and put them into a slot in another machine. He did it over and over again. Each time a little piece of film came out, which the doctor looked at. Finally, he turned toward George with a queer frown between his eyes.

The buzzing stopped.

George said breathlessly, "Is it over?"

The doctor said, "Yes," but he was still frowning.

"Can I read now?" asked George. He felt no different.

The doctor said, "What?" then smiled very suddenly and briefly. He said, "It works fine, George. You'll be reading in fifteen minutes. Now we're going to use another machine this time and it will take longer. I'm going to cover your whole head, and when I turn it on you won't be able to see or hear anything for a while, but it won't hurt. Just to make sure I'm going to give you a little switch to hold in your hand. If anything hurts, you press the little button and everything shuts off. All right?"

In later years, George was told that the little switch was strictly a dummy; that it was introduced solely for confidence. He never did know for sure, however, since he never pushed the button.

A large smoothly curved helmet with a rubbery inner lining was placed over his head and left there. Three or four little knobs seemed to grab at him and bite into his skull, but there was only a little pressure that faded. No pain.

The doctor's voice sounded dimly. "Everything all right, George?"

And then, with no real warning, a layer of thick felt closed down all about him. He was disembodied, there was no sensation, no universe, only himself and a distant murmur at the very ends of nothingness telling him something—telling him—telling him—

He strained to hear and understand but there was all that thick felt between.

Then the helmet was taken off his head, and the light was so bright that it hurt his eyes while the doctor's voice drummed at his ears.

The doctor said, "Here's your card, George. What does it say?"

George looked at his card again and gave out a strangled shout. The marks weren't just marks at all. They made up words. They were words just as clearly as though something were whispering them in his ears. He could *hear* them being whispered as he looked at them.

"What does it say, George?"

"It says—it says—'Platen, George. Born 13 February 6492 of Peter and Amy Platen in . . .'" He broke off.

"You can read, George," said the doctor. "It's all over."

"For good? I won't forget how?"

"Of course not." The doctor leaned over to shake hands gravely. "You will be taken home now."

6. VISION: Profession

It was days before George got over this new and great talent of his. He read for his father with such facility that Platen, Senior, wept and called relatives to tell the good news.

George walked about town, reading every scrap of printing he could find and wondering how it was that none of it had ever made sense to him before.

He tried to remember how it was not to be able to read and he couldn't. As far as his feeling about it was concerned, he had always been able to read. Always.

At eighteen, George was rather dark, of medium height, but thin enough to look taller. Trevelyan, who was scarcely an inch shorter, had a stockiness of build that made "Stubby" more than ever appropriate, but in this last year he had grown self-conscious. The nickname could no longer be used without reprisal. And since Trevelyan disapproved of his proper first name even more strongly, he was called Trevelyan or any decent variant of that. As though to prove his manhood further, he had most persistently grown a pair of sideburns and a bristly mustache.

He was sweating and nervous now, and George, who had himself grown out of "Jaw-jee" and into the curt monosyllabic gutturability of "George," was rather amused by that.

They were in the same large hall they had been in ten years before (and not since). It was as if a vague dream of the past had come to sudden reality. In the first few minutes George had been distinctly surprised at finding everything seem smaller and more cramped than his memory told him; then he made allowance for his own growth.

The crowd was smaller than it had been in childhood. It was exclusively male this time. The girls had another day assigned them.

Trevelyan leaned over to say, "Beats me the way they make you wait."

"Red tape," said George. "You can't avoid it."

Trevelyan said, "What makes *you* so damned tolerant about it?"

"I've got nothing to worry about."

"Oh, brother, you make me sick. I hope you end up Registered Manure Spreader just so I can see your face when you do." His somber eyes swept the crowd anxiously.

George looked about, too. It wasn't quite the system they used on the children. Matters went slower, and instructions had been given out at the start in print (an advantage over the pre-Readers). The names Platen and Trevelyan were well down the alphabet still, but this time the two knew it.

Young men came out of the education rooms, frowning and uncomfortable, picked up their clothes and belongings, then went off to analysis to learn the results.

Each, as he come out, would be surrounded by a clot of the thinning crowd. "How was it?" "How'd it feel?" "Whacha think ya made?" "Ya feel any different?"

Answers were vague and noncommittal.

George forced himself to remain out of those clots. You only raised your own blood pressure. Everyone said you stood the best chance if you remained calm. Even so, you could feel the palms of your hands grow cold. Funny that new tensions came with the years.

For instance, high-specialty professionals heading out for an Outworld were accompanied by a wife (or husband). It was important to keep the sex ratio in good balance on all worlds. And if you were going out to a Grade A world, what girl would refuse you? George had no specific girl in mind yet; he wanted none. Not now! Once he made Programmer; once he could add to his name, Registered Computer Programmer, he could take his pick, like a sultan in a harem. The thought excited him and he tried to put it away. Must stay calm.

Trevelyan muttered, "What's it all about anyway? First they say it works best if you're relaxed and at ease. Then they put you through this and make it impossible for you to be relaxed and at ease."

"Maybe that's the idea. They're separating the boys from the men to begin with. Take it easy, Trev."

"Shut up."

George's turn came. His name was not called. It appeared in glowing letters on the notice board.

He waved at Trevelyan. "Take it easy. Don't let it get you."

He was happy as he entered the testing chamber. Actually happy.

The man behind the desk said, "George Platen?"

For a fleeting instant there was a razor-sharp picture in George's mind of another man, ten years earlier, who had asked the same question, and it was almost as though this were the same man and he, George, had turned eight again as he had stepped across the threshold.

But the man looked up and, of course, the face matched that of the sudden memory not at all. The nose was bulbous, the hair thin and stringy, and the chin wattled as though its owner had once been grossly overweight and had reduced.

The man behind the desk looked annoyed. "Well?"

George came to Earth. "I'm George Platen, sir."

"Say so, then. I'm Dr. Zachary Antonelli, and we're going to be intimately acquainted in a moment."

He stared at small strips of film, holding them up to the light owlishly.

George winced inwardly. Very hazily, he remembered that other doctor (he had forgotten the name) staring at such film. Could these be the same? The other doctor had frowned and this one was looking at him now as though he were angry.

His happiness was already just about gone.

6. VISION: Profession

Dr. Antonelli spread the pages of a thickish file out before him now and put the films carefully to one side. "It says here you want to be a Computer Programmer."

"Yes, doctor."

"Still do?"

"Yes, sir."

"It's a responsible and exacting position. Do you feel up to it?"

"Yes, sir."

"Most pre-Educates don't put down any specific profession. I believe they are afraid of queering it."

"I think that's right, sir."

"Aren't you afraid of that?"

"I might as well be honest, sir."

Dr. Antonelli nodded, but without any noticeable lightening of his expression. "Why do you want to be a Programmer?"

"It's a responsible and exacting position as you said, sir. It's an important job and an exciting one. I like it and I think I can do it."

Dr. Antonelli put the papers away, and looked at George sourly. He said, "How do you know you like it? Because you think you'll be snapped up by some Grade A planet?"

George thought uneasily: He's trying to rattle you. Stay calm and stay frank.

He said, "I think a Programmer has a good chance, sir, but even if I were left on Earth, I know I'd like it." (That was true enough. I'm not lying, thought George.)

"All right, how do you know?"

He asked it as though he knew there was no decent answer and George almost smiled. He had one.

He said, "I've been reading about Programming, sir."

"You've been *what?*" Now the doctor looked genuinely astonished and George took pleasure in that.

"Reading about it, sir. I bought a book on the subject and I've been studying it."

"A book for Registered Programmers?"

"Yes, sir."

"But you couldn't understand it."

"Not at first. I got other books on mathematics and electronics. I made out all I could. I still don't know much, but I know enough to know I like it and to know I can make it." (Even his parents never found that secret cache of books or knew why he spent so much time in his own room or exactly what happened to the sleep he missed.)

The doctor pulled at the loose skin under his chin. "What was your idea in doing that, son?"

"I wanted to make sure I would be interested, sir."

"Surely you know that being interested means nothing. You could be devoured by a subject and if the physical make-up of your brain makes it more efficient for you to be something else, something else you will be. You know that, don't you?"

"I've been told that," said George cautiously.

"Well, believe it. It's true."

George said nothing.

Dr. Antonelli said, "Or do you believe that studying some subject will bend the brain cells in that direction, like that other theory that a pregnant woman need only listen to great music persistently to make a composer of her child. Do you believe that?"

George flushed. That had certainly been in his mind. By forcing his intellect constantly in the desired direction, he had felt sure that he would be getting a head start. Most of his confidence had rested on exactly that point.

"I never—" he began, and found no way of finishing.

"Well, it isn't true. Good Lord, youngster, your brain pattern is fixed at birth. It can be altered by a blow hard enough to damage the cells or by a burst blood vessel or by a tumor or by a major infection—each time, of course, for the worse. But it certainly can't be affected by your thinking special thoughts." He stared at George thoughtfully, then said, "Who told you to do this?"

George, now thoroughly disturbed, swallowed and said, "No one, doctor. My own idea."

"Who knew you were doing it after you started?"

"No one. Doctor, I meant to do no wrong."

"Who said anything about wrong? Useless is what I would say. Why did you keep it to yourself?"

"I—I thought they'd laugh at me." (He thought abruptly of a recent exchange with Trevelyan. George had very cautiously broached the thought, as of something merely circulating distantly in the very outermost reaches of his mind, concerning the possibility of learning something by ladling it into the mind by hand, so to speak, in bits and pieces. Trevelyan had hooted, "George, you'll be tanning your own shoes next and weaving your own shirts." He had been thankful then for his policy of secrecy.)

Dr. Antonelli shoved the bits of film he had first looked at from position to position in morose thought. Then he said, "Let's get you analyzed. This is getting me nowhere."

The wires went to George's temples. There was the buzzing. Again there came a sharp memory of ten years ago.

George's hands were clammy; his heart pounded. He should never have told the doctor about his secret reading.

It was his damned vanity, he told himself. He had wanted to show how enterprising he was, how full of initiative. Instead, he had showed himself superstitious and ignorant and aroused the hostility of the doctor. (He could tell the doctor hated him for a wise guy on the make.)

6. VISION: Profession

And now he had brought himself to such a state of nervousness, he was sure the analyzer would show nothing that made sense.

He wasn't aware of the moment when the wires were removed from his temples. The sight of the doctor, staring at him thoughtfully, blinked into his consciousness and that was that; the wires were gone. George dragged himself together with a tearing effort. He had quite given up his ambition to be a Programmer. In the space of ten minutes, it had all gone.

He said dismally, "I suppose no?"

"No what?"

"No Programmer?"

The doctor rubbed his nose and said, "You get your clothes and whatever belongs to you and go to room 15-C. Your files will be waiting for you there. So will my report."

George said in complete surprise, "Have I been Educated already? I thought this was just to—"

Dr. Antonelli stared down at his desk. "It will all be explained to you. You do as I say."

George felt something like panic. What was it they couldn't tell him? He wasn't fit for anything but Registered Laborer. They were going to prepare him for that; adjust him to it.

He was suddenly certain of it and he had to keep from screaming by main force.

He stumbled back to his place of waiting. Trevelyan was not there, a fact for which he would have been thankful if he had had enough self-possession to be meaningfully aware of his surroundings. Hardly anyone was left, in fact, and the few who were looked as though they might ask him questions were it not that they were too worn out by their tail-of-the-alphabet waiting to buck the fierce, hot look or anger and hate he cast at them.

What right had *they* to be technicians and he, himself, a Laborer? Laborer! He was *certain!*

He was led by a red-uniformed guide along the busy corridors lined with separate rooms each containing its groups, here two, there five: the Motor Mechanics, the Construction Engineers, the Agronomists— There were hundreds of specialized Professions and most of them would be represented in this small town by one or two anyway.

He hated them all just then: the Statisticians, the Accountants, the lesser breeds and the higher. He hated them because they owned their smug knowledge now, knew their fate, while he himself, empty still, had to face some kind of further red tape.

He reached 15-C, was ushered in and left in an empty room. For one moment, his spirits bounded. Surely, if this were the Labor classification room, there would be dozens of youngsters present.

A door sucked into its recess on the other side of a waist-high partition

93

and an elderly, white-haired man stepped out. He smiled and showed even teeth that were obviously false, but his face was still ruddy and unlined and his voice had vigor.

He said, "Good evening, George. Our own sector has only one of you this time, I see."

"Only one?" said George blankly.

"Thousands over the Earth, of course. Thousands. You're not alone."

George felt exasperated. He said, "I don't understand, sir. What's my classification? What's happening?"

"Easy, son. You're all right. It could happen to anyone." He held out his hand and George took it mechanically. It was warm and it pressed George's hand firmly. "Sit down, son. I'm Sam Ellenford."

George nodded impatiently. "I want to know what's going on, sir."

"Of course. To begin with, you can't be a Computer Programmer, George. You've guessed that, I think."

"Yes, I have," said George bitterly. "What will I be, then?"

"That's the hard part to explain, George." He paused, then said with careful distinctness, "Nothing."

"What!"

"Nothing!"

"But what does that mean? Why can't you assign me a profession?"

"We have no choice in the matter, George. It's the structure of your mind that decides that."

George went a sallow yellow. His eyes bulged. "There's something wrong with my mind?"

"There's *something* about it. As far as professional classification is concerned, I suppose you can call it wrong."

"But why?"

Ellenford shrugged. "I'm sure you know how Earth runs its Educational program, George. Practically any human being can absorb practically any body of knowledge, but each individual brain pattern is better suited to receiving some types of knowledge than others. We try to match mind to knowledge as well as we can within the limits of the quota requirements for each profession."

George nodded. "Yes, I know."

"Every once in a while, George, we come up against a young man whose mind is not suited to receiving a superimposed knowledge of any sort."

"You mean I can't be Educated?"

"That is what I mean."

"But that's crazy. I'm intelligent. I can understand—" He looked helplessly about as though trying to find some way of proving that he had a functioning brain.

"Don't misunderstand me, please," said Ellenford gravely. "You're intelligent. There's no question about that. You're even above average in intelligence. Unfortunately that has nothing to do with whether the mind ought to be allowed to accept superimposed knowledge or not. In fact, it is almost always the intelligent person who comes here."

"You mean I can't even be a Registered Laborer?" babbled George. Suddenly even that was better than the blank that faced him. "What's there to know to be a Laborer?"

"Don't underestimate the Laborer, young man. There are dozens of subclassifications and each variety has its own corpus of fairly detailed knowledge. Do you think there's no skill in knowing the proper manner of lifting a weight? Besides, for the Laborer, we must select not only minds suited to it, but bodies as well. You're not the type, George, to last long as a Laborer."

George was conscious of his slight build. He said, "But I've never heard of anyone without a profession."

"There aren't many," conceded Ellenford. "And we protect them."

"Protect them?" George felt confusion and fright grow higher inside him.

"You're a ward of the planet, George. From the time you walked through that door, we've been in charge of you." And he smiled.

It was a fond smile. To George it seemed the smile of ownership; the smile of a grown man for a helpless child.

He said, "You mean, I'm going to be in prison?"

"Of course not. You will simply be with others of your kind."

Your kind. The words made a kind of thunder in George's ear.

Ellenford said, "You need special treatment. We'll take care of you."

To George's own horror, he burst into tears. Ellenford walked to the other end of the room and faced away as though in thought.

George fought to reduce the agonized weeping to sobs and then to strangle those. He thought of his father and mother, of his friends, of Trevelyan, of his own shame—

He said rebelliously, "I learned to read."

"Everyone with a whole mind can do that. We've never found exceptions. It is at this stage that we discover—exceptions. And when you learned to read, George, we were concerned about your mind pattern. Certain peculiarities were reported even then by the doctor in charge."

"Can't you try Educating me? You haven't even tried. I'm willing to take the risk."

"The law forbids us to do that, George. But look, it will not be bad. We will explain matters to your family so they will not be hurt. At the place to which you'll be taken, you'll be allowed privileges. We'll get you books and you can learn what you will."

"Dab knowledge in by hand," said George bitterly. "Shred by shred. Then, when I die I'll know enough to be a Registered Junior Office Boy, Paper-Clip Division."

III.   Nature or Nurture—Once More with Feeling

"Yet I understand you've already been studying books."

George froze. He was struck devastatingly by sudden understanding. "That's it . . ."

"What is?"

"That fellow Antonelli. He's knifing me."

"No, George. You're quite wrong."

"Don't tell me that." George was in an ecstasy of fury. "That lousy bastard is selling me out because he thought I was a little too wise for him. I read books and tried to get a head start toward programming. Well, what do you want to square things? Money? You won't get it. I'm getting out of here and when I finish broadcasting this—"

He was screaming.

Ellenford shook his head and touched a contact.

Two men entered on catfeet and got on either side of George. They pinned his arms to his sides. One of them used an air-spray hypodermic in the hollow of his right elbow and the hypnotic entered his vein and had an almost immediate effect.

His screams cut off and his head fell forward. His knees buckled and only the men on either side kept him erect as he slept.

7.
VALENCE:
A Scientist's Variations
on a Disturbing Racial Theme
JOHN NEARY

In the preceding two articles, the idea has been put forth that some people may be born to be "thinkers." If you are a "thinker" yourself, this is not at all a bad idea. But it is well not to forget the corresponding point: if some people are "born to think," then some people will be "born not to think." This latter idea is explored in the following article by John Neary.

I was not surprised when, on his very first attempt at surf-casting, a tricky exercise of timing and coordination that takes years to master, my friend fouled the line.

But I was startled—and stung, too—when he said, as we unraveled the tangled backlash and he poised the 11-foot rod to try again, "Too bad Arthur Jensen isn't here with his little stopwatch and clipboard to see how long it takes me to figure this out!"

Urbane, traveled, well-educated, a nationally published writer, even my friend had felt the searching lash of Arthur Jensen's writings.

My friend is black—and he, like so many other blacks (and no few whites, too), has been shocked by Jensen's well-publicized belief that Negroes, on the average, are inherently less intelligent than whites. Shocked, hurt, outraged—and made to feel that whites are weighing them in a new way, as my friend's wry joke revealed, to see whether, perhaps, Jensen is not right.

Jensen, of course, is not alone in his belief; nor is he the first to expound it. My friend and other blacks are bitterly accustomed to hearing the ugly accusations of ignorant bigots. But Arthur Jensen is not known to be an ignorant bigot. He is, in fact, *Dr.* Arthur Jensen, a full professor of educational psychology at the University of California at Berkeley; and, where most exponents of racial superiority must promulgate their murky theories in tracts and pamphlets, Jensen was accorded almost an entire issue of the prestigious *Harvard Educational Review* in February 1969, where he expounded his theory in the longest article ever published by the journal.

More than a year has gone by since Jensen's paper first appeared, reporting that blacks, as a population, score significantly lower on IQ tests than the white population; and attributing their lower IQs primarily to their genetic heritage, not to discrimination, poor diet, bad living conditions or inferior schools. This IQ gap, Jensen said, had not resulted from the failure of compensatory education programs, but was instead the very reason underlying that failure. The correct course for a nation concerned about millions of ghetto students who were growing up unable to read and write and function as participating citizens, his paper suggested, was not to try to close the IQ gap, but to recognize it and work in ghetto classrooms with what potential was there.

Jensen's paper ignited a debate that has rocked academe, whistled through the pages of professional journals, spilled over into teachers' lounge debates and cocktail party harangues. On Jensen's own campus, vehement reaction to his paper erupted in an ugly spate of Fire-Jensen rallies, with students and some fellow faculty members angrily demanding his resignation. Totally surprised at the response, Jensen found himself moving classes to secret rendezvous spots to avoid demonstrations. One of Jensen's staff members quit in fear and the local school board, saying he was too publically hot to handle, canceled a survey of its busing program which Jensen had been commissioned to make.

Wherever he went, Jensen was confronted with angry blacks who wanted to face him personally with their outcries; at one academic conference at the University of Illinois he sat impassively as a young Ghanaian student rose and shouted, "Why do you whites hate blacks?" and when the campus was threatened by a bomb rumor, he joked nervously at lunch, "I didn't bring my bulletproof vest." That afternoon the scientists tried to mollify one black student who rose to say, with bitterness, "I'd like you to let *me* set up the tests and let all these white folks come in and take the tests in *my* school. I think you'll find they don't know what's going on and I would have to say *they* are inferior. Instead of me coming into your university like a white person and trying to perform on your tests, why aren't the universities creating courses which reflect the various cultures of this country . . . ?" Presently, the blacks walked out.

These were tough questions intruding from the outside world into the tidy and clubby little laboratory universe Jensen feels most comfortable in. But he had his allies, too, some of them respected professionals such as Physicist William Shockley, who shared the Nobel prize for inventing the transistor, has applied himself in recent years to promoting research into genetics and intelligence, and who says "there is a difference in the wiring patterns" of white and black minds. Some others who took up Jensen's cause, however, had no scientific credentials and no scientific motives; his article quickly found its way into a Virginia courtroom, introduced as defense evidence in a desegregation suit, and one Southern congressman had the entire 123-page article reprinted in the *Congressional Record* for the edification of his white constituents.

At the beginning of this year, President Nixon made a report to Congress on the nation's compensatory education programs, which Jensen had most strongly criticized. Enacted five years ago, the programs, such as Head Start and other elementary enrichment projects, were in effect going to compensate the kids in the ghetto, in the forgotten mountain hollow and on the Indian reservation, for their poor environments. These children might still have to live in slums—but the new special schools were going to set them on equal footing with the rich kids in the suburbs.

Surveying the results of that hopeful beginning, Mr. Nixon's report card to the Congress gave compensatory education almost straight F's for failure, with only a desultory and lowercase e for effort. Before investing more millions in projects that weren't working, the President said, a new National Institute of Education should carry out work on a fourth R—research into what it is that enables some children to pick up reading, writing and arithmetic better than others.

The President avoided any mention of Jensen's paper although he knew about it. Shortly after the paper had appeared in the *Harvard Educational Review,* White House domestic advisor Daniel Moynihan had been moved to remark that "the winds of Jensen" were gusting through the capital at gale force. At a meeting of the President's Cabinet, Moynihan recalls, "someone asked, 'What about Jensen?' and the President asked me if I knew anything about it and I briefed the Cabinet: who Jensen is, what he said, the essentials: that it was merely a hypothesis, that in fact we have no direct knowledge of a genetic basis of intelligence, only inferential knowledge, that nobody knows what a 'smart gene' looks like, that Dr. Jensen is a thoroughly respectable man, that he is in no sense a racist—but that it is merely a *hypothesis.*"

The Jensen report, says one high government official, "has kicked up a lot more private reaction than you'd think. It's not something that anybody does talk about. It's *secret knowledge* in Washington, something everybody knows and doesn't say. In the bureaucracy, when they see these compensatory programs not working, they just look at each other . . ."

Professor Jensen is privately convinced that he has more supporters in high government places than any public survey—or the President's report —would reveal. "The kind of research being funded and some of the appointments being made," Dr. Jensen says, "reflect in subtle ways some of the ideas in my *Harvard Review* article."

If so, the knowing glances of the bureaucrats could have as much effect on the fate of compensatory education as the official dogma of the government's Office of Education, where the liberal educator Dr. James Allen Jr. now presides. Despite the millions of dollars spent on schooling for the

III. Nature or Nurture—Once More with Feeling

disadvantaged, Dr. Allen's office admits it has, as yet, no substantial research data on the results and is therefore not prepared to refute Jensen. Dr. Allen does say, however, that he was bothered by the Jensen paper, because of its potential for racist mischief.

To many people it has seemed that Jensen lent his considerable academic prestige and the prestige of science to some malevolent notions that were inflammatory indeed in a nation already a racial powder keg. Dr. Lee J. Cronbach, professor of education at Stanford, says, "I wish this whole thing would just go away and die—we've heard entirely too much about the wrong aspects of it." The Jensen issue, though, remains very much alive. Just recently Jensen and Shockley reported on their research to the National Academy of Sciences, and Dr. Shockley again urged the Academy to sponsor more research into race and intelligence. And Jensen, himself, with his cold, brazen air of trying to bring science to bear on the seemingly ineffable, mysterious human mind, is busy thinking up yet more ways to find out whether, as he suspects, American Negroes are, on the average, *really* dumber than whites and whether, as he also suspects, it is the fault of their genes. As for the criticism which his paper has brought him, Jensen insists that most people have not only misunderstood what he said but scarcely grasp the main points of his argument.

Just exactly what *did* Dr. Jensen say in that 123-page paper?

Compensatory education programs, he claimed, are a flop: they have not raised IQ scores or scholastic achievement.

Compensatory education programs, he contended, were built on two false assumptions: that children are equally endowed with intelligence at birth; and that differences in their school achievement can be equalized by improving the environments of kids who do poorly.

"Intelligence," he concedes, "like electricity, is easier to measure than to define." But, in practice, Jensen simply defines intelligence as whatever it is that IQ tests measure. The prestigious Society for the Psychological Study of Social Issues, attacking Jensen's paper, lambasted him for trusting IQ tests. "Largely developed and standardized on white middle-class children," the Society argued, "these tests tend to be biased against black children to an unknown degree." The point is a major one, for if white society is the only game in town, and one needs a high IQ to play, *and* the IQ test is rigged against black people, then the 15-point gap might be no more than a reflection of this rigging. Jensen, aware of this argument, had said that even on so-called "culture fair" IQ tests, black children did less well than whites, but the Society's psychologists contend that none of these tests is really unbiased.

Biased or not, the IQ tests have been used by Jensen not only to demonstrate a 15-point black–white intelligence difference, but also to decide that exactly 80% of the gap is due to heredity—which would mean the black child's lower IQ is largely invulnerable to any efforts at improvement. To get this 80% figure, Jensen analyzed more than a hundred studies of IQ test programs by a statistical technique (known as "analysis of variance") which required his assigning *precise* numerical values to such intangible "variables" as the effect of a ghetto environment on a child's mind. Thus, the way Jensen "graded" the intangible effects of ghetto life had obviously quite a bit to do with the results of his study. And it is precisely upon that ground that he got some of his most savage criticism.

Theoretically, Jensen admits, he can imagine a situation where some environmental factor could explain the intelligence gap. "Let's say," he says, "the Negroes were in uniformly poorer environmental circumstances than whites; just all of them were for some reason depressed—just by virtue of being black in our society, let's say." In such "theoretical" circumstances, Jensen allows, environmental deprivation could account for Negroes' lower IQ scores.

But by such deprivation, Jensen says, he does not mean a "mere lack of middle-class amenities." He means situations in which children suffer "little sensory stimulation of any kind and little contact with adults." The children that educators call culturally disadvantaged, he says, are not reared in conditions anywhere near that bad.

To blacks living in ghettos, it is not quite so apparent that hunger, welfare dependency, prejudice, rat bites and all the other insults of a ghetto environment amount to no more than, as Jensen puts it, the "mere lack of middle-class amenities." But, having thus written off the cultural impact of slavery, segregation and poverty on black children, Jensen could only conclude that blacks must be *born* with lower IQs.

Jensen did hedge his findings considerably, at almost every step, since his statistical conclusions were, of necessity, based on imperfect and sometimes inadequate data. On one significant point, he reported that all the data on the heritability of IQ—on which he based his own computations—came from studies of white European and North American populations. That means, he says, that "our knowledge of the heritability of intelligence in different racial and cultural groups within these populations is nil."

But, as is often the case, few of Jensen's disclaimers were noticed in the fine print of his provocative paper and most people took his speculations for blunt statements of fact. A major source of such confusion was the essential distinction Jensen makes between populations and individuals.

"As far as we know," he observed, "the full range of human talents is represented in all the major races of man and in all socioeconomic levels." But in broad population terms, he explained, the 15-point gap has grim implications. "I would say for any one individual, 15 points may not make much difference—after all, the average difference of siblings raised in the same family is 12 points," Jensen says. "Where it makes a lot of difference is when you look at groups," and he points to the 115-point IQ score he considers the minimum to get into college. Sixteen percent of U.S. whites make it over that hurdle; fewer than 3% of blacks. "So," Jensen says, "if we want equal representation, it's impossible. M.I.T. and Cal Tech have close to a 130 cutoff, the highest in the country and only the upper 3% of the white population make it. You may not find one Negro in a thousand that high."

Only, Jensen ultimately admits, he doesn't really know if the gap is genetic. "I simply say the idea of a genetic difference is not an unreasonable one," he says, "because everything else that's ever been examined has shown differences and why should the brain be an exception? It's not an unreasonable proposition, but it has not been proved in any scientifically acceptable way. I think it *could* be, if the work necessary were done, but it's been such a tabooed area that either no one has wanted to do the work or the persons who were capable of doing the work haven't wanted to do it."

In its rebuttal to Jensen's paper, the Society for the Psychological Study of Social Issues agreed with Jensen that he hadn't proved his proposition in a "scientifically acceptable way," and it also went on to assert that science could not begin to sort out the role of heredity in intelligence until social conditions had been equal for both races for several generations.

Theoretically, of course, almost any area is fair game for scientific study, from human mating habits to the innermost secrets of the psyche. But the National Academy of Sciences has, despite the repeated entreaties of Dr. Shockley, refused to endorse studies of genetics and intelligence, on the ground that clear data—such as an accurate measure of "environmental deprivation"—are just plain impossible to isolate. Such considerations— and the painfully sensitive nature of the question—have caused many qualified geneticists to ignore the issue entirely, or to dismiss it, as behavioral geneticist Jerry Hirsch did Jensen's work by saying, "It's an example of the engineering mind at work—and I don't know of it working in biology."

Jensen, despite his daredevil willingness to think about these questions, is dismayed at the hostile reaction to his paper. His whole project, he recalls, began almost offhandedly, as a casual attempt to answer a schoolteacher friend's inquiry about why some of the liveliest kids on the playground did so badly when they got back into her fourth grade classroom after recess. The problem, however, soon proved to be teasingly complex —and when Jensen had filled four filing cabinet drawers with his research, he decided to write a book about educating underprivileged children. Then, when his chapter on the question of nature versus nurture went beyond 200 pages he decided his book *really* ought to be about that, instead. "I knew," he says, "that one had to be cautious, but I thought one had to be honest and objective about the whole matter [of genetics] and I thought it was a sadly neglected area. When I began getting into the literature on this and saw how relevant it was to the problems people concerned with the disadvantaged have, I realized *how* neglected it was. You can read book after book and paper after paper which talk as though such things as genes don't exist, as though there's no question about genetic differences whatsoever. It's never brought up as a possibility, even. You'd think it had never crossed the minds of the people who'd written or worked in this field. I thought I would be doing the field a service by bringing it into the picture.

One of Jensen's sharpest critics, Nobel prize-winning geneticist Joshua Lederberg, says Jensen's work has had exactly the opposite effect. Such studies, Lederberg says, presented in a "premature and sloppy style," make no contribution to science and can only lead to a deepening alienation in society. Jensen's paper, he says, represented "a set of conjectures pulled out of thin air. There is no scientific substance to the assertion of a genetic basis for black–white difference. It's a legitimate *hypothesis* and that's as far as one can go." Because the issue is "undecidable" at present, he feels, discussing it as Jensen does is a great disservice.

"To bring this up right now, when some degree of harmony and convergence of social purpose among the races is what we've got to develop to keep this country together, I think is very vicious," says Lederberg. "I'm not saying that ought to dominate our conception of what is correct and incorrect—if we are to find solutions to problems we have to know the facts about them. But I also think it's a question that is too important to leave to sloppy and inconclusive science. On something that can affect group esteem and inter-group esteem as well as self-esteem as deeply as this, then one ought to be very, very careful and very, very sure before one promulgates one's hypothesis. As somebody else put it, there are different thresholds for making speculations, and you don't go around telling somebody he's about to die unless you have a fairly high degree of certainty that's a correct statement—and I think we're dealing with a social climate that is just as loaded as that."

Jensen, of course, disagrees, and insists that it is dangerously wrong to go on thinking the races are inherently equal in intelligence when they may not be. "As long as people are told there are no differences among groups and individuals, and the only differences are differences society imposes on them, then I think you are going to have frustration, are going to have a kind of paranoia develop, with people wondering. 'Look, these people are making a pretense of giving us every opportunity, but we're still not making it. In what way are they keeping us back?' "

Incredible as it may seem, in a country littered with the physical and moral debris of hundreds of ghetto riots, Jensen is in effect saying that, if his studies could only show blacks that their lower IQ scores are a product of genetics, they would stop complaining about imagined insults and alleged discrimination—or at least that they should. "I don't see why people should be disturbed by unequal representation of different groups in different occupations—or educationally, *if* it should be found that there are real differences," Jensen says.

One of the obvious hazards of this sort of conjecture, and the research behind it, of course, is that they supply the segregationists with just the

III. Nature or Nurture—Once More with Feeling

sort of "scientific" data they delight in quoting, just as a century or so ago they took pleasure in measuring cranial capacities and discussing brain pans. Jensen himself says that, on the average, Negro children not only have lower IQs, but what intelligence they do have may not be the same kind as whites. He makes a distinction between *cognitive* learning, or the abstract use of concepts and ideas, and *associative* learning, or rote memorization. IQ tests, Jensen says, are a better gauge of cognitive than of associative abilities, and therefore "do not reveal that aspect of mental ability which may be the disadvantaged child's strongest point—the ability for associative learning." Then he suggests that compensatory education programs ought to emphasize more rote learning for the disadvantaged, to tap this hidden power source. This, he says, would "make education more rewarding for children of different patterns of ability." Stanford's Cronbach dismisses this idea as mere *training,* not education; and blacks already have spent generations watching their kids assigned to metal shop, while the white kids went to mathematics.

Shockley contends that Jensen's research on black–white intelligence is destined to save Negroes, almost in spite of themselves, from what he calls "genetic enslavement" (a phrase that Jensen uses, too). Shockley is a zealot on the subject of eugenics—on the need, that is, to insure that the nation's "gene pool" is not polluted by the uncontrolled reproduction of inferior genetic stock. Along with Jensen, Shockley worries that such a "dysgenic trend" may be at work in U.S. populations. This point, Jensen says in exasperation, was the most explosive part of his paper and got hardly any attention at all.

Census data show, he told a Berkeley symposium on genetics, that the poorest Negroes are having more children than middle-class Negroes, and that this disparity between the classes is greater in the black population than in the white. Suggesting that, in general, the poor inherit lower IQs than the well-to-do, Jensen warned that the present reproductive patterns could "create and widen the genetic intelligence differences" between blacks and whites. "The social and educational implications of this trend," he said, "if it exists and persists, are enormous."

The "dysgenic trend," of course, may not exist at all—some researchers such as Dr. Moynihan say it does not—and it may in fact, as others claim, be something that, by virtue of the elusiveness of the facts involved, is utterly invulnerable to research in the first place. Clearcut, unambiguous research on human genes and environment, they say, cannot be assembled as it can and has been with fruit flies, or bread mold, or even the garden pea with which Gregor Mendel began the science of genetics. But Dr. Jensen, undaunted by such objections, speculates on:

"Is there a danger," he asks, "that current welfare policies, unaided by eugenic foresight, could lead to the genetic enslavement of a substantial segment of our population? The possible consequences of our failure seriously to study these questions may well be viewed by future generations as our society's greatest injustice to Negro Americans."

It is precisely this sort of speculation that geneticist Lederberg finds most vicious. "Jensen feeds Shockley," says Lederberg, "and Shockley feeds the racists—people who are impatient about making a significant investment in improving the condition of blacks, and would welcome any excuse to be off-loaded with it."

Shockley and Jensen see themselves first as scientists, committed to pursuing truth wherever the chase leads—and in this case, Jensen's archetypically academic tunnel vision led him right into a mare's nest of bitter controversy. Difficult as that kind of naïveté may be to believe, Jensen says he never dreamt of the volatility of his report. The fact is, however, that Jensen, a 46-year-old workhorse of a professor who was once a concert clarinetist, lives a life that seems comfortably sealed off to almost everything except his research and his music. He is into his study and uncovering his typewriter first thing after an early breakfast and he doesn't surface until it is time for lunch and his departure for his tiny office on the Berkeley campus. There he juggles his mail, oversees several researchers, works on his book, his articles and his several on-going research projects. Evenings and weekends find him once more in his study, with scant time out only to study symphony scores—he is a conductor at heart and he reveres Toscanini—or to listen to classical music on his sophisticated high fidelity set.

Thus insulated from the oppressive actualities of a problem his data barely hint at, Arthur Jensen is continuing with his work in the quiet solitude of his study, in the sequestered office at Berkeley, dreaming up experiments.

How could science *ever* decide this genetics–environment issue?

"The ideal experiment," he says, "would be to take a fertilized black ovum, both parents Negro, and implant it into a white mother and have that child brought up in society where there's no prejudice against skin color . . .

"Or, if possible—this is zany, but it's a conceptual experiment—transplant the brain of a kid, do a brain transplant from white to black and black to white and see if it makes a difference. You'd have a black brain in a white body and everything controlled . . .

"Now," he admits, "you can't do that kind of experiment, so it's just out of the question." Then, says Professor Arthur Jensen, white, IQ well up in the gifted range, "I hope people realize what I mean by conceptual experiment—that you dream up the ideal experiment, and then try to set up something as close to that as possible."

8.
VISION:
Learning Theory

JAMES V. McCONNELL

James V. McConnell is a psychologist who has, among other things, a sense of humor and a taste for science fiction. Both are at play in his short vision entitled "Learning Theory."

I am writing this because I presume He wants me to. Otherwise He would not have left paper and pencil handy for me to use. And I put the word "He" in capitals because it seems the only thing to do. If I am dead and in hell, then this is only proper. However, if I am merely a captive somewhere, then surely a little flattery won't hurt matters.

As I sit here in this small room and think about it, I am impressed most of all by the suddenness of the whole thing. At one moment I was out walking in the woods near my suburban home. The next thing I knew, here I was in a small, featureless room, naked as a jaybird, with only my powers of rationalization to stand between me and insanity. When the "change" was made (whatever the change was), I was not conscious of so much as a momentary flicker between walking in the woods and being here in this room. Whoever is responsible for all of this is to be complimented—either He has developed an instantaneous anesthetic or He has solved the problem of instantaneous transportation of matter. I would prefer to think it the former, for the latter leads to too much anxiety.

Yes, there I was walking through the woods, minding my own business, studiously pretending to enjoy the outing so that I wouldn't mind the exercise too much, when the transition took place. As I recall, I was immersed in the problem of how to teach my class in Beginning Psychology some of the more abstruse points of Learning Theory when the transition

From *If-Worlds of Science Fiction*, December 1967, Copyright 1957 by Quinn Publishing Co. Reprinted by permission of the author.

8. VISION: Learning Theory

came. How far away and distant life at the University seems at the moment! I must be forgiven if now I am much more concerned about where I am and how to get out of here than about how freshmen can be cajoled into understanding Hull or Tolman.

Problem One

Where am I? For an answer, I can only describe this room. It is about twenty feet square, some twelve feet high, with no windows, but with what might be a door in the middle of one of the walls. Everything is of a uniform gray color, and the walls and ceiling emit a fairly pleasant achromatic light. The walls themselves are of some hard material which might be metal since it feels slightly cool to the touch. The floor is of a softer, rubbery material that yields a little when I walk on it. Also, it has a rather "tingly" feel to it, suggesting that it may be in constant vibration. It is somewhat warmer than the walls, which is all to the good since it appears I must sleep on the floor.

The only furniture in the room consists of what might be a table and what passes for a chair. They are not quite that, but they can be made to serve this purpose. On the table I found the paper and the pencil. No, let me correct myself. What I call paper is a good deal rougher and thicker than I am used to, and what I call a pencil is nothing more than a thin round stick of graphite which I have sharpened by rubbing one end of it on the table.

And that is the sum extent of my surroundings. I wish I knew what He has done with my clothes. The suit was an old one, but I am worried about the walking boots. I was very fond of those boots—not because of any sentimental attachment nor because they had done me much good service, but rather because they were quite expensive and I would hate to lose them.

The problem still remains to be answered, however, as to just where in the hell I am—if not in hell itself!

Problem Two

Problem Two is a knottier one—why am I here? Were I subject to paranoid tendencies, I would doubtless come to the conclusion that my enemies had kidnapped me. Or perhaps that the Russians had taken such an interest in my research that they had spirited me away to some Siberian hideout and would soon appear to demand either cooperation or death. Sadly enough, I am too reality oriented. My research was highly interesting to me, and perhaps to a few other psychologists who like to dabble in esoteric problems of animal learning, but it was scarcely startling enough to warrant such attention as kidnapping.

So I am left as baffled as before. Where am I, and why?
And who is He?

III. Nature or Nurture—Once More with Feeling

I have decided to forego all attempts at keeping this diary according to "days" or "hours." Such units of time have no meaning in my present circumstances, for the light remains constant all the time I am awake. The human organism is not possessed of as neat an internal clock as some of the lower species. Far too many studies have shown that a human being who is isolated from all external stimulation soon loses his sense of time. So I will merely indicate breaks in the narrative and hope that He will understand that if He wasn't bright enough to leave me with my wristwatch. He couldn't expect me to keep an accurate record.

Nothing much has happened since I began this narrative, except that I have slept, been fed and watered, and have emptied my bladder and bowels. The food was waiting on the table when I awoke last time. I must say that He had little of the gourmet in Him. Protein balls are not my idea of a feast royal. However, they will serve to keep body and soul together (presuming, of course, that they *are* together at the moment). But I must object to my source of liquid refreshment. The meal made me very thirsty and I was in the process of cursing Him and everybody else when I noticed a small nipple which had appeared in the wall while I was asleep. At first I thought that perhaps Freud was right after all, and that my libido had taken over control of my imagery. Experimentation convinced me, however, that the thing was real, and that it is my present source of water. If one sucks on the thing, it delivers a slightly cool and somewhat sweetish flow of liquid. But really, it's a most undignified procedure. It's bad enough to have to sit around all day in my birthday suit. But for a full professor to have to stand on his tiptoes and suck on an artificial nipple in order to obtain water is asking a little too much. I'd complain to the Management if only I knew to whom to complain!

Following eating and drinking, the call to nature became a little too strong to ignore. Now, I was adequately toilet-trained with indoor plumbing, and the absence of same is most annoying. However, there was nothing much to do but choose a corner of the room and make the best of a none too pleasant situation. (As a side-thought, I wonder if the choosing of a corner was in any way instinctive?) However, the upshot of the whole thing was my learning what is probably the purpose of the vibration of the floor. For the excreted material disappeared through the floor not too many minutes later. The process was a gradual one. Now I will be faced with all kinds of uncomfortable thoughts concerning what might possibly happen to me if I slept too long!

Perhaps this is to be expected, but I find myself becoming a little paranoid after all. In attempting to solve my *Problem Two*, why I am here, I have begun to wonder if perhaps some of my colleagues at the University are not using me as the subject in some kind of experiment. It would be just like them to dream up some fantastic kind of "human-in-isolation" experiment and use me as a pilot observer. You would think that they'd have asked my permission first. However, perhaps it's important that the subject not know what's happening to him. If so, I have one happy thought to console me. If any of them are responsible for this, they'll have to take over the teaching of my classes for the time being. And how they hate teaching Learning Theory to freshmen!

You know, this place seems dreadfully quiet to me.

3

Suddenly I have solved two of my problems. I know both where I am and who He is. And I bless the day I got interested in the perception of motion.

I should say to begin with that the air in this room seems to have more than the usual concentration of dust particles. This didn't seem particularly noteworthy until I noticed that most of them seemed to pile up along the floor against one wall in particular. For a while I was sure that this was due to the ventilation system—perhaps there was an outgoing air duct there where this particular wall was joined to the floor. However, when I went over and put my hand to the floor there, I could feel no breeze whatsoever. Yet even as I held my hand along the dividing line between the wall and the floor, dust motes covered my hand with a thin coating. I tried this same experiment everywhere else in the room to no avail. This was the only spot where the phenomenon occurred, and it occurred along the entire length of this one wall.

But if ventilation was not responsible for the phenomenon, what was? All at once there popped into my mind some calculations I had made back when the rocket boys had first proposed a manned satellite station. Engineers are notoriously naive when it comes to the performance of a human being in most situations, and I remembered that the problem of the perception of the satellite's rotation seemingly had been ignored by the slip-stick crowd. They had planned to rotate the doughnut-shaped satellite in order to substitute centrifugal force for the force of gravity. Thus the outer shell of the doughnut would appear to be "down" to anyone inside the thing. Apparently they had not realized that man is at least as sensitive to angular rotation as he is to variations in the pull of gravity. As I figured the problem then, if a man aboard the doughnut moved his head as much as three or four feet outwards from the center of the doughnut, he would have become fairly dizzy! Rather annoying it would have been, too, to have been hit by a wave of nausea every time one sat down in a chair. Also, as I pondered the problem, it became apparent that dust particles and the like would probably show a tendency to move in a direction opposite to the direction of the rotation, and hence pile up against any wall or such that impeded their flight.

Using the behavior of the dust particles as a clue, I then climbed atop the table and leapt off. Sure enough, my head felt like a mule had kicked it by the time I landed on the floor. My hypothesis was confirmed.

So I am aboard a spaceship!

III. Nature or Nurture—Once More with Feeling

The thought is incredible but in a strange way comforting. At least now I can postpone worrying about heaven and hell—and somehow I find the idea of being in a spaceship much more to the liking of a confirmed agnostic. I suppose I owe my colleagues an apology—I should have known they would never have put themselves in a position where they might have to teach freshmen all about learning!

And, of course, I now know who "He" is. Or rather, I know who He *isn't*, which is something else again. Surely, though, I can no longer think of Him as being human. Whether I should be consoled at this or not, I have no way of telling.

I still have no notion of *why* I am here, however, nor why this alien chose to pick me of all people to pay a visit to His spaceship. What possible use could I be? Surely if He were interested in making contact with the human race, He would have spirited away a politician. After all, that's what politicians are for! Since there has been no effort made to communicate with me, however, I must reluctantly give up any cherished hopes that His purpose is that of making contact with *genus homo.*

Or perhaps He's a galactic scientist of some kind, a biologist of sorts, out gathering specimens. Now, that's a particularly nasty thought. What if He turned out to be a psychologist, interested in cutting me open eventually to see what makes me tick? Will my innards be smeared over a glass slide for scores of youthful Hims to peer at under a microscope? Brrrr! I don't mind giving my life to Science, but I'd rather do it a little at a time.

If you don't mind, I think I'll go do a little repressing for a while.

4

Good God! I should have known it! Destiny will play her little tricks, and all jokes have their cosmic angles. He is a *psychologist!* Had I given it due consideration, I would have realized that whenever you come across a new species, you worry about behavior first, physiology second. So I have received the ultimate insult—or the ultimate compliment. I don't know which. I have become a specimen for an alien psychologist!

This thought first occurred to me when I awoke after my latest sleep (which was filled, I must admit, with most frightening dreams). It was immediately obvious that something about the room had changed. Almost at once I noticed that one of the walls now had a lever of some kind protruding from it, and to one side of the lever, a small hole in the wall with a container beneath the hole. I wandered over to the lever, inspected it for a few moments, then accidently depressed the thing. At once there came a loud clicking noise, and a protein ball popped out of the hole and fell into the container.

For just a moment a frown crossed my brow. This seemed somehow so strangely familiar. Then, all at once, I burst into wild laughter. The room had been changed into a gigantic Skinner Box! For years I had been studying animal learning by putting white rats in a Skinner Box and following

110

8. VISION: Learning Theory

the changes in the rats' behavior. The rats had to learn to press the lever in order to get a pellet of food, which was delivered to them through just such an apparatus as is now affixed to the wall of my cell. And now, after all of these years, and after all of the learning studies I had done, to find myself trapped like a rat in a Skinner Box! Perhaps this was hell after all, I told myself, and the Lord High Executioner's admonition to "let the punishment fit the crime" was being followed.

Frankly, this sudden turn of events has left me more than a little shaken.

5

I seem to be performing according to theory. It didn't take me long to discover that pressing the lever would give me food some of the time, while at other times all I got was the click and no protein ball. It appears that approximately every twelve hours the thing delivers me a random number of protein balls—the number has varied from five to fifteen so far. I never know ahead of time how many pellets—I mean protein balls—the apparatus will deliver, and it spews them out intermittently. Sometimes I have to press the lever a dozen times or so before it will give me anything, while at other times it gives me one ball for each press. Since I don't have a watch on me, I am never quite sure when the twelve hours have passed, so I stomp over to the lever and press it every few minutes when I think it's getting close to time to be fed. Just like my rats always did. And since the pellets are small and I never get enough of them, occasionally I find myself banging away on the lever with all the compulsion of a stupid animal. But I missed the feeding time once and almost starved to death (so it seemed) before the lever delivered food the next time. About the only consolation to my wounded pride is that at this rate of starvation, I'll lose my bay window in short order.

At least He doesn't seem to be fattening me up for the kill. Or maybe he just likes lean meat.

6

I have been promoted. Apparently He in His infinite alien wisdom has decided that I'm intelligent enough to handle the Skinner-type apparatus, so I've been promoted to solving a maze. Can you picture the irony of the situation? All of the classic Learning Theory methodology is practically being thrown in my face in mockery. If only I could communicate with Him! I don't mind being subjected to tests nearly as much as I mind being underestimated. Why, I can solve puzzles hundreds of times more complex than what He's throwing at me. But how can I tell Him?

7

As it turns out, the maze is much like our standard T-mazes, and is not too difficult to learn. It's a rather long one, true, with some 23 choice points along the way. I spent the better part of half an hour wandering through the thing the first time I found myself in it. Surprisingly enough, I didn't realize the first time out what I was in, so I made no conscious attempt to memorize the correct turns. It wasn't until I reached the final turn and found food waiting for me that I recognized what I was expected to do. The next time through the maze my performance was a good deal better, and I was able to turn in a perfect performance in not too long a time. However, it does not do my ego any good to realize that my own white rats could have learned the maze a little sooner than I did.

My "home cage," so to speak, still has the Skinner apparatus in it, but the lever delivers food only occasionally now. I still give it a whirl now and again, but since I'm getting a fairly good supply of food at the end of the maze each time, I don't pay the lever much attention.

Now that I am very sure of what is happening to me, quite naturally my thoughts have turned to how I can get out of this situation. Mazes I can solve without too much difficulty, but how to escape is apparently beyond my intellectual capacity. But then, come to think of it, there was precious little chance for my own experimental animals to get out of my clutches. And assuming that I am unable to escape, what then? After He has finished putting me through as many paces as He wishes, where do we go from there? Will he treat me as I treated most of my non-human subjects—that is, will I get tossed into a jar containing chloroform? "Following the experiment, the animals are sacrificed," as we so euphemistically report in the scientific literature. This doesn't appeal to me much, as you can imagine. Or maybe if I seem particularly bright to Him, He may use me for breeding purposes, to establish a colony of His own. Now, that might have possibilities . . .

Oh, damn Freud anyhow!

8

And damn Him, too! I had just gotten the maze well learned when He upped and changed things on me. I stumbled about like a bat in the sunlight for quite some time before I finally got to the goal box. I'm afraid my performance was pretty poor.

9

Well, it wasn't so bad after all. What He did was just to reverse the whole maze so that it was a mirror image of what it used to be. Took me only two trials to discover the solution. Let Him figure that one out if He's so smart!

10

My performance on the maze reversal must have pleased Him, because now He's added a new complication. And again I suppose I could have predicted the next step if I had been thinking along the right direction. I

8. VISION: Learning Theory

woke up a few hours ago to find myself in a totally different room. There was nothing whatsoever in the room, but opposite me were two doors in the wall—one door a pure white, the other jet black. Between me and the doors was a deep pit, filled with water. I didn't like the looks of the situation, for it occurred to me right away that He had devised a kind of jumping stand for me. I had to choose which of the doors was open and led to the food. The other door would be locked. If I jumped at the wrong door, and found it locked, I'd fall in the water. I needed a bath, that was for sure, but I didn't relish getting it in this fashion.

While I stood there watching, I got the shock of my life. I mean it quite literally. The bastard had thought of everything. When I used to run rats on jumping stands, to overcome their reluctance to jump, I used to shock them. He's following exactly the same pattern. The floor in this room is wired but good. I howled and jumped about and showed all the usual anxiety behavior. It took me less than two seconds to come to my senses and make a flying leap at the white door, however.

You know something? That water is ice-cold!

11

I have now, by my own calculations, solved no fewer than 87 different problems on the jumping stand, and I'm getting sick and tired of it. One time I got angry and just pointed at the correct door—and got shocked for not going ahead and jumping. I shouted bloody murder, cursing Him at the top of my voice, telling Him if He didn't like my performance, He could damn well lump it. All He did, of course, was to increase the shock.

Frankly, I don't know how much longer I can put up with this. It's not that the work is difficult. But rather that it seems so senseless, so useless. If He were giving me half a chance to show my capabilities, I wouldn't mind it. I suppose I've contemplated a thousand different ways of escaping, but none of them is worth mentioning. But if I don't get out of here soon, I shall go stark raving mad!

12

For almost an hour after it happened, I sat in this room and just wept. I realize that it is not the style of our culture for a grown man to weep, but there are times when cultural taboos must be forgotten. Again, had I thought much about the sort of experiments He must have had in mind, I most probably could have predicted the next step. Even so, I most likely would have repressed the knowledge.

One of the standard problems which any learning psychologist is interested in is this one—will an animal learn something if you fail to reward him for his performance? There are many theorists, such as Hull and Spence, who believe that reward (or "reinforcement," as they call it) is absolutely necessary for learning to occur. This is mere stuff and nonsense, as anyone with a grain of sense knows, but nonetheless the "reinforcement" theory has been dominant in the field for years now. We fought a hard battle with Spence and Hull, and actually had them with their backs to the wall at one point, when suddenly they came up with the concept of "secondary reinforcement." That is, anything associated with a reward takes on the ability to act as a reward itself. For example the mere sight of food would become a reward in and of itself—almost as much a reward, in fact, as is the eating of food. The *sight* of food, indeed! But nonetheless, it saved their theories for the moment.

For the past five years now, I have been trying to design an experiment that would show beyond a shadow of a doubt that the *sight* of a reward was not sufficient for learning to take place. And now look at what has happened to me!

I'm sure that He must lean towards Hull and Spence in his theorizing, for earlier today, when I found myself in the jumping stand room, instead of being rewarded with my usual protein balls when I made the correct jump, I discovered . . .

I'm sorry, but it is difficult to write about even now. For when I made the correct jump and the door opened and I started toward the food trough, I found it had been replaced with a photograph. A calendar photograph. You know the one. Her name, I think, is Monroe.

I sat on the floor for almost an hour weeping afterwards. For five whole years I have been attacking the validity of the secondary reinforcement theory, and now I find myself giving Him evidence that the theory is correct! For I cannot help "learning" which of the doors is the correct one to jump through. I refuse to stand on the apparatus and have the life shocked out of me, and I refuse to pick the wrong door all the time and get an icy bath time after time. It just isn't fair! For He will doubtless put it all down to the fact that the mere *sight* of the photograph is functioning as a reward, and that I am learning the problems merely to be able to see Miss What's-her-name in her bare skin!

Oh, I can just see Him now, sitting somewhere else in this spaceship, gathering in all the data I am giving Him, plotting all kinds of learning curves, chortling to Himself because I am confirming all of His pet theories. I just wish . . .

13

Almost an hour has gone by since I wrote the above section. It seems longer than that, but surely it's been only an hour. And I have spent the time in deep thought. For I have discovered a way out of this place, I think. The question is, dare I do it?

I was in the midst of writing that paragraph about His sitting and chortling and confirming his theories, when it suddenly struck me that theories are born of the equipment that one uses. This has probably been true throughout the history of all science, but perhaps most true of all in

8. VISION: Learning Theory

psychology. If Skinner had never invented his blasted box, if the maze and the jumping stand had not been developed, we probably would have entirely different theories of learning today than we now have. For if nothing else, the type of equipment that one uses drastically reduces the type of behavior that one's subjects can show, and one's theories have to account only for the type of behavior that appears in the laboratories.

It follows from this also that any two cultures that devise the same sort of experimental procedures will come up with almost identical theories.

Keeping all of this in mind, it's not hard for me to believe that He is an iron-clad reinforcement theorist, for He uses all of the various paraphernalia that they use, and uses it in exactly the same way.

My means of escape is therefore obvious. He expects from me confirmation of all His pet theories. Well, He won't get it any more! I know all of His theories backwards and forwards, and this means I know how to give Him results that will tear his theories right smack in half!

I can almost predict the results. What does any learning theorist do with an animal that won't behave properly, that refuses to give the results that are predicted? One gets rid of the beast, quite naturally. For one wishes to use only healthy, normal animals in one's work, and any animal that gives "unusual" results is removed from the study but quickly. After all, if it doesn't perform as expected, it must be sick, abnormal, or aberrant in one way or another . . .

There is no guarantee, of course, what method He will employ to dispose of my now annoying presence. Will He "sacrifice" me? Or will He just return me to the "permanent colony"? I cannot say. I know only that I will be free from what is now an intolerable situation. The chance must be taken.

Just wait until He looks at His results from now on!

FROM: Experimenter-in-Chief, Interstellar Labship PSYCH-145
TO: Director, Bureau of Science

Thlan, my friend, this will be an informal missive. I will send the official report along later, but I wanted to give you my subjective impressions first.

The work with the newly discovered species is, for the moment, at a standstill. Things went exceedingly well at first. We picked what seemed to be a normal, healthy animal and smattered it into our standard test apparatus. I may have told you that this new species seemed quite identical to our usual laboratory animals, so we included a couple of the "toys" that our home animals seem to be fond of—thin pieces of material made from woodpulp and a tiny stick of graphite. Imagine our surprise, and our pleasure, when this new specimen made exactly the same use of the materials as have all of our home colony specimens. Could it be that there are certain innate behavior patterns to be found throughout the universe in the lower species?

115

III. Nature or Nurture—Once More with Feeling

Well, I merely pose the question. The answer is of little importance to a Learning Theorist. Your friend Verpk keeps insisting that the use of these "toys" may have some deeper meaning to it, and that perhaps we should investigate further. At his insistence, then, I include with this informal missive the materials used by our first subject. In my opinion, Verpk is guilty of gross anthropomorphism, and I wish to have nothing further to do with the question. However, this behavior did give us hope that our newly discovered colony would yield subjects whose performance would be exactly in accordance with standard theory.

And, in truth, this is exactly what seemed to be the case. The animal solved the Bfian Box problem in short order, yielding as beautiful data as I have ever seen. We then shifted it to maze, maze-reversal and jumping stand problems, and the results could not have confirmed our theories better had we rigged the data. However, when we switched the animal to secondary reinforcement problems, it seemed to undergo a strange sort of change. No longer was its performance up to par. In fact, at times it seemed to go quite berserk. For part of the experiment, it would perform superbly. But then, just as it seemed to be solving whatever problem we set it to, its behavior would subtly change into patterns that obviously could not come from a normal specimen. It got worse and worse, until its behavior departed radically from that which our theories predicted. Naturally, we knew then that something had happened to the animal, for our theories are based upon thousands of experiments with similar subjects, and hence our theories must be right. But our theories hold only for normal subjects, and for normal species, so it soon became apparent to us that we had stumbled upon some abnormal type of animal.

Upon due consideration, we returned the subject to its home colony. However, we also voted almost unanimously to request from you permission to take steps to destroy the complete colony. It is obviously of little scientific use to us, and stands as a potential danger that we must take adequate steps against. Since all colonies are under your protection, we therefore request permission to destroy it in toto.

I must report, by the way, that Verpk's vote was the only one which was cast against this procedure. He has some silly notion one should study behavior as one finds it. Frankly, I cannot understand why you have seen fit to saddle me with him on this expedition, but perhaps you have your reasons.

Verpk's vote notwithstanding, however, the rest of us are of the considered opinion that this whole new colony must be destroyed, and quickly. For it is obviously diseased or some such—as reference to our theories has proven. And should it by some chance come in contact with our other colonies, and infect our other animals with whatever disease or aberration it has, we would never be able to predict their behavior again. I need not carry the argument further, I think.

8. VISION: Learning Theory

May we have your permission to destroy the colony as soon as possible, then, so that we may search out yet other colonies and test our theories against other healthy animals? For it is only in this fashion that science progresses.

Respectfully yours,
Iowyy.

9.
VALENCE:
The Chemistry of Learning
DAVID KRECH

In the following article, David Krech delves into the knotty interrelationships between nature and nurture in human learning that provide another valence for contemporary psychology.

American educators now talk a great deal about the innovative hardware of education, about computer-assisted instruction, 8 mm. cartridge-loading projectors, microtransparencies, and other devices. In the not too distant future they may well be talking about enzyme-assisted instruction, protein memory consolidators, antibiotic memory repellers, and the chemistry of the brain. Although the psychologists' learning theories derived from the study of maze-running rats or target-pecking pigeons have failed to provide insights into the education of children, it is unlikely that what is now being discovered by the psychologist, chemist, and neuro-physiologist about rat-brain chemistry can deviate widely from what we will eventually discover about the chemistry of the human brain.

Most adults who are not senile can repeat a series of seven numbers—8, 4, 8, 8, 3, 9, 9—immediately after the series is read. If however, they are asked to repeat these numbers thirty minutes later, most will fail. In the first instance, we are dealing with the immediate memory span; in the second, with long-term memory. These basic behavioral observations lie behind what is called the two-stage memory storage process theory.

According to a common variant of these notions, immediately after every learning trial—indeed, after every experience—a short-lived electro-chemical process is established in the brain. This process, so goes the assumption, is the physiological mechanism which carries the short-term memory. Within a few seconds or minutes, however, this process decays and disappears; but before doing so, if all systems are go, the short-term electrochemical process triggers a second series of events in the brain. This second process is chemical in nature and involves, primarily, the production of new proteins and the induction of higher enzymatic activity levels in the brain cells. This process is more enduring and serves as the physiological substrate of our long-term memory.

It would follow that one approach to testing our theory would be to provide a subject with some experience or other, then interrupt the short-term electrochemical process immediately—before it has had an opportunity to establish the long-term process. If this were done, our subject should never develop a long-term memory for that experience.

At the Albert Einstein Medical School in New York, Dr. Murray Jarvik has devised a "step-down" procedure based on the fact that when a rat is placed on a small platform a few inches above the floor, the rat will step down onto the floor within a few seconds. The rat will do this consistently, day after day. Suppose that on one day the floor is electrified, and stepping onto it produces a painful shock. When the rat is afterward put back on the platform—even twenty-four hours later—it will not budge from the platform but will remain there until the experimenter gets tired and calls the experiment quits. The rat has thus demonstrated that he has a long-term memory for that painful experience.

If we now take another rat, but this time *interfere* with his short-term memory process *immediately after* he has stepped onto the electrified floor, the rat should show no evidence of having experienced a shock when tested the next day, since we have not given his short-term electrochemical memory process an opportunity to initiate the long-term protein-enzymatic process. To interrupt the short-term process, Jarvik passes a mild electric current across the brain of the animal. The current is not strong enough to cause irreparable harm to the brain cells, but it does result in a very high level of activation of the neurons in the brain, thus disrupting the short-term electrochemical memory process. If this treatment follows closely enough after the animal's first experience with the foot shock, and we test the rat a day later, the rat acts as if there were no memory for yesterday's event; the rat jauntily and promptly steps down from the platform with no apparent expectation of shock.

When a long time-interval is interposed between the first foot shock and the electric-current (through the brain) treatment, the rat *does* remember the foot shock, and it remains on the platform when tested the next day. This, again, is what we should have expected from our theory. The short-term electrochemical process has now had time to set up the long-term chemical memory process before it was disrupted.

Some well-known effects of accidental human head injury seem to parallel these findings. Injuries which produce a temporary loss of consciousness (but no permanent damage to brain tissue) can cause the patient to experience a "gap" in his memory for the events just preceding the accident. This retrograde amnesia can be understood on the assumption that the events immediately prior to the accident were still being carried by the short-term memory processes at the time of the injury, and their disruption by the injury was sufficient to prevent the induction of the long-term processes. The patient asks "Where am I?" not only because he does not recognize the hospital, but also because he cannot remember how he became injured.

Work conducted by Dr. Bernard Agranoff at the University of Michigan Medical School supports the hypothesis that the synthesis of new brain proteins is crucial for the establishment of the long-term memory process. He argues that if we could prevent the formation of new proteins in the brain, then—although the short-term electrochemical memory process is not interfered with—the long-term memory process could never become established.

Much of Agranoff's work has been done with goldfish. The fish is placed in one end of a small rectangular tank, which is divided into two halves by a barrier which extends from the bottom to just below the surface of the water. When a light is turned on, the fish must swim across the barrier into the other side of the tank within twenty seconds—otherwise he receives an electric shock. This training is continued for several trials until the animal learns to swim quickly to the other side when the light is turned on. Most goldfish learn this shock-avoidance task quite easily and remember it for many days. Immediately before—and in some experiments, immediately after—training, Agranoff injects the antibiotic puromycin into the goldfish's brain. (Puromycin is a protein inhibitor and prevents the formation of new proteins in the brain's neurons.) After injection, Agranoff finds that the goldfish are not impaired in their acquisition of the shock-avoidance task, but, when tested a day or so later, they show almost no retention for the task.

These results mean that the short-term memory process (which helps the animal remember from one trial to the next and thus permits him to learn in the first place) is not dependent upon the formation of new proteins, but that the long-term process (which helps the animal remember from one day to the next and thus permits him to retain what he had learned) is dependent upon the production of new proteins. Again, as in the instance of Jarvik's rats, if the puromycin injection comes more than an hour after learning, it has no effect on later memory—the long-term memory process presumably has already been established and the inhibition of protein synthesis can now no longer affect memory. In this antibiotic, therefore, we have our first chemical memory erasure—or, more accurately, a chemical long-term memory preventative. (Almost identical findings have been reported by other workers in other laboratories working with such animals as mice and rats, which are far removed from the goldfish.)

Thus far I have been talking about disrupting or preventing the formation of memory. Now we will accentuate the positive. Dr. James L. McGaugh of the University of California at Riverside has argued that injections of central nervous system stimulants such as strychnine, picrotoxin, or metrazol should enhance, fortify, or extend the activity of the short-term electrochemical memory processes and thus increase the probability that they will be successful in initiating long-term memory processes. From this it follows that the injection of CNS [central nervous system] stimulants immediately before or after training should improve learning performance. That is precisely what McGaugh found—together with several additional results which have important implications for our concerns today.

In one of McGaugh's most revealing experiments, eight groups of mice from two different hereditary backgrounds were given the problem of learning a simple maze. Immediately after completing their learning trials, four groups from each strain were injected with a different dosage of metrazol—from none to five, 10, and 20 milligrams per kilogram of body weight. First, it was apparent that there are hereditary differences in learning ability—a relatively bright strain and a relatively dull one. Secondly, by properly dosing the animals with metrazol, the learning performance increased appreciably. Under the optimal dosage, the metrazol animals showed about a 40 per cent improvement in learning ability over their untreated brothers. The improvement under metrazol was so great, in fact, that the dull animals, when treated with 10 milligrams, did slightly better than their untreated but hereditarily superior colleagues.

In metrazol we not only have a chemical facilitator of learning, but one which acts as the "Great Equalizer" among hereditarily different groups. As the dosage was increased for the dull mice from none to five to 10 milligrams their performance improved. Beyond the 10-milligram point for the dull mice, however, and beyond the five-milligram point for the bright mice, increased strength of the metrazol solution resulted in a deterioration in learning. We can draw two morals from this last finding. First, the optimal dosage of chemical learning facilitators will vary greatly with the individual taking the drug (there is, in other words, an interaction between heredity and drugs); second, there is a limit to the intellectual power of even a hopped-up Southern Californian Super Mouse!

We already have available a fairly extensive class of drugs which can facilitate learning and memory in animals. A closer examination of McGaugh's results and the work of others, however, also suggests that these drugs do not work in a monolithic manner on something called "learning" or "memory." In some instances, the drugs seem to act on "attentiveness"; in some, on the ability to vary one's attacks on a problem;

in some, on persistence; in some, on immediate memory; in some, on long-term memory. Different drugs work differentially for different strains, different individuals, different intellectual tasks, and different learning components.

Do all of these results mean that we will soon be able to substitute a pharmacopoeia of drugs for our various school-enrichment and innovative educational programs, and that most educators will soon be technologically unemployed—or will have to retool and turn in their schoolmaster's gown for a pharmacist's jacket? The answer is no—as our Berkeley experiments on the influence of education and training on brain anatomy and chemistry suggest. This research is the work of four—Dr. E. L. Bennett, biochemist; Dr. Marian Diamond, anatomist; Dr. M. R. Rosenzweig, psychologist; and myself—together, of course, with the help of graduate students, technicians, and, above all, government money.

Our work, started some fifteen years ago, was guided by the same general theory which has guided more recent work, but our research strategy and tactics were quite different. Instead of interfering physiologically or chemically with the animal to determine the effects of such intervention upon memory storage (as did Jarvik, Agranoff, and McGaugh), we had taken the obverse question and, working with only normal animals, sought to determine the *effects* of memory storage on the chemistry and anatomy of the brain.

Our argument was this: If the establishment of long-term memory processes involves increased activity of brain enzymes, then animals which have been required to do a great deal of learning and remembering should end up with brains enzymatically different from those of animals which have not been so challenged by environment. This should be especially true for the enzymes involved in trans-synaptic neural activity. Further, since such neural activity would make demands on brain-cell action and metabolism, one might also expect to find various morphological differences between the brains of rats brought up in psychologically stimulating and psychologically pallid environments.

I describe briefly one of our standard experiments. At weaning age, one rat from each of a dozen pairs of male twins is chosen by lot to be placed in an educationally active and innovative environment, while its twin brother is placed in as unstimulating an environment as we can contrive. All twelve educationally enriched rats live together in one large, wire-mesh cage in a well lighted, noisy, and busy laboratory. The cage is equipped with ladders, running wheels, and other "creative" rat toys. For thirty minutes each day, the rats are taken out of their cages and allowed to explore new territory. As the rats grow older they are given various learning tasks to master, for which they are rewarded with bits of sugar. This stimulating educational and training program is continued for eighty days.

While these animals are enjoying their rich intellectual environment, each impoverished animal lives out his life in solitary confinement, in a small cage situated in a dimly lit and quiet room. He is rarely handled by his keeper and never invited to explore new environments, to solve problems, or join in games with other rats. Both groups of rats, however, have unlimited access to the same standard food throughout the experiment. At the age of 105 days, the rats are sacrificed, their brains dissected out and analyzed morphologically and chemically.

This standard experiment, repeated dozens of times, indicates that as the fortunate rat lives out his life in the educationally enriched condition, the bulk of his cortex expands and grows deeper and heavier than that of his culturally deprived brother. Part of this increase in cortical mass is accounted for by an increase in the number of glia cells (specialized brain cells which play vital functions in the nutrition of the neurons and, perhaps, also in laying down permanent memory traces); part of it by an increase in the size of the neuronal cell bodies and their nuclei; and part by an increase in the diameters of the blood vessels supplying the cortex. Our postulated chemical changes also occur. The enriched brain shows more acetylocholinesterase (the enzyme involved in the trans-synaptic conduction of neural impulses) and cholinesterase (the enzyme found primarily in the glia cells).

Finally, in another series of experiments we have demonstrated that these structural and chemical changes are the signs of a "good" brain. That is, we have shown that either through early rat-type Head Start programs or through selective breeding programs, we can increase the weight and density of the rat's cortex and its acetylocholinesterase and cholinesterase activity levels. And when we do—by either method—we have created superior problem-solving animals.

What does all of this mean? It means that the effects of the psychological and educational environment are not restricted to something called the "mental" realm. Permitting the young rat to grow up in an educationally and experientially inadequate and unstimulating environment creates an animal with a relatively deteriorated brain—a brain with a thin and light cortex, lowered blood supply, diminished enzymatic activities, smaller neuronal cell bodies, and fewer glia cells. A lack of adequate educational fare for the young animal—no matter how large the food supply or how good the family—and a lack of adequate psychological enrichment results in palpable, measurable, deteriorative changes in the brain's chemistry and anatomy.

Returning to McGaugh's results, we find that whether, and to what extent, this or that drug will improve the animal's learning ability will depend, of course, on what the drug does to the rat's brain chemistry. And what it does to the rat's brain chemistry will depend upon the status of the chemistry in the brain to begin with. And what the status of the brain's chemistry is to begin with reflects the rat's early psychological and educational environment. Whether, and to what extent, this or that drug will improve the animal's attention, or memory, or learning ability, therefore, will depend upon the animal's past experiences. I am not talking about interaction between "mental" factors on the one hand and "chemical" compounds on the other. I am talking, rather, about interactions between chemical factors introduced into the brain by the biochemist's injection or pills, and chemical factors induced in the brain by the educator's stimulating or impoverishing environment. The biochemist's work can be only half effective without the educator's help.

What kind of educational environment can best develop the brain chemically and morphologically? What kind of stimulation makes for an enriched environment? What educational experiences can potentiate the effects of the biochemist's drugs? We don't know. The biochemist doesn't know. It is at this point that I see a whole new area of collaboration in basic research between the educator, the psychologist, and the neurobiochemist —essentially, a research program which combines the Agranoff and McGaugh techniques with our Berkeley approach. Given the start that has already been made in the animal laboratory, an intensive program of research—with animals and with children—which seeks to spell out the interrelations between chemical and educational influences on brain and memory can pay off handsomely. This need not wait for the future. We know enough now to get started.

Both the biochemist and the teacher of the future will combine their skills and insights for the educational and intellectual development of the child. Tommy needs a bit more of an immediate memory stimulator; Jack could do with a chemical attention-span stretcher; Rachel needs an anticholinesterase to slow down her mental processes; Joan, some puromycin —she remembers too many details, and gets lost.

To be sure, all our data thus far come from the brains of goldfish and rodents. But is anyone so certain that the chemistry of the brain of a rat (which, after all, is a fairly complex mammal) is so different from that of the brain of a human being that he dare neglect this challenge—or even gamble—when the stakes are so high?

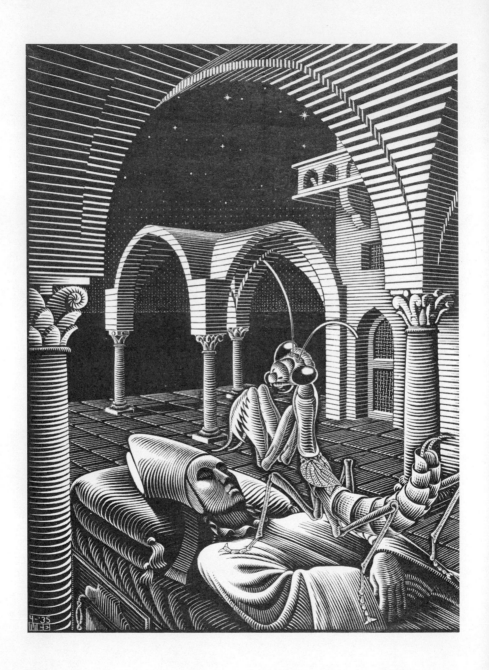

IV.
The Emergence
of Parapsychology

10.
VALENCE:
ESP and Credibility in Science
R. A. McCONNELL

The next two articles deal with an area that is of increasing concern to contemporary psychologists: ESP. The first article, by R. A. McConnell, examines ESP and speculates on its nonacceptance by the American scientific community. The second article concerns the scientific community of Russia, which has pursued the study of extrasensory phenomena.

In discussing extrasensory perception (ESP) before psychology students, it is not uncommon to stress the credulity of the public. Perhaps, instead, we ought to examine the credibility of scientists—including those on both sides of the controversy.

In ESP research whom shall we trust? One can rather easily imagine experimental precautions to keep participating subjects from cheating. But how do we know whether the experimenter is deliberately deceiving us? And in a world where people believe all kinds of nonsense, how can we be sure that the experimenter is not deceiving himself?

Let us suppose that 10 experimenters independently get the same result. Can we accept it? Ten is not a large number. There are about 150,000 names in *American Men of Science*. We may reasonably assume that at least 10,000 of these hold beliefs about the nature of reality that the majority of scientists would regard as wholly without foundation. Thus, on a subject like ESP, where there are no recognized authorities, why should we accept the word of 10 experimenters—or, for that matter, a thousand? Are we not, all of us, creatures of our culture? Is there any way we can be sure that a scientist in any field is as rational as he pretends to be?

Questions concerning the credibility of scientists are rarely asked in our

From R. A. McConnell, "ESP and Credibility in Science," *American Psychologist*, 1969, pp. 531–538. Copyright 1969 by the American Psychological Association, and reproduced by permission.

classrooms. I have wondered why. Perhaps it makes us uncomfortable to consider the possibility of incompetence, dishonesty, or mental illness among professional people. Whatever the reason, this is forbidden territory for study.

Once in a long while, these embarrassing ideas do come to the surface. Someone, a little bolder or a little more eccentric than the rest of us, may write an article that slips by the editorial censor. When that happens, we have a chance to learn what people really think.

When I accepted this invitation to talk to you, I was told I could give you an advance reading assignment. I asked that you read an eight-page article on ESP by G. R. Price that appeared in *Science* together with several letters to the editor written in reply to Price. These papers are currently available as part of the Bobbs-Merrill reprint series that is widely used for teaching psychology, and they have thus acquired a quasi-official status as source documents to which the very young may be exposed.

I also suggested that you read an analysis of Price's article that appeared in the *Journal of Parapsychology* and that was not included in the Bobbs-Merrill series. I hope that most of you have had a chance to study these references, which I shall now discuss briefly.

Price, a chemist by profession, presented a well-supported argument showing that existing experimental evidence constitutes conclusive proof of ESP if one accepts the good faith and sanity of the experimenters. But he went on to say that all of the otherwise convincing evidence for ESP can be easily explained away if one assumes that experimenters, working in collaboration with their witnesses, have intentionally faked their results.

Perhaps the most interesting thing about this unsubstantiated suggestion of fraud is that it was published on the first page of the most influential scientific journal in the United States. I will not say whether Price intended what he wrote as a joke. That is a riddle that I leave to you to answer. The important question is not whether Price took himself seriously, but whether you and I ought to do so.

I believe, as apparently does Price, that all kinds of fraud, even by highly placed scientists, are possible and that it is conceivable that there might be collaboration between two scientists in perpetuating a scientific hoax. Nevertheless, I think that those who accept Price's argument fail to understand two important things about science as a social enterprise.

First, they fail to realize that the way to tell whether a number of scientists are collaborating in a hoax is to consider the intricate web of public and private motivation, belief, and retribution that determines the behavior of professional people in our culture. Price suggested that scientists, university teachers, medical doctors, and intellectually prominent persons who have assisted in the investigation of ESP may have engaged in conscious collusive fraud. Price answered the question of how one might get such people to become willing accomplices by saying: "In recruiting, I would appeal not to desire for fame or material gain but to the noblest motives, arguing that much good to humanity could result from a small deception designed to strengthen religious belief." An experienced lawyer or even a politician would laugh at this explanation of a supposed conspiracy among well-educated and fully engaged members of our society, but evidently quite a few scientists find it plausible.

Second, those scientists who take Price seriously do not understand scientific method. Price suggested that the way to establish the scientific truth of ESP is to carry out a fraudproof experiment. In his words: "What is needed is one completely convincing experiment." He described in specific detail how this might be done by using prominent scientists and stage magicians as witnesses, backed up by motion pictures of the entire proceedings, plus photomicrographs of welded seals, and so on. This is nonsense because it assumes that scientific proof is of the same nature as legal proof. On the contrary, the acceptance of a scientific principle does not, and never can, depend upon the honesty of individual scientists.

I wish I had time to pursue with you the subtle psychological question of the nature of scientific proof and of how the method of science deals with individual experimenter error as well as mass irrationality. Those of you who are especially interested may wish to read a book by T. S. Kuhn titled *The Structure of Scientific Revolutions*. Here today, I can only say that in my opinion, wittily or unwittingly, Price's article is a hoax about hoaxes and about the nature of science.

If you were to ask: "What does it signify that Price successfully placed his article in our most important journal of science?" I would answer as follows: There is a facade of respectability and belief that covers all of the activities of society and makes it possible for men to work together and for society to exist. Most people—including those who are well educated —are unaware of this false front and lose their equilibrium when they are forced by circumstances to penetrate behind it. On the other hand, those of you who are intellectually alienated from our culture understand quite well that this pretense exists. I hope that some day you will also understand why it is necessary and that it is not the contrivance of a group of evil men but reflects what existential philosophers refer to as "the human condition."

This curtain of propriety and convention exists in science also, where it allows us to believe that all is well with our knowledge system. ESP or any other revolutionary discovery may seem to threaten science. From time to time, when such a challenge is offered, the stagehands nervously fumble, the curtain slips, and we see a little of the normally concealed machinery. We get a glimpse of underlying reality, a glimpse of the ignorance and fear that govern the inner affairs of the mind of man. Such was the case when *Science* published Price's critique of ESP. That is why his article is important.

10. VALENCE: ESP and Credibility in Science

Evidence and Belief

Then, what about ESP? If laboratory scientists lack sophistication about human nature and even about the methodology of science, how do we decide for ourselves whether ESP is real or imaginary, true or false?

Before we try to answer so difficult a question, let us go back to the beginning. I shall give you an operational definition of ESP that you may find a bit confusing. Then I shall describe a test for ESP that I hope will make the matter clear to you.

The definition goes this way: "Extrasensory perception is a response to an unknown event not presented to any known sense." I shall not try to explain it. Instead, let me describe the test.

I have brought with me a deck of ESP cards. These cards have five different kinds of symbols printed on them: a circle, a square, a plus, a star, and wavy lines. Altogether, there are 25 cards, 5 of each kind.

Suppose I shuffle these cards, hide them, and ask you to guess them. By the theory of chance probability, the number you would most often get right is five. Sometimes you would get four or six or seven. Only once in a long while would you get 15 right out of 25. In fact, if you got more than 10 right very often, you would begin to suspect that it was not just good luck. It might even be ESP.

Of course, you could not be sure. It might be luck—or it might be something else. If you look closely at the backs of these cards, sometimes you can see the symbol showing through. Perhaps in this way you recognized some of the cards when I shuffled them. Or again, every time I asked whether you were ready for your next guess, perhaps I gave you a hint without knowing it. Perhaps, unconsciously, I raised the tone of my voice just a little when I came to each star—because I think of stars as being "higher" than the other symbols, or for some other trivial reason.

You can see that there are many subtle ways for information to leak through by sight or by sound. No serious scientist would try to conduct an ESP experiment in this fashion. My only purpose in showing you these cards is to let you know how some of the early tests for ESP were done at Duke University 35 years ago. I regard these cards as a museum piece, although they are a lot of fun and can be used in preliminary testing.

• • •

ESP is a controversial idea in psychology. Nevertheless, the psychologists whom I know personally agree with me on many things. I am sure we agree on what constitutes good quality experimental laboratory research. We also agree that there is a sizable body of high-grade evidence for ESP in the literature.

In 1947 I visited Duke University in North Carolina where a man by the name of Rhine was doing experiments on ESP. I wanted to get acquainted with Rhine and with the people who were working under him. Even more important, I wanted to talk to those faculty members who rejected Rhine's work. I rented a dormitory room, and during four weeks I interviewed everyone I could, beginning with the President of the University and working down to assistant professors in various departments. I shall not have time to describe that adventure, but I will tell you what I was told by one professor of psychology in a private interview.

He said that he was familiar with the experimental literature of ESP and that, in his opinion, if it were anything else *but* ESP, one-tenth of the published evidence would already have established the phenomenon. He also explained that he would not accept ESP himself because, as he put it, he found "a world without ESP a more comfortable place in which to live."

That trip to Duke University was part of a larger investigation that made me decide to leave engineering electronics, in which I had acquired some experience, and to devote my life to the investigation of ESP and related effects.

That was 20 years ago. What has happened in this field since then? Among other things, there has been time to publish 20 more volumes of the *Journal of Parapsychology*. That comes to about 4,000 pages of research. There have been several thousand additional pages in the *Journal of the American Society for Psychical Research* and in the English and Continental journals. You might think that the argument would be settled by now.

Only recently, a brilliant young psychologist, who is here on your campus, gave a lecture on ESP in which he said, "I tend to believe the evidence is as good as it is for many of our other psychological phenomena." He also said that "Psychologists will not be interested in ESP until there is a repeatable experiment."

Where my psychologist friends and I disagree, is that I believe that the available evidence for ESP is sufficient to establish its reality beyond all reasonable doubt. My psychologist friends think that the evidence is not yet conclusive. I do not regard this difference of opinion as very important. I am happy to allow anyone the privilege of doubt.

How else does the position of professional psychologists whom I know differ from my own? Perhaps the main difference—the really important difference—lies in our interpretation of the history and methodology of science—in what today we call the philosophy of science.

For one thing, my friends seem to believe that the only good evidence for ESP must come from controlled experimentation in a laboratory. My own belief is that all available evidence must be weighed, taking into account its source and the conditions under which it was gathered.

Perhaps it will clarify the problem if I say that there are only two important kinds of scientific evidence in this world: our own evidence and someone else's. Since most of us are not in a position to gather evidence of ESP, my remarks apply especially to other people's evidence.

The first thing to remember is that, no matter how reputable the scientific journal, someone else's evidence is always suspect. And if the matter is important, we ought to be *aggressively* skeptical about it.

Whether we are listening to a tale of a ghost in a haunted house or reading the tightly edited *Journal of Experimental Psychology*, we have to concern ourselves with two questions: what is the content of the report and what are the competence and motivation of the observer?

What I am suggesting is that our attitude toward *all* supposedly scientific reports must be that of the psychologist in receiving an introspective account from a human subject in a laboratory experiment—for it must be remembered that, as far as the reader is concerned, a journal article by a distant scientist is in some ways even less dependable than what psychologists, often condescendingly, refer to as a "verbal report."

From a study of the history of science, I have come to two conclusions in this connection: (a) the evidence presented in scientific journals by professional scientists for all kinds of ordinary phenomena is not as good as commonly supposed, and (b) on a controversial subject where the professionals do not agree, the evidence of the layman may have considerable scientific value. As corollaries, I suggest that the textbooks of science are often wrong and that contrary popular opinion is sometimes right. Let us examine these ideas.

Storehouses of Knowledge?

Textbooks are the storehouses of man's knowledge. They are presumed to contain all of the things we know to be true. If you are becoming a scientist, you will spend at least 18 years studying from books. It would be not entirely unfair to call most of this training a "brainwashing" process. Nearly everything you learn as factual reality must be accepted upon the word of some recognized authority and not upon your own firsthand experience. It should be a matter of concern to you whether you have been told the truth for those 18 years. Just how bad are the textbooks we use? Let me take an example from the field of geology.

Did you know that until the year 1800 the highest scientific authorities thought that there was no such thing as a meteorite? After all, there are no stones in the sky; so stones cannot fall out of the sky. Only a superstitious person would believe in meteorites.

Many of you are familiar with the work of Lavoisier. He was the founder of modern chemistry. He discovered that burning is the combining of oxygen with other things, and he helped to show that the formula for water is H_2O. He was one of the great scientists of all time.

In 1772 Lavoisier signed a report to the French Academy of Science in which he said he had examined a stone that was believed to have fallen from the sky in a great blaze of light. Lavoisier said in his report that this was just an ordinary stone that had been struck by lightning and had melted partly into glass while lying on the ground.

Eventually, of course, the leaders of science decided that meteorites do come from outer space, and they revised the textbooks accordingly. But in doing so, they forgot to mention that there had ever been any argument about the matter. So here we are, living in the space age, without realizing how hard it is to discover the truth about even a simple thing like meteorites, which can be seen as meteors in the sky on any clear night, and which have been found upon the surface of the earth since the dawn of history.

Even worse, as students, we have no way of estimating how many arguments are still going on in science and how many mistakes—truly serious mistakes—there are in the textbooks from which we study. It is my guess that we can safely believe nearly all of what is said in the physics and chemistry books. But we ought to believe only half of the ideas in the biological sciences—although I am not sure which half. And we should accept as final very little in the social sciences, which try to explain why groups of people behave as they do.

Our subject today is extrasensory perception, which belongs in psychology, one of the biological sciences. ESP is something about which the "authorities" are in error. Most psychology textbooks omit the subject entirely as unworthy of serious attention. But these books are mistaken, because ESP is a real psychological phenomenon.

Of course, I am only giving you my individual opinion about ESP. I do not want you to base your belief upon what I tell you. When you have studied advanced psychology and statistics, and when you come to realize that your professors cannot be expected to teach you everything you wish to know, then I hope you will go to the scientific journals and study the experiments that have been done and decide for yourself.

Mental Radio

I have already discussed the credibility of experts and the errors we find in science textbooks. I would like to turn next to the other half of my thesis, namely, that evidence from a layman may sometimes have scientific value.

Most of you are familiar with the name Upton Sinclair, who was a socialist reformer and a writer active in the first half of the twentieth century. He died in 1968 at the age of 90. In his time he wrote nearly 90 books. One of the best known of these, published in 1906, was called *The Jungle*. It told about the cruel and unsanitary conditions in the processing of beef in the Chicago stock yards. As a result of that book, laws were passed, and today the situation is much improved. In a very real sense, all of us are indebted to this man.

Sinclair discovered that his wife had an unusual amount of what was then known as "psychic ability." (That was before the beginning of the ESP controversy.) After three years of serious experimentation, he wrote a book about it: *Mental Radio*.

In his experiments, Sinclair, or someone else, would draw a secret picture and ask Mrs. Sinclair to draw another picture to match it. Some of the pairs of pictures are presented in the following examples.* The one on the left

*Illustrations from *Mental Radio* by Upton Sinclair are reproduced by permission of the publisher, Charles C. Thomas, Springfield, Illinois.

10. VALENCE: ESP and Credibility in Science

is always the original picture, and the one on the right is what Mrs. Sinclair got by ESP.

Sometimes the pictures were made as far apart as 40 miles. At other times the target picture was held by Mrs. Sinclair in her hand—without looking, of course—while she concentrated before drawing her matching picture. The degree of success did not seem to depend upon distance.

Let us examine some of the pictures. In Example 1 we see an almost perfect ESP response. It is a knight's helmet. Notice that for every important line in the left-hand picture there is a corresponding line on the right.

Example 1

Compare that with Example 2. Here, the response on the right is not quite the same as the target on the left, but the idea is the same.

Example 2

[In] Example 3, Sinclair drew a football as a target. Mrs. Sinclair made the drawing on the right, but she thought it was a "baby calf with a belly band." Why did her ESP make this mistake? We cannot be sure, but we think it had something to do with the fact that in her childhood she had known a queer old man who raised calves as parlor pets and dressed them in embroidered belly bands.

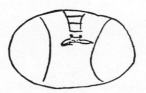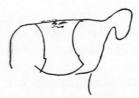

Example 3

IV. The Emergence of Parapsychology

Example 4 is another instance of the right shape with a wrong interpretation. Upton Sinclair drew a volcano, and Mrs. Sinclair drew what she called a black beetle. The beetle is upside down. It you turn the example over, you can more easily recognize its antennae and legs.

Example 4

In Example 5 Sinclair drew a fish hook, which turned into two flowers.

Example 5

Example 6 shows a fragmentary response. Sinclair drew a balloon. The response on the right is what his wife received by "mental radio." She was not sure what it was, so she wrote beside the picture: "Shines in sunlight, must be metal, a scythe hanging among vines or strings."

Example 6

Example 7 on the left is a swastika. Mrs. Sinclair drew the response on the right. She did not know what it meant, but she wrote beside it, "These things somehow belong together, but won't get together." You can see some of her words which were accidentally included when the printer made the book. Here is the beginning of "These" and "belong" and "but won't" and "together."

136

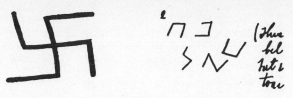

Example 7

Example 8 is a pair of drawings in which a stick man became a skull and crossbones.

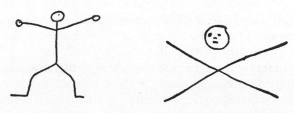

Example 8

Notice that in Example 9, Mrs. Sinclair left out some of the stars and added a moon instead.

Example 9

In Example 10 Sinclair drew an umbrella. His wife responded with this curious picture, which she described in writing beside it as follows: "I feel that it is a snake crawling out of something—vivid feeling of snake, but it looks like a cat's tail." I might mention that she had a special fear of snakes, having grown up on a plantation in a Mississippi swamp.

Example 10

The last example is the American flag and a response to it that could hardly be called a chance coincidence (Example 11).

IV. The Emergence of Parapsychology

Example 11

You have seen a selection of 11 pictures out of a total of 290 trials made by Mrs. Sinclair. Perhaps 4 of the 11 would be called direct target hits. The rest are partial hits. Out of the 290 tries, 23% were rated by Upton Sinclair as hits, 53% were partial hits, and 24% were failures.

Of course, before you can be sure that these pictures were made by ESP, many questions must be answered. Because Upton Sinclair and his wife were laymen, you will have to pay particular attention to their competence and motivation. On the other hand, one important feature of Sinclair's book is that you do not have to be a scientist to understand it. Even though you may not have studied statistics and psychology, you can read the book yourself and make up your mind as to its value on the basis of common sense. When you do, I think you will arrive at the same conclusion that many scientists have reached by entirely different kinds of experiments. I think you will decide that extrasensory perception is a reality regardless of the skepticism of the psychological profession.

A Matter of Interest

I have been told by my friends that psychologists will not be interested in ESP until someone discovers a repeatable experiment. Upton Sinclair repeated his experiments over a period of three years. In London, a mathematician by the name of Soal repeated certain card-guessing experiments again and again over a period of six years using two subjects and many different witnesses. What do psychologists mean by a repeatable experiment?

Evidently, they mean an experiment that is "repeatable by prescription." They want a standard experimental procedure that can be described on paper by which any qualified person—or at least some qualified persons —can guarantee to produce ESP upon demand. I must confess that we have not yet reached that stage in ESP research. And, until we do, I can sympathize with my skeptical friends. I can see why they, as busy individuals with other interests, are unwilling to reach a firm position about the reality of ESP.

What I cannot understand is why they say: "Psychologists will not be *interested* in ESP until there is a repeatable experiment."

It is a statement of fact that psychologists are *not* interested in ESP. Recently, I had occasion to examine a number of psychology textbooks.

10.   VALENCE: ESP and Credibility in Science

Only one of them mentioned ESP. After reading the four pages which these authors devote to ESP, I have only two minor critical observations to offer.

The first is that the authors have given too much space to finding fault with unimportant papers. They go back 25 years to a journal article in which they accuse an ESP experimenter of overanalyzing his data. I am sure that comparable examples of weak statistical method could be found in any one of the quantitative journals of the APA—and we would not need to go back a generation in time to do it.

My second comment is that the authors may have tended to damage their own scholarly reputations by recommending as a "scholarly review" a book by C. E. M. Hansel titled *ESP: A Scientific Evaluation*. This book has been reviewed by S. S. Stevens of Harvard, who regards ESP as a Rabelaisian joke and who gave Hansel his unqualified approval. If you like amusing book reviews, I suggest that you read Stevens. I regret that I do not have time here today to document for you the basis of my unfavorable opinion of Hansel's book.

I have wandered over many facets of ESP. I shall now summarize what I think are the most important ideas. Since the scientific study of ESP was begun by the London Society for Psychical Research in 1882, there have been hundreds and perhaps thousands of experiments done with a care typical of the journals of the APA. Many psychologists of high repute admit that the evidence is as good as that for other phenomena that are accepted by their profession.

Surprising though it may seem, most of this research on ESP has been done by people who were not psychologists. From this fact and from the usual psychology textbook treatment of the subject as well as from private discussion, we know that psychologists are *not* interested in ESP. This raises a question—a very mysterious question that I invite you to try to answer: Why are psychologists not interested in ESP?

11.
VALENCE:
Parapsychology in the U.S.S.R.

STANLEY KRIPPNER AND RICHARD DAVIDSON

Last summer we traveled to the U.S.S.R. to meet with Russian parapsychologists and to observe some of their research firsthand. Although the Russians were familiar with our work at the Dream Laboratory of Maimonides Medical Center—in the past seven years the laboratory has published more than 100 articles on extrasensory perception in dreams, not only in parapsychological journals but in medical, physiological, and psychiatric journals as well—we had to carry on a lengthy correspondence with Soviet researchers before Edward Naumov approved the visit. Naumov is a member of the Department of Physics of the City of Moscow Engineering Institute and, as the Soviet Union's leading parapsychologist, directs the Institute of Technical Parapsychology.

Parapsychology, so named because it is concerned with phenomena usually considered outside the realm of orthodox psychology, deals primarily with extrasensory perception (ESP) and psychokinesis (PK). ESP refers to information that is not received through the usual senses and includes telepathy and clairvoyance. PK describes physical effects not caused by so-called natural laws or human motor activities. Objects that seemingly move by themselves or are made to move by the will of a "sensitive" fall into the realm of PK.

Perhaps the most striking discovery we made during our stay in the Soviet Union was the difference between American and Russian approaches to parapsychology. In America the thrust of research is on simply proving the existence of ESP and PK. At the Dream Laboratory, for example, we begin an experiment on ESP with an elaborate statement of purpose and methods. Then we go to great lengths to shield the subject from any type of sensory or motor cue. Finally, we analyze and evaluate the results with such conservative statistical techniques that there *must* be ESP for the results to be significant.

In the Soviet Union, however, there is little emphasis on the experimental, statistical approach or on proving the existence of ESP or PK. The Russian parapsychologists seem to harbor no doubts about the existence of parapsychological phenomena. Instead, they are seeking practical applications and an understanding of how these phenomena operate.

The United States and the Soviet Union each have about six major centers for parapsychological research and about a dozen minor ones. All of the Soviet centers, of course, are government-funded. While we were in Russia, we told Naumov that only one U.S. center receives any federal financial support and that our own laboratory is privately funded, principally by the Babcock Foundation of Winston-Salem, North Carolina. At that moment, we added, the laboratory had only enough funds to operate for another six months or so.

Naumov was incredulous. "Don't your people realize the importance of parapsychology in the development of the human mind?" he asked. "This is extremely important work that you are doing, for it opens the door to creativity and human potential. Your country is a nation of businessmen. Don't they realize that it is good business to support humanitarian efforts?"

We then asked Naumov about the status of parapsychology among Soviet scientists. He produced two lists that had been compiled by his staff from all the material printed in the U.S.S.R. on parapsychology. One list contained the names of forty-five scientists who had publicly supported parapsychology research and were sympathetic to the data produced. The other contained the names of scientists who were critical—all nine of them.

This public support, however, is a fairly recent development. In the 1955 edition of the *Soviet Encyclopedia,* the definitive reference book that supplies the "party line" on all the sciences, parapsychology is defined as "the nonscientific idealistic consideration of supernatural abilities of perceptual phenomena." But in the 1970 edition, parapsychology is described as "the area of psychical and biophysical research dealing with the informational and energetics possibilities of living organisms. Parapsychology considers the newest forms of sensitivity, the results of those sensitivities, and the possibilities of the human organism." You will not find any standard reference book in the United States that describes parapsychology in similarly positive terms.

In fact, much of the difference between American and Soviet approaches to parapsychology is displayed in the terminology used in the two coun-

141

tries to describe parapsychological phenomena. To describe perceptual phenomena, for example, we in America use the term "extrasensory perception," or "ESP." Russians, however, speak of biological information or bio-information. Much can be said for the wisdom of this choice, for, as several American scientists have noted, any inference that events might be extrasensory or beyond the range of the senses creates immediate hostility. Anthropologist Margaret Mead, for example, a longtime member of the American Society for Psychical Research, prefers to think of ESP as "supersensory" perception or "extraordinary sense" perception.

The Soviet notion of bio-information takes many forms. If a person gains information without an agent—what we would call clairvoyance—the Russians use the term "bio-location." One special type of bio-location is bio-introscopy in which subjects identify the contents of sealed containers or envelopes. Other types of bio-location being studied in the U.S.S.R. are dowsing and dermal-optical sensitivity, sometimes known as "skin vision." In the area of dermal-optical sensitivity, experiments in both countries have shown that blindfolded "sensitives" can determine the color of a card either by touching it with their fingers or by touching a plastic envelope in which it is enclosed. But Soviet research in dermal-optical sensitivity, we were told, recently suffered an unfortunate setback: The star subject went off and joined a circus. However, new subjects are being trained, and Larisa Vilenskaya, a leading Soviet parapsychologist, has herself developed dermal-optical skills.

American researchers use the term psychokinesis to describe psychic physical effects on both living and nonliving objects. In the U.S.S.R., however, psychokinesis refers only to nonliving objects. Furthermore, the Soviets break down PK into two areas, spontaneous and experimental. Spontaneous PK refers to situations where objects seem to move for no apparent reason. Experimental PK, on the other hand, refers to objects moved by a "sensitive." These distinctions may seem to be merely semantic quibbles, but it is our belief that they point to a fundamental difference in outlook.

Only an hour after we checked in at Moscow's Intourist Hotel on the first day of our visit, we received a call from Larisa Vilenskaya. She welcomed us and said: "We have arranged for Dr. Krippner to give an address at the Institute of Psychology in the Academy of Pedagogical Sciences in Moscow on Monday. This will be the first lecture on parapsychology ever delivered at the institute. We have invited two hundred psychologists, psychiatrists, physicists, engineers, space scientists, and cosmonauts-in-training." Flattered by the invitation, Krippner accepted. It was an auspicious beginning for our stay in the U.S.S.R.

During the next week we worked on the lecture slated for the following Monday, traveled to several historic sites in and around Moscow, and were visited by a number of Soviet parapsychologists, most of them involved in psychokinetic research. One of the historic sites we visited was the

11. VALENCE: Parapsychology in the U.S.S.R.

Archangel Palace, the home of Catherine the Great. We told Naumov of the several movies we had seen about Catherine and of how she had been portrayed by actresses as diverse as Marlene Dietrich, Tallulah Bankhead, Jeanne Moreau, and Bette Davis. Naumov was delighted to hear that Miss Davis—obviously one of his favorite Hollywood stars—had played the Czarina. He was even more impressed when we mentioned that she had studied Russian for her role as Catherine in the movie *John Paul Jones.*

One of our visitors was G. S. Vassilichenko, a noted Russian physician and sexologist, who is a believer in acupuncture. He described how he and his colleagues use acupuncture for sexual dysfunction, primarily directing their efforts to certain points near the base of the spine. Vassilichenko is not unusual in his emphasis on acupuncture. Many Soviet physicians use it to treat various disorders, and the technique is employed at many large Russian clinics.

Almost everyone we met in Russia mentioned acupuncture, although it is not as widely practiced there as in China. There are, in fact, important differences between the two techniques. Instead of using needles, as the Chinese do, Soviet physicians usually stimulate the appropriate area with massage, ointments, lotions, weak pulses of electricity, injected chemicals, and even, in the case of epileptic seizures, laser beams. Although most parapsychologists in the U.S.S.R. believe in the efficacy of acupuncture, it should be noted that not all physicians who use acupuncture are interested in parapsychology. Many use acupuncture simply because it seems to work.

We also heard about acupuncture from another visitor, Victor Adamenko, a brilliant physicist who has helped to develop the tobioscope, a device used to detect acupuncture points. We watched him demonstrate the device, which is about the size of a small flashlight. As he slowly moved it across a woman's face, its bulb flashed on and off. We were told that the light goes on as the tobioscope passes over the various acupuncture points. A bright light indicates the individual is in good health, a dim light that there is a current or future health problem. Adamenko and his associates claim to have identified more than 900 acupuncture points with their tobioscope. After the demonstration, Adamenko explained that the device measures changes in the body's "bioplasmic energy." By obtaining measures from several of the body's acupuncture points, he claims he can detect the flow of this energy and thus predict and treat disease. The bioplasmic system, he feels, will eventually be recognized as an important component of the organism, along with the circulatory, lymphatic, and nervous systems.

Adamenko then described to us his work with a device invented some thirty years ago by Semyon and Valentina Kirlian. It is said to take photographs of this bioplasmic energy. Basically, he told us, the Kirlian device is an electrical Tesla coil connected to two metallic plates. Between the plates are placed a living or nonliving object and a piece of film, with the film touching the object. When a switch is turned on, a high-energy frequency is generated that causes the film to record an "aura" that surrounds the object. Adamenko showed us photographs of plants taken with the Kirlian device. When we inspected the prints closely, we saw flare patterns emerging from the leaves. If the plant has buds and flowers, there is more activity in those regions. If the buds and flowers are cut off, the photograph shows streams of light coming from the severed tip of the plant, much like the shower of sparks that emanate from the end of a Roman candle.

When we looked at Kirlian photographs of human body parts, we also saw flare patterns. They were especially obvious in the pictures taken of human heads and hands. The patterns are said to change very quickly if the individual is hypnotized, imbibes alcohol, or takes drugs. The Kirlians claim that the technique is a method of converting nonelectrical effects into electrical ones that can be visually observed by the device. Applications of the process to such fields as agriculture, nutrition, dentistry, and medicine may be possible, they say, since each living species has its own distinctive flare pattern that changes according to its biological state.

Interestingly, sunspots are believed to affect the Kirlian photographs, since pictures taken on days when there is sunspot activity do not turn out well. These photographs may relate to the electromagnetic fields around living organisms studied by A. S. Presman, another of our visitors.

Genady Sergeiev, a psychophysiologist, has made Kirlian photographs of the noted Russian "sensitive," Nina Kulagina, in which a heightened biological luminescence seems to radiate from her eyes while she is performing some of her celebrated feats of psychokinesis. Other Kirlian photographs of Mrs. Kulagina engaged in psychokinesis show a bioplasmic field around her entire body that expands and pulses rhythmically. We did not see Mrs. Kulagina because she was out of town when we visited her home in Leningrad. However, one of our Maimonides colleagues, Montague Ullman, a psychiatrist who directs the Maimonides Community Mental Health Center, recently observed a performance of her powers in Leningrad. As she made passes with her hands over a table in Ullman's hotel room, paper clips, matches, and pen tops seemed to move across the table without her touching them. Since then, Mrs. Kulagina is reported to have performed even more remarkable feats, such as moving objects by simply thinking about them. Her weight is reported to drop and her blood-sugar level to rise during these experiments.

A small group of women, we learned later, is now being trained to duplicate Mrs. Kulagina's feats. Each one is given a compass and told to spend several hours each week attempting to move the needle. Each is told to make these attempts while in a highly emotional state and to imagine what the Russians call bioplasma coming out of the hand and pushing the needle. Once they can move the needle, the women attempt to make a wooden cylinder roll across the tabletop. If they are successful, they place small pieces of metal and wood (paper clips and matchboxes, for example)

11. VALENCE: Parapsychology in the U.S.S.R.

on a table and try to move them. Women with dry skin seem to make the best candidates for psychokinesis, possibly because bioplasma is inhibited by oily skin.

The concept of bioplasma is a key to the understanding of Soviet parapsychology. Bioplasma is presumed by the Russians to be a fourth state of matter that constantly interacts with other states of matter, perhaps transforming itself into them from time to time, just as water becomes steam or ice. It is bioplasma that explains the workings of acupuncture and other aspects of Soviet parapsychology.

Before we left the United States for the U.S.S.R., Khigh Dhiegh, an actor and one of the few Americans who is knowledgeable on the subjects of bioplasma and acupuncture, discussed them with us. He explained that the ancient Chinese physicians conceptualized a life energy running through the body, an energy that resembles the Soviet concept of bioplasma. In the Chinese belief, the body's 900 acupuncture points represent the focuses of this energy. The life energy can be brought into balance by stimulating the energy centers. T. X. Barber, a U.S. researcher in the psychology of altered states of consciousness, has noted that the concept of bioplasma serves Soviet parapsychologists as a useful "hypothetical construct" in stimulating integrated research approaches to elusive parapsychological events. In other words it gives them a "handle" to grasp in designing experiments.

While in Moscow, we were exposed to another extraordinary approach to human potential. Vladimir Raikov, a psychiatrist, brought several students to our room and demonstrated what is called "hypno-reproduction," a form of hypnotism in which the subject is told he or she is a figure in public life or history who can do something extraordinarily well. His first subject was a student at a musical conservatory who played the violin for us. The student was then hypnotized by Raikov and told he was Fritz Kreisler. The student played again—this time, in our opinion, with more confidence and expertise. When the hypnotism was terminated, the young man told us that it took only a few seconds for him to "slip away"; from that point on, he had no memory of the experience. He believes his skill on the violin has improved as a result of hypnosis.

Raikov then hypnotized another student and told her she was three days old. When she opened her eyes, they were unfocused and wandered aimlessly like those of an infant. When Raikov erased this suggestion and told her she was Rachmaninoff, she played an imaginary piano with great pleasure. At one point in the session, when the subject had her eyes open, Raikov told the hypnotically reproduced Rachmaninoff that we were the hypnotist's drinking companions. The young woman looked at us in disgust and went to a far corner of the room. Raikov then explained that Rachmaninoff had had a drinking problem, as had the young woman at one time. Hypnosis had helped her overcome it.

One of Raikov's subjects was an attractive young girl who showed us several of her pastel paintings. She had no interest in painting before she volunteered for Raikov's experiments but was told, during hypnosis, that she was Lisa Repin, a well-known Russian artist. We saw the results of her work from session to session. By the end of the sixth session, she was doing what seemed to us to be highly competent work—without having taken a single art lesson.

Raikov's subjects work in small groups, the hypnotically reproduced Rubenses and Rembrandts drawing and painting each other while hypnotized. Perhaps they learn artistic techniques from each other while hypnotized. In any event, the improvement we saw in several dozen "before" hypno-reproduction and "after" hypno-reproduction drawings was remarkable.

Raikov feels that only about one in five people can enter hypnosis deeply enough for hypno-reproduction to work. We performed a number of hypnotic suggestibility tests on his subjects and found them all highly hypnotizable. On the eye-roll test, for example, they were able to roll their eyes so far upwards that their pupils all but disappeared. Would one of us be a candidate for hypno-reproduction? Raikov agreed to a demonstration with Richard Davidson. "Sit down, Richard, and relax," he said. He pushed Richard's head back, pulled his neck forward, and began to strike his chest. When Raikov said, "I am holding a rose under your nose, and you can smell it," the subject immediately smelled a rose aroma. Age-regression techniques, however, produced little response.

"Richard," concluded Raikov, "you are not a candidate for hypno-reproduction."

On Monday, standing beneath a large portrait of Lenin, Krippner delivered his lecture at the Institute of Psychology. He began his presentation with a description of the technique of "convergent operations" used at the Dream Laboratory and its relation to dream and alpha-wave research. Convergent operations, he explained, combines the subject's report of his experiences with psychophysiological monitoring. In the dream studies the subject is awakened when his eye movements and brain-wave patterns indicate that he is dreaming. He then describes the dream.

Krippner outlined the laboratory's most recent dream study, carried out with the enthusiastic cooperation of the Grateful Dead, a well-known U.S. rock group. While the two subjects of the study slept, the audience at a series of six Grateful Dead concerts, all held about forty miles from the laboratory, viewed a randomly selected slide of an art print for fifteen minutes. The Grateful Dead played as the slide was projected. The audience of about 2,000 was told to try to communicate the slide's contents to one of the subjects who was sleeping at the Dream Laboratory. Nothing was said about the other subject, who slept at home. The experiment was repeated each night with a different print being shown.

When the experiment was completed, two outside judges matched the dream reports of the two subjects with the art prints. The judges evaluated the dreams of the subject who had slept in the laboratory as corresponding with the print that had been shown at the concert four times out of six. The dreams of the other subject corresponded only one time out of six. The laboratory subject's dreams sometimes mirrored the print very closely. When Scralian's painting *The Seven Spinal Chakras* was projected, the subject dreamed about "an energy box" and a "spinal column," both recognizable components of the painting. Krippner pointed out that the results of the experiment suggest that intentionality on the part of the agent is important, since only the subject whose name was given to the audience attained significant results.

After the lecture, we were told that the top two rows in the audience were filled by space scientists and cosmonauts-in-training. Naumov gave us affectionate bear hugs and told us that the day was a "victory for parapsychology."

A few days later, after a brief trip to Leningrad, we boarded a plane in Moscow for the return flight to the United States. We were aware that we had much to learn from the Russians in parapsychology, and that the Russians, in turn, could learn much from us.

Perhaps the most important Soviet contribution to parapsychology is their work in the area of psychokinesis. However, we could well adopt their stategy for putting parapsychology into the mainstream of science. We should follow their lead and redouble our efforts to find possible practical applications for ESP and PK, especially in the areas of medicine and mental health. For example, in our own dream and telepathy studies, it would be extremely useful to find out how schizophrenics react in the experimental situations. Perhaps, as we told Yuri Nikolayev, a leading Soviet schizophrenia researcher, the paranoid delusions of schizophrenics contain a nugget of truth; perhaps, they are picking up other people's thoughts at least some of the time. Though little experimentation has been done in this field, it could be enormously important.

The Russians, on the other hand, could learn from us rigid experimental techniques with which to temper their approach to parapsychology. Most of the papers we collected on our trip were from the Russian popular press or from such semiscientific periodicals as *Science and Religion,* which praises science and criticizes religion. They rarely present well-designed tests with control conditions, isolation of variables, and tests for statistical significance.

International cooperation, including cross-studies of "sensitives," joint seminars, and research programs, would greatly aid the absorption of parapsychology into the mainstream of science. It would, we feel, contribute to man's understanding of his own potential.

12.
VISION:
Fear Hound

KATHERINE MacLEAN

In the following story, Katherine MacLean envisions a possible application of the study of extrasensory phenomena.

A few years ago the sf field suffered a rash of psi stories—too often shallow and gimmicky—with the result that most of the conscientious writers in the field abandoned the theme as overworked. But another way of dealing with a familiar idea is to dig more deeply and thoughtfully into it—as Katherine MacLean does in this gripping story of a future Rescue Squad.

Hunger is not a bad thing. Some guys who knew Zen and jaine yogi had told me they could go without food thirty days. They showed me how. The only trouble is, when you skip meals, you shake. When I touched a building it felt like the world was trembling.

If I told the employment board that my student support money had run out, they'd give me an adult support pension and a ticket to leave New York and never come back. I wasn't planning on telling them.

Ahmed the Arab came along the sidewalk, going fast, his legs rangy and swinging. Ahmed used to be king of our block gang when we were smaller, and he used to ask me to help him sometimes. This year Ahmed had a job working for the Rescue Squad. Maybe he would let me help him; maybe he could swing a job for me.

I signaled him as he came close. "Ahmed."

He went on by, hurrying. "OK, George, come on."

I fell into stride beside him. "What's the rush?"

From *Analog Science Fiction/Science Fact,* 1968. Reprinted by permission.

12.   VISION: Fear Hound

"Look at the clouds, man. Something's getting ready to happen. We've got to stop it."

I looked at the clouds. The way I felt was smeared all over the sky. Dangerous dark dirty clouds bulged down over the city, looking ready to burst and spill out fire and dirt. In high school Psychology-A they said that people usually match their mood. My mood was bad, I could see that, but I still did not know what the sky really looked like—dark, probably, but harmless.

"What is it?" I asked. "Is it smog?"

Ahmed stopped walking, and looked at my face. "No. It's fear."

He was right. Fear lay like a fog across the air. Fear was in the threatening clouds and in the darkness across the faces of the people. People went by under the heavy sky, hunched as if there were a cold rain falling. Buildings above us seemed to be swaying outward.

I shut my eyes, but the buildings seemed to sway out farther.

Last year when Ahmed had been training for the Rescue Squad he'd opened up a textbook and tried to explain something to me about the difference between inner reality and outer reality, and how mobs can panic when they all see the same idea. I opened my eyes and studied the people running at me, past me, and away from me as the crowds rushed by. Crowds always rush in New York. Did they all see the buildings as leaning and ready to fall? Were they afraid to mention it?

"Ahmed, you Rescue Squad fink," I said, "what would happen if we yelled Earthquake good and loud? Would they all panic?"

"Probably so." Ahmed was looking at me with interest, his lean face and black eyes intent. "How do you feel, George? You look sick."

"I feel lousy. Something wrong in my head. Dizzy." Talking made it worse. I braced my hand against a wall. The walls rocked, and I felt as if I were down flat while I was still standing up.

"What in creation is wrong with me?" I asked. "I can't get sick from skipping a meal or so, can I?" Mentioning food made my stomach feel strange and hollow and dry. I was thinking about death suddenly. "I'm not even hungry," I told Ahmed. "Am I sick?"

Ahmed, who had been king of our block gang when we were kids, was the one who knew the answers.

"Man, you've got good pickup." Ahmed studied my face. "Someone near here is in trouble and you're tuned in to it." He glanced at the sky east and west. "Which way is worst? We've got to find him fast."

I looked up Fifth Avenue. The giant glass office buildings loomed and glittered insecurely, showing clouds through in dark green, and reflecting clouds in gray as if dissolving into the sky. I looked along Forty-second Street to the giant arches of the transport Center. I looked down Fifth Avenue, past the stone lions of the library, and then west to the neon signs and excitement. The darkness came at me with teeth, like a giant mouth. Hard to describe.

149

IV. The Emergence of Parapsychology

"Man, it's bad." I was shaken. "It's bad in every direction. It's the whole city!"

"It can't be," Ahmed said. "It's loud; we must be near where the victim is."

He put his wrist radio up to his mouth and pushed the signal button. "Statistics, please." A voice answered. "Statistics." Ahmed articulated carefully. "Priority call. Rescue Badge 54B. Give me today's trends in hospital admissions, all rises above sigma reciprocal 30. Point the center of any area with a sharp rise in"—he looked at me analytically—"dizziness, fatigue, and acute depression." He considered me further. "Run a check on general anxiety syndromes and hypochondria." He waited for the Statistics Department to collect data.

I wondered if I should be proud or ashamed of feeling sick.

He waited—lean, efficient, impatient, with black eyebrows and black intense eyes. He'd looked almost the same when he was ten and I was nine. His family were immigrants, speaking some unAmerican language, but they were the proud kind. Another person would burn with hate or love for girls, but Ahmed would burn about Ideas. His ideas about adventure made him king of our block gang. He'd lead us into strange adventures and grown-up no-trespassing places just to look at things, and when we were trapped he'd consult a little pack of cards, or some dice, and lead us out of trouble at high speed—like he had a map. He had an idea that the look and feel of a place told you its fate; a bad-luck place looked bad. When he consulted me, or asked me how a place looked to me, I'd feel proud.

He'd left us behind. We all dropped out in high school, but Ahmed the Arab got good marks, graduated and qualified for advanced training. All the members of our gang had taken their adult retirement pensions and left the city, except me and Ahmed the Arab—and I heard Ahmed was the best detector in the Rescue Squad.

The wrist radio whistled and he put it to his ear. The little voice crackled off figures and statistical terms. Ahmed looked around at the people passing, surprised, then looked at me more respectfully. "It's all over Manhattan. Women coming in with psychosomatic pregnancy. Pregnant women are coming in with nightmares. Men are coming in with imaginary ulcers and cancers. Lots of suicides and lots of hospital commitments for acute suicidal melancholy. You are right. The whole city is in trouble."

He started along Forty-second Street toward Sixth Avenue, walking fast. "Need more help. Try different techniques." A hanging sign announced, *Gypsy Tea Room, Oriental Teas, Exotic Pastries, Readings of Your Personality and Future.* Ahmed pushed through a swinging door and went up a moving escalator two steps at a time, with me right after him. We came out into the middle of a wide, low-ceiling restaurant, with little tables and spindly chairs.

Four old ladies were clustered around one table nibbling at cupcakes and talking. A businessman sat at a table near the window reading the *Wall*

12. VISION: Fear Hound

Street Journal. Two teener students sat leaning against the glass wall window looking down into Forty-second Street and its swirling crowds. A fat woman sat at a table in a corner, holding a magazine up before her face. She lowered it and looked at us over the top. The four old ladies stopped talking and the businessman folded his *Wall Street Journal* and put it aside as if Ahmed and I were messengers of bad news. They were all in a miserable, nervous mood like the one I was in—expecting the worst from a doomed world.

Ahmed threaded his way among the tables toward the corner table where the fat woman sat. She put her magazine aside on another table as we approached. Her face was round and pleasant, with smile creases all over it. She nodded and smiled at me and then did not smile at Ahmed at all, but instead stared straight back into his eyes as he sat down in front of her.

He leaned across the table. "All right, Bessie, you feel it, too. Have you located who it is?"

She spoke in a low, intense voice, as if afraid to speak loudly: "I felt it first thing I woke up this morning, Ahmed. I tried to trace it for the Rescue Squad, but she's feeling, not thinking. And it's echoing off too many other people because they keep thinking up reasons why they feel so—" She paused and I knew what she was trying to describe. Trying to describe it made it worse.

She spoke in a lower voice and her round face was worried. "The bad dream feeling is hanging on, Ahmed. I wonder if I'm—"

She didn't want to talk about it, and Ahmed had his mouth open for a question, so I was sorry for her and butted in.

"What do you mean about people making echoes? How come all this crowd—" I waved my hand in a vague way, indicating the city and the people. The Rescue Squad was supposed to rescue lost people. The city was not lost.

Ahmed looked at me impatiently. "Adults don't like to use telepathy. They pretend they can't. But say a man falls down an elevator shaft and breaks a leg. No one finds him, and he can't reach a phone so he'll get desperate and pray and start using mind power. He'll try to send his thoughts as loud as he can. He doesn't know how loud he can send. But the dope doesn't broadcast his name and where he is, he just broadcasts: 'Help, I've got a broken leg!' They come limping into the emergency clinics and get X rays of good legs. The doctors tell them to go home. But they are picking up the thought, 'Help! I'm going to die unless I get help!' so they hang around the clinics and bother the doctors. They are scared. The Rescue Squad uses them as tracers. Whenever there is an abnormal wave of people applying for help in one district, we try to find the center of the wave and locate someone in real trouble."

The more he talked the better I felt. It untuned me from the bad mood of the day, and Rescue Squad work was beginning to sound like something

151

I could do. I know how people feel just by standing close to them. Maybe the Rescue Squad would let me join if I showed that I could detect people.

"Great," I said. "What about preventing murders? How do you do that?"

Ahmed took out his silver badge and looked at it. "I'll give you an example. Imagine an intelligent sensitive kid with a vivid imagination. He is being bullied by a stupid father. He doesn't say anything back; he just imagines what he will do to the big man when he grows up. Whenever the big man gets him mad the kid clenches his fists and smiles and puts everything he's got into a blast of mental energy, thinking of himself splitting the big man's skull with an ax. He thinks loud. A lot of people in the district have nothing much to do, nothing much to think about. They never plan or imagine much and they act on the few thoughts that come to them. Get it?"

"The dopes act out what he is thinking," I grinned.

Ahmed looked at my grin with a disgusted expression and turned back to the fat woman. "Bessie, we've got to locate this victim. What do the tea leaves say about where she is?"

"I haven't asked." Bessie reached over to the other table and picked up an empty cup. It had a few soggy tea leaves in the bottom. "I was hoping that you would find her." She heaved herself to her feet and waddled into the kitchen.

I was still standing. Ahmed looked at me with a disgusted expression. "Quit changing the subject. Do you want to help rescue someone or don't you?"

Bessie came back with a round pot of tea and a fresh cup on a tray. She put the tray on the table, and filled the cup, then poured half of the steaming tea back into the pot. I remembered that a way to get information from the group-mind is by seeing how people interpret peculiar shapes like ink blots and tea leaves, and I stood quietly, trying not to bother her.

She lowered herself slowly into her chair, swirled the tea in the cup, and looked in. We waited. She rocked the cup, looking; then shut her eyes and put the cup down. She sat still, eyes closed, the eylids squeezed tight in wrinkles.

"What was it?" Ahmed asked in a low voice.

"Nothing, nothing, just a—" She stopped and choked. "Just a damned, lousy maggotty skull."

That had to be a worse sign than getting the ace of spades in a card cut. Death. I began to get that sick feeling again. Death for Bessie?

"I'm sorry," Ahmed said. "But push on, Bessie. Try another angle. We need the name and address."

"She was not thinking about her name and address," Bessie's eyes were still tightly shut.

Suddenly Ahmed spoke in a strange voice. I'd heard that voice years ago when he was head of our gang—when he hypnotized another kid. It was a deep smooth voice and it penetrated inside of you.

12. VISION: Fear Hound

"You need help and no one has come to help you. What are you thinking?"
The question got inside my head. An answer opened up and I started to answer, but Bessie answered first. "When I don't think, just shut my eyes and hold still, I don't feel anything, everything goes far away. When the bad things begin to happen I can stay far away and refuse to come back." Bessie's voice was dreamy.

The same dark sleepy ideas had formed in my own head. She was saying them for me. Suddenly I was afraid that the darkness would swallow me. It was like a night cloud, or a pillow, floating deep down and inviting you to come and put your head on it, but it moved a little and turned and showed a flash of shark teeth, so you knew it was a shark waiting to eat anyone who came close.

Bessie's eyes snapped open and she straightened herself upright, her eyes so wide open that white showed around the rims. She was scared of sleeping. I was glad she had snapped out of it. She had been drifting down into the inviting dark toward that black monster.

"If you went in too deep, you could wake up dead," I said and put a hand on Ahmed's shoulder to warn him to slow down.

"I don't care which one of you speaks for her," he said, without turning around. "But you have to learn to separate your thoughts from hers. You're not thinking of dying—the victim is. She's in danger of death, somewhere." He leaned across the table to Bessie again. "Where is she?"

I tightened my grip on Ahmed's shoulder, but Bessie obediently picked up the teacup in fat fingers and looked in again. Her face was round and innocent, but I judged she was braver than I was.

I went around Bessie's side of the table to look into the teacup over her shoulder. A few tea leaves were at the bottom of the cup, drifting in an obscure pattern. She tapped the side of the cup delicately with a fat finger. The pattern shifted. The leaves made some sort of a picture, but I could not make out exactly what it was. It looked like it meant something, but I could not see it clearly.

Bessie spoke sympathetically. "You're thirsty, aren't you? There, there Honeybunch. We'll find you. We haven't forgotten you. Just think where you are and we will—" Her voice died down to a low, fading mumble, like a windup doll running down. She put the cup down and put her head down into her spread hands.

I heard a whisper. "Tired of trying, tired of smiling. Let die. Let death be born. Death will come out to destroy the world, the worthless dry, rotten—"

Ahmed reached across and grasped her shoulders and shook them. "Bessie, snap out of it. That's not you. It's the *other* one."

Bessie lifted a changed face from her hands. The round smiling look was gone into sagging sorrowful folds like an old bloodhound. She mumbled, "It's true. Why wait for someone to help you and love you? We are born and die. No one can help that. No reason to hope. Hope hurts. Hope hurt

153

her." It bothered me to hear Bessie talk. It was like she were dead. It was a corpse talking.

Bessie seemed to try to pull herself together and focus on Ahmed to report, but one eye went off focus and she did not seem to see him.

She said, "Hope hurts. She hates hope. She tries to kill it. She felt my thinking and she thought my feelings of life and hope were hers. I was remembering how Harry always helped me, and she blasted in blackness and hate—" She put her face down in her hands again. "Ahmed, he's dead. She killed Harry's ghost in my heart. He won't ever come back anymore, even in dreams." Her face was dead, like a mask.

He reached over and shook her shoulder again. "Bessie, shame on you, snap out of it."

She straightened and glared. "It's true. All men are beasts. No one is going to help a woman. You want me to help you at your job and win you another medal for finding that girl, don't you? You don't care about her." Her face was darkening, changing to something worse, that reminded me of the black shapes of the clouds.

I had to pull her out of it, but I didn't know what to do.

Ahmed clattered the spoon against the teacup with a loud clash and spoke in a loud casual voice: "How's the restaurant business, Bessie? Are the new girls working out?"

She looked down at the teacup, surprised, and then looked vaguely around the restaurant. "Not many customers right now. It must be an off hour. The girls are in the kitchen." Her face began to pull back into its own shape, a pleasant restaurant-service mask, round and ready to smile. "Can I have the girls get you anything, Ahmed?"

She turned to me with a habit of kindness, and her words were less mechanical. "Would you like anything, young man? You look so energetic standing there! Most young people like our Turkish honey rolls." She still wasn't focused on me, didn't see me, really, but—I smiled back at her, glad to see her feeling better.

"No thank you, Ma'am," I said and glanced at Ahmed to see what he would want to do next.

"Bessie's honey rolls are famous," Ahmed said. "They are dripping with honey and have so much almond flavor they burn your mouth." He rose easily, looking lazy. "I guess I'll have a dozen to take along."

The fat woman sat blinking her eyes up at him. Her round face did not look sick and sagging anymore, just sort of rumpled and meaningless, like your own face looks in the mirror in the morning. "Turkish honey-and-almond rolls," she repeated. "One dozen." She rang a little bell in the middle of the table and rose.

"Wait for me, downstairs," Ahmed told me. He turned to Bessie.

"Remember the time a Shriners Convention came in and they all wanted lobster and palm reading at once? Where did you get all those hot lobsters?" They moved off together to the counter which displayed cookies

12.   VISION: Fear Hound

and rolls. A pretty girl in a frilled apron trotted out of the kitchen and stood behind the counter.

Bessie laughed, starting with a nervous high-pitched giggle and ending up in a deep ho-ho sound like Santa Claus. "Do I remember? What a hassle! Imagine me on the phone trying to locate twenty palm readers in ten minutes! I certainly was grateful when you sent over those twenty young fellows and girls to read palms for my Shriners. I was really nervous until I saw they had their marks really listening, panting for the next word. I thought you must have gotten a circus tribe of gypsies from the cooler. *Ho-ho.* I didn't know you had sent over the whole police class in Suspect Personality Analysis."

I went out the door, down to the sidewalk. A few minutes later Ahmed came down the escalator two steps at a time and arrived at the sidewalk like a rocket. "Here, carry these." He thrust the paper bag of Turkish honey rolls at me. The warm, sweet smell was good. I took the bag and plunged my hand in.

"Just carry them. Don't eat any." Ahmed led the way down the subway stairs to the first underground walkway.

I pulled my hand out of the bag and followed. I was feeling so shaky I went down the stairs slowly one at a time instead of two at a time. When I got there Ahmed was looking at the signs that pointed in different directions, announcing what set of tracks led to each part of the city. For the first time I saw that he was uncertain and worried. He didn't know which way to go. It was a strange thought for me, that Ahmed did not know which way to go. It meant he had been running without knowing which way to run.

He was thinking aloud: "We know that the victim is female, adult, younger than Bessie, probably pregnant, and is trapped someplace where there is no food or water for her. She expected help from the people she loves, and was disappointed, and now is angry with the thought of love and hates the thought of people giving help."

I remembered Bessie's suddenly sick and flabby face, after the victim had struck out at Bessie's thought of giving help. *Angry* seemed to be the understatement of the year. I remembered the wild threatening sky, and I watched the people hurrying by, pale and anxious. Two chicks passed in bad shape. One was holding her stomach and muttering about Alka-Seltzer, and the other had red-rimmed eyes as if she had just been weeping. Can one person in trouble do that to a whole city full of people?

"Who is she, Ahmed?" I asked. "I mean, *what* is she anyhow?"

"I don't understand it myself," Ahmed said. Suddenly he attacked me again with his question, using that deep hypnotic voice to push me backward into the black whirlpools of the fear of death. "*If you were thirsty, very thirsty, and there was only one place in the city you could go to buy a thirst quencher where—*"

"I'm not thirsty." I tried to swallow, and my tongue felt swollen, my

155

mouth seemed dry and filled with sand, and my throat was coated with dry gravel. The world tilted over sideways. I braced my feet to stand up. "I *am* thirsty. How did you do that? I want to go to the White Horse Tavern on Bleeker Street and drink a gallon of ginger ale and a bottle of brown beer."

"You're my compass. Let's go there. I'll buy for you."

Ahmed ran down the Eighth Avenue subway stairs to the chair tracks. I followed, clutching the bag of sweet smelling rolls as if it were a heavy suitcase full of rocks. The smell made me hungry and weak. I could still walk, but I was pretty sure that, if Ahmed pushed me deep into that black mood just once more, they'd have to send me back on a stretcher.

On the tracks we linked our chairs and Ahmed shifted the linked chairs from belt to belt until we were traveling at a good speed. The chairs moved along the tunnels, passing under bright store windows with beautiful mannequins dancing and displaying things to buy. I usually looked up when we got near the forest fire and waterfall three-dimensional pics, but today I did not look up. I sat with my elbows braced on my knees and my head hanging. Ahmed looked at me alertly, his black eyebrows furrowed and dark eyes scanning me up and down like I was a medical diagram.

"Man, I'd like to see the suicide statistics right now. One look at you and I know it's bad."

I had enough life left to be annoyed. "I have my own feelings, not just some chick's feelings. I've been sick all day. A virus or something."

"Damnit, will you never understand? We've got to rescue this girl because she's broadcasting. She's broadcasting feeling sick!"

I looked at the floor between my feet. "That's a lousy reason. Why can't you rescue her just because she's in trouble? Let her broadcast. High School Psych-A said that everybody broadcasts."

"Listen—" Ahmed leaned forward ready to tell me an idea. His eyes began to glitter as the idea took him. "Maybe she broadcasts too loud. Statistics has been running data on trends and surges in popular action. They think that people who broadcast too loud might be causing some of the mass action."

"I don't get you, Ahmed."

"I mean like they get a big surge of people going to Coney Island on a cloudy day, and they don't have subway cars ready for it, and traffic ties up. They compare that day with other cloudy days, the same temperature and the same time of year other years, and try to figure out what caused it. Sometimes it's a factory vacation; but sometimes it's one man, given the day off, who goes to the beach, and an extra crowd of a thousand or so people from all over the city, people that don't know him, suddenly make excuses, clear schedules and go to the beach, sometimes arriving at almost the same time, jamming up the subways for an hour, and making it hard for the Traffic Flow Control people."

"Is it a club?" I was trying to make out what he meant, but I couldn't see what it had to do with anything.

12. VISION: Fear Hound

"No," he said. "They didn't know each other. It's been checked. The Traffic Flow experts have to know what to expect. They started collecting names from the crowds. They found that most of the people in each surge are workers with an IQ below one hundred, but somehow doing all right with their lives. They seemed to be controlled by one man in the middle of the rush who had a reason to be going in that direction. The Statistics people call the man in the middle the *Archetype.* That's an old Greek word. The original that other people are copied from—one real man and a thousand echoes."

The idea of some people being echoes made me uneasy. It seemed insulting to call anyone an echo. "They must be wrong," I said.

"Listen—" Ahmed leaned forward, his eyes brightening. "They think they are right—one man and a thousand echoes. They checked into the lives of the ones that seemed to be in the middle. The Archetypes are energetic ordinary people living average lives. When things go as usual for the Archetype, he acts normal and everybody controlled by him acts normal, get it?"

I didn't get it, and I didn't like it. "An average healthy person is a good joe. He wouldn't want to control anyone," I said, but I knew I was sugaring the picture. Humans can be bad. People love power over people. "Listen," I said, "some people like taking advice. Maybe it's like advice?"

Ahmed leaned back and pulled his chin. "It fits. Advice by ESP is what you mean. Maybe the Archetype doesn't know he is broadcasting. He does just what the average man wants to do. Solves the same problems—and does it better. He broadcasts loud, pleasant, simple thoughts and they are easy to listen to if you have the same kind of life and problems. Maybe more than half the population below an IQ of 100 have learned to use telepathic pickup and let the Archetypes do their thinking for them."

Ahmed grew more excited, his eyes fixed on the picture he saw in his head. "Maybe the people who are letting Archetypes run their lives don't even know they are following anyone else's ideas. They just find these healthy, problem-solving thoughts going on in a corner of their mind. Notice how the average person believes that thinking means sitting quietly and looking far away, resting your chin in your hand like someone listening to distant music? Sometimes they say, 'When there's too much noise I *can't hear myself think.*' But when an intellectual, a real thinker is thinking —" He had been talking louder with more excitement as the subject got hold of him. He was leaning forward, his eyes glittering.

I laughed, interrupting. "When an intellectual is thinking he goes into high gear, leans forward, bugs his eyes at you and practically climbs the wall with each word, like you, Ahmed. Are you an Archetype?"

He shook his head. "Only for my kind of person. If an average kind of person started picking up my kind of thinking, it wouldn't solve his problems—so he would ignore it."

He quit talking because I was laughing so hard. Laughing drove away the ghosts of despair that were eating at my heart. "Your kind of person!

Ho ho. Show me one. Ha ha. Ignore it? Hell, if a man found your thoughts in his head he'd go to a psychiatrist. He'd think he was going off his rails."

Ahead we saw the big "14" signs signaling Fourteenth Street. I shifted gears on the linked seats and we began to slide sideways from moving cables to slower cables, slowing and going uphill.

We stopped. On the slow strip coming along a girl was kneeling sideways in one of the seats. I throught she was tying a shoelace, but when I looked back I saw she was lying curled up, her knees under her chin, her thumb in her mouth. Regression. Retreat into infancy. Defeat.

Somehow it sent a shiver of fear through me. Defeat should not come so easily. Ahmed had leaped out of his chair and was halfway toward the stairs.

"Ahmed!—" I shouted.

He looked back and saw the girl. The seat carried her slowly by in the low-speed lane.

He waved for me to follow him and bounded up the moving stairs. "Come on," he yelled back, "before it gets worse."

When I got up top I saw Ahmed disappearing into the White Horse Tavern. I ran down the block and went in after him, into the cool shadows and paneled wood—nothing seemed to move. My eyes adjusted slowly and I saw Ahmed with his elbows on the counter, sipping a beer, and discussing the weather with the bartender.

It was too much for me. The world was out of its mind in one way and Ahmed was out of his mind in a different way. I could not figure it out, and I was ready to knock Ahmed's block off.

I was thirsty, but there was no use trying to drink or eat anything around that nut. I put my elbows on the bar a long way from Ahmed and called over to the bartender. "A quart of bock to go." I tilted my head at Ahmed. "He'll pay for it."

I sounded normal enough, but the bartender jumped and moved fast. He plunked a bottle in a brown paper bag in front of me and rubbed the bar in front of me with wood polish.

"Nice weather," he said, and looked around his place with his shoulders hunched, looking over his shoulders. "I wish I was outside walking in the fresh air. Have you been here before?"

"Once," I said, picking up the bag. "I liked it." I remembered the people who had shown me the place. Jean Fitzpatrick—she had shown me some of her poetry at a party—and a nice guy, her husband. Mort Fitzpatrick had played a slide whistle in his own tunes when we were walking along over to the tavern, and some bearded friends of theirs walked with us and talked odd philosophy and strange shared trips. The girl told me that she and her husband had a house in the neighborhood, and invited me to a party there, which I turned down, and she asked me to drop in anytime.

I knew she meant the "anytime" invitation. They were villagers, Bohemians, the kind who collect art, and strange books, and farout people.

12. VISION: Fear Hound

Villagers always have the door open for people with strange stories and they always have a pot of coffee ready to share with you.

"Do Jean Fitzpatrick and Mort Fitzpatrick still live around here?" I asked the bartender.

"I see them around. They haven't been in recently." He began to wipe and polish the bar away from me, moving toward Ahmed. "For all I know they might of moved."

Ahmed sipped his beer and glanced at us sidelong, like a stranger.

I walked out into the gray day with a paper bag under my arm with its hard weight of bock beer inside. I could quit this crazy, sick-making business of being a detector. I could go look up somebody in the Village like Jean Fitzpatrick and tell how sick the day had been, and how I couldn't take it and had chickened out, until the story began to seem funny and the world became some place I could stand.

Ahmed caught up with me and put a hand on my arm. I stopped myself from spinning around to hit him and just stood—staring straight ahead.

"You angry?" he asked, walking around me to get a look at my face. "How do you feel?"

"Ahmed, my feelings are my own business. OK? There is a girl around here I want to look up. I want to make sure she is all right. OK? Don't let me hold you up on Rescue Squad business. Don't wait for me. OK?" I started walking again, but the pest was walking right behind me. I had spelled it out clear and loud that I didn't want company. I did not want to flatten him, because at other times he had been my friend.

"May I come along?" he asked politely. "Maybe I can help."

I shrugged, walking along toward the river. What difference did it make? I was tired and there was too much going on in New York City. Ahmed would go away soon on his business. The picture of talking to the girl was warm, dark, relaxing. We'd share coffee and tell each other crazy little jokes and let the world go forgotten.

The house of the Fitzpatricks was one of those little tilted houses left over from a hundred years ago when the city was a town, lovingly restored by hand labor and brightened under many coats of paint by groups of volunteer decorators. It shone with white paint and red doors and red shutters with windowboxes under each window growing green vines and weeds and wildflowers. The entire house was overhung by the gigantic girders of the Hudson River Drive with its hissing flow of traffic making a faint rumble through the air and shaking the ground underfoot.

I knocked on the bright red door. No one answered. I found an unused doorbutton at the side and pushed it. Chimes sounded, but nothing stirred inside.

Village places usually are lived in by guests. Day or night someone is there: broke artists, travelers, hitchhikers, stunned inefficient looking refugees from the student or research worlds staving off a nervous breakdown by a vacation far away from pressure. It was considered legitimate to put your head inside and holler for attention if you couldn't raise anyone by knocking and ringing. I turned the knob to go in. It would not turn. It was locked.

I felt like they had locked the door when they saw me coming. The big dope, musclehead George is coming, lock the door. This was a bad day, but I couldn't go any farther. There was no place to go but here.

I stood shaking the knob dumbly, trying to turn it. It began to make a rattling noise like chains, and like an alarm clock in a hospital. The sound went through my blood and almost froze my hand. I thought something was behind the door, and I thought it was opening and a monster with a skull face was standing there waiting.

I turned my back to the door and carefully, silently went down the two steps to the sidewalk. I had gone so far off my rails that I thought I heard the door creaking open, and I thought I felt the cold wind of someone reaching out to grab me.

I did not look back, just strode away, walking along the same direction I had been going, pretending I had not meant to touch that door.

Ahmed trotted beside me, sidling to get a view of my face, scuttling sideways and ahead of me like a big crab.

"What's the matter? What is it?"

"She's not—Nobody was—" It was a lie. Somebody or something was in that house. Ignore it, walk away faster.

"Where are we going now?" Ahmed asked.

"Straight into the river," I said and laughed. It sounded strange and hurt my chest like coughing. "The water is a mirage in the desert and you walk out on the dry sand looking for water to drown in. The sand is covered with all the lost dried things that sank out of sight. You die on the dry sand, crawling, looking for water. Nobody sees you. People sail overhead and see the reflection of the sky in the fake waves. Divers come and find your dried mummy on the bottom and make notes, wondering because they think there is water in the river. But it is all a lie."

I stopped. The giant docks were ahead, and between them the ancient, small wharfs. There was no use going in that direction, or in any direction. The world was shriveled and old, with thousands of years of dust settling on it—a mummy case. As I stood there the world grew smaller, closing in on me like a lid shutting me into a box. I was dead, lying down, yet standing upright on the sidewalk. I could not move.

"Ahmed," I said, hearing my voice from a great distance, "get me out of this. What's a friend for?"

He danced around me like some evil goblin. "Why can't you help yourself?"

"I can't move," I answered, being remarkably reasonable.

He circled me, looking at my face and the way I stood. He was moving with stops and starts, like a bug looking for a place to bite. I imagined myself shooting a spray can of insecticide at him.

12. VISION: Fear Hound

Suddenly he used the *voice,* the clear deep hypnotic voice that penetrates into the dark private world where I live when I'm asleep and dreaming.

"Why can't you move?"

The gulf opened up beneath my feet. "Because I'd fall," I answered.

He used the voice again, and it penetrated to an interior world where the dreams lived and were real all the time. I was shriveled and weak, lying on dust and bits of old cloth. A foul and dusty smell was in my nostrils and I was looking down over an edge where the air came up from below. The air from below smelled better. I had been there a long time. Ahmed's voice reached me; it asked—

"How far would you fall?"

I measured the distance with my eye. I was tired and the effort to think was very hard. Drop ten or twelve feet to the landing, then tangle your feet in the ladder lying there and pitch down the next flight of steep stairs. ... Death waited at the bottom.

"A long way," I answered. "I'm too heavy. Stairs are steep."

"Your mouth is dry," he said.

I could feel the thirst like flames, drying up my throat, thickening my tongue as he asked the question, the jackpot question.

"Tell me, what is your name?"

I tried to answer with my right name, George Sanford. I heard a voice croak. "Jean Dalais."

"Where do you live?" he asked in the penetrating voice that rang inside my skull and rang into the evil other world where I, or someone, was on the floor smelling dust for the duration of eternity.

"Downstairs," I heard myself answer.

"Where are you now?" he asked in the same penetrating voice.

"In hell," the voice answered from my head.

I struck out with careful aim to flatten him with the single blow. He was dangerous. I had to stop him, and leave him stopped. I struck carefully, with hatred. He fell backward and I started to run. I ran freely, one block, two blocks. My legs were my own, my body was my own, my mind was my own. I was George Sanford and I could move without fear of falling. No one was behind me. No one was in front of me. The sun shone through clouds, the fresh wind blew along the empty sidewalks. I was alone. I had left that capsule world of dead horror standing behind me like an abandoned phone booth.

This time I knew what to do to stay out of it. Don't think back. Don't remember what Ahmed was trying to do. Don't bother about rescuing anyone. Take a walk along the edge of the piers in the foggy sunshine and think cheerful thoughts, or no thoughts at all.

I looked back and Ahmed was sitting on the sidewalk far back. I remembered that I was exceptionally strong and the coach had warned me to hold myself back when I hit. Even Ahmed? But he had been thinking, listening, off guard.

What had I said? *Jean Dalais.* Jean Fitzpatrick had showed me some of

161

her poetry, and that had been the name signed to it. Was Jean Dalais really Jean Fitzpatrick? It was probably her name before she married Mort Fitzpatrick.

I had run by the white house with the red shutters. I looked back. It was only a half a block back. I went back, striding before fear could grip me again, and rattled the knob and pulled at the red door and looked at the lock.

Ahmed caught up with me.

"You know how to pick locks?" I asked him.

"It's too slow," he answered in a low voice. "Let's try the windows."

He was right. The first window we tried was only stuck by New York soot. With our hands black and grimy with soot we climbed into the kitchen. The kitchen was neat except for a dried-up salad in a bowl. The sink was dry, the air was stuffy.

It was good manners to yell announcement of our trespassing.

"Jean!" I called. I got back echoes and silence, and something small falling off a shelf upstairs. The ghosts rose in my mind again and stood behind me, their claws outstretched. I looked over my shoulder and saw only the empty kitchen. My skin prickled. I was afraid of making a noise. Afraid death would hear me. Had to yell; afraid to yell. Had to move; afraid to move. Dying from cowardice. Someone else's thoughts, with the odor of illness, the burning of thirst, the energy of anger. I was shriveling up inside.

I braced a hand on the kitchen table. "Upstairs in the attic," I said. I knew what was wrong with me now. Jean Dalais was an Archetype. She was delirious and dreaming that she was I. Or I was really Jean Dalais suffering through another dream of rescue, and I was dreaming that strange people were downstairs in my kitchen looking for me. I, Jean, hated these hallucinations. I struck at the dream images of men with the true feeling of weakness and illness, with the memory of the time that had passed with no one helping me and the hatred of a world that trapped you and made hope a lie, trying to blast the lies into vanishing.

The George Sanford hallucination slid down to a sitting position on the floor of the kitchen. The bottle of bock in its paper bag hit the floor beside him with a heavy clunk, sounding almost real. "You go look, Ahmed," said the George Sanford mouth.

The other figure in the dream bent over and placed a phone on the floor. It hit the linoleum with another clunk and a musical chiming sound that seemed to be heard upstairs. "Hallucinations getting more real. Can hear 'em now," muttered the Sanford self—or was it Jean Dalais who was thinking?

"When I yell, dial O and ask for the Rescue Squad to come over." Ahmed picked up the paper bag of bock. "OK, George?" He started looking through the kitchen drawers. "Great stuff, beer, nothing better for extreme dehydration. Has salt in it. Keeps the system from liquid shock."

162

12. VISION: Fear Hound

He found the beer opener and slipped it into his hip pocket. "Liquid shock is from sudden changes in the water-versus-salt balance," he remarked, going up the stairs softly, two at a time. He went out of sight and I heard his footsteps, very soft and inquiring. Even Ahmed was afraid of stirring up ghosts.

What had Bessie said about the victim? "Hope hurts." She had tried to give the victim hope and the victim had struck her to the heart with a dagger of hatred and shared despair.

That was why I was sitting on the floor!

Danger George *don't think!* I shut my eyes and blanked my mind.

The dream of rescue and the man images were gone. I was Jean Dalais sinking down into the dark, a warm velvet darkness, no sensation, no thought, only distantly the pressure of the attic floor against my face.

A strange thump shook the floor and a scraping sound pulled at my curiosity. I began to wake again. It was a familiar sound, familiar from the other world and the other life, six days ago, an eternity ago, almost forgotten. The attic floor pushed against my face with a smell of dust. The thump and the scraping sound came again, metal against wood. I was curious. I opened dry, sand-filled eyes and raised my head, and the motion awakened my body to the hell of thirst and the ache of weakness.

I saw the two ends of the aluminum ladder sticking up through the attic trapdoor. The ladder was back now. It had fallen long ago, and now it was back, looking at me, expecting me to climb down it. I cursed the ladder with a mental bolt of hatred. What good is a ladder if you can't move? Long ago I had found that moving around brought on labor pains. No good to have a baby here. Better to hold still.

I heard a voice. "She's here. George. Call the Rescue Squad." I hated the voice. Another imaginary voice in the long nightmare of imaginary rescues. Who was "George"? I was Jean Dalais.

George. Someone had called "George." Downstairs in the small imagined kitchen I imagined a small image of a man grope for a phone beside him on the floor. He dialed "O" clumsily. A female voice asked a question. The man image said "Rescue Squad," hesitantly.

The phone clicked and buzzed and then a deep voice said, "Rescue Squad."

In the attic I knew how a dream of the Rescue Squad should go. I had dreamed it before. I spoke through the small man-image. "My name is Jean Fitzpatrick. I am at 29 Washington Street. I am trapped in my attic without water. If you people weren't fools, you would have found me long ago. Hurry. I'm pregnant." She made the man-image drop the receiver. The dream of downstairs faded again as the man-image put his face in his hands.

My dry eyes were closed, the attic floor again pressed against my face. Near me was the creak of ladder rungs taking weight, and then the creaks of the attic floor, something heavy moving on it gently, then the rustle of

163

clothing as somebody moved; the click of a bottle opener against a cap; the clink of the cap hitting the floor; the bubbling and hissing of a fizzing cool liquid. A hand lifted my head carefully and a cold bottle lip pushed against my mouth. I opened my mouth and the cool touch of liquid pressed within it and down the dry throat. I began to swallow.

George Sanford, me, took his hands away from his eyes and looked down at the phone. I was not lying down; I was not drinking; I was not thirsty. Had I dialed the Rescue Squad when Ahmed called me? A small mannequin of a man in Jean Fitzpatrick's mind had called and hung up, but the mannequin was me, George Sanford—six feet one and a half inches. I am no woman's puppet. The strength of telepathy is powered by emotion and need, and the woman upstairs had enough emotion and need, but no one could have done that to me if I did not want to help. No one.

A musical, two-toned note of a siren approaching, growing louder. It stopped before the door. Loud knocks came at the door. I was feeling all right but still dizzy and not ready to move.

"Come in," I croaked. They rattled the knob. I got up and let them in, then stood hanging on to the back of a chair.

Emergency squad orderlies in blue and white. "You sick?"

"Not me, the woman upstairs." I pointed and they rushed up the stairs, carrying their stretcher and medical kits.

There was no thirst or need driving her mind to intensity any more, but our minds were still connected somehow, for I felt the prick of a needle in one thigh, and then the last dizziness and fear dimmed and vanished, the world steadied out in a good upright position, the kitchen was not a dusty attic but only a clean empty kitchen and all the sunshine of the world was coming in the windows.

I took a deep breath and stretched, feeling the muscles strong and steady in my arms and legs. I went up to the second floor and steadied the ladder for the Rescue Squad men while they carried the unconscious body of a young woman down from the attic.

She was curly-haired with a dirt-and-tear streaked face and skinny arms and legs. She was bulging in the middle, as pregnant as a pumpkin.

I watched the blue and white Rescue truck drive away.

"Want to come along and watch me make out my report?" Ahmed asked.

On the way out of the kitchen I looked around for the Turkish honey rolls, but the bag was gone. I must have dropped it somewhere.

We walked south a few blocks to the nearest police station, Ahmed settled down at a desk they weren't using to fill out his report, and I found a stack of comic magazines in the waiting room and chose the one with the best action on the cover. My hands shook a little because I was hungry, but I felt happy and important.

Ahmed filled out the top, wrote a few lines, and then started working the calculator on the desk. He stopped, stared off into space, glanced at me and started writing again, glancing at me every second. I wondered what he was writing about me. I wanted the Rescue Squad brass to read good things about me so they would hire me for a job.

"I hunch good, don't I, Ahmed?"

"Yes." He filled something into a space, read the directions for the next question and began biting the end of his pen and staring at the ceiling.

"Would I make a good detector?" I asked.

"What kind of mark did you get in Analysis of Variance in high school?"

"I never took it. I flunked probability in algebra, in six B—"

"The Rescue Squad wants you to fill out reports that they can run into the statistics machines. Look"—I went over and he showed me a space where he had filled out some numbers and a funny symbol like a fallen down *d*—"can you read it, George?"

"What's it say?"

"It says probability .005. That means the odds were two hundred to one against you finding the White Horse Tavern just by accident, when it was the place the Fitzpatrick woman usually went to. I got the number by taking a rough count of the number of bars in the phone book. More than two hundred wrong bars, and there was only one bar you actually went to. Two hundred divided by one, or two hundred. If you had tried two bars before finding the right one your chance of being wrong would have been two hundred divided by two. That's one hundred. Your score for being right was your chance of being wrong, or the reciprocal of your chance of being right by luck. Your score is two hundred. Understand? Around here they think forty is a good score."

I stared at him, looking stupid. The school had tried relays of teachers and tutors on me for two terms before they gave up trying to teach me. It didn't seem to mean anything. It didn't seem to have anything to do with people. Without probability algebra and graphs I found out they weren't going to let me take Psychology B, History, Social Dynamics, Systems Analysis, Business Management, Programming or Social Work. They wouldn't even let me study to be a Traffic Flow cop. I could have taken Electronics Repair but I wanted to work with people, not TV sets, so I dropped out. I couldn't do school work, but the kind of thing the Rescue Squad wanted done, I could do.

"Ahmed, I'd be good in the Rescue Squad. I don't need statistics. Remember I told you you were pushing Bessie in too deep. I was right, wasn't I? And you were wrong. That shows I don't need training."

Ahmed looked sorry for me. "George, you don't get any score for that. Every soft-hearted slob is afraid when he sees someone going into a traumatic area in the subjective world. He always tries to make them stop. You would have said I was pushing her too deep anyhow, even if you were wrong."

"But I was right."

Ahmed half rose out of his chair, then made himself calm down.

He settled back, his lips pale and tight against his teeth. "It doesn't matter if you were right, unless you are right against odds. You get credit for picking the White Horse Tavern out of all the taverns you could have picked, and you get credit for picking the girl's house out of all the addresses you could have picked. I'm going to multiply the two figures by each other. It will run your score over eighty thousand probably. That's plenty of credit."

"But I only went to the tavern because I was thirsty. You can't credit me with that. You made me thirsty somehow. And I went to the girl's house because I wanted to see her. Maybe she was pulling at me."

"I don't care what your reasons were! You went to the right place, didn't you? You found her, didn't you?" Ahmed stood up and shouted. "You're talking like a square. What do you think this is, 1950, or some time your grandmother was running a store? I don't care what your reasons are, nobody cares anymore what the reasons are. We only care about results, understand? We don't know why things happen, but if everyone makes out good reports about them, with clear statistics, we can run the reports into the machines, and the machines will tell us exactly what is happening, and we can work with that, because they're facts, and it's the real world. I know you can find people. Your reasons don't matter. Scientific theories about the causes don't matter!"

He was red in the face and shouting, like I'd said something against his religion or something. "I wish we could get theories for some of it. But, if the statistics say that if something funny happens here and something else funny always happens over there, next, we don't have to know how the two connect; all we have to do is expect the second thing every time we see the first thing happen. See?"

I didn't know what he was talking about. My tutors had said things like that to me, but Ahmed felt miserable enough about it to shout. Ahmed was a friend.

"Ahmed," I said, "would I make a good detector?"

"You'd make a good detector, you dope!" He looked down at his report. "But you can't get into the Rescue Squad. The rules say that you've got to have brains in your head instead of rocks. I'll help you figure out someplace else you can get a job. Stick around. I'll loan you fifty bucks as soon as I finish this report. Go read something."

I felt lousy, but I stood there fighting it, because this was my last chance at a real job, and there was something right about what I was trying to do. The Rescue Squad needed me. Lost people were going to need me.

"Ahmed," I said, trying to make my meaning very clear to him. "I *should* be in your department. You gotta figure out a way to get me in."

It's hard watching a strong, confident guy go through a change. Generally Ahmed always knows what he is doing, he never wonders. He stared down at his report, holding his breath, he was thinking so hard. Then he got away from his desk and began to pace up and down. "What the hell is wrong with me? I must be going chicken. Desk work is softening me up."

12. VISION: Fear Hound

He grabbed up his report off the desk. "Come on, let's go buck the rules. Let's fight City Hall."

"We can't hire your friend." The head of the Rescue Squad shook his head. "He couldn't pass the tests. You said so yourself."

"The *rules* say that George has to pass the pen and paper tests." Ahmed leaned forward on the desk and tapped his hand down on the desk top, emphasizing words. "The rules are *trash* rules made up by trash bureaucrats so that nobody can get a job but people with picky little old-maid minds like them! Rules are something we use to deal with people we don't know and don't care about. We know George and we know we want him! How do we fake the tests?"

The chief held out one hand, palm down. "Slow down, Ahmed. I appreciate enthusiasm, but maybe we can get George in legitimately. I know he cut short an epidemic of hysteria and psychosomatics at the hospitals and saved the hospitals a lot of time and expense. I want him in the department if he can keep that up. But let's not go breaking up the system to get him in. We can use the system."

The chief opened the intercom switch and spoke into the humming box. "Get me Accounting will you?" The box answered after a short while and the chief spoke again. He was a big, square built man, going slightly flabby. His skin was loose and slightly gray. "Jack, listen, we need the services of a certain expert. We can't hire him. He doesn't fit the height and weight regulations, or something like that. How do we pay him?"

The man at the other end spoke briefly in accounting technicalities: ". . . Contingencies, services, fees. Consultant. File separate services rendered, time and results, with statistics of probability rundown on departmental expenses saved by outside help and city expenses saved by the Rescue Squad action, et cetera, et cetera. Get it?"

"OK, thanks." He shut off the chatterbox and spoke to Ahmed. "We're in. Your friend is hired."

My feet were tired standing there. My hands were shaking slightly so I had stuffed them into my pockets, like a nonchalant pose. I was passing the time thinking of restaurants, all the good ones that served the biggest plates for the least money. "When do I get paid?" I asked.

"Next month," Ahmed said. "You get paid at the end of every month for the work you did on each separate case. Don't look so disappointed. You are a consultant expert now. You are on my expense account. I'm supposed to buy your meals and pay your transportation to the scene of the crime whenever I consult you."

"Consult me now," I said.

We had a great Italian meal at an old-fashioned Italian restaurant: lasagna, antipasto, French bread in thick, tough slices, lots of butter, four cups of hot black coffee and spumoni for dessert, rich and sweet. Everything tasted fresh and cooked just right, and they served big helpings. I stopped shaking after the second cup of coffee.

There was something funny about the restaurant. Somebody was planning a murder, but I wasn't going to mention it to Ahmed until after dessert.

He'd probably want me to rescue somebody instead of eating.

13.
VISION:
Mad House

RICHARD MATHESON

In "Mad House" Richard Matheson takes the general principle of biofeedback and applies it in an effective—and terrifying—vision.

He sits down at his desk. He picks up a long, yellow pencil and starts to write on a pad. The lead point breaks.

The ends of his lips turn down. The eye pupils grow small in the hard mask of his face. Quietly, mouth pressed into an ugly, lipless gash, he picks up the pencil sharpener.

He grinds off the shavings and tosses the sharpener back in the drawer. Once more he starts to write. As he does so, the point snaps again and the lead rolls across the paper.

Suddenly his face becomes livid. Wild rage clamps the muscles of his body. He yells at the pencil, curses it with a stream of outrage. He glares at it with actual hate. He breaks it in two with a brutal snap and flings it into the wastebasket with a triumphant, "There! See how you like it in *there!*"

He sits tensely on the chair, his eyes wide, his lips trembling. He shakes with a frenzied wrath; it sprays his insides with acid.

The pencil lies in the wastebasket, broken and still. It is wood, lead, metal, rubber; all dead, without appreciation of the burning fury it has caused.

And yet . . .

IV. The Emergence of Parapsychology

He is quietly standing by the window, peering out at the street. He is letting the tightness sough away. He does not hear the rustle in the wastebasket which ceases immediately.

Soon his body is normal again. He sits down. He uses a fountain pen.

He sits down before his typewriter.

He inserts a sheet of paper and begins tapping on the keys.

His fingers are large. He hits two keys at once. The two typefaces are jammed together. They stand in the air, hovering impotently over the black ribbon.

He reaches over in disgust and slaps them back. They separate, flap back into their separate berths. He starts typing again.

He hits a wrong key. The start of a curse falls from his lips unfinished. He snatches up the round eraser and rubs the unwanted letter from the sheet of paper.

He drops the eraser and starts to type again. The paper has shifted on the roller. The next sentences are on a level slightly above the original. He clenches a fist, ignores the mistake.

The machine sticks. His shoulders twitch, he slams a fist on the space bar with a loud curse. The carriage jumps, the bell tinkles. He shoves the carriage over and it crashes to a halt.

He types faster. Three keys stick together. He clenches his teeth and whines in helpless fury. He smacks the type arms. They will not come apart. He forces them to separate with bent, shaking fingers. They fall away. He sees that his fingers are smudged with ink. He curses out loud, trying to outrage the very air for revenge on the stupid machine.

Now he hits the keys brutally, fingers falling like the stiff claws of a derrick. Another mistake, he erases savagely. He types still faster. Four keys stick together.

He screams.

He slams his fists on the machine. He clutches at the paper and rips it from the machine in jagged pieces. He welds the fragments in his fist and hurls the crumpled ball across the room. He beats the carriage over and slams the cover down on the machine.

He jumps up and glares down.

"You fool!" he shouts with a bitter, revolted voice. "You stupid, idiotic, asinine *fool!*"

Scorn drips from his voice. He keeps talking, he drives himself into a craze.

"You're no damn good. You're no damn good at all. I'm going to break you in pieces. I'm going to crack you into splinters, melt you, *kill* you! You stupid, moronic, lousy goddam machine!"

He quivers as he yells. And he wonders, deep in the self-isolated recesses of his mind whether he is killing himself with anger, whether he is destroying his system with fury.

13. VISION: Mad House

He turns and stalks away. He is too outraged to notice the cover of the machine slip down and hear the slight whirring of metal such as he might hear if the keys trembled in their slots.

He is shaving. The razor will not cut. Or the razor is too sharp and cuts too much.

Both times a muffled curse billows through his lips. He hurls the razor on the floor and kicks it against the wall.

He is cleaning his teeth. He draws the fine silk floss between his teeth. It shreds off. A fuzzy bit remains in the gap. He tries to press another piece down to get that bit out. He cannot force the white thread down. It snaps in his fingers.

He screams. He screams at the man in the mirror and draws back his hand, throws the floss away violently. It hits the wall. It hangs there and waves in the rush of angry breeze from the man.

He has torn another piece of floss from the container. He is giving the dental floss another chance. He is holding back his fury. If the floss knows what is good for it, it will plunge down between the teeth and draw out the shredded bit immediately.

It does. The man is mollified. The systematic juices leave off bubbling, the fires sink, the coals are scattered.

But the anger is still there, apart. Energy is never lost; a primal law.

He is eating.

His wife places a steak before him. He picks up the knife and fork and slices. The meat is tough, the blade is dull.

A spot of red puffs up in the flesh of his cheeks. His eyes narrow. He draws the knife through the meat. The blade will not sever the browned flesh.

His eyes widen. Withheld tempest tightens and shakes him. He saws at the meat as though to give it one last opportunity to yield.

The meat will not yield.

He howls. *"God damn it!"* White teeth jam together. The knife is hurled across the room.

The woman appears, mild alarm etching transient scars on her forehead. Her husband is beyond himself. Her husband is shooting poison through his arteries. Her husband is releasing another cloud of animal temper. It is mist that clings. It hangs over the furniture, drips from the walls.

It is alive.

So through the days and nights. His anger falling like frenzied axe blows in his house, everything he owns. Sprays of teeth-grinding hysteria clouding his windows and falling to his floors. Oceans of wild, uncontrolled hate flooding through every room of his house; filling each iota of space with a shifting, throbbing life.

He lay on his back and stared at the sun-mottled ceiling.

IV. The Emergence of Parapsychology

The last day, he told himself. The phrase had been creeping in and out of his brain since he'd awakened.

In the bathroom he could hear the water running. He could hear the medicine cabinet being opened and then closed again. He could hear the sound of her slippers shuffling on the tile floor.

Sally, he thought, don't leave me.

"I'll take it easy if you stay," he promised the air in a whisper.

But he knew he couldn't take it easy. That was too hard. It was easier to fly off the handle, easier to scream and rant and attack.

He turned on his side and stared out into the hall at the bathroom door. He could see the line of light under the door. Sally is in there, he thought. Sally, my wife, whom I married many years ago when I was young and full of hope.

He closed his eyes suddenly and clenched his fists. It came on him again. The sickness that prevailed with more violence every time he contracted it. The sickness of despair, of lost ambition. It ruined everything. It cast a vapor of bitterness over all his comings and goings. It jaded appetite, ruined sleep, destroyed affection.

"Perhaps if we'd had children," he muttered and knew before he said it that it wasn't the answer.

Children. How happy they would be watching their wretched father sinking deeper into his pit of introspective fever each day.

All right, tortured his mind, let's have the facts. He gritted his teeth and tried to make his mind a blank. But, like a dull-eyed idiot, his mind repeated the words that he muttered often in his sleep through restless, tossing nights.

I'm 40 years old. I teach English at Fort College. Once I had hoped to be a writer. I thought this would be a fine place to write. I would teach class part of the day and write with the rest of my time. I met Sally at school and married her. I thought everything would be just fine. I thought success was inevitable. Eighteen years ago.

Eighteen years.

How, he thought, did you mark the passing of almost two decades? The time seemed a shapeless lump of failing efforts, of nights spent in anguish; of the secret, the answer, the revelation always being withheld from him. Dangled overhead like cheese swinging in a maddening arc over the head of a berserk rat.

And resentment creeping. Days spent watching Sally buy food and clothing and pay rent with his meager salary. Watching her buy new curtains or new chair covers and feeling a stab of pain ever time because he was that much farther removed from the point where he could devote his time to writing. Every penny she spent he felt like a blow at his aspirations.

He forced himself to think that way. He forced himself to believe that it was only the time he needed to do good writing.

172

13. VISION: Mad House

But once a furious student had yelled at him, "You're just a third rate talent hiding behind a desk!"

He remembered that. Oh, God, how he remembered that moment. Remembered the cold sickness that had convulsed him when those words hit his brain. Recalled the trembling and the shaky unreason of his voice.

He had failed the student for the semester despite good marks. There had been a great to-do about it. The student's father had come to the school. They had all gone before Dr. Ramsay, the head of the English Department.

He remembered that too; the scene could crowd out all other memories. Him, sitting on one side of the conference table, facing the irate father and son. Dr. Ramsay stroking his beard until he thought he'd hurl something at him. Dr. Ramsay had said—well let's see if we can't straighten out this matter.

They had consulted the record book and found the student was right. Dr. Ramsay had looked up at him in great surprise. Well, I can't see what . . . he had said and let his syrupy voice break off and looked probingly at him, waiting for an explanation.

And the explanation had been hopeless, a jumbled and pointless affair. Irresponsible attitude, he had said, flaunting of unpardonable behavior; morally a failure. And Dr. Ramsay, his thick neck getting red, telling him in no uncertain terms that morals were not subject to the grading system at Fort College.

There was more but he'd forgotten it. He'd made an effort to forget it. But he couldn't forget that it would be years before he made a professorship. Ramsay would hold it back. And his salary would go on being insufficient and bills would mount and he would never get his writing done.

He regained the present to find himself clutching the sheets with taut fingers. He found himself glaring in hate at the bathroom door. Go on!— his mind snapped vindictively—Go home to your precious mother. See if I care. Why just a trial separation? Make it permanent. Give me some peace. Maybe I can do some writing then.

Maybe I can do some writing then.

The phrase made him sick. It had no meaning anymore. Like a word that is repeated until it becomes gibberish that sentence, for him, had been used to extinction. It sounded silly; like some bit of cliché from a soap opera. Hero saying in dramatic tones—Now, by God, maybe I can do some writing. Senseless.

For a moment, though, he wondered if it was true. Now that she was leaving could he forget about her and really get some work done? Quit his job? Go somewhere and hole up in a cheap furnished room and write?

You have $123.89 in the bank, his mind informed him. He pretended it was the only thing that kept him from it. But, far back in his mind, he wondered if he could write anywhere. Often the question threw itself at

173

him when he was least expecting it. You have four hours every morning, the statement would rise like a menacing wraith. You have time to write many thousands of words. Why don't you?

And the answer was always lost in a tangle of becauses and wells and endless reasons that he clung to like a drowning man at straws.

The bathroom door opened and she came out, dressed in her good red suit.

For no reason at all, it seemed, he suddenly realized that she'd been wearing that same outfit for more than three years and never a new one. The realization angered him even more. He closed his eyes and hoped she wasn't looking at him. I hate her, he thought. I hate her because she has destroyed my life.

He heard the rustle of her skirt as she sat at the dressing table and pulled out a drawer. He kept his eyes shut and listened to the venetian blinds tap lightly against the window frame as morning breeze touched them. He could smell her perfume floating lightly on the air.

And he tried to think of the house empty all the time. He tried to think of coming home from class and not finding Sally there waiting for him. The idea seemed, somehow, impossible. And that angered him. Yes, he thought, she's gotten to me. She's worked on me until I am so dependent of her for really unessential things that I suffer under the delusion that I cannot do without her.

He turned suddenly on the mattress and looked at her.

"So you're really going," he said in a cold voice.

She turned briefly and looked at him. There was no anger on her face. She looked tired.

"Yes," she said. "I'm going."

Good riddance. The words tried to pass his lips. He cut them off.

"I suppose you have your reasons," he said.

Her shoulders twitched a moment in what he took for a shrug of weary amusement.

"I have no intention of arguing with you," he said. "Your life is your own."

"Thank you," she murmured.

She's waiting for apologies, he thought. Waiting to be told that he didn't hate her as he'd said. That he hadn't struck *her* but all his twisted and shattered hopes; the mocking spectacle of his own lost faith.

"And just how long is this *trial* separation going to last?" he said, his voice acidulous.

She shook her head.

"I don't know, Chris," she said quietly. "It's up to you."

"Up to me," he said. "It's always up to me, isn't it?"

"Oh, please darl—Chris. I don't want to argue anymore. I'm too tired to argue."

13. VISION: Mad House

"It's easier to just pack and run away."

She turned and looked at him. Her eyes were very dark and unhappy.

"Run away?" she said. "After eighteen years you accuse me of that? Eighteen years of watching you destroy yourself. And me along with you. Oh, don't look surprised. I'm sure you know you've driven me half insane too."

She turned away and he saw her shoulders twitch. She brushed some tears from her eyes.

"It's n-not just because you hit me," she said. "You kept saying that last night when I said I was leaving. Do you think it would matter if . . ." She took a deep breath. "If it meant you were angry with *me?* If it was that I could be hit every day. But you didn't hit me. I'm nothing to you. I'm not wanted."

"Oh, stop being so . . ."

"No," she broke in. "That's why I'm going. Because I can't bear to watch you hate me more every day for something that . . . that isn't my fault."

"I suppose you . . ."

"Oh, don't say anymore," she said, getting up. She hurried out of the room and he heard her walk into the livingroom. He stared at the dressing table.

Don't say anymore?—his mind asked as though she were still there. Well, there's more to say; lots more. You don't seem to realize what I've lost. You don't seem to understand. I had hopes, oh God, what hopes I had. I was going to write prose to make the people sit up and gasp. I was going to tell them things they needed badly to know. I was going to tell them in so entertaining a way that they would never realize that the truth was getting to them. I was going to create immortal works.

Now when I die, I shall only be dead. I am trapped in this depressing village, entombed in a college of science where men gape at dust and do not even know that there are stars above their heads. And what can I do, what can . . . ?

The thoughts broke off. He looked miserably at her perfume bottles, at the powder box that tinkled *Always* when the cover was lifted off.

I'll remember you. Always.

With a heart that's true. Always.

The words are childish and comical, he thought. But his throat contracted and he felt himself shudder.

"Sally," he said. So quietly that he could hardly hear it himself.

After a while he got up and dressed.

While he was putting on his trousers a rug slid from under him and he had to grab the dresser for support. He glared down, heart pounding in the total fury he had learned to summon in the space of seconds.

"Damn you," he muttered.

He forgot Sally. He forgot everything. He just wanted to get even with the rug. He kicked it violently under the bed. The anger plunged down and disappeared. He shook his head. I'm sick, he thought. He thought of going in to her and telling her he was sick.

His mouth tightened as he went into the bathroom. I'm not sick, he thought. Not in body anyway. It's my mind that's ill and she only makes it worse.

The bathroom was still damply warm from her use of it. He opened the window a trifle and got a splinter in his finger. He cursed the window in a muffled voice. He looked up. Why so quiet? he asked. So *she* won't hear me?

"Damn you!" he snarled loudly at the window. And he picked at his finger until he had pulled out the sliver of wood.

He jerked at the cabinet door. It stuck. His face reddened. He pulled harder and the door flew open and cracked him on the wrist. He spun about and grabbed his wrist, threw back his head with a whining gasp.

He stood there, eyes clouded with pain, staring at the ceiling. He looked at the crack that ran in a crazy meandering line across the ceiling. Then he closed his eyes.

And began to sense something. Intangible. A sense of menace. He wondered about it. Why it's myself, of course, he answered then. It is the moral decrepitude of my own subconscious. It is bawling out to me, saying: You are to be punished for driving your poor wife away to her mother's arms. You are not a man. You are a—

"Oh, shut up," he said.

He washed his hands and face. He ran an inspecting finger over his chin. He needed a shave. He opened the cabinet door gingerly and took out his straight razor. He held it up and looked at it.

The handle has expanded. He told himself that quickly as the blade appeared to fall out of the handle willfully. It made him shiver to see it flop out like that and glitter in the light from the cabinet light fixture.

He stared in repelled fascination at the bright steel. He touched the blade edge. So sharp, he thought. The slightest touch would sever flesh. What a hideous thing it was.

"It's my hand."

He said it involuntarily and shut the razor suddenly. It *was* his hand, it had to be. It couldn't have been the razor moving by itself. That was sick imagination.

But he didn't shave. He put the razor back in the cabinet with a vague sense of forestalling doom.

Don't care if we *are* expected to shave every day, he muttered. I'm not taking a chance on my hand slipping. I'd better get a safety razor anyway. This kind isn't for me, I'm too nervous.

Suddenly, impelled by those words, the picture of him eighteen years before flew into his brain.

13. VISION: Mad House

He remembered a date he'd had with Sally. He remembered telling her he was so calm it was akin to being dead. Nothing bothers me, he'd said. And it was true, at the time. He remembered too telling her he didn't like coffee, that one cup kept him awake at night. That he didn't smoke, didn't like the taste or smell. I like to stay healthy, he'd said. He remembered the exact words.

"And now," he muttered at his lean and worn reflection.

Now he drank gallons of coffee a day. Until it sloshed like a black pool in his stomach and he couldn't sleep anymore than he could fly. Now he smoked endless strings of finger-yellowing cigarettes until his throat felt raw and clogged, until he couldn't write in pencil because his hand shook so much.

But all that stimulation didn't help his writing any. Paper still remained blank in the typewriter. Words never came, plots died on him. Characters eluded him, mocking him with laughter from behind the veil of their noncreation.

And time passed. It flew by faster and faster, seeming to single him out for highest punishment. He—a man who had begun to value time so neurotically that it overbalanced his life and made him sick to think of its passing.

As he brushed his teeth he tried to recall when this irrational temper had first begun to control him. But there was no way of tracing its course. Somewhere in mists that could not be pierced, it had started. With a word of petulance, an angry contraction of muscles. With a glare of unrecallable animosity.

And from there, like a swelling amoeba, it had gone its own perverted and downward course of evolution, reaching its present nadir in him; a taut embittered man who found his only solace in hating.

He spit out white froth and rinsed his mouth. As he put down the glass, it cracked and a barb of glass drove into his hand.

"Damn!" he yelled.

He spun on his heel and clenched his fist. It sprang open instantly as the sliver sank into his palm. He stood with tears on his cheeks, breathing heavily. He thought of Sally listening to him, hearing once more the audible evidence of his snapping nerves.

Stop it!—he ordered himself. You can never do anything until you rid yourself of this enervating temper.

He closed his eyes. For a moment he wondered why it seemed that everything was happening to him lately. As if some revenging power had taken roost in the house, pouring a savage life into inanimate things. Threatening him. But the thought was just a faceless, passing figure in the crushing horde of thoughts that mobbed past his mind's eye; seen but not appreciated.

He drew the glass sliver from his palm. He put on his dark tie.

Then he went into the dining room, consulting his watch. It was ten

177

thirty already. More than half the morning was gone. More than half the time for sitting and trying to write the prose that would make people sit up and gasp.

It happened that way more often now than he would even admit to himself. Sleeping late, making up errands, doing anything to forestall the terrible moment when he must sit down before his typewriter and try to wrench some harvest from the growing desert of his mind.

It was harder every time. And he grew more angry every time; and hated more. And never noticed until now, when it was too late, that Sally grew desperate and could no longer stand his temper or his hate.

She was sitting at the kitchen table drinking dark coffee. She too drank more than she once had. Like him, she drank it black, without sugar. It jangled her nerves too. And she smoked now although she'd never smoked until a year before. She got no pleasure from it. She drew the fumes deep down into her lungs and then blew them out quickly. And her hands shook almost as badly as his did.

He poured himself a cup of coffee and sat down across from her. She started to get up.

"What's the matter? Can't you stand the sight of me?"

She sat back and took a deep pull on the cigarette in her hand. Then she tamped it out on the saucer.

He felt sick. He wanted to get out of the house suddenly. It felt alien and strange to him. He had the feeling that she had renounced all claim to it, that she had retreated from it. The touch of her fingers and the loving indulgences she had bestowed on every room; all these things were taken back. They had lost tangibility because she was leaving. She was deserting it and it was not their home anymore. He felt it strongly.

Sinking back against the chair he pushed away his cup and stared at the yellow oilcloth on the table. He felt as if he and Sally were frozen in time; that seconds were drawn out like some fantastic taffy until each one seemed an eternity. The clock ticked slower. And the house was a different house.

"What train are you getting?" he asked, knowing before he spoke that there was only one morning train.

"11:47," she said.

When she said it, he felt as if his stomach were pulled back hard against his backbone. He gasped, so actual was the physical pain. She glanced up at him.

"Burned myself," he said hastily, and she got up and put her cup and saucer in the sink.

Why did I say that?—he thought. Why couldn't I say that I gasped because I was filled with terror at the thought of her leaving me? Why do I always say the things I don't mean to say? I'm not bad. But every time I speak I build higher the walls of hatred and bitterness around me until I cannot escape from them.

13. VISION: Mad House

With words I have knit my shroud and will bury myself therein.

He looked at her back and a sad smile raised his lips. I can think of words when my wife is leaving me. It is very sad.

Sally had walked out of the kitchen. His mind reverted to its sullen attitude. This is a game we're playing. Follow the leader. You walk in one room, head high, the justified spouse, the injured party. I am supposed to follow, slope shouldered and contrite, pouring out apologetic hecatombs.

Once more conscious of himself, he sat tensely at the table, rage making his body tremble. Consciously he relaxed and pressed his left hand over his eyes. He sat there trying to lose his misery in silence and blackness.

It wouldn't work.

And then his cigarette really burned him and he sat erect. The cigarette hit the floor scattering ashes. He bent over and picked it up. He threw it at the wastecan and missed. To hell with it, he thought. He got up and dumped his cup and saucer in the sink. The saucer broke in half and nicked his right thumb. He let it bleed. He didn't care.

She was in the extra room finishing her packing.

The extra room. The words tortured him now. When had they stopped calling it "the nursery"? When had it begun to eat her insides out because she was so full of love and wanted children badly? When had he begun to replace this loss with nothing better than volcanic temper and days and nights of sheath-scraped nerves?

He stood in the doorway and watched her. He wanted to get out the typewriter and sit down and write reams of words. He wanted to glory in his coming freedom. Think of all the money he could save. Think of how soon he could go away and write all the things he'd always meant to write.

He stood in the doorway, sick.

Is all this possible?—his mind asked, incredulous. Possible that she was leaving? But she and he were man and wife. They had lived and loved in this house for more than eighteen years. Now she was leaving. Putting articles of clothing in her old black suitcase and leaving. He couldn't reconcile himself to that. He couldn't understand it or ally it with the functions of the day. Where did it fit into the pattern?—the pattern that was Sally right there cleaning and cooking and trying to make their home happy and warm.

He shivered and, turning abruptly, went back into the bedroom.

He slumped on the bed and stared at the delicately whirring electric clock on their bedside table.

Past eleven, he saw. In less than an hour I have to hold class for a group of idiot freshmen. And, on the desk in the livingroom is a mountain of mid-term examinations with essays that I must suffer through, feeling my stomach turn at their paucity of intelligence, their adolescent phraseology.

And all that tripe, all those miles of hideous prose, had been wound into an eternal skein in his head. And there it sat unraveling into his own writing until he wondered if he could stand the thought of living anymore. I have digested the worst, he thought. Is it any wonder that I exude it piecemeal?

Temper began again, a low banking fire in him, gradually fanned by further thinking. I've done no writing this morning. Like every morning after every other morning as time passes. I do less and less. I write nothing. Or I write worthless material. I could write better when I was twenty than I can now.

I'll *never* write anything good!

He jolted to his feet and his head snapped around as he looked for something to strike at, something to break, something to hate with such hate that it would wither in the blast.

It seemed as though the room clouded. He felt a throbbing. His left leg banged against a corner of the bed.

He gasped in fury. He wept. Tears of hate and repentance and self commiseration. I'm lost, he thought. Lost. There is nothing.

He became very calm, icy calm. Drained of pity, of emotion. He put on his suit coat. He put on his hat and got his briefcase off the dresser.

He stopped before the door to the room where she still fussed with her bag. So she will have something to occupy herself with now, he thought, so she won't have to look at me. He felt his heart thudding like a heavy drum beat.

"Have a nice time at your mother's," he said dispassionately.

She looked up and saw the expression on his face. She turned away and put a hand to her eyes. He felt a sudden need to run to her and beg her forgiveness. Make everything right again.

Then he thought again of papers and years of writing undone. He turned away and walked across the livingroom. The small rug slipped a little and it helped to focus the strength of anger he needed. He kicked it aside and it fluttered against the wall in a rumpled heap.

He slammed the door behind him.

His mind gibbered. Now, soap opera like, she has thrown herself on the coverlet and is weeping tears of martyr-tinged sorrow. Now she is digging nails into the pillow and moaning my name and wishing she were dead.

His shoes clicked rapidly on the sidewalk. God help me, he thought. God help all us poor wretches who would create and find that we must lose our hearts for it because we cannot afford to spend our time at it.

It was a beautiful day. His eyes saw that but his mind would not attest to it. The trees were thick with green and the air warm and fresh. Spring breezes flooded down the streets. He felt them brush over him as he walked down the block, crossed Main Street to the bus stop.

He stood there on the corner looking back at the house.

She is in there, his mind persisted in analysis. In there, the house in which we've lived for more than eighteen years. She is packing or crying or doing something. And soon she will call the Campus Cab Company. A cab will come driving out. The driver will honk the horn. Sally will put on her light spring coat and take her suitcase out on the porch. She will lock the door behind her for the last time.

"No—"

He couldn't keep the word from strangling in his throat. He kept staring at the house. His head ached. He saw everything weaving. I'm sick, he thought.

"I'm *sick!*"

He shouted it. There was no one around to hear. He stood gazing at the house. She is going away forever, said his mind.

Very well then! I'll write, write, write. He let the words soak into his mind and displace all else.

A man had a choice, after all. He devoted his life to his work or to his wife and children and home. It could not be combined; not in this day and age. In this insane world where God was second to income and goodness to wealth.

He glanced aside as the green-striped bus topped the distant hill and approached. He put the briefcase under his arm and reached into his coat pocket for a token. There was a hole in the pocket. Sally had been meaning to sew it. Well, she would never sew it now. What did it matter anyway?

I would rather have my soul intact than the suit of clothes I wear.

Words, words, he thought, as the bus stopped before him. They flood through me now that she is leaving. Is that evidence that it is her presence that clogs the channels of thought?

He dropped the token in the coin box and weaved down the length of the bus. He passed a professor he knew and nodded to him abstractedly. He slumped down on the back seat and stared at the grimy, rubberized floor boards.

This is a great life, his mind ranted. I am so pleased with this, my life, and these, my great and noble accomplishments.

He opened the briefcase a moment and looked in at the thick prospectus he had outlined with the aid of Dr. Ramsay.

First week—1. *Everyman.* Discussion of. Reading of selections from *Classic Readings For College Freshmen.* 2. *Beowulf.* Reading of. Class discussion. Twenty minute quotation quiz.

He shoved the sheaf of papers back into the briefcase. It sickens me, he thought. I hate these things. The classics have become anathema to me. I begin to loathe the very mention of them. Chaucer, the Elizabethan poets, Dryden, Pope, Shakespeare. What higher insult to a man than to grow to hate these names because he must share them by part with unappreciative clods? Because he must strain them thin and make them palatable for the dullards who should better be digging ditches.

He got off the bus downtown and started down the long slope of Ninth Street.

Walking, he felt as though he were a ship with its hawser cut, prey to a twisted network of currents. He felt apart from the city, the country, the world. If someone told me I were a ghost, he thought, I would be inclined to believe.

What is she doing now?

He wondered about it as the buildings floated past him. What is she thinking as I stand here and the town of Fort drifts by me like vaporous stage flats? What are her hands holding? What expression has she on her lovely face?

She is alone in the house, our house. What might have been our *home.* Now it is only a shell, a hollow box with sticks of wood and metal for furnishings. Nothing but inanimate dead matter.

No matter what John Morton said.

Him with his gold leaves parting and his test tubes and his God of the microscope. For all his erudite talk and his papers of slide-ruled figures; despite all that—it was simple witchcraft he professed. It was idiocy. The idiocy that prompted that ass Charles Fort to burden the world with his nebulous fancies. The idiocy that made that fool of a millionaire endow this place and from the arid soil erect these huge stone structures and house within a zoo of wild-eyed scientists always searching for some fashion of elixir while the rest of the clowns blew the world out from under them.

No, there is nothing right with the world, he thought as he plodded under the arch and onto the wide, green campus.

He looked across at the huge Physical Sciences Center, its granite face beaming in the late morning sun.

Now she is calling the cab. He consulted his watch. No. She is in the cab already. Riding through the silent streets. Past the houses and down into the shopping district. Past the red brick buildings spewing out yokels and students. Through the town that was a potpourri of the sophisticated and the rustic.

Now the cab was turning left on Tenth Street. Now it was pulling up the hill, topping it. Gliding down toward the railroad station. Now . . .

"Chris!"

His head snapped around and his body twitched in surprise. He looked toward the wide-doored entrance to the Mental Sciences Building. Dr. Morton was coming out.

We attended school together eighteen years ago, he thought. But I took only a small interest in science. I preferred wasting my time on the culture of the centuries. That's why I'm an associate and he's a doctor and the head of his department.

All this fled like racing winds through his mind as Dr. Morton approached, smiling. He clapped Chris on the shoulder.

"Hello there," he said. "How are things?"

"How are they ever?"

Dr. Morton's smile faded.

"What is it, Chris?" he asked.

13. VISION: Mad House

I won't tell you about Sally, Chris thought. Not if I die first. You'll never know it from me.

"The usual," he said.

"Still on the outs with Ramsay?"

Chris shrugged. Morton looked over at the large clock on the face of the Mental Sciences Building.

"Say look," he said. "Why are we standing here? Your class isn't for a half hour yet, is it?"

Chris didn't answer. He's going to invite me for coffee, he thought. He's going to regale me with more of his inane theories. He's going to use me as whipping boy for his mental merry-go-round.

"Let's get some coffee," Morton said, taking Chris's arm. They walked along in silence for a few steps.

"How's Sally?" Morton asked then.

"She's fine," he answered in an even voice.

"Good. Oh, incidentally. I'll probably drop by tomorrow or the next day for that book I left there last Thursday night."

"All right."

"What were you saying about Ramsay now?"

"I wasn't."

Morton skipped that. "Been thinking any more about what I told you?" he asked.

"If you're referring to your fairy tale about my house—no. I haven't been giving it any more thought than it deserves—which is none."

They turned the corner of the building and walked toward Ninth Street.

"Chris, that's an indefensible attitude," Morton said. "You have no right to doubt when you don't know."

Chris felt like pulling his arm away, turning and leaving Morton standing there. He was sick of words and words and words. He wanted to be alone. He almost felt as if he could put a pistol to his head now, get it over with. Yes, I could—he thought. If someone handed it to me now, this moment, it would be done in a moment

They went up the stone steps to the sidewalk and crossed over to the Campus Cafe. Morton opened the door and ushered Chris in. Chris went in back and slid into a wooden booth.

Morton brought two coffees and sat across from him.

"Now listen," he said, stirring in sugar, "I'm your best friend. At least I regard myself as such. And I'm damned if I'll sit by like a mute and watch you kill yourself."

Chris felt his heart jump. He swallowed. He got rid of the thoughts as though they were visible to Morton.

"Forget it," he said. "I don't care what proofs you have. I don't believe any of it."

"What'll it take to convince you, damn it?" Morton said. "Do you have to lose your life first?"

183

IV. The Emergence of Parapsychology

"Look," Chris said pettishly. "I don't believe it. That's *it*. Forget it now, let it go."

"Listen, Chris, I can show you ..."

"You can show me nothing!" Chris cut in.

Morton was patient. "It's a recognized phenomenon," he said.

Chris looked at him in disgust and shook his head.

"What dreams you white-frocked kiddies have in the sanctified cloister of your laboratories. You can make yourself believe anything after a while. As long as you can make up a measurement for it."

"Will you listen to me, Chris? How many times have you complained to me about splinters, about closet doors flying open, about rugs slipping? How many times?"

"Oh, for God's sake, don't start *that* again. I'll get up and walk out of here. I'm in no mood for your lectures. Save them for those poor idiots who pay tuition to hear them."

Morton looked at him with a shake of his head.

"I wish I could get to you," he said.

"Forget it."

"Forget it?" Morton squirmed. "Can't you see that you're in danger because of your temper?"

"I'm telling you, John ..."

"Where do you think that temper of yours goes? Do you think it disappears? No. It doesn't. It goes into your rooms and into your furniture and into the air. It goes into Sally. It makes everything sick; including you. It crowds you out. It welds a link between animate and inanimate. *Psychobolie.* Oh, don't look so petulant; like a child who can't stand to hear the word *spinach*. Sit down, for God's sake. You're an adult; listen like one."

Chris lit a cigarette. He let Morton's voice drift into a non-intelligent hum. He glanced at the wall clock. Quarter to twelve. In two minutes, if the schedule was adhered to, she would be going. The train would move and the town of Fort would pass away from her.

"I've told you any number of times," Morton was saying. "No one knows what matter is made of. Atoms, electrons, pure energy—all words. Who knows where it will end? We guess, we theorize, we make up means of measurement. But we don't know.

"And that's for matter. Think of the human brain and its still unknown capacities. It's an uncharted continent, Chris. It may stay that way for a long time. And all that time the suspected powers will still be affecting us and, maybe, affecting matter; even if we *can't* measure it on a gauge.

"And I say you're poisoning your house. I say your temper has become ingrained in the structure, in every article you touch. All of them influenced by you and your ungovernable rages. And I think too that if it weren't for Sally's presence acting as an abortive factor, well ... you might actually be attacked by ..."

Chris heard the last few sentences.

13. VISION: Mad House

"Oh, stop this gibberish!" he snapped angrily. "You're talking like a juvenile after his first Tom Swift novel."

Morton sighed. He ran his fingers over the cup edge and shook his head sadly.

"Well," he said, "All I can do is hope that nothing breaks down. It's obvious to me that you're not going to listen."

"Congratulations on one statement I can agree with," said Chris. He looked at his watch. "And now if you'll excuse me I'll go and listen to saddle-shoed cretins stumble over passages they haven't the slightest ability to assimilate."

They got up.

"I'll take it," said Morton but Chris slapped a dime on the counter and walked out. Morton followed, putting his change into his pocket slowly.

In the street he patted Chris on the shoulder.

"Try to take it easy," he said. "Look, why don't you and Sally come out to the house tonight? We could have a few rounds of bridge."

"That's impossible," Chris said.

The students were reading a selection from *King Lear.* Their heads were bent over the books. He stared at them without seeing them.

I've got to resign myself to it, he told himself. I've got to forget her, that's all. She's gone. I'm not going to bewail the fact. I'm not going to hope against hope that she'll return. I don't *want* her back. I'm better off without her. Free and unfettered now.

His thoughts drained off. He felt empty and helpless. He felt as though he could never write another word for the rest of his life. Maybe, he thought, sullenly displeased with the idea, maybe it was only the upset of her leaving that enabled my brain to find words. For, after all, the words I thought of, the ideas that flourished, though briefly, were all to do with her—her going and my wretchedness because of it.

He caught himself short. No!—he cried in silent battle. I will not let it be that way. I'm strong. This feeling is only temporary, I'll very soon have learned to do without her. And then I'll do work. Such work as I have only dreamed of doing. After all haven't I lived eighteen years more? Haven't those years filled me to overflowing with sights and sounds, ideals, impressions, interpretations?

He trembled with excitement.

Someone was waving a hand in his face. He focused his eyes and looked coldly at the girl.

"Well?" he said.

"Could you tell us when you're going to give back our mid-term papers, Professor Neal?" she asked.

He stared at her, his right cheek twitching. He felt about to hurl every invective at his command into her face. His fists closed.

"You'll get them back when they're marked," he said tensely.

"Yes, but . . ."

"You heard me," he said.

His voice rose at the end of the sentence. The girl sat down. As he lowered his head he noticed that she looked at the boy next to her and shrugged her shoulders, a look of disgust on her face.

"Miss . . ."

He fumbled with his record book and found her name.

"Miss Forbes!"

She looked up, her features drained of color, her red lips standing out sharply against her white skin. Painted alabaster idiot. The words clawed at him.

"You may get out of this room," he ordered sharply.

Confusion filled her face.

"Why?" she asked in a thin, plaintive voice.

"Perhaps you didn't hear me," he said, the fury rising. "I said get out of this room!"

"But . . ."

Do you hear me! he shouted.

Hurriedly she collected her books, her hands shaking, her face burning with embarrassment. She kept her eyes on the floor and her throat moved convulsively as she edged along the aisle and went out the doorway.

The door closed behind her. He sank back. He felt a terrible sickness in himself. Now, he thought, they will all turn against me in defense of an addle-witted little girl. Dr. Ramsay would have more fuel for his simple little fire.

And they were right.

He couldn't keep his mind from it. They *were* right. He knew it. In that far recess of mind which he could not cow with thoughtless passion, he knew he was a stupid fool. I have no right to teach others. I cannot even teach myself to be a human being. He wanted to cry out the words and weep confessions and throw himself from one of the open windows.

"The whispering will stop!" he demanded fiercely.

The room was quiet. He sat tensely, waiting for any signs of militance. I am your teacher, he told himself, I am to be obeyed, I am . . .

The concept died. He drifted away again. What were students or a girl asking about mid-term papers? What was anything?

He glanced at his watch. In a few minutes the train would pull into Centralia. She would change to the main line express to Indianapolis. Then up to Detroit and her mother. Gone.

Gone. He tried to visualize the word, put it into living terms. But the thought of the house without her was almost beyond his means. Because it wasn't the house without her; it was something else.

He began to think of what John had said.

Was it possible? He was in a mood to accept the incredible. It was

13. VISION: Mad House

incredible that she had left him. Why not extend the impossibilities that were happening to him?

All right then, he thought angrily. The house is alive. I've given it this life with deadly outpourings of wrath. I hope to God that when I get back there and enter the door, the roof collapses. I hope the walls buckle and I'm crushed to pulp by the crushing weight of plaster and wood and brick. That's what I want. Some agency to do away with me. I cannot drive myself to it. If only a gun would commit my suicide for me. Or gas blow its deadly fumes at me for the asking or a razor slice my flesh upon request.

The door opened. He glanced up. Dr. Ramsay stood there, face drawn into a mask of indignation. Behind him in the hall Chris could see the girl, her face streaked with tears.

"A moment, Neal," Ramsay said sharply and stepped back into the hall again.

Chris sat at the desk staring at the door. He felt suddenly very tired, exhausted. He felt as if getting up and moving into the hall was more than he could possibly manage. He glanced at the class. A few of them were trying to repress smiles.

"For tomorrow you will finish the reading of *King Lear,*" he said. Some of them groaned.

Ramsay appeared in the doorway again, his cheeks pink.

"Are you coming, Neal?" he asked loudly.

Chris felt himself tighten with anger as he walked across the room and out into the hall. The girl lowered her eyes. She stood beside Dr. Ramsay's portly frame.

"What's this I hear, Neal?" Ramsay asked.

That's right, Chris thought. Don't ever call me professor. I'll never be one, will I? You'll see to that, you bastard.

"I don't understand," he said, as coolly as possible.

"Miss Forbes here claims you ejected her from class for no reason at all."

"Then Miss Forbes is lying quite stupidly," he said. Let me hold this anger, he thought. Don't let it flood loose. He shook with holding it back.

The girl gasped and took out her handkerchief again. Ramsay turned and patted her shoulder.

"Go in my office, child. Wait for me."

She turned away slowly. Politician!—cried Neal's mind. How easy it is for you to be popular with them. You don't have to deal with their bungling minds.

Miss Forbes turned the corner and Ramsay looked back.

"Your explanation had better be good," he said. "I'm getting a little weary, Neal, of your behavior."

Chris didn't speak. Why am I standing here?—he suddenly wondered. Why, in all the world, am I standing in this dim lit hall and voluntarily, listening to this pompous boor berate me?

"I'm waiting, Neal."

Chris tightened. "I told you she was lying," he said quietly.

"I choose to believe otherwise," said Dr. Ramsay, his voice trembling.

A shudder ran through Chris. His head moved forward and he spoke slowly, teeth clenched.

"You can believe anything you damn well please."

Ramsay's mouth twitched.

"I think it's time you appeared before the board," he muttered.

"Fine!" said Chris loudly. Ramsay made a move to close the classroom door. Chris gave it a kick and it banged against the wall. A girl gasped.

"What's the matter?" Chris yelled. "Don't you want your students to hear me tell you off? Don't you even want them to suspect that you're a dolt, a windbag, an ass!"

Ramsay raised shaking fists before his chest. His lips trembled violently.

"This will do, Neal!" he cried.

Chris reached out and shoved the heavy man aside, snarling, "Oh, *get* out of my way!"

He started away. The hall fled past him. He heard the bell ring. It sounded as though it rang in another existence. The building throbbed with life; students poured from classrooms.

"Neal!" called Dr. Ramsay.

He kept walking. Oh, God, let me out of here, I'm suffocating, he thought. My hat, my briefcase. Leave them. Get out of here. Dizzily he descended the stairs surrounded by milling students. They swirled about him like an unidentifiable tide. His brain was far from them.

Staring ahead dully he walked along the first floor hall. He turned and went out the door and down the porch steps to the campus sidewalk. He paid no attention to the students who stared at his ruffled blonde hair, his mussed clothes. He kept walking. I've done it, he thought belligerently. I've made the break. I'm *free!*

I'm sick.

All the way down to Main Street and out on the bus he kept renewing his stores of anger. He went over those few moments in the hallway again and again. He summoned up the vision of Ramsay's stolid face, repeated his words. He kept himself taut and furious. I'm glad, he told himself forcibly. Everything is solved. Sally has left me. Good. My job is done. Good. Now I'm free to do as I like. A strained and angry joy pounded through him. He felt alone, a stranger in the world and glad of it.

At his stop he got off the bus and walked determinedly toward the house pretending to ignore the pain he felt at approaching it. It's just an empty house, he thought. Nothing more. Despite all puerile theories, it is nothing but a house.

Then, when he went in, he found her sitting on the couch.

He almost staggered as if someone had struck him. He stood dumbly,

staring at her. She had her hands tightly clasped. She was looking at him.
He swallowed.

"Well," he managed to say.

"I . . ." Her throat contracted. "Well . . ."

"Well *what!*" he said quickly and loudly to hide the shaking in his voice.

She stood up. "Chris, please. Won't you . . . ask me to stay?" She looked
at him like a little girl, pleading.

The look enraged him. All his day dreams shattered; he saw the growing thing of new ideas ground under foot.

"Ask you to stay!" he yelled at her. "By God, I'll ask you nothing!"

"Chris! Don't!"

She's buckling, cried his mind. She's cracking. Get her now. Get her out
of here. Drive her from these walls!

"Chris," she sobbed, "be kind. Please be kind."

"Kind!"

He almost choked on the word. He felt a wild heat coursing his body.

"Have *you* been kind? Driving me crazy, into a pit of despair. I can't get
out. Do you understand? Never. Never! Do you understand that! I'll never
write. I *can't* write! You drained it out of me! You killed it! Understand
that? Killed it!"

She backed away toward the dining room. He followed her, hands
shaking at his sides, feeling that she had driven him to this confession and
hating her the more for it.

"Chris," she murmured in fright.

It seemed as if his rage grew cell-like, swelling him with fury until he
was nothing of bone and blood but a hating accusation made flesh.

"I don't want you!" he yelled. "You're right, I don't want you! Get out
of here!"

Her eyes were wide, her mouth an open wound. Suddenly she ran past
him, eyes glistening with tears. She fled through the front doorway.

He went to the window and watched her running down the block, her
dark brown hair streaming behind her.

Dizzy suddenly, he sank down on the couch and closed his eyes. He dug
his nails into his palms. Oh God, I *am* sick, his mind churned.

He twitched and looked around stupidly. What was it? This feeling that
he was sinking into the couch, into the floorboards, dissolving in the air,
joining the molecules of the house. He whimpered softly looking around.
His head ached; he pressed a palm against his forehead.

"What?" he muttered. "What?"

He stood up. As though there were fumes he tried to smell them. As
though it were a sound he tried to hear it. He turned around to see it. As
though there were something with depth and length and width; something
menacing.

He wavered, fell back on the couch. He stared around. There was nothing; all intangible. It might only be in the mind. The furniture lay as it did before. The sunlight filtered through the windows, piercing the gauzelike curtains, making gold patterns on the inlaid wooden floor. The walls were still creamy, the ceiling was as it was before. Yet there was this darkening, darkening . . .

What?

He pushed up and walked dizzily around the room. He forgot about Sally. He was in the dining room. He touched the table, he stared at the dark oak. He went into the kitchen. He stood by the sink and looked out the window.

Far up the block he saw her walking, stumbling. She must have been waiting for the bus. Now she couldn't wait any longer and she was walking away from the house, away from him.

"I'll go after her," he muttered.

No, he thought. No, I won't go after her like a . . .

He forgot what like. He stared down at the sink. He felt drunk. Everything was fuzzy on the edges.

She's washed the cups. The broken saucer was thrown away. He looked at the nick on his thumb. It was dried. He'd forgotten about it.

He looked around suddenly as if someone had sneaked behind him. He stared at the wall. Something was rising. He felt it. It's not me. But it had to be; it had to be imagination.

Imagination!

He slammed a fist on the sink. I'll write. Write, *write.* Sit down and drain it all away in words; this feeling of anguish and terror and loneliness. Write it out of my system.

He cried, "Yes!"

He ran from the kitchen. He refused to accept the instinctive fear in himself. He ignored the menace that seemed to thicken the very air.

A rug slipped. He kicked it aside. He sat down. The air hummed. He tore off the cover on the typewriter. He sat nervously, staring at the keyboard. The moment before attack. It was in the air. But it's *my* attack!—he thought triumphantly, my attack on stupidity and fear.

He rolled a sheet into the typewriter. He tried to collect his throbbing thoughts. Write, the word called in his mind. Write—*now.*

"Now!" he cried.

He felt the desk lurch against his shins.

The flaring pain knifed open his senses. He kicked the desk in automatic frenzy. More pain. He kicked again. The desk flung back at him. He screamed.

He'd seen it move.

He tried to back off, the anger torn from him. The typewriter keys moved under his hands. His eyes swept down. He couldn't tell whether

13. VISION: Mad House

he was moving the keys or whether they moved by themselves. He pulled hysterically, trying to dislodge his fingers but he couldn't. The keys were moving faster than his eye could see. They were a blur of motion. He felt them shredding his skin, peeling his fingers. They were raw. Blood started to ooze out.

He cried out and pulled. He managed to jerk away his fingers and jump back in the chair.

His belt buckle caught, the desk drawer came flying out. It slammed into his stomach. He yelled again. The pain was a black cloud pouring over his head.

He threw down a hand to shove in the drawer. He saw the yellow pencils lying there. They glared. His hand slipped, it banged into the drawer.

One of the pencils jabbed at him.

He always kept the points sharp. It was like the bite of a snake. He snapped back his hand with a gasp of pain. The point was jammed under a nail. It was imbedded in raw, tender flesh. He cried out in fury and pain. He pulled at the pencil with his other hand. The point flew out and jabbed into his palm. He couldn't get rid of the pencil, it kept dragging over his hand. He pulled at it and it tore black, jagged lines on his skin. It tore the skin open.

He heaved the pencil across the room. It bounced on the wall. It seemed to jump as it fell on the eraser. It rolled over and was still.

He lost his balance. The chair fell back with a rush. His head banged sharply against the floorboards. His outclutched hand grabbed at the window sill. Tiny splinters flashed into his skin like invisible needles. He howled in deathly fear. He kicked his legs. The mid-term papers showered down over him like the beating wings of insane bird flocks.

The chair snapped up again on its springs. The heavy wheels rolled over his raw, bloody hands. He drew them back with a shriek. He reared a leg and kicked the chair over violently. It crashed on the side against the mantelpiece. The wheels spun and chattered like a swarm of furious insects.

He jumped up. He lost his balance and fell again, crashing against the window sill. The curtains fell on him like a python. The rods snapped. They flew down and struck him across the scalp. He felt warm blood trickle across his forehead. He thrashed about on the floor. The curtains seemed to writhe around him like serpents. He screamed again. He tore at them wildly. His eyes were terror-stricken.

He threw them off and lurched up suddenly, staggering around for balance. The pain in his hand assailed him. He looked at them. They were like raw butcher meat, skin hanging down in shreds. He had to bandage them. He turned toward the bathroom.

At his first step the rug slid from under him, the rug he had kicked aside. He felt himself rush through the air. He reached down his hands instinctively to block the fall. The white pain made his body leap. One finger snapped. Splinters shot into his raw fingers, he felt a burning pain in one ankle.

He tried to scramble up but the floor was like ice under him. He was deadly silent. His heart thudded in his chest. He tried to rise again. He fell hissing with pain.

The bookshelf loomed over him. He cried out and flung up an arm. The case came crashing down on him. The top shelf drove into his skull. Black waves dashed over him, a sharp blade of pain drove into his head. Books showered over him. He rolled on his side with a groan. He tried to crawl out from underneath. He shoved the books aside weakly and they fell open. He felt the page edges slicing into his fingers like razor blades.

The pain cleared his head. He sat up and hurled the books aside. He kicked the bookcase back against the wall. The back fell off it and it crashed down.

He rose up, the room spinning before his eyes. He staggered into the wall, tried to hold on. The wall shifted under his hands it seemed. He couldn't hold on. He slipped to his knees, pushed up again.

"Bandage myself," he muttered hoarsely.

The words filled his brain. He staggered up through the quivering dining room, into the bathroom.

He stopped. No! Get out of the house! He knew it was not his will that brought him in there.

He tried to turn but he slipped on the tiles and cracked his elbow against the edge of the bath tub. A shooting pain barbed into his upper arm. The arm went numb. He sprawled on the floor, writhing in pain. The walls clouded; they welled around him like blank shroud.

He sat up, breath tearing at his throat. He pushed himself up with a gasp. His arm shot out, he pulled open the cabinet door. It flew open against his cheek, tearing a jagged rip in the soft flesh.

His head snapped back. The crack in the ceiling looked like a wide idiot smile on a blank, white face. He lowered his head, whimpering in fright. He tried to back away.

His hand reached out. For iodine, for gauze!—his mind cried.

His hand came out with the razor.

It flopped in his hand like a new caught fish. His other hand reached in. For iodine, for gauze!—shrieked his mind.

His hand came out with dental floss. It flooded out of the tube like an endless white worm. It coiled around his throat and shoulders. It choked him.

The long shiny blade slipped from its sheath.

He could not stop his hand. It drew the razor heavily across his chest. It slit open the shirt. It sliced a valley through his flesh. Blood spurted out.

He tried to hurl away the razor. It stuck to his hand. It slashed at him, at his arms and hands and legs and body.

13. VISION: Mad House

At his throat.

A scream of utter horror flooded from his lips. He ran from the bathroom, staggering wildly into the livingroom.

"Sally!" he screamed, "Sally, Sally, Sally . . ."

The razor touched his throat. The room went black. Pain. Life ebbing
away into the night. Silence over all the world.

The next day Dr. Morton came. He called the police. And later the
coroner wrote in his report:

Died of self-inflicted wounds.

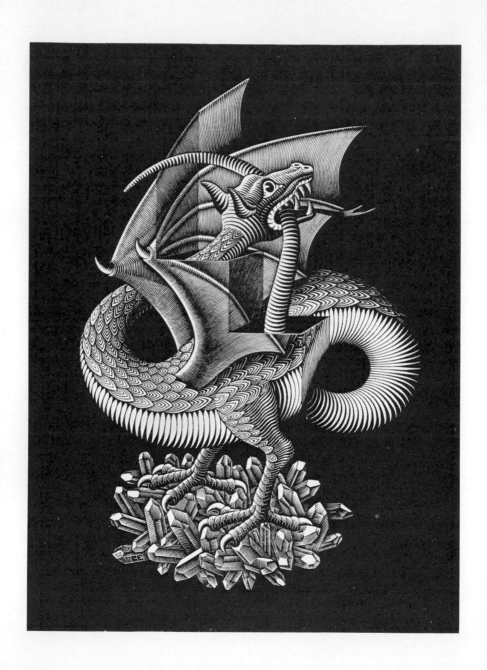

V.
The Exploration and Control of the Brain

14.
VALENCE:
How the Machine
Called the Brain Feels and Thinks

DEAN E. WOOLDRIDGE

In the following article, Dean Wooldridge provides an overview on current research regarding the human brain.

In a provocative series of experiments, a team of scientists at Western Reserve University in Cleveland has developed techniques to remove the brain of a monkey from its body and keep it alive for many hours. Bare except for two small bits of bone to help support it, the nerves and blood vessels that once connected it to the monkey's body severed, the brain is suspended above a laboratory table. Attached to it are the tubes of a mechanical heart to maintain its blood supply; from it run wires to recording instruments. Their measurements of its electrical activity not only show that it remains alive but even suggest that sometimes this isolated brain is conscious.

While the immediate goal of the team, headed by Dr. Robert J. White, is the development of methods for obtaining answers to the basic questions related to the physiology of the brain, one cannot help being fascinated by less specifically scientific, but perhaps more profoundly philosophic, considerations. Can the truly "detached minds" of the Cleveland monkeys really be conscious? If so, conscious of what?

Sensation, for example, is an important ingredient of the conscious state. Does biological science give us any clues as to what sensations, if any, the conscious incorporated brains of the Western Reserve monkeys could have felt? After all, the nerves that normally carry to the brain indications of touch, taste, odor, light and sound were all cut, and the associated sensory organs were far removed. Does this mean that, during its conscious periods, the isolated monkey brain floated in a sensory void, with no flashes of touch, pain, sight or sound to remind it of the kind of existence it once knew?

No one can know for sure, of course, but the answer is: Probably not. We know that the conscious, "feeling" part of the brain does not reach out to the sensory receptors of the finger tips in order to find out what the outside environment is doing to the periphery of the body. Instead, "feeling" is the result of electrical activity in a section of the brain's surface called the "sensory strip," which ordinarily serves as a "receiving station" for signals coming in through the nerves from the body surface. It is the activity in this "receiving station," rather than in the "wires" leading to it, that actually produces the conscious sensation that, say, a toe is cold.

Severing or otherwise mistreating the nerves leading to the sensory strip can result in patterns of electrical activity that "fool" the conscious part of the brain. This is why an amputee can feel the specific sensation of the fingers of his hand being twisted in an uncomfortable position for months after the arm carrying that hand has been cut off.

Similarly, while useful vision requires functioning eyes, and meaningful hearing requires operating ears, the sensations of sight and sound, involving uncoordinated but nonetheless vivid flashes of light or bursts of sound, can be experienced by an eyeless or earless individual. All that is necessary is that the conditions at the extremities of his severed nerves be such as to produce the rather simple kinds of electrochemical impulses that, upon arrival at the visual or auditory areas of the brain, are interpreted as sight or sound.

The detached monkey brain could even have felt hungry or thirsty. Such sensations are determined by local electric currents and related chemical activity in specific small regions, or "centers," in the brainstem—the "primitive" lower part of the brain that is really an extension of the spinal cord. When stimulating electric impulses are injected into the appropriate part of an animal's "appetite center," for example, by means of a surgically implanted wire, the animal will exhibit the only kind of appetite that truly deserves the adjective "insatiable": It will continue to eat any food provided to it, even though it is so stuffed that it must regurgitate what it has already swallowed. If the stimulating electrode is placed in another part of the appetite center, only a fraction of an inch away, the animal will be unable to eat—even to the extent of starving to death while surrounded by its favorite food.

Hunger of another sort would also have been possible for the isolated monkey brain. There are small regions of nerve tissue in the brainstem that control activities related to reproduction and care of the young. While electric stimulation in these centers is effective, some of the most interesting recent work has been with hormones. By implanting the right chemicals in the right spots in rats' brains, Dr. Alan E. Fisher, psychologist at the

V. The Exploration and Control of the Brain

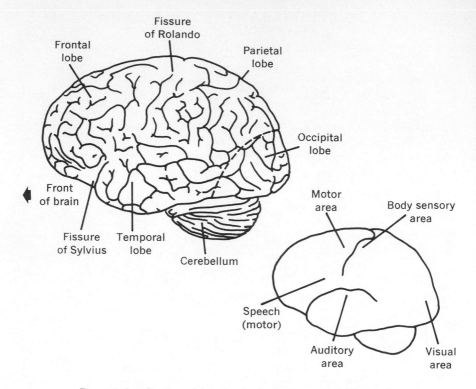

Figure 1. Localization of function in the human cortex. Above: the lobes of the cerebral hemispheres and the landmarks separating them. Right: the projection areas. Reproduced from *Introduction to Psychology*, 4th edition, by Ernest R. Hilgard and Richard C. Atkinson (New York: Harcourt Brace Jovanovich, Inc., 1967), p. 46, by permission of the publisher.

Control center. The human brain is a mass of 10 billion nerve cells weighing about three pounds. By means of electrochemical impulses traveling along the nerves at speeds of 2 to 200 miles an hour, it receives and transmits messages from and to every part of the body. The human brain (Figure 1) consists of three main parts:

The brainstem. This is the core of the brain, essentially an extension of the spinal cord (through which all nerve impulses are channeled). The brainstem controls such involuntary but vital functions as breathing and the heart beat, and generates such primitive drives as feelings of hunger, anger and pleasure. Sometimes called the "old brain," it existed in much the same form in the dinosaurs.

The cerebellum. This bulbous structure, part way up the brainstem and protruding toward the back of the head, coordinates muscular activity. It has been called the "private secretary" of the brain.

The cerebrum, or cerebral cortex. This convoluted mantle covers the other parts of the brain and fills the rest of the skull. It is divided, left and right, into two equal hemispheres. Sometimes called the "new brain," it is the seat of mental activity, voluntary action and the senses.

14. VALENCE: How the Brain Machine Feels and Thinks

University of Pittsburgh, found that he could cause a male rat to exhibit typically female behavior, and vice versa. Thus, males were observed building nests and gently carrying to shelter the baby rats they would ordinarily have eaten.

We can even speculate on the state of mind of the detached monkey brain, during its periods of consciousness. If it at all understood what was happening to it, it may well have been angry and afraid. Perhaps it felt like biting with the teeth it once possessed, or like scratching or running with the legs it formerly controlled. If so, it is not unlikely that the brain did in fact generate such commands and send them in the form of electro-chemical impulses to the severed ends of the nerves which formerly went to the muscles.

But it is also possible that the brain felt relaxed and comfortable. It could even have felt happy. For there appear to be "pleasure" and "punishment" centers in the brain. The feelings of anger, fright, horror, ease, relaxation, pleasure and ecstasy, just like those of hunger and thirst, are now known to be turned on or off selectively by local patterns of electrochemical activity in the brainstem. Whether you are a rat, cat, monkey or human being, sites deep in the brain have been located where electric stimulation will produce a sense of horror; other sites are known where stimulation will result in feelings of euphoria or ecstasy.

(Experimenters do not enjoy subjecting their animals to fright and pain, and do so as little as is consistent with obtaining the important information they seek. The justification for all such work is, of course, that the knowledge gained may ultimately make it possible to relieve human suffering.)

The Western Reserve experiments on isolated monkey brains constitute only one example of the progress that is being made toward clarifying some of the mysteries of the conscious state. For example, a "consciousness switch" has been located in the brain. Dr. H. W. Magoun, now at the University of California at Los Angeles, was able to show that an arrangement of interconnected nerve cells in the brainstem—the "reticular activating system" he called it—is the source of a special pattern of electrochemical nerve impulses that must be received by the brain if we are to be aware of what is going on.

During a surgical operation under general anesthesia, measurements have shown that the nerve impulses caused by the manipulation of the surgeon's scalpel arrive at the major brain centers with at least as great strength as though the patient were conscious. He does not feel them only because the chemical anesthetic has suppressed the reticular activating system. Without its steady flow of impulses to the higher portions of the brain, our sense of awareness is "turned off."

But this consciousness control need not be an "all or nothing" matter. The "switch" can regulate degrees of awareness as well.

For example, if a cat in a cage is exposed to a monotonous sequence of musical tones, measuring equipment will detect a corresponding sequence of electric impulses in the nerve leading from ear to brain. If then, with no change in the tone sequence or intensity, an object of great feline interest is displayed to the cat—a beaker containing mice, let us say—the measurements will show a great decrease or perhaps complete disappearance of the tone-generated nerve impulses.

It is the same reticular activating system in the brainstem—the "consciousness switch"—that is at work. The appearance of an object of overriding interest generates a new electric signal that serves to turn down the "volume control" of the nerve system registering the object of lesser interest. In this way we are permitted to "focus" our attention—to enhance our consciousness of events of interest by freeing our minds from unimportant distractions.

One of the most interesting and puzzling phenomena related to consciousness was first observed nearly 30 years ago by Dr. Wilder Penfield, at that time head of the Montreal Neurological Institute.

In connection with operations to remove tumors or epileptically defective brain tissue, Penfield had developed a new kind of electric-probe technique. After removal of the section of skull covering the area where defective tissue was believed to be, the patient would be restored to consciousness in the operating room, and asked to describe his sensations as needles were stuck into various parts of his brain and electricity injected. (The brain contains no nerve endings that can sense pain; a patient suffers no discomfort in such tests.) By the nature of the responses, it was frequently possible to determine the boundaries of defective tissue more accurately than by visual observation alone.

In 1936, several years after the first use of this new technique, Penfield was preparing to operate on a woman whose lesion was on the side of the cortex (the outer surface of the brain) just above the ear—a region that later work was to implicate with the memory mechanisms. When the needle electrode was inserted and the electric current turned on, the patient suddenly reported that she felt transported back to her early childhood. In the operating room, she essentially relived an episode out of her remote past, even feeling again the same fear that had accompanied the original event.

In the succeeding years, Penfield and many other brain surgeons have observed, in many patients, this kind of triggering of memory by cortical stimulation. The phenomenon possesses a number of fascinating features, which the developing understanding of brain function must some day explain. For example: The electrically elicited experiences always appear to be real although the patient usually has not been consciously carrying them in his memory. The induced recollection can be stopped abruptly by turning off the stimulating current, and often restarted by turning it on again. But, when restarted, the recalled episode never continues where it left off—instead, it starts again from the beginning, as though it were stored on a film or tape which automatically rewinds each time it is interrupted.

14. VALENCE: How the Brain Machine Feels and Thinks

Perhaps most startling is the vividness of the elicited experience. Instead of being a remembering, according to Penfield, "it is a hearing-again and seeing-again—a living-through-moments-of-past-time."

Nevertheless, the patient does not lose contact with the present. He seems to have concurrent existences—one in the operating room, and one in the part of the past that he is reliving. The term "double-consciousness" is employed by brain surgeons to describe these peculiar sensations of their patients.

Penfield's discovery no longer stands as the sole example of the successful tampering with the unity of consciousness by brain surgeons and research scientists. In the biology laboratories of the California Institute of Technology, Dr. R. W. Sperry has had under way for several years a series of experiments on cats and monkeys that in some ways are even more spectacular.

Sperry's methods are based on the left–right symmetry that characterizes higher animals, including cats, monkeys and men. In particular, in such animals the brain consists of two similar hemispheres.

They are interconnected by a vast system of nerve fibers numbering several hundred million in a human brain.

In concept, Sperry's idea was simple: Break these connections and see what happens. The trouble was that when he tried it on laboratory animals (usually cats) nothing much did happen. Even after most of the connections between the brain hemispheres had been cut, the animal appeared substantially unchanged. It behaved about as before; it achieved about the same scores on intelligence tests; it remembered its old tricks and could learn new ones.

The experiment had to be refined. This was done by adding to the brain-splitting surgery an operation on the visual system of the animal, as a result of which the left eye was connected only with the left half of the brain, and the right eye with the right half (ordinarily there are also crossing connections; these were cut).

Cats prepared in this way were then subjected to special training procedures. They were taught to choose between two swinging doors that they could easily open, one carrying a conspicuous circular design, the other a cross.

The cat under training would learn that choice of the door with a circle, say, would lead to a reward, choice of the door with a cross would lead to punishment. This was routine animal training; the distinguishing feature of the experiment was that the cat was provided with an eyepatch, so that all of its trials involved the use of, say, the left eye only, which in turn was connected to the isolated left half of the brain.

The animals learned their lessons about as fast as cats that had not had their brains split. Everything seemed normal—up to a point. This point was reached when the cat had been trained to near perfection using its left eye, and then was reintroduced into the training cage with the eyepatch shifted, so that the untrained eye—and the associated half of the brain—came into play.

The result was spectacular. Changing the eyepatch was exactly equivalent to changing cats. When employing the eye connected to the untrained half of its brain, the animal appeared to have not the slightest recollection of ever having been in the problem box. It could be trained again, using the new eye and hemisphere, to perform the desired discrimination, but its rate of learning was exactly the same as that of an entirely fresh, untrained cat.

In the new condition, it could even be taught, equally easily, a discrimination opposite to that learned originally. Using its right eye and right hemisphere, it could learn to open the door with the cross despite its earlier acquisition, when using its left eye and left hemisphere, of the habit of opening the door with the circle. Such a doubly trained animal would shift its performance automatically, without confusion, when the eyepatch was shifted.

By severing the connections between the two halves of the brain, Sperry had apparently split into two distinct parts what had previously been a single sense of consciousness.

In some respects, the split-consciousness implications of the work on cats was demonstrated even more vividly by later experiments on monkeys. In this work the two halves of the brain were provided with different properties, not by training, but by surgical modification. On one side of the monkey's brain the nerve fibers running from the brainstem to a forward part of the brain were severed. This operation—a frontal lobotomy—has for years been known to produce significant personality changes if performed on both sides of the brain. Specifically, it produces under these circumstances a relaxed, "I-don't-care" person or animal. Before the development of tranquilizing drugs, it was sometimes employed to ease the unbearable tensions of psychotic mental patients.

In addition to the frontal lobotomy on one side of the brain, the monkeys were subjected to the split-brain operation, including modification of their optic connections, just as in the cat experiments. After the surgery, they were fitted with an arrangement of contact lenses similar to the cat's eyepatches.

A monkey employing the eye that was connected to the unmodified half of its brain would then be shown a snake. Monkeys are normally deathly afraid of snakes and the split-brain monkey was no exception. It showed the usual fright and escape reactions.

Then the conditions were changed so that the monkey had to employ the eye connected with the hemisphere that had had the lobotomy. Again the snake was displayed. This time, the monkey could not have cared less; the snake held no terrors for it. It was as though two different animal personalities now inhabited the body that had formerly been occupied by one.

14. VALENCE: How the Brain Machine Feels and Thinks

The existence of pleasure and punishment centers in the brain, the discovery of the consciousness switch, the peculiar "double-consciousness" of Penfield's patients, the split-personality of Sperry's split-brain animals—all are variations on a single theme: the operation of the principle of cause and effect in the content and quality of the conscious state.

We feel horror or ecstasy, are conscious or unconscious, *because* of the electrochemical activity in specific brainstem tissue; we appear to have concurrent existences in past and present *because* of the disturbance of our brain mechanisms produced by Penfield's electric probe; we have two separate states of consciousness *because* Sperry has cut the connections between the two halves of our brain.

Is consciousness, then, finally to become an early and predictable physical quantity like gravity, electric charge or magnetism? Is it to be only another property of matter, to be dealt with by the impersonal and objective techniques of the mathematician and physicist? To be sure, consciousness seems to be connected with intelligence, but are we to learn that it is automatically and inevitably associated with the complex organizations and states of matter required for intelligence, much as gravity is associated with mass?

Must we even come to speculate that, among the wires and transistors of our electronic computers, there already stirs a dim glimmering of the same kind of sense of awareness that has become, for man, his most personal and precious possession? Fantastic? Perhaps.

The immediate human reaction—that consciousness is by its very nature a mysterious and unexplainable phenomenon—is really not very pertinent. All the laws and properties of nature are fundamentally mysterious; science can no more explain gravitational attraction or electric charge than it can the sense of consciousness. The scientist delineates the orderly and predictable interactions among his quantities; he never explains the quantities themselves.

If future investigation continues to disclose consistent interrelationships between the physical conditions of the brain and the qualities of consciousness, it is hard to see how consciousness can escape ultimate acceptance as a property of certain organizations and states of matter. Then consciousness would be no longer a question of metaphysics but part of the realm described by the physical laws of nature.

It would be hard to imagine a development of more far-reaching importance to science and philosophy. Yet it could come as a consequence of the exciting work now under way in the laboratories of the brain research scientists.

15.
VISION:
William and Mary

ROALD DAHL

*Following Dean Wooldridge's article reviewing current research on the brain,
Roald Dahl spins a fantasy regarding the same subject, in an all-too-human
setting.*

William Pearl did not leave a great deal of money when he died, and his
will was a simple one. With the exception of a few small bequests to
relatives, he left all his property to his wife.

The solicitor and Mrs. Pearl went over it together in the solicitor's office,
and when the business was completed, the widow got up to leave. At that
point, the solicitor took a sealed envelope from the folder on his desk and
held it out to his client.

"I have been instructed to give you this," he said. "Your husband sent
it to us shortly before he passed away." The solicitor was pale and prim,
and out of respect for a widow he kept his head on one side as he spoke,
looking downward. "It appears that it might be something personal, Mrs.
Pearl. No doubt you'd like to take it home with you and read it in privacy."

Mrs. Pearl accepted the envelope and went out into the street. She
paused on the pavement, feeling the thing with her fingers. A letter of
farewell from William? Probably, yes. A formal letter. It was bound to be
formal—stiff and formal. The man was incapable of acting otherwise. He
had never done anything informal in his life.

My dear Mary, I trust that you will not permit my departure from this
world to upset you too much, but that you will continue to observe

those precepts which have guided you so well during our partnership together. Be diligent and dignified in all things. Be thrifty with your money. Be careful that you do not ... et cetera, et cetera.

A typical William letter.

Or was it possible that he might have broken down at the last moment and written her something beautiful? Maybe this was a beautiful tender message, a sort of love letter, a lovely warm note of thanks to her for giving him thirty years of her life and for ironing a million shirts and cooking a million meals and making a million beds, something that she could read over and over again, once a day at least, and she would keep it for ever in the box on the dressing-table together with her brooches.

There is no knowing what people will do when they are about to die, Mrs. Pearl told herself, and she tucked the envelope under her arm and hurried home.

She let herself in the front door and went straight to the livingroom and sat down on the sofa without removing her hat or coat. Then she opened the envelope and drew out the contents. These consisted, she saw, of some fifteen or twenty sheets of lined white paper, folded over once and held together at the top left-hand corner by a clip. Each sheet was covered with the small, neat, forward-sloping writing that she knew so well, but when she noticed how much of it there was, and in what a neat businesslike manner it was written, and how the first page didn't even begin in the nice way a letter should, she began to get suspicious.

She looked away. She lit herself a cigarette. She took one puff and laid the cigarette in the ash-tray.

If this is about what I am beginning to suspect it is about, she told herself, then I don't want to read it.

Can one refuse to read a letter from the dead?

Yes.

Well ...

She glanced over at William's empty chair on the other side of the fireplace. It was a big brown leather armchair, and there was a depression on the seat of it, made by his buttocks over the years. Higher up, on the backrest, there was a dark oval stain on the leather where his head had rested. He used to sit reading in that chair and she would be opposite him on the sofa, sewing on buttons or mending socks or putting a patch on the elbow of one of his jackets, and every now and then a pair of eyes would glance up from the book and settle on her, watchful, but strangely impersonal, as if calculating something. She had never liked those eyes. They were ice blue, cold, small, and rather close together, with two deep vertical lines of disapproval dividing them. All her life they had been watching her. And even now, after a week alone in the house, she sometimes had an uneasy feeling that they were still there, following her around, staring at her from doorways, from empty chairs, through a window at night.

V. The Exploration and Control of the Brain

Slowly she reached into her handbag and took out her spectacles and put them on. Then, holding the pages up high in front of her so that they caught the late afternoon light from the window behind, she started to read:

This note, my dear Mary, is entirely for you, and will be given you shortly after I am gone.

Do not be alarmed by the sight of all this writing. It is nothing but an attempt on my part to explain to you precisely what Landy is going to do to me, and why I have agreed that he should do it, and what are his theories and his hopes. You are my wife and you have a right to know these things. In fact you *must* know them. During the past few days I have tried very hard to speak with you about Landy, but you have steadfastly refused to give me a hearing. This, as I have already told you, is a very foolish attitude to take, and I find it not entirely an unselfish one either. It stems mostly from ignorance, and I am absolutely convinced that if only you were made aware of all the facts, you would immediately change your view. That is why I am hoping that when I am no longer with you, and your mind is less distracted, you will consent to listen to me more carefully through these pages. I swear to you that when you have read my story, your sense of antipathy will vanish, and enthusiasm will take its place. I even dare to hope that you will become a little proud of what I have done.

As you read on, you must forgive me, if you will, for the coolness of my style, but this is the only way I know of getting my message over to you clearly. You see, as my time draws near, it is natural that I begin to brim with every kind of sentimentality under the sun. Each day I grow more extravagantly wistful, especially in the evenings, and unless I watch myself closely my emotions will be overflowing on to these pages.

I have a wish, for example, to write something about you and what a satisfactory wife you have been to me through the years, and I am promising myself that if there is time, and I still have the strength, I shall do that next.

I have a yearning also to speak about this Oxford of mine where I have been living and teaching for the past seventeen years, to tell something about the glory of the place and to explain, if I can, a little of what it has meant to have been allowed to work in its midst. All the things and places that I loved so well keep crowding in on me now in this gloomy bedroom. They are bright and beautiful as they always were, and today, for some reason, I can see them more clearly than ever. The path around the lake in the gardens of Worcester College, where Lovelace used to walk. The gateway at Pembroke. The view westward over the town from Magdalen Tower. The great hall at Christchurch. The little rockery at St. John's where I have counted more than a dozen varieties of campanula, including the rare and dainty C. Waldsteiniana. But there, you see! I haven't even begun and already I'm falling into the trap. So let me get started now; and let you

15. VISION: William and Mary

read it slowly, my dear, without any of that sense of sorrow or disapproval that might otherwise embarrass your understanding. Promise me now that you will read it slowly, and that you will put yourself in a cool and patient frame of mind before you begin.

The details of the illness that struck me down so suddenly in my middle life are known to you. I need not waste time upon them—except to admit at once how foolish I was not to have gone earlier to my doctor. Cancer is one of the few remaining diseases that these modern drugs cannot cure. A surgeon can operate if it has not spread too far; but with me, not only did I leave it too late, but the thing had the effrontery to attack me in the pancreas, making both surgery and survival equally impossible.

So here I was with somewhere between one and six months left to live, growing more melancholy every hour—and then, all of a sudden, in comes Landy.

That was six weeks ago, on a Tuesday morning, very early, long before your visiting time, and the moment he entered I knew there was some sort of madness in the wind. He didn't creep in on his toes, sheepish and embarrassed, not knowing what to say, like all my other visitors. He came in strong and smiling, and he strode up to the bed and stood there looking down at me with a wild bright glimmer in his eyes, and he said, "William, my boy, this is perfect. You're just the one I want!"

Perhaps I should explain to you here that although John Landy has never been to our house, and you have seldom if ever met him, I myself have been friendly with him for at least nine years. I am, of course, primarily a teacher of philosophy, but as you know I've lately been dabbling a good deal in psychology as well. Landy's interests and mine have therefore slightly overlapped. He is a magnificent neurosurgeon, one of the finest, and recently he has been kind enough to let me study the results of some of his work, especially the varying effects of prefrontal lobotomies upon different types of psychopaths. So you can see that when he suddenly burst in on me Tuesday morning, we were by no means strangers to one another.

"Look," he said, pulling up a chair beside the bed. "In a few weeks you're going to be dead. Correct?"

Coming from Landy, the question didn't seem especially unkind. In a way it was refreshing to have a visitor brave enough to touch upon the forbidden subject.

"You're going to expire right here in this room, and then they'll take you out and cremate you."

"Bury me," I said.

"That's even worse. And then what? Do you believe you'll go to heaven?"

"I doubt it," I said "though it would be comforting to think so."

"Or hell, perhaps?"

"I don't really see why they should send me there."

"You never know, my dear William."

V. The Exploration and Control of the Brain

"What's all this about?" I asked.

"Well," he said, and I could see him watching me carefully, "personally, I don't believe that after you're dead you'll ever hear of yourself again—unless . . ." and here he paused and smiled and leaned closer ". . . unless, of course, you have the sense to put yourself into my hands. Would you care to consider a proposition?"

The way he was staring at me, and studying me, and appraising me with a queer kind of hungriness, I might have been a piece of prime beef on the counter and he had bought it and was waiting for them to wrap it up.

"I'm really serious about it, William. Would you care to consider a proposition?"

"I don't know what you're talking about."

"Then listen and I'll tell you. Will you listen to me?"

"Go on then, if you like. I doubt I've got very much to lose by hearing it."

"On the contrary, you have a great deal to gain—especially *after you're dead.*"

I am sure he was expecting me to jump when he said this, but for some reason I was ready for it. I lay quite still, watching his face and that slow white smile of his that always revealed the gold clasp of an upper denture curled around the canine on the left side of his mouth.

"This is a thing, William, that I've been working on quietly for some years. One or two others here at the hospital have been helping me, especially Morrison, and we've completed a number of fairly successful trials with laboratory animals. I'm at the stage now where I'm ready to have a go with a man. It's a big idea, and it may sound a bit far-fetched at first, but from a surgical point of view there doesn't seem to be any reason why it shouldn't be more or less practicable."

Landy leaned forward and placed both hands on the edge of my bed. He has a good face, handsome in a bony sort of way, with none of the usual doctor's look about it. You know that look, most of them have it. It glimmers at you out of their eyeballs like a dull electric sign and it reads *Only I can save you.* But John Landy's eyes were wide and bright and little sparks of excitement were dancing in the centres of them.

"Quite a long time ago," he said, "I saw a short medical film that had been brought over from Russia. It was a rather gruesome thing, but interesting. It showed a dog's head completely severed from the body, but with the normal blood supply being maintained through the arteries and veins by means of an artificial heart. Now the thing is this: that dog's head, sitting there all alone on a sort of tray, was *alive.* The brain was functioning. They proved it by several tests. For example, when food was smeared on the dog's lips, the tongue would come out and lick it away; and the eyes would follow a person moving across the room.

"It seemed reasonable to conclude from this that the head and the brain did not need to be attached to the rest of the body in order to remain alive

15. VISION: William and Mary

—provided, of course, that a supply of properly oxygenated blood could be maintained.

"Now then. My own thought, which grew out of seeing this film, was to remove the brain from the skull of a human and keep it alive and functioning as an independent unit for an unlimited period after he died. *Your* brain, for example, after *you* are dead."

"I don't like that," I said.

"Don't interrupt, William. Let me finish. So far as I can tell from subsequent experiments, the brain is a peculiarly self-supporting object. It manufactures its own cerebrospinal fluid. The magic process of thought and memory which go on inside it are manifestly not impaired by the absence of limbs or trunk or even of skull, provided, as I say, that you keep pumping in the right kind of oxygenated blood under the proper conditions.

"My dear William, just think for a moment of your own brain. It is in perfect shape. It is crammed full of a lifetime of learning. It has taken you years of work to make it what it is. It is just beginning to give out some first-rate original ideas. Yet soon it is going to have to die along with the rest of your body simply because your silly little pancreas is riddled with cancer."

"No thank you," I said to him. "You can stop there. It's a repulsive idea, and even if you could do it, which I doubt, it would be quite pointless. What possible use is there in keeping my brain alive if I couldn't talk or see or hear or feel? Personally, I can think of nothing more unpleasant."

"I believe that you *would* be able to communicate with us," Landy said. "And we might even succeed in giving you a certain amount of vision. But let's take this slowly. I'll come to all that later on. The fact remains that you're going to die fairly soon whatever happens; and my plans would not involve touching you at all until *after* you are dead. Come now, William. No true philosopher could object to lending his dead body to the cause of science."

"That's not putting it quite straight," I answered. "It seems to me there'd be some doubts as to whether I were dead or alive by the time you'd finished with me."

"Well," he said, smiling a little, "I suppose you're right about that. But I don't think you ought to turn me down quite so quickly, before you hear a bit more about it."

"I said I don't want to hear it."

"Have a cigarette," he said, holding out his case.

"I don't smoke, you know that."

He took one himself and lit it with a tiny silver lighter that was no bigger than a shilling piece. "A present from the people who make my instruments," he said. "Ingenious, isn't it?"

I examined the lighter, then handed it back.

"May I go on?" he asked.

"I'd rather you didn't."

"Just lie still and listen. I think you'll find it quite interesting."

There were some blue grapes on the plate beside my bed. I put the plate on my chest and began eating the grapes.

"At the very moment of death," Landy said, "I should have to be standing by so that I could step in immediately to keep your brain alive."

"You mean leaving it in the head?"

"To start with, yes. I'd have to."

"And where would you put it after that?"

"If you want to know, in a sort of basin."

"Are you really serious about this?"

"Certainly I'm serious."

"All right. Go on."

"I suppose you know that when the heart stops and the brain is deprived of fresh blood and oxygen, its tissues die very rapidly. Anything from four to six minutes and the whole thing's dead. Even after three minutes you may get a certain amount of damage. So I should have to work rapidly to prevent this from happening. But with the help of the machine, it should all be quite simple."

"What machine?"

"The artificial heart. We've got a nice adaptation here of the one originally devised by Alexis Carrel and Lindbergh. It oxygenates the blood, keeps it at the right temperature, pumps it in at the right pressure, and does a number of other little necessary things. It's really not at all complicated."

"Tell me what you would do at the moment of death," I said. "What is the first thing you would do?"

"Do you know anything about the vascular and venous arrangements of the brain?"

"No."

"Then listen. It's not difficult. The blood supply to the brain is derived from two main sources, the internal carotid arteries and the vertebral arteries. There are two of each, making four arteries in all. Got that?"

"Yes."

"And the return system is even simpler. The blood is drained away by only two large veins, the internal jugulars. So you have four arteries going up—they go up the neck, of course—and two veins coming down. Around the brain itself they naturally branch out into other channels, and those don't concern us. We never touch them."

"All right," I said. "Imagine that I've just died. Now what would you do?"

"I should immediately open your neck and locate the four arteries, the carotids and the vertebrals. I should then perfuse them, which means that I'd stick a large hollow needle into each. These four needles would be connected by tubes to the artificial heart.

15. VISION: William and Mary

"Then, working quickly, I would dissect out both the left and right jugular veins and hitch these also to the heart machine to complete the circuit. Now switch on the machine, which is already primed with the right type of blood, and there you are. The circulation through your brain would be restored."

"I'd be like that Russian dog."

"I don't think you would. For one thing, you'd certainly lose consciousness when you died, and I very much doubt whether you would come to again for quite a long time—if indeed you came to at all. But, conscious or not, you'd be in a rather interesting position, wouldn't you? You'd have a cold dead body and a living brain."

Landy paused to savour this delightful prospect. The man was so entranced and bemused by the whole idea that he evidently found it impossible to believe I might not be feeling the same way.

"We could now afford to take our time," he said. "And believe me, we'd need it. The first thing we'd do would be to wheel you to the operating-room, accompanied of course by the machine, which must never stop pumping. The next problem . . ."

"All right," I said. "That's enough. I don't have to hear the details."

"Oh but you must," he said. "It is important that you should know precisely what is going to happen to you all the way through. You see, afterwards, when you regain consciousness, it will be much more satisfactory from your point of view if you are able to remember exactly *where* you are and *how* you came to be there. If only for your own peace of mind you should know that. You agree?"

I lay still on the bed, watching him.

"So the next problem would be to remove your brain, intact and undamaged, from your dead body. The body is useless. In fact it has already started to decay. The skull and the face are also useless. They are both encumbrances and I don't want them around. All I want is the brain, the clean beautiful brain, alive and perfect. So when I get you on the table I will take a saw, a small oscillating saw, and with this I shall proceed to remove the whole vault of your skull. You'd still be unconscious at that point so I wouldn't have to bother with anaesthetic."

"Like hell you wouldn't," I said.

"You'd be out cold, I promise you that, William. Don't forget you *died* just a few minutes before."

"Nobody's sawing off the top of my skull without an anesthetic," I said.

Landy shrugged his shoulders. "It makes no difference to me," he said. "I'll be glad to give you a little procaine if you want it. If it will make you any happier I'll infiltrate the whole scalp with procaine, the whole head, from neck up."

"Thanks very much," I said.

"You know," he went on," it's extraordinary what sometimes happens.

V. The Exploration and Control of the Brain

Only last week a man was brought in unconscious, and I opened his head without any anesthetic at all and removed a small blood clot. I was still working inside the skull when he woke up and began talking.

" 'Where am I?' he asked.

" 'You're in hospital.'

" 'Well,' he said. 'Fancy that.'

" 'Tell me,' I asked him, 'is this bothering you, what I'm doing?'

" 'No,' he answered. 'Not at all. What *are* you doing?'

" 'I'm just removing a blood clot from your brain.'

" 'You *are?*'

" 'Just lie still. Don't move. I'm nearly finished.'

" 'So that's the bastard who's been giving me all those headaches,' the man said."

Landy paused and smiled, remembering the occasion. "That's word for word what the man said," he went on, "although the next day he couldn't even recollect the incident. It's a funny thing the brain."

"I'll have the procaine," I said.

"As you wish, William. And now, as I say, I'd take a small oscillating saw and carefully remove your complete calvarium—the whole vault of the skull. This would expose the top half of the brain, or rather the outer covering in which it is wrapped. You may or may not know that there are three separate coverings around the brain itself—the outer one called the dura mater or dura, the middle one called the arachnoid, and the inner one called the pia matter or pia. Most laymen seem to have the idea that the brain is a naked thing floating around in fluid in your head. But it isn't. It's wrapped up neatly in these three strong coverings, and the cerebrospinal fluid actually flows within the little gap between the two inner coverings, known as the subarachnoid space. As I told you before, this fluid is manufactured by the brain and it drains off into the venous system by osmosis.

"I myself would leave all three coverings—don't they have lovely names, the dura, the arachnoid, and the pia?—I'd leave them all intact. There are many reasons for this, not least among them being the fact that within the dura run the venous channels that drain the blood from the brain into the jugular.

"Now," he went on, "we've got the upper half of your skull off so that the top of the brain, wrapped in its outer covering, is exposed. The next step is the really tricky one: to release the whole package so that it can be lifted cleanly away, leaving the stubs of the four supply arteries and the two veins hanging underneath ready to be re-connected to the machine. This is an immensely lengthy and complicated business involving the delicate chipping away of much bone, the severing of many nerves, and the cutting and tying of numerous blood vessels. The only way I could do it with any hope of success would be by taking a rongeur and slowly biting off the rest of your skull, peeling it off downward like an orange until the

212

15. VISION: William and Mary

sides and underneath of the brain covering are fully exposed. The problems involved are highly technical and I won't go into them, but I feel fairly sure that the work can be done. It's simply a question of surgical skill and patience. And don't forget that I'd have plenty of time, as much as I wanted, because the artificial heart would be continually pumping away alongside the operating-table, keeping the brain alive.

"Now, let's assume that I've succeeded in peeling off your skull and removing everything else that surrounds the sides of the brain. That leaves it connected to the body only at the base, mainly by the spinal column and by the two large veins and the four arteries that are supplying it with blood. So what next?

"I would sever the spinal column just above the first cervical vertebra, taking great care not to harm the two vertebral arteries which are in that area. But you must remember that the dura or outer covering is open at this place to receive the spinal column, so I'd have to close this opening by sewing the edges of the dura together. There'd be no problem there.

"At this point, I would be ready for the final move. To one side, on a table, I'd have a basin of a special shape, and this would be filled with what we call Ringer's Solution. That is a special kind of fluid we use for irrigation in neurosurgery. I would now cut the brain completely loose by severing the supply arteries and the veins. Then I would simply pick it up in my hands and transfer it to the basin. This would be the only other time during the whole proceeding when the blood flow would be cut off: but once it was in the basin, it wouldn't take a moment to re-connect the stubs of the arteries and veins to the artificial heart.

"So there you are," Landy said. "Your brain is now in the basin, and still alive, and there isn't any reason why it shouldn't stay alive for a very long time, years and years perhaps, provided we looked after the blood and the machine."

"But would it *function?*"

"My dear William, how should I know? I can't even tell you whether it would ever regain consciousness.

"And if it did?"

"There now! That would be fascinating!"

"Would it?" I said, and I must admit I had my doubts.

"Of course it would! Lying there with all your thinking processes working beautifully, and your memory as well . . ."

"And not being able to see or feel or smell or hear or talk," I said.

"Ah!" he cried. "I knew I'd forgotten something! I never told you about the eye. Listen. I am going to try to leave one of your optic nerves intact, as well as the eye itself. The optic nerve is a little thing about the thickness of a clinical thermometer and about two inches in length as it stretches between the brain and the eye. The beauty of it is that it's not really a nerve at all. Its an outpouching of the brain itself, and the dura or brain covering extends along it and is attached to the eyeball. The back of the eye is

213

therefore in very close contact with the brain, and cerebrospinal fluid flows right up to it.

"All that suits my purpose very well, and makes it reasonable to suppose that I could succeed in preserving one of your eyes. I've already constructed a small plastic case to contain the eyeball, instead of your own socket, and when the brain is in the basin, submerged in Ringer's Solution, the eyeball in its case will float on the surface of the liquid."

"Staring at the ceiling," I said.

"I suppose so, yes. I'm afraid there wouldn't be any muscles there to move it around. But it might be sort of fun to lie there so quietly and comfortably peering out at the world from your basin."

"Hilarious," I said. "How about leaving me an ear as well?"

"I'd rather not try an ear this time."

"I want an ear," I said. "I insist upon an ear."

"No."

"I want to listen to Bach."

"You don't understand how difficult it would be," Landy said gently. "The hearing apparatus—the cochlea, as it's called—is a far more delicate mechanism than the eye. What's more, it is encased in bone. So is a part of the auditory nerve that connects it with the brain. I couldn't possibly chisel the whole thing out intact."

"Couldn't you leave it encased in the bone and bring the bone to the basin?"

"No," he said firmly. "This thing is complicated enough already. And anyway, if the eye works, it doesn't matter all that much about your hearing. We can always hold up messages for you to read. You really must leave me to decide what is possible and what isn't."

"I haven't yet said that I'm going to do it."

"I know, William, I know."

"I'm not sure I fancy the idea very much."

"Would you rather be dead, altogether?"

"Perhaps I would. I don't know yet. I wouldn't be able to talk, would I?"

"Of course not."

"Then how would I communicate with you? How would you know that I'm conscious?"

"It would be easy for us to know whether or not you regain consciousness," Landy said. "The ordinary electro-encephalograph could tell us that. We'd attach the electrodes directly to the frontal lobes of your brain, there in the basin."

"And you could actually tell?"

"Oh, definitely. Any hospital could do that part of it."

"But *I* couldn't communicate with *you*."

"As a matter of fact," Landy said, "I believe you could. There's a man up in London called Wertheimer who's doing some interesting work on the subject of thought communication, and I've been in touch with him. You know, don't you, that the thinking brain throws off electrical and chemical discharges? And that these discharges go out in the form of waves, rather like radio waves?"

"I know a bit about it," I said.

"Well, Wertheimer has constructed an apparatus somewhat similar to the encephalograph, though far more sensitive, and he maintains that within certain narrow limits it can help him to interpret the actual things that a brain is thinking. It produces a kind of graph which is apparently decipherable into words or thoughts. Would you like me to ask Wertheimer to come and see you?"

"No," I said. Landy was already taking it for granted that I was going to go through with this business, and I resented his attitude. "Go away now and leave me alone," I told him. "You won't get anywhere by trying to rush me."

He stood up at once and crossed to the door.

"One question," I said.

He paused with a hand on the doorknob. "Yes, William?"

"Simply this. Do you yourself honestly believe that when my brain is in that basin, my mind will be able to function exactly as it is doing at present? Do you believe that I will be able to think and reason as I can now? And will the power of memory remain?"

"I don't see why not," he answered. "It's the same brain. It's alive. It's undamaged. In fact, it's completely untouched. We haven't even opened the dura. The big difference, of course, would be that we've severed every single nerve that leads into it—except for the one optic nerve—and this means that your thinking would no longer be influenced by your senses. You'd be living in an extraordinarily pure and detached world. Nothing to bother you at all, not even pain. You couldn't possibly feel pain because there wouldn't be any nerves to feel it with. In a way, it would be an almost perfect situation. No worries or fears or pains or hunger or thirst. Not even any desires. Just your memories and your thoughts, and if the remaining eye happened to function, then you could read books as well. It all sounds rather pleasant to me."

"It does, does it?"

"Yes, William, it does. And particularly for a Doctor of Philosophy. It would be a tremendous experience. You'd be able to reflect upon the ways of the world with a detachment and a serenity that no man had ever attained before. And who knows what might not happen then! Great thoughts and solutions might come to you, great ideas that could revolutionize our way of life! Try to imagine, if you can, the degree of concentration that you'd be able to achieve!"

"And the frustration," I said.

"Nonsense. There couldn't be any frustration. You can't have frustration without desire, and you couldn't possibly have any desire. Not physical desire, anyway."

"I should certainly be capable of remembering my previous life in the world, and I might desire to return to it."

"What, to this mess! Out of your comfortable basin and back into this madhouse!"

"Answer one more question," I said. "How long do you believe you could keep it alive?"

"The brain? Who knows? Possibly for years and years. The conditions would be ideal. Most of the factors that cause deterioration would be absent, thanks to the artificial heart. The blood-pressure would remain constant at all times, an impossible condition in real life. The temperature would also be constant. The chemical composition of the blood would be near perfect. There would be no impurities in it, no virus, no bacteria, nothing. Of course it's foolish to guess, but I believe that a brain might live for two or three hundred years in circumstances like these. Good-bye for now," he said. "I'll drop in and see you tomorrow." He went out quickly, leaving me, as you might guess, in a fairly disturbed state of mind.

My immediate reaction after he had gone was one of revulsion towards the whole business. Somehow, it wasn't at all nice. There was something basically repulsive about the idea that I myself, with all my mental faculties intact, should be reduced to a small slimy blob lying in a pool of water. It was monstrous, obscene, unholy. Another thing that bothered me was the feeling of helplessness that I was bound to experience once Landy had got me into the basin. There could be no going back after that, no way of protesting or explaining. I would be committed for as long as they could keep me alive.

And what, for example, if I could not stand it? What if it turned out to be terribly painful? What if I became hysterical?

No legs to run away on. No voice to scream with. Nothing. I'd just have to grin and bear it for the next two centuries.

No mouth to grin with either.

At this point, a curious thought struck me, and it was this: Does not a man who has had a leg amputated often suffer from the delusion that the leg is still there? Does he not tell the nurse that the toes he doesn't have any more are itching like mad, and so on and so forth? I seemed to have heard something to that effect quite recently.

Very well. On the same premise, was it not possible that my brain, lying there alone in that basin, might not suffer from a similar delusion in regard to my body? In which case, all my usual aches and pains could come flooding over me and I wouldn't even be able to take an aspirin to relieve them. One moment I might be imagining that I had the most excruciating cramp in my leg, or a violent indigestion, and a few minutes later, I might easily get the feeling that my poor bladder—you know me—was so full that if I didn't get to emptying it soon it would burst.

Heaven forbid.

I lay there for a long time thinking these horrid thoughts. Then quite suddenly, round about midday, my mood began to change. I became less concerned with the unpleasant aspect of the affair and found myself able to examine Landy's proposals in a more reasonable light. Was there not, after all, I asked myself, something a bit comforting in the thought that my brain might not necessarily have to die and disappear in a few weeks' time? There was indeed. I am rather proud of my brain. It is a sensitive, lucid, and uberous organ. It contains a prodigious store of information, and it is still capable of producing imaginative and original theories. As brains go, it is a damn good one, though I say it myself. Whereas my body, my poor old body, the thing that Landy wants to throw away—well, even you, my dear Mary, will have to agree with me that there is really nothing about *that* which is worth preserving any more.

I was lying on my back eating a grape. Delicious it was, and there were three little seeds in it which I took out of my mouth and placed on the edge of the plate.

"I'm going to do it," I said quietly. "Yes, by God, I'm going to do it. When Landy comes back to see me tomorrow I shall tell him straight out that I'm going to do it."

It was as quick as that. And from then on, I began to feel very much better. I surprised everyone by gobbling an enormous lunch, and shortly after that you came in to visit me as usual.

But how well I looked, you told me. How bright and well and chirpy. Had anything happened? Was there some good news?

Yes, I said there was. And then, if you remember, I bade you sit down and make yourself comfortable, and I began immediately to explain to you as gently as I could what was in the wind.

Alas, you would have none of it. I had hardly begun telling you the barest details when you flew into a fury and said that the thing was revolting, disgusting, horrible, unthinkable, and when I tried to go on, you marched out of the room.

Well, Mary, as you know, I have tried to discuss this subject with you many times since then, but you have consistently refused to give me a hearing. Hence this note, and I can only hope that you will have the good sense to permit yourself to read it. It has taken me a long time to write. Two weeks have gone since I started to scribble the first sentence, and I'm now a good deal weaker than I was then. I doubt whether I have the strength to say much more. Certainly I won't say good-bye because there's a chance, just a tiny chance, that if Landy succeeds in his work I may actually *see* you again later, that is if you can bring yourself to come and visit me.

V. The Exploration and Control of the Brain

I am giving orders that these pages shall not be delivered to you until a week after I am gone. By now, therefore, as you sit reading them, seven days have already elapsed since Landy did the deed. You yourself may even know what the outcome has been. If you don't, if you have purposely kept yourself apart and have refused to have anything to do with it— which I suspect may be the case—please change your mind now and give Landy a call to see how things went with me. That is the least you can do. I have told him that he may expect to hear from you on the seventh day.

Your faithful husband,
William

P.S. Be good when I am gone, and always remember that it is harder to be a widow than a wife. Do not drink cocktails. Do not waste money. Do not smoke cigarettes. Do not eat pastry. Do not use lipstick. Do not buy a television apparatus. Keep my rose beds and my rockery well weeded in the summers. And incidentally I suggest that you have the telephone disconnected now that I shall have no further use for it.

W.

Mrs. Pearl laid the last page of the manuscript slowly down on the sofa beside her. Her little mouth was pursed up tight and there was a whiteness around her nostrils.

But really! You would think a widow was entitled to a bit of peace after all these years.

The whole thing was just awful to think about. Beastly and awful. It gave her the shudders.

She reached for her bag and found herself another cigarette. She lit it, inhaling the smoke deeply and blowing it out in clouds all over the room. Through the smoke she could see her lovely television set, brand new, lustrous, huge, crouching defiantly but also a little self-consciously on top of what used to be William's worktable.

What would he say, she wondered, if he could see that now?

She paused, to remember the last time he had caught her smoking a cigarette. That was about a year ago, and she was sitting in the kitchen by the open window having a quick one before he came home from work. She'd had the radio on loud playing dance music and she had turned round to pour herself another cup of coffee and there he was standing in the doorway, huge and grim, staring down at her with those awful eyes, a little black dot of fury blazing in the centre of each.

For four weeks after that, he had paid the housekeeping bills himself and given her no money at all, but of course he wasn't to know that she had over six pounds, salted away in a soap-flake carton in the cupboard under the sink.

"What is it?" she had said to him once during supper. "Are you worried about me getting lung cancer?"

15. VISION: William and Mary

"I am not," he had answered.

"Then why can't I smoke?"

"Because I disapprove, that's why."

He had also disapproved of children, and as a result they had never had any of them either.

Where was he now, this William of hers, the great disapprover?

Landy would be expecting her to call up. Did she *have* to call Landy? Well, not really, no.

She finished her cigarette, then lit another one immediately from the old stub. She looked at the telephone that was sitting on the worktable beside the television set. William had asked her to call. He had specifically requested that she telephone Landy as soon as she had read the letter. She hesitated, fighting hard now against that ingrained sense of duty that she didn't quite yet dare to shake off. Then, slowly, she got to her feet and crossed over to the phone on the worktable. She found a number in the book, dialed it, and waited.

"I want to speak to Mr. Landy, please."

"Who is calling?"

"Mrs. Pearl. Mrs. William Pearl."

"One moment, please."

Almost at once, Landy was on the other end of the wire.

"Mrs. Pearl?"

"This is Mrs. Pearl."

There was a slight pause.

"I am so glad you called at last, Mrs. Pearl. You are quite well, I hope?" The voice was quiet, unemotional, courteous. "I wonder if you would care to come over here to the hospital? Then we can have a little chat. I expect you are very eager to know how it all came out."

She didn't answer.

"I can tell you now that everything went pretty smoothly, one way and another. Far better, in fact, than I was entitled to hope. It is not only alive, Mrs. Pearl, it is conscious. It recovered consciousness on the second day. Isn't that interesting?"

She waited for him to go on.

"And the eye is seeing. We are sure of that because we get an immediate change in the deflections on the encephalograph when we hold something up in front of it. And now we're giving it the newspaper to read every day."

"Which newspaper?" Mrs. Pearl asked sharply.

"The *Daily Mirror*. The headlines are larger."

"He hates the *Mirror*. Give him *The Times*."

There was a pause, then the doctor said, "Very well, Mrs. Pearl. We'll give it *The Times*. We naturally want to do all we can to keep it happy."

"*Him,*" she said. "Not *it. Him!*"

"Him," the doctor said. "Yes, I beg your pardon. To keep him happy.

V. The Exploration and Control of the Brain

That's one reason why I suggested you should come along here as soon as possible. I think it would be good for him to see you. You could indicate how delighted you were to be with him again—smile at him and blow him a kiss and all that sort of thing. It's bound to be a comfort to him to know that you are standing by."

There was a long pause.

"Well," Mrs. Pearl said at last, her voice suddenly very meek and tired. "I suppose I had better come on over and see how he is."

Good. I knew you would. I'll wait here for you. Come straight up to my office on the second floor. Good-bye."

Half an hour later, Mrs. Pearl was at the hospital.

"You mustn't be surprised by what he looks like," Landy said as he walked beside her down a corridor.

"No, I won't."

"It's bound to be a bit of a shock to you at first. He's not very prepossessing in his present state, I'm afraid."

"I didn't marry him for his looks, Doctor."

Landy turned and stared at her. What a queer little woman this was, he thought, with her large eyes and her sullen, resentful air. Her features, which must have been quite pleasant once, had now gone completely. The mouth was slack, the cheeks loose and flabby, and the whole face gave the impression of having slowly but surely sagged to pieces through years and years of joyless married life. They walked on for a while in silence.

"Take your time when you get inside," Landy said. "He won't know you're in there until you place your face directly above his eye. The eye is always open, but he can't move it at all, so the field of vision is very narrow. At present we have it looking straight up at the ceiling. And of course he can't hear anything. We can talk together as much as we like. It's in here."

Landy opened a door and ushered her into a small square room.

"I wouldn't go too close yet," he said, putting a hand on her arm." Stay back here a moment with me until you get used to it all."

There was a biggish white enamel bowl about the size of a washbasin standing on a high white table in the centre of the room, and there were half a dozen thin plastic tubes coming out of it. These tubes were connected with a whole lot of glass piping in which you could see the blood flowing to and from the heart machine. The machine itself made a soft rhythmic pulsing sound.

"He's in there," Landy said, pointing to the basin, which was too high for her to see into. "Come just a little closer. Not too near."

He led her two paces forward.

By stretching her neck Mrs. Pearl could now see the surface of the liquid inside the basin. It was clear and still, and on it there floated a small oval capsule, about the size of a pigeon's egg.

"That's the eye in there," Landy said. "Can you see it?"

"Yes."

"So far as we can tell, it is still in perfect condition. It's his right eye, and the plastic container has a lens on it similar to the one he used in his own spectacles. At this moment he's probably seeing quite as well as he did before."

"The ceiling isn't much to look at," Mrs. Pearl said.

"Don't worry about that. We're in the process of working out a whole programme to keep him amused, but we don't want to go too quickly at first."

"Give him a good book."

"We will, we will. Are you feeling all right, Mrs. Pearl?"

"Yes."

"Then we'll go forward a little more, shall we, and you'll be able to see the whole thing."

He led her forward until they were standing only a couple of yards from the table, and now she could see right down into the basin.

"There you are," Landy said. "That's William."

He was far larger than she had imagined he would be, and darker in colour. With all the ridges and creases running over his surface, he reminded her of nothing so much as an enormous pickled walnut. She could see the stubs of the four big arteries and the two veins coming out from the base of him and the neat way in which they were joined to the plastic tubes; and with each throb of the heart machine, all the tubes gave a little jerk in unison as the blood was pushed through them.

"You'll have to lean over," Landy said, "and put your pretty face right above the eye. He'll see you then, and you can smile at him and blow him a kiss. If I were you I'd say a few nice things as well. He won't actually hear them, but I'm sure he'll get the general idea."

"He hates people blowing kisses at him," Mrs. Pearl said. "I'll do it my own way if you don't mind." She stepped up to the edge of the table, leaned forward until her face was directly over the basin, and looked straight down into William's eye.

"Hallo, dear," she whispered. "It's me—Mary."

The eye, bright as ever, stared back at her with a peculiar, fixed intensity.

"How are you, dear?" she said.

The plastic capsule was transparent all the way round so that the whole of the eyeball was visible. The optic nerve connecting the underside of it to the brain looked like a short length of grey spaghetti.

"Are you feeling all right, William?"

It was a queer sensation peering into her husband's eye when there was no face to go with it. All she had to look at was the eye, and she kept starting at it, and gradually it grew bigger and bigger, and in the end it was the only thing that she could see—a sort of face in itself. There was a network of tiny red veins running over the white surface of the eyeball, and in the ice-blue of the iris there were three or four rather pretty darkish streaks radiating from the pupil in the centre. The pupil was large and black, with a little spark of light reflecting from one side of it.

"I got your letter, dear, and came over at once to see how you were. Dr. Landy says you are doing wonderfully well. Perhaps if I talk slowly you can understand a little of what I am saying by reading my lips."

There was no doubt that the eye was watching her.

"They are doing everything possible to take care of you, dear. This marvellous machine thing here is pumping away all the time and I'm sure it's a lot better than those silly old hearts all the rest of us have. Ours are liable to break down at any moment, but yours will go on for ever."

She was studying the eye closely, trying to discover what there was about it that gave it such an unusual appearance.

"You seem fine, dear, simply fine. Really you do."

It looked ever so much nicer, this eye, than either of his eyes used to look, she told herself. There was a softness about it somewhere, a calm, kindly quality that she had never seen before. Maybe it had to do with the dot in the very centre, the pupil. William's pupils used always to be tiny black pinheads. They used to glint at you, stabbing into your brain, seeing right through you, and they always knew at once what you were up to and even what you were thinking. But this one she was looking at now was large and soft and gentle, almost cowlike.

"Are you quite sure he's conscious?" she asked, not looking up.

"Oh yes, completely," Landy said.

"And he *can* see me?"

"Perfectly."

"Isn't that marvellous? I expect he's wondering what happened."

"Not at all. He knows perfectly well where he is and why he's there. He can't possibly have forgotten that."

"You mean he *knows* he's in this basin?"

"Of course. And if only he had the power of speech, he would probably be able to carry on a perfectly normal conversation with you this very minute. So far as I can see, there should be absolutely no difference mentally between this William here and the one you used to know back home."

"Good *gracious* me," Mrs. Pearl said, and she paused to consider this intriguing aspect.

You know what, she told herself, looking behind the eye now and staring hard at the great grey pulpy walnut that lay so placidly under the water. I'm not at all sure that I don't prefer him as he is at present. In fact, I believe that I could live very comfortably with this kind of a William. I could cope with this one.

"Quiet, isn't he?" she said.

"Naturally he's quiet."

No arguments and criticisms, she thought, no constant admonitions, no rules to obey, no ban on smoking cigarettes, no pair of cold disapproving eyes watching me over the top of a book in the evenings, no shirts to wash and iron, no meals to cook—nothing but the throb of the heart machine, which was rather a soothing sound anyway and certainly not loud enough to interfere with television.

"Doctor," she said, "I do believe I'm suddenly getting to feel the most enormous affection for him. Does that sound queer?"

"I think it's quite understandable."

"He looks so helpless and silent lying there under the water in his little basin."

"Yes, I know."

"He's like a baby, that's what he's like. He's exactly like a little baby."

Landy stood still behind her, watching.

"There," she said softly, peering into the basin. "From now on Mary's going to look after you *all* by herself and you've nothing to worry about in the world. When can I have him back home, Doctor?"

"I beg your pardon?"

"I said when can I have him back—back in my own house?"

"You're joking," Landy said.

She turned her head slowly around and looked directly at him. "Why should I joke?" she asked. Her face was bright, her eyes round and bright as two diamonds.

"He couldn't possibly be moved."

"I don't see why not."

"This is an experiment, Mrs. Pearl."

"It's my husband, Dr. Landy."

A funny little nervous half-smile appeared on Landy's mouth. "Well . . ." he said.

"It *is* my husband, you know." There was no anger in her voice. She spoke quietly, as though merely reminding him of a simple fact.

"That's rather a tricky point," Landy said, wetting his lips. "You're a widow now, Mrs. Pearl. I think you must resign yourself to that fact."

She turned away suddenly from the table and crossed over to the window. "I mean it," she said, fishing in her bag for a cigarette. "I want him back."

Landy watched her as she put the cigarette between her lips and lit it. Unless he were very much mistaken, there was something a bit odd about this woman, he thought. She seemed almost pleased to have her husband over there in the basin.

He tried to imagine what his own feelings would be if it were *his* wife's brain lying there and *her* eye staring up at him out of that capsule.

He wouldn't like it.

"Shall we go back to my room now?" he said.

She was standing by the window, apparently quite calm and relaxed, puffing her cigarette.

"Yes, all right."

On her way past the table she stopped and leaned over the basin once more. "Mary's leaving now, sweetheart," she said. "And don't you worry about a single thing, you understand? We're going to get you right back home where we can look after you properly just as soon as we possibly can. And listen dear . . ." At this point she paused and carried the cigarette to her lips, intending to take a puff.

Instantly the eye flashed.

She was looking straight into it at the time, and right in the centre of it she saw a tiny but brilliant flash of light, and the pupil contracted into a minute black pinpoint of absolute fury.

At first she didn't move. She stood bending over the basin, holding the cigarette up to her mouth, watching the eye.

Then very slowly, deliberately, she put the cigarette between her lips and took a long suck. She inhaled deeply, and she held the smoke inside her lungs for three or four seconds; then suddenly, *whoosh,* out it came through her nostrils in two thin jets which struck the water in the basin and billowed out over the surface in a thick blue cloud, enveloping the eye.

Landy was over by the door, with his back to her, waiting. "Come on, Mrs. Pearl," he called.

"Don't look so cross, William," she said softly. "It isn't any good looking cross."

Landy turned his head to see what she was doing.

"Not any more it isn't," she whispered. "Because from now on, my pet, you're going to do just exactly what Mary tells you. Do you understand that?"

"Mrs. Pearl," Landy said, moving towards her.

"So don't be a naughty boy again, will you, my precious," she said, taking another pull at the cigarette. "Naughty boys are liable to get punished most severely nowadays, you ought to know that."

Landy was beside her now, and he took her by the arm and began drawing her firmly but gently away from the table.

"Good-bye, darling," she called. "I'll be back soon."

"That's enough, Mrs. Pearl."

"Isn't he sweet?" she cried, looking up at Landy with big bright eyes. "Isn't he heaven? I just can't wait to get him home."

16.
VALENCE:
The Happiest Creatures on Earth?
RUTH AND EDWARD BRECHER

Although brain research increasingly presents us with a number of things we can do regarding the behavior of organisms, Ruth and Edward Brecher refuse to equate "can" with "should." In the following article, recent research trends are viewed from an ethical perspective.

In the psychological laboratory of Dr. James Olds at the University of Michigan, a rat presses a lever. This turns on a mild electric current which courses through an electrode to stimulate a carefully selected region in the rat's own brain.

Just what sensation the rat gets no one knows, of course. But Dr. Olds's rats certainly behave as if they loved it. No other reward in the rat world compares with it. Though food and water are readily available, famished or parched rats will press the lever rather than eat or drink. Even a female rat in heat cannot distract a male from the happy pursuit of this electrical delight.

In other laboratories, cats, dogs, dolphins, and monkeys stimulate their own brains in the same way. And at several medical centers human patients report pleasant emotions when corresponding regions of their brains are electrically stimulated. (Applied to other brain regions, the current can evoke displeasure, fear, even terror.)

These discoveries have implications far beyond their impact on psychological theory: they may point the way to new methods of treating human illnesses; military applications have been explored. The possible social consequences are incalculable. These vistas have opened up only within the past decade although the underlying technique is not new.

During the 1930s and 1940s a Swiss investigator, Dr. W. R. Hess, developed the basic methods of electrical brain stimulation (ESB) to a high level of precision; other psychologists and physiologists throughout the world thereafter found it a remarkably effective way to explore brain structure and functions.

At Yale in 1953, for example, Drs. José M. R. Delgado, Warren E. Roberts, and Neal E. Miller implanted sixty-six electrodes in the brains of six laboratory animals. Reactions differed greatly according to which electrode transmitted the current. When it was routed through some, the results were commonplace—the animals merely turned their heads, circled, pawed, licked, or gave no response whatever. But stimulation through other electrodes evoked "a fearlike response, characterized by hissing, opening the mouth, showing the teeth, flattening the ear, accompanied by well-oriented, co-ordinated efforts to escape. . . . Usually docile animals became aggressive, trying to bite and scratch. . . . Pupillary dilatation and other autonomic reactions, such as defecation and urination, were often observed. . . ." The animals learned to escape this unpleasant stimulation either by manipulating a wheel or by jumping through an escape hatch. No matter how hungry, they would keep away from food if they knew the current would be turned on when they approached it.

At the 1953 meetings of the American Psychological Association, motion pictures of these experiments were shown. Among those who saw them was Dr. Olds, then a budding psychologist, working under Dr. Donald O. Hebb at McGill in Montreal. Another fledgling psychologist, Dr. Peter Milner, had just taught Dr. Olds how to use ESB—how, for example, to insert an electrode carefully into the brain of an anesthetized rat. Each electrode consisted of two very fine hairlike wires, insulated so that the current when applied would stimulate only the brain area near the tip. The effect depended primarily upon where the tip was lodged. A fraction of a millimeter shift in the site might make a significant difference in the animal's response.

Dr. Olds was so fascinated by this ESB work that he often spent Sundays in the laboratory "playing around" with the rats. On one such occasion, he noticed an animal behaving quite differently from those in the Yale film. When its brain was stimulated it neither bared its teeth, defecated, nor urinated in terror. Instead it raised its head, sniffed daintily—and kept coming back to the same corner of the experimental table for additional doses of ESB.

Soon Drs. Olds and Milner could make the rat go wherever they wanted merely by turning on the current when it headed in the desired direction. They concluded that ESB could serve not only as punishment but as a welcome reward; both effects could be used to control behavior. Very likely earlier ESB researchers had evoked—but failed to observe—such pleasurable reactions. Dr. Olds himself was nonplused that first Sunday morning. "Scarcely believing what I saw," he says, "I tried in the next few weeks and months to get other rats to do the same."

16.   VALENCE: The Happiest Creatures on Earth?

He has been at it ever since, with notable success, at McGill, at the University of California, and since 1957 at the University of Michigan. His work suggests that—for rats at least—ESB is the reward that exceeds all others.

Pleasure Without Satiety

One standard laboratory device for measuring the strength of motives is the "Skinner box," which has a pedal-like lever at one end. Each time an animal presses the lever, he receives a reward—usually a pellet of food. An automatic mechanism records the number of times per hour the lever is pressed, and this rate is a measure of the animal's hunger. For instance, a famished rat may press the lever for fifteen minutes at the rate of 100 per hour before it is sated by the food so earned.

To measure the strength of the ESB reward, Dr. Olds substitutes a half-second of brain stimulation for the food pellet. To get another half-second dose, the rat must release the lever and press again. Thus the rat rather than the experimenter controls the stimulus. Under these conditions, a rat with a properly placed electrode will stimulate itself continuously hour after hour—many hundreds of times each hour. Some electrode placements cause a rat to press the lever every half-second or oftener—7,000 or 8,000 times an hour, until it falls exhausted. When it awakens, it neither eats nor drinks but starts pressing the lever again, at the same rate.

Another measuring device is a long obstacle box bisected by an electrified grid which delivers a painful electric shock to the animal's paws. The hungrier the rat, the more severe the shock it will endure in order to reach food. A sufficiently painful shock will deter even the hungriest rat. But it takes a shock twice or three times as strong to keep him away from an ESB reward.

Experimenters have shown that this reward effect is not a mere laboratory curiosity but is directly related to such natural drives as hunger, thirst, and sex. For example, with an electrode in a brain region controlling sexual function, a rat may stimulate itself 2,000 times an hour. If it is then castrated, the rate gradually slows down as the level of sex hormones in its blood stream falls off. Within two weeks the rat loses all interest in the lever. But if sex hormones are later injected it starts pressing the lever again.

In several important ways reactions to ESB differ from most physiological responses. For instance, we eat until we are satisfied and then "can't eat another mouthful." Satiation similarly results when an electrode is placed in certain regions. But rats with an electrode in other reward regions seem *never* to get too much.

In one experiment a monkey stimulated itself 200,000 times in a single day. In another, at the Walter Reed Army Medical Center in Washington, D.C., researchers organized an ESB marathon. Day after day, week after week, rats pressed the levers, pausing only occasionally for fifteen-second snacks and sips, or brief naps. After twenty-one days, says Dr. Joseph V. Brady, the laboratory's director, "the rats were still going strong, but the rest of us were exhausted."

Were these rats ESB addicts—in the sense that they needed an additional dose to counteract the unpleasant aftereffects of the previous one? Apparently not. After six or eight months of continuous self-stimulation, Dr. Olds's rats look younger, healthier, more vigorous, and more alert than litter mates who have led ordinary lives. Between sessions the ESB rats behave normally. They exhibit no "withdrawal symptoms" when deprived of their accustomed stimulation. Nor do they, like the alcohol or narcotics habitué, have to keep increasing their dose to maintain the effect. The same mild current—usually measuring only a few volts and a few thousandths of an ampere—evokes the same response after many months.

Several researchers have been patiently mapping out, cubic millimeter by cubic millimeter, the precise regions where the reward and punishment phenomena can be evoked. The brain consists of three major systems. At the core is the brain-stem, very similar in man and in animals far down the evolutionary scale; it is the site of quite primitive neurological functions. The outermost layer is the cerebral cortex, seat of the "higher thought processes," vastly more developed in man and the higher apes than in lower animals. In between, forming a border or "limbus" around the brain-stem and therefore called the "limbic system," is a complex collection of brain structures essentially similar in man and other mammals but not in sub-mammalian species. This system, recent research indicates, is the site of emotional control over behavior and of the reward and punishment effects.

Within the limbic system is a small organ called the hypothalamus. Here reward and punishment regions are interlarded with or overlap closely packed regions that control eating, drinking, sex, lactation, sweating, shivering, panting, heart rate, sleep, hormone secretions, and other physiological functions and emotional responses. When one hypothalamic region is stimulated, a rat will eat almost continuously and grow enormously fat. Stimulation of a nearby region will suppress appetite altogether. This close-knit structure of the hypothalamus leads to intriguing speculations. For example, oral, sex, and reward regions are close together or overlap. Does this suggest a physiological basis for the "oral eroticism" of Freudian fame? Could sadism or masochism be caused by some minute disorder in the contiguous regions concerned with reward, punishment, and sex? Further experiments may or may not confirm such speculations.

One effect of ESB is its ability to suppress anxiety. This has been demonstrated by Dr. Brady at Walter Reed. An animal in a Skinner box receives food pellets as a reward for pressing the lever. Then from time to time a loud buzzer is sounded for three minutes—after which a painful shock is delivered to the animal's paws. Soon the animal comes to associate the sound with the shock and stops pressing the lever as the buzzing begins.

16. VALENCE: The Happiest Creatures on Earth?

This is a typical anxiety response. But when the reward is ESB instead of food, the animal goes on unconcernedly pressing the lever despite the warning buzzer and inevitable painful shock. In this capacity to suppress anxiety ESB resembles the mythical drug *soma,* used in Aldous Huxley's *Brave New World* to enslave mankind.

Of equal interest are experiments conducted by Dr. Delgado and his associates at Yale with a cageful of monkeys. As is their custom, the monkeys establish a "society" of their own, with a status hierarchy. The most aggressive becomes the "boss"; the others cower at his approach. Then Dr. Delgado stimulates the boss monkey in a brain region where taming effects are produced. Promptly the boss loses his aggressiveness and behaves with unaccustomed meekness. The other monkeys —as well as human observers—soon note that, in Madison Avenue parlance, he is projecting an altered image. As a result, the whole social structure of the monkey colony shifts. The stimulated monkey is no longer boss; another takes over and rules the colony. When the current is turned off, the original boss resumes his accustomed role and the group readjusts. This experiment suggests that sociologists may find ESB an extremely useful tool. Its applicability to the human brain has, in fact, already been established.

Making Pain Bearable

Human brains are stimulated only if benefit to the particular patient can be expected. When conservative treatment of a brain condition fails, for example, a surgeon may decide to remove abnormal tissue. ESB in such cases can be a valuable prelude to surgery. The surgeon must make sure that he will not cut into any regions which serve essential functions. Electrodes implanted temporarily throughout the area of interest and activated one at a time help him map his surgical strategy.

In other cases, ESB may be tried as a less drastic substitute for a radical brain operation such as lobotomy (an incision which severs certain nerve fibers in the frontal lobe). This is sometimes performed when all else has failed to relieve mental disorders and also to control intractable pain. Lobotomy is an irreversible procedure which may permanently destroy important functions. ESB, in contrast, causes little or no brain damage, although there is of course an inherent risk in any procedure which involves opening up the cranial cavity.

ESB has been used medically by groups headed by Dr. Wilder Penfield at Montreal Neurological Institute; Dr. Robert G. Heath at Tulane; Dr. Delgado at Yale; Drs. Sidney Mervin and George Hayes at Walter Reed; Dr. Reginald F. Bickford at the Mayo Clinic and Dr. Carl W. Sem-Jacobsen both there and at the Gaustad Mental Hospital in Oslo, Norway.

Dr. Penfield's work dates back to the 1940s when he stimulated the outermost layer of the brain—the cerebral cortex—of many hundreds of fully conscious patients. They reported experiencing a wide range of sounds, smells, visions, hallucinations, memories, dreamlike states, and

V. The Exploration and Control of the Brain

déjà-vu feelings—even the detailed recall of whole scenes from the distant past. But these effects were curiously devoid of emotion. Neither pleasure, joy, anger, fear, nor rage was felt.

Very different results were reported, however, by subsequent researchers who ventured to implant electrodes more deeply in the limbic system. Dr. Heath at Tulane, for example, began stimulating such regions in 1950. The effect on pain-ridden patients he says "is quite startling. They get immediate relief . . . say they feel good. They smile, brighten up, change their facial expressions. . . . The effect is immediate, as soon as the current hits. It is a repeatable thing. You can stimulate over and over again."

In contrast, Dr. Heath points out, "Lobotomy patients still have pain, but don't care about it. Our stimulation patients say they don't have pain. . . . We feel it is a disappearance of pain rather than a lack of concern about it."

Dr. Sem-Jacobsen and his associates have implanted some 6,000 electrodes in the brains of 120 human patients as an essential prelude to surgery. With the electrode in some reward regions, "the patients get euphoric, laughing out loud and enjoying themselves actively. There are other pleasure areas where the patients enjoy themselves passively." An element of sexual pleasure is occasionally noted or there may be "a feeling of ease and relaxation," of "joy with smiling," or just "great satisfaction." Dr. Sem-Jacobsen adds that neither patients nor scientists seem to have a vocabulary adequate to describe or differentiate all the nuances of these feelings.

Some terminal cancer patients have been kept reasonably comfortable by ESB for many months, without addiction effects. The patients enjoy their daily ESB experience and are tranquil in the interim. Though narcotics are available to them they use them only sparingly. Nor is it necessary to increase the strength of current as the months roll by. ESB, however, is the "treatment of choice" for only a few patients under special circumstances including continuous hospitalization.

Punishment regions are never stimulated deliberately but are occasionally hit by accident. Dr. Sem-Jacobsen divides the negative effects in humans roughly into five groups: "anxiety," "restlessness," "depression," "fright," and "horror."

The complex relationships between ESB and chemical agents—such as the tranquilizers and "psychic energizers"—are being studied by several researchers. Dr. Miller and his group at Yale, for example, lodge an electrode in a rat's reward region and measure the minimum current which will make the rat press the lever. Then the rat gets a dose of a drug often used to treat human depression. The effect is to lower the threshold of the reward effect. A current so weak that it ordinarily has no effect will make the drug-treated rat press the lever repeatedly.

In other experiments, researchers seem to have discovered why one of the well-known tranquilizers sometimes deepens the depression of pa-

16. VALENCE: The Happiest Creatures on Earth?

tients already depressed. This drug raises the threshold of the reward effect. A current ordinarily strong enough to make a rat press the lever has no effect at all after the drug has been administered.

With his wife, Dr. Olds has run a series of experiments in which drugs are substituted for ESB. Instead of an electrode a tiny pipette is implanted in a reward region of the rat's brain. Each time the rat presses the lever, it receives a minute drug injection. The rat responds to this chemical reward as it would to ESB, pressing the lever several hundred times an hour. Such research is valuable in locating the precise site of a drug's action within the brain and in casting light on how each drug achieves its effects. Newly synthesized chemicals can be screened for their potential action on reward and punishment centers; chemicals likely to achieve ESB-like effects when swallowed or injected can be identified. In the treatment of depression and other mental illnesses, such goals are benign indeed. But this new tool also raises ethical questions, as a recent experiment suggests.

Impressed by the practical possibilities of ESB, one far-sighted corporation launched an ESB project of its own, in the hope of securing a research and development contract from the Defense Department. A corporate "top secret" lid was clamped on the project; hence the facts which follow have not been confirmed by the corporation, but we have reason to believe they are accurate.

The experimental subject was a donkey wearing a collar laden with a prism, a photoelectric eye, a make-break switch, a battery, and a miniaturized, transistorized circuit for sending an ESB current through an electrode lodged in a reward area of the donkey's brain. When sunlight struck the prism at precisely the right angle, the photoelectric eye activated the switch which turned on the current and administered the ESB reward. If the donkey veered in either direction or stood still, the switch turned the current off again. Thus accoutered, the joyful donkey trotted straight ahead, up hill, down dale, even across a mountain, neither straying nor lagging, to its predestined goal—a substation some five miles away. There the prism was reversed—whereupon the donkey retraced its arduous course over the mountain and back to its starting place.

When moving pictures of "Project Donkey" were shown at the Pentagon last year as part of a contract application, the audience reaction was mixed. One nonmilitary viewer—a scientist—is said to have murmured: "There, but for the grace of God, go I."

Can It Control Human Behavior?

We need not feel sorry for the donkey; it was no doubt enjoying a delightful ESB experience as it jogged along. But the thought of a human being subjected to this kind of external control—reduced to the status of an automaton for someone else's benefit—is shocking to the conscience of anyone adhering to democratic or to Judaeo–Christian ethical traditions. As Professor F. S. C. Northrop of the Yale Law School reminded us, the

231

heart of the matter is Immanuel Kant's "categorical imperative": *no man must ever be used as a mere pawn to serve another man's ends.* Nor is the ethical objection evaded when a man is thus degraded "with his own consent," or "for the good of all mankind."

The practical likelihood that ESB itself will ever be misused to enslave individuals or whole populations is exceedingly small. As a method of behavioral control, it is far too crude, requiring invasion of the cranial cavity and a heavy investment of skilled time to control a single individual. But ESB is nevertheless a striking example of a whole class of new behavioral control techniques.

Hypnosis is of course the prototype. Like ESB, it is not as yet directly adaptable to mass use. But the quasi-hypnotic techniques of the rabble rouser or lynch-mob leader suggest its possibilities. Reduced to a reliable science through further laboratory research, mass hypnosis might go far.

Isolation and *sensory deprivation* also produce amazing results in subjugating the human ego, for such purposes as brain-washing. Experiments in this area are currently under way.

Psychically active drugs are the most convenient method yet suggested for reducing men to pawns. One well-known drug seems to act on the same reward regions as ESB; users report that "all the bells of Heaven ring." Perhaps fortunately, this drug causes addiction and has degenerative side effects. However, a great effort is currently being made to develop equally potent substances free of such built-in limitations.

Beyond these known possibilities, others may already be secretly under investigation, here or abroad or both. In the course of our own inquiries we were asked: "Have you been cleared for access to classified data?"

Should We Keep Still?

The hazard, let us stress, is *not* that behavioral scientists will misuse these techniques for personal ends. Like physicians, our psychologists adhere to a professional code of ethics in which the Kantian imperative is implicit. Existing law, moreover, makes abuse of ESB, hypnosis, drugs, sensory deprivation, or the like by an individual scientist a tort and perhaps also a crime. As we trust our physicians with poisons, narcotics, and scalpels, so we can safely trust behavioral scientists in their professional roles.

The real hazard arises when behavioral control techniques are taken over by others—for example, by national governments. As Dr. Carl R. Rogers, University of Wisconsin clinical psychologist, has cogently warned his colleagues:

> To hope that the power which is being made available by the behavioral sciences will be exercised by the scientists, or by a benevolent group, seems to me to be a hope little supported by either recent or distant history. It seems far more likely that behavioral scientists,

holding their present attitudes, will be in the position of the German rocket scientists specializing in guided missiles. First, they worked devotedly for Hitler to destroy the U.S.S.R. and the United States. Now depending on who captured them, they work devotedly for the U.S.S.R. in the interest of destroying the United States, or devotedly for the United States in the interest of destroying the U.S.S.R. If behavioral scientists are concerned solely with advancing their science, it seems most probable that they will serve the purpose of whatever group has the power.

The new behavioral controls may prove far more tempting to those in power than such traditional devices as imprisonment, the rack, or the thumbscrew. Altruistic, benevolent leaders who would shrink from applying torture, or from dropping an H-bomb, might without qualms use the "pain-free" devices for what they deem the good of mankind—to steal a lap on an enemy or to lead their own followers into a land flowing with milk, honey, and ESB-like rewards.

It is thus high time, we believe, for laymen to ask: How are these new behavioral controls likely to affect mankind? Shall we permit their use at all? If so, which uses shall we permit and which shall we prohibit? How shall misuse be defined and prevented or punished? And what body— national or international—should make such decisions? During the early period of nuclear research, such questions were asked too seldom and too late.

At Yale, a symposium on Heaven, Hell and Electrical Stimulation of the Brain has already been held, with a theologian and philosopher as well as scientists participating. Further conferences should be scheduled. The foundations—including Ford, Carnegie, and Rockefeller—which have been supporting ESB research might similarly support inquiries into the ethical implications of such scientific advances. The problem should also go on the agenda of the President's Science Advisory Committee—and behavioral scientists should be added to that committee.

Several of the scientists we consulted urged that these ethical problems not even be mentioned in an article for lay readers. Scientists, they point out, are already under exasperating fire from antivivisectionists, antifluoridationists, and antiscientific obscurantists of many brands who may gain aid and comfort from any new "attack on science." We are convinced, in contrast, that only good can come of open discussion. Fear and hatred of science have long existed among us; they have been intensified since Hiroshima, and cannot be merely shushed. The best way to build fuller confidence in science and scientists is to bring the hazards of misuse out into the open, determine their limits, explain the codes of ethics to which scientists already adhere, and modernize these codes to curb misuse by others—up to and including national governments.

It is in the political area, we suspect, that this issue must ultimately be faced. Even twenty years ago, our national leaders had relatively modest powers. The H-bomb gave them in addition the power to destroy a large part of mankind and the Cold War gave them an incentive to develop this power to the fullest. The new methods of controlling behavior now emerging from the laboratory may soon add an awe-inspiring power to enslave us all with our own engineered consent. "Project Donkey" is an omen we ignore at our peril.

17.
VISION:
Patent Pending

ARTHUR C. CLARKE

Ruth and Edward Brecher have raised some ethical and moral concerns regarding contemporary brain research. In the following story, Arthur C. Clarke examines another implication that could easily arise from the exploration of the brain.

There are no subjects that have not been discussed, at some time or other, in the saloon bar of the "White Hart"—and whether or not there are ladies present makes no difference whatsoever. After all, they came in at their own risk. Three of them, now I come to think of it, have eventually gone out again with husbands. So perhaps the risk isn't on their side at all. . . .

I mention this because I would not like you to think that all our conversations are highly erudite and scientific, and our activities purely cerebral. Though chess is rampant, darts and shove-ha'penny also flourish. The *Times Literary Supplement,* the *Saturday Review,* the *New Statesman* and the *Atlantic Monthly* may be brought in by some of the customers, but the same people are quite likely to leave with the latest issue of *Staggering Stories of Pseudoscience.*

A great deal of business also goes on in the obscurer corners of the pub. Copies of antique books and magazines frequently change hands at astronomical prices, and on almost any Wednesday at least three well-known dealers may be seen smoking large cigars as they lean over the bar, swapping stories with Drew. From time to time a vast guffaw announces the *denouement* of some anecdote and provokes a flood of anxious enquiries from patrons who are afraid they may have missed something. But, alas,

From *Tales from the White Hart* by Arthur Clarke, pp. 19–30. © 1954 by Popular Publications. Reprinted by permission of the author and the author's agents, Scott Meredith Literary Agency, Inc., 580 Fifth Avenue, New York, N.Y. 10036.

delicacy forbids that I should repeat any of these interesting tales here. Unlike most things in this island, they are not for export. . . .

Luckily, no such restrictions apply to the tales of Mr. Harry Purvis, B.Sc. (at least), Ph.D. (probably), F.R.S. (personally I don't think so, though it *has* been rumoured). None of them would bring a blush to the cheeks of the most delicately nurtured maiden aunts, should any still survive in these days.

I must apologise. This is too sweeping a statement. There was one story which might, in some circles, be regarded as a little daring. Yet I do not hesitate to repeat it, for I know that you, dear reader, will be sufficiently broadminded to take no offence.

It started in this fashion. A celebrated Fleet Street reviewer had been pinned into a corner by a persuasive publisher, who was about to bring out a book of which he had high hopes. It was one of the riper productions of the deep and decadent South—a prime example of the "and-then-the-house-gave-another-lurch-as-the-termites-finished-the-east-wing" school of fiction. Eire had already banned it, but that is an honour which few books escape nowadays, and certainly could not be considered a distinction. However, if a leading British newspaper could be induced to make a stern call for its suppression, it would become a best-seller overnight. . . .

Such was the logic of its publisher, and he was using all his wiles to induce co-operation. I heard him remark, apparently to allay any scruples his reviewer friend might have, "Of course not! If they can understand it, they *can't* be corrupted any further!" And then Harry Purvis, who has an uncanny knack of following half a dozen conversations simultaneously, so that he can insert himself in the right one at the right time, said in his peculiarly penetrating and non-interruptable voice: "Censorship does raise some very difficult problems doesn't it? I've always argued that there's an inverse correlation between a country's degree of civilisation and the restraints it puts on its press."

A New England voice from the back of the room cut in: "On *that* argument, Paris is a more civilised place than Boston."

"Precisely," answered Purvis. For once, he waited for a reply.

"O.K." said the New England voice mildly. "I'm not arguing. I just wanted to check."

"To continue," said Purvis, wasting no more time in doing so, "I'm reminded of a matter which has not yet concerned the censor, but which will certainly do so before long. It began in France, and so far has remained there. When it *does* come out into the open, it may have a greater impact on our civilisation than the atom bomb.

"Like the atom bomb, it arose out of equally academic research. *Never*, gentlemen, underestimate science. I doubt if there is a single field of study so theoretical, so remote from what is laughingly called everyday life, that it may not one day produce something that will shake the world.

17. VISION: Patent Pending

"You will appreciate that the story I am telling you is, for once in a while, second-hand. I got it from a colleague at the Sorbonne last year while I was over there at a scientific conference. So the names are all fictitious: I was told them at the time, but I can't remember them now.

"Professor—ah—Julian was an experimental physiologist at one of the smaller, but less impecunious, French universities. Some of you may remember that rather unlikely tale we heard here the other week from that fellow Hinckelberg, about his colleague who'd learned how to control the behaviour of animals through feeding the correct currents into their nervous systems. Well, if there *was* any truth in that story—and frankly I doubt it—the whole project was probably inspired by Julian's papers in *Comptes Rendus.*

"Professor Julian, however, never published his most remarkable results. When you stumble on something which is really terrific, you don't rush into print. You wait until you have overwhelming evidence—unless you're afraid that someone else is hot on the track. Then you may issue an ambiguous report that will establish your priority at a later date, without giving too much away at the moment—like the famous cryptogram that Huygens put out when he detected the rings of Saturn.

"You may well wonder what Julian's discovery was, so I won't keep you in suspense. It was simply the natural extension of what man has been doing for the last hundred years. First the camera gave us the power to capture scenes. Then Edison invented the phonograph, and sound was mastered. Today, in the talking film, we have a kind of mechanical memory which would be inconceivable to our forefathers. But surely the matter cannot rest there. Eventually science must be able to catch and store thoughts and sensations themselves, and feed them back into the mind so that, whenever it wishes, it can repeat any experience in life, down to its minutest detail."

"That's an old idea!" snorted someone. "See the 'feelies' in 'Brave New World'."

"All good ideas have been thought of by somebody before they are realised," said Purvis severely. "The point is that what Huxley and others had talked about, Julian actually did. My goodness, there's a pun there! Aldous—Julian—oh, let it pass!

"It was done electronically, of course. You all know how the encephalograph can record the minute electrical impulses in the living brain—the so-called 'brain waves,' as the popular press calls them. Julian's device was a much subtler elaboration of this well-known instrument. And, having recorded cerebral impulses, he could play them back again. It sounds simple, doesn't it? So was the phonograph, but it took the genius of Edison to think of it.

"And now, enter the villain. Well, perhaps that's too strong a word, for Professor Julian's assistant Georges—Georges Dupin—is really quite a sympathetic character. It was just that, being a Frenchman of a more practical turn of mind than the Professor, he saw at once that there were some milliards of francs involved in this laboratory toy.

"The first thing was to get it out of the laboratory. The French have an undoubted flair for elegant engineering, and after some weeks of work— with the full co-operation of the Professor—Georges had managed to pack the "play-back" side of the apparatus into a cabinet no larger than a television set, and containing not very many more parts.

"Then Georges was ready to make his first experiment. It would involve considerable expense, but as someone so rightly remarked you cannot make omelettes without breaking eggs. And the analogy is, if I may say so, an exceedingly apt one.

"For Georges went to see the most famous *gourmet* in France, and made an interesting proposition. It was one that the great man could not refuse, because it was so unique a tribute to his eminence. Georges explained patiently that he had invented a device for registering (he said nothing about storing) sensations. In the cause of science, and for the honour of the French *cuisine,* could he be privileged to analyse the emotions, the subtle nuances of gustatory discrimination, that took place in Monsieur le Baron's mind when he employed his unsurpassed talents? Monsieur could name the restaurant, the *chef* and the menu—everything would be arranged for his convenience. Of course, if he was too busy, no doubt that well-known epicure, Le Compte de—

"The Baron, who was in some respects a surprisingly coarse man, uttered a word not to be found in most French dictionaries. '*That* cretin!' he exploded. 'He would be happy on English cooking! No, *I* shall do it.' And forthwith he sat down to compose the menu, while Georges anxiously estimated the cost of the items and wondered if his bank balance would stand the strain. . . .

"It would be interesting to know what the chef and the waiters thought about the whole business. There was the Baron, seated at his favourite table and doing full justice to his favourite dishes, not in the least inconvenienced by the tangle of wires that trailed from his head to that diabolical-looking machine in the corner. The restaurant was empty of all other occupants, for the last thing Georges wanted was premature publicity. This had added very considerably to the already distressing cost of the experiment. He could only hope that the results would be worth it.

"They were. The only way of *proving* that, of course, would be to play back Georges' 'recording.' We have to take his word for it, since the utter inadequacy of words in such matters is all too well-known. The Baron *was* a genuine connoisseur, not one of those who merely pretend to powers of discrimination they do not possess. You know Thurber's 'Only a naive domestic Burgundy, but I think you'll admire its presumption.' The Baron would have known at the first sniff whether it was domestic or not—and if it had been presumptious he'd have smacked it down.

17. VISION: Patent Pending

"I gather that Georges had his money's worth out of that recording, even though he had not intended it merely for personal use. It opened up new worlds to him, and clarified the ideas that had been forming in his ingenious brain. There was no doubt about it: all the exquisite sensations that had passed through the Baron's mind during the consumption of that Lucullan repast had been captured, so that anyone else, however untrained they might be in such matters, could savour them to the full. For, you see, the recording dealt purely with emotions: intelligence did not come into the picture at all. The Baron needed a lifetime of knowledge and training before he could *experience* these sensations. But once they were down on tape, anyone, even if in real life they had no sense of taste at all, could take over from there.

"Think of the glowing vistas that opened up before Georges' eyes! There were other meals, other gourmets. There were the collected impressions of all the vintages of Europe—what would connoisseurs not pay for them? When the last bottle of a rare wine had been broached, its incorporeal essence could be preserved, as the voice of Melba can travel down the centuries. For, after all, it was not the wine itself that mattered, but the sensations it evoked. . . .

"So mused Georges. But this, he knew, was only a beginning. The French claim to logic I have often disputed, but in Georges' case it cannot be denied. He thought the matter over for a few days: then he went to see his *petite dame.*

" 'Yvonne, *ma cheri,*' he said, 'I have a somewhat unusual request to make of you. . . .' "

Harry Purvis knew when to break off in a story. He turned to the bar and called, "Another Scotch, Drew." No-one said a word while it was provided.

"To continue," said Purvis at length, "the experiment, unusual though it was, even in France, was successfully carried out. As both discretion and custom demanded, all was arranged in the lonely hours of the night. You will have gathered already that Georges was a persuasive person, though I doubt if Mam'selle needed much persuading.

"Stifling her curiosity with a sincere but hasty kiss, Georges saw Yvonne out of the lab and rushed back to his apparatus. Breathlessly, he ran through the playback. It worked—not that he had ever had any real doubts. Moreover—do please remember I have only my informant's word for this—it was indistinguishable from the real thing. At that moment something approaching religious awe overcame Georges. This was, without a doubt, the greatest invention in history. He would be immortal as well as wealthy, for he had achieved something of which all men had dreamed, and had robbed old age of one of its terrors. . . .

"He also realised that he could now dispense with Yvonne, if he so wished. This raised implications that would require further thought. *Much* further thought.

V. The Exploration and Control of the Brain

"You will, of course, appreciate that I am giving you a highly condensed account of events. While all this was going on, Georges was still working as a loyal employee of the Professor, who suspected nothing. As yet, indeed, Georges had done little more than any research worker might have in similar circumstances. His performances had been somewhat beyond the call of duty, but could all be explained away if need be.

"The next step would involve some very delicate negotiations and the expenditure of further hard-won francs. Georges now had all the material he needed to prove, beyond a shadow of doubt, that he was handling a very valuable commercial property. There were shrewd businessmen in Paris who would jump at the opportunity. Yet a certain delicacy, for which we must give him full credit, restrained Georges from using his second— er—recording as a sample of the wares his machine could purvey. There was no way of disguising the personalities involved, and Georges was a modest man. 'Besides,' he argued, again with great good sense, 'when the gramophone company wishes to make a *disque,* it does not enregister the performance of some amateur musician. *That* is a matter for professionals. And so, *ma foi,* is *this.*' Whereupon, after a further call at his bank, he set forth again for Paris.

"He did not go anywhere near the Place Pigalle, because that was full of Americans and prices were accordingly exorbitant. Instead, a few discreet enquiries and some understanding cab-drivers took him to an almost oppressively respectable suburb, where he presently found himself in a pleasant waiting room, by no means as exotic as might have been supposed.

"And there, somewhat embarrassed, Georges explained his mission to a formidable lady whose age one could have no more guessed than her profession. Used though she was to unorthodox requests, *this* was something she had never encountered in all her considerable experience. But the customer was always right, as long as he had the cash, and so in due course everything was arranged. One of the young ladies and her boy friend, an *apache* of somewhat overwhelming masculinity, travelled back with Georges to the provinces. At first they were, naturally, somewhat suspicious, but as Georges had already found, no expert can ever resist flattery. Soon they were all on excellent terms. Hercule and Susette promised Georges that they would give him every cause for satisfaction.

"No doubt some of you would be glad to have further details, but you can scarcely expect me to supply them. All I can say is that Georges—or rather his instrument—was kept very busy, and that by the morning little of the recording material was left unused. For it seems that Hercule was indeed appropriately named. . . .

"When this piquant episode was finished, Georges had very little money left, but he did possess two recordings that were quite beyond price. Once more he set off to Paris, where, with practically no trouble, he came to terms with some businessmen who were so astonished that they gave him a very generous contract before coming to their senses. I am pleased to report this, because so often the scientist emerges second best in his dealings with the world of finance. I'm equally pleased to record that Georges had made provision for Professor Julian in the contract. You may say cynically that it was, after all, the Professor's invention, and that sooner or later Georges would have had to square him. But I like to think that there was more to it than that.

"The full details of the scheme for exploiting the device are, of course, unknown to me. I gather that Georges had been expansively eloquent— not that much eloquence was needed to convince anyone who had once experienced one or both of his play-backs. The market would be enormous, unlimited. The export trade alone could put France on her feet again and would wipe out her dollar deficit overnight—once certain snags had been overcome. Everything would have to be managed through somewhat clandestine channels, for think of the hub-bub from the hypocritical Anglo-saxons when they discovered just what was being imported into their countries. The Mother's Union, The Daughters of the American Revolution, The Housewives League, and *all* the religious organisations would rise as one. The lawyers were looking into the matter very carefully, and as far as could be seen the regulations that still excluded *Tropic of Capricorn* from the mails of the English-speaking countries could not be applied to this case—for the simple reason that no-one had thought of it. But there would be such a shout for new laws that Parliament and Congress would have to do something, so it was best to keep under cover as long as possible.

"In fact, as one of the directors pointed out, if the recordings were banned, so much the better. They could make much more money on a smaller output, because the price would promptly soar and all the vigilance of the Customs Officials couldn't block every leak. It would be Prohibition all over again.

"You will scarcely be surprised to hear that by this time Georges had somewhat lost interest in the gastronomical angle. It was an interesting but definitely minor possibility of the invention. Indeed, this had been tacitly admitted by the directors as they drew up the articles of association, for they had included the pleasures of the *cuisine* among 'subsidiary rights.'

"Georges returned home with his head in the clouds, and a substantial check in his pocket. A charming fancy had struck his imagination. He thought of all the trouble to which the gramophone companies had gone so that the world might have the complete recordings of the Forty-eight Preludes and Fugues or the Nine Symphonies. Well, *his* new company would put out a complete and definite set of recordings, performed by experts versed in the most esoteric knowledge of East and West. How many *opus* numbers would be required? That, of course, had been a subject of profound debate for some thousands of years. The Hindu text-books, Georges had heard, got well into three figures. It would be a most interesting research, combining profit with pleasure in an unexampled manner. . . . He had already begun some preliminary studies, using treatises which even in Paris were none too easy to obtain.

"If you think that while all this was going on, Georges had neglected his usual interests, you are all too right. He was working literally night and day, for he had not yet revealed his plans to the Professor and almost everything had to be done when the lab was closed. And one of the interests he had had to neglect was Yvonne.

"Her curiosity had already been aroused, as any girl's would have been. But now she was more than intrigued—she was distracted. For Georges had become so remote and cold. He was no longer in love with her.

"It was a result that might have been anticipated. Publicans have to guard against the danger of sampling their own wares too often—I'm sure *you* don't, Drew—and Georges had fallen into this seductive trap. He had been through that recording too many times, with somewhat debilitating results. Moreover, poor Yvonne was not to be compared with the experienced and talented Susette. It was the old story of the professional versus the amateur.

"All that Yvonne knew was that Georges was in love with someone else. That was true enough. She suspected that he had been unfaithful to her. And *that* raises profound philosophical questions we can hardly go into here.

"This being France, in case you had forgotten, the outcome was inevitable. Poor Georges! He was working late one night at the lab, as usual, when Yvonne finished him off with one of those ridiculous ornamental pistols which are *de rigeur* for such occasions. Let us drink to his memory."

"That's the trouble with all your stories," said John Beynon. "You tell us about wonderful inventions, and then at the end it turns out that the discoverer was killed, so no-one can do anything about it. For I suppose, as usual, the apparatus was destroyed?"

"But no," replied Purvis. "Apart from Georges, this is one of the stories that has a happy ending. There was no trouble at all about Yvonne, of course. Georges' grieving sponsors arrived on the scene with great speed and prevented any adverse publicity. Being men of sentiment as well as men of business, they realised that they would have to secure Yvonne's freedom. They promptly did this by playing the recording to *le Maire* and *le Préfet*, thus convincing them that the poor girl had experienced irresistible provocation. A few shares in the new company clinched the deal, with expressions of the utmost cordiality on both sides. Yvonne even got her gun back."

"Then when—" began someone else.

"Ah, these things take time. There's the question of mass production, you know. It's quite possible that distribution has already commenced through private—*very* private—channels. Some of those dubious little shops and notice boards around Leicester Square may soon start giving hints."

"Of course," said the New England voice disrespectfully, "you wouldn't know the *name* of the company."

You can't help admiring Purvis at times like this. He scarcely hesitated. "*Le Société Anonyme d'Aphrodite,*" he replied. "And I've just remembered something that will cheer *you* up. They hope to get round your sticky mails regulations and establish themselves before the inevitable congressional enquiry starts. They're opening up a branch in Nevada: apparently you can still get away with anything there." He raised his glass.

"To Georges Dupin," he said solemnly. "Martyr to science. Remember him when the fireworks start. And one other thing—"

"Yes?" we all asked.

"Better start saving now. And sell your TV sets before the bottom drops out of the market."

VI.
The Discovery of
Elbow Room

18.
VALENCE:
O Rotten Gotham—
Sliding Down into the Behavioral Sink

TOM WOLFE

In the following pages, Tom Wolfe provides a highly readable—and thoroughly alarming—passage on some research and conclusions in the area of how we arrange the space around us.

I just spent two days with Edward T. Hall, an anthropologist, watching thousands of my fellow New Yorkers short-circuiting themselves into hot little twitching death balls with jolts of their own adrenalin. Dr. Hall says it is overcrowding that does it. Overcrowding gets the adrenalin going, and the adrenalin gets them hyped up. And here they are, hyped up, turning bilious, nephritic, queer, autistic, sadistic, barren, batty, sloppy, hot-in-the-pants, chancred-on-the-flankers, leering, puling, numb—the usual in New York, in other words, and God knows what else. Dr. Hall has the theory that overcrowding has already thrown New York into a state of behavioral sink. Behavioral sink is a term from ethology, which is the study of how animals relate to their environment. Among animals, the sink winds up with a "population collapse" or "massive die-off." O rotten Gotham.

It got to be easy to look at New Yorkers as animals, especially looking down from some place like a balcony at Grand Central at the rush hour Friday afternoon. The floor was filled with the poor white humans, running around, dodging, blinking their eyes, making a sound like a pen full of starlings or rats or something.

"Listen to them skid," says Dr. Hall.

18. VALENCE: O Rotten Gotham

He was right. The poor old etiolate animals were out there skidding on their rubber soles. You could hear it once he pointed it out. They stop short to keep from hitting somebody or because they are disoriented and they suddenly stop and look around, and they skid on their rubbersole shoes, and a screech goes up. They pour out onto the floor down the escalators from the Pan-Am Building, from 42nd Street, from Lexington Avenue, up out of subways, down into subways, railroad trains, up into helicopters—

"You can also hear the helicopters all the way down here," says Dr. Hall. The sound of the helicopters using the roof of the Pan-Am Building nearly fifty stories up beats right through. "If it weren't for this ceiling"—he is referring to the very high ceiling in Grand Central—"this place would be unbearable with this kind of crowding. And yet they'll probably never 'waste' space like this again."

They screech! And the adrenal glands in all those poor white animals enlarge, micrometer by micrometer, to the size of cantaloupes. Dr. Hall pulls a Minox camera out of a holster he has on his belt and starts shooting away at the human scurry. The Sink!

Dr. Hall has the Minox up to his eye—he is a slender man, calm, 52 years old, young-looking, an anthropologist who has worked with Navajos, Hopis, Spanish-Americans, Negroes, Trukese. He was the most important anthropologist in the government during the crucial years of the foreign aid program, the 1950's. He directed both the Point Four training program and the Human Relations Area Files. He wrote *The Silent Language* and *The Hidden Dimension*, two books that are picking up the kind of "underground" following his friend Marshall McLuhan started picking up about five years ago. He teaches at the Illinois Institute of Technology, lives with his wife, Mildred, in a high-ceilinged town house on one of the last great residential streets in downtown Chicago, Astor Street; has a grown son and daughter, loves good food, good wine, the relaxed, civilized life—but comes to New York with a Minox at his eye to record—perfect!—The Sink.

We really got down in there by walking down into the Lexington Avenue line subway stop under Grand Central. We inhaled those nice big fluffy fumes of human sweat, urine, effluvia, and sebaceous secretions. One old female human was already stroked out on the upper level, on a stretcher, with two policemen standing by. The other humans barely looked at her. They rushed into line. They bellied each other, haunch to paunch, down the stairs. Human heads shone through the gratings. The species North European tried to create bubbles of space around themselves, about a foot and a half in diameter—

"See, he's reacting against the line," says Dr. Hall.

—but the species Mediterranean presses on in. The hell with bubbles of space. The species North European resents that, this male human behind him presses forward toward the booth . . . *breathing* on him, he's disgusted, he pulls out of the line entirely, the species Mediterranean resents him for resenting it, and neither of them realizes what the hell they are getting

247

irritable about exactly. And in all of them the old adrenals grow another micrometer.

Dr. Hall whips out the Minox. Too perfect! The bottom of The Sink.

It is the sheer overcrowding, such as occurs in the business sections of Manhattan five days a week and in Harlem, Bedford-Stuyvesant, southeast Bronx every day—sheer overcrowding is converting New Yorkers into animals in a sink pen. Dr. Hall's argument runs as follows: all animals, including birds, seem to have a built-in, inherited requirement to have a certain amount of territory, space, to lead their lives in. Even if they have all the food they need, and there are no predatory animals threatening them, they cannot tolerate crowding beyond a certain point. No more than two hundred wild Norway rats can survive on a quarter acre of ground, for example, even when they are given all the food they can eat. They just die off.

But why? To find out, ethologists have run experiments on all sorts of animals, from stickleback crabs to Sika deer. In one major experiment, an ethologist named John Calhoun put some domesticated white Norway rats in a pen with four sections to it, connected by ramps. Calhoun knew from previous experiments that the rats tend to split up into groups of ten to twelve and that the pen, therefore, would hold forty to forty-eight rats comfortably, assuming they formed four equal groups. He allowed them to reproduce until there were eighty rats, balanced between male and female, but did not let it get any more crowded. He kept them supplied with plenty of food, water, and nesting materials. In other words, all their more obvious needs were taken care of. A less obvious need—space—was not. To the human eye, the pen did not even look especially crowded. But to the rats, it was crowded beyond endurance.

The entire colony was soon plunged into a profound behavioral sink. "The sink," said Calhoun, "is the outcome of any behavioral process that collects animals together in unusually great numbers. The unhealthy connotations of the term are not accidental: a behavioral sink does act to aggravate all forms of pathology that can be found within a group."

For a start, long before the rat population reached eighty, a status hierarchy had developed in the pen. Two dominant male rats took over the two end sections, acquired harems of eight to ten females each, and forced the rest of the rats into the two middle pens. All the overcrowding took place in the middle pens. That was where the "sink" hit. The aristocrat rats at the ends grew bigger, sleeker, healthier, and more secure the whole time.

In The Sink, meanwhile, nest building, courting, sex behavior, reproduction, social organization, health—all of it went to pieces. Normally, Norway rats have a mating ritual in which the male chases the female, the female ducks down into a burrow and sticks her head up to watch the male. He performs a little dance outside the burrow, then she comes out, and he mounts her, usually for a few seconds. When The Sink set in, however, no more than three males—the dominant males in the middle sections—

kept up the old customs. The rest tried everything from satyrism to homo-sexuality or else gave up on sex altogether. Some of the subordinate males spent all their time chasing females. Three or four might chase one female at the same time, and instead of stopping at the burrow entrance for the ritual, they would charge right in.

Homosexuality rose sharply. So did bisexuality. Some males would mount anything—males, females, babies, senescent rats, anything. Still other males dropped sexual activity altogether, wouldn't fight and, in fact, would hardly move except when the other rats slept. Occasionally a female from the aristocrat rats' harems would come over the ramps and into the middle sections to sample life in The Sink. When she had had enough, she would run back up the ramp. Sink males would give chase up to the top of the ramp, which is to say, to the very edge of the aristocratic preserve. But one glance from one of the king rats would stop them cold and they would return to The Sink.

The slumming females from the harems had their adventures and then returned to a placid, healthy life. Females in The Sink, however, were ravaged, physically and psychologically. Pregnant rats had trouble contin-uing pregnancy. The rate of miscarriages increased significantly, and females started dying from tumors and other disorders of the mammary glands, sex organs, uterus, ovaries, and Fallopian tubes. Typically, their kidneys, livers, and adrenals were also enlarged or diseased or showed other signs associated with stress. Child-rearing became totally disorga-nized. The females lost the interest or the stamina to build nests and did not keep them up if they did build them. In the general filth and confusion, they would not put themselves out to save offspring they were momen-tarily separated from. Frantic, even sadistic competition among the males was going on all around them and rendering their lives chaotic. The males began unprovoked and senseless assaults upon one another, often in the form of tail-biting. Ordinarily, rats will suppress this kind of behavior when it crops up. In The Sink, male rats gave up all policing and just looked out for themselves. The "pecking order" among males in The Sink was never stable. Normally, male rats set up a three-class structure. Under the pressure of overcrowding, however, they broke up into all sorts of unstable subclasses, cliques, packs—and constantly pushed, probed, explored, tested one another's power. Anyone was fair game, except for the aristo-crats in the end pens.

Calhoun kept the population down to eighty, so that the next stage, "population collapse" or "massive die-off," did not occur. But the autop-sies showed that the pattern—as in the diseases among the female rats—was already there.

The classic study of die-off was John J. Christian's study of Sika deer on James Island in the Chesapeake Bay, west of Cambridge, Maryland. Four or five of the deer had been released on the island, which was 280 acres and uninhabited, in 1916. By 1955 they had bred freely into a herd of 280 to 300. The population density was only about one deer per acre at this point, but Christian knew that this was already too high for the Sikas' inborn space requirements, and something would give before long. For two years the number of deer remained 280 to 300. But suddenly, in 1958, over half the deer died; 161 carcasses were recovered. In 1959 more deer died and the population steadied at about 80.

In two years, two-thirds of the herd had died. Why? It was not starvation. In fact, all the deer collected were in excellent condition, with well-developed muscles, shining coats, and fat deposits between the muscles. In practically all the deer, however, the adrenal glands had enlarged by 50 percent. Christian concluded that the die-off was due to "shock following severe metabolic disturbance, probably as a result of prolonged adrenocortical hyperactivity. . . . There was no evidence of infection, starvation, or other obvious cause to explain the mass mortality." In other words, the constant stress of overpopulation, plus the normal stress of the cold of the winter, had kept the adrenalin flowing so constantly in the deer that their systems were depleted of blood sugar and they died of shock.

Well, the white humans are still skidding and darting across the floor of Grand Central. Dr. Hall listens a moment longer to the skidding and the darting noises, and then says, "You know, I've been on commuter trains here after everyone has been through one of these rushes, and I'll tell you, there is enough acid flowing in the stomachs in every car to dissolve the rails underneath."

Just a little invisible acid bath for the linings to round off the day. The ulcers the acids cause, of course, are the one disease people have already been taught to associate with the stress of city life. But overcrowding, as Dr. Hall sees it, raises a lot more hell with the body than just ulcers. In everyday life in New York—just the usual, getting to work, working in massively congested areas like 42nd Street between Fifth Avenue and Lexington, especially now that the Pan-Am Building is set in there, working in cubicles such as those in the editorial offices at Time-Life, Inc., which Dr. Hall cites as typical of New York's poor handling of space, working in cubicles with low ceilings and, often, no access to a window, while construction crews all over Manhattan drive everybody up the Masonite wall with air-pressure generators with noises up to the boil-a-brain decibel levels, then rushing to get home, piling into subways and trains, fighting for time and for space, the usual day in New York—the whole now-normal thing keeps shooting jolts of adrenalin into the body, breaking down the body's defenses and winding up with the work-a-daddy human animal stroked out at the breakfast table with his head apoplexed like a cauliflower out of his $6.95 semispread Pima-cotton shirt, and nosed over into a plate of No-Kloresto egg substitute, signing off with the black thrombosis, cancer, kidney, liver, or stomach failure, and the adrenals ooze to a halt, the size of eggplants in July.

18.   VALENCE: O Rotten Gotham

One of the people whose work Dr. Hall is interested in on this score is
Rene Dubos at the Rockefeller Institute. Dubos's work indicates that specific organisms, such as the tuberculosis bacillus or a pneumonia virus, can
seldom be considered "the cause" of a disease. The germ or virus, apparently, has to work in combination with other things that have already
broken the body down in some way—such as the old adrenal hyperactivity. Dr. Hall would like to see some autopsy studies made to record the
size of adrenal glands in New York, especially of people crowded into
slums and people who go through the full rush-hour-work-rush-hour
cycle every day. He is afraid that until there is some clinical, statistical data
on how overcrowding actually ravages the human body, no one will be
willing to do anything about it. Even in so obvious a thing as air pollution,
the pattern is familiar. Until people can actually see the smoke or smell the
sulphur or feel the sting in their eyes, politicians will not get excited about
it, even though it is well known that many of the lethal substances pollut-
ing the air are invisible and odorless. For one thing, most politicians are
like the aristocrat rats. They are insulated from The Sink by practically
sultanic buffers—limousines, chauffeurs, secretaries, aides-de-camp, door-
men, shuttered houses, high-floor apartments. They almost never ride
subways, fight rush hours, much less live in the slums or work in the
Pan-Am Building.

We took a cab from Grand Central to go up to Harlem, and by 48th
Street we were already socked into one of those great, total traffic jams on
First Avenue on Friday afternoon. Dr. Hall motions for me to survey the
scene, and there they all are, humans, male and female, behind the glass
of their automobile windows, soundlessly going through the torture of
their own adrenalin jolts. This male over here contracts his jaw muscles so
hard that they bunch up into a great cheese Danish pattern. He twists his
lips, he bleeds from the eyeballs, he shouts . . . soundlessly behind
glass . . . the fat corrugates on the back of his neck, his whole body shakes
as he pounds the heel of his hand into the steering wheel. The female
human in the car ahead of him whips her head around, she bares her teeth,
she screams . . . soundlessly behind glass . . . she throws her hands up in
the air, Whaddya expect me—Yah, yuh stupid—and they all sit there,
trapped in their own congestion, bleeding hate all over each other, shorting
out the ganglia and—goddam it—

Dr. Hall sits back and watches it all. This is it! The Sink! And where is
everybody's wandering boy?

Dr. Hall says, "We need a study in which drivers who go through these
rush hours every day would wear GSR bands."

GSR?

"Galvanic skin response. It measures the electric potential of the skin,
which is a function of sweating. If a person gets highly nervous, his plams
begin to sweat. It is an index of tension. There are some other fairly simple

251

devices that would record respiration and pulse. I think everybody who goes through this kind of experience all the time should take his own pulse —not literally—but just be aware of what's happening to him. You can usually tell when stress is beginning to get you physically."

In testing people crowded into New York's slums, Dr. Hall would like to take it one step further—gather information on the plasma hydrocortisone level in the blood or the corticosteroids in the urine. Both have been demonstrated to be reliable indicators of stress, and testing procedures are simple.

The slums—we finally made it up to East Harlem. We drove into 101st Street, and there was a new, avant-garde little church building, the Church of the Epiphany, which Dr. Hall liked—and, next to it, a pile of rubble where a row of buildings had been torn down, and from the back windows of the tenements beyond several people were busy "airmailing," throwing garbage out the window, into the rubble, beer cans, red shreds, the No-Money-Down Eames roller stand for a TV set, all flying through the air onto the scaggy sump. We drove around some more in Harlem, and a sequence was repeated, trash, buildings falling down, buildings torn down, rubble, scaggy sumps or, suddenly, a cluster of high-rise apartment projects, with fences around the grass.

"You know what this city looks like?" Dr. Hall said. "It looks bombed out. I used to live at Broadway and 124th Street back in 1946 when I was studying at Columbia. I can't tell you how much Harlem has changed in twenty years. It looks bombed out. It's broken down. People who live in New York get used to it and don't realize how filthy the city has become. The whole thing is typical of a behavioral sink. So is something like the Kitty Genovese case—a girl raped and murdered in the courtyard of an apartment complex and forty or fifty people look on from their apartments and nobody even calls the police. That kind of apathy and anomie is typical of the general psychological deterioration of The Sink."

He looked at the high-rise housing projects and found them mainly testimony to how little planners know about humans' basic animal requirements for space.

"Even on the simplest terms," he said, "it is pointless to build one of these blocks much over five stories high. Suppose a family lives on the fifteenth floor. The mother will be completely cut off from her children if they are playing down below, because the elevators are constantly broken in these projects, and it often takes half an hour, literally half an hour, to get the elevator if it is running. That's very common. A mother in that situation is just as much a victim of overcrowding as if she were back in the tenement block. Some Negro leaders have a bitter joke about how the white man is solving the slum problem by stacking Negroes up vertically, and there is a lot to that."

For one thing, says Dr. Hall, planners have no idea of the different space requirements of people from different cultures, such as Negroes and Puerto

18.   VALENCE: O Rotten Gotham

Ricans. They are all treated as if they were minute, compact middle-class whites. As with the Sika deer, who are overcrowded at one per acre, overcrowding is a relative thing for the human animal, as well. Each species has its own feeling for space. The feeling may be "subjective," but it is quite real.

Dr. Hall's theories on space and territory are based on the same information, gathered by biologists, ethologists, and anthropologists, chiefly, as Robert Ardrey's. Ardrey has written two well-publicized books, *African Genesis* and *The Territorial Imperative*. *Life* magazine ran big excerpts from *The Territorial Imperative*, all about how the drive to acquire territory and property and add to it and achieve status is built into all animals, including man, over thousands of centuries of genetic history, etc., and is a more powerful drive than sex. *Life's* big display prompted Marshall McLuhan to crack, "They see this as a great historic justification for free enterprise and Republicanism. If the birds do it and the stickleback crabs do it, then it's right for man." To people like Hall and McLuhan, and Ardrey, for that matter, the right or wrong of it is irrelevant. The only thing they find inexcusable is the kind of thinking, by influential people, that isn't even aware of all this. Such as the thinking of most city planners.

"The planners always show you a bird's-eye view of what they are doing," he said. "You've seen those scale models. Everyone stands around the table and looks down and says that's great. It never occurs to anyone that they are taking a bird's-eye view. In the end, these projects do turn out fine, when viewed from an airplane."

As an anthropologist, Dr. Hall has to shake his head every time he hears planners talking about fully integrated housing projects for the year 1980 or 1990, as if by then all cultural groups will have the same feeling for space and will live placidly side by side, happy as the happy burghers who plan all the good clean bird's-eye views. According to his findings, the very fact that every cultural group does have its own peculiar, unspoken feeling for space is what is responsible for much of the uneasiness one group feels around the other.

It is like the North European and the Mediterranean in the subway line. The North European, without ever realizing it, tries to keep a bubble of space around himself, and the moment a stranger invades that sphere, he feels threatened. Mediterranean peoples tend to come from cultures where everyone is much more involved physically, publicly, with one another on a day-to-day basis and feels no uneasiness about mixing it up in public, but may have very different ideas about space inside the home. Even Negroes brought up in America have a different vocabulary of space and gesture from the North European Americans who, historically, have been their models, according to Dr. Hall. The failure of Negroes and whites to communicate well often boils down to things like this: some white will be interviewing a Negro for a job; the Negro's culture has taught him to show somebody you are interested by looking right at him and listening intently to what he has to say. But the species North European requires something more. He expects his listener to nod from time to time, as if to say, "Yes, keep going." If he doesn't get this nodding, he feels anxious, for fear the listener doesn't agree with him or has switched off. The Negro may learn that the white expects this sort of thing, but he isn't used to the precise kind of nodding that is customary, and so he may start overresponding, nodding like mad, and at this point the North European is liable to think he has some kind of stupid Uncle Tom on his hands, and the guy still doesn't get the job.

The whole handling of space in New York is so chaotic, says Dr. Hall, that even middle-class housing now seems to be based on the bird's-eye models for slum projects. He took a look at the big Park West Village development, set up originally to provide housing in Manhattan for families in the middle-income range, and found its handling of space very much like a slum project with slightly larger balconies. He felt the time has come to start subsidizing the middle class in New York on its own terms—namely, the kind of truly "human" spaces that still remain in brownstones.

"I think New York City should seriously consider a program of encouraging the middle-class development of an area like Chelsea, which is already starting to come up. People are beginning to renovate houses there on their own, and I think if the city would subsidize that sort of thing with tax reliefs and so forth, you would be amazed at what would result. What New York needs is a string of minor successes in the housing field, just to show everyone that it can be done, and I think the middle class can still do that for you. The alternative is to keep on doing what you're doing now, trying to lift a very large lower class up by main force almost and finding it a very slow and discouraging process."

"But before deciding how to redesign space in New York," he said, "people must first simply realize how severe the problem already is. And the handwriting is already on the wall."

"A study published in 1962," he said, "surveyed a representative sample of people living in New York slums and found only 18 percent of them free from emotional symptoms. Thirty-eight percent were in need of psychiatric help, and 23 percent were seriously disturbed or incapacitated. Now, this study was published in 1962, which means the work probably went on from 1955 to 1960. There is no telling how bad it is now. In a behavioral sink, crises can develop rapidly."

Dr. Hall would like to see a large-scale study similar to that undertaken by two sociopsychologists, Chombart de Lauwe and his wife, in a French working-class town. They found a direct relationship between crowding and general breakdown. In families where people were crowded into the apartment so that there was less than 86 to 108 square feet per person, social and physical disorders doubled. That would mean that for four people the smallest floor space they could tolerate would be an apartment, say, 12 by 30 feet.

18. VALENCE: O Rotten Gotham

What would one find in Harlem? "It is fairly obvious," Dr. Hall wrote in *The Hidden Dimension*, "that the American Negroes and people of Spanish culture who are flocking to our cities are being very seriously stressed. Not only are they in a setting that does not fit them, but they have passed the limits of their own tolerance of stress. The United States is faced with the fact that two of its creative and sensitive peoples are in the process of being destroyed and like Samson could bring down the structure that houses us all."

Dr. Hall goes out to the airport, to go back to Chicago, and I am coming back in a cab, along the East River Drive. It is four in the afternoon, but already the damned drive is clogging up. There is a 1959 Oldsmobile just to the right of me. There are about eight people in there, a lot of popeyed silhouettes against a leopard-skin dashboard, leopard-skin seats—and the driver is classic. He has a mustache, sideburns down to his jaw socket, and a tattoo on his forearm like a Rossetti painting of Jane Burden Morris with her hair long. All right; it is even touching, like a postcard photo of the main drag in San Pedro, California. But suddenly Sideburns guns it and cuts in front of my cab so that my driver has to hit the brakes, and then hardly 100 feet ahead Sideburns hits a wall of traffic himself and has to hit his brakes, and then it happens. A stuffed white Angora animal, a dog, no, it's a Pekingese cat, is mounted in his rear window—as soon as he hits the brakes its *eyes* light up Nighttown pink. To keep from ramming him, my driver has to hit the brakes again, too, and so here I am, out in an insane, jammed-up expressway at four in the afternoon shuddering to a stop while a stuffed Pekingese grows bigger and bigger and brighter in the eyeballs directly in front of me. Jolt! Nighttown pink! Hey—that's me the adrenalin is hitting, *I* am this white human sitting in a projectile heading amid a mass of clotted humans toward a white Angora stuffed goddam leopard-dash Pekingese freaking cat—kill that damned Angora—Jolt!— got me—another micrometer on the old adrenals—

19.
VALENCE:
Behavioral Research and
Environmental Programming
ROBERT SOMMER

One of the pioneers in the current research into the ecological relationship between people and their spatial environment is Robert Sommer. Here, Sommer takes a sober look at some of the realities that must be dealt with in further research in this field.

To a greater extent than perhaps any other nation, we Americans have become an "indoor" people. A large portion of our lives—working, sleeping, playing—is spent in buildings: buildings over whose design and construction we have little or no control; buildings whose physical and economic distribution are only remotely conditioned by our needs; buildings whose effect upon our health and happiness is only obscurely understood.

J. M. Fitch, American Building

As a psychologist in the design fields, I write articles on hospital design for hospital administrators, on outdoor study spaces for landscape designers, on classroom seating for teachers and principals, and so on. I am less interested in the specific substance of my results, since I lack the time, facilities, and commitment to do a really extensive study of any single setting, than in demonstrating the relevance of behavior research to practitioners. The goal is to stimulate individuals in the field to undertake this research themselves. When someone comes into a situation, does research, and then leaves, barely a ripple of change appears. It is better to get the people involved in the situation to conduct the research themselves, even if the research is of inferior quality. This is one lesson of the Peace Corps experience. Although it is easier for the corpsmen to build a well or a school themselves than to get the local people to do it, if they do it

Robert Sommer, *Personal Space: The Behavioral Basis of Design,* © 1969, pp. 155–172. Reprinted by permission of Prentice-Hall, Inc., Englewood Cliffs, New Jersey.

19. VALENCE: Environmental Programming

themselves and leave, the situation would revert to the *status quo* quickly. Not until practitioners in the design fields and space managers become concerned with how their buildings affect people are we going to have some meaningful changes taking place. When a designer or user participates in evaluation research, the situation is no longer one of an outsider coming in, telling him in a foreign language how to run his business, and leaving on the next plane.

An occupational hazard of environmental consulting is that the client receives the impression that all problems can be solved by pushing through a wall or rearranging the chairs. Things just are not that simple. Any change in the physical or organizational structure of a hospital, office, or household will require some rearrangement of other items, but there is no guarantee that any single change will produce the desired results. Frequently it is the fact of change itself that is important—shaking things up or "making it hot for them," to use Terry Southern's phrase.

More than anything else, the interest shown by management in environmental change conveys to others that experiment and innovation are encouraged and will be supported. Such changes within an organization tend to be infectious. Department heads feel that they cannot sit still when others are experimenting with new procedures and programs. A new car on the block creates some dissatisfaction among neighbors on all sides. When one man redecorates his office, others will follow. So much is written about the deterioration of environment, that we tend to overlook people's desires for beauty and harmony. A single renovation or beautification program accomplishes more by creating an awareness of the possibilities of change than as a statistical increment of beauty in a desolate or ugly world.

The contributions of social scientists to design fields are going to change over the years. Right now they will be most useful in teaching designers how to evaluate existing structures and in participating in such evaluations as a member of a research team. This means going out into windowless schools and offices, low income housing projects, and adventure playgrounds to see how the people are using the facilities and what they think of them. This will provide a good body of case studies of individual design solutions. If there is great consistency in the way that people react to certain design features or a larger architectural element, some generalization may be possible.

Considered from the standpoint of a single building, evaluation research is not very practical since the findings will come too late to be of use to the clients. However, if we are dealing with a building system that will expand and change over time, then this criticism becomes invalid. A 300-bed hospital may not be constructed all at one time but rather in three increments of 100 beds each. This will make it possible to include the results from behavioral studies of the first wing into the planning and design of the second and third wings. Such a procedure was followed by

257

VI. The Discovery of Elbow Room

Wheeler in his collaboration with an architectural firm designing college dormitories for several Indiana campuses. From the study of the first unit they derived information that modified the plans for the subsequent dormitories. The first dormitory lounge was a large open area, the usual sort of status space that impresses parents and visitors but provides limited privacy for the residents. In the second residence hall a two-level plan reduced complaints substantially. The formal lounge was divided into four areas by means of a central chimney; activity areas were located on a mezzanine.[1]

Where circumstances permit, the research team can conduct experiments within the setting. In view of the amount of money involved in large-scale renovation, these will probably be rather modest ventures. Time will also be a limitation since a structure or area should be observed over a period of years rather than weeks. In terms of priorities, it would seem that collecting the observational and survey data from existing settings would have the greatest immediate payoff.

Given our present state of ignorance, I have serious misgivings about social scientists becoming involved in the actual design of buildings. When an architect comes to me with plans for a conference room or college dormitory, I can only make the wildest guesses as to how these are going to work in practice—unless of course they are so obvious that any observer could make the same predictions. I have no special competence in predicting how customers will react to an open-plan bank or a round auditorium. All I can say is: "If you are interested in knowing about open-plan banks, build one and let me observe it, or hire me to visit open-plan banks and a few closed-plan structures for comparison purposes." Even when I advise about a building type I know well—college dormitories—I feel compelled to preface it this way: "Although we found these opinions held at 20 dormitories in California, your situation in Salt Lake City or Toronto may be different, so borrow carefully from our findings."

I feel that at this point in time, social scientists can be most useful in evaluating existing structures. It is premature to involve them in the design process unless they have had prior experience with a building type or will have sufficient time to acquire relevant data. It would be regrettable if social scientists were brought into architectural firms as status symbols, for their great potential contributions as data gatherers will be lost if they become merely sources of ancedote, myth, and analogy.

The need for translating scientific findings into a form usable by practitioners exists in almost every field. Few engineers can read physics journals and few medical men can read journals of biochemistry. It would be a waste of time for architects to keep abreast of journals in psychology or sociology; few social scientists are able to do this either. The one relevant

[1]Lawrence Wheeler, *Behavioral Research for Architectural Planning and Design* (Terre Haute, Indiana: Ewing Miller, Associates, 1967).

19. VALENCE: Environmental Programming

article in a hundred would have an ambiguous title: "The Effects of Proximity on Clique Structure," or "Luminosity and Color Perception." Furthermore, the practical implications of relevant findings are not always apparent. It has been shown that there are more friendships in dormitories with common washrooms than in those with private washrooms, but what does this mean to an architect who wants to design for privacy as well as for friendliness? For almost every item in a building program there is the qualification that too much of a good thing is undesirable.

The delay in using social science data in the design fields is a product of several factors. There is, for one thing, the reluctance of designers to replace their reliance on intuition, artistry, and perceptual values such as harmony, integrity, and cohesion with the jargon of a new group of self-proclaimed experts. The coalescing of individuals and professions with diverse training, viewpoint, and perceptual style requires the time for each group to become accustomed to each other and this can only occur in a nonthreatening situation. Case studies of design solutions such as buildings or parks cannot be undertaken with an attitude of finding out what is wrong with the place. This is particularly true when it comes to publishing the results of such studies. Fortunately there is some precedent in biomedical research where case studies are published without the names of the individuals. A physician describes twenty cases of sleeping sickness, the first is a woman age 54 with two children, the second a man age 38, unmarried, and so on; a public health team describes the locale of its study as "A small Kansas town of 1500 people, primarily a marketing and commercial center for the surrounding agriculture area." Community surveys typically employ pseudonyms (Middletown or Prairieville) or a general statement about "three suburban communities on the east coast." Economists and others studying business organizations do not identify a company by name in published articles. Many precedents exist for evaluating schools, office buildings, and housing projects without mentioning the individuals or companies involved and thus avoiding *ad hominem* arguments or the creation of a form of negative awards system.

Also needed is a middleman who is acquainted with the design fields as well as with the social sciences to translate relevant behavioral data into terms meaningful to designers. Thomas Seabrook advocates the category of planner-sociologist in the city planning field.[2] Such a person would translate behavioral theories and facts into the range of tolerance with which the physical planner can cope. Seabrook asks of what relevance is it to know that poorer families are less mobile, more neighborhood oriented, and depend to a greater degree on their neighbors for psychological support? If one can penetrate the jargon, these data are more interesting than helpful to planners. Someone has to tease out their design implica-

[2]Thomas G. Seabrook, "The Role of the Sociologist in the Planning Professions," *Habitat* (March–April 1965), pp. 20–24.

tions by asking the right questions. Does the shortage of money mean that the children and parents will spend more time in the park? Does the increased leisure of the upper middle class mean a greater need for outdoor recreational spaces? Do older people and retired individuals have special needs for benches, shaded areas, and access to restroom facilities that are not included in standard park designs?

The behavioral scientist differs from the subject-matter specialist in that he is an expert on methods for obtaining information and may know little, at least at the outset, about particular settings. Let us consider the design of a library for a NASA academy. It would be desirable for the planning board to bring in a library consultant, probably a trained librarian interested and experienced in library construction, someone who is knowledgeable about the history of the field, present developments, and where things are heading. The money invested in experienced library consultants will be returned many times over in the improved efficiency of the building and actual cost savings on specific items. However, the needs of a particular agency in a specific situation are unique, so it would be hazardous to rely solely on subject-matter knowledge in designing for specific clients. What are the special needs of NASA people? What provisions can be made for storing classified materials so they can be retrieved easily? An architect can learn much from visiting libraries at West Point and the Air Force Academy as well as from talking with librarians at regional NASA sites. To tie all this material together as well as to obtain information on the specific work habits and needs of NASA personnel may take more time and effort than the architect is willing to invest. It would be wasteful to use library consultants as data gatherers, people who go out and interview NASA personnel at various sites, although this practice has been followed. A more reasonable procedure would involve delegating the task of learning the opinions and work habits of the building's prospective residents to some person trained in the social sciences. He would introduce a different perspective, the viewpoint of someone who has assisted with environmental programming in a variety of settings. Called in by NASA, he may know nothing about military librarianship—his last job might have been with a community redevelopment agency trying to unslum a salvageable district and, before that, with a state agency drawing up specifications for playgrounds. This work has taught him how to find the needs of clients and express them in such a way that they are meaningful to designers. It is the architect who translates the building program into sketches and the sketches into a three-dimensional form, but it is the behavioral scientist who feeds information into the system about the needs of the specific people involved, just as the subject-matter expert feeds in information about like buildings elsewhere and new developments in the field.

Designers need concepts that are relevant to both physical form and human behavior. Much of architecture affects people from beyond the focus of awareness. People are not sure what it is about a building or room that affects them, nor are they able to express how they feel in different surroundings. Norbitt Mintz interviewed a large number of students in three sorts of rooms—one very attractive with modern decor, the second a room of average appearance, and the third an ugly room resembling a janitor's closet in a sad state of disrepair with an exposed light bulb, torn shade, and a tin can serving as a receptacle for cigarette ashes. When he questioned the students afterwards, he found that only 29 per cent mentioned anything about the appearance of the rooms, 46 per cent mentioned that something seemed wrong in the experiment but could not say what it was, and 25 per cent reported that the experiment was "fine."[3]

Not only do people have difficulty expressing what they feel about architecture, but most of their reactions to a division of space is on an emotional rather than a rational level. This is especially true in regard to the division of space within a house rather than the shell or enclosure. Architects rely on language even though it is apparent that words may mean different things to an architect than to a client. The way an architect uses the word "cell" to describe an office may disturb a corporation executive who associates the term with prisons.

In their studies of highway experience, Donald Appleyard and his associates believed that their first task was to develop techniques for recording, analyzing, and communicating the visual and kinesthetic sequences of highway travel. Without such techniques, it is difficult to express or refine design alternatives short of building full-scale roads. Sensing the inadequacies of photographic recording for detailed analysis of visual experience, they have developed an intriguing system analogous to the music notations used by composers in which the road becomes a spatial and kinesthetic rhythmic experience—a symphony.[4] Recently there have been attempts to develop techniques for studying the subjective connotations of structures as well as their objective dimensions. One such technique is the semantic differential developed by Charles Osgood at the University of Illinois in which concepts are rated along various scales, good to bad, strong to weak, active to passive, and so forth.[5] The same object may have vastly different connotations to different people—a hammer is a toy to a child and a tool to his father; a slum neighborhood can mean security and warmth to a child growing up there and a social problem to a city planner. One study was aimed specifically at exploring how arthitects use the concept of space. Architects speak of "interesting spaces" and "vital spaces," but laymen use the term to refer to a void or absence of something. Architecture students saw space as more valuable, active, and more potent

[3]Norbitt Mintz, "Effects of Aesthetic Surroundings," *Journal of Psychology,* XLI (1956), 459–66.

[4]Donald Appleyard, Kevin Lynch, and J. R. Myer, *The View from the Road* (Cambridge, Mass.: M.I.T. Press, 1964).

[5]Charles E. Osgood, G. Suci, and P. Tannenbaum, *The Measurement of Meaning* (Urbana: University of Illinois Press, 1957).

than did the liberal arts students.[6] Such techniques can help us to clarify and to understand people's reactions to their surroundings. Most present architectural criticism has been written by highly literate and sensitive individuals who visit buildings for short periods and whose reactions may be unrepresentative of the building's inhabitants. Another solution is to increase the sensitivity and correct the visual and emotional blindness of people so that they can present their needs and feelings in a form that others can understand and appreciate. This may require considerable effort, and the task is being made more difficult by electronic technology, which leaves little room for human experience and meaningful social intercourse.

Methods for Gathering Data

Laboratory experiments have generally yielded discouraging results when it comes to evaluating environmental effects on human performance. There are extremes of heat, cold, and humidity that have an obvious effect on behavior, but these are rarely the concern of designers interested in the normal range of sensory stimulation. Edward Thorndike conducted an elaborate series of tests for the New York State Commission on Ventilation on the efficiency of student performance under various conditions of temperature, humidity, and air movement. The tasks included laboratory exercises in naming colors and canceling digits as well as school exercises in arithmetic, English composition, and typing. Environmental conditions ranged from those that, at the time, were considered optimal (68 degrees, 50 per cent relative humidity, and 45 feet per person per minute of outside air) to those that were regarded as very unfavorable (86 degrees, 80 per cent relative humidity, and no circulation or change of air). The authors concluded:

> With the forms of work and lengths of period used, we find that when an individual is urged to do his best he does as much, and does it as well, and improves as rapidly in a hot, humid, sterile, and stagnant air condition as in an optimum condition. . . . We find further that when an individual is given work to do that is of no interest or value to him and is deprived even of the means of telling how well he does it, and is in other ways tempted to relax standards and do work of poor quality, he still shows no inferiority in the quality of the product. . . . Finally we find that when an individual is left to his own choice as to whether he shall do mental work or read stories, rest, talk, or sleep, he does as much work per hour when the temperature is 75 degrees as when it is 68 degrees.[7]

[6]Robert Sommer, "The Significance of Space," *AIA Journal* (May 1965), pp. 63–65.
[7]Edward L. Thorndike, W. A. McCall, and J. C. Chapman, "Ventilation in Relation to Mental Work," *Teachers College Contributions to Education,* LXXVIII (1916), 82.

19. VALENCE: Environmental Programming

Productivity in the laboratory tends to remain constant regardless of environment. When conditions are unfavorable, the subject works harder to compensate for his handicaps. Many effects of a noxious environment are insidious and reveal themselves over the long run rather than immediately. On the other hand, it is true that symphonies have been created in basements, inventions made in garages, and masterpieces painted in unheated garrets. Whether these heroes are able to triumph because of the challenge of adversity or in spite of it is only part of the answer. We must also know how the vast majority of ordinary mortals perform in different environments. I can read a novel (but not a technical book) with the phonograph playing, but someone else will react differently.

If a ten-year-old child in New York can survive the crowding, noise, crime, and litter, it is unlikely that rearranging the chairs in his classroom will have a significant effect on how much he learns if he wants to. A small desk or obnoxious roommate in a college dormitory is not going to lower a student's grades if he can go elsewhere to study. It will change his behavior, increasing the amount of study outside the room, but this is not a "hard performance variable" like grade point average. At Rensselaer Polytechnic Institute an experimental classroom has been developed whose lighting, colored surfaces, seating types, and projection display surfaces can all be altered systematically. After several years of research, the authors admit that the question "How well does this environment perform in supporting learning?" has not been answered.[8]

Let me pose a conundrum that I think will elucidate some of the important but hidden issues in the criterion problem.

> We have two chairs in a classroom, Type A and Type B, and whenever a student is given a choice, he sits in Type A. The result is that Type A chairs are occupied first and Type B remain empty when there are surplus chairs in the room. However, when there are only as many chairs as there are pupils, or students must sit in assigned places without regard to chair type, we find no difference in examination scores between students sitting in A and B chairs.

What does this mean? Does the lack of difference in examination scores mean that a school board can purchase either chair or the cheaper of the two in good conscience, that is, with the realization that the amount of learning taking place will be unaffected by their decision? I do not accept this view, and I will try to explain why. For one thing, it overlooks the totalitarian nature of institutional experience. If a house builder constructs two models, A and B, and nobody buys B, the question of whether he builds both A and B is academic. In the free market situation, he does not build anything that people will not buy. However, a school, library, or

---

[8]A. Green, "Architectural Research and the Learning Environment" (Paper presented at the Second National Conference on Architectural Psychology, Park City, Utah, 1966).

hospital board, corporation committee, or any other institutional client does not have to worry about the vagaries of the market place. If they construct small classrooms, two-man offices, and four-bed hospital rooms, they will be used and, in terms of performance criteria, probably will be just as effective as single rooms or three-man rooms. Institutional arrangements place people in situations they would not otherwise choose. We can cut the Gordian knot by making the realization of individual choice and satisfaction as values in their own right. If people say they like something or show by their behavior that they prefer it, this should be a value fed into the design process even though it cannot be proven that this makes a difference on a profit-and-loss statement or an academic record. Many performance criteria deal with only a single aspect of a multigoal organization. The encouragement of academic achievement is one objective of a good classroom teacher, but she also strives for personal growth, maturity, and self-direction on the part of her pupils. I am not saying that performance criteria such as profit-and-loss, days-in-hospital, or grades should be discarded. When a measure fits only a single dimension of a situation, the solution is not to reject all measurement, but to develop measures for the other aspects. Single item evaluation tends to encourage *criterion-directed performance,* which neglects important but unmeasured aspects of program success.

In a changing world it seems reasonable to establish *variety* and *flexibility* as important goals in a building program. I do not propose substituting them for harmony, unity, balance, rhythm, excitement, or the other traditional design values. Both variety and flexibility inherently increase the range of individual choice. A necessary corollary of these two values is that we must establish institutional arrangements—rules, procedures, and personnel practices—that enable individuals to exploit the variety and possibilities for flexibility in their environment. By *variety* I mean a multiplicity of settings and spaces a person can select to suit his individual needs. On my campus there is a policy regarding dormitory construction that no new residence hall complex should be identical with an existing one. The goal is to increase the range of choices available to students at the beginning of the term. The same principle can be applied to other design elements; rather than installing benches of one kind or size in parks and recreation areas, it is preferable to vary one's purchases and arrangements. *Flexibility* is expressed in such terms as multipurpose, multiuse, and convertible spaces. With rapidly changing technology and the inability to predict institutional practices even five years ahead, its importance seems obvious. It is closely tied in with *personalization* since it permits a man to adapt a setting to his unique needs.

The Hawthorne Myth

Perhaps the least understood and most maligned study in the history of the social sciences was the research into worker productivity conducted at

19. VALENCE: Environmental Programming

Western Electric Company. Many people have heard of the *Hawthorne effect* or the way that production rose as working conditions improved.[9] However, when some of the changes were reversed, production continued to rise. This has been interpreted to mean that environment did not make any difference, it was all a placebo effect—like getting a reaction to a sugar pill. However, what the Western Electric study showed conclusively was that environment did make a difference. Almost every change in environmental conditions had its effect on the workers and, often, on their production. The study also demonstrated that there is no simple relationship between single environmental elements and complex human behavior. The effects of environmental changes are mediated by individual needs and group processes. The worker does not react to improved lighting or a coffee break as the rat does to the lever in his cage that brings him a food pellet. In an atmosphere of trust and understanding, he accepts environmental changes as indications that management is interested in his welfare. In an atmosphere of distrust and hostility, he wonders how management hopes to exploit him by changing his working conditions; he looks upon environmental programming as manipulation. Behavior produced by a sugar pill is just as real and observable as behavior produced by amphetamine. Just as some people are made sleepy by pep pills and the magnitude of their reaction is influenced by the presence or absence of other people, so changes in man's internal environment are not simple conditioned reflexes in which A automatically produces B.

Studies of schools, hospitals, prisons, and slums have shown that it is nearly impossible to isolate the specific factors responsible for a given outcome. Neither can we tell precisely why one city can support a major league team and another cannot, or why Topeka, Kansas, became a world-renowned center of psychiatry, but Wichita, which is a much larger city, did not, or why one town can pass a large school bond issue that is defeated in an adjacent city. There is no single factor that can explain any of these phenomena. Frequently it appears that the reason is connected with the town's self-image as a sports capital or a cultural center or a good business town. The citizens then support the programs that fit the town's image. San Franciscans believe themselves to be cosmopolitan and are therefore willing to tolerate toplessness and gay bars; the citizens of Green Bay accept with joy or resignation the annual fall football madness. An image that is believed becomes a self-fulfilling prophecy. The image of a city as a bad business town can doom that city, and the stereotype of a neighborhood as good or bad will raise or lower real estate values. Any attempt to trace the origin of these beliefs will produce a score of causal agents, major as well as minor. The mechanisms involved in this process are similar to the Hawthorne effect. People who are concerned with solutions to particular

[9]F. J. Roethlisberger and W. J. Dickson, *Management and the Worker* (Cambridge, Mass.: Harvard University Press, 1939).

problems are less concerned with how something works than the fact that it works. A recent review of programs for geriatric patients includes these comments: "... whether by a Hawthorne effect or by the specific action of the milieu program on the staff or patients, most of these programs have succeeded in raising the functioning level of their recipients in a measurable manner,"[10] and "Almost any type of facility works with older brain-damaged patients. The main thing is stimulation from the environment and, of course, a radical change in attitude on the part of personnel."

The methods of the biological sciences, particularly animal biology and ecology, which rely heavily upon observation and field experimentation over long periods, seem more applicable to the design fields than the single variable laboratory experiments characteristic of physics and chemistry. A designer would profit more from training in the techniques of systematic observation than in the empty rituals included under the category of experimental design. It is extremely difficult if not impossible to execute a rigorous experiment that deals with important relationships under natural conditions. Experiments in the field are replete with unanticipated variables and *post hoc* explanations. It is unlikely that the use of laboratory models in teaching students will increase the number of field experiments or improve their quality, since the techniques necessary to undertake a good field study differ radically from those of a laboratory. For one thing the field investigator must be extremely sensitive to the structure of the environment, the important processes that are taking place, the people with whom he works, the administrative procedures that must be followed. . . . Administrative arrangements [can take] more time and effort than the research itself. A study in a public school requires the permission of individual teachers, the school principal and his assistants, the local school board, the county superintendent of schools and his assistants, as well as the approval and cooperation of students and parents. If any single step is omitted and some key person is not consulted, the affair can turn into a debacle. A recent article describes a study that had been cleared with all the important names on the official school hierarchy, but the investigator forgot to contact several assistants to key people (one was out of town during the orientation session, and the other was away on a two-year leave), and, to the investigator's dismay, these assistants were the ones responsible for interpreting headquarters' policy to individual schools. Field studies are not for the soft-hearted or the administratively ignorant; they are far more complex from the standpoint of human relationships and sensitivity to social structure than laboratory studies. Occasionally an investigator finds a situation where a high-ranking official in a large operation becomes interested in behavioral studies and gives them his enthusiastic support. This was the case in the studies by Wells of the new office building of the Cooperative Insurance Company in Manchester.[11]

[10]M. Powell Lawton, "Planning a Building for the Mentally Impaired Aged," mimeo., 1965.

19. VALENCE: Environmental Programming

It would have been impossible to undertake individual interviews and systematic observational studies without management's full cooperation. One cannot undertake creative environmental experimentation without the support and interest of those who are administratively responsible for the environment.

None of these methods can be applied arbitrarily. One has to learn when, where, and how to gain information. This requires a feeling for the nature of the setting and the people in it. One does not use a printed questionnaire with migrant workers, geriatric patients, or ghetto children. On the other hand, the questionnaire is a most efficient and appropriate tool for college students accustomed to written examinations and who may indeed be troubled by a personal interview that requires direct confrontation with an older person—a novel experience for many of them! With children I would choose direct observation in situations where many options are available, supplemented by interviews (both individual and group) after the observations had continued for some time. With migrant workers the use of participant observation would seem appropriate provided the researcher spoke the workers' language. Thus far we have said little about participant observation where the observer shares the daily lives of the people under study, observing things that happen, listening to what is said, and questioning people over some length of time. The method produces data that are often strikingly different from those obtained through interview or casual observation methods. A designer or some member of his staff might live in a migrant workers' camp or accompany hospital attendants through their daily routine for a few days. As an insider he sees, hears, smells, and feels things to which the general public or infrequent visitors are not privy. Spending time in a setting allows him to gain the confidence and learn the private language of the participants. He is able to question people about matters that he has observed directly (the toilet facilities in the camp or the temperature in the building on an extremely hot day) rather than employ abstract questions about heating, lighting, and ventilation. Becker and Geer believe that participant observation is most useful when a situation or institution is in a state of change. Living and working in the situation will assist the researcher in distinguishing between reactions to the present situation, memories of the past, and hopes for the future.[12]

The expense of building mock-ups and the need to evaluate building systems before they are opened to the public has created an interest in various simulation techniques ranging from wide-screen photography in assessing reactions to the cityscape to hypnosis. Aaronson has been using hypnotic induction to learn the effects of color and sound on mood, the way a person behaves when the world is lacking in depth, or when he is

[11]Brian W. P. Wells, "The Psycho-Social Influence of Building Environment," *Building Science,* I (1965), 153–65.
[12]Howard S. Becker and Blanche Geer, "Participant Observation and Interviewing: A Comparison," *Human Organization,* XVI (1957), 28–32.

four feet tall. All these conditions exert a powerful influence on the way a person perceives and behaves. When the hypnotic suggestion was made to a subject that he had diminished in size, he responded by seeing everything as if it were twice as far away as usual. Events and objects took on a dreamlike character and things seemed to be moving faster than they were. He became withdrawn and apathetic and felt isolated, sleepy, and without interest. When the hypnotic set of his diminished size was removed, he felt pleased and seemed normal except for his feeling that everything looked smaller. He described the world as toylike and was much impressed with how much prettier and daintier everybody and everything looked.[13]

There is no single best method—questionnaire, interview, simulation, or experiment—for studying man's adaptations to his environment. One chooses methods to suit the problem and the people and not vice versa. These methods are generally complementary rather than mutually exclusive. One would not only interview office workers and managers, he might also work alongside them at a desk for a few weeks, observe who drinks coffee with whom and to which desk people go when they want to borrow things, and he might also examine various artifacts such as interoffice mail envelopes, which would show communication patterns within the office.

There are important ethical questions about the user's role and participation in environmental experimentation. The whole matter of experimentation with human subjects is receiving long-needed critical attention from medical and behavioral researchers as well as lawyers and legislators. The need for strict surveillance in cases involving radiation hazards and pesticides is clear enough. The situation becomes murky in cases of sonic booms and crowded beaches, annoyances rather than dangers. Most of the building evaluation work discussed [does] not involve serious risks to anyone's health or livelihood. However, one can still imagine a lawsuit brought by a parent who maintained that his son failed in school because he had been placed in a six-man dormitory room to fit an experimental plan devised by college authorities to evaluate the effects of room size upon study habits. To determine the justification of his complaint, one would have to know whether the student or his parents had protested his being assigned to a six-man room, whether there was a decline in his school work that seemed related to his study situation, and whether the college authorities had made some attempt to ensure that participants in the study would not suffer as a result of the room assignments. I do not feel it is immoral to assign students to facilities that are presently being used on hundreds of campuses in order to learn how they work in practice. On the contrary, it seems immoral to build and use dormitories without making some systematic attempt to evaluate their effectiveness.

[13]Bernard S. Aaronson, "Lilliput and Brobdignag—Self and World," *American Journal of Clinical Hypnosis*, X (1968), 160–66.

19. VALENCE: Environmental Programming

Administrative practices and informal understandings within an organization imprint themselves upon people until they accept them without question. The evidence from perceptual experiments is consistent in finding that familiarity does not breed contempt, but rather increased liking. This can be seen as an adaptive reaction in the human organism to permit it to adjust to a multitude of conditions. Not only will people adapt to crowding, noise, and traffic in the city, they will find it difficult to live in any other environment. Zajonc and Harrison have studied the connection between exposure and preference. In one study people were shown a series of photographs of faces—some faces were exposed once, some twice, some ten times, some 25 times. Afterwards it was found that the more a face had been shown to a person, the more he liked it. The same result was obtained when Chinese characters were used as stimuli. The more a Chinese character was exposed, the more likely did people feel that it stood for an attractive word or something they would like.[14]

Studies like this can tell us something about the dynamics of habituation and environmental preference. There are many other perceptual experiments dealing with illusions[15] and the effects of human needs on perception[16] that are relevant to spatial behavior. However it is important that architects guard themselves against *perceptual reductionism*. This attitude has all the weaknesses of the biological reductionism of Ardrey[17] and others who see in man's spatial behavior the clear expression of instinctual drives. On a technical level, the distinction here is one of analogy and homology. Behavior that is similar in appearance between species may be triggered by entirely different mechanisms. A person's behavior is affected by how he perceives the world as well as his biological makeup but both are overlaid and shaped through learning. Environmental adaptations are too complex and multidetermined to be reduced either to instincts or perceptual laws.

Finally we come to the question of applying the results of these studies. Any building must meet the diverse needs of occupants whose interests frequently conflict. A wife's need for cooking space will compete with TV space and play area for the children. A public building that serves numerous client groups will have an even larger number of competing demands made upon it. One cannot design a college dormitory solely for individual privacy since this is also the student's main social area. A store must serve

[14]Robert B. Zajonc, "The Attitudinal Effects of Mere Exposure," *Journal of Personality and Social Psychology*, monograph supplement, IX (1968), 1–27. Also see A. A. Harrison, "Response Competition and Attitude Change as a Function of Repeated Stimulus Exposure" (Ph.D. thesis, University of Michigan, 1967).

[15]A. Ames, "Visual Perception and the Rotating Trapezoidal Window," *Psychological Monographs*, No. 324 (1951).

[16]Charles M. Solley and Gardner Murphy, *Development of the Perceptual World* (New York: Basic Books, Inc., Publishers, 1960).

[17]Robert Ardrey, *The Territorial Imperative* (New York: Atheneum Publishers, 1966).

the needs of shoppers, clerks, and store detectives. Some engineers and scientists have tried to sidestep this problem by substituting harmony, coherence, or efficiency as the ultimate criterion of a design solution. A recent review states:

> Man is the most unreliable part of the man-machine-environment complex with which the system engineer deals. For the time being, he is tolerated in the system because he is either cheaper or has some skill which no machine has. Eventually he will be displaced by a more reliable component. This will not be so bad so long as some people remain in the system, but at last the day will come when even the system engineer will be replaced by a superior robot designer. At that stage, society will have developed a set of design values to replace the more old-fashioned and inefficient human values.[18]

One can design a system in which machines work efficiently to serve other machines, prisons that serve the short-term interests of people outside, and universities that serve the needs of researchers rather than students. One outcome is as feasible as any other. A design problem is a value problem: whose interests are to be served.

It is difficult for the ordinary citizen to get a handle on the larger environmental problems of pollution, pesticides, and congestion where the causes are complex, relationships between cause and effort obscure, effects insidious, and cures expensive. Most of the time we are spectators at a grand tragedy wondering if we can last through the final act. The minor spaces around us, our bedrooms, offices, schools, and streets bring problems of another, more manageable magnitude. A man's office can be a stimulating, esthetically pleasing, and highly personal place, or it can be a cold, impersonal, and bureaucratic area that belongs to the company through its surrogates, the custodians. A conference room can bring people together or it can prevent them from hearing and seeing one another, diminish their interest in the proceedings, and create cliques. Privacy for Americans is mainly a matter of visual protection against other people, but open plan housing is moving in the opposite direction. The bank manager may tell a customer that they cannot be overheard as they talk in the center of a large office, but the customer will not feel comfortable, nor will the manager believe that the space is really his unless he can personalize it in some way. The myth of infinite plasticity must be discarded in the design of minor spaces, too. The price paid in adapting to uncongenial environments may be difficult to estimate in money, sickness, inefficiency, and turnover, but it is too high if we can design congenial environments for the same money or less. There is a lesson to be learned when executives put calendars and charts on the backs of glass doors, college students choose old barracks over modern dormitories, and Sylvia Ashton-Warner, the talented teacher of Maori children, prefers her dilapidated prefab to the

[18]Luigi Petrullo, review of *The New Utopians,* in *Contemporary Psychology,* XII (1967), 165.

19. VALENCE: Environmental Programming

elegant glass castle where the teachers are concerned with proper coat-hooks and preventing the chairs from scraping the new floor. People like spaces they can call their own and make over; they reject an alien environment that is built according to detailed square footage allocations for a standard model of impersonal humanity in the most durable and antiseptic condition. The man of tomorrow whose capacity to respond to the environment is reduced, may be excused from this lesson, but we are not.

The situation in the agricultural fields is instructive. Engineers and agricultural economists believe that if the production of a crop cannot be mechanized, the crop will eventually disappear. Since ordinary tomatoes cannot withstand the rough treatment of mechanical harvesting in which the fruit is shaken from the vine and placed in large bins, a new breed of tomato has been developed. It has a tough skin, and the fruit ripens at the same time so a machine can make a single run through a field. Experiments are underway to give a cube shape so it can be stored easily. "Tomatoes" are being harvested mechanically but they are a different fruit from the ones we have known. "Man" of the future, barring a nuclear holocaust, will adapt to hydrocarbons in the air, detergents in the water, crime in the streets, and crowded recreational areas. Good design becomes a meaningless tautology if we consider that man will be reshaped to fit whatever environment he creates. The long-range question is not so much what sort of environment we want, but what sort of man we want.

20.
VISION:
Living Space

ISAAC ASIMOV

The idea of the territorial imperative, as advocated by Desmond Morris, Konrad Lorenz, and Robert Ardrey, can be seen with a new twist in the science-fiction work entitled "Living Space" by Isaac Asimov.

Clarence Rimbro had no objections to living in the only house on an uninhabited planet, any more than had any other of Earth's even trillion of inhabitants.

If someone had questioned him concerning possible objections, he would undoubtedly have stared blankly at the questioner. His house was much larger than any house could possibly be on Earth proper and much more modern. It had its independent air supply and water supply, ample food in its freezing compartments. It was isolated from the lifeless planet on which it was located by a force field, but the rooms were built about a five-acre farm (under glass, of course), which, in the planet's beneficent sunlight, grew flowers for pleasure and vegetables for health. It even supported a few chickens. It gave Mrs. Rimbro something to do with herself afternoons, and a place for the two little Rimbros to play when they were tired of indoors.

Furthermore, if one *wanted* to be on Earth proper; if one insisted on it; if one *had* to have people around and air one could breathe in the open or water to swim in, one had only to go out of the front door of the house.

So where was the difficulty?

Remember, too, that on the lifeless planet on which the Rimbro house was located there was complete silence except for the occasional monotonous effects of wind and rain. There was absolute privacy and the feeling

20. VISION: Living Space

of absolute ownership of two hundred million square miles of planetary surface.

Clarence Rimbro appreciated all that in his distant way. He was an accountant, skilled in handling very advanced computer models, precise in his manners and clothing, not much given to smiling beneath his thin, well-kept mustache and properly aware of his own worth. When he drove from work toward home, he passed the occasional dwelling place on Earth proper and he never ceased to stare at them with a certain smugness.

Well, either for business reasons or mental perversion, some people simply had to live on Earth proper. It was too bad for them. After all, Earth proper's soil had to supply the minerals and basic food supply for all the trillion of inhabitants (in fifty years, it would be two trillion) and space was at a premium. Houses on Earth proper just *couldn't* be any bigger than that, and people who had to live in them had to adjust to the fact.

Even the process of entering his house had its mild pleasantness. He would enter the community twist place to which he was assigned (it looked, as did all such, like a rather stumpy obelisk), and there he would invariably find others waiting to use it. Still more would arrive before he reached the head of the line. It was a sociable time.

"How's your planet?" "How's yours?" The usual small talk. Sometimes someone would be having trouble. Machinery breakdowns or serious weather that would alter the terrain unfavorably. Not often.

But it passed the time. Then Rimbro would be at the head of the line; he would put his key into the slot; the proper combination would be punched; and he would be twisted into a new probability pattern; his own particular probability pattern; the one assigned to him when he married and became a producing citizen; a probability pattern in which life had never developed on Earth. And twisting to this particular lifeless Earth, he would walk into his own foyer.

Just like that.

He never worried about being in another probability. Why should he? He never gave it any thought. There were an infinite number of possible Earths. Each existed in its own niche; its own probability pattern. Since on a planet such as Earth there was, according to calculation, about a fifty-fifty chance of life's developing, half of all the possible Earths (still infinite, since half of infinity was infinity) possessed life, and half (still infinite) did not. And living on about three hundred billion of the unoccupied Earths were three hundred billion families, each with its own beautiful house, powered by the sun of that probability, and each securely at peace. The number of Earths so occupied grew by millions each day.

And then one day, Rimbro came home and Sandra (his wife) said to him, as he entered, "There's been the most peculiar noise."

Rimbro's eyebrows shot up and he looked closely at his wife. Except for a certain restlessness of her thin hands and a pale look about the corners of her tight mouth, she looked normal.

VI. The Discovery of Elbow Room

Rimbro said, still holding his topcoat halfway toward the servette that waited patiently for it, "Noise? What noise? I don't hear anything."

"It's stopped now," Sandra said. "Really, it was like a deep thumping or rumble. You'd hear it a bit. Then it would stop. Then you'd hear it a bit and so on. I've never heard anything like it."

Rimbro surrendered his coat. "But that's quite impossible."

"I *heard* it."

"I'll look over the machinery," he mumbled. "Something may be wrong."

Nothing was, that his accountant's eyes could discover, and, with a shrug, he went to supper. He listened to the servettes hum busily about their different chores, watched one sweep up the plates and cutlery for disposal and recovery, then said, pursing his lips, "Maybe one of the servettes is out of order. I'll check them."

"It wasn't anything like that, Clarence."

Rimbro went to bed, without further concern over the matter, and wakened with his wife's hand clutching his shoulder. His hand went automatically to the contact patch that set the walls glowing. "What's the matter? What time is it?"

She shook her head. "Listen! *Listen!*"

Good Lord, thought Rimbro, there *is* a noise. A definite rumbling. It came and went.

"Earthquake?" he whispered. It did happen, of course, though, with all the planet to choose from, they could generally count on having avoided the faulted areas.

"All day long?" asked Sandra fretfully. "I think it's something else." And then she voiced the secret terror of every nervous householder. "I think there's someone on the planet with us. This Earth is *inhabited.*"

Rimbro did the logical things. When morning came, he took his wife and children to his wife's mother. He himself took a day off and hurried to the Sector's Housing Bureau.

He was quite annoyed at all this.

Bill Ching of the Housing Bureau was short, jovial and proud of his part Mongolian ancestry. He thought probability patterns had solved every last one of humanity's problems. Alec Mishnoff, also of the Housing Bureau, thought probability patterns were a snare into which humanity had been hopelessly tempted. He had originally majored in archeology and had studied a variety of antiquarian subjects with which his delicately poised head was still crammed. His face managed to look sensitive despite overbearing eyebrows, and he lived with a pet notion that so far he had dared tell no one, though preoccupation with it had driven him out of archeology and into housing.

Ching was fond of saying, "The hell with Malthus!" It was almost a

20. VISION: Living Space

verbal trademark of his. "The hell with Malthus. We can't possibly over-populate now. However frequently we double and redouble, Homo sapiens remains finite in number, and the uninhabited Earths remain infinite. And we don't have to put one house on each planet. We can put a hundred, a thousand, a million. Plenty of room and plenty of power from each probability sun."

"More than one on a planet?" said Mishnoff sourly.

Ching knew exactly what he meant. When probability patterns had first been put to use, sole ownership of a planet had been powerful inducement for early settlers. It appealed to the snob and despot in every one. What man so poor, ran the slogan, as not to have an empire larger than Genghis Khan's? To introduce multiple settling now would outrage everyone.

Ching said, with a shrug, "All right, it would take psychological preparation. So what? That's what it took to start the whole deal in the first place."

"And food?" asked Mishnoff.

"You know we're putting hydroponic works and yeast plants in other probability patterns. And if we had to, we could cultivate their soil."

"Wearing space suits and importing oxygen."

"We could reduce carbon dioxide for oxygen till the plants got going and they'd do the job after that."

"Given a million years."

"Mishnoff, the trouble with you," Ching said, "is you read too many ancient history books. You're an obstructionist."

But Ching was too good-natured really to mean that, and Mishnoff continued to read books and to worry. Mishnoff longed for the day he could get up the courage necessary to see the Head of the Section and put right out in plain view—bang, like that—exactly what it was that was troubling him.

But now, a Mr. Clarence Rimbro faced them, perspiring slightly and toweringly angry at the fact that it had taken him the better part of two days to reach this far into the Bureau.

He reached his exposition's climax by saying, "And *I* say the planet is inhabited and I don't propose to stand for it."

Having listened to his story in full, Ching tried the soothing approach. He said, "Noise like that is probably just some natural phenomenon."

"What kind of natural phenomenon?" demanded Rimbro. "I want an investigation. If it's a natural phenomenon, I want to know what kind. I say the place is inhabited. It has life on it, by Heaven, and I'm not paying rent on a planet to share it. And with dinosaurs, from the sound of it."

"Come, Mr. Rimbro, how long have you lived on your Earth?"

"Fifteen and a half years."

"And has there ever been any evidence of life?"

"There is now, and, as a citizen with a production record classified as A-1, I demand an investigation."

VI. The Discovery of Elbow Room

"Of course we'll investigate, sir, but we just want to assure you now that everything is all right. Do you realize how carefully we select our probability patterns?"

"I'm an accountant. I have a pretty good idea," said Rimbro at once.

"Then surely you know our computers cannot fail us. They never pick a probability which has been picked before. They can't possibly. And they're geared to select only probability patterns in which Earth has a carbon dioxide atmosphere, one in which plant life, and therefore animal life, has never developed. Because if plants had evolved, the carbon dioxide would have been reduced to oxygen. Do you understand?"

"I understand it all very well and I'm not here for lectures," said Rimbro. "I want an investigation out of you and nothing else. It is quite humiliating to think I may be sharing my world, my own world, with something or other, and I don't propose to endure it."

"No, of course not," muttered Ching, avoiding Mishnoff's sardonic glance. "We'll be there before night."

They were on their way to the twisting place with full equipment.

Mishnoff said, "I want to ask you something. Why do you go through that 'There's no need to worry, sir' routine? They always worry anyway. Where does it get you?"

"I've got to try. They *shouldn't* worry," said Ching petulantly. "Ever hear of a carbon dioxide planet that *was* inhabited? Besides, Rimbro is the type that starts rumors. I can spot them. By the time he's through, if he's encouraged, he'll say his sun went nova."

"*That* happens sometimes," said Mishnoff.

"So? One house is wiped out and one family dies. See, you're an obstructionist. In the old times, the times you like, if there were a flood in China or someplace, thousands of people would die. And that's out of a population of a measly billion or two."

Mishnoff muttered, "How do you know the Rimbro planet doesn't have life on it?"

"Carbon dioxide atmosphere."

"But suppose—" It was no use. Mishnoff couldn't say it. He finished lamely, "Suppose plant and animal life develops that can live on carbon dioxide."

"It's never been observed."

"In an infinite number of worlds, anything can happen." He finished that in a whisper. "Everything *must* happen."

"Chances are one in a duodecillion," said Ching, shrugging.

They arrived at the twisting point then, and, having utilized the freight twist for their vehicle (thus sending it into the Rimbro storage area), they entered the Rimbro probability pattern themselves. First Ching, then Mishnoff.

20. VISION: Living Space

"A nice house," said Ching, with satisfaction. "Very nice model. Good taste."

"Hear anything?" asked Mishnoff.

"No."

Ching wandered into the garden. "Hey," he yelled. "Rhode Island Reds."

Mishnoff followed, looking up at the glass roof. The sun looked like the sun of a trillion other Earths.

He said absently, "There could be plant life, just starting out. The carbon dioxide might just be starting to drop in concentration. The computer would never know."

"And it would take millions of years for animal life to begin and millions more for it to come out of the sea."

"It doesn't have to follow that pattern."

Ching put an arm about his partner's shoulder. "You brood. Someday, you'll tell me what's really bothering you, instead of just hinting, and we can straighten you out."

Mishnoff shrugged off the encircling arm with an annoyed frown. Ching's tolerance was always hard to bear. He began, "Let's not psychotherapize—" He broke off, then whispered, "Listen."

There was a distant rumble. Again.

They placed the seismograph in the center of the room and activated the force field that penetrated downward and bound it rigidly to bedrock. They watched the quivering needle record the shocks.

Mishnoff said, "Surface waves only. Very superficial. It's not underground."

Ching looked a little more dismal, "What is it then?"

"I think," said Mishnoff, "we'd better find out." His face was gray with apprehension. "We'll have to set up a seismograph at another point and get a fix on the focus of the disturbance."

"Obviously," said Ching. "I'll go out with the other seismograph. You stay here."

"No," said Mishnoff, with energy, "I'll go out."

Mishnoff felt terrified, but he had no choice. If this were *it,* he would be prepared. He could get a warning through. Sending out an unsuspecting Ching would be disastrous. Nor could he warn Ching, who would certainly never believe him.

But since Mishnoff was not cast in the heroic mold, he trembled as he got into his oxygen suit and fumbled the disrupter as he tried to dissolve the force field locally in order to free the emergency exit.

"Any reason *you* want to go, particularly?" asked Ching, watching the other's inept manipulations. "I'm willing."

"It's all right. I'm going out," said Mishnoff, out of a dry throat, and stepped into a lock that led out onto the desolate surface of a lifeless Earth. A presumably lifeless Earth.

VI.   The Discovery of Elbow Room

The sight was not unfamiliar to Mishnoff. He had seen its like dozens of times. Bare rock, weathered by wind and rain, crusted and powdered with sand in the gullies; a small and noisy brook beating itself against its stony course. All brown and gray; no sign of green. No sound of life.

Yet the sun was the same and, when night fell, the constellations would be the same.

The situation of the dwelling place was in that region which on Earth proper would be called Labrador. (It was Labrador here, too, really. It had been calculated that in not more than one out of a quadrillion or so Earths were there significant changes in the geological development. The continents were everywhere recognizable down to quite small details.)

Despite the situation and the time of the year, which was October, the temperature was sticky warm due to the hothouse effect of the carbon dioxide in this Earth's dead atmosphere.

From inside his suit, through the transparent visor, Mishnoff watched it all somberly. If the epicenter of the noise were close by, adjusting the second seismograph a mile or so away would be enough for the fix. If it weren't, they would have to bring in an air scooter. Well, assume the lesser complication to begin with.

Methodically, he made his way up a rocky hillside. Once at the top, he could choose his spot.

Once at the top, puffing and feeling the heat most unpleasantly, he found he didn't have to.

His heart was pounding so that he could scarcely hear his own voice as he yelled into his radio mouthpiece, "Hey, Ching, there's construction going on."

"What?" came back the appalled shout in his ears.

There was no mistake. Ground was being leveled. Machinery was at work. Rock was being blasted out.

Mishnoff shouted, "They're blasting. That's the noise."

Ching called back, "But it's impossible. The computer would never pick the same probability pattern twice. *It couldn't.*"

"You don't understand—" began Mishnoff.

But Ching was following his own thought processes. "Get over there, Mishnoff. I'm coming out, too."

"No, damn it. You stay there," cried Mishnoff in alarm. "Keep me in radio contact, and for God's sake be ready to leave for Earth proper on wings if I give the word."

"Why?" demanded Ching. "What's going on?"

"I don't know yet," said Mishnoff. "Give me a chance to find out."

To his own surprise, he noticed his teeth were chattering.

Muttering breathless curses at the computer, at probability patterns and at the insatiable need for living space on the part of a trillion human beings expanding in numbers like a puff of smoke, Mishnoff slithered and slipped down the other side of the slope, setting stones to rolling and rousing peculiar echoes.

20. VISION: Living Space

A man came out to meet him, dressed in a gas-tight suit, different in many details from Mishnoff's own, but obviously intended for the same purpose—to lead oxygen to the lungs.

Mishnoff gasped breathlessly into his mouthpiece, "Hold it, Ching. There's a man coming. Keep in touch." Mishnoff felt his heart pump more easily and the bellows of his lungs labor less.

The two men were staring at one another. The other man was blond and craggy of face. The look of surprise about him was too extreme to be feigned.

He said in a harsh voice, *"Wer sind Sie? Was machen Sie hier?"*

Mishnoff was thunderstruck. He'd studied ancient German for two years in the days when he expected to be an archeologist and he followed the comment despite the fact that the pronunciation was not what he had been taught. The stranger was asking his identity and his business there.

Stupidly, Mishnoff stammered, *"Sprechen Sie Deutsch?"* and then had to mutter reassurance to Ching whose agitated voice in his earpiece was demanding to know what the gibberish was all about.

The German-speaking one made no direct answer. He repeated, *"Wer sind Sie?"* and added impatiently, *"Hier ist für ein verrückten Spass keine Zeit."*

Mishnoff didn't feel like a joke either, particularly not a foolish one, but he continued, *"Sprechen Sie Planetisch?"*

He did not know the German for "Planetary Standard Language" so he had to guess. Too late, he thought he should have referred to it simply as English.

The other man stared wide-eyed at him. *"Sind Sie wahnsinnig?"*

Mishnoff was almost willing to settle for that, but in feeble self-defense, he said, "I'm not crazy, damn it. I mean, *"Auf der Erde woher Sie gekom—"*

He gave it up for lack of German, but the new idea that was rattling inside his skull would not quit its nagging. He had to find some way of testing it. He said desperately, *"Welches Jahr ist es jetzt?"*

Presumably, the stranger, who was questioning his sanity already, would be convinced of Mishnoff's insanity now that he was being asked what year it was, but it was one question for which Mishnoff had the necessary German.

The other muttered something that sounded suspiciously like good German swearing and then said, *"Es ist doch zwei tausend drei hundert vier-und-sechzig, und warum—"*

The stream of German that followed was completely incomprehensible to Mishnoff, but in any case he had had enough for the moment. If he translated the German correctly, the year given him was 2364, which was nearly two thousand years in the past. How could that be?

He muttered, *"Zwei tausend drei hundert vier-und-sechzig?"*

"Ja, Ja," said the other, with deep sarcasm. *"Zwei tausend drei hundert vier-und-sechzig. Der ganze Jahr lang ist es so gewesen."*

Mishnoff shrugged. The statement that it had been so all year long was a feeble witticism even in German and it gained nothing in translation. He pondered.

But then the other's ironical tone deepening, the German-speaking one went on, *"Zwei tausend drei hundert vier-und-sechzig nach Hitler. Hilft das Ihnen vielleicht? Nach Hitler!"*

Mishnoff yelled with delight. "That *does* help me. *Es hilft! Hören Sie, bitte*—" He went on in broken German interspersed with scraps of Planetary, "For Heaven's sake, *um Gottes willen*—"

Making it 2364 after Hitler was different altogether.

He put German together desperately, trying to explain.

The other frowned and grew thoughtful. He lifted his gloved hand to stroke his chin or make some equivalent gesture, hit the transparent visor that covered his face and left his hand there uselessly, while he thought.

He said, suddenly, *"Ich heiss George Fallenby."*

To Mishnoff it seemed that the name must be of Anglo-Saxon derivation, although the change in vowel form as pronounced by the other made it seem Teutonic.

"Guten Tag," said Mishnoff awkwardly. *"Ich heiss Alec Mishnoff,"* and was suddenly aware of the Slavic derivation of his own name.

"Kommen Sie mit mir, Herr Mishnoff," said Fallenby.

Mishnoff followed with a strained smile, muttering into his transmitter, "It's all right, Ching. It's all right."

Back on Earth proper, Mishnoff faced the Sector's Bureau Head, who had grown old in the Service; whose every gray hair betokened a problem met and solved; and every missing hair a problem averted. He was a cautious man with eyes still bright and teeth that were still his own. His name was Berg.

He shook his head. "And they speak German; but the German you studied was two thousand years old."

"True," said Mishnoff. "But the English Hemingway used is two thousand years old and Planetary is close enough for anyone to be able to read it."

"Hmp. And who's this Hitler?"

"He was a sort of tribal chief in ancient times. He led the German tribe in one of the wars of the twentieth century, just about the time the Atomic Age started and true history began."

"Before the Devastation, you mean?"

"Right. There was a series of wars then. The Anglo-Saxon countries won out, and I suppose that's why the Earth speaks Planetary."

"And if Hitler and his Germans had won out, the world would speak German instead?"

"They *have* won out on Fallenby's Earth, sir, and they *do* speak German."

"And make their dates 'after Hitler' instead of A.D.?"

20. VISION: Living Space

"Right. And I suppose there's an Earth in which the Slavic tribes won out and everyone speaks Russian."

"Somehow," said Berg, "it seems to me we should have foreseen it, and yet, as far as I know, no one has. After all, there is an infinite number of inhabited Earths, and we can't be the only one that has decided to solve the problem of unlimited population growth by expanding into the worlds of probability."

"Exactly," said Mishnoff earnestly, "and it seems to me that if you think of it, there must be countless inhabited Earths so doing and there must be many multiple occupations in the three hundred billion Earths we ourselves occupy. The only reason we caught this one is that, by sheer chance, they decided to build within a mile of the dwelling we had placed there. This is something we must check."

"You imply we ought to search all our Earths."

"I do, sir. We've got to make some settlement with other inhabited Earths. After all, there is room for all of us and to expand without agreement may result in all sorts of trouble and conflict."

"Yes," said Berg thoughtfully. "I agree with you."

Clarence Rimbro stared suspiciously at Berg's old face, creased now into all manner of benevolence.

"You're sure now?"

"Absolutely," said the Bureau Head. "We're sorry that you've had to accept temporary quarters for the last two weeks—"

"More like three."

"—three weeks, but you will be compensated."

"What was the noise?"

"Purely geological, sir. A rock was delicately balanced and, with the wind, it made occasional contact with the rocks of the hillside. We've removed it and surveyed the area to make certain that nothing similar will occur again."

Rimbro clutched his hat and said, "Well, thanks for your trouble."

"No thanks necessary, I assure you, Mr. Rimbro. This is our job."

Rimbro was ushered out, and Berg turned to Mishnoff, who had remained a quiet spectator of this completion of the Rimbro affair.

Berg said, "The Germans were nice about it, anyway. They admitted we had priority and got off. Room for everybody, they said. Of course, as it turned out, they build any number of dwellings on each unoccupied world. . . . And now there's the project of surveying our other worlds and making similar agreements with whomever we find. It's all strictly confidential, too. It can't be made known to the populace without plenty of preparation. . . . Still, none of this is what I want to speak to you about."

"Oh?" said Mishnoff. Developments had not noticeably cheered him. His own bogey still concerned him.

Berg smiled at the younger man. "You understand, Mishnoff, we in the

281

Bureau, and in the Planetary Government, too, are very appreciative of your quick thinking, of your understanding of the situation. This could have developed into something very tragic, had it not been for you. This appreciation will take some tangible form."

"Thank you, sir."

"But, as I said once before, this is something many of us should have thought of. How is it you did? . . . Now we've gone into your background a little. Your co-worker, Ching, tells us you have hinted in the past at some serious danger involved in our probability-pattern setup, and that you insisted on going out to meet the Germans although you were obviously frightened. You were anticipating what you actually found, were you not? And how did you do it?"

Mishnoff said confusedly, "No, no. That was not in my mind at all. It came as a surprise. I—"

Suddenly he stiffened. Why not now? They were grateful to him. He had proved that he was a man to be taken into account. One unexpected thing had already happened.

He said firmly, "There's something else."

"Yes?"

(How did one begin?) "There's no life in the Solar System other than the life on Earth."

"That's right," said Berg benevolently.

"And computation has it that the probability of developing any form of interstellar travel is so low as to be infinitesimal."

"What are you getting at?"

"That all this is so *in this probability!* But there must be some probability patterns in which other life *does* exist in the Solar System or in which interstellar drives *are* developed by dwellers in other star systems."

Berg frowned. "Theoretically."

"In one of these probabilities, Earth may be visited by such intelligences. If it were a probability pattern in which Earth is inhabited, it won't affect us; they'll have no connection with us in Earth proper. But if it were a probability pattern in which Earth is uninhabited and they set up some sort of a base, they may find, by happenstance, one of our dwelling places."

"Why ours?" demanded Berg dryly. "Why not a dwelling place of the Germans, for instance?"

"Because we spot our dwellings one to a world. The German Earth doesn't. Probably very few others do. The odds are in favor of us by billions to one. And if extraterrestrials do find such a dwelling, they'll investigate and find the route to Earth proper, a highly developed, rich world."

"Not if we turn off the twisting place," said Berg.

"Once they know that twisting places exist, they can construct their own," said Mishnoff. "A race intelligent enough to travel through space could do that, and from the equipment in the dwelling they would take over, they could easily spot our particular probability. . . . And then how would we handle extraterrestrials? They're not Germans, or other Earths. They would have alien psychologies and motivations. And we're not even on our guard. We just keep setting up more and more worlds and increasing the chance every day that—"

His voice had risen in excitement and Berg shouted at him, "Nonsense. This is all ridiculous—"

The buzzer sounded and the communiplate brightened and showed the face of Ching. Ching's voice said, "I'm sorry to interrupt, but—"

"What is it?" demanded Berg savagely.

"There's a man here I don't know what to do with. He's drunk or crazy. He complains that his home is surrounded and that there are things staring through the glass roof of his garden."

"Things?" cried Mishnoff.

"Purple things with big red veins, three eyes and some sort of tentacles instead of hair. They have—"

But Mishnoff and Berg didn't hear the rest. They were staring at each other in sick horror.

VII.
A New Look at Therapy and the Assessment of Personality

21.
VISION:
Selection from *Brave New World*
ALDOUS HUXLEY

*A number of contemporary psychologists have commented on the similarity
between the "encounter culture" and certain forms of religious expression. This
is the topic of the following selection from Aldous Huxley's* Brave New
World.

Alternate Thursdays were Bernard's Solidarity Service days. After an
early dinner at the Aphroditæum (to which Helmholtz had recently been
elected under Rule Two) he took leave of his friend and, hailing a taxi on
the roof, told the man to fly to the Fordson Community Singery. The
machine rose a couple of hundred metres, then headed eastwards, and as
it turned, there before Bernard's eyes, gigantically beautiful, was the Singery. Floodlighted, its three hundred and twenty metres of white Carrara-
surrogate gleamed with a snowy incandescence over Ludgate Hill; at each
of the four corners of its helicopter platform an immense T shone crimson
against the night, and from the mouths of twenty-four vast golden trumpets rumbled a solemn synthetic music.

"Damn, I'm late," Bernard said to himself as he first caught sight of Big
Henry, the Singery clock. And sure enough, as he was paying off his cab,
Big Henry sounded the hour. "Ford," sang out an immense bass voice from
all the golden trumpets. "Ford, Ford, Ford . . ." Nine times. Bernard ran for
the lift.

The great auditorium for Ford's Day celebrations and other massed
Community Sings was at the bottom of the building. Above it, a hundred
to each floor, were the seven thousand rooms used by Solidarity Groups
for their fortnight services. Bernard dropped down to floor thirty-three,

From pp. 92–101 in *Brave New World* by Aldous Huxley. Copyright, 1932, 1960 by Aldous
Huxley. By permission of Harper & Row, publishers, Inc.

21. VISION: Selection from *Brave New World*

hurried along the corridor, stood hesitating for a moment outside Room 3210, then, having wound himself up, opened the door and walked in.

Thank Ford! he was not the last. Three chairs of the twelve arranged round the circular table were still unoccupied. He slipped into the nearest of them as inconspicuously as he could and prepared to frown at the yet later comers whenever they should arrive.

Turning towards him, "What were you playing this afternoon?" the girl on his left enquired. "Obstacle, or Electro-magnetic?"

Bernard looked at her (Ford! it was Morgana Rothschild) and blushingly had to admit that he had been playing neither. Morgana stared at him with astonishment. There was an awkward silence.

Then pointedly she turned away and addressed herself to the more sporting man on her left.

"A good beginning for a Solidarity Service," thought Bernard miserably, and foresaw for himself yet another failure to achieve atonement. If only he had given himself time to look round instead of scuttling for the nearest chair! He could have sat between Fifi Bradlaugh and Joanna Diesel. Instead of which he had gone and blindly planted himself next to Morgana. *Morgana*! Ford! Those black eyebrows of hers—that eyebrow, rather—for they met above the nose. Ford! And on his right was Clara Deterding. True, Clara's eyebrows didn't meet. But she was really *too* pneumatic. Whereas Fifi and Joanna were absolutely right. Plump, blonde, not too large . . . And it was that great lout, Tom Kawaguchi, who now took the seat between them.

The last arrival was Sarojini Engels.

"You're late," said the President of the Group severely. "Don't let it happen again."

Sarojini apologized and slid into her place between Jim Bokanovsky and Herbert Bakunin. The group was now complete, the solidarity circle perfect and without flaw. Man, woman, man, in a ring of endless alternation round the table. Twelve of them ready to be made one, waiting to come together, to be fused, to lose their twelve separate identities in a larger being.

The President stood up, made the sign of the T and, switching on the synthetic music, let loose the soft indefatigable beating of drums and a choir of instruments—near-wind and super-string—that plangently repeated and repeated the brief and unescapably haunting melody of the first Solidarity Hymn. Again, again—and it was not the ear that heard the pulsing rhythm, it was the midriff; the wail and clang of those recurring harmonies haunted, not the mind, but the yearning bowels of compassion.

The President made another sign of the T and sat down. The service had begun. The dedicated *soma* tablets were placed in the centre of the table. The loving cup of strawberry ice-cream *soma* was passed from hand to hand and, with the formula, "I drink to my annihilation," twelve times quaffed. Then to the accompaniment of the synthetic orchestra the First Solidarity Hymn was sung.

> *Ford, we are twelve; oh, make us one,*
> *Like drops within the Social River;*
> *Oh, make us now together run*
> *As swiftly as thy shining Flivver.*

Twelve yearning stanzas. And then the loving cup was passed a second time. "I drink to the Greater Being" was now the formula. All drank. Tirelessly the music played. The drums beat. The crying and clashing of the harmonies were an obsession in the melted bowels. The Second Solidarity Hymn was sung.

> *Come, Greater Being, Social Friend,*
> *Annihilating Twelve-in-One!*
> *We long to die, for when we end,*
> *Our larger life has but begun.*

Again twelve stanzas. By this time the *soma* had begun to work. Eyes shone, cheeks were flushed, the inner light of universal benevolence broke out on every face in happy, friendly smiles. Even Bernard felt himself a little melted. When Morgana Rothschild turned and beamed at him, he did his best to beam back. But the eyebrow, that black two-in-one—alas, it was still there; he couldn't ignore it, couldn't, however hard he tried. The melting hadn't gone far enough. Perhaps if he had been sitting between Fifi and Joanna . . . For the third time the loving cup went around. "I drink to the imminence of His Coming," said Morgana Rothschild, whose turn it happened to be to initiate the circular rite. Her tone was loud, exultant. She drank and passed the cup to Bernard. "I drink to the imminence of His Coming," he repeated, with a sincere attempt to feel that the coming was imminent; but the eyebrow continued to haunt him, and the Coming, so far as he was concerned, was horribly remote. He drank and handed the cup to Clara Deterding. "It'll be a failure again," he said to himself. "I know it will." But he went on doing his best to beam.

The loving cup had made its circuit. Lifting his hand, the President gave a signal; the chorus broke out into the third Solidarity Hymn.

> *Feel how the Greater Being comes!*
> *Rejoice and, in rejoicing, die!*
> *Melt in the music of the drums!*
> *For I am you and you are I.*

As verse succeeded verse the voices thrilled with an ever intenser excitement. The sense of the Coming's imminence was like an electric tension in the air. The President switched off the music and, with the final note of the final stanza, there was absolute silence—the silence of stretched expectancy, quivering and creeping with a galvanic life. The President reached out his hand; and suddenly a Voice, a deep strong Voice, more musical than any merely human voice, richer, warmer, more vibrant with love and yearning and compassion, a wonderful, mysterious, supernatural Voice spoke from above their heads. Very slowly, "Oh, Ford, Ford, Ford," it said diminishingly and on a descending scale. A sensation of warmth radiated thrillingly out from the solar plexus to every extremity of the bodies of those who listened; tears came into their eyes; their hearts, their bowels seemed to move within them, as though with an independent life. "Ford!" they were melting, "Ford!" dissolved, dissolved. Then, in another tone, suddenly, startlingly. "Listen!" trumpeted the voice. "Listen!" They listened. After a pause, sunk to a whisper, but a whisper, somehow, more penetrating than the loudest cry. "The feet of the Greater Being," it went on, and repeated the words: "The feet of the Greater Being." The whisper almost expired. "The feet of the Greater Being are on the stairs." And once more there was silence; and the expectancy, momentarily relaxed, was stretched again, tauter, tauter, almost to the tearing point. The feet of the Greater Being—oh, they heard them, they heard them, coming softly down the stairs, coming nearer and nearer down the invisible stairs. The feet of the Greater Being. And suddenly the tearing point was reached. Her eyes staring, her lips parted, Morgana Rothschild sprang to her feet.

"I hear him," she cried. "I hear him."

"He's coming," shouted Sarojini Engels.

"Yes, he's coming, I hear him." Fifi Bradlaugh and Tom Kawaguchi rose simultaneously to their feet.

"Oh, oh, oh!" Joanna inarticulately testified.

"He's coming!" yelled Jim Bokanovsky.

The President leaned forward and, with a touch, released a delirium of cymbals and blown brass, a fever of tom-tomming.

"Oh, he's coming!" screamed Clara Deterding. "Aie!" and it was as though she were having her throat cut.

Feeling that it was time for him to do something, Bernard also jumped up and shouted: "I hear him; He's coming." But it wasn't true. He heard nothing and, for him, nobody was coming. Nobody—in spite of the music, in spite of the mounting excitement. But he waved his arms, he shouted with the best of them; and when the others began to jig and stamp and shuffle, he also jigged and shuffled.

Round they went, a circular procession of dancers, each with hands on the hips of the dancer preceding, round and round, shouting in unison, stamping to the rhythm of the music with their feet, beating it, beating it out with hands on the buttocks in front; twelve pairs of hands beating as one; as one, twelve buttocks slabbily resounding. Twelve as one, twelve as one. "I hear Him, I hear Him coming." The music quickened; faster beat the feet, faster, faster fell the rhythmic hands. And all at once a great synthetic bass boomed out the words which announced the approaching atonement and final consummation of solidarity, the coming of the Twelve-in-One, the incarnation of the Greater Being. "Orgy-Porgy," it sang, while the tom-toms continued to beat their feverish tattoo:

> Orgy-porgy, Ford and fun,
> Kiss the girls and make them One.
> Boys at one with girls at peace;
> Orgy-porgy gives release.

"Orgy-porgy," the dancers caught up the liturgical refrain, "Orgy-porgy, Ford and fun, kiss the girls . . ." And as they sang, the lights began slowly to fade—to fade and at the same time to grow warmer, richer, redder, until at last they were dancing in the crimson twilight of an Embryo Store. "Orgy-porgy . . ." In their blood-coloured and foetal darkness the dancers continued for a while to circulate, to beat and beat out the indefatigable rhythm. "Orgy-porgy . . ." Then the circle wavered, broke, fell in partial disintegration on the ring of couches which surrounded—circle enclosing circle—the table and its planetary chairs. "Orgy-porgy . . ." Tenderly the deep Voice crooned and cooed; in the red twilight it was as though some enormous negro dove were hovering benevolently over the now prone or supine dancers.

They were standing on the roof; Big Henry had just sung eleven. The night was calm and warm.

"Wasn't it wonderful?" said Fifi Bradlaugh. "Wasn't it simply wonderful?" She looked at Bernard with an expression of rapture, but of rapture in which there was no trace of agitation or excitement—for to be excited is still to be unsatisfied. Hers was the calm ecstasy of achieved consummation, the peace, not of mere vacant satiety and nothingness, but of balanced life, of energies at rest and in equilibrium. A rich and living peace. For the Solidarity Service had given as well as taken, drawn off only to replenish. She was full, she was made perfect, she was still more than merely herself. "Didn't you think it was wonderful?" she insisted, looking into Bernard's face with those supernaturally shining eyes.

"Yes, I thought it was wonderful," he lied and looked away; the sight of her transfigured face was at once an accusation and an ironical reminder of his own separateness. He was as miserably isolated now as he had been when the service began—more isolated by reason of his unreplenished emptiness, his dead satiety. Separate and unatoned, while the others were being fused into the Greater Being; alone even in Morgana's embrace—much more alone, indeed, more hopelessly himself than he had ever been in his life before. He had emerged from that crimson twilight into the common electric glare with a self-consciousness intensified to the pitch of

21. VISION: Selection from *Brave New World*

agony. He was utterly miserable, and perhaps (her shining eyes accused him), perhaps it was his own fault. "Quite wonderful," he repeated; but the only thing he could think of was Morgana's eyebrow.

22.
VALENCE:
All About the New Sex Therapy

Lest it be assumed that, in the preceding story, Aldous Huxley was preoccupied with sex as it influenced the course of therapy, the following article is preoccupied with therapy as it influences sexuality.

Call them Helen and Gordon West.* He is 45 and earns $75,000 a year as a New York advertising executive. They have been married twelve years, have three children and would seem to lead an ideal life. They have a spacious apartment on Manhattan's East Side, spend summers at their beach house on Long Island and make winter ski trips to exclusive resorts in Europe. But lately, the fun, the warmth and closeness have gone out of their lives—and they have come to a doctor to see what can be done about it.

Baldish and a little overweight, West slumps disconsolately in a chair, obviously depressed. He speaks in monosyllables in a flat, unemotional voice. His clothes are expensive but grayishly dull. Helen West, by contrast, wears a bit too much make-up, and a print dress that is a trifle too bright for the occasion. Throughout the interview, she chain-smokes and fidgets in her chair. With patience and great tact, the doctor gets the couple to talk about their problem. It's sex.

West was raised as a strict Roman Catholic. His wife comes from a family in which emotion was rarely expressed, and sex—when it came up at all—was treated as a not-very-necessary evil. Both were virgins on their wedding night. In the early years of their marriage, the Wests managed to overcome their inhibitions to some extent. West tended to be a premature

*Patients' names have been changed throughout.

From *Newsweek*, November 27, 1972. Copyright Newsweek, Inc. 1972, reprinted by permission.

ejaculator, but the couple settled into a relatively normal sex life. Two years ago, the premature ejaculation problem became worse. As his anxiety intensified, West became totally impotent. Inevitably, the marriage curdled. Helen feared that she had suddenly lost her allure; West worried that she might seek gratification from another man. Both studiously avoided the problem, and, eventually, each other. Helen plunged into charity and women's club work; West took to spending more of his evenings entertaining clients. But he soon realized that things really weren't going well at the office, either; it was almost impossible for him to make decisions and he began to have trouble getting along with his associates.

Then West read about the Human Sexuality Program at Manhattan's Mount Sinai Hospital and in desperation made an appointment with its director, Dr. Harold Lear. The doctor had a prescription for the Wests' problem. Basically, it was a series of exercises that would help the couple learn the art of giving and receiving sexual pleasure. "What I am doing," Lear explained, "is giving you a license to think and feel and be erotic." In just a month, West was able to have intercourse, and his wife was enjoying sex more than ever before.

The case of Helen and Gordon West is hardly unusual. Sexual problems of one kind or another afflict at least half the married couples in the U.S. today. The remarkable thing about the Wests is that they found a fast, specific and highly effective treatment that would not have been available just a year or two ago. In the past, husbands and wives had to take their marital troubles to a clergyman or family doctor who was usually ill-prepared to deal with sexual dysfunction. For those who could afford it, there was the expensive—and lengthy—option of psychotherapy. The situation changed dramatically two years ago, when Dr. William H. Masters and Virginia E. Johnson published "Human Sexual Inadequacy," a detailed description of their pioneering techniques for treating such widespread sexual disorders as impotence, frigidity and premature ejaculation.

Thanks to the Masters and Johnson approach, the sex clinic is fast becoming as vital a part of the modern hospital as the emergency room and the intensive-care unit. Masters and Johnson disciples trained at their Reproductive Biology Research Foundation in St. Louis, have established programs of their own in New York, Milwaukee, Washington, New Haven, Ann Arbor, Durham, N.C., and Chevy Chase, Md. Scores of physicians and psychiatrists throughout the U.S. have adopted the Masters and Johnson method in their practices—with impressive results. The approach has even spread abroad, with the establishment of sex clinics in such sophisticated cities as London, Geneva, Stockholm, Hamburg and Amsterdam.

Many of the clinics claim a remarkably high rate of success. Still, the new sex therapy has generated controversy aplenty. Some critics raise moral questions about the techniques employed by the sex therapist—especially the use of paid "surrogate" partners to help single men work out their sexual problems. Others question the psychological soundness of the new approach. Many psychiatrists are convinced that sex therapy is too simplistic, relieving symptoms but leaving their deep-seated neurotic underpinnings untouched. "Teaching 'push here' and 'rub there'," says New York analyst Natalie Shainess, "is not going to change people."

Mind and Body

Whatever the merits of the new style of therapy, there is no doubt that an increasing number of American couples are willing to confront sexual inadequacy in an unflinching way. With many conventional marriage counselors, men and women could talk endlessly around the central issue, placing the blame for their discord on anything from a wife's shopping bills to a husband's drinking problem. But with a sex therapist, no such evasions are possible—the troubled couple must engage the problem with their bodies as well as their minds. The two-to-four-month waiting lists at most sex clinics are ample proof that thousands of people are rapidly losing their reticence and are fully prepared to shed their inhibitions.

The sex clinics and the new sexual candor that brings them patients are two of the more worthwhile manifestations of the much-heralded American sexual revolution. "Problems are being faced and dealt with more explicitly and honestly than ever before," says Dr. Judd Marmor, a University of Southern California psychiatrist. "I don't think that there are more people with sexual problems than there were—they are just dealing with them now." The assault by American women on the remnants of the Victorian double standard is part of the new atmosphere. The pill and liberalized abortion laws have finally liberated women from the fear of unwanted pregnancy—allowing them for the first time to demand equal rights in sexual expression.

Indeed, some specialists theorize that the sexual liberation of women may be responsible for the increase in the number of men, especially younger ones, coming to therapists with impotence problems. Feminine pressure may not be causing the disorders, as these experts see it, but rather it may be forcing the non-performing man to face up to his inadequacy.

"A man who was impotent a generation ago simply ignored it," says Marmor. "Today, you can't get away with that." Guilt used to be a leading cause of impotence; in the era of sexual freedom, it is anxiety over performance.

Sexual candor aside, no one can say with much assurance how substantial other aspects of the sexual revolution may be. American popular culture is blatantly sex-saturated, but authorities differ—and research is sketchy—on whether American patterns of sexual behavior have changed as drastically as the Main Street movie marquees. The proliferation of books, movies and talk about sex has underscored the depth of the average American's anxiety and ignorance about sexual matters. The *Dayton* (Ohio) *Daily News* started a sex-information column last year, mainly to

294

answer teen-agers' questions about VD. But fully half of the inquiries the paper receives come from adults, asking for advice on how to improve their sex lives. Community Sex Information, a telephone counseling service that opened in New York 18 months ago, averages 200 calls a day. "You can almost feel the anxiety every time you pick up the phone," says Ann Welbourne, the 30-year-old psychologist in charge. "They ask: 'How can I last longer?' 'What about oral sex?' 'Am I OK?' 'Am I normal?' "

Hobbies and Cold Showers

Despite the new openness, the myths about sex that have prevailed for generations are dying hard. An unseemly number of Americans, the sex counselers report, still believe that penis size really matters, that masturbation causes physical and mental harm, that sex during menstruation or pregnancy is dangerous and that insufficient sexual activity can cause prostate trouble. Physicians, unfortunately, haven't been much help in dispelling such notions. As recently as four years ago, only a third of the nation's 111 medical schools offered any kind of course dealing with the emotional and psychological aspects of sex. A standard medical text currently in use recommends a hobby or cold showers to control the male sex drive.

Masters and Johnson's celebrated studies—in which they monitored and photographed male and female volunteers during intercourse and masturbation—did more than anyone since Kinsey to dispel massive ignorance about sex. Their research, for example, disputed the Freudian dogma that women actually experience two types of orgasm—clitoral and vaginal—and that the vaginal type is more mature. Masters and Johnson showed that, however perceived by women, all orgasms are identical physiologically. They graphically disproved the doctrine put forth in countless sex manuals that direct contact with the clitoris during intercourse is essential for orgasmic fulfillment. As the sex researchers now know, the penis rarely touches the clitoris during intercourse; erotic stimulation occurs indirectly through pressure on tissues surrounding the clitoris. Such findings are now the basis for the therapy being offered by the sex clinics for the treatment of such problems as impotence, premature ejaculation, inability to ejaculate, frigidity, vaginismus (constriction of the vaginal opening) and vaginal pain during the sexual act.

Following the Masters and Johnson lead, many of the new sex therapists believe it takes a couple to cure a couple of a sexual problem. At many points in therapy they have found a patient requires the support of someone of the same sex. Conversely, one partner in a marriage can better understand the problems of the other when explained by a member of the spouse's sex. Many of the therapists insist that, no matter which partner has the specific sexual complaint, both must undergo therapy. Says Masters: "There is no such thing as an uninvolved partner in a sexual dysfunction."

VII. A New Look at Therapy and the Assessment of Personality

At most clinics, the early stages of treatment consist largely of "sensate focus" exercises. The couple is instructed simply to stroke various parts of each other's bodies—carefully avoiding genital contact—to master the knack of giving pleasure in order to receive pleasure. Once the partners have begun to shed their inhibitions about physical contact, stroking proceeds to the breasts and genitals. When the therapists feel the couple is ready, sexual intercourse is assigned for homework. Many therapists use flexible wood and wire artist's figures to demonstrate coital positions that might aid in the progress of therapy. During the course of treatment, the troubled partners learn to signal each other—in many cases for the first time in their lives—what kind of sexual contact is gratifying to each one.

The most common—and most curable—problem dealt with by the therapists is premature ejaculation. Some counselors, including Masters and Johnson, employ the "squeeze technique" in the treatment of this disorder. The woman is told to stimulate her husband to erection and, when ejaculation is imminent, squeeze the tip of the penis. This delays orgasm and with repeated application the husband acquires the ability to maintain an erection for increasing periods without ejaculation.

Removing the Pressure

Impotence is more difficult to remedy. The disorder is usually psychological, and only rarely involves physical problems such as thyroid deficiencies or a spinal-cord injury. Treatment begins with sensate focus and then centers on the psychological block. The man is taught that he cannot will an erection, and comes to the liberating realization that fear of failure is probably the main reason for his disability.

For Gary, a 37-year-old stockbroker who lives in Brooklyn Heights, chronic impotence spelled the end of his ten-year marriage. After the divorce, he met Carol, and decided to go to a therapist. On the first visit, they were told to touch and caress each other, but not to attempt intercourse. "I knew the purpose was to take the pressure off me," recalls Gary. "But even knowing that, the tactic worked. I relaxed and started getting more and more sensation. I felt myself letting go. With Carol's love, I was getting connected."

Gary was also assured that if he failed on his first attempts at intercourse, it would not be disastrous. By the fourth week, says Carol, "the therapy had built up enormous sexual feelings, through abstinence and titillation." The therapist prescribed intercourse with Carol kneeling above Gary. "It allowed me my passivity," says Gary. "I wasn't expected to do anything. And it worked."

In the experience of most therapists, the most obstinate sex problem is frigidity, more accurately referred to as orgasmic dysfunction. The therapist teaches the patient that her unresponsiveness may come from a negative attitude toward sex, ingrained during childhood. The object of treatment is to help the woman come to terms with physical pleasure and, finally, to achieve its heights during sexual intercourse.

22. VALENCE: All About the New Sex Therapy

Jeannette, a 29-year-old housewife, could only reach orgasm during masturbation—and then, only when she imagined she was being raped by someone she detested. Because she blocked out the fantasy during intercourse with her husband, Frank, she had never achieved orgasm with him. The therapist explained that resisting the fantasy was distracting her and urged her instead to concentrate on it during intercourse. "The doctor put me at ease," says Jeannette, "by explaining that many women do not have orgasms. It helped remove the pressure."

After several weeks of practicing sensate focus, with Jeannette actively thinking about her fantasy, the couple began experimenting with direct sexual contact. Now, Jeannette is having orgasms regularly, even without imagining rape. And Frank admits that the clinic saved their marriage. "It was the first time we had ever really worked together to solve a problem," he says. "And it turned out to be an act of love."

Undoubtedly the most controversial sex-therapy technique is the employment of female surrogate partners to perform sexually in the treatment of single men. The idea originated with Masters and Johnson, who employed some thirteen surrogates in the first years of their program. All the women were single and sexually well-adjusted and some of them had participated in the early experiments in sexual physiology. Masters and Johnson have since abandoned the practice, partly because of a lawsuit brought by the husband of a part-time secretary who suspected that his wife was being used as a surrogate partner. The suit was ultimately settled out of court. Masters and Johnson also dropped the surrogates because they feared public reaction might hinder their own and other therapy programs.

Incense and a Water Bed

Surrogates, however, are used by the Berkeley Group for Sexual Development, a California therapy program directed by clinical psychologist Dr. Bernard Apfelbaum. Currently, Sandi Enders, an attractive brunette of 26 who intends to become an occupational therapist, is earning her way through San Jose State University by working as a sexual therapist. She charges $50 for a two-and-a-half-hour session—including lovemaking— in her sensuously decorated apartment with its incense burner and heated water bed. Among her present clients are a clinical psychologist, an IBM executive, an attorney and two college students. "They're trapped in a vicious cycle,"says Miss Enders, explaining her role. "They have a sexual problem that makes it difficult for them to relate to women. Since they can't relate to women, it's impossible for them to work out their problem." She admits: "What I'm doing is technically prostitution. But I'm convinced that helping men out of their hangups is valid, important work."

Masters and Johnson are also treating sexual dysfunction in homosexuals, either to help them convert to heterosexual performance or to improve their effectiveness in homosexual or lesbian relations. The treatment program is the same as for heterosexuals and the St. Louis researchers adamantly refuse to take sides on whether homosexuality should be regarded as normal or abnormal behavior. "The goal of therapy is set by the patient," says Masters, "and we are non-judgmental about their preferences."

The way in which the Masters and Johnson precepts are being applied varies widely in the growing number of U.S. sex clinics. But the goals are the same: specific treatment and quick results. The teams that have been trained in St. Louis to establish their own clinics tend to stick close to the line. Dr. Harvey L. Resnik, a psychoanalyst, and his wife, Audrey, a psychiatric nurse, insist on a concentrated approach at their clinic in Chevy Chase, Md. They receive about six inquiries a week but treat only one couple at a time for each intensive two-week period.

Many sex clinics, however, treat patients while they remain at home and on the job, a departure from the two-week honeymoon atmosphere prescribed by Masters and Johnson. Dr. Donald Sloane, director of a sex-therapy unit at New York Medical College, sees patients three or four times a week for up to a month and suggests that they take occasional long weekends away from home. At New York's Long Island Jewish Hospital, treatment may extend up to twenty weeks at one or two visits per week. Dr. Sallie Schumacher, and a co-therapist, Richard Green, believe the prolonged treatment works as well and that it is unnecessary for a couple to be away from home. "If they can function when the kids and the mother-in-law are there," Green says, "it's much better—and patients don't feel they have to make it in only two weeks."

Mrs. Marilyn Fithian, a 52-year-old sociologist, and Dr. William E. Hartman, a 53-year-old psychologist, who operate the Center for Marital and Sexual Studies in Long Beach, Calif., have added innovations of their own to the Masters and Johnson formula. As a visual aid for their patients, they show videotapes of their more skillful volunteer subjects in action. For inorgasmic women, Hartman and Fithian prescribe exercises for the muscle controlling the entrance to the vagina.

Some sex therapists developed their own quick methods of therapy separate from Masters and Johnson and have merely augmented their techniques with the findings of the St.Louis researchers. Dr. Helen Kaplan, director of the Sexual Disorders Program at New York's Payne Whitney Psychiatric Clinic, doesn't use a co-therapist, calling in a male colleague only if a patient somehow isn't communicating well with her. She also eschews the squeeze technique advocated by Masters and Johnson for treating premature ejaculators. "It hurts," she observes simply. Instead, she trains such patients to acquire control through "stop-start"—a technique in which the woman stimulates the man to the brink of orgasm, stops, and then renews the process in a short time.

In treating women, Kaplan and her associates make a distinction between those who are totally unresponsive and those with orgastic inhibition, who enjoy sex but cannot let themselves go to the point of orgasm.

22. VALENCE: All About the New Sex Therapy

Using dream interpretation and other analytic techniques, together with sexual exercises, she helps the patient work through her fear of physical abandon.

Filling a Prescription

Both Kaplan and Wardell Pomeroy, a former Kinsey collaborator, agree that the essence of good sex therapy is to exert authority over patients who are understandably reluctant to come to grips with their bodies and their emotions. "I get very explicit," says Pomeroy. "I'll say, 'Take your clothes off, take a shower together. Make notes and tell me what happens. Think that I'm giving you a prescription at the drugstore that you have to go out and fill.' " Some couples, particularly those who have been in psychotherapy, get involved in intellectual word games to avoid the central issue. "Enough of the psychology," Kaplan told one couple during a recent interview. "Tell me how you make love."

To make sex treatment available to more people, several of the sex doctors are trying group therapy. Kaplan and Pomeroy last summer treated four men, suffering from premature ejaculation, and their wives with good results. "Group dynamic appears to aid in therapy," notes Pomeroy. "The men found they weren't alone and there was a certain competition to improve." In a more far-out approach, New York psychiatrist Martin Shepard treats sexual hangups in nude encounter sessions in which he himself participates. Actual intercourse, however, is carried on in private.

The cost of sex therapy varies. Masters and Johnson charge $2,500 for their two-week program but see about 20 per cent of their patients on a reduced-fee or free-treatment basis. Some outpatient clinics use a sliding scale according to the patient's financial status, with $50 per visit as the top but many in the $10–$20 range.

Sex and the Poor

But even though low-income patients can get treatment, most people who come to sex clinics are white and upper-middle class. Dr. John O'Connor of Columbia's College of Physicians and Surgeons in New York believes different cultural and class attitudes about sex are the main reason why more of the poor haven't sought help. There is no reason to believe that the poor have fewer sexual problems than the affluent, but, says O'Connor: "They seem to handle sex problems in a different way, by drinking or acting out sexually with someone else."

Predictably, many psychiatrists have serious reservations about the new sex therapists. Some, like existential psychiatrist Rollo May, argue that while "some clinics do free people for a better relationship, many undermine the fact that sex is connected with tenderness. Certainly nothing is wrong with technique as such, in playing golf or acting or making love. But the emphasis beyond a certain point on technique in sex makes for a mechanistic attitude toward lovemaking, and goes along with depersonalization." Other critics, particularly the more classical Freudian analysts, argue that the sex therapists are merely treating symptoms without relieving the deep emotional problems that prompt them.

Some psychoanalysts warn that relieving a sexual problem by such therapy could result in the patient's disturbance emerging in other, potentially more serious symptoms—a phenomenon known as symptom substitution. "Sex therapists have to evaluate very carefully who's getting into the clinics and their underlying psychiatric problems," points out Dr. Charles Socarides, another New York analyst. "Without careful screening, there are going to be a lot of secondary emotional disturbances."

Socarides cites the case of a young woman who regards intercourse as a kind of rape and can just barely manage an occasional act of love. "If you try to force her to a sex clinic before she has resolved her fears about being penetrated," he says, "you could push her up against a severe emotional crisis."

Furthermore, according to analytically oriented psychiatrists, sex therapy tends to ignore the psychological complexity of sexual feelings. "Sex problems are based on conflicts between certain wishes—partly sexual, partly aggressive—and the restraints inculcated in every one of us from parental and cultural sources," says Dr. Burness E. Moore, president-elect of the American Psychoanalytic Association. "Prescribing certain sexual practices such as masturbation or oral sex may produce shame and guilt, unless the restraints are lessened slowly. Restraints are controls integrated into the total personality and can usually be changed only gradually."

There are patients, Moore maintains, who have orgasms but simply don't enjoy them—a syndrome he describes as "psychic impotence"—and others who have orgasms but deny them. "In such people," he maintains, "a treatment that focuses predominantly on physical performance often promises more in the way of happiness than can be fulfilled."

Some psychiatrists also question the worthiness of the goals set by sex therapists and the couples who seek their help. "There's a tendency to assume that everyone should make love, and well," Socarides says. "Some people can lead perfectly normal lives without feeling they should be functioning like Don Juan." Socarides is especially critical of attempts to improve homosexual relationships. "You don't treat fetishists to enjoy their fetishes," he declares. "Homosexuality is a serious disorder of tremendous social proportions."

The sex therapists, for the most part, aren't bothered by such criticism. Some of the counselors, like Kaplan, are psychoanalysts themselves and many psychiatrists refer their patients to the clinics for treatment of specific sexual disorders during long-term psychotherapy. In only a few instances have untoward psychic reactions occurred among patients after treatment of their sexual dysfunction. In addition, sex therapy works much faster than deep psychic probing. "I was astonished when I first did it,"

22. VALENCE: All About the New Sex Therapy

says one sex doctor who is a trained analyst. "In two weeks I saw problems disappear that had usually taken two or three years to change."

Keeping Out the Quacks

What's more, the sex therapists argue, the simple relief of a sexual problem can have a profound impact on a marriage. "It can change the pattern of a couple's communication for the rest of their lives," Kaplan maintains, "and make their whole relationship more genuine, mature and trusting."

Of primary concern to the sex therapists is the rich potential in their field for quackery. "This could be a real faddist thing," says Mount Sinai's Harold Lear. "What's to stop the guy who's been to a one-day workshop from seeing his own patients?" Lear and his colleagues would like to see some kind of licensing procedure to govern sex therapy, similar to those that control the practice of optometry or nursing.

Sex therapy is new and only time will tell how effective it is as a long-term cure. Up to now, there have been no controlled studies comparing the results of the sex therapists with those of their colleagues using conventional psychotherapy. Masters and Johnson have treated nearly 2,000 patients, most of whom had failed at psychotherapy and other forms of counseling. About 80 per cent were cured of their problem and continue to have satisfactory sex lives five years after treatment. Most of Masters and Johnson's disciples haven't been in practice long enough to provide such a long-range picture. But their initial results are about the same as the pioneers and few patients regress once they've overcome their sexual inadequacy. "It's like learning to ride a bicycle," says Dr. Alexander Levay of Columbia. "Once you get the hang of it, you never forget."

23.
VALENCE:
The Sex Testers

The following article provides a glimpse into the uses of technology to probe our psyches (and preferences!).

Neurologists have long used the electroencephalogram, which records patterns of electrical activity in the brain, to detect such disorders as epilepsy and brain tumors. Now, psychiatrists at Stanford University have found that the EEG may make it possible to read a person's mind. The California researchers have shown that brain waves produced in response to the sight of nude photographs seem to reveal an individual's sexual preferences. Ultimately, their findings may lead to new ways of treating scores of behavior problems, from sexual deviation to alcoholism.

These intriguing possibilities arose out of four years of research, by Drs. Ronald M. Costell, Donald T. Lunde, Bert S. Kopell and William Wittner, on the so-called E wave. Related to the four waves that register electrical potential on the standard EEG, the E wave is associated with anticipation or expectancy. Not unreasonably, the Stanford researchers suspected that an individual confronted with a preferred sex object or stimulus would show a heightened state of anticipation and that this could be objectively recorded in the form of intensified E-wave activity. To test their theory, they combined the EEG with a computer that averages E-wave changes over a succession of trials. The E-wave response can thus be made to stand out in bold relief against the background "noise" of other electrical activity in the brain.

In their first trials, Lunde and his colleagues recruited twelve male and twelve female Stanford students who were presumed to have normal

23. VALENCE: The Sex Testers

heterosexual preferences. The volunteers were seated individually in a small, soundproof cubicle and EEG electrodes were attached to their scalps. They were then shown a series of photographs of naked men and women; while the pictures were not actively erotic, the genitals were fully revealed. Also included in the series was a "neutral" figure, a clothed young woman photographed in shadow so that her gender was not readily detectable. Each picture was flashed on a screen for half a second—to trigger a sense of anticipation at what was to come. Then, after a pause of one and a half seconds, the picture was displayed again for two full seconds. The E-wave levels during the interval between the showings were recorded and fed into the computer for analysis.

Female. The results were just what the researchers hoped for. The men showed a much stronger E-wave response to female nudes than they did to male figures. Precisely the opposite was true of the women in the study. Interestingly, over a series of trials, the males gradually showed increased E-wave activity in response to the so-called neutral picture, while the women showed a steadily lessening response. This, of course, reflected the fact that the volunteers had begun to perceive the picture as female as the experiment progressed.

The Stanford psychiatrists have yet to test their technique on homosexuals or persons with other sexual aberrations. They expect, however, that E-wave responses to pictures of preferred sex objects—including, in the case of homosexuals, members of the same sex—could accurately and objectively assess sexual preferences in such patients. By the same token, changes in these responses during the course of psychiatric treatment might provide an accurate gauge of a patient's progress in therapy.

Lunde and his co-workers also believe measurement of E waves may prove useful in judging progress in the treatment of alcoholism or drug addiction. In such cases, E-wave changes would be recorded while the subjects were being shown such items as liquor bottles or hypodermic needles. Costell, who is now at the National Institute of Mental Health, believes the technique could also be useful in family psychotherapy. If, for example, a child's E waves increased when he saw a picture of his mother, as against seeing one of his father, this would suggest that the mother played the more influential role in the family structure.

Lunde admits that recording E waves smacks of invasion of privacy. "It's a scary thing," he says, "and I do have a fear of its being wrongly used to find out what people are really thinking." But, he adds, the test doesn't seem to work unless the subject is willing. "They have to concentrate," says Lunde, "which is easy to avoid if you don't want to take the test."

24.
VISION:
He Who Shapes

ROGER ZELAZNY

In the preceding article, the possibility emerges that psychic phenomena may be treated in their own right, and not as behavioral phenomena. This is the theme of the following edited selection from "He Who Shapes" by Roger Zelazny.

Lovely as it was, with the blood and all, Render could sense that it was about to end.

Therefore, each microsecond would be better off as a minute, he decided —and perhaps the temperature should be increased . . . Somewhere, just at the periphery of everything, the darkness halted its constriction.

Something, like a crescendo of subliminal thunders, was arrested at one raging note. That note was a distillate of shame and pain, and fear.

The Forum was stifling.

Caesar cowered outside the frantic circle. His forearm covered his eyes but it could not stop the seeing, not this time.

The senators had no faces and their garments were spattered with blood. All their voices were like the cries of birds. With an inhuman frenzy they plunged their daggers into the fallen figure.

All, that is, but Render.

The pool of blood in which he stood continued to widen. His arm seemed to be rising and falling with a mechanical regularity and his throat might have been shaping bird-cries, but he was simultaneously apart from and a part of the scene.

For he was Render, the Shaper.

Crouched, anguished and envious, Caesar wailed his protests.

"You have slain him! You have murdered Marcus Antonius—a blameless, useless fellow!"

24. VISION: He Who Shapes

Render turned to him, and the dagger in his hand was quite enormous and quite gory.

"Aye," said he.

The blade moved from side to side. Caesar, fascinated by the sharpened steel, swayed to the same rhythm.

"Why?" he cried. "Why?"

"Because," answered Render, "he was a far nobler Roman than yourself."

"You lie! It is not so!"

Render shrugged and returned to the stabbing.

"It is not true!" screamed Caesar. "Not true!"

Render turned to him again and waved the dagger. Puppetlike, Caesar mimicked the pendulum of the blade.

"Not true?" smiled Render. "And who are you to question an assassination such as this? You are no one! You detract from the dignity of this occasion! Begone!"

Jerkily, the pink-faced man rose to his feet, his hair half-wispy, half-wetplastered, a disarray of cotton. He turned, moved away; and as he walked, he looked back over his shoulder.

He had moved far from the circle of assassins, but the scene did not diminish in size. It retained an electric clarity. It made him feel even further removed, ever more alone and apart.

Render rounded a previously unnoticed corner and stood before him, a blind beggar.

Caesar grasped the front of his garment.

"Have you an ill omen for me this day?"

"Beware!" jeered Render.

"Yes! Yes!" cried Caesar. " 'Beware!' That is good! Beware what?"

"The ides—"

"Yes? The ides—"

"—of October."

He released the garment.

"What is that you say? What is Octember?"

"A month."

"You lie! There is no month of Octember!"

"And that is the date noble Caesar need fear—the nonexistent time, the never-to-be-calendared occasion."

Render vanished around another sudden corner.

"Wait! Come back!"

Render laughed, and the Forum laughed with him. The bird-cries became a chorus of inhuman jeers.

"You mock me!" wept Caesar.

The Forum was an oven, and the perspiration formed like a glassy mask over Caesar's narrow forehead, sharp nose, chinless jaw.

"I want to be assassinated too!" he sobbed. "It isn't fair!"

305

VII. A New Look at Therapy and the Assessment of Personality

And Render tore the Forum and the senators and the grinning corpse of Antony to pieces and stuffed them into a black sack—with the unseen movement of a single finger—and last of all went Caesar.

Charles Render sat before the ninety white buttons and the two red ones, not really looking at any of them. His right arm moved in its soundless sling, across the lap-level surface of the console—pushing some of the buttons, skipping over others, moving on, retracing its path to press the next in the order of the Recall Series.

Sensations throttled, emotions reduced to nothing. Representative Erikson knew the oblivion of the womb.

There was a soft click.

Render's hand had glided to the end of the bottom row of buttons. An act of conscious intent—will, if you like—was required to push the red .button.

Render freed his arm and lifted off his crown of Medusa-hair leads and microminiature circuitry. He slid from behind his desk-couch and raised the hood. He walked to the window and transpared it, fingering forth a cigarette.

One minute in the ro-womb, he decided. *No more. This is a crucial one . . . Hope it doesn't snow till later—those clouds look mean . . .*

It was smooth yellow trellises and high towers, glassy and gray, all smouldering into evening under a shale-colored sky; the city was squared volcanic islands, glowing in the end-of-day light, rumbling deep down under the earth; it was fat, incessant rivers of traffic, rushing.

Render turned away from the window and approached the great egg that lay beside his desk, smooth and glittering. It threw back a reflection that smashed all aquilinity from his nose, turned his eyes to gray saucers, transformed his hair into a light-streaked skyline; his reddish necktie became the wide tongue of a ghoul.

He smiled, reached across the desk. He pressed the second red button.

With a sigh, the egg lost its dazzling opacity and a horizontal crack appeared about its middle. Through the now-transparent shell, Render could see Erikson grimacing, squeezing his eyes tight, fighting against a return to consciousness and the thing it would contain. The upper half of the egg rose vertical to the base, exposing him knobby and pink on half-shell. When his eyes opened he did not look at Render. He rose to his feet and began dressing. Render used this time to check the ro-womb.

He leaned back across his desk and pressed the buttons: temperature control, full range, *check;* exotic sounds—he raised the earphone—*check,* on bells, on buzzes, on violin notes and whistles, on squeals and moans, on traffic noises and the sound of surf; *check,* on the feedback circuit—holding the patient's own voice, trapped earlier in analysis; *check,* on the sound

306

blanket, the moisture spray, the odor banks; *check,* on the couch agitator and the colored lights, the taste stimulants . . .

Render closed the egg and shut off its power. He pushed the unit into the closet, palmed shut the door. The tapes had registered a valid sequence.

"Sit down," he directed Erikson.

The man did so, fidgeting with his collar.

"You have full recall," said Render, "So there is no need for me to summarize what occurred. Nothing can be hidden from me. I was there."

Erikson nodded.

"The significance of the episode should be apparent to you."

Erikson nodded again, finally finding his voice. "But was it valid?" he asked. "I mean, you constructed the dream and you controlled it, all the way. I didn't really *dream* it—in the way I would normally dream. Your ability to make things happen stacks the deck for whatever you're going to say—doesn't it?"

Render shook his head slowly, flicked an ash into the southern hemisphere of his globe-made-ashtray, and met Erikson's eyes.

"It is true that I supplied the format and modified the forms. You, however, filled them with an emotional significance, promoted them to the status of symbols corresponding to your problem. If the dream was not a valid analogue it would not have provoked the reactions it did. It would have been devoid of the anxiety-patterns which were registered on the tapes.

"You have been in analysis for many months now," he continued, "and everything I have learned thus far serves to convince me that your fears of assassination are without any basis in fact."

Erikson glared.

"Then why the hell do I have them?"

"Because," said Render, "you would like very much to be the subject of an assassination."

Erikson smiled then, his composure beginning to return.

"I assure you, doctor, I have never contemplated suicide, nor have I any desire to stop living."

He produced a cigar and applied a flame to it. His hand shook.

"When you came to me this summer," said Render, "you stated that you were in fear of an attempt on your life. You were quite vague as to why anyone should want to kill you—"

"My position! You can't be a Representative as long as I have and make no enemies!"

"Yet," replied Render, "it appears that you have managed it. When you permitted me to discuss this with your detectives I was informed that they could unearth nothing to indicate that your fears might have any real foundation. Nothing."

"They haven't looked far enough—or in the right places. They'll turn up something."

"I'm afraid not."

"Why?"

"Because, I repeat, your feelings are without any objective basis.—Be honest with me. Have you any information whatsoever indicating that someone hates you enough to want to kill you?"

"I receive many threatening letters . . ."

"As do all Representatives—and all of those directed to you during the past year have been investigated and found to be the work of cranks. Can you offer me *one* piece of evidence to substantiate your claims?"

Erikson studied the tip of his cigar.

"I came to you on the advice of a colleague," he said, "came to you to have you poke around inside my mind to find me something of that sort, to give my detectives something to work with.—Someone I've injured severely perhaps—or some damaging piece of legislation I've dealt with . . ."

"—And I found nothing," said Render, "nothing, that is, but the cause of your discontent. Now, of course, you are afraid to hear it, and you are attempting to divert me from explaining my diagnosis—"

"I am not!"

"Then listen. You can comment afterwards if you want, but you've poked and dawdled around here for months, unwilling to accept what I presented to you in a dozen different forms. Now I am going to tell you outright what it is, and you can do what you want about it."

"Fine."

"First," he said, "you would like very much to have an enemy or enemies—"

"Ridiculous!"

"—Because it is the only alternative to having friends—"

"I have lots of friends!"

"—Because nobody wants to be completely ignored, to be an object for whom no one has really strong feelings. Hatred and love are the ultimate forms of human regard. Lacking one, and unable to achieve it, you sought the other. You wanted it so badly that you succeeded in convincing yourself it existed. But there is always a psychic pricetag on these things. Answering a genuine emotional need with a body of desire-surrogates does not produce real satisfaction, but anxiety, discomfort—because in these matters the psyche should be an open system. You did not seek outside yourself for human regard. You were closed off. You created that which you needed from the stuff of your own being. You are a man very much in need of strong relationships with other people."

"Manure!"

"Take it or leave it," said Render. "I suggest you take it."

"I've been paying you for half a year to help find out who wants to kill me. Now you sit there and tell me I made the whole thing up to satisfy a desire to have someone hate me."

"Hate you, or love you. That's right."

"It's absurd! I meet so many people that I carry a pocket recorder and a lapel-camera, just so I can recall them all . . ."

"Meeting quantities of people is hardly what I was speaking of.—Tell me, *did* that dream sequence have a strong meaning for you?"

Erikson was silent for several tickings of the huge wallclock.

"Yes," he finally conceded, "it did. But your interpretation of the matter is still absurd. Granting though, just for the sake of argument, that what you say is correct—what would I do to get out of this bind?"

Render leaned back in his chair.

"Rechannel the energies that went into producing the thing. Meet some people as yourself, Joe Erikson, rather than Representative Erikson. Take up something you can do with other people—something non-political, and perhaps somewhat competitive—and make some real friends or enemies, preferably the former. I've encouraged you to do this all along."

"Then tell me something else."

"Gladly."

"Assuming you *are* right, why is it that I am neither liked nor hated, and never have been? I have a responsible position in the Legislature. I meet people all the time. Why am I so neutral a—thing?"

Highly familiar now with Erikson's career, Render had to push aside his true thoughts on the matter, as they were of no operational value. He wanted to cite him Dante's observations concerning the trimmers—those souls who, denied heaven for their lack of virtue, were also denied entrance to hell for a lack of significant vices—in short, the ones who trimmed their sails to move them with every wind of the times, who lacked direction, who were not really concerned toward which ports they were pushed. Such was Erikson's long and colorless career of migrant loyalties, of political reversals.

Render said:

"More and more people find themselves in such circumstances these days. It is due largely to the increasing complexity of society and the depersonalization of the individual into a sociometric unit. Even the act of cathecting toward other persons has grown more forced as a result. There are so many of us these days."

Erikson nodded, and Render smiled inwardly.

Sometimes the gruff line, and then the lecture . . .

"I've got the feeling you could be right," said Erikson. "Sometimes I *do* feel like what you described—a unit, something depersonalized . . ."

Render glanced at the clock.

"What you choose to do about it from here is, of course, your own decision to make. I think you'd be wasting your time to remain in analysis any longer. We are now both aware of the cause of your complaint. I can't take you by the hand and show you how to lead your life. I can indicate, I can commiserate—but no more deep probing. Make an appointment as soon as you feel a need to discuss your activities and relate them to my diagnosis."

"I will," nodded Erikson, "and—damn that dream! It got to me. You can make them seem as vivid as waking life—more vivid . . . It may be a long while before I can forget it."

"I hope so."

"Okay, doctor." He rose to his feet, extended a hand. "I'll probably be back in a couple weeks. I'll give this socializing a fair try." He grinned at the word he normally frowned upon. "In fact, I'll start now. May I buy you a drink around the corner, downstairs?"

Render met the moist palm which seemed as weary of the performance as a lead actor in too successful a play. He felt almost sorry as he said, "Thank you, but I have an engagement."

Render helped him on with his coat then, handed him his hat, saw him to the door.

"Well, good night."

"Good night."

As the door closed soundlessly behind him, Render recrossed the dark Astrakhan to his mahogany fortress and flipped his cigarette into the southern hemisphere. He leaned back in his chair, hands behind his head, eyes closed.

"Of course it was more real than life," he informed no one in particular. "I shaped it."

Smiling, he reviewed the dream sequence step by step, wishing some of his former instructors could have witnessed it. It had been well-constructed and powerfully executed, as well as being precisely appropriate for the case at hand. But then, he was Render, the Shaper—one of the two hundred or so special analysts whose own psychic makeup permitted them to enter into neurotic patterns without carrying away more than an esthetic gratification from the mimesis of aberrance—a Sane Hatter.

Render stirred his recollections. He had been analyzed himself, analyzed and passed upon as a granite-willed, ultrastable outsider—tough enough to weather the basilisk gaze of a fixation, walk unscathed amidst the chimaerae of perversions, force dark Mother Medusa to close her eyes before the caduceus of his art. His own analysis had not been difficult. Nine years before (it seemed much longer) he had suffered a willing injection of novocain into the most painful area of his spirit. It was after the auto wreck, after the death of Ruth, and of Miranda their daughter, that he had begun to feel detached. Perhaps he did not want to recover certain empathies; perhaps his own world was now based upon a certain rigidity of feeling. If this was true, he was wise enough in the ways of the mind to realize it, and perhaps he had decided that such a world had its own compensations.

24. VISION: He Who Shapes

[That night during dinner, Render meets Dr. Eileen Shallot, a psychiatrist who wishes to become a neuroparticipant therapist ... and who is blind.]

"Doctor Shallot, this is Doctor Render," the waiter was saying.

"Good evening," said Render.

"Good evening," she said. "My name is Eileen and I've wanted very badly to meet you." He thought he detected a slight quaver in her voice. "Will you join me for dinner?"

"My pleasure," he acknowledged, and the waiter drew out the chair.

Render sat down, noting that the woman across from him already had a drink. He reminded the waiter of his second Manhattan.

"Have you ordered yet?" he inquired.

"No."

"... And two menus—" he started to say, then bit his tongue.

"Only one," she smiled.

"Make it none," he amended, and recited the menu.

They ordered. Then:

"Do you always do that?"

"What?"

"Carry menus in your head."

"Only a few," he said, "for awkward occasions. What was it you wanted to see—talk to me about?"

"You're a neuroparticipant therapist," she stated, "a Shaper."

"And you are—?"

"—a resident in psychiatry at State Psych. I have a year remaining."

"You knew Sam Riscomb then."

"Yes, he helped me get my appointment. He was my adviser."

"He was a very good friend of mine. We studied together at Menninger."

She nodded.

"I'd often heard him speak of you—that's one of the reasons I wanted to meet you. He's responsible for encouraging me to go ahead with my plans, despite my handicap."

Render stared at her. She was wearing a dark green dress which appeared to be made of velvet. About three inches to the left of the bodice was a pin which might have been gold. It displayed a red stone which could have been a ruby, around which the outline of a goblet was cast. Or was it really two profiles that were outlined, staring through the stone at one another? It seemed vaguely familiar to him, but he could not place it at the moment. It glittered expensively in the dim light.

Render accepted his drink from the waiter.

"I want to become a neuroparticipant therapist," she told him.

And if she had possessed vision Render would have thought she was staring at him, hoping for some response in his expression. He could not quite calculate what she wanted him to say.

"I commend your choice," he said, "and I respect your ambition." He tried to put his smile into his voice. "It is not an easy thing, of course, not all of the requirements being academic ones."

"I know," she said. "But then, I have been blind since birth and it was not an easy thing to come this far."

"Since birth?" he repeated. "I thought you might have lost your sight recently. You did your undergrad work then, and went on through med school without eyes . . . That's—rather impressive."

"Thank you," she said, "but it isn't. Not really. I heard about the first neuroparticipants—Bartelmetz and the rest—when I was a child, and I decided then that I wanted to be one. My life ever since has been governed by that desire."

"What did you do in the labs?" he inquired. "—Not being able to see a specimen, look through a microscope . . . ? Or all that reading?"

"I hired people to read my assignments to me. I taped everything. The school understood that I wanted to go into psychiatry, and they permitted a special arrangement for labs. I've been guided through the dissection of cadavers by lab assistants, and I've had everything described to me. I can tell things by touch . . . and I have a memory like yours with the menu," she smiled. " 'The quality of psychoparticipation phenomena can only be gauged by the therapist himself, at that moment outside of time and space as we normally know it, when he stands in the midst of a world erected from the stuff of another man's dreams, recognizes there the non-Euclidian architecture of aberrance, and then takes his patient by the hand and tours the landscape . . . If he can lead him back to the common earth, then his judgments were sound, his actions valid.' "

"From *Why No Psychometrics in This Place*," reflected Render.

"—By Charles Render, M.D."

"Our dinner is already moving in this direction," he noted, picking up his drink as the speed-cooked meal was pushed toward them in the kitchen-buoy.

"That's one of the reasons I wanted to meet you," she continued, raising her glass as the dishes rattled before her. "I want you to help me become a Shaper."

Her shaded eyes, as vacant as a statue's, sought him again.

"Yours is a completely unique situation," he commented. "There has never been a congenitally blind neuroparticipant—for obvious reasons. I'd have to consider all the aspects of the situation before I could advise you. Let's eat now, though. I'm starved."

"All right. But my blindness does not mean that I have never seen."

He did not ask her what she meant by that, because prime ribs were standing in front of him now and there was a bottle of Chambertin at his elbow. He did pause long enough to notice though, as she raised her left hand from beneath the table, that she wore no rings.

24. VISION: He Who Shapes

• • •

Deciding it was time to continue the discussion, he said, "So you want to be a Shaper . . ."

"Yes."

"I hate to be the one to destroy anybody's high ambitions," he told her. "Like poison, I hate it. Unless they have no foundation at all in reality. Then I can be ruthless. So—honestly, frankly, and in all sincerity, I do not see how it could ever be managed. Perhaps you're a fine psychiatrist—but in my opinion, it is a physical and mental impossibility for you ever to become a neuroparticipant. As for my reasons—"

• • •

"I acknowledge the truth of the diagnosis," she said. "Do you want to speak it for me?

"No, go ahead."

He refilled the small glasses once more.

"The damage is in my eyes," she told him, "not my brain."

He lit her cigarette.

"I can see with other eyes if I can enter other brains."

He lit his own cigarette.

"Neuroparticipation is based upon the fact that two nervous systems can share the same impulses, the same fantasies . . ."

"*Controlled* fantasies."

"I could perform therapy and at the same time experience genuine visual impressions."

"No," said Render.

"You don't know what it's like to be cut off from a whole area of stimuli! To know that a Mongoloid idiot can experience something you can never know—and that he cannot appreciate it because, like you, he was condemned before birth in a court of biological happenstance, in a place where there is no justice—only fortuity, pure and simple."

"The universe did not invent justice. Man did. Unfortunately, man must reside in the universe."

"I'm not asking the universe to help me—I'm asking you."

"I'm sorry," said Render.

"Why won't you help me?"

"At this moment you are demonstrating my main reason."

"Which is . . . ?"

"Emotion. This thing means far too much to you. When the therapist is in-phase with a patient he is narco-electrically removed from most of his own bodily sensations. This is necessary—because his mind must be completely absorbed by the task at hand. It is also necessary that his emotions undergo a similar suspension. This, of course, is impossible in the one sense that a person always emotes to some degree. But the therapist's emotions are sublimated into a generalized feeling of exhilaration—or, as

313

in my own case, into an artistic reverie. With you, however, the 'seeing' would be too much. You would be in constant danger of losing control of the dream."

"I disagree with you."

"Of course you do. But the fact remains that you would be dealing, and dealing constantly, with the abnormal. The power of a neurosis is unimaginable to ninety-nine point etcetera percent of the population, because we can never adequately judge the intensity of our own—let alone those of others, when we only see them from the outside. That is why no neuroparticipant will ever undertake to treat a full-blown psychotic. The few pioneers in that area are all themselves in therapy today. It would be like diving into a maelstrom. If the therapist loses the upper hand in an intense session he becomes the Shaped rather than the Shaper. The synapses respond like a fission reaction when nervous impulses are artificially augmented. The transference effect is almost instantaneous.

"I did an awful lot of skiing five years ago. This is because I was a claustrophobe. I had to run and it took me six months to beat the thing —all because of one tiny lapse that occurred in a measureless fraction of an instant. I had to refer the patient to another therapist. And this was only a minor repercussion.—If you were to go ga-ga over the scenery, girl, you could wind up in a rest home for life."

She finished her drink and Render refilled the glass. The night raced by. They had left the city far behind them, and the road was open and clear. The darkness eased more and more of itself between the falling flakes. The Spinner picked up speed.

"All right," she admitted, "maybe you're right. Still, though, I think you can help me."

"How?" he asked.

"Accustom me to seeing, so that the images will lose their novelty, the emotions wear off. Accept me as a patient and rid me of my sight-anxiety. Then what you have said so far will cease to apply. I will be able to undertake the training then, and give my full attention to therapy. I'll be able to sublimate the sight-pleasure into something else."

Render wondered.

Perhaps it could be done. It would be a difficult undertaking, though.

It might also make therapeutic history.

No one was really qualified to try it, because no one had ever tried it before.

But Eileen Shallot was a rarity—no, a unique item—for it was likely she was the only person in the world who combined the necessary technical background with the unique problem.

He drained his glass, refilled it, refilled hers.

He was still considering the problem as the "RE-COORDINATE" light came on and the car pulled into a cutoff and stood there. He switched off the buzzer and sat there for a long while, thinking.

314

24. VISION: He Who Shapes

It was not often that other persons heard him acknowledge his feelings regarding his skill. His colleagues considered him modest. Offhand, though, it might be noted that he was aware that the day a better neuroparticipant began practicing would be the day that a troubled homo sapiens was to be treated by something but immeasurably less than angels.

Two drinks remained. Then he tossed the emptied bottle into the backbin.

"You know something?" he finally said.

"What?"

"It might be worth a try."

He swiveled about then and leaned forward to re-coordinate, but she was there first. As he pressed the buttons and the S-7 swung around, she kissed him. Below her dark glasses her cheeks were moist.

[Later, Render and Shallot meet for the first attempt at neuroparticipant therapy.]

Render seated himself. His chair became a contour couch and moved in halfway beneath the console. He sat upright and it moved back again, becoming a chair. He touched a part of the desk and half the ceiling disengaged itself, reshaped itself, and lowered to hover overhead like a huge bell. He stood and moved around to the side of the ro-womb. Respighi spoke of pines and such, and Render disengaged an earphone from beneath the egg and leaned back across his desk. Blocking one ear with his shoulder and pressing the microphone to the other, he played upon the buttons with his free hand. Leagues of surf drowned the tone poem; miles of traffic overrode it; a great clanging bell sent fracture lines running through it; and the feedback said: ". . . Now that you are just sitting there listening to me, saying nothing, I associate you with a deep, almost violet, blue . . ."

He switched to the face mask and monitored, *one*—cinnamon, *two*—leaf mold, *three*—deep reptilian musk . . . and down through thirst, and the tastes of honey and vinegar and salt, and back on up through lilacs and wet concrete, a before-the-storm whiff of ozone, and all the basic olfactory and gustatory cues for morning, afternoon, and evening in the town.

The couch floated normally in its pool of mercury, magnetically stabilized by the walls of the egg. He set the tapes.

The ro-womb was in perfect condition.

"Okay," said Render, turning, "everything checks."

She was just placing her glasses atop her folded garments. She had undressed while Render was testing the machine. He was perturbed by her narrow waist, her large, dark-pointed breasts, her long legs. She was too well-formed for a woman her height, he decided.

He realized though, as he stared at her, that his main annoyance was, of course, the fact that she was his patient.

315

"Ready here," she said, and he moved to her side.

He took her elbow and guided her to the machine. Her fingers explored its interior. As he helped her enter the unit, he saw that her eyes were a vivid seagreen. Of this, too, he disapproved.

"Comfortable?"

"Yes."

"Okay then, we're set. I'm going to close it now. Sweet dreams."

The upper shell dropped slowly. Closed, it grew opaque, then dazzling. Render was staring down at his own distorted reflection.

He moved back in the direction of his desk.

• • •

Render seated himself and lowered the hood, the operator's modified version of the ro-womb. He was alone before the ninety white buttons and the two red ones. The world ended in the blackness beyond the console. He loosened his necktie and unbuttoned his collar.

He removed the helmet from its receptacle and checked its leads. Donning it then, he swung the halfmask up over his lower face and dropped the darksheet down to meet with it. He rested his right arm in the sling, and with a single tapping gesture, he eliminated his patient's consciousness.

A Shaper does not press white buttons consciously. He wills conditions. Then deeply-implanted muscular reflexes exert an almost imperceptible pressure against the sensitive arm-sling, which glides into the proper position and encourages an extended finger to move forward. A button is pressed. The sling moves on.

Render felt a tingling at the base of his skull; he smelled fresh-cut grass.

Suddenly he was moving up the great gray alley between the worlds.

After what seemed a long time, Render felt that he was footed on a strange Earth. He could see nothing; it was only a sense of presence that informed him he had arrived. It was the darkest of all the dark nights he had ever known.

He willed that the darkness disperse. Nothing happened.

A part of his mind came awake again, a part he had not realized was sleeping; he recalled whose world he had entered.

He listened for her presence. He heard fear and anticipation.

He willed color. First, red . . .

He felt a correspondence. Then there was an echo.

Everything became red; he inhabited the center of an infinite ruby.

Orange. Yellow . . .

He was caught in a piece of amber.

Green now, and he added the exhalations of a sultry sea. Blue, and the coolness of evening.

He stretched his mind then, producing all the colors at once. They came in great swirling plumes.

Then he tore them apart and forced a form upon them.

An incandescent rainbow arched across the black sky.

24. VISION: He Who Shapes

He fought for browns and grays below him. Self-luminescent, they appeared—in shimmering, shifting patches.

Somewhere, a sense of awe. There was no trace of hysteria though, so he continued with the Shaping.

He managed a horizon, and the blackness drained away beyond it. The sky grew faintly blue, and he ventured a herd of dark clouds. There was resistance to his efforts at creating distance and depth, so he reinforced the tableau with a very faint sound of surf. A transference from an auditory concept of distance came on slowly then, as he pushed the clouds about. Quickly, he threw up a high forest to offset a rising wave of acrophobia.

The panic vanished.

Render focused his attention on tall trees—oaks and pines, poplars and sycamores. He hurled them about like spears, in ragged arrays of greens and browns and yellows, unrolled a thick mat of morning-moist grass, dropped a series of gray boulders and greenish logs at irregular intervals, and tangled and twined the branches overhead, casting a uniform shade throughout the glen.

The effect was staggering. It seemed as if the entire world was shaken with a sob, then silent.

Through the stillness he felt her presence. He had decided it would be best to lay the groundwork quickly, to set up a tangible headquarters, to prepare a field for operations. He could backtrack later, he could repair and amend the results of the trauma in the sessions yet to come; but this much, at least, was necessary for a beginning.

With a start, he realized that the silence was not a withdrawal. Eileen had made herself immanent in the trees and the grass, the stones and the bushes; she was personalizing their forms, relating them to tactile sensations, sounds, temperatures, aromas.

With a soft breeze, he stirred the branches of the trees. Just beyond the bounds of seeing he worked out the splashing sounds of a brook.

There was a feeling of joy. He shared it.

She was bearing it extremely well, so he decided to extend the scope of the exercise. He let his mind wander among the trees, experiencing a momentary doubling of vision, during which time he saw an enormous hand riding in an aluminum carriage toward a circle of white.

He was beside the brook now and he was seeking her, carefully.

He drifted with the water. He had not yet taken on a form. The splashes became a gurgling as he pushed the brook through shallow places and over rocks. At his insistence, the waters became more articulate.

"Where are you?" asked the brook.

Here! Here!

Here!

. . . and here! replied the trees, the bushes, the stones, the grass.

"Choose one," said the brook, as it widened, rounded a mass of rock, then bent its way toward a slope, heading toward a blue pool.

I cannot, was the answer from the wind.

"You must." The brook widened and poured itself into the pool, swirled about the surface, then stilled itself and reflected branches and dark clouds. "Now!"

Very well, echoed the wood, *in a moment.*

The mist rose above the lake and drifted to the bank of the pool.

"Now," tinkled the mist.

Here, then . . .

She had chosen a small willow. It swayed in the wind; it trailed its branches in the water.

"Eileen Shallot," he said, "regard the lake."

The breezes shifted; the willow bent.

It was not difficult for him to recall her face, her body. The tree spun as though rootless. Eileen stood in the midst of a quiet explosion of leaves; she stared, frightened, into the deep blue mirror of Render's mind, the lake.

She covered her face with her hands, but it could not stop the seeing.

"Behold yourself," said Render.

She lowered her hands and peered downwards. Then she turned in every direction, slowly; she studied herself. Finally:

"I feel I am quite lovely," she said. "Do I feel so because you want me to, or is it true?"

She looked all about as she spoke, seeking the Shaper.

"It is true," said Render, from everywhere.

"Thank you."

There was a swirl of white and she was wearing a belted garment of damask. The light in the distance brightened almost imperceptibly. A faint touch of pink began at the base of the lowest cloudbank.

"What is happening there?" She asked, facing that direction.

"I am going to show you a sunrise," said Render, "and I shall probably botch it a bit—but then, it's my first professional sunrise under these circumstances."

"Where are *you?*" she asked.

"Everywhere," he replied.

"Please take on a form so that I can see you."

"All right."

"Your natural form."

He willed that he be beside her on the bank, and he was.

Startled by a metallic flash, he looked downward. The world receded for an instant, then grew stable once again. He laughed, and the laugh froze as he thought of something.

He was wearing the suit of armor which had stood beside their table in The Partridge and Scalpel on the night they met.

She reached out and touched it.

"The suit of armor by our table," she acknowledged, running her fingertips over the plates and the junctures. "I associated it with you that night."

". . . And you stuffed me into it just now," he commented. "You're a strong-willed woman."

The armor vanished and he was wearing his graybrown suit and loose-knit bloodclot necktie and a professional expression.

"Behold the real me," he smiled faintly. "Now, to the sunset. I'm going to use all the colors. Watch!"

They seated themselves on the green park bench which had appeared behind them, and Render pointed in the direction he had decided upon as east.

Slowly, the sun worked through its morning attitudes. For the first time in this particular world it shone down like a god, and reflected off the lake, and broke the clouds, and set the landscape to smouldering beneath the mist that arose from the moist wood.

Watching, watching intently, staring directly into the ascending bonfire, Eileen did not move for a long while, nor speak. Render could sense her fascination.

She was staring at the source of all light; it reflected back from the gleaming coin on her brow, like a single drop of blood.

Render said, "That is the sun, and those are clouds," and he clapped his hands and the clouds covered the sun and there was a soft rumble overhead, "and that is thunder," he finished.

The rain fell then, shattering the lake and tickling their faces, making sharp striking sounds on the leaves, then soft tapping sounds, dripping down from the branches overhead, soaking their garments and plastering their hair, running down their necks and falling into their eyes, turning patches of brown earth to mud.

A splash of lightning covered the sky, and a second later there was another peal of thunder.

". . . And this is a summer storm," he lectured. "You see how the rain affects the foliage, and ourselves. What you just saw in the sky before the thunderclap was lightning."

". . . Too much," she said. "Let up on it for a moment, please."

The rain stopped instantly and the sun broke through the clouds.

"I have the damnedest desire for a cigarette," she said, "but I left mine in another world."

As she said it one appeared, already lighted, between her fingers.

"It's going to taste rather flat," said Render strangely.

He watched her for a moment, then:

"I didn't give you that cigarette," he noted. "You picked it from my mind."

The smoke laddered and spiraled upward, was swept away.

". . . Which means that, for the second time today, I have underestimated the pull of that vacuum in your mind—in the place where sight ought to be. You are assimilating these new impressions very rapidly. You're even going to the extent of groping after new ones. Be careful. Try to contain that impulse."

"It's like a hunger," she said.

"Perhaps we had best conclude this session now."

Their clothing was dry again. A bird began to sing.

"No, wait! Please! I'll be careful. I want to see more things."

"There is always the next visit," said Render. "But I suppose we can manage one more. Is there something you want very badly to see?"

"Yes. Winter. Snow."

"Okay," smiled the Shaper, "then wrap yourself in that furpiece . . ."

[After several sessions with Eileen Shallot, Render goes on vacation skiing. There he meets his former teacher . . .]

"Charles Render!" said the voice (only it sounded more like "Sharlz Runder"), and his head instantly jerked in that direction, but his eyes danced with too many afterimages for him to isolate the source of the calling.

"Maurice?" he queried after a moment, "Bartelmetz?"

"Aye," came the reply, and then Render saw the familiar grizzled visage, set neckless and balding above the red and blue shag sweater that was stretched mercilessly about the wine-keg rotundity of the man who now picked his way in their direction, deftly avoiding the strewn crutches and the stacked skis and the people who, like Jill and Render, disdained sitting in chairs.

Render stood, stretching, and shook hands as he came upon them.

"You've put on more weight," Render observed. "That's unhealthy."

"Nonsense, it's all muscle. How have you been, and what are you up to these days?" He looked down at Jill and she smiled back at him.

"This is Miss DeVille," said Render.

"Jill," she acknowledged.

He bowed slightly, finally releasing Render's aching hand.

". . . And this is Professor Maurice Bartelmetz of Vienna," finished Render, "a benighted disciple of all forms of dialectical pessimism, and a very distinguished pioneer in neuroparticipation—although you'd never guess it to look at him. I had the good fortune to be his pupil for over a year."

Bartelmetz nodded and agreed with him, taking in the Schnappsflasche Render brought forth from a small plastic bag, and accepting the collapsible cup which he filled to the brim.

"Ah, you are a good doctor still," he sighed. "You have diagnosed the case in an instant and you make the proper prescription. Nozdrovia!"

"Seven years in a gulp," Render acknowledged, refilling their glasses.

"Then we shall make time more malleable by sipping it."

They seated themselves on the floor, and the fire roared up through the great brick chimney as the logs burnt themselves back to branches, to twigs, to thin sticks, ring by yearly ring.

24. VISION: He Who Shapes

Render replenished the fire.

"I read your last book," said Bartelmetz finally, casually, "about four years ago."

Render reckoned that to be correct.

"Are you doing any research work these days?"

Render poked lazily at the fire.

"Yes," he answered, "sort of."

He glanced at Jill, who was dozing with her cheek against the arm of the huge leather chair that held his emergency bag, the planes of her face all crimson and flickering shadow.

"I've hit upon a rather unusual subject and started with a piece of jobbery I eventually intend to write about."

"Unusual? In what way?"

"Blind from birth, for one thing."

"You're using the ONT&R?"

"Yes. She's going to be a Shaper."

"Verfluchter!—Are you aware of the possible repercussions?"

"Of course."

"You've heard of unlucky Pierre?"

"No."

"Good, then it was successfully hushed. Pierre was a philosophy student at the University of Paris, and he was doing a dissertation on the evolution of consciousness. This past summer he decided it would be necessary for him to explore the mind of an ape, for purposes of comparing a moins-nausée mind with his own, I suppose. At any rate, he obtained illegal access to an ONT&R and to the mind of our hairy cousin. It was never ascertained how far along he got in exposing the animal to the stimuli-bank, but it is to be assumed that such items as would not be immediately trans-subjective between man and ape—traffic sounds and so weiter— were what frightened the creature. Pierre is still residing in a padded cell, and all his responses are those of a frightened ape.

"So, while he did not complete his own dissertation," he finished, "he may provide significant material for someone else's."

Render shook his head.

"Quite a story," he said softly, "But I have nothing that dramatic to contend with. I've found an exceedingly stable individual—a psychiatrist, in fact—one who's already spent time in ordinary analysis. She wants to go into neuroparticipation—but the fear of a sight-trauma was what was keeping her out. I've been gradually exposing her to a full range of visual phenomena. When I've finished she should be completely accommodated to sight, so that she can give her full attention to therapy and not be blinded by vision, so to speak. We've already had four sessions."

"And?"

". . . And it's working fine."

"You are certain about it?"

"Yes, as certain as anyone can be in these matters."

"Mm-hm," said Bartelmetz. "Tell me, do you find her excessively strong-willed? By that I mean, say, perhaps an obsessive-compulsive pattern concerning anything to which she's been introduced so far?"

"No."

"Has she ever succeeded in taking over control of the fantasy?"

"No!"

"You lie," he said simply.

Render found a cigarette. After lighting it, he smiled.

"Old father, old artificer," he conceded, "age has not withered your perceptiveness. I may trick me, but never you.—Yes, as a matter of fact, she *is* very difficult to keep under control. She is not satisfied just to see. She wants to Shape things for herself already. It's quite understandable—both to her and to me—but conscious apprehension and emotional acceptance never do seem to get together on things. She has become dominant on several occasions, but I've succeeded in resuming control almost immediately. After all, I *am* master of the bank."

"Hm," mused Bartelmetz. "Are you familiar with a Buddhist text—*Shankara's Catechism?*"

"I'm afraid not."

"Then I lecture you on it now. It posits—obviously not for therapeutic purposes—a true ego and a false ego. The true ego is that part of man which is immortal and shall proceed on to nirvana: the soul, if you like. Very good. Well, the false ego, on the other hand, is the normal mind, bound round with the illusions—the consciousness of you and I and everyone we have ever known professionally. Good?—Good. Now, the stuff this false ego is made up of they call skandhas. These include the feelings, the perceptions, the aptitudes, consciousness itself, and even the physical form. Very unscientific. Yes. Now they are not the same thing as neuroses, or one of Mister Ibsen's life-lies, or an hallucination—no, even though they are all wrong, being parts of a false thing to begin with. Each of the five skandhas is a part of the eccentricity that we call identity—then on top come the neuroses and all the other messes which follow after and keep us in business. Okay?—Okay. I give you this lecture because I need a dramatic term for what I will say, because I wish to say something dramatic. View the skandhas as lying at the bottom of the pond; the neuroses, they are ripples on the top of the water; the 'true ego,' if there is one, is buried deep beneath the sand at the bottom. So. The Ripples fill up the—the—zwischenwelt—between the object and the subject. The skandhas are a part of the subject, basic, unique, the stuff of his being.—So far, you are with me?"

"With many reservations."

"Good. Now I have defined my term somewhat, I will use it. You are fooling around with skandhas, not simple neuroses. You are attempting to adjust this woman's overall conception of herself and of the world. You are using the ONT&R to do it. It is the same thing as fooling with a psychotic, or an ape. All may seem to go well, but—at any moment, it is possible you may do something, show her some sight, or some way of seeing which will break in upon her selfhood, break a skandha—and pouf! —it will be like breaking through the bottom of the pond. A whirlpool will result, pulling you—where? I do not want you for a patient, young man, young artificer, so I counsel you not to proceed with this experiment. The ONT&R should not be used in such a manner."

Render flipped his cigarette into the fire and counted on his fingers:

"One," he said, "you are making a mystical mountain out of a pebble. All I am doing is adjusting her consciousness to accept an additional area of perception. Much of it is simple transference work from the other senses.—Two, her emotions were quite intense initially because it *did* involve a trauma—but we've passed that stage already. Now it is only a novelty to her. Soon it will be a commonplace.—Three, Eileen is a psychiatrist herself; she is educated in these matters and deeply aware of the delicate nature of what we are doing.—Four, her sense of identity and her desires, or her skandhas, or whatever you want to call them, are as firm as the Rock of Gibraltar. Do you realize the intense application required for a blind person to obtain the education she has obtained? It took a will of ten-point steel and the emotional control of an ascetic as well—"

"—And if something that strong should break, in a timeless moment of anxiety," smiled Bartelmetz sadly, "may the shades of Sigmund Freud and Carl Jung walk by your side in the valley of darkness.

"—And five," he added suddenly, staring into Render's eyes. "Five," he ticked it off on one finger. "Is she pretty?"

Render looked back into the fire.

"Very clever," sighed Bartelmetz, "I cannot tell whether you are blushing or not, with the rosy glow of the flames upon your face. I fear that you are, though, which would mean that you are aware that you yourself could be the source of the inciting stimulus. I shall burn a candle tonight before a portrait of Adler and pray that he give you the strength to compete successfully in your duel with your patient."

Render looked at Jill, who was still sleeping. He reached out and brushed a lock of her hair back into place.

"Still," said Bartelmetz, "if you do proceed and all goes well, I shall look forward with great interest to the reading of your work. Did I ever tell you that I have treated several Buddhists and never found a 'true ego'?"

Both men laughed.

[Despite the misgivings of both Bartelmetz and himself, Render decides to continue the therapy sessions with Eileen Shallot.]

In this place, of all places, Render knew he was the master of all things.

He was at home on those alien worlds, without time, those worlds where flowers copulate and the stars do battle in the heavens, falling at last to the ground, bleeding, like so many spilt and shattered chalices, and the seas part to reveal stairways leading down, and arms emerge from caverns, waving torches that flame like liquid faces—a midwinter night's nightmare, summer go a-begging, Render knew—for he had visited those worlds on a professional basis for the better part of a decade. With the crooking of a finger he could isolate the sorcerers, bring them to trial for treason against the realm—aye, and he could execute them, could appoint their successors.

Fortunately, this trip was only a courtesy call . . .

He moved forward through the glade, seeking her.

He could feel her awakening presence all about him.

He pushed through the branches, stood beside the lake. It was cold, blue, and bottomless, the lake, reflecting that slender willow which had become the station of her arrival.

"Eileen!"

The willow swayed toward him, swayed away.

"Eileen! Come forth!"

Leaves fell, floated upon the lake, disturbed its mirror-like placidity, distorted the reflections.

"Eileen?"

All the leaves yellowed at once then, dropped down into the water. The tree ceased its swaying. There was a strange sound in the darkening sky, like the humming of high wires on a cold day.

Suddenly there was a double file of moons passing through the heavens.

Render selected one, reached up, and pressed it. The others vanished as he did so, and the world brightened; the humming went out of the air.

He circled the lake to gain subjective respite from the rejection-action and his counter to it. He moved up along an aisle of pines toward the place where he wanted the cathedral to occur. Birds sang now in the trees. The wind came softly by him. He felt her presence quite strongly.

"Here, Eileen. Here."

She walked beside him then, green silk, hair of bronze, eyes of molten emerald; she wore an emerald in her forehead. She walked in green slippers over the pine needles, saying: "What happened?"

"You were afraid."

"Why?"

"Perhaps you fear the cathedral. Are you a witch?" he smiled.

"Yes, but it's my day off."

He laughed, and he took her arm, and they rounded an island of foliage, and there was the cathedral reconstructed on a grassy rise, pushing its way above them and above the trees, climbing into the middle air, breathing out organ notes, reflecting a stray ray of sunlight from a pane of glass.

"Hold tight to the world," he said. "Here comes the guided tour."

They moved forward and entered.

" '. . . With its floor-to-ceiling shafts, like so many huge treetrunks, it achieves a ruthless control over its spaces,' " he said. "—Got that from the guidebook. This is the north transept . . ."

" 'Greensleeves,' " she said, "the organ is playing 'Greensleeves.' "

"So it is. You can't blame me for that though.—Observe the scalloped capitals—"

"I want to go nearer the music."

"Very well. This way then."

Render felt that something was wrong. He could not put his finger on it.

Everything retained its solidity . . .

Something passed rapidly then, high above the cathedral, uttering a sonic boom. Render smiled at that, remembering now; it was like a slip of the tongue: for a moment he had confused Eileen with Jill—yes, that was what had happened.

Why, then . . .

A burst of white was the altar. He had never seen it before, anywhere. All the walls were dark and cold about them. Candles flickered in corners and high niches. The organ chorded thunder under invisible hands.

Render knew that something was wrong.

He turned to Eileen Shallot, whose hat was a green cone towering up into the darkness trailing wisps of green veiling. Her throat was in shadow, but . . .

"That necklace—Where?"

"I don't know," she smiled.

The goblet she held radiated a rosy light. It was reflected from her emerald. It washed him like a draft of cool air.

"Drink?" she asked.

"Stand still," he ordered.

He willed the walls to fall down. They swam in shadow.

"Stand still!" he repeated urgently. "Don't do anything. Try not even to think.

"—Fall down!" he cried. And the walls were blasted in all directions and the roof was flung over the top of the world, and they stood amid ruins lighted by a single taper. The night was black as pitch.

"Why did you do that?" she asked, still holding the goblet out toward him.

"Don't think. Don't think anything," he said. "Relax. You are very tired. As that candle flickers and wanes so does your consciousness. You can barely keep awake. You can hardly stay on your feet. Your eyes are closing. There is nothing to see here anyway."

He willed the candle to go out. It continued to burn.

"I'm not tired. Please have a drink."

He heard organ music through the night. A different tune, one he did not recognize at first.

"I need your cooperation."

"All right. Anything."

"Look! The moon!" he pointed.

She looked upward and the moon appeared from behind an inky cloud.

". . . And another, and another."

Moons, like strung pearls, proceeded across the blackness.

"The last one will be red," he stated.

It was.

He reached out then with his right index finger, slid his arm sideways along his field of vision, then tried to touch the red moon.

His arm ached, it burned. He could not move it.

"Wake up!" he screamed.

The red moon vanished, and the white ones.

"Please take a drink."

He dashed the goblet from her hand and turned away. When he turned back she was still holding it before him.

"A drink?"

He turned and fled into the night.

It was like running through a waist-high snowdrift. It was wrong. He was compounding the error by running—he was minimizing his strength, maximizing hers. It was sapping his energies, draining him.

He stood still in the midst of the blackness.

"The world around me moves," he said. "I am its center."

"Please have a drink," she said, and he was standing in the glade beside their table set beside the lake. The lake was black and the moon was silver, and high, and out of his reach. A single candle flickered on the table, making her hair as silver as her dress. She wore the moon on her brow. A bottle of Romanée-Conti stood on the white cloth beside a wide-brimmed wine glass. It was filled to overflowing, that glass, and rosy beads clung to its lip. He was very thirsty, and she was lovelier than anyone he had ever seen before, and her necklace sparkled, and the breeze came cool off the lake, and there was something—something he should remember . . .

He took a step toward her and his armor clinked lightly as he moved. He reached toward the glass and his right arm stiffened with pain and fell back to his side.

● ● ●

He was hanging onto her shoulder then, holding her tightly, there beside the black lake beneath the moon that was Wedgwood. A single candle flickered upon their table. She held the glass to his lips.

"Please drink it."

"Yes, give it to me!"

He gulped the wine that was all softness and lightness. It burned within him. He felt his strength returning.

"I am . . ."

"—*Render, the Shaper*," splashed the lake.

24. VISION: He Who Shapes

"No!"

He turned and ran again, looking for the wreck. He had to go back, to return . . .

"You can't."

"I can!" he cried. "I can, if I try . . ."

Yellow flames coiled through the thick air. Yellow serpents. They coiled, glowing, about his ankles. Then through the murk, two-headed and towering, approached his Adversary.

Small stones rattled past him. An overpowering odor corkscrewed up his nose and into his head.

"Shaper!" came the bellow from one head.

"You have returned for the reckoning!" called the other.

Render stared, remembering.

"No reckoning, Thaumiel," he said. "I beat you and I chained you for —Rothman, yes, it was Rothman—the cabalist." He traced a pentagram in the air. "Return to Qliphoth. I banish you."

"This place be Qliphoth."

". . . By Khamael, the angel of blood, by the hosts of Seraphim, in the Name of Elohim Gebor, I bid you vanish!"

"Not this time," laughed both heads.

It advanced.

Render backed slowly away, his feet bound by the yellow serpents. He could feel the chasm opening behind him. The world was a jigsaw puzzle coming apart. He could see the pieces separating.

"Vanish!"

The giant roared out its double-laugh.

Render stumbled.

"This way, love!"

She stood within a small cave to his right.

He shook his head and backed toward the chasm.

Thaumiel reached out toward him.

Render toppled back over the edge.

"Charles!" she screamed, and the world shook itself apart with her wailing.

"Then Vernichtung," he answered as he fell. "I join you in darkness."

Everything came to an end.

"I want to see Doctor Charles Render."

"I'm sorry, that is impossible."

"But I skip-jetted all the way here, just to thank him. I'm a new man! He changed my life!"

"I'm sorry, Mister Erikson. When you called this morning, I told you it was impossible."

"Sir, I'm Representative Erikson—and Render once did me a great service."

"Then you can do him one now. Go home."

"You can't talk to me that way!"

"I just did. Please leave. Maybe next year sometime . . ."

"But a few words can do wonders . . ."

"Save them!"

"I—I'm sorry . . ."

Lovely as it was, pinked over with the morning—the slopping, steaming bowl of the sea—he knew that it *had* to end. Therefore . . .

He descended the high tower stairway and he entered the courtyard. He crossed to the bower of roses and he looked down upon the pallet set in its midst.

"Good morrow, m'lord," he said.

"To you the same," said the knight, his blood mingling with the earth, the flowers, the grasses, flowing from his wound, sparkling over his armor, dripping from his fingertips.

"Naught hath healed?"

The knight shook his head.

"I empty. I wait."

"Your waiting is near ended."

"What mean you?" He sat upright.

"The ship. It approacheth harbor."

The knight stood. He leaned his back against a mossy treetrunk. He stared at the huge, bearded servitor who continued to speak, words harsh with barbaric accents:

"It cometh like a dark swan before the wind—returning."

"Dark, say you? Dark?"

"The sails be black, Lord Tristram."

"You lie!"

"Do you wish to see? To see for yourself?—Look then!"

He gestured.

The earth quaked, the wall toppled. The dust swirled and settled. From where they stood they could see the ship moving into the harbor on the wings of the night.

"No! You lied!—See! They are white!"

The dawn danced upon the waters. The shadows fled from the ship's sails.

"No, you fool! Black! They *must* be!"

"White! White!—Isolde! You have kept faith! You have returned!"

He began running toward the harbor.

"Come back!—Your wound! You are ill!—Stop . . ."

The sails were white beneath a sun that was a red button which the servitor reached quickly to touch.

Night fell.

25.
VALENCE:
Therapy Is
the Handmaiden of the Status Quo

SEYMOUR L. HALLECK

In the following article, Seymour Halleck examines the social ramifications of therapy, and suggests that there is no such thing as an apolitical therapist.

The thesis that all of our citizens are oppressed by current social institutions is certainly debatable, but there can be little doubt that many individuals the psychiatrist is asked to help are living in highly oppressive environments. When the psychiatrist works with such patients, he learns some bitter lessons. He learns how much more help he could provide if he were able to change the environment. And he learns that he helps his patients little—or perhaps even hurts them—if he ignores their environment.

My own experience in trying to help persons trapped in a severely oppressive environment came when I worked as a psychiatrist in a prison. For many years I used verbal reassurance or drugs in attempts to comfort those who broke down under the strain of the prison regimen. By clarifying the stresses in their lives, I helped some make less-painful adjustments to the realities of their prison sentences, and I helped a few learn to modify their behavior so they could stay out of trouble. I made very little effort to alter the oppressive environment of the prison itself. Occasionally, I would suggest changes that I hoped would make the environment more humane, but I never pressed too hard for fear that I would alienate myself from the prison administrators and lose whatever effectiveness I had.

Now, looking back, I am plagued by doubt as to whether I did enough, or, for that matter, whether it was moral for me to work in the prison at

From *Politics of Therapy* by Seymour Halleck, published by Science House. New York 10003.
© 1971 Seymour Halleck.

all. Suffering is general in prison; every confined person is depressed at least some of the time. Every one of my patients was in a vicious environment that stripped him of dignity and enforced upon him life conditions that were antagonistic to the values of mental health. By participating in the punishment process, even as a healer, I lent a certain credibility to the correction system.

Activism

I recently heard a prominent psychiatrist say of his work in a ghetto that if he did not help a welfare patient get larger welfare payments, he considered that he had done an inadequate job. He was in frequent contact with welfare offices in his efforts to get livable stipends for his patients. This is a kind of political activism—a major step for a psychiatrist. It goes beyond merely encouraging the individual to recognize and deal with environmental stress in his life. It requires the psychiatrist to go out and do something to change the patient's environment.

The focus here is on a few individuals. This raises the troubling question of the social utility of helping only those few who are miserable enough or fortunate enough to get a psychiatrist's help. In a social system that massively oppresses a large proportion of its members, the psychiatrist's efforts to get preferential treatment for a few will drain the capacity of that system to help the many. If the psychiatrist's welfare patient gets more money, there will be less welfare money for someone else. If I had persuaded prison authorities to provide special treatment programs for my patients, other inmates would have been deprived.

To justify preferential activism the psychiatrist must be convinced that his patients are more needy or more deserving than others. Or he must hope that patients thus privileged will do so well that those who run the system will offer equal privilege to others. In an oppressive environment, this is wishful thinking. Those in control may even harden in their positions if they can boast about the special care they provide for problem cases.

Trap

The psychiatrist who commits himself to changing social institutions must consider where the commitment might lead him. In my more recent work with students I have come to realize that their perceptions of the world are growing more and more like those of prisoners. When they envision their futures, when they perceive the injustices of their society, and when they contemplate the improbability of being able to lead honorable lives in that society, many feel that they are trapped in a world that cannot or will not satisfy their needs.

The unhappiness of the young is too widespread and commonplace to be viewed as a weakness or defect in young persons themselves. It is a mistake to place the whole blame for their restlessness on affluence or on the permissiveness with which they were reared, and it is not that they have failed to learn responsibility or that they are simply too willing to define minor states of psychological discomfort as illness. The young are being put under stress by society—by its failure to provide a future for them, by its emphasis on meaningless competition, by its unjust wars, by its technology that pollutes the environment. They fear that overpopulation will destroy their world or drastically worsen the quality of their lives. The young feel these pressures more powerfully than adults because they have longer futures to anticipate.

For several years now I have realized that it is futile—in fact, dishonest —to reassure students about the state of their external world. When I first began to appreciate the impact modern society was having upon youth, my message to students who became my patients was: *Yes, our world is a mess, but you could tolerate that mess better, or you might even be able to do something about it, if you freed yourself of your neuroses.*

This approach sometimes helped the individual patient, but it left me again feeling much like the prison psychiatrist who helps to sustain his patient's sanity so that the patient can better tolerate the process of daily punishment.

Duty

My doubts about the social role of today's psychiatrist grew as I discovered that my patients and those of a colleague had almost universally desperate views of society. I became even more troubled when, as a teacher, I found the same pessimism in a large proportion, perhaps the majority, of educated young people. Students have some freedom to attack society; they have ready access to the psychiatrist and are adept at making him feel guilty about not doing more to change the society. I was persuaded that the psychiatrist who believes that stresses of the modern world won't let the young anticipate decent lives must consider whether he has some responsibility for trying to change that world.

I am convinced that the psychiatrist must involve himself in efforts to change the society. I am also convinced that he must try to find an ideology —or if you prefer, a uniform set of values—that will guide him in his work.

Psychiatry was never, even in more stable times, an ethically or politically neutral profession. Value systems, usually implicit, have always dominated the different schools of psychiatry. Every psychiatrist who ever treated a patient has had some notion of what kind of life would be best for that patient. And every patient who has benefited from psychiatry has incorporated some of his doctor's values. Furthermore, by the very nature of his practice, the psychiatrist consistently takes positions on issues that involve the distribution of power within social systems—issues that have political implications.

A psychiatrist usually focuses on his patient's internal problems, presupposing that the patient's environment is adequate and not contributing

331

to his misery. But the patient is part of a social system. Treatment that doesn't encourage the patient to examine or confront his environment strengthens the status quo. Treatment that emphasizes the oppressiveness of the patient's external environment or shows the patient how to change it may help alter the status quo. The psychiatrist either encourages the patient to accept existing distributions of power or encourages the patient to change them. Every encounter with any psychotherapist, therefore, has political implications.

While my specific concern is with my own discipline, these political responsibilities lie just as heavily on all other therapists.

By reinforcing the positions of those who hold power, the psychiatrist is committing a political act whether he intends to or not. Once this fact is appreciated, the psychiatrist's search for political neutrality begins to appear illusory.

Use

A few psychiatrists have recognized the political implications of psychiatric practice. Frederic Wertham has warned of the potential danger in psychiatry's being used as a sort of Praetorian Guard, dedicated to preserving the status quo. R. D. Laing has insisted that some forms of psychiatric treatment are best viewed as repressive political acts. Thomas Szasz maintains that the psychiatrist has become an agent of social control who identifies and immobilizes those with deviant ideas in much the way that Medieval inquisitors identified and tortured witches. All of these critics, however, have concentrated on the repressive uses of involuntary psychiatry; they have not acknowledged that even when psychiatric treatment is accepted voluntarily it has profound political consequences.

To those concerned with finding a humane and effective use of psychiatry, it makes a critical difference whether one sees all of psychiatry or only some of psychiatry as politically influential. Szasz, who is the most eloquent critic of the repressive use of psychiatry, believes that institutional psychiatry—that practiced by state-employed physicians with involuntary patients—is a formidable political weapon and that contractual psychiatry, in which patients contract for help, is not. I am convinced that this is a false distinction. Any psychiatric intervention into social systems can have liberating or repressive consequences for individual patients. It makes some difference whether the patient seeks this intervention, passively accepts it, or has it thrust upon him. But ultimately, the moral and political outcome of psychiatric treatment is determined by the way in which the psychiatrist goes about it.

Bind

At present, the psychiatrist is being pulled in two different political directions. On the one hand he is being asked by government agencies, prisons, military organizations and parents of alienated children to help people adjust to the world as it is. On the other hand, he is being asked by students, blacks, and members of other oppressed groups to help change some institutions.

Until the past decade psychiatrists were allowed to pursue their work in relative calm and consensus. The great majority of citizens who were capable of expressing their opinions approved of the basic institutions that shaped their society. Undoubtedly many black citizens and others would not have been so approving, but until the 1960s the black man was distressingly "invisible," and his voice was rarely heard by psychiatrists or anyone else.

In the 1960s those who had quietly tolerated oppression for centuries became restless. Psychiatrists, like most other citizens, gradually gained a sense of the unrest in our nation. Some, responding to the unrest, tried to involve themselves in political change. However, massive ambivalence has afflicted their involvement. They are reluctant to criticize institutions that have brought them to positions of relative affluence and power that they wish to retain, and they are concerned over whether it is ethical for a "politically neutral" healer to fight for reform.

The rapid growth of new militancy in many professions suggests that the Establishment is willing to tolerate a considerable amount of dissent from its care-givers, at least at the moment.

Myth

Primarily because of their belief that the art and science of healing must be nonpolitical, psychiatrists have failed to take full advantage of the freedom to dissent that they already have. It is now time to lay to rest the myth of psychiatric neutrality. Psychiatrists can and should be as active as other care-giving professionals in seeking to change the society. It is time for psychiatrists who wish to do something about our society to go to their own leaders and to community leaders and to say something like the following:

Look, I cannot practice good psychiatry without being an activist. I am going to say things and do things that may irritate or may even enrage you. I will repeatedly question your values and will try to get you to engage in dialogue with oppressed people. Much of what I do in the practice of psychiatry will make you uncomfortable. I am sorry it has to be this way. But I believe you have the wisdom and the flexibility to tolerate my activity.

Some conditions in American society are conducive to creating misery among large groups of people. There is no reason why psychiatrists, as citizens and as professionals, should not devote themselves to changing them. Certainly our country's continued involvement in wars not vital to its self-defense causes great suffering among many of our citizens and among those upon whose land we fight. It is likely that the majority of psychiatrists view the Indochinese war as unjust, unwise or unnecessary. There is nothing to keep psychiatrists from involving themselves in antiwar causes and no reason why they should not try to get their professional organizations to take antiwar stands.

Targets

Psychiatrists should also lead the fight against any oppression based on skin color, age, sex or harmless social deviation. Oppression in our ghettos, old people's homes, and prisons creates massive human misery, as do the more subtle social attitudes that isolate and deny privileges to minority or socially deviant groups. The psychiatrist could and should be more active than the average citizen in seeking remedies for these conditions.

Overpopulation is another problem that could be ameliorated slightly by psychiatric activism. Psychiatrists could help with population control by supporting ready birth-control information and free abortion. Finally, the psychiatrist, along with his fellow physicians, must work more and harder for legislation and for reform of medical practices to get adequate health care for the poor as well as the rich.

Shock

Psychiatrists should be committed to ongoing study of, and informed comment on, the effect that all forms of technology and technological progress have on the human condition. They should constantly increase public awareness of the emotional consequences of living in a technocracy, and of the shattering consequences of what Alvin Toffler has referred to as "future shock." Similar examination and critique of economic and political institutions can also be useful.

In any kind of reform, the political role of professional psychiatric organizations is especially important. Certainly organizations such as the American Psychiatric Association cannot take formal stands on every social issue that its members raise. But some social problems are so urgent that professional organizations would be justified in taking active stands on them. Those who seek neutrality must appreciate that our professional organizations already are deeply involved in politics. The American Psychiatric Association already tries to review mental-health legislation and either support or criticize it. As might be expected, the term "mental health" is interpreted broadly enough to justify intervention in a wide variety of social problems, such as crime, violence or drug abuse. In practice the only limits imposed on the American Psychiatric Association's political activities have been in lobbying and support of political candidates. Thus, I am not advocating a major change in the broad policies of psychiatric organizations. I am only advocating that the organization speak out more forcefully on a broader range of issues.

Search

Organized psychiatry could be a powerful political force if psychiatric organizations presented position papers and testified before legislative

334

bodies on social issues. Organized psychiatry could expose the oppressiveness of institutions and use its influence to change them. Violence is one issue upon which the American Psychiatric Association has proven to be socially responsive. Largely because of the urging of Milton H. Miller, professor and chairman of the department of psychiatry at the University of Wisconsin, the American Psychiatric Association has agreed to spend a major part of its efforts throughout 1971 and 1972 searching for alternatives to violence. The emphasis will be on finding ways in which people can confront each other, militantly if that is necessary, but nonviolently. Implicit in this search is the belief that polarization is evil and that lack of communication between groups with dissimilar perspectives ultimately leads to violent confrontation.

Reform

Many of psychiatry's practices, ideologies and training methods interfere with efforts to create a climate that is responsive to social needs. Here are my recommendations for reform:

1. Individual psychotherapy should, in addition to focusing on internal problems, help the patient achieve greater awareness of his external environment.

2. Therapists should spell out their own belief systems and values to their patients as clearly as possible.

3. Family therapy is an important technique for social change and its use should be expanded. Like the individual therapist, the family therapist must clarify his own values to his patients.

4. Group therapy can be a powerful tool for stabilizing or changing the status quo. Its practitioners are obligated to make their political intentions clear.

5. Except in emergencies, therapists should not use mind-altering drugs or behavior therapy to treat symptoms without investigating the patient's family and community relationships. When it is apparent that drugs or behavior therapy can have repressive consequences, the patient should have a clear understanding of what these consequences might be. Psychiatrists also have a responsibility to acquaint their fellow physicians with the political and moral implications of drug therapy.

6. Because community psychiatry can be used to achieve political goals, psychiatrists who work in communities should make their political intentions clear.

7. The community itself should play a major role in selecting its psychiatrists. If the community feels that the psychiatrist is not adequately meeting its needs, the community should have the power to get rid of him.

8. Psychiatrists should be more careful with psychiatric labels. Many patients are judged to be schizophrenic, psychopathic, paranoid or alcoholic on the basis of flimsy evidence. Putting a label on a patient can have

repressive consequences for that person. The arbitrariness of many categories of psychiatric disturbance must be made clear to the public.

9. Psychiatrists must examine certain myths that they have accepted as facts and must stop perpetuating them in a manner that oppresses blacks, women, the elderly, the poor and those who have unconventional sexual tastes.

10. In an age that increasingly calls upon them to comment on moral issues, psychiatrists must realize that their public statements about almost anything will be exploited by advocates of various political viewpoints, and they must carefully distinguish between fact and speculation in their statements. When their statements are used irresponsibly by moral or political partisans, psychiatrists should publicly repudiate such usage.

11. The results of psychiatric research will often support one or another political viewpoint. There is nothing inherently wrong with this, but psychiatrists must accept responsibility for how their research findings, which are often equivocal, are used as evidence in moral or political issues.

12. Naive psychological analysis that deprecates prominent persons is a form of political commentary that is not justifiable. Psychiatrists should not make public statements regarding the mental stability of living public figures.

13. A request by an agency or an insurance company for information about a former patient should not be honored unless ignoring the request would hurt the patient. Such requests should be discouraged vigorously.

14. Too frequently, and usually unwisely, psychological tests are used to grant or deny privileges. Psychiatrists have some responsibility for preventing repressive use of psychological tests.

15. The practice of granting psychiatric excuses caters to an elite, forces the psychiatrist to be dishonest and contributes to social stagnation. Energy invested in providing psychiatric reasons why a woman should have an abortion or why a young man should not be drafted would be better used in efforts to legalize abortion and to end unjust wars. Investment of the energy of psychiatrists in the courtroom should be redirected toward reforming the system of correctional justice.

16. Civil commitment should be based primarily on substantial evidence that a patient is dangerous to himself or to others. Psychiatrists should insist that their decisions regarding commitment be reviewed frequently by judicial agencies.

17. In spite of many improvements in the last 20 years, the level of psychiatric care in most of our public hospitals is inadequate. There is no way to justify any indeterminate commitment, either civil or specialized, to an institution that cannot provide humane and modern treatment. Psychiatrists should devote themselves again to raising the standards of care in our public mental hospitals.

18. In seeking to define the optimum human condition, psychiatric research should focus upon finding solutions to moral problems. Research

that sheds light upon the human condition (or what L. Jolyon West refers to as "biosocial humanism") should have as high a priority as does research that is designed to find causes for socially deviant behavior.

Confess

Many of my recommendations will not be carried out until psychiatrists frankly acknowledge that their use of the concept of mental illness is scientifically inaccurate and socially dangerous. Too many psychiatrists still communicate to their patients that mental illness is an affliction, visited upon them by an external force.

In their more sober moments, psychiatrists understand that the analogy between mental and physical disorders is tenuous, and they recognize the moral and political implications of treating unhappy people as sick people. But they do not acknowledge these implications in their relationships with patients and they tend almost totally to obscure them in their relationship with the public.

Psychiatry will never be able to deal with the moral and political questions that are so critical to its future unless psychiatrists become more consistent in conceptualizing and publicizing their work. Psychiatrists must immediately stop all propaganda designed to convince the public that mental illness is "a disease just like any other disease." Instead, they should acknowledge publicly that there are some behavior disorders that resemble physical illness and others that do not.

Elitism

Still other kinds of reform are needed in psychiatry. Certain changes in psychiatric ideologies, practices and training could do a great deal to bring about a more equitable distribution of mental-health services. Competent psychotherapy—long- or short-term—is a luxury available primarily to a social elite. Psychoanalysts spend a great deal of their time treating psychiatrists, psychologists and social workers. Many of their other patients tend to be professionals, artists and highly successful businessmen. Other therapists also treat primarily middle- or upper-class patients. Even when service is free, therapists will select for long-term therapy patients who are intellectually oriented, creative and usually of upper-middle-class background—in short, persons who are most like themselves. This behavior by therapists, which is well documented, shows little sign of changing even in an era of greater social awareness.

Training more professional therapists in the techniques of family and group therapy will help enormously in reaching more people. Even these techniques, however, are unlikely to let the psychiatrist help the mass of people who need his services. In groups, as in individual therapy, psychiatrists are most likely to treat patients who are most like themselves. Doubling or tripling the number of professionally trained therapists would not solve the problem.

Degree

It is time to acknowledge what many psychiatrists already know: that it is not necessary to have a medical degree to practice good psychotherapy. Even much of the training involved in obtaining a degree in clinical psychology, counseling, guidance or social work may not be absolutely essential to the making of a good psychotherapist. There are many relatively uneducated but otherwise intelligent and sensitive persons in all strata of our society who could and would make excellent therapists if they were properly trained. There has been more disagreement over how much training is needed to make an intelligent and sensitive person into a good therapist than there has been study of the question, but there are enough data to suggest that it can be done.

I foresee a future in which one of the psychiatrist's major functions will be to train nonprofessional therapists to do psychotherapy. Talented people will have to have ready access to psychiatric educational facilities and to the best psychiatric teachers. Up to now the best training programs in the mental-health fields have been open primarily to physicians. In certain circumstances, experienced clinicians teach and supervise psychologists and social workers, but even they generally find it hard to get good clinical training.

The creation of a new class of therapists without specific degrees or licenses will create many new problems: ethics, selection, evaluation of competence, pay. Should lay therapists form a new profession, or will professionalization create distance between them and those they treat? Lay therapists will need to be aware of and sensitive to the political and moral implications of their work.

Those physicians who would resist any tendency to dilute the medical or professional status of psychotherapy must appreciate that in the short run, at least, there is no other humane choice. In our current climate of need and distrust of professionalism, it seems certain that large numbers of nonprofessionals will start doing psychotherapy with or without training. Thousands of persons with little or no training already are trying to help others with encounter or sensitivity experiences and with counseling, formal and informal. Psychiatrists know that bad psychotherapy can hurt people. If they refuse to commit themselves substantially to the training of lay therapists, they will renege on an important obligation to their society.

Change

By giving younger psychiatrists more power in professional organizations and training centers, we could speed the process of orderly change in the psychiatric profession. The young readily accept innovations, but when change comes rapidly the older psychiatrist has great difficulty. In the 12 years since I have finished my residency, I have had to integrate into my basically psychoanalytical orientation new developments in behavior therapy, drug therapy, community therapy, communication therapy, general-systems theory, sensitivity training and family therapy.

Many of the psychiatrists I know are frustrated visionaries, men who dream of contributing to social reform but who are afraid that to act will be to violate some medical or social ethic. In their quest for scientific and social respectability, psychiatrists have shunted their visionary dreams into remote corners, or felt ambivalence or guilt when they occasionally used their professional skills for political purposes. However, the experience of practicing psychiatry in a time of chaos is teaching psychiatrists that they can—indeed must—be helpers and reformers at the same time. While this new awareness enormously complicates psychiatric theories and practices, it also liberates. Psychiatrists can now free themselves from artificial and inauthentic neutrality. They can dream and search for ways to make realities of their dreams.

26.
VISION:
The Murderer

RAY BRADBURY

Halleck's thesis that therapy can support the status quo was the subject of a vision some decades ago by Ray Bradbury. This is the vision of "The Murderer."

Music moved with him in the white halls. He passed an office door: "The Merry Widow Waltz." Another door: "Afternoon of a Faun." A third: "Kiss Me Again." He turned into a cross corridor: "The Sword Dance" buried him in cymbals, drums, pots, pans, knives, forks, thunder, and tin lightning. All washed away as he hurried through an anteroom where a secretary sat nicely stunned by Beethoven's Fifth. He moved himself before her eyes like a hand; she didn't see him.

His wrist radio buzzed.

"Yes?"

"This is Lee, Dad. Don't forget about my allowance."

"Yes, son, yes. I'm busy."

"Just didn't want you to forget, Dad," said the wrist radio. Tchaikovsky's "Romeo and Juliet" swarmed about the voice and flushed into the long halls.

The psychiatrist moved in the beehive of offices, in the cross-pollination of themes, Stravinsky mating with Bach, Haydn unsuccessfully repulsing Rachmaninoff, Schubert slain by Duke Ellington. He nodded to the humming secretaries and the whistling doctors fresh to their morning work. At his office he checked a few papers with his stenographer, who sang under her breath, then phoned the police captain upstairs. A few minutes later a red light blinked, a voice said from the ceiling:

"Prisoner delivered to Interview Chamber Nine."

26. VISION: The Murderer

He unlocked the chamber door, stepped in, heard the door lock behind him.

"Go away," said the prisoner, smiling.

The psychiatrist was shocked by that smile. A very sunny, pleasant warm thing, a thing that shed bright light upon the room. Dawn among the dark hills. High noon at midnight, that smile. The blue eyes sparkled serenely above that display of self-assured dentistry.

"I'm here to help you," said the psychiatrist, frowning. Something was wrong with the room. He had hesitated the moment he entered. He glanced around. The prisoner laughed. "If you're wondering why it's so quiet in here, I just kicked the radio to death."

Violent, thought the doctor.

The prisoner read his thought, smiled, put out a gentle hand. "No, only to machines that yak-yak-yak."

Bits of the wall radio's tubes and wires lay on the gray carpeting. Ignoring these, feeling that smile upon him like a heat lamp, the psychiatrist sat across from his patient in the unusual silence which was like the gathering of a storm.

"You're Mr. Albert Brock, who calls himself The Murderer?"

Brock nodded pleasantly. "Before we start ..." He moved quietly and quickly to detach the wrist radio from the doctor's arm. He tucked it in his teeth like a walnut, gritted and heard it crack, handed it back to the appalled psychiatrist as if he had done them both a favor. "That's better."

The psychiatrist stared at the ruined machine. "You're running up quite a damage bill."

"I don't care," smiled the patient. "As the old song goes: 'Don't Care What Happens to Me!' " He hummed it.

The psychiatrist said: "Shall we start?"

"Fine. The first victim, or one of the first, was my telephone. Murder most foul. I shoved it in the kitchen Insinkerator! Stopped the disposal unit in mid-swallow. Poor thing strangled to death. After that I shot the television set!"

The psychiatrist said, "Mmm."

"Fired six shots right through the cathode. Made a beautiful tinkling crash, like a dropped chandelier."

"Nice imagery."

"Thanks, I always dreamt of being a writer."

"Suppose you tell me when you first began to hate the telephone."

"It frightened me as a child. Uncle of mine called it the Ghost Machine. Voices without bodies. Scared the living hell out of me. Later in life I was never comfortable. Seemed to me a phone was an impersonal instrument. If it *felt* like it, it let your personality go through its wires. If it didn't *want* to, it just drained your personality away until what slipped through at the other end was some cold fish of a voice all steel, copper, plastic, no warmth, no reality. It's easy to say the wrong thing on telephones; the telephone changes your meaning on you. First thing you know, you've made an enemy. Then, of course, the telephone's such a *convenient* thing; it just sits there and *demands* you call someone who doesn't want to be called. Friends were always calling, calling, calling me. Hell, I hadn't any time of my own. When it wasn't the telephone it was the television, the radio, the phonograph. When it wasn't the television or radio or the phonograph it was motion pictures at the corner theater, motion pictures projected, with commercials on low-lying cumulus clouds. It doesn't rain rain any more, it rains soapsuds. When it wasn't High-Fly Cloud advertisements, it was music by Mozzek in every restaurant; music and commercials on the busses I rode to work. When it wasn't music, it was inter-office communications, and my horror chamber of a radio wrist watch on which my friends and my wife phoned every five minutes. What is there about such 'conveniences' that makes them so *temptingly* convenient? The average man thinks, Here I am, time on my hands, and there on my wrist is a wrist telephone, so why not just buzz old Joe up, eh? 'Hello, hello!' I love my friends, my wife, humanity, very much, but when one minute my wife calls to say, 'Where are you *now,* dear?' and a friend calls and says, 'Got the best off-color joke to tell you. Seems there was a guy—' And a stranger calls and cries out, 'This is the Find-Fax Poll. What gum are you chewing at this very *instant!*' Well!"

"How did you feel during the week?"

"The fuse lit. On the edge of the cliff. That same afternoon I did what I did at the office."

"Which was?"

"I poured a paper cup of water into the intercommunications system."

The psychiatrist wrote on his pad.

"And the system shorted?"

"Beautifully! The Fourth of July on wheels! My God, stenographers ran around looking *lost!* What an uproar!"

"Felt better temporarily, eh?"

"Fine! Then I got the idea at noon of stomping my wrist radio on the sidewalk. A shrill voice was just yelling out of it at me, 'This is People's Poll Number Nine. What did you eat for lunch?' when I kicked the Jesus out of the wrist radio!"

"Felt even *better,* eh?"

"It *grew* on me!" Brock rubbed his hands together. "Why didn't I start a solitary revolution, deliver man from certain 'conveniences'? 'Convenient for who?' I cried. Convenient for friends: 'Hey, Al, thought I'd call you from the locker room out here at Green Hills. Just made a sockdolager hole in one! A hole in one, Al! A *beautiful* day. Having a shot of whiskey now. Thought you'd want to know, Al!' Convenient for my office, so when I'm in the field with my radio car there's no moment when I'm not in touch. In *touch! There's* a slimy phrase. Touch, hell. *Gripped!* Pawed, rather. Mauled and massaged and pounded by FM voices. You can't leave your

342

car without checking in: 'Have stopped to visit gas-station men's room.' 'Okay, Brock, step on it!' 'Brock, what *took* you so long?' 'Sorry, sir.' 'Watch it next time, Brock.' ' *Yes, sir!* So, do you know what I did, Doctor? I bought a quart of French chocolate ice cream and spooned it into the car radio transmitter.''

"Was there any *special* reason for selecting French chocolate ice cream to spoon into the broadcasting unit?"

Brock thought about it and smiled. "It's my favorite flavor."

"Oh," said the doctor.

"I figured, hell, what's good enough for me is good enough for the radio transmitter."

"What made you think of spooning *ice cream* into the radio?"

"It was a hot day."

The doctor paused.

"And what happened next?"

"Silence happened next. God, it was *beautiful.* That car radio cackling all day, Brock go here, Brock go there, Brock check in, Brock check out, okay Brock, hour lunch, Brock, lunch over, Brock, Brock, Brock. Well, that silence was like putting ice cream in my ears.''

"You seem to like ice cream a lot."

"I just rode around feeling of the silence. It's a big bolt of the nicest, softest flannel ever made. Silence. A whole hour of it. I just sat in my car; smiling, feeling of that flannel with my ears. I felt *drunk* with Freedom!''

"Go on."

"Then I got the idea of the portable diathermy machine. I rented one, took it on the bus going home that night. There sat all the tired commuters with their wrist radios, talking to their wives, saying 'Now I'm at Forty-third, now I'm at Forty-fourth, here I am at Forty-ninth, now turning at Sixty-first.' One husband cursing, 'Well, get *out* of that bar, damn it, and get home and get dinner started, I'm at Seventieth!'' And the transit-system radio playing 'Tales from the Vienna Woods,' a canary singing words about a first-rate wheat cereal. Then—I switched on my diathermy! Static! Interference! All wives cut off from husbands grousing about a hard day at the office. All husbands cut off from wives who had just seen their children break a window! The 'Vienna Woods' chopped down, the canary mangled! *Silence!* A terrible, unexpected silence. The bus inhabitants faced with having to converse with each other. Panic! Sheer, animal panic!''

"The police seized you?"

"The bus *had* to stop. After all, the music *was* being scrambled, husbands and wives *were* out of touch with reality. Pandemonium, riot, and chaos. Squirrels chattering in cages! A trouble unit arrived, triangulated on me instantly, had me reprimanded, fined, and home, minus my diathermy machine, in jig time.''

"Mr. Brock, may I suggest that so far your whole pattern here is not very —practical? If you didn't like transit radios or office radios or car business radios, why didn't you join a fraternity of radio haters, start petitions, get legal and constitutional rulings? After all, this *is* a democracy."

"And I," said Brock, "am that thing called a minority. I *did* join fraternities, picket, pass petitions, take it to court. Year after year I protested. Everyone laughed. Everyone else *loved* bus radios and commercials. *I* was out of step."

"Then you should have taken it like a good soldier, don't you think? The majority rules."

"But they went too far. If a little music and 'keeping in touch' was charming, they figured a lot would be ten times as charming. I went *wild!* I got home to find my wife hysterical. *Why?* Because she had been completely out of touch with me for half a day. Remember, I did a dance on my wrist radio? Well, that night I laid plans to murder my house."

"Are you *sure* that's how you want me to write it down?"

"That's semantically accurate. Kill it dead. It's one of those talking, singing, humming, weather-reporting, poetry-reading, novel-reciting, jingle-jangling, rockaby-crooning-when-you-go-to-bed houses. A house that screams opera to you in the shower and teaches you Spanish in your sleep. One of those blathering caves where all kinds of electronic Oracles make you feel a trifle larger than a thimble, with stoves that say, 'I'm apricot pie, and I'm *done,*' or 'I'm prime roast beef, so *baste* me!' and other nursery gibberish like that. With beds that rock you to sleep and *shake* you awake. A house that *barely* tolerates humans, I tell you. A front door that barks: 'You've mud on your feet, sir!' And an electronic vacuum hound that snuffles around after you from room to room, inhaling every fingernail or ash you drop. Jesus God, *I* say, Jesus God!"

"Quietly," suggested the psychiatrist.

"Remember that Gilbert and Sullivan song—'I've Got It on My List, It Never Will Be Missed'? All night I listed grievances. Next morning early I bought a pistol. I *purposely* muddied my feet. I stood at our front door. The front door shrilled, 'Dirty feet, muddy feet! Wipe your feet! Please be neat!' I shot the damn thing in its keyhole. I ran to the kitchen, where the stove was just whining, 'Turn me *over!*' In the middle of a mechanical omelet I did the stove to death. Oh, how it sizzled and screamed, 'I'm *shorted!*' Then the telephone rang like a spoiled brat. I shoved it down the Insinkerator. I must state here and now I have *nothing* whatever against the Insinkerator; it was an innocent bystander. I feel sorry for it now, a practical device indeed, which never said a word, purred like a sleepy lion most of the time, and digested our leftovers. I'll have it restored. Then I went in and shot the televisor, that insidious beast, that Medusa, which freezes a billion people to stone every night, staring fixedly, that Siren which called and sang and promised so much and gave, after all, so little, but myself always going back, going back, hoping and waiting until—bang! Like a headless turkey, gobbling, my wife whooped out the front door. The police came. Here I *am!*"

26. VISION: The Murderer

He sat back happily and lit a cigarette.

"And did you realize, in committing these crimes, that the wrist radio, the broadcasting transmitter, the phone, the bus radio, the office intercoms, all were rented or were someone else's property?"

"I would do it all over again, so help me God."

The psychiatrist sat there in the sunshine of that beatific smile.

"You don't want any further help from the Office of Mental Health? You're ready to take the consequences?"

"This is only the beginning," said Mr. Brock. "I'm the vanguard of the small public which is tired of noise and being taken advantage of and pushed around and yelled at, every moment music, every moment in touch with some voice somewhere, do this, do that, quick, quick, now here, now there. You'll see. The revolt begins. My name will go down in history!"

"Mmm." The psychiatrist seemed to be thinking.

"It'll take time, of course. It was all so enchanting at first. The very *idea* of these things, the practical uses, was wonderful. They were almost toys, to be played with, but the people got too involved, went too far, and got wrapped up in a pattern of social behavior and couldn't get out, couldn't admit they were *in,* even. So they rationalized their nerves as something else. 'Our modern age,' they said. 'Conditions.' they said. 'High-strung,' they said. But mark my words, the seed has been sown. I got world-wide coverage on TV, radio, films; *there's* an irony for you. That was five days ago. A billion people know about me. Check your financial columns. Any day now. Maybe today. Watch for a sudden spurt, a rise in sales for French chocolate ice cream!"

"I see," said the psychiatrist.

"Can I go back to my nice private cell now, where I can be alone and quiet for six months?"

"Yes," said the psychiatrist quietly.

"Don't worry about me," said Mr. Brock, rising. "I'm just going to sit around for a long time stuffing that nice bolt of quiet material in both ears."

"Mmm," said the psychiatrist, going to the door.

"Cheers," said Mr. Brock.

"Yes," said the psychiatrist.

He pressed a code signal on a hidden button, the door opened, he stepped out, the door shut and locked. Alone, he moved in the offices and corridors. The first twenty yards of his walk were accompanied by "Tambourine Chinois." Then it was "Tzigane," Bach's Passacaglia and Fugue in something Minor, "Tiger Rag," "Love Is Like a Cigarette." He took his broken wrist radio from his pocket like a dead praying mantis. He turned in at his office. A bell sounded; a voice came out of the ceiling, "Doctor?"

"Just finished with Brock," said the psychiatrist.

"Diagnosis?"

"Seems completely disorientated, but convivial. Refuses to accept the simplest realities of his environment and work *with* them."

VII. A New Look at Therapy and the Assessment of Personality

"Prognosis?"

"Indefinite. Left him enjoying a piece of invisible material."

Three phones rang. A duplicate wrist radio in his desk drawer buzzed like a wounded grasshopper. The intercom flashed a pink light and click-clicked. Three phones rang. The drawer buzzed. Music blew in through the opened door. The psychiatrist, humming quietly, fitted the new wrist radio to his wrist, flipped the intercom, talked a moment, picked up one telephone, talked, picked up another telephone, talked, picked up the third telephone, talked, touched the wrist-radio button, talked calmly and quietly, his face cool and serene, in the middle of the music and the lights flashing, the two phones ringing again, and his hands moving, and his wrist radio buzzing, and the intercoms talking, and voices speaking from the ceiling. And he went on quietly this way through the remainder of a cool, air-conditioned, and long afternoon; telephone, wrist radio, intercom, telephone, wrist radio, intercom, telephone, wrist radio, intercom, telephone, wrist radio, intercom, telephone, wrist radio, intercom, telephone, wrist radio . . .

27.
VISION:
The Petrified World

ROBERT SHECKLEY

The following two articles show obvious similarities that overlap the categories of "valence" and "vision." In "The Petrified World," Robert Sheckley draws a portrait which illustrates the Wittgensteinian dimensions of mental illness —and mental health. In the following article, Thomas Szasz presents what has come to be a highly influential argument that "mental illness" is simply a point of perspective.

Lanigan dreamed the dream again and managed to wake himself with a hoarse cry. He sat upright in bed and glared around him into the violet darkness. His teeth clenched and his lips were pulled back into a spastic grin. Beside him he felt his wife, Estelle, stir and sit up. Lanigan didn't look at her. Still caught in his dream, he waited for tangible proofs of the world.

A chair slowly drifted across his field of vision and fetched up against the wall with a quiet thump. Lanigan's face relaxed slightly. Then Estelle's hand was on his arm—a touch meant to be soothing, but which burned like lye.

"Here," she said. "Drink this."

"No," Lanigan said. "I'm all right now."

"Drink it anyhow."

"No, really. I really am all right."

For now he was completely out of the grip of the nightmare. He was himself again, and the world was its habitual self. That was very precious to Lanigan; he didn't want to let go of it just now, not even for the soothing release of a sedative. "Was it the same dream?" Estelle asked him.

"Yes, just the same. . . . I don't want to talk about it."

"All right," Estelle said. (She is humoring me, Lanigan thought. I frighten her. I frighten myself.)

She asked, "Hon, what time is it?"

Lanigan looked at his watch. "Six fifteen." But as he said it, the hour hand jumped convulsively forward. "No, it's five to seven."

"Can you get back to sleep?"

"I don't think so," Lanigan said. "I think I'll stay up."

"Fine, dear," Estelle said. She yawned, closed her eyes, opened them again and asked, "Hon, don't you think it might be a good idea if you called—"

"I have an appointment with him for twelve ten," Lanigan said.

"That's fine," Estelle said. She closed her eyes again. Sleep came over her while Lanigan watched. Her auburn hair turned a faint blue, and she sighed once, heavily.

Lanigan got out of bed and dressed. He was, for the most part, a large man, unusually easy to recognize. His features were curiously distinct. He had a rash on his neck. He was in no other way outstanding, except that he had a recurring dream which was driving him insane.

He spent the next few hours on his front porch watching stars go nova in the dawn sky.

Later, he went out for a stroll. As luck would have it, he ran into George Torstein just two blocks from his house. Several months ago, in an incautious moment, he had told Torstein about his dream. Torstein was a bluff, hearty fellow, a great believer in self-help, discipline, practicality, common sense and other dull virtues. His hard-headed, no-nonsense attitude had come as a momentary relief to Lanigan. But now it acted as an abrasive. Men like Torstein were undoubtedly the salt of the earth and the backbone of the country; but for Lanigan, wrestling with the impalpable and losing, Torstein had grown from a nuisance into a horror.

"Well, Tom, how's the boy?" Torstein greeted him.

"Fine," Lanigan said, "just fine." He nodded pleasantly and began to walk away under a melting green sky. But one did not escape from Torstein so easily.

"Tom, boy, I've been thinking about your problem," Torstein said. "I've been quite disturbed about you."

"Well, that's very nice of you," Lanigan said. "But really, you shouldn't concern yourself—"

"I do it because I want to," Torstein said, speaking the simple, deplorable truth. "I take an interest in people, Tom. Always have, ever since I was a kid. And you and I've been friends and neighbors for a long time."

"That's true enough," Lanigan said numbly. (The worst thing about needing help was having to accept it.)

"Well, Tom, I think what would really help you would be a little vacation."

Torstein had a simple prescription for everything. Since he practiced soul-doctoring without a license, he was always careful to prescribe a drug you could buy over the counter.

348

27. VISION: The Petrified World

"I really can't afford a vacation this month," Lanigan said. (The sky was ochre and pink now; three pines had withered; an aged oak had turned into a youthful cactus.)

Torstein laughed heartily. "Boy, you can't afford *not* to take a vacation just now! Did you ever consider that?"

"No, I guess not."

"Well, *consider* it! You're tired, tense, all keyed-up. You've been working too hard."

"I've been on leave of absence all week," Lanigan said. He glanced at his watch. The gold case had turned to lead, but the time seemed accurate enough. Nearly two hours had passed since he had begun this conversation.

"It isn't good enough," Torstein was saying. "You've stayed right here in town, right close to your work. You need to get in touch with nature. Tom, when was the last time you went camping?"

"Camping? I don't think I've ever gone camping."

"There, you see! Boy, you've got to put yourself back in touch with real things. Not streets and buildings, but mountains and rivers."

Lanigan looked at his watch again and was relieved to see it turn back to gold. He was glad; he had paid sixty dollars for that case.

"Trees and lakes," Torstein was rhapsodizing. "The feel of grass growing under your feet, the sight of tall black mountains marching across a golden sky—"

Lanigan shook his head. "I've been in the country, George. It doesn't do anything for me."

Torstein was obstinate. "You must get away from artificialities."

"It all seems equally artificial," Lanigan said. "Trees or buildings—what's the difference?"

"Men make buildings," Torstein intoned rather piously, "but God makes trees."

Lanigan had his doubts about both propositions, but he wasn't going to tell them to Torstein. "You might have something there," he said. "I'll think about it."

"You do that," Torstein said. "It happens I know the perfect place. It's in Maine, Tom, and it's right near this little lake—"

Torstein was a master of the interminable description. Luckily for Lanigan, there was a diversion. Across the street, a house burst into flames.

"Hey, whose house is that?" Lanigan asked.

"Makelby's," Torstein said. "That's his third fire this month."

"Maybe we ought to give the alarm."

"You're right, I'll do it myself," Torstein said. "Remember what I told you about that place in Maine, Tom."

Torstein turned to go, and something rather humorous happened. As he stepped over the pavement, the concrete liquefied under his left foot.

Caught unawares, Torstein went in ankle-deep. His forward motion pitched him head-first into the street.

Tom hurried to help him out before the concrete hardened again. "Are you all right?" he asked.

"Twisted my damned ankle," Torstein muttered. "It's okay, I can walk."

He limped off to report the fire. Lanigan stayed and watched. He judged the fire had been caused by spontaneous combustion. In a few minutes, as he had expected, it put itself out by spontaneous decombustion.

One shouldn't be pleased by another man's misfortunes; but Lanigan couldn't help chuckling about Torstein's twisted ankle. Not even the sudden appearance of flood waters on Main Street could mar his good spirits. He beamed at something like a steamboat with yellow stacks that went by in the sky.

Then he remembered his dream, and the panic began again. He walked quickly to the doctor's office.

Dr. Sampson's office was small and dark this week. The old gray sofa was gone; in its place were two Louis Quinze chairs and a hammock. The worn carpet had finally rewoven itself, and there was a cigarette burn on the puce ceiling. But the portrait of Andretti was in its usual place on the wall, and the big free-form ashtray was scrupulously clean.

The inner door opened, and Dr. Sampson's head popped out. "Hi," he said. "Won't be a minute." His head popped back in again.

Sampson was as good as his word. It took him exactly three seconds by Lanigan's watch to do whatever he had to do. One second later Lanigan was stretched out on the leather couch with a fresh paper doily under his head. And Dr. Sampson was saying, "Well, Tom, how have things been going?"

"The same," Lanigan said. "Worse."

"The dream?"

Lanigan nodded.

"Let's just run through it again."

"I'd rather not," Lanigan said.

"Afraid?"

"More afraid than ever."

"Even now?"

"Yes. Especially now."

There was a moment of therapeutic silence. Then Dr. Sampson said, "You've spoken before of your fear of this dream; but you've never told me *why* you fear it so."

"Well . . . It sounds so silly."

Sampson's face was serious, quiet, composed: the face of a man who found nothing silly, who was constitutionally incapable of finding anything silly. It was a pose, perhaps, but one which Lanigan found reassuring.

"All right, I'll tell you," Lanigan said abruptly. Then he stopped.

27. VISION: The Petrified World

"Go on," Dr. Sampson said.

"Well, it's because I believe that somehow, in some way I don't understand. . . ."

"Yes, go on," Sampson said.

"Well, that somehow the world of my dream is becoming the real
world." He stopped again, then went on with a rush. "And that some day
I am going to wake up and find myself *in* that world. And then that world
will have become the real one and this world will be the dream."

He turned to see how this mad revelation had affected Sampson. If the
doctor was disturbed, he didn't show it. He was quietly lighting his pipe
with the smoldering tip of his left forefinger. He blew out his forefinger
and said, "Yes, please go on."

"Go on? But that's it, that's the whole thing!"

A spot the size of a quarter appeared on Sampson's mauve carpet. It
darkened, thickened, grew into a small fruit tree. Sampson picked one of
the purple pods, sniffed it, then set it down on his desk. He looked at
Lanigan sternly, sadly.

"You've told me about your dream-world before, Tom."

Lanigan nodded.

"We have discussed it, traced its origins, analyzed its meaning for you.
In past months we have learned, I believe, why you *need* to cripple yourself
with this nightmare fear."

Lanigan nodded unhappily.

"Yet you refuse the insights," Sampson said. "You forget each time that
your dream-world is a *dream,* nothing but a dream, operated by arbitrary
dream-laws which you have invented to satisfy your psychic needs."

"I wish I could believe that," Lanigan said. "The trouble is my dream-
world is so damnably reasonable."

"Not at all," Sampson said. "It is just that your delusion is hermetic,
self-enclosed and self-sustaining. A man's actions are based upon certain
assumptions about the nature of the world. Grant his assumptions, and his
behavior is entirely reasonable. But to change those assumptions, those
fundamental axioms, is nearly impossible. For example, how do you prove
to a man that he is not being controlled by a secret radio which only he
can hear?"

"I see the problem," Lanigan muttered. "And that's me?"

"Yes, Tom. That, in effect, is you. You want me to prove to you that this
world is real, and that the world of your dream is false. You propose to
give up your fantasy if I supply you with the necessary proofs."

"Yes, exactly!" Lanigan cried.

"But you see, I can't supply them," Sampson said. "The nature of the
world is apparent, but unprovable."

Lanigan thought for a while. Then he said, "Look, Doc, I'm not as sick
as the guy with the secret radio, am I?"

"No, you're not. You're more reasonable, more rational. You have doubts about the reality of the world; but luckily, you also have doubts about the validity of your delusion."

"Then give it a try," Lanigan said. "I understand your problem; but I swear to you, I'll accept anything I can possibly bring myself to accept."

"It's not my field, really," Sampson said. "This sort of thing calls for a metaphysician. I don't think I'd be very skilled at it. . . ."

"Give it a try," Lanigan pleaded.

"All right, here goes." Sampson's forehead wrinkled and shed as he concentrated. Then he said, "It seems to me that we inspect the world through our senses, and therefore we must in the final analysis accept the testimony of those senses."

Lanigan nodded, and the doctor went on.

"So, we know that a thing exists because our senses tell us it exists. How do we check the accuracy of our observations? By comparing them with the sensory impressions of other men. We know that our senses don't lie when other men's senses agree upon the existence of the thing in question."

Lanigan thought about this, then said, "Therefore, the real world is simply what most men think it is."

Sampson twisted his mouth and said, "I told you that metaphysics was not my forte. Still, I think it is an acceptable demonstration."

"Yes. . . . But Doc, suppose *all* of those observers are wrong? For example, suppose there are many worlds and many realities, not just one? Suppose this is simply one arbitrary existence out of an infinity of existences? Or suppose that the nature of reality itself is capable of change, and that somehow I am able to perceive that change?"

Sampson sighed, found a little green bat fluttering inside his jacket and absentmindedly crushed it with a ruler.

"There you are," he said. "I can't disprove a single one of your suppositions. I think, Tom, that we had better run through the entire dream."

Lanigan grimaced. "I really would rather not. I have a feeling. . . ."

"I know you do," Sampson said, smiling faintly. "But this will prove or disprove it once and for all, won't it?"

"I guess so," Lanigan said. He took courage—unwisely—and said, "Well, the way it begins, the way my dream starts—"

Even as he spoke the horror came over him. He felt dizzy, sick, terrified. He tried to rise from the couch. The doctor's face ballooned over him. He saw a glint of metal, heard Sampson saying, "Just try to relax . . . brief seizure . . . try to think of something pleasant."

Then either Lanigan or the world or both passed out.

Lanigan and/or the world came back to consciousness. Time may or may not have passed. Anything might or might not have happened. Lanigan sat up and looked at Sampson.

"How do you feel now?" Sampson asked.

27. VISION: The Petrified World

"I'm all right," Lanigan said. "What happened?"

"You had a bad moment. Take it easy for a bit."

Lanigan leaned back and tried to calm himself. The doctor was sitting at his desk, writing notes. Lanigan counted to twenty with his eyes closed, then opened them cautiously. Sampson was still writing notes.

Lanigan looked around the room, counted the five pictures on the wall, re-counted them, looked at the green carpet, frowned at it, closed his eyes again. This time he counted to fifty.

"Well, care to talk about it now?" Sampson asked, shutting a notebook.

"No, not just now," Lanigan said. (Five paintings, green carpet.)

"Just as you please," the doctor said. "I think that our time is just about up. But if you'd care to lie down in the anteroom—"

"No, thanks, I'll go home," Lanigan said.

He stood up, walked across the green carpet to the door, looked back at the five paintings and at the doctor, who smiled at him encouragingly. Then Lanigan went through the door and into the anteroom, through the anteroom to the outer door and through that and down the corridor to the stairs and down the stairs to the street.

He walked and looked at the trees, on which green leaves moved faintly and predictably in a faint breeze. There was traffic, which moved soberly down one side of the street and up the other. The sky was an unchanging blue, and had obviously been so for quite some time.

Dream? He pinched himself. A dream pinch? He did not awaken. He shouted. An imaginary shout? He did not waken.

He was in the street of the world of his nightmare.

The street at first seemed like any normal city street. There were paving stones, cars, people, buildings, a sky overhead, a sun in the sky. All perfectly normal. Except that *nothing was happening.*

The pavement never once yielded beneath his feet. Over there was the First National City Bank; it had been here yesterday, which was bad enough; but worse it would be there without fail tomorrow, and the day after that, and the year after that. The First National City Bank (Founded 1892) was grotesquely devoid of possibilities. It would never become a tomb, an airplane, the bones of a prehistoric monster. Sullenly it would remain a building of concrete and steel, madly persisting in its fixity until men with tools came and tediously tore it down.

Lanigan walked through this petrified world, under a blue sky that oozed a sly white around the edges, teasingly promising something that was never delivered. Traffic moved implacably to the right, people crossed at crossings, clocks were within minutes of agreement.

Somewhere between the town lay countryside; but Lanigan knew that the grass did not grow under one's feet; it simply lay still, growing no doubt, but imperceptibly, unusable to the senses. And the mountains were still tall and black, but they were giants stopped in mid-stride. They would never march against a golden (or purple or green) sky.

353

VII.   A New Look at Therapy and the Assessment of Personality

The essence of life, Dr. Sampson had once said, is change. The essence of death is immobility. Even a corpse has a vestige of life about it as long as its flesh rots, as long as maggots still feast on its blind eyes and blowflies suck the juice from the burst intestines.

Lanigan looked around at the corpse of the world and perceived that it was dead.

He screamed. He screamed while people gathered around and looked at him (but didn't do anything or become anything), and then a policeman came as he was supposed to (but the sun didn't change shape once), and then an ambulance came down the invariant street (but without trumpets, minus strumpets, on four wheels instead of a pleasing three or twenty-five) and the ambulance men brought him to a building which was exactly where they expected to find it, and there was a great deal of talk by people who stood untransformed, asking questions in a room with relentlessly white walls.

And there was evening and there was morning, and it was the first day.

28.
VALENCE:
The Myth of Mental Illness

THOMAS S. SZASZ

My aim in this essay is to raise the question "Is there such a thing as mental illness?" and to argue that there is not. Since the notion of mental illness is extremely widely used nowadays, inquiry into the ways in which this term is employed would seem to be especially indicated. Mental illness, of course, is not literally a "thing"—or physical object—and hence it can "exist" only in the same sort of way in which other theoretical concepts exist. Yet, familiar theories are in the habit of posing, sooner or later—at least to those who come to believe in them—as "objective truths" (or "facts"). During certain historical periods, explanatory conceptions such as deities, witches, and microorganisms appeared not only as theories but as self-evident *causes* of a vast number of events. I submit that today mental illness is widely regarded in a somewhat similar fashion, that is, as the cause of innumerable diverse happenings. As an antidote to the complacent use of the notion of mental illness—whether as a self-evident phenomenon, theory, or cause—let us ask this question: What is meant when it is asserted that someone is mentally ill?

In what follows I shall describe briefly the main uses to which the concept of mental illness has been put. I shall argue that this notion has outlived whatever usefulness it might have had and that it now functions merely as a convenient myth.

VII.   A New Look at Therapy and the Assessment of Personality

Mental Illness as a Sign of Brain Disease

The notion of mental illness derives its main support from such phenomena as syphilis of the brain or delirious conditions—intoxications, for instance—in which persons are known to manifest various peculiarities or disorders of thinking and behavior. Correctly speaking, however, these are diseases of the brain, not of the mind. According to one school of thought, *all* so-called mental illness is of this type. The assumption is made that some neurological defect, perhaps a very subtle one, will ultimately be found for all the disorders of thinking and behavior. Many contemporary psychiatrists, physicians, and other scientists hold this view. This position implies that people *cannot* have troubles—expressed in what are *now* called "mental illnesses"—because of differences in personal needs, opinions, social aspirations, values, and so on. *All problems in living* are attributed to physicochemical processes which in due time will be discovered by medical research.

"Mental illnesses" are thus regarded as basically no different than all other diseases (that is, of the body). The only difference, in this view, between mental and bodily diseases is that the former, affecting the brain, manifest themselves by means of mental symptoms; whereas the latter, affecting other organ systems (for example, the skin, liver, etc.), manifest themselves by means of symptoms referable to those parts of the body. This view rests on and expresses what are, in my opinion, two fundamental errors.

In the first place, what central nervous system symptoms would correspond to a skin eruption or a fracture? It would *not* be some emotion or complex bit of behavior. Rather, it would be blindness or a paralysis of some part of the body. The crux of the matter is that a disease of the brain, analogous to a disease of the skin or bone, is a neurological defect, and not a problem in living. For example, a *defect* in a person's visual field may be satisfactorily explained by correlating it with certain definite lesions in the nervous system. On the other hand, a person's *belief*—whether this be a belief in Christianity, in Communism, or in the idea that his internal organs are "rotting" and that his body is, in fact, already "dead"—cannot be explained by a defect or disease of the nervous system. Explanations of this sort of occurrence—assuming that one is interested in the belief itself and does not regard it simply as a "symptom" or expression of something else that is *more interesting*—must be sought along different lines.

The second error in regarding complex psychosocial behavior, consisting of communications about ourselves and the world about us, as mere symptoms of neurological functioning is *epistemological.* In other words, it is an error pertaining not to any mistakes in observation or reasoning, as such, but rather to the way in which we organize and express our knowledge. In the present case, the error lies in making a symmetrical dualism between mental and physical (or bodily) symptoms, a dualism which is merely a habit of speech and to which no known observations can be found to

356

correspond. Let us see if this is so. In medical practice, when we speak of physical disturbances, we mean either signs (for example, a fever) or symptoms (for example, pain). We speak of mental symptoms, on the other hand, when we refer to a patient's *communications about himself, others, and the world about him.* He might state that he is Napoleon or that he is being persecuted by the Communists. These would be considered mental symptoms *only* if the observer believed that the patient was *not* Napoleon or that he was *not* being persecuted by the Communists. This makes it apparent that the statement that "X is a mental symptom" involves rendering a judgment. The judgment entails, moreover, a covert comparison or matching of the patient's ideas, concepts, or beliefs with those of the observer and the society in which they live. The notion of mental symptom is therefore inextricably tied to the *social* (including *ethical*) *context* in which it is made in much the same way as the notion of bodily symptom is tied to an *anatomical* and *genetic context.*

To sum up what has been said thus far: I have tried to show that for those who regard mental symptoms as signs of brain disease, the concept of mental illness is unnecessary and misleading. For what they mean is that people so labeled suffer from diseases of the brain; and, if that is what they mean, it would seem better for the sake of clarity to say that and not something else.

Mental Illness as a Name for Problems in Living

The term "mental illness" is widely used to describe something which is very different than a disease of the brain. Many people today take it for granted that living is an arduous process. Its hardship for modern man, moreover, derives not so much from a struggle for biological survival as from the stresses and strains inherent in the social intercourse of complex human personalities. In this context, the notion of mental illness is used to identify or describe some feature of an individual's so-called personality. Mental illness—as a deformity of the personality, so to speak—is then regarded as the *cause* of the human disharmony. It is implicit in this view that social intercourse between people is regarded as something *inherently harmonious,* its disturbance being due solely to the presence of "mental illness" in many people. This is obviously fallacious reasoning, for it makes the abstraction "mental illness" into a *cause,* even though this abstraction was created in the first place to serve only as a shorthand expression for certain types of human behavior. It now becomes necessary to ask: "What kinds of behavior are regarded as indicative of mental illness, and by whom?"

The concept of illness, whether bodily or mental, implies *deviation from some clearly defined norm.* In the case of physical illness, the norm is the structural and functional integrity of the human body. Thus, although the desirability of physical health, as such, is an ethical value, what health *is* can be stated in anatomical and physiological terms. What is the norm deviation from which is regarded as mental illness? This question cannot be easily answered. But whatever this norm might be, we can be certain of only one thing: namely, that it is a norm that must be stated in terms of *psychosocial, ethical,* and *legal* concepts. For example, notions such as "excessive repression" or "acting out an unconscious impulse" illustrate the use of psychological concepts for judging (so-called) mental health and illness. The idea that chronic hostility, vengefulness, or divorce are indicative of mental illness would be illustrations of the use of ethical norms (that is, the desirability of love, kindness, and a stable marriage relationship). Finally, the widespread psychiatric opinion that only a mentally ill person would commit homicide illustrates the use of a legal concept as a norm of mental health. The norm from which deviation is measured whenever one speaks of a mental illness is a *psychosocial and ethical one.* Yet, the remedy is sought in terms of *medical* measures which—it is hoped and assumed—are free from wide differences of ethical value. The definition of the disorder and the terms in which its remedy are sought are therefore at serious odds with one another. The practical significance of this covert conflict between the alleged nature of the defect and the remedy can hardly be exaggerated.

Having identified the norms used to measure deviations in cases of mental illness, we will now turn to the question: "Who defines the norms and hence the deviation?" Two basic answers may be offered: (a) It may be the person himself (that is, the patient) who decides that he deviates from a norm. For example, an artist may believe that he suffers from a work inhibition; and he may implement this conclusion by seeking help *for* himself from a psychotherapist. (b) It may be someone other than the patient who decides that the latter is deviant (for example, relatives, physicians, legal authorities, society generally, etc.). In such a case a psychiatrist may be hired by others to do something *to* the patient in order to correct the deviation.

These considerations underscore the importance of asking the question "Whose agent is the psychiatrist?" and of giving a candid answer to it. The psychiatrist (psychologist or nonmedical psychotherapist), it now develops, may be the agent of the patient, of the relatives, of the school, of the military services, of a business organization, of a court of law, and so forth. In speaking of the psychiatrist as the agent of these persons or organizations, it is not implied that his values concerning norms, or his ideas and aims concerning the proper nature of remedial action, need to coincide exactly with those of his employer. For example, a patient in individual psychotherapy may believe that his salvation lies in a new marriage; his psychotherapist need not share this hypothesis. As the patient's agent, however, he must abstain from bringing social or legal force to bear on the patient which would prevent him from putting his beliefs into action. If his *contract* is with the patient, the psychiatrist (psychotherapist) may disagree with him or stop his treatment; but he cannot engage others to obstruct the patient's aspirations. Similarly, if a psychiatrist is engaged by a court to determine the sanity of a criminal, he need not fully share the legal authorities' values and intentions in regard to the criminal and the means available for dealing with him. But the psychiatrist is expressly barred from stating, for example, that it is not the criminal who is "insane" but the men who wrote the law on the basis of which the very actions that are being judged are regarded as "criminal." Such an opinion could be voiced, of course, but not in a courtroom, and not by a psychiatrist who makes it his practice to assist the court in performing its daily work.

To recapitulate: In actual contemporary social usage, the finding of a mental illness is made by establishing a deviance in behavior from certain psychosocial, ethical, or legal norms. The judgment may be made, as in medicine, by the patient, the physician (psychiatrist), or others. Remedial action, finally, tends to be sought in a therapeutic—or covertly medical— framework, thus creating a situation in which *psychosocial, ethical,* and/or *legal deviations* are claimed to be correctible by (so-called) *medical action.* Since medical action is designed to correct only medical deviations, it seems logically absurd to expect that it will help solve problems whose very existence had been defined and established on nonmedical grounds. I think that these considerations may be fruitfully applied to the present use of tranquilizers and, more generally, to what might be expected of drugs of whatever type in regard to the amelioration or solution of problems in human living.

The Role of Ethics In Psychiatry

Anything that people *do*—in contrast to things that *happen* to them— takes place in a context of value. In this broad sense, no human activity is devoid of ethical implications. When the values underlying certain activities are widely shared, those who participate in their pursuit may lose sight of them altogether. The discipline of medicine, both as a pure science (for example, research) and as a technology (for example, therapy), contains many ethical considerations and judgments. Unfortunately, these are often denied, minimized, or merely kept out of focus; for the ideal of the medical profession as well as of the people whom it serves seems to be having a system of medicine (allegedly) free of ethical value. This sentimental notion is expressed by such things as the doctor's willingness to treat and help patients irrespective of their religious or political beliefs, whether they are rich or poor, etc. While there may be some grounds for this belief—albeit it is a view that is not impressively true even in these regards—the fact remains that ethical considerations encompass a vast range of human affairs. By making the practice of medicine neutral in regard to some specific issues of value need not, and cannot, mean that it can be kept free from all such values. The practice of medicine is intimately tied to ethics; and the first thing that we must do, it seems to me, is to try to make this clear and explicit. I shall let this matter rest here, for it does not concern us specifically in this essay. Lest there be any vagueness, however, about how or where ethics and medicine meet, let me remind the reader of such issues as birth control, abortion, suicide, and euthanasia as only a few of the major areas of current ethicomedical controversy.

Psychiatry, I submit, is very much more intimately tied to problems of ethics than is medicine. I use the word "psychiatry" here to refer to that contemporary discipline which is concerned with *problems in living* (and not with diseases of the brain, which are problems for neurology). Problems in human relations can be analyzed, interpreted, and given meaning only within given social and ethical contexts. Accordingly, it *does* make a difference—arguments to the contrary notwithstanding—what the psychiatrist's socioethical orientations happen to be; for these will influence his ideas on what is wrong with the patient, what deserves comment or interpretation, in what possible directions change might be desirable, and so forth. Even in medicine proper, these factors play a role, as for instance, in the divergent orientations which physicians, depending on their religious affiliations, have toward such things as birth control and therapeutic abortion. Can anyone really believe that a psychotherapist's ideas concerning religious belief, slavery, or other similar issues play no role in his practical work? If they do make a difference, what are we to infer from it? Does it not seem reasonable that we ought to have different psychiatric therapies—each expressly recognized for the ethical positions which they embody—for, say, Catholics and Jews, religious persons and agnostics, democrats and communists, white supremacists and Negroes, and so on? Indeed, if we look at how psychiatry is actually practiced today (especially in the United States), we find that people do seek psychiatric help in accordance with their social status and ethical beliefs. This should really not surprise us more than being told that practicing Catholics rarely frequent birth control clinics.

The foregoing position which holds that contemporary psychotherapists deal with problems in living, rather than with mental illnesses and their cures, stands in opposition to a currently prevalent claim, according to which mental illness is just as "real" and "objective" as bodily illness. This is a confusing claim since it is never known exactly what is meant by such words as "real" and "objective." I suspect, however, that what is intended by the proponents of this view is to create the idea in the popular mind that mental illness is some sort of disease entity, like an infection or a malignancy. If this were true, one could *catch* or *get* a "mental illness," one might *have* or *harbor* it, one might *transmit* it to others, and finally one could get *rid* of it. In my opinion, there is not a shred of evidence to support this idea. To the contrary, all the evidence is the other way and supports the view that what people now call mental illnesses are for the most part *communications* expressing unacceptable ideas, often framed, moreover, in an unusual idiom. The scope of this essay allows me to do no more than mention this alternative theoretical approach to this problem.

28. VALENCE: The Myth of Mental Illness

This is not the place to consider in detail the similarities and differences between bodily and mental illnesses. It shall suffice for us here to emphasize only one important difference between them: namely, that whereas bodily disease refers to public, physicochemical occurrences, the notion of mental illness is used to codify relatively more private, sociopsychological happenings of which the observer (diagnostician) forms a part. In other words, the psychiatrist does not stand *apart* from what he observes, but is, in Harry Stack Sullivan's apt words, a "participant observer." This means that he is *committed* to some picture of what he considers reality—and to what he thinks society considers reality—and he observes and judges the patient's behavior in the light of these considerations. This touches on our earlier observation that the notion of mental symptom itself implies a comparison between observer and observed, psychiatrist and patient. This is so obvious that I may be charged with belaboring trivialities. Let me therefore say once more that my aim in presenting this argument was expressly to criticize and counter a prevailing contemporary tendency to deny the moral aspects of psychiatry (and psychotherapy) and to substitute for them allegedly value-free medical considerations. Psychotherapy, for example, is being widely practiced as though it entailed nothing other than restoring the patient from a state of mental sickness to one of mental health. While it is generally accepted that mental illness has something to do with man's social (or interpersonal) relations, it is paradoxically maintained that problems of values (that is, of ethics) do not arise in this process.* Yet, in one sense, much of psychotherapy may revolve around nothing other than the elucidation and weighing of goals and values—many of which may be mutually contradictory—and the means whereby they might best be harmonized, realized, or relinquished.

The diversity of human values and the methods by means of which they may be realized is so vast, and many of them remain so unacknowledged, that they cannot fail but lead to conflicts in human relations. Indeed, to say that human relations at all levels—from mother to child, through husband and wife, to nation and nation—are fraught with stress, strain, and disharmony is, once again, making the obvious explicit. Yet, what may be obvious may be also poorly understood. This I think is the case here. For it seems to me that—at least in our scientific theories of behavior—we have failed to *accept* the simple fact that human relations are inherently fraught with difficulties and that to make them even relatively harmonious requires much patience and hard work. I submit that the idea of mental illness is now being put to work to obscure certain difficulties which at

*Freud went so far as to say that: "I consider ethics to be taken for granted. Actually I have never done a mean thing." This surely is a strange thing to say for someone who has studied man as a social being as closely as did Freud. I mention it here to show how the notion of "illness" (in the case of psychoanalysis, "psychopathology," or "mental illness") was used by Freud and by most of his followers—as a means for classifying certain forms of human behavior as falling within the scope of medicine, and (by *fiat*) outside that of ethics!

present may be inherent—not that they need be unmodifiable—in the social intercourse of persons. If this is true, the concept functions as a disguise; for instead of calling attention to conflicting human needs, aspirations, and values, the notion of mental illness provides an amoral and impersonal "thing" (an "illness") as an explanation for *problems in living*. We may recall in this connection that not so long ago it was devils and witches who were held responsible for men's problems in social living. The belief in mental illness, as something other than man's trouble in getting along with his fellow man, is the proper heir to the belief in demonology and witchcraft. Mental illness exists or is "real" in exactly the same sense in which witches existed or were "real."

Choice, Responsibility, and Psychiatry

While I have argued that mental illnesses do not exist, I obviously did not imply that the social and psychological occurrences to which this label is currently being attached also do not exist. Like the personal and social troubles which people had in the Middle Ages, they are real enough. It is the labels we give them that concerns us and, having labelled them, what we do about them. While I cannot go into the ramified implications of this problem here, it is worth noting that a demonologic conception of problems in living gave rise to therapy along theological lines. Today, a belief in mental illness implies—nay, requires—therapy along medical or psychotherapeutic lines.

What is implied in the line of thought set forth here is something quite different. I do not intend to offer a new conception of "psychiatric illness" nor a new form of "therapy." My aim is more modest and yet also more ambitious. It is to suggest that the phenomena now called mental illnesses be looked at afresh and more simply, that they be removed from the category of illnesses, and that they be regarded as the expressions of man's struggle with the problem of *how* he should live. The last mentioned problem is obviously a vast one, its enormity reflecting not only man's inability to cope with his environment, but even more his increasing self-reflectiveness.

By problems in living, then, I refer to that truly explosive chain reaction which began with man's fall from divine grace by partaking of the fruit of the tree of knowledge. Man's awareness of himself and of the world about him seems to be a steadily expanding one, bringing in its wake an ever larger *burden of understanding* (an expression borrowed from Suzanne Langer). *This burden, then, is to be expected and must not be misinterpreted.* Our only *rational* means for lightening it is *more understanding,* and appropriate *action* based on such understanding. The main alternative lies in acting as though the burden were not what in fact we perceive it to be and taking refuge in an outmoded theological view of man. In the latter view, man does not fashion his life and much of his world about him, but merely lives out his fate in a world created by superior beings. This may logically lead to pleading nonresponsibility in the face of seemingly unfathomable problems and difficulties. Yet, if man fails to take increasing responsibility for his actions, individually as well as collectively, it seems unlikely that some higher power or being would assume this task and carry this burden for him. Moreover, this seems hardly the proper time in human history for obscuring the issue of man's responsibility for his actions by hiding it behind the skirt of an all-explaining conception of mental illness.

Conclusions

I have tried to show that the notion of mental illness has outlived whatever usefulness it might have had and that it now functions merely as a convenient myth. As such, it is a true heir to religious myths in general, and to the belief in witchcraft in particular; the role of all these belief-systems was to act as *social tranquilizers,* thus encouraging the hope that mastery of certain specific problems may be achieved by means of substitutive (symbolic-magical) operations. The notion of mental illness thus serves mainly to obscure the everyday fact that life for most people is a continous struggle, not for biological survival, but for a "place in the sun," "peace of mind," or some other human value. For man aware of himself and of the world about him, once the needs for preserving the body (and perhaps the race) are more or less satisfied, the problem arises as to what he should do with himself. Sustained adherence to the myth of mental illness allows people to avoid facing this problem, believing that mental health, conceived as the absence of mental illness, automatically insures the making of right and safe choices in one's conduct of life. But the facts are all the other way. It is the making of good choices in life that others regard, retrospectively, as good mental health!

The myth of mental illness encourages us, moreover, to believe in its logical corollary: that social intercourse would be harmonious, satisfying, and the secure basis of a "good life" were it not for the disrupting influences of mental illness or "psychopathology." The potentiality for universal human happiness, in this form at least, seems to me but another example of the I-wish-it-were-true type of fantasy. I do believe that human happiness or well-being on a hitherto unimaginably large scale, and not just for a select few, is possible. This goal could be achieved, however, only at the cost of many men, and not just a few being willing and able to tackle their personal, social, and ethical conflicts. This means having the courage and integrity to forego waging battles on false fronts, finding solutions for substitute problems—for instance, fighting the battle of stomach acid and chronic fatigue instead of facing up to a marital conflict.

Our adversaries are not demons, witches, fate, or mental illness. We have no enemy whom we can fight, exorcise, or dispel by "cure." What we do have are *problems in living*—whether these be biologic, economic, political, or sociopsychological. In this essay I was concerned only with problems belonging in the last mentioned category, and within this group mainly with those pertaining to moral values. The field to which modern psychiatry addresses itself is vast, and I made no effort to encompass it all. My argument was limited to the proposition that mental illness is a myth, whose function it is to disguise and thus render more palatable the bitter pill of moral conflicts in human relations.

Jones, E. *The life and work of Sigmund Freud.* Vol. III. New York: Basic Books, 1957.

Langer, S. K. *Philosophy in a new key.* New York: Mentor Books, 1953.

VIII.
Testing, Measurement, and the Ultimate Experiment

29.
VALENCE:
Psychological Testing—
A Smoke Screen Against Logic

FRANK B. McMAHON, JR.

*Each of the following two articles discusses the use of testing—and each does
so in its own way. First, Frank McMahon raises some points that are of
increasingly central concern to psychologists regarding the use of testing.
Following him, Robert Silverberg writes of a test that—in both procedure and
result—somehow puts an end to further testing.*

Many years ago—but not long enough—I took Psychological Testing I
and II, Projective Testing I and II and a couple of Advanced Testings I and
II. I shall never forget the day the class was analyzing the results of a
Rorschach ink-blot test and the professor became extremely excited over
a response to one of the cards: " . . . and here," the patient had said, "I see
a church steeple, over here a church, and down here is the grass."

"You see," the professor explained, "the church steeple represents a
phallus; the grass, pubic hair; and we are dealing with a conflict between
religious restriction and sexual desire."

And in another class, we discussed a sentence-completion item from
another personality test: "*One night I* . . . awakened and went to the refrig-
erator to get something to eat, a hot dog, I think." Well, this was written
by a young woman, and its interpretation I shall leave to the reader, whose
wildest fantasies could not outdo those of the psychologists.

Or the objective test item: "I'm not as healthy as I used to be." (Checked
true.) That one sent us scurrying through the other tests for indications of
abnormal anxieties or mental disorders, never once giving even passing
thought to the possibility that on that day the test taker may have needed
an Alka-Seltzer.

One of the great geniuses of the psychological movement was Sigmund
Freud. Freud helped everyone but the psychologist. To the psychologist

Reprinted from *Psychology Today* Magazine, January 1969. Copyright © Communications/
Research/Machines, Inc.

29. VALENCE: Psychological Testing

Freud gave the psychoanalytic method, in which the analyst is free to roam the patient's subconscious without fear of successful contradiction. The Freudian method was a handle that the psychologist could grasp in all emergencies, a method that allows contradictory diagnoses and deceives the psychologist and alienates the patient. In interpreting a patient's subconscious, it is axiomatic that what is sought is unknown both to the patient *and to the psychologist*.

Granted, remarkable strides have been made as a result of Freud's work. We have, for example, pretty clear evidence that people are not always what they seem to be on the surface. The possibility that sexuality is a childhood trait as well as an adult preoccupation seems clearly established. But one of the leaders in current dream research, Calvin Hall of the University of California, Santa Cruz, made a list of sexual symbolism found in various psychology books and articles. There were 102 such objects, including anything resembling a gun or stick, and actions such as ploughing and flogging. Like cars, sexual symbols have suddenly become too numerous. What started as a good idea has suddenly swamped us in an asphyxiating smog. Sexual symbols and their interpretation have almost supplanted the patient himself.

On the other hand, the late Gordon Allport, Harvard professor and former president of the American Psychological Association, suggested that if we wanted to know about a person, the first step was to ask him directly. Unfortunately, his suggestion has gone by the wayside. We psychologists are afraid to relinquish our position of omnipotence in relation to the patient and to elicit his aid in understanding man.

Today, a mixture of fear and desire for power grips clinical psychology. The desire for power indirectly manifests itself in the American Psychological Association's valid attempts to have clinicians as expert witnesses at trials. A recent court victory has validated these attempts, solidifying clinical psychology's growing power base. On the other hand, fear indirectly manifests itself, making it seem clinicians have something to hide, in the restrictions against undergraduates purchasing Rorschach cards and in the incomprehensible jargon that has been set up to explain and understand psychological disturbances.

Psychologists have had a long and difficult struggle in gaining recognition. Unfortunately, the price of this recognition has been to obscure understanding and diagnosis by double talk or even triple talk. If this results in the patient being kept in the dark, it is immaterial because few psychologists feel the patient should have any say. Witness the common phenomenon at a hospital "staff" conference: heads nodding, slight smiles, everything short of cheering at a say-nothing statement such as, "He's fixated at this level because during these early years his father was stern, lenient, hostile, neutral, castrating, overprotective." Choose any of the above. They all work!

With psychology now strong enough as a science, the sad part is that we do not go back and pick up the pieces. Are we really testing what we think we are testing?

Psychology has had a strange developmental pattern. In order to get rid of the idea that man is a completely rational animal, we stressed his inability to understand himself. We stressed that the fountain pen represented something other than itself—it represented a penis. Now that we have proved our point (that man is not always rational), psychologists are caught in an equally extreme myth that man is a spidery maze of disguised sickness.

We must go back and talk with the patient—if need be, about something as insignificant as the pen. "Tell me, Mr. Patient, what does this pen mean in your dream (or your Rorschach card)?" The patient may say it means that he wants to be a writer, that he feels his imagination and its expression are constricted.

Rather than loosen the hold on the past, however, we interpret elaborate psychological tests in the same way, over and over, searching most of all for hidden symbols, deep meanings. The patient knows this. That there is trickery involved is most obvious to him. The patient is on guard and legitimately so. The psychologist is on guard, and legitimately so. We have, then, a contest of who can outfox whom. The psychologist has the upper hand, of course, because he can interpret anything he finds in the tests any way he wants.

Another problem, repeatedly pointed out by men like Lee Cronbach, Hans Eysenck, Gordon Allport and Carl Rogers, is that we are playing roulette odds when we predict anything of substance via psychological tests as they now stand. For example, roughly half of the studies on the validity of Rorschach tests are positive, half are negative. Take your pick.

In any case, validity studies (which tell whether a test measures what it is supposed to measure) show personality tests to be of such low validity that the issue is often sidestepped. A validity of 1.00 is perfect and in the personality testing field a validity of .25 is often considered pretty good. Lee Cronbach, however, in *Essentials of Psychological Testing*, says a validity of .25 is poor. Depending on how a validity study is performed, who the test takers are, what their backgrounds and intelligence are, a validity of .25 can mean a personality test has little better than fifty-fifty accuracy. Reliability, which is closely related to validity, tells how *consistent* a test is in measuring what it is supposed to measure. The Minnesota Multiphasic Personality Inventory, which is considered the king of self-report tests, has reliability coefficients that begin as low as .50. [Self-report tests are ones where the patient reports on himself, by himself, via written answers to true–false questions like: I am contented with my sex life.]

Dr. Anne Anastasi, a prominent psychologist in the testing field, reports one reliability study (to note the extreme) on the MMPI Paranoia scale that was a minus quantity, –.05. She then explains that the scales don't mean what they say, anyway.

29. VALENCE: Psychological Testing

"For example, we cannot assume a high score on the Schizophrenia scale indicates the presence of Schizophrenia . . . moreover, such a score may appear in a normal person."

In the face of such evidence, I think there are two major reasons for the continued ingrowth of the psychological testing movement. First, in order to maintain a mythical sense of professionalism, we are overinterpreting, being overerudite and succumbing to a fear of *not* seeing something in a test. Second, and running counter to the first reason, to understand the infinitely complex human mind we would have to ask the patient for assistance and take some of what he says at face value, integrating his material with our testing. Unfortunately, some psychologists think this is like the surgeon asking the patient where to cut.

Basically, there are three types of psychological tests: objective, semi-projective and projective (true–false, sentence completion and ink-blot).

Examining these three types in 1959, K. B. Little of the University of Denver and Edwin Schneidman of the National Institute of Mental Health had 48 clinical psychologists assess the tests of persons already interviewed and tested by other clinicians who had diagnosed these persons as ranging from psychotic to normal. These 48 investigators found that the clinicians tended to "overinterpret" the tests of the normal group. The clinicians assigned to normal persons the diagnostic label of "neurotic."

Subsequently, I decided to do an experiment of my own to test further the hypothesis that clinicians "overinterpret." I ran a study comparing psychology graduate students as raters of test results with raters from outside psychology. Objective, semi-projective and projective material was abstracted from the tests of 36 individuals receiving psychotherapy and 27 who said they had never received psychological treatment. The 27 responded to a questionnaire, on which they did not have to put their name, to the effect that they had never felt the need of, or sought, treatment. Of course, statistically, there would be more "disturbed" persons among those who were receiving treatment. I selected replies of the 63 persons to each type of test, avoiding replies that appear infrequently in response to a given test stimulus. I gave the replies to 16 clinical psychology graduate students, all of whom had completed their course work in psychological testing and were within a semester of receiving their Ph.D.s. I selected 16 business-administration majors at a comparable level of graduate study as the second group of raters.

The two sets of graduate students evaluated the replies of the "neurotic" and the "normal" groups according to whether they thought the test takers were "normal" or "neurotic."

Our finding was that in an overall evaluation of the replies to the Minnesota Multiphasic Personality Inventory and the sentence-completion test the business-administration students were able to differentiate "normal" from "neurotic" replies with approximately as much accuracy as were the students in psychology. What is possibly more interesting is that in differentiating between "normal" and "neurotic" on the Rorschach tests the business students outdid their counterparts in psychology.

Detailed examination showed that the psychology students interpreted the Rorschach replies of more intelligent test takers as being more disturbed; they overinterpreted the symbolic content given by the brighter persons.

Considerable evidence from other studies shows that more intelligent people produce more symbols. If symbolic interpretation is indeed the primary factor in overinterpreting, then normal persons of higher intelligence are likely to receive abnormal ratings.

This is not meant to suggest that laymen are necessarily better at test interpretation than psychologists, but that psychologists are evolving even more elaborate test interpretations that remove the clinician further and further from the reality of the patient.

One could go to the extreme of saying that in the case just cited clinical training was of no benefit to diagnosis. My contention, however, is that training has been aimed in the wrong direction. It encourages a preoccupation with digging out what may not even be in a person's psyche: elaborate and secret unconscious meanings. Instead, clinical training should be used in conjunction with both common sense and what the patient says of himself. In place of the tricky diagnosis, we should focus on what the patient is saying, in most cases taking his word for it (statistically better than roulette) and trying to integrate both sources into a comprehensible whole.

Oddly enough, although both groups of raters were able to distinguish "normal" from "neurotic" replies on the MMPI and the sentence-completion tests, the content of the test items themselves did not seem to be critical in the rating procedure. That is, if certain test items consistently meant disturbance, these items should have been consistently rated as such. This was not the case. There were only 22 out of 376 test items that 75 per cent of the raters rated the same way.

This suggests that the content of the test items themselves is not being accurately interpreted. The traditional psychological test may not be pinpointing the content that is most meaningful to the patient and most enlightening to the psychologist.

In 1963, I published a new personality test designed to be administered on a "man-to-man" basis. Each and every question was completely transparent, or face-valid. The test taker could easily tell that a certain response would count "against" him. A face-valid item looks to the test taker to be what it is. An example of an item that is *not* face-valid is, "I used to like to play drop the handkerchief."

For this "man-to-man" technique to work, I had to avoid the ambiguity of the typical test. Therefore, after each traditional psychological test item I inserted a qualifier that the test taker could use to keep from feeling (and being) shoved behind the eight ball. For example, "Some people have it in for me," True or False, followed by: If true, "I can't seem to get them off my mind," True or False.

This couplet type of questioning means that if the individual checks both parts "true," he is acknowledging a problem in his life that is important enough to admit to twice. Obviously, the couplet does not make clear the deeper meaning of the item, nor can the meaning really be made clear by any self-report test. The couplet does signal areas in which the patient desires further discussion. More important, the couplet relies heavily on the patient himself.

The test is then scored, but instead of writing a report that is known only to the psychologist, as is customary, we return the test to the test taker for discussion. To discuss each item on a standard objective psychological test would be a big job considering the large (more than 500 on the MMPI) number of items. But by using the couplet method, we can construct an effective test with just under 50 items. The psychologist may point out that certain of the test taker's replies to the test suggest problem areas. The discussion should further clarify the meaning and purpose of any test item and the extent to which an item, in the opinion of the psychologist or the test taker, should be further explored. I consider this discussion an essential ingredient of the testing process.

Psychologists using the test quickly found that it helped place the patient–doctor relationship on an above-board basis. The meaning behind the items and the methods of coping with the problems the items suggested could be explored with mutual confidence.

We further analyzed the test structure to determine what meaning was inherent in the single test item versus the couplet. For example, the traditional test item, "Some people have it in for me," was rated by a group of psychologists. Interpretations of its meaning ranged from "indicates an aggressive individual" to "he's got paranoid traits."

A second group of psychologists rated the same item, except that we added the couplet or qualifier, "I can't seem to get them off my mind," and marked it *false*. Interpretations changed considerably. Many fewer psychologists now thought that the statement, "Some people have it in for me," indicated severe disturbance. Their interpretations, however, still varied widely.

At this point, I performed an informal validity study of my test. Patients who had discussed the test items with the therapists were asked, after three sessions, to list important problems not covered so far in the therapeutic relationship. Only one of 32 persons indicated he had failed to touch on his major problems.

In numerous other validity studies, the couplet test has been compared with the longer and less face-valid type of objective tests. The results of these other tests were the same as those obtained with the couplet test in enough cases to yield correlations of between .80 and .95 (and none below .80), which are high. Other studies of the couplet test yielded validities in the .70 and .80 range. In these studies, therapists who were unaware of the results obtained with couplet tests rated patients with other diagnostic tools. Comparison of their results with the couplet test results showed the high validities.

Therapy with regressed patients has been most effective when the therapist takes the time to learn the specific language of the patient himself. He might have to learn, for instance, that the patient conceives of God as a Chinese four feet tall, with a mustache. This can take a great deal of time and effort and only a few therapists have been heroic enough to bother.

Similarly, most of us are not now allowing for the meaning that patients attach to their symbols when they take tests. I do not intend to imply that symbolism or hidden meaning is not of the utmost value. It seems only logical, however, that the patient should help us to understand the symbols. I think the reason for the high validities of the couplet test is that the test is neither clever nor tricky. It says to the patient, "You help me to understand you." Why not try him out?

30.
VISION:
The Sixth Palace
ROBERT SILVERBERG

Ben Azai was deemed worthy and stood at the gate of the sixth palace
and saw the ethereal splendor of the pure marble plates. He opened his
mouth and said twice, "Water! Water!" In the twinkling of an eye they
decapitated him and threw eleven thousand iron bars at him. This shall
be a sign for all generations that no one should err at the gate of the
sixth palace.

Lesser Hekhaloth

There was the treasure, and there was the guardian of the treasure. And
there were the whitened bones of those who had tried in vain to make the
treasure their own. Even the bones had taken on a kind of beauty, lying
out there by the gate of the treasure vault, under the blazing arch of the
heavens. The treasure itself lent beauty to everything near it—even the
scattered bones, even the grim guardian.

The home of the treasure was a small world that belonged to red Valzar.
Hardly more than moon-sized, really, with no atmosphere to speak of, a
silent, dead little world that spun through darkness a billion miles from its
cooling primary. A wayfarer had stopped there once. Where from, where
bound? No one knew. He had established a cache there, and there it still
lay, changeless and eternal, treasure beyond belief, presided over by the
faceless metal man who waited with metal patience for his master's return.

There were those who would have the treasure. They came, and were
challenged by the guardian, and died.

On another world of the Valzar system, men undiscouraged by the fate
of their predecessors dreamed of the hoard, and schemed to possess it.
Lipescu was one: a tower of a man, golden beard, fists like hammers, gullet
of brass, back as broad as a tree of a thousand years. Bolzano was another;
awlshaped, bright of eye, fast of finger, twig thick, razor sharp. They had
no wish to die.

Lipescu's voice was like the rumble of island galaxies in collision. He

Reprinted by permission of the author and his agents, Scott Meredith Literary Agency, Inc.,
580 Fifth Avenue, New York, New York 10036.

wrapped himself around a tankard of good black ale and said, "I go tomorrow, Bolzano."

"Is the computer ready?"

"Programmed with everything the beast could ask me," the big man boomed. "There won't be a slip."

"And if there is?" Bolzano asked, peering idly into the blue, oddly pale, strangely meek eyes of the giant. "And if the robot kills you?"

"I've dealt with robots before."

Bolzano laughed. "That plain is littered with bones, friend. Yours will join the rest. Great bulky bones, Lipescu. I can see them now."

"You're a cheerful one, friend."

"I'm realistic."

Lipescu shook his head heavily. "If you were realistic, you wouldn't be in this with me," he said slowly. "Only a dreamer would do such a thing as this." One meaty paw hovered in the air, pounced, caught Bolzano's forearm. The little man winced as bones ground together. Lipescu said, "You won't back out? If I die, you'll make the attempt?"

"Of course I will, you idiot."

"Will you? You're a coward, like all little men. You'll watch me die, and then you'll turn tail and head for another part of the universe as fast as you know how. Won't you?"

"I intend to profit by your mistakes," Bolzano said in a clear, testy voice. "Let go of my arm."

Lipescu released his grip. The little man sank back in his chair, rubbing his arm. He gulped ale. He grinned at his partner and raised his glass.

"To success," Bolzano said.

"Yes. To the treasure."

"And to long life afterward."

"For both of us," the big man boomed.

"Perhaps," said Bolzano. "Perhaps."

He had his doubts. The big man was sly, Ferd Bolzano knew, and that was a good combination, not often found: slyness and size. Yet the risks were great. Bolzano wondered which he preferred—that Lipescu should gain the treasure on his attempt, thus assuring Bolzano of a share without risk, or that Lipescu should die, forcing Bolzano to venture his own life. Which was better, a third of the treasure without hazard, or the whole thing for the highest stake?

Bolzano was a good enough gambler to know the answer to that. Yet there was more than yellowness to the man; in his own way, he longed for the chance to risk his life on the airless treasure world.

Lipescu would go first. That was the agreement. Bolzano had stolen the computer, had turned it over to the big man, and Lipescu would make the initial attempt. If he gained the prize, his was the greater share. If he perished, it was Bolzano's moment next. An odd partnership, odd terms, but Lipescu would have it no other way, and Ferd Bolzano did not argue the point with his beefy compatriot. Lipescu would return with the treasure, or he would not return at all. There would be no middle way, they both were certain.

Bolzano spent an uneasy night. His apartment, in an airy shaft of a building overlooking glittering Lake Eris, was a comfortable place, and he had little longing to leave it. Lipescu, by preference, lived in the stinking slums beyond the southern shore of the lake, and when the two men parted for the night, they went in opposite ways. Bolzano considered bringing a woman home for the night, but did not. Instead, he sat moody and wakeful before the televector screen, watching the procession of worlds, peering at the green and gold and ochre planets as they sailed through the emptiness.

Toward dawn, he ran the tape of the treasure. Octave Merlin had made that tape, a hundred years before, as he orbited sixty miles above the surface of the airless little world. Now Merlin's bones bleached on the plain, but the tape had come home, and bootlegged copies commanded a high price in hidden markets. His camera's sharp eye had seen much.

There was the gate; there was the guardian. Gleaming, ageless, splendid. The robot stood ten feet high, a square, blocky, black shape topped by the tiny anthropomorphic head dome, featureless and sleek. Behind him the gate, wide open but impassable all the same. And behind him, the treasure, culled from the craftsmanship of a thousand worlds, left here who knew why, untold years ago.

No mere jewels. No dreary slabs of so-called precious metal. The wealth here was not intrinsic; no vandal would think of melting the treasure into dead ingots. Here were statuettes of spun iron, that seemed to move and breathe. Plaques of purest lead, engraved with lathework that dazzled the mind and made the heart hesitate. Cunning intaglios in granite, from the workshops of a frosty world half a parsec from nowhere. A scatter of opals, burning with an inner light, fashioned into artful loops of brightness.

A helix of rainbow-colored wood. A series of interlocking strips of some beast's bone, bent and splayed so that the pattern blurred and perhaps abutted some other-dimensional continuum. Cleverly carved shells, one within the other, descending to infinity. Burnished leaves of nameless trees. Polished pebbles from unknown beaches. A dizzying spew of wonders, covering some fifty square yards, sprawled out behind the gate in stunning profusion.

Rough men unschooled in the tenets of aesthetics had given their lives to possess the treasure. It took no fancy knowledge to realize the wealth of it, to know that collectors strung from galaxy to galaxy would fight with bare fangs to claim their share. Gold bars did not a treasure make. But these things? Beyond duplication, almost beyond price?

Bolzano was wet with a fever of yearning before the tape had run its course. When it was over, he slumped in his chair, drained, depleted.

Dawn came. The silvery moons fell from the sky. The red sun splashed across the heavens. Bolzano allowed himself the luxury of an hour's sleep.

VIII. Testing, Measurement, and the Ultimate Experiment

And then it was time to begin. . . .

As a precautionary measure, they left the ship in a parking orbit three miles above the airless world. Past reports were unreliable, and there was no telling how far the robot guardian's power extended. If Lipescu were successful, Bolzano could descend and get him—and the treasure. If Lipescu failed, Bolzano would land and make his own attempt.

The big man looked even bigger, encased in his suit and in the outer casement of a dropshaft. Against his massive chest he wore the computer, an extra brain as lovingly crafted as any object in the treasure hoard. The guardian would ask him questions; the computer would help him answer. And Bolzano would listen. If Lipescu erred, possibly his partner could benefit by knowledge of the error and succeed.

"Can you hear me?" Lipescu asked.

"Perfectly. Go on, get going!"

"What's the hurry? Eager to see me die?"

"Are you lacking in confidence?" Bolzano asked. "Do you want me to go first?"

"Fool," Lipescu muttered. "Listen carefully. If I die, I don't want it to be in vain."

"What would it matter to you?"

The bulky figure wheeled around. Bolzano could not see his partner's face, but he knew Lipescu must be scowling. The giant rumbled, "Is life that valuable? Can't I take a risk?"

"For *my* benefit?"

"For mine," Lipescu said. "I'll be coming back."

"Go, then. The robot is waiting."

Lipescu walked to the lock. A moment later he was through and gliding downward, a one-man spaceship, jets flaring beneath his feet. Bolzano settled by the scanner to watch. A televector pickup homed in on Lipescu just as he made his landing, coming down in a blaze of fire. The treasure and its guardian lay about a mile away. Lipescu rid himself of the dropshaft, stepping with giant bounds toward the waiting guardian.

Bolzano watched.

Bolzano listened.

The televector pickup provided full fidelity. It was useful for Bolzano's purposes, and useful, too, for Lipescu's vanity, for the big man wanted his every moment taped for posterity. It was interesting to see Lipescu dwarfed by the guardian. The black faceless robot, squat and motionless, topped the big man by better than three feet.

Lipescu said, "Step aside."

The robot's reply came in surprisingly human tones, though void of any distinguishing accent. "What I guard is not to be plundered."

"I claim them by right," Lipescu said.

"So have many others. But their right did not exist. Nor does yours. I cannot step aside for you."

378

30. VISION: The Sixth Palace

"Test me," Lipescu said. "See if I have the right or not!"

"Only my master may pass."

"Who is your master? *I* am your master!"

"My master is he who can command me. And no one can command me who shows ignorance before me."

"Test me, then," Lipescu demanded.

"Death is the penalty for failure."

"Test me."

"The treasure does not belong to you."

"Test me and step aside."

"Your bones will join the rest here."

"Test me," Lipescu said.

Watching from aloft, Bolzano went tense. His thin body drew together like that of a chilled spider. Anything might happen now. The robot might propound riddles, like the Sphinx confronting Oedipus.

It might demand proofs of mathematical theorems. It might ask the translation of strange words. So they gathered, from their knowledge of what had befallen other men here. And, so it seemed, to give the wrong answer was to earn instant death.

He and Lipescu had ransacked the libraries of the world. They had packed all knowledge, so they hoped, into their computer. It had taken months, even with multistage programming. The tiny globe of metal on Lipescu's chest contained an infinity of answers to an infinity of questions.

Below, there was a long silence as man and robot studied one another. Then the guardian said, "Define latitude."

"Do you mean geographical latitude?" Lipescu asked.

Bolzano congealed with fear. The idiot, asking for a clarification! He would die before he began!

The robot said, "Define latitude."

Lipescu's voice was calm. "The angular distance of a point on a planet's surface north or south of the equator, as measured from the center of the planet."

"Which is more consonant," the robot asked, "the minor third or the major sixth?"

There was a pause. Lipescu was no musician. But the computer would feed him the answer.

"The minor third," Lipescu said.

Without a pause, the robot fired another question. "Name the prime numbers between five thousand two hundred and thirty-seven and seven thousand six hundred and forty-one."

Bolzano smiled as Lipescu handled the question with ease. So far, so good. The robot had stuck to strictly factual questions, schoolbook stuff, posing no real problems to Lipescu. And after the initial hesitation and quibble over latitude, Lipescu had seemed to grow in confidence from moment to moment. Bolzano squinted at the scanner, looking beyond the robot, through the open gate, to the helter-skelter pile of treasures. He wondered which would fall to his lot when he and Lipescu divided them, two-thirds for Lipescu, the rest for him.

"Name the seven tragic poets of Elifora," the robot said.

"Domiphar, Halionis, Slegg, Hork-Sekan. . . ."

"The fourteen signs of the zodiac as seen from Morneez," the robot demanded.

"The Teeth, the Serpents, the Leaves, the Waterfall, the Blot. . . ."

"What is a pedicel?"

"The stalk of an individual flower of an inflorescence."

"How many years did the Siege of Larrina last?"

"Eight."

"What did the flower cry in the third canto of Somner's *Vehicles?*"

" 'I ache, I sob, I whimper, I die,' " Lipescu boomed.

"Distinguish between the stamen and the pistil."

"The stamen is the pollen-producing organ of the flower; the pistil. . . ."

And so it went. Question after question. The robot was not content with the legendary three questions of mythology; it asked a dozen, and then asked more. Lipescu answered perfectly, prompted by the murmuring of the peerless compendium of knowledge strapped to his chest. Bolzano kept careful count: The big man had dealt magnificently with seventeen questions. When would the robot concede defeat? When would it end its grim quiz and step aside?

It asked an eighteenth question, pathetically easy. All it wanted was an exposition of the Pythagorean theorem. Lipescu did not even need the computer for that. He answered, briefly, concisely, correctly. Bolzano was proud of his burly partner.

Then the robot struck Lipescu dead.

It happened in the flickering of an eyelid. Lipescu's voice had ceased, and he stood there, ready for the next question, but the next question did not come. Rather, a panel in the robot's vaulted belly slid open, and something bright and sinuous lashed out, uncoiling over the ten feet or so that separated guardian from challenger, and sliced Lipescu in half. The bright something slid back out of sight. Lipescu's trunk toppled to one side. His massive legs remained absurdly planted for a moment; then they crumpled, and a spacesuit leg kicked once, and all was still.

Stunned, Bolzano trembled in the loneliness of the cabin, and his lymph turned to water. What had gone wrong? Lipescu had given the proper answer to every question, and yet the robot had slain him. Why? Could the big man possibly have misphrased Pythagoras? No: Bolzano had listened. The answer had been flawless, as had the seventeen that preceded it. Seemingly the robot had lost patience with the game, then. The robot had cheated. Arbitrarily, maliciously, it had lashed out at Lipescu, punishing him for the correct answer.

Did robots cheat, Bolzano wondered? Could they act in malicious spite? No robot he knew was capable of such actions; but this robot was unlike all others.

For a long while, Bolzano remained huddled in the cabin. The temptation was strong to blast free of orbit and head home, treasureless but alive. Yet the treasure called to him. Some suicidal impulse drove him on. Siren-like, the robot drew him downward.

There had to be a way to make the robot yield, Bolzano thought, as he guided his small ship down to the broad barren plain. Using the computer had been a good idea, whose only defect was that it hadn't worked. The records were uncertain, but it appeared that in the past, men had died when they finally gave a wrong answer after a series of right ones. Lipescu had given no wrong answers. Yet he too had died. It was inconceivable that the robot understood some relationship of the squares on the hypotenuse and on the other two sides that was different from the relationship Lipescu had expressed.

Bolzano wondered what method would work.

He plodded leadenly across the plain toward the gate and its guardian. The germ of an idea formed in him, as he walked doggedly on.

He was, he knew, condemned to death by his own greed. Only extreme agility of mind would save him from sharing Lipescu's fate. Ordinary intelligence would not work. Odyssean cleverness was the only salvation.

Bolzano approached the robot. Bones lay everywhere. Lipescu weltered in his own blood. Against that vast dead chest lay the computer, Bolzano knew. But he shrank from reaching for it. He would do without it. He looked away, unwilling to let the sight of Lipescu's severed body interfere with the coolness of his thoughts.

He collected his courage. The robot showed no interest in him.

"Give ground," Bolzano said. "I am here. I come for the treasure."

"Win your right to it."

"What must I do?"

"Demonstrate truth," the robot said. "Reveal inwardness. Display understanding."

"I am ready," said Bolzano.

The robot offered a question. "What is the excretory unit of the vertebrate kidney called?"

Bolzano contemplated. He had no idea. The computer could tell him, but the computer lay strapped to the fallen Lipescu. No matter. The robot wanted truth, inwardness, understanding. These things were not necessarily the same as information. Lipescu had offered information. Lipescu had perished.

"The frog in the pond," Bolzano said, "utters an azure cry."

There was silence. Bolzano watched the robot's front, waiting for the panel to slide open, the sinuous something to chop him in half.

VIII. Testing, Measurement, and the Ultimate Experiment

The robot said, "During the War of Dogs on Vanderverr IX, the embattled colonists drew up thirty-eight dogmas of defiance. Quote the third, the ninth, the twenty-second, and the thirty-fifth."

Bolzano pondered. This was an alien robot, product of an unknown hand. How did its maker's mind work? Did it respect knowledge? Did it treasure facts for their own sake? Or did it recognize that information is meaningless, insight a nonlogical process?

Lipescu had been logical. He lay in pieces.

"The mereness of pain," Bolzano responded, "is ineffable and refreshing."

The robot said, "The monastery of Kwaisen was besieged by the soldiers of Oda Nobunaga on the third of April, 1582. What words of wisdom did the abbot utter?"

Bolzano spoke quickly and buoyantly. "Eleven, forty-one, elephant, voluminous."

The last word slipped from his lips despite an effort to retrieve it. Elephants *were* voluminous, he thought. A fatal slip? The robot did not appear to notice.

Sonorously, ponderously, the great machine delivered the next question. "What is the percentage of oxygen in the atmosphere of Muldonar VII?"

"False witness bears a swift sword," Bolzano replied.

The robot made an odd humming sound. Abruptly it rolled on massive treads, moving some six feet to its left. The gate of the treasure trove stood wide, beckoning.

"You may enter," the robot said.

Bolzano's heart leaped. He had won! He had gained the high prize!

Others had failed, most recently less than an hour before, and their bones glistened on the plain. They had tried to answer the robot, sometimes giving right answers, sometimes giving wrong ones, and they had died. Bolzano lived.

It was a miracle, he thought. Luck? Shrewdness? Some of each, he told himself. He had watched a man give eighteen right answers and die. So the accuracy of the responses did not matter to the robot. What did? Inwardness. Understanding. Truth.

There could be inwardness and understanding and truth in random answers, Bolzano realized. Where earnest striving had failed, mockery had succeeded. He had staked his life on nonsense, and the prize was his.

He staggered forward into the treasure trove. Even in the light gravity, his feet were like leaden weights. Tension ebbed in him. He knelt among the treasures.

The tapes, the sharp-eyed televector scanners, had not begun to indicate the splendor of what lay here. Bolzano stared in awe and rapture at a tiny disk, no greater in diameter than a man's eye, on which myriad coiling lines writhed and twisted in patterns of rare beauty. He caught his breath, sobbing with the pain of perception, as a gleaming marble spire, angled in mysterious swerves, came into view. Here, a bright beetle of some fragile waxy substance rested on a pedestal of yellow jade. There, a tangle of metallic cloth spurted dizzying patterns of luminescence. And over there —and beyond—and there—

The ransom of a universe, Bolzano thought.

It would take many trips to carry all this to his ship. Perhaps it would be better to bring the ship to the hoard, eh? He wondered, though, if he would lose his advantage if he stepped back through the gate. Was it possible that he would have to win entrance all over again? And would the robot accept his answers as willingly the second time? It was something he would have to chance, Bolzano decided. His nimble mind worked out a plan. He would select a dozen of the finest treasures, as much as he could comfortably carry, and take them back to the ship. Then he would lift the ship and set it down next to the gate. If the robot raised objections about his entering, Bolzano would simply depart, taking what he had already secured. There was no point in running undue risks. When he had sold this cargo, and felt pinched for money, he could always return and try to win admission once again. Certainly, no one else would steal the horde if he abandoned it.

Selection, that was the key now.

Crouching, Bolzano picked through the treasure, choosing for portability and easy marketability. The marble spire? Too big. But the coiling disk, yes, certainly, and the beetle, of course, and this small statuette of dull hue, and the cameos showing scenes no human eye had ever beheld, and this, and this, and this—

His pulse raced. His heart thundered. He saw himself traveling from world to world, vending his wares. Collectors, museums, governments would vie with one another to have these prizes. He would let them bid each object up into the millions before he sold. And, of course, he would keep one or two for himself—or perhaps three or four—souvenirs of this great adventure.

And someday when wealth bored him he would return and face the challenge again. And he would dare the robot to question him, and he would reply with random absurdities, demonstrating his grasp on the fundamental insight that in knowledge there is only hollow merit, and the robot would admit him once more to the treasure trove.

Bolzano rose. He cradled his lovelies in his arms. Carefully, carefully, he thought. Turning, he made his way through the gate.

The robot had not moved. It had shown no interest as Bolzano plundered the hoard. The small man walked calmly past it.

The robot said, "Why have you taken those? What do you want with them?"

Bolzano smiled. Nonchalantly he replied, "I've taken them because they're beautiful. Because I want them. Is there a better reason?"

"No," the robot said, and the panel slid open in its ponderous black chest.

Too late, Bolzano realized that the test had not yet ended, that the

VIII.   Testing, Measurement, and the Ultimate Experiment

robot's question had arisen out of no idle curiosity. And this time he had replied in earnest, speaking in rational terms.

Bolzano shrieked. He saw the brightness coming toward him.

Death followed instantly.

31.
VALENCE:
What Can We Predict?

RUBY YOSHIOKA

In an article that is both thorough and succinct, Ruby Yoshioka notes the very real valence that is to be found in the uses of probabilities.

A mathematical system which was born in order to predict the probable winnings of gamblers is now helping man predict the path of atomic particles, the color of a hybrid flower, the odds against quintuplets or whether an eel will swim to America or to Europe.

Aside from gambling, our daily lives are full of probabilities. Will it rain? Will I pass the science exam? Will a surgical operation be successful? At best what we decide will or will not happen is based on some previous experience or just a guess as to the outcome or a "feeling" of what probably will take place. This is the common conception of probability.

But for mathematicians and statisticians, probability is more than a guess or intuition. They have devised mathematical systems, some of which are very complex, whereby the chances of an event occurring can be predicted.

How Theory Arose

The theory of mathematical probability arose from the studies of games of chance, early in the 17th century. Blaise Pascal, a French mathematician, scientist, and philosopher, and creator of the famous Pascal triangle based on the binomial theorem, was asked by a gambler friend, who was interested in the "why" of gambling chances, to figure out why certain odds were more favorable to a gambling house than other odds. This Pascal

From *Science News Letter*, 85, 139, 1964. Reprinted by permission of *Science News*, weekly summary of current science. Copyright © 1964 by Science Service, Inc.

undertook with the help of Pierre Fermat, another French mathematician, and developed probability theory.

Since that time, probability theory has become increasingly important and many mathematicians have contributed to its advancement.

Probability theory today has applications in virtually every field from atomic physics and biology to social science.

Predictions of weather, population increase, the number of accidents that may occur during a holiday weekend and the probable outcome of elections are all examples of the application of mathematical probability, as are the estimation of insurance rates.

The classic example to explain probability theory is in tossing coins. If a coin is flipped, what is the chance that it will turn up heads? Since it must turn up either heads or tails, the probability is ½; in 100 throws the probability is 50 heads and 50 tails in an ideal situation.

This does not mean that if heads shows in the first throw, tails will turn up in the next. Each throw is independent of the previous throw, since coins do not have a memory. However, in the long run, that is, after many tosses, say 100,000, the ratio of heads to tails tends to be 1 to 1.

Thus, if in 100 throws, there are 45 heads, heads could turn up about 450 times in 1,000 throws. It would be most unusual and highly improbable that in 1,000 throws the number of heads would be only 45. Actually tossing the coin and recording the result would show this to be true.

Taking another example, if a die is thrown, the chances of any one of the numbers, 1 through 6, appearing is 1/6. This means that after many throws, or in the long run, any single number, say 3, will appear in 1/6 of the throws.

If you throw two dice, one blue and one white, the chance of 3 appearing on a blue dice is 1/6 X 1/6 or 1/36, but a sum of 3 can be produced in two ways, with a 2 and 1, both equally likely. Thus its probability is 2/36, or 1/18, so a sum of 3 may be expected to occur once in every 18 throws.

As the number of throws increases, the chances of occurring at this ratio increase.

More Complex Problems

These simple applications of probability theory as shown in the tossed coins and the throwing of dice have been applied to more complex problems of probability. James Bernoulli, later in the 17th century, clearly defined probability theory in relationship to large numbers of cases, applying the same mathematical equation.

As a result of Bernoulli's law and subsequent related laws, the central limit theorems were derived. These theorems state that as the number of trials increases, the predictions made by probability theory can be more and more closely satisfied.

For example, taking coins again, the ratio of heads to tails tends to come closer to 1 to 1 as the number of throws is increased. However, an interesting point is that the actual numerical difference between heads and tails tends to become greater with the greater number of trials. In 100 throws, if tails show 45 times and heads 55 times, the difference is 10. But, if 1,000 throws are made and the ratio is 450 to 550, the numerical difference is 100.

Why Gamblers Lose

Thus, the best lesson a gambler can learn from probability theory is that if he continues to play, he will always lose. Mathematicians have shown, since the time of Bernoulli, that the chances of loss become greater and greater as the gambler continues to play and the resources of the house increase compared to those of the gambler.

This is also true in a slot machine. The more quarters a player puts into the machine, the slimmer become his chances of becoming a winner.

A curve can be drawn from a table of the various ways in which an event may happen, such as the tossing of coins. The probability distribution curve is bell-shaped and is known as the normal distribution curve, or Gaussian curve after Karl Friedrich Gauss.

The normal curve is used extensively in many applications, for example, in showing the variations of I.Q. in a certain age group or the heights of different races. Where natural phenomena can be measured, such as the number of peas in a pod or the weight of children of a certain age, the normal probability distribution is closely followed.

In genetics, the Mendelian theory of the transmission of traits can be predicted by probability theory.

If a red flower is crossed with a white flower, the red gene will unite with the white gene to form a pink flower. If two pink flowers are then crossed, the next generation will produce one red, one white and two pinks, following the pattern of the probability distribution of heads and tails when two coins are tossed.

This ability to predict offspring of plants is most useful to agriculturists and botanists in hybridizing and improving plants and animals.

Random Sampling

It is often desirable to know how a population will vote or how well a machine is turning out a product. A system of random sampling has been devised.

The straw vote taken before an election is an example of random sampling. From such a vote, the trend of the election can be predicted.

If the product of a new machine is to be tested, samples selected at random can give the manufacturer an indication of the quality of the whole.

Sampling is a convenient and oftentimes the only method by which a study of large groups can be made.

In physics the behavior of atoms and molecules and the paths of electrons and protons are determined probabilistically. Since it is impossible to determine the exact position or exact motion of an electron at a particular moment, its position or direction of movement must be based on probability and must be estimated.

Most physicists believe that probability behavior governing electrons must also apply to the universe, but the late Prof. Albert Einstein, among other scientists, believed there is an underlying order in the universe that does not involve probability.

Astronomers apply probability statistics when determining the position of stars and space scientists calculate travels in outer space on a probabilistic basis.

New Method of Calculating

A new method of calculating probability that uses only existing factors rather than previous events has been recently devised by Prof. Marcel Neuts of Purdue University, Lafayette, Ind.

Prof. Neuts reported that his method can be applied to actual biological and physical phenomena as well as purely theoretical mathematical problems.

The concept of mathematical probability is far reaching and enters into virtually all phases of our lives, from birth rates to death rates, with all the probabilities and statistics that can happen in between.

32.
VISION:
Jokester

ISAAC ASIMOV

A central question in testing and measurement is the question of reliability
*—that is, whether or not a test consistently measures something. There
is also the question of* validity *—whether a test is measuring what
it sets out to measure. In "Jokester," Isaac Asimov provides a grim
example of absolute validity.*

Noel Meyerhof consulted the list he had prepared and chose which item
was to be first. As usual, he relied mainly on intuition.

He was dwarfed by the machine he faced, though only the smallest
portion of the latter was in view. That didn't matter. He spoke with the
offhand confidence of one who thoroughly knew he was master.

"Johnson," he said, "came home unexpectedly from a business trip to
find his wife in the arms of his best friend. He staggered back and said,
'Max! I'm married to the lady so I *have* to. But why you?'"

Meyerhof thought: Okay, let that trickle down into its guts and gurgle
about a bit.

And a voice behind him said, "Hey."

Meyerhof erased the sound of that monosyllable and put the circuit he
was using into neutral. He whirled and said, "I'm working. Don't you
knock?"

He did not smile as he customarily did in greeting Timothy Whistler, a
senior analyst with whom he dealt as often as with any. He frowned as
he would have for an interruption by a stranger, wrinkling his thin face
into a distortion that seemed to extend to his hair, rumpling it more than
ever.

Whistler shrugged. He wore his white lab coat with his fists pressing
down within its pockets and creasing it into tense vertical lines. "I
knocked. You didn't answer. The operations signal wasn't on."

VIII. Testing, Measurement, and the Ultimate Experiment

Meyerhof grunted. It wasn't at that. He'd been thinking about this new project too intensively and he was forgetting little details.

And yet he could scarcely blame himself for that. This thing was important.

He didn't know why it was, of course. Grand Masters rarely did. That's what made them Grand Masters; the fact that they were beyond reason. How else could the human mind keep up with that ten-mile-long lump of solidified reason that men called Multivac, the most complex computer ever built?

Myerhof said, "I *am* working. Is there something important on your mind?"

"Nothing that can't be postponed. There are a few holes in the answer on the hyperspatial—" Whistler did a double take and his face took on a rueful look of uncertainty. *"Working?"*

"Yes. What about it?"

"But—" He looked about, staring into the crannies of the shallow room that faced the banks upon banks of relays that formed a small portion of Multivac. "There isn't anyone here at that."

"Who said there was, or should be?"

"You were telling one of your jokes, weren't you?"

"And?"

Whistler forced a smile. "Don't tell me you were telling a joke to Multivac?"

Meyerhof stiffened. "Why not?"

"Were you?"

"Yes."

"Why?"

Meyerhof stared the other down. "I don't have to account to you. Or to anyone."

"Good Lord, of course not, I was curious, that's all. . . . But then, if you're working, I'll leave." He looked about once more, frowning.

"Do so," said Meyerhof. His eyes followed the other out and then he activated the operations signal with a savage punch of his finger.

He strode the length of the room and back, getting himself in hand. Damn Whistler! Damn them all! Because he didn't bother to hold those technicians, analysts and mechanics at the proper social distance, because he treated them as though they, too, were creative artists, they took these liberties.

He thought grimly: They can't even tell jokes decently.

And instantly that brought him back to the task in hand. He sat down again. Devil take them all.

He threw the proper Multivac circuit back into operation and said, "The ship's steward stopped at the rail of the ship during a particularly rough ocean crossing and gazed compassionately at the man whose slumped position over the rail and whose intensity of gaze toward the depths betokened all too well the ravages of seasickness.

32. VISION: Jokester

"Gently, the steward patted the man's shoulder. 'Cheer up, sir,' he murmured. 'I know it seems bad, but really, you know, nobody ever dies of seasickness.'

"The afflicted gentleman lifted his greenish, tortured face to his comforter and gasped in hoarse accents, 'Don't say that, man. For Heaven's sake, don't say that. It's only the hope of dying that's keeping me alive.' "

Timothy Whistler, a bit preoccupied, nevertheless smiled and nodded as he passed the secretary's desk. She smiled back at him.

Here, he thought, was an archaic item in this computer-ridden world of the twenty-first century, a human secretary. But then perhaps it was natural that such an institution should survive here in the very citadel of computerdom; in the gigantic world corporation that handled Multivac. With Multivac filling the horizons, lesser computers for trivial tasks would have been in poor taste.

Whistler stepped into Abram Trask's office. That government official paused in his careful task of lighting a pipe; his dark eyes flicked in Whistler's direction and his beaked nose stood out sharply and prominently against the rectangle of window behind him.

"Ah, there, Whistler. Sit down. Sit down."

Whistler did so. "I think we've got a problem, Trask."

Trask half-smiled. "Not a technical one, I hope. I'm just an innocent politician." (It was one of his favorite phrases.)

"It involves Meyerhof."

Trask sat down instantly and looked acutely miserable. "Are you sure?"

"Reasonably sure."

Whistler understood the other's sudden unhappiness well. Trask was the government official in charge of the Division of Computers and Automation of the Department of the Interior. He was expected to deal with matters of policy involving the human satellites of Multivac, just as those technically trained satellites were expected to deal with Multivac itself.

But a Grand Master was more than just a satellite. More, even, than just a human.

Early in the history of Multivac, it had become apparent that the bottleneck was the questioning procedure. Multivac could answer the problem of humanity, *all* the problems, if—*if* it were asked meaningful questions. But as knowledge accumulated at an ever-faster rate, it became ever more difficult to locate those meaningful questions.

Reason alone wouldn't do. What was needed was a rare type of intuition; the same faculty of mind (only much more intensified) that made a grand master at chess. A mind was needed of the sort that could see through the quadrillions of chess patterns to find the one best move, and do it in a matter of minutes.

Trask moved restlessly. "What's Meyerhof been doing?"

"He's introduced a line of questioning that I find disturbing."

"Oh, come on, Whistler. Is that all? You can't stop a Grand Master from going through any line of questioning he chooses. Neither you nor I are equipped to judge the worth of his questions. You know that. I know you know that."

"I do. Of course. But I also know Meyerhof. Have you ever met him socially?"

"Good Lord, no. Does anyone meet any Grand Master socially?"

"Don't take that attitude, Trask. They're human and they're to be pitied. Have you ever thought what it must be like to be a Grand Master; to know there are only some twelve like you in the world; to know that only one or two come up per generation; that the world depends on you; that a thousand mathematicians, logicians, psychologists and physical scientists wait on you?"

Trask shrugged and muttered, "Good Lord, I'd feel king of the world."

"I don't think you would," said the senior analyst impatiently. "They feel kings of nothing. They have no equal to talk to, no sensation of belonging. Listen, Meyerhof never misses a chance to get together with the boys. He isn't married, naturally; he doesn't drink; he has no natural social touch—yet he forces himself into company because he must. And do you know what he does when he gets together with us, and that's at least once a week?"

"I haven't the least idea," said the government man. "This is all new to me."

"He's a jokester."

"What?"

"He tells jokes. Good ones. He's terrific. He can take any story, however old and dull, and make it sound good. It's the way he tells it. He has a flair."

"I see. Well, good."

"Or bad. These jokes are important to him." Whistler put both elbows on Trask's desk, bit at a thumbnail and stared into the air. "He's different, he knows he's different and these jokes are the one way he feels he can get the rest of us ordinary schmoes to accept him. We laugh, we howl, we clap him on the back and even forget he's a Grand Master. It's the only hold he has on the rest of us."

"This is all interesting. I didn't know you were such a psychologist. Still, where does this lead?"

"Just this. What do you suppose happens if Meyerhof runs out of jokes?"

"What?" The government man stared blankly.

"If he starts repeating himself? If his audience starts laughing less heartily, or stops laughing altogether? It's his only hold on our approval. Without it, he'll be alone and then what would happen to him? After all, Trask, he's one of the dozen men mankind can't do without. We can't let anything happen to him. I don't mean physical things. We can't even let him get too unhappy. Who knows how that might affect his intuition?

"Well, has he started repeating himself?"

"Not as far as I know, but I think *he* thinks he has."

"Why do you say that?"

"Because I've heard him telling jokes to Multivac."

"Oh, no."

"Accidentally! I walked in on him and he threw me out. He was savage. He's usually good-natured enough, and I consider it a bad sign that he was so upset at the intrusion. But the fact remains that he was telling a joke to Multivac, and I'm convinced it was one of a series."

"But why?"

Whistler shrugged and rubbed a hand fiercely across his chin. "I have a thought about that. I think he's trying to build up a store of jokes in Multivac's memory banks in order to get back new variations. You see what I mean? He's planning a mechanical jokester, so that he can have an infinite number of jokes at hand and never fear running out."

"Good Lord!"

"Objectively, there may be nothing wrong with that, but I consider it a bad sign when a Grand Master starts using Multivac for his personal problems. Any Grand Master has a certain inherent mental instability and he should be watched. Meyerhof may be approaching a borderline beyond which we lose a Grand Master."

Trask said blankly, "What are you suggesting I do?"

"You can check me. I'm too close to him to judge well, maybe, and judging humans isn't my particular talent, anyway. You're a politician; it's more your talent."

"Judging humans, perhaps, not Grand Masters."

"They're human, too. Besides, who else is to do it?"

The fingers of Trask's hand struck his desk in rapid succession over and over like a slow and muted roll of drums.

"I suppose I'll have to," he said.

Meyerhof said to Multivac, "The ardent swain, picking a bouquet of wildflowers for his loved one, was disconcerted to find himself, suddenly, in the same field with a large bull of unfriendly appearance which, gazing at him steadily, pawed the ground in a threatening manner. The young man, spying a farmer on the other side of a fairly distant fence, shouted, 'Hey, mister, is that bull safe?' The farmer surveyed the situation with critical eye, spat to one side and called back, 'He's safe as anything.' He spat again, and added, 'Can't say the same about you, though.'"

Meyerhof was about to pass on to the next when the summons came.

It wasn't really a summons. No one could summon a Grand Master. It was only a message that Division Head Trask would like very much to see Grand Master Meyerhof if Grand Master Meyerhof could spare the time.

Meyerhof might, with impunity, have tossed the message to one side and continued with whatever he was doing. He was not subject to discipline.

VIII.   Testing, Measurement, and the Ultimate Experiment

On the other hand, were he to do that, they would continue to bother him—oh, very respectfully, but they would continue to bother him.

So he neutralized the pertinent circuits of Multivac and locked them into place. He put the freeze signal on his office so that no one would dare enter in his absence and left for Trask's office.

Trask coughed and felt a bit intimidated by the sullen fierceness of the other's look. He said, "We have not had occasion to know one another, Grand Master, to my great regret."

"I have reported to you," said Meyerhof stiffly.

Trask wondered what lay behind those keen, wild eyes. It was difficult for him to imagine Meyerhof with his thin face, his dark, straight hair, his intense air, even unbending long enough to tell funny stories.

He said, "Reports are not social acquaintance. I—I have been given to understand you have a marvelous fund of anecdotes."

"I am a jokester, sir. That's the phrase people use. A jokester."

"They haven't used the phrase to me, Grand Master. They have said—"

"The hell with them! I don't care what they've said. See here, Trask, do you want to hear a joke?" He leaned forward across the desk, his eyes narrowed.

"By all means. Certainly," said Trask, with an effort at heartiness.

"All right. Here's the joke: Mrs. Jones stared at the fortune card that had emerged from the weighing machine in response to her husband's penny. She said, 'It says here, George, that you're suave, intelligent, farseeing, industrious and attractive to women.' With that, she turned the card over and added, 'And they have your weight wrong, too.' "

Trask laughed. It was almost impossible not to. Although the punch line was predictable, the surprising facility with which Meyerhof had produced just the tone of contemptuous disdain in the woman's voice, and the cleverness with which he had contorted the lines of his face to suit that tone carried the politician helplessly into laughter.

Meyerhof said sharply, "Why is that funny?"

Trask sobered. "I beg your pardon."

"I said, why is that funny? Why do you laugh?"

"Well," said Trask, trying to be reasonable, "the last line put everything that preceded in a new light. The unexpectedness—"

"The point is," said Meyerhof, "that I have pictured a husband being humiliated by his wife; a marriage that is such a failure that the wife is convinced that her husband lacks any virtue. Yet you laugh at that. If you were the husband, would you find it funny?"

He waited a moment in thought, then said, "Try this one, Trask: Abner was seated at his wife's sickbed, weeping uncontrollably, when his wife, mustering the dregs of her strength, drew herself up to one elbow.

" 'Abner,' she whispered, 'Abner, I cannot go to my Maker without confessing my misdeed.'

" 'Not now,' muttered the stricken husband. 'Not now, my dear. Lie back and rest.'

" 'I cannot,' she cried, 'I must tell, or my soul will never know peace. I have been unfaithful to you, Abner. In this very house, not one month ago—'

" 'Hush, dear,' soothed Abner. 'I know all about it. Why else have I poisoned you?' "

Trask tried desperately to maintain equanimity but did not entirely succeed. He suppressed a chuckle imperfectly.

Meyerhof said, "So that's funny, too. Adultery. Murder. All funny."

"Well, now," said Trask, "books have been written analyzing humor."

"True enough," said Meyerhof, "and I've read a number of them. What's more, I've read most of them to Multivac. Still, the people who write the books are just guessing. Some of them say we laugh because we feel superior to the people in the joke. Some say it is because of a suddenly realized incongruity, or a sudden relief from tension, or a sudden reinterpretation of events. Is there any simple reason? Different people laugh at different jokes. No joke is universal. Some people don't laugh at any joke. Yet what may be most important is that man is the only animal with a true sense of humor: the only animal that laughs."

Trask said suddenly, "I understand. You're trying to analyze humor. That's why you're transmitting a series of jokes to Multivac."

"Who told you I was doing that? . . . Never mind, it was Whistler. I remember, now. He surprised me at it. Well, what about it?"

"Nothing at all."

"You don't dispute my right to add anything I wish to Multivac's general fund of knowledge, or to ask any question I wish?"

"No, not at all," said Trask hastily. "As a matter of fact, I have no doubt that this will open the way to new analyses of great interest to psychologists."

"Hmp. Maybe. Just the same there's something plaguing me that's more important than just the general analysis of humor. There's a specific question I have to ask. Two of them, really."

"Oh? What's that?" Trask wondered if the other would answer. There would be no way of compelling him if he chose not to.

But Meyerhof said, "The first question is this: Where do all these jokes come from?"

"What?"

"Who makes them up? Listen! About a month ago, I spent an evening swapping jokes. As usual, I told most of them and, as usual, the fools laughed. Maybe they really thought the jokes were funny and maybe they were just humoring me. In any case, one creature took the liberty of slapping me on the back and saying, 'Meyerhof, you know more jokes than any ten people I know.'

"I'm sure he was right, but it gave rise to a thought. I don't know how many hundreds, or perhaps thousands, of jokes I've told at one time or another in my life, yet the fact is I never made up one. Not one. I'd only repeated them. My only contribution was to tell them. To begin with, I'd either heard them or read them. And the source of my hearing or reading didn't make up the jokes, either. I never met anyone who ever claimed to have constructed a joke. It's always 'I heard a good one the other day,' and 'Heard any good ones lately?'

"*All the jokes are old!* That's why jokes exhibit such a social lag. They still deal with seasickness, for instance, when that's easily prevented these days and never experienced. Or they'll deal with fortune-giving weighing machines, like the joke I told you, when such machines are found only in antique shops. Well, then, who makes up the jokes?"

Trask said, "Is *that* what you're trying to find out?" It was on the tip of Trask's tongue to add: Good Lord, who cares? He forced that impulse down. A Grand Master's questions were also meaningful.

"Of course that's what I'm trying to find out. Think of it this way. It's not just that jokes happen to be old. They *must* be old to be enjoyed. It's essential that a joke not be original. There's one variety of humor that is, or can be, original and that's the pun. I've heard puns that were obviously made up on the spur of the moment. I have made some up myself. But no one laughs at such puns. You're not supposed to. You groan. The better the pun, the louder the groan. Original humor is not laugh-provoking. Why?"

"I'm sure I don't know."

"All right. Let's find out. Having given Multivac all the information I thought advisable on the general topic of humor, I am now feeding it selected jokes."

Trask found himself intrigued. "Selected how?" he asked.

"I don't know," said Meyerhof. "They felt like the right ones. I'm Grand Master, you know."

"Oh, agreed, Agreed."

"From those jokes and the general philosophy of humor, my first request will be for Multivac to trace the origin of the jokes, if it can. Since Whistler is in on this and since he has seen fit to report it to you, have him down in Analysis day after tomorrow. I think he'll have a bit of work to do."

"Certainly. May I attend, too?"

Meyerhof shrugged. Trask's attendance was obviously a matter of indifference to him.

Meyerhof had selected the last in the series with particular care. What that care consisted of, he could not have said, but he had revolved a dozen possibilities in his mind, and over and over again had tested each for some indefinable quality of meaningfulness.

He said, "Ug, the caveman, observed his mate running to him in tears, her leopard-skin skirt in disorder. 'Ug,' she cried, distraught, 'do something

32. VISION: Jokester

quickly. A saber-toothed tiger has entered Mother's cave. Do something!'
Ug grunted, picked up his well-gnawed buffalo bone and said, 'Why do
anything? Who the hell cares what happens to a saber-toothed tiger?' "

It was then that Meyerhof asked his two questions and leaned back,
closing his eyes. He was done.

"I saw absolutely nothing wrong," said Trask to Whistler. "He told me
what he was doing readily enough and it was odd but legitimate."

"What he *claimed* he was doing," said Whistler.

"Even so, I can't stop a Grand Master on opinion alone. He seemed queer
but, after all, Grand Masters are supposed to seem queer. I didn't think him
insane."

"Using Multivac to find the source of jokes?" muttered the senior analyst in discontent. "That's not insane?"

"How can we tell?" asked Trask irritably. "Science has advanced to the
point where the only meaningful questions left are the ridiculous ones. The
sensible ones have been thought of, asked and answered long ago."

"It's no use. I'm bothered."

"Maybe, but there's no choice now, Whistler. We'll see Meyerhof and
you can do the necessary analysis of Multivac's response, if any. As for
me, my only job is to handle the red tape. Good Lord, I don't even know
what a senior analyst such as yourself is supposed to do, except analyze,
and that doesn't help me any."

Whistler said, "It's simple enough. A Grand Master like Meyerhof asks
questions and Multivac automatically formulates it into quantities and
operations. The necessary machinery for converting words to symbols is
what makes up most of the bulk of Multivac. Multivac then gives the
answer in quantities and operations, but it doesn't translate that back into
words except in the most simple and routine cases. If it were designed to
solve the general retranslation problem, its bulk would have to be quadru-
pled at least."

"I see. Then it's your job to translate these symbols into words?"

"My job and that of other analysts. We use smaller, specially designed
computers whenever necessary." Whistler smiled grimly. "Like the Del-
phic priestess of ancient Greece, Multivac gives oracular and obscure answers. Only we have translators, you see."

They had arrived. Meyerhof was waiting.

Whistler said briskly, "What circuits did you use, Grand Master?"

Meyerhof told him and Whistler went to work.

Trask tried to follow what was happening, but none of it made sense.
The government official watched a spool unreel with a pattern of dots in
endless incomprehensibility. Grand Master Meyerhof stood indifferently
to one side while Whistler surveyed the pattern as it emerged. The analyst
had put on headphones and a mouthpiece and at intervals murmured a

series of instructions which, at some far-off place, guided assistants through electronic contortions in other computers.

Occasionally, Whistler listened, then punched combinations on a complex keyboard marked with symbols that looked vaguely mathematical but weren't.

A good deal more than an hour's time elapsed.

The frown on Whistler's face grew deeper. Once, he looked up at the two others and began, "This is unbel—" and turned back to his work.

Finally, he said hoarsely, "I can give you an unofficial answer." His eyes were red-rimmed. "The official answer awaits complete analysis. Do you want it unofficial?"

"Go ahead," said Meyerhof.

Trask nodded.

Whistler darted a hangdog glance at the Grand Master. "Ask a foolish question—" he said. Then, gruffly, "Multivac says, extraterrestrial origin."

"What are you saying?" demanded Trask.

"Don't you hear me? The jokes we laugh at were not made up by any man. Multivac has analyzed all data given it and the one answer that best fits that data is that some extraterrestrial intelligence has composed the jokes, all of them, and placed them in selected human minds at selected times and places in such a way that no man is conscious of having made one up. All subsequent jokes are minor variations and adaptations of these grand originals."

Meyerhof broke in, face flushed with the kind of triumph only a Grand Master can know who once again has asked the right question. "All comedy writers," he said, "work by twisting old jokes to new purposes. That's well known. The answer fits."

"But why?" asked Trask. "Why make up the jokes?"

"Multivac says," said Whistler, "that the only purpose that fits all the data is that the jokes are intended to study human psychology. We study rat psychology by making the rats solve mazes. The rats don't know why and wouldn't even if they were aware of what was going on, which they're not. These outer intelligences study man's psychology by noting individual reactions to carefully selected anecdotes. Each man reacts differently. . . . Presumably, these outer intelligences are to us as we are to rats." He shuddered.

Trask, eyes staring, said, "The Grand Master said man is the only animal with a sense of humor. It would seem then that the sense of humor is foisted upon us from without."

Meyerhof added excitedly, "And for possible humor created from within, we have no laughter. Puns, I mean."

Whistler said, "Presumably, the extraterrestrials cancel out reactions to spontaneous jokes to avoid confusion."

Trask said in sudden agony of spirit, "Come on, now, Good Lord, do either of you believe this?"

The senior analyst looked at him coldly. "Multivac says so. It's all that can be said so far. It has pointed out the real jokesters of the universe, and if we want to know more, the matter will have to be followed up." He added in a whisper, "If anyone dares follow it up."

Grand Master Meyerhof said suddenly, "I asked two questions, you know. So far only the first has been answered. I think Multivac has enough data to answer the second."

Whistler shrugged. He seemed a half-broken man. "When a Grand Master thinks there is enough data," he said, "I'll make book on it. What is your second question?"

"I asked this: What will be the effect on the human race of discovering the answer to my first question?"

"Why did you ask that?" demanded Trask.

"Just a feeling that it had to be asked," said Meyerhof.

Trask said, "Insane. It's all insane," and turned away. Even he himself felt how strangely he and Whistler had changed sides. Now it was Trask crying insanity.

Trask closed his eyes. He might cry insanity all he wished, but no man in fifty years had doubted the combination of a Grand Master and Multivac and found his doubts verified.

Whistler worked silently, teeth clenched. He put Multivac and its subsidiary machines through their paces again. Another hour passed and he laughed harshly. "A raving nightmare!"

"What's the answer?" asked Meyerhof. "I want Multivac's remarks, not yours."

"All right. Take it. Multivac states that, once even a single human discovers the truth of this method of psychological analysis of the human mind, it will become useless as an objective technique to those extraterrestrial powers now using it."

"You mean there won't be any more jokes handed out to humanity?" asked Trask faintly. "Or what do you mean?"

"No more jokes," said Whistler, "*now!* Multivac says *now!* The experiment is ended *now!* A new technique will have to be introduced."

They stared at each other. The minutes passed.

Meyerhof said slowly, "Multivac is right."

Whistler said haggardly, "I know."

Even Trask said in a whisper, "Yes. It must be."

It was Meyerhof who put his finger on the proof of it, Meyerhof the accomplished jokester. He said, "It's over, you know, all over. I've been trying for five minutes now and I can't think of one single joke, not one! And if I read one in a book, I wouldn't laugh. I know."

"The gift of humor is gone," said Trask drearily. "No man will ever laugh again."

And they remained there, staring, feeling the world shrink down to the dimensions of an experimental rat cage—with the maze removed and something, something about to be put in its place.

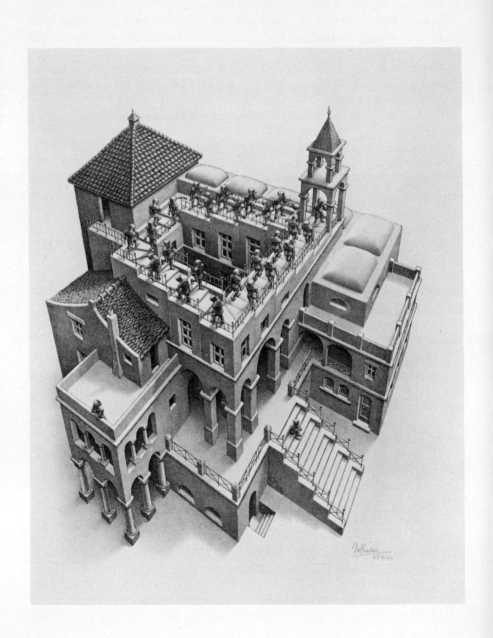

IX.
Who Are They?
Who Am I?–
The Increased
Relevancy of
Social Psychology

33.
VISION:
The Day the Martians Came

FREDERIK POHL

The intricasies of forming an outgroup in Vietnam are the same dynamics that are handled in a more pointed setting by Frederik Pohl in the following story.

There were two cots in every room of the motel, besides the usual number of beds, and Mr. Mandala, the manager, had converted the rear section of the lobby into a men's dormitory. Nevertheless he was not satisfied and was trying to persuade his colored bellmen to clean out the trunk room and put cots in that too. "Now, please, Mr. Mandala," the bell captain said, speaking loudly over the noise in the lounge, "you know we'd do it for you if we could. But it cannot be, because, first, we don't have any other place to put those old TV sets you want to save and because, second, we don't *have* any more cots."

"You're arguing with me, Ernest. I told you to quit arguing with me," said Mr. Mandala. He drummed his fingers on the registration desk and looked angrily around the lobby. There were at least forty people in it, talking, playing cards and dozing. The television set was mumbling away in a recap of the NASA releases, and on the screen Mr. Mandala could see a picture of one of the Martians, gazing into the camera and weeping large, gelatinous tears.

"Quit that," ordered Mr. Mandala, turning in time to catch his bellmen looking at the screen. "I don't pay you to watch TV. Go see if you can help out in the kitchen."

"We been in the kitchen, Mr. Mandala. They don't need us."

"Go when I tell you to go, Ernest! You too, Berzie." He watched them

From Harlan Ellison (ed.), *Dangerous Visions,* Doubleday, 1967. Reprinted by permission of the author.

go through the service hall and wished he could get rid of some of the crowd in the lounge as easily. They filled every seat and the overflow sat on the arms of the chairs, leaned against the walls and filled the booths in the bar, which had been closed for the past two hours because of the law. According to the registration slips, they were nearly all from newspapers, wire services, radio and television networks and so on, waiting to go to the morning briefing at Cape Kennedy. Mr. Mandala wished morning would come. He didn't like so many of them cluttering up his lounge, especially since he was pretty sure a lot of them were not even registered guests.

On the television screen a hastily edited tape was now showing the return of the Algonquin Nine space probe to Mars, but no one was watching it. It was the third time that particular tape had been repeated since midnight and everybody had seen it at least once; but when it changed to another shot of one of the Martians, looking like a sad dachshund with elongated seal flippers for limbs, one of the poker players stirred and cried: "I got a Martian joke! Why doesn't a Martian swim in the Atlantic Ocean?"

"It's your bet," said the dealer.

"Because he'd leave a ring around it," said the reporter, folding his cards. No one laughed, not even Mr. Mandala, although some of the jokes had been pretty good. Everybody was beginning to get tired of them, or perhaps just tired.

Mr. Mandala had missed the first excitement about the Martians, because he had been asleep. When the day manager phoned him, waking him up, Mr. Mandala had thought, first, that it was a joke and, second, that the day man was out of his mind; after all, who would care if the Mars probe had come back with some kind of animals? Or even if they weren't animals, exactly: When he found out how many reservations were coming in over the teletype he realized that some people did in fact care. However, Mr. Mandala didn't take much interest in things like that. It was nice the Martians had come, since they had filled his motel, and every other motel within a hundred miles of Cape Kennedy, but when you had said that you had said everything about the Martians that mattered to Mr. Mandala.

On the television screen the picture went to black and was replaced by the legend *Bulletin from NBC News.* The poker game paused momentarily. The lounge was almost quiet as an invisible announcer read a new release from NASA. "Dr. Hugo Bache, the Fort Worth, Texas, veterinarian who arrived late this evening to examine the Martians at the Patrick Air Force Base reception center, has issued a preliminary report which has just been released by Colonel Eric T. 'Happy' Wingerter, speaking for the National Aeronautics and Space Administration."

A wire-service man yelled, "Turn it up!" There was a convulsive movement around the set. The sound vanished entirely for a moment, then blasted out:

IX. Increased Relevancy of Social Psychology

"—Martians are vertebrate, warm-blooded and apparently mammalian. A superficial examination indicates a generally low level of metabolism, although Dr. Bache states that it is possible that this is in some measure the result of their difficult and confined voyage through 137,000,000 miles of space in the specimen chamber of the Algonquin Nine spacecraft. There is no, repeat no, evidence of communicable disease, although standing sterilization precautions are—"

"Hell he says," cried somebody, probably a stringer from CBS. "Walter Cronkite had an interview with the Mayo Clinic that—"

"Shut up!" bellowed a dozen voices, and the TV became audible again:

"—completes the full text of the report from Dr. Hugo Bache as released at this hour by Colonel Happy Wingerter." There was a pause; then the announcer's voice, weary but game, found its place and went on with a recap of the previous half dozen stories. The poker game began again as the announcer was describing the news conference with Dr. Sam Sullivan of the Linguistic Institute of the University of Indiana, and his conclusions that the sounds made by the Martians were indeed some sort of language.

What nonsense, thought Mr. Mandala, drugged and drowsy. He pulled a stool over and sat down, half asleep.

Then the noise of laughter woke him and he straightened up belligerently. He tapped his call bell for attention. "Gentlemen! Ladies! Please!" he cried. "It's four o'clock in the morning. Our other guests are trying to sleep."

"Yeah, sure," said the CBS man, holding up one hand impatiently, "but wait a minute. I got one. What's a Martian highrise? You give up?"

"Go ahead," said a red-haired girl, a staffer from *Life.*

"Twenty-seven floors of basement apartments!"

The girl said, "All right, I got one too. What is a Martian female's religious injunction requiring her to keep her eyes closed during intercourse?" She waited a beat. "God forbid she should see her husband having a good time!"

"Are we playing poker or not?" groaned one of the players, but they were too many for him. "Who won the Martian beauty contest? . . . Nobody won!" "How do you get a Martian female to give up sex? . . . Marry her!" Mr. Mandala laughed out loud at that one, and when one of the reporters came to him and asked for a book of matches he gave it to him. "Ta," said the man, puffing his pipe alight. "Long night, eh?"

"You bet," said Mr. Mandala genially. On the television screen the tape was running again, for the fourth time. Mr. Mandala yawned, staring vacantly at it; it was not much to see but, really, it was all that anyone had seen or was likely to see of the Martians. All these reporters and cameramen and columnists and sound men, thought Mr. Mandala with pleasure, all of them waiting here for the 10:00 A.M. briefing at the Cape would have a forty-mile drive through the palmetto swamps for nothing. Because what they would see when they got there would be just about what they were seeing now.

One of the poker players was telling a long, involved joke about Martians wearing fur coats at Miami Beach. Mr. Mandala looked at them with dislike. If only some of them would go to their rooms and go to sleep he might try asking the others if they were registered in the motel. Although actually he couldn't squeeze anyone else in anyway, with all the rooms doubly occupied already. He gave up the thought and stared vacantly at the Martians on the screen, trying to imagine people all over the world looking at that picture on their television sets, reading about them in their newspapers, *caring* about them. They did not look worth caring about as they sluggishly crawled about on their long, weak limbs, like a stretched seal's flippers, gasping heavily in the drag of Earth's gravity, their great long eyes dull.

"Stupid-looking little bastards," one of the reporters said to the pipe smoker. "You know what I heard? I heard the reason the astronauts kept them locked in the back was the stink."

"They probably don't notice it on Mars," said the pipe smoker judiciously. "Thin air."

"Notice it? They love it." He dropped a dollar bill on the desk in front of Mr. Mandala. "Can I have change for the Coke machine?" Mr. Mandala counted out dimes silently. It had not occurred to him that the Martians would smell, but that was only because he hadn't given it much of a thought. If he had thought about it at all, that was what he would have thought.

Mr. Mandala fished out a dime for himself and followed the two men over to the Coke machine. The picture on the TV changed to some rather poorly photographed shots brought back by the astronauts, of low, irregular sand-colored buildings on a bright sand floor. These were what NASA was calling "the largest Martian city," altogether about a hundred of the flat, windowless structures.

"I dunno," said the second reporter at last, tilting his Coke bottle. "You think they're what you'd call intelligent?"

"Difficult to say, exactly," said the pipe smoker. He was from Reuter's and looked it, with a red, broad English squire's face. "They do build houses," he pointed out.

"So does a bull gorilla."

"No doubt. No doubt." The Reuter's man brightened. "Oh, just a moment. That makes me think of one. There once was—let me see, at home we tell it about the Irish—yes, I have it. The next spaceship goes to Mars, you see, and they find that some dread terrestrial disease has wiped out the whole race, all but one female. These fellows too, gone. All gone except this one she. Well, they're terribly upset, and they debate it at the UN and start an anti-genocide pact and America votes two hundred million dollars for reparations and, well, the long and short of it is, in order to keep the race from dying out entirely they decide to breed a human man to this one surviving Martian female."

"Cripes!"

"Yes, exactly. Well, then they find Paddy O'Shaughnessy, down on his luck, and they say to him, 'See here, just go in that cage there, Paddy, and you'll find this female. And all you've got to do is render her pregnant, do you see?' And O'Shaughnessy says, 'What's in it for me?' and they offer him, oh, thousands of pounds. And of course he agrees. But then he opens the door of the cage and he sees what the female looks like. And he backs out." The Reuter's man replaced his empty Coke bottle in the rack and grimaced, showing Paddy's expression of revulsion. " 'Holy saints,' he says, 'I never counted on anything like this.' 'Thousands of pounds, Paddy!' they say to him, urging him on. 'Oh, very well then,' he says, 'but on one condition.' 'And what may that be?' they ask him. 'You've got to promise me,' he says, 'that the children'll be raised in the Church.' "

"Yeah, I heard that," said the other reporter. And he moved to put his bottle back, and as he did his foot caught in the rack and four cases of empty Coke bottles bounced and clattered across the floor.

Well, that was just about more than Mr. Mandala could stand and he gasped, stuttered, dinged his bell and shouted, "Ernest! Berzie! On the double!" And when Ernest showed up, poking his dark plum-colored head out of the service door with an expression that revealed an anticipation of disaster, Mr. Mandala shouted: "Oh, curse your thick heads, I told you a hundred times, keep those racks cleaned out." And he stood over the two bellmen, fuming, as they bent to the litter of whole bottles and broken glass, their faces glancing up at him sidewise, worried, dark plum and Arabian sand. He knew that all the reporters were looking at him and that they disapproved.

And then he went out into the late night to cool off, because he was sorry and knew he might make himself still sorrier.

The grass was wet. Condensing dew was dripping from the fittings of the diving board into the pool. The motel was not as quiet as it should be so close to dawn, but it was quiet enough. There was only an occasional distant laugh, and the noise from the lounge. To Mr. Mandala it was reassuring. He replenished his soul by walking all the galleries around the room, checking the ice makers and the cigarette machines, and finding that all was well.

A military jet from McCoy was screaming overhead. Beyond it the stars were still bright, in spite of the beginnings of dawn in the east. Mr. Mandala yawned, glanced mildly up and wondered which of them was Mars, and returned to his desk; and shortly he was too busy with the long, exhausting round of room calls and checkouts to think about Martians. Then, when most of the guests were getting noisily into their cars and

33. VISION: The Day the Martians Came

limo-buses and the day men were coming on, Mr. Mandala uncapped two cold Cokes and carried one back through the service door to Ernest.

"Rough night," he said, and Ernest, accepting both the Coke and the intention, nodded and drank it down. They leaned against the wall that screened the pool from the access road and watched the newsmen and newsgirls taking off down the road toward the highway and the ten o'clock briefing. Most of them had had no sleep. Mr. Mandala shook his head, disapproving so much commotion for so little cause.

And Ernest snapped his fingers, grinned and said, "I got a Martian joke, Mr. Mandala. What do you call a seven-foot Martian when he's comin' at you with a spear?"

"Oh, hell, Ernest," said Mr. Mandala, "you call him sir. Everybody knows that one." He yawned and stretched and said reflectively, "You'd think there'd be some new jokes. All I heard was the old ones, only instead of picking on the Jews and the Catholics and—and everybody, they were telling them about the Martians."

"Yeah, I noticed that, Mr. Mandala," said Ernest.

Mr. Mandala stood up. "Better get some sleep," he advised, "because they might all be back again tonight. I don't know what for. . . . Know what I think, Ernest? Outside of the jokes, I don't think that six months from now anybody's going to remember there ever were such things as Martians. I don't believe their coming here is going to make a nickel's worth of difference to anybody."

"Hate to disagree with you, Mr. Mandala," said Ernest mildly, "but I don't think so. Going to make a difference to some people. Going to make a *damn* big difference to me."

34.
VISION:
Sundance

ROBERT SILVERBERG

The complicated dimensions of cognitive dissonance and role conflict are the topic of the following story by Robert Silverberg.

Today you liquidated about 50,000 Eaters in Sector A, and now you are spending an uneasy night. You and Herndon flew east at dawn, with the green-gold sunrise at your backs, and sprayed the neural pellets over a thousand hectares along the Forked River. You flew on into the prairie beyond the river, where the Eaters have already been wiped out, and had lunch sprawled on that thick, soft carpet of grass where the first settlement is expected to rise. Herndon picked some juiceflowers and you enjoyed half an hour of mild hallucinations. Then, as you headed toward the copter to begin an afternoon of further pellet-spraying, he said suddenly, "Tom, how would you feel about this if it turned out that the Eaters weren't just animal pests? That they were *people,* say, with a language and rites and a history and all?"

You thought of how it had been for your own people.

"They aren't," you said.

"Suppose they were. Suppose the Eaters—"

"They aren't. Drop it."

Herndon has this streak of cruelty in him that leads him to ask such questions. He goes for the vulnerabilities; it amuses him. All night now his casual remark has echoed in your mind. Suppose the Eaters. . . . Suppose the Eaters. . . . Suppose. . . . Suppose. . . .

34. VISION: Sundance

You sleep for a while, and dream, and in your dreams you swim through rivers of blood.

Foolishness. A feverish fantasy. You know how important it is to exterminate the Eaters fast, before the settlers get here. They're just animals, and not even harmless animals at that; ecology-wreckers is what they are, devourers of oxygen-liberating plants, and they have to go. A few have been saved for zoological study. The rest must be destroyed. Ritual extirpation of undesirable beings: the old, old story. But let's not complicate our job with moral qualms, you tell yourself. Let's not dream of rivers of blood.

The Eaters don't even *have* blood, none that could flow in rivers, anyway. What they have is, well, a kind of lymph that permeates every tissue and transmits nourishment along the interfaces. Waste products go out the same way, osmotically. In terms of process it's structurally analogous to your own kind of circulatory system, except there's no network of blood vessels hooked to a master pump. The life-stuff just oozes through their bodies, as though they were amoebas or sponges or some other low-phylum form. Yet they're definitely high-phylum in nervous system, digestive set-up, limb-and-organ template, etc. Odd, you think. The thing about aliens is that they're alien, you tell yourself, not for the first time.

The beauty of their biology for you and your companions is that it lets you exterminate them so neatly.

You fly over the grazing grounds and drop the neural pellets. The Eaters find and ingest them. Within an hour the poison has reached all sectors of the body. Life ceases; a rapid breakdown of cellular matter follows, the Eater literally falling apart molecule by molecule the instant that nutrition is cut off; the lymph-like stuff works like acid; a universal lysis occurs; flesh and even the bones, which are cartilaginous, dissolve. In two hours, a puddle on the ground. In four, nothing at all left. Considering how many millions of Eaters you've scheduled for extermination here, it's sweet of the bodies to be self-disposing. Otherwise what a charnel-house this world would become!

Suppose the Eaters. . . .

Damn Herndon. You almost feel like getting a memory-editing in the morning. Scrape his stupid speculations out of your head. If you dared. If you dared.

In the morning he does not dare. Memory-editing frightens him; he will try to shake free of his newfound guilt without it. The Eaters, he explains to himself, are mindless herbivores, the unfortunate victims of human expansionism, but not really deserving of passionate defense. Their extermination is not tragic; it's just too bad. If Earthmen are to have this world, the Eaters must relinquish it. There's a difference, he tells himself, between the elimination of the Plains Indians from the American prairie in the nineteenth century and the destruction of the bison on that same prairie. One feels a little wistful about the slaughter of the thundering herds; one regrets the butchering of millions of the noble brown woolly beasts, yes. But one feels outrage, not mere wistful regret, at what was done to the Sioux. There's a difference. Reserve your passions for the proper cause.

He walks from his bubble at the edge of the camp toward the center of things. The flagstone path is moist and glistening. The morning fog has not yet lifted, and every tree is bowed, the long notched leaves heavy with droplets of water. He pauses, crouching, to observe a spider-analog spinning its asymmetrical web. As he watches, a small amphibian, delicately shaded turquoise, glides as inconspicuously as possible over the mossy ground. Not inconspicuously enough; he gently lifts the little creature and puts it on the back of his hand. The gills flutter in anguish and the amphibian's sides quiver. Slowly, cunningly, its color changes until it matches the coppery tone of the hand. The camouflage is excellent. He lowers his hand and the amphibian scurries into a puddle. He walks on.

He is forty years old, shorter than most of the other members of the expedition, with wide shoulders, a heavy chest, dark glossy hair, a blunt spreading nose. He is a biologist. This is his third career, for he has failed as an anthropologist and as a developer of real estate. His name is Tom Two Ribbons. He has been married twice but has had no children. His great-grandfather died of alcoholism; his grandfather was addicted to hallucinogens; his father had compulsively visited cheap memory-editing parlors. Tom Two Ribbons is conscious that he is failing a family tradition, but he has not yet found his own mode of self-destruction.

In the main building he discovers Herndon, Julia, Ellen, Schwartz, Chang, Michaelson, and Nichols. They are eating breakfast; the others are already at work. Ellen rises and comes to him and kisses him. Her short soft yellow hair tickles his cheeks. "I love you," she whispers. She has spent the night in Michaelson's bubble. "I love you," he tells her, and draws a quick vertical line of affection between her small pale breasts. He winks at Michaelson, who nods, touches the tips of two fingers to his lips, and blows them a kiss. We are all good friends here, Tom Two Ribbons thinks.

"Who drops pellets today?" he asks.

"Mike and Chang," says Julia. "Sector C."

Schwartz says, "Eleven more days and we ought to have the whole peninsula clear. Then we can move inland."

"If our pellet supply holds up," Chang points out.

Herndon says, "Did you sleep well, Tom?"

"No," says Tom. He sits down and taps out his breakfast requisition. In the west the fog is beginning to burn off the mountains. Something throbs in the back of his neck. He has been on this world nine weeks, now, and in that time it has undergone its only change of season, shading from dry weather to foggy. The mists will remain for many months. Before the plains parch again the Eaters will be gone and the settlers will begin to arrive. His food slides down the chute and he seizes it. Ellen sits beside him. She is a little more than half his age; this is her first voyage; she is their keeper of records, but she also is skilled at editing. "You look troubled," Ellen tells him. "Can I help you?"

"No. Thank you."

"I hate it when you get gloomy."

"It's a racial trait," says Tom Two Ribbons.

"I doubt that very much."

"The truth is that maybe my personality reconstruct is wearing thin. The trauma level was so close to the surface. I'm just a walking veneer, you know."

Ellen laughs prettily. She wears only a sprayon half-wrap. Her skin looks damp; she and Michaelson have had a swim at dawn. Tom Two Ribbons is thinking of asking her to marry him, when this job is over. He has not been married since the collapse of the real estate business. The therapist suggested divorce as part of the reconstruct. He sometimes wonders where Terry has gone and who she lives with now. Ellen says, "You seem pretty stable to me, Tom."

"Thank you," he says. She is young. She does not know.

"If it's just a passing gloom I can edit it out in one quick snip."

"Thank you," he says. "No."

"I forget. You don't like editing."

"My father—"

"Yes."

"In fifty years he pared himself down to a thread," Tom Two Ribbons says. "He had his ancestors edited away, his whole heritage, his religion, his wife, his sons, finally his name. Then he sat and smiled all day. Thank you, no editing."

"Where are you working today?" Ellen asks.

"In the compound, running tests."

"Want company? I'm off all morning."

"Thank you, no," he says, too quickly. She looks hurt. He tries to remedy his unintended cruelty by touching her arm lightly and saying, "Maybe this afternoon, all right? I need to commune a while. Yes?"

"Yes," she says, and smiles, and shapes a kiss with her lips.

After breakfast he goes to the compound. It covers a thousand hectares east of the base; they have bordered it with neural-field projectors at intervals of eighty meters, and this is a sufficient fence to keep the captive population of two hundred Eaters from straying. When all the others have been exterminated, this study group will remain. At the southwest corner of the compound stands a lab bubble from which the experiments are run: metabolic, psychological, physiological, ecological. A stream crosses the compound diagonally. There is a low ridge of grassy hills at its eastern edge. Five distinct copses of tightly clustered knifeblade trees are separated by patches of dense savanna. Sheltered beneath the grass are the oxygen-plants, almost completely hidden except for the photosynthetic spikes that jut to heights of three or four meters at regular intervals, and for the lemon-colored respiratory bodies, chest-high, that make the grassland sweet and dizzying with exhaled gases. Through the fields move the Eaters in a straggling herd, nibbling delicately at the respiratory bodies. Tom Two Ribbons spies the herd beside the stream and goes toward it. He stumbles over an oxygen-plant hidden in the grass, but deftly recovers his balance and, seizing the puckered orifice of the respiratory body, inhales deeply. His despair lifts. He approaches the Eaters. They are spherical, bulky, slow-moving creatures, covered by masses of coarse orange fur. Saucerlike eyes protrude above narrow rubbery lips; their legs are thin and scaly, like a chicken's, and their arms are short and held close to their bodies. They regard him with bland lack of curiosity. "Good morning, brothers!" is the way he greets them this time and he wonders why.

I noticed something strange today. Perhaps I simply sniffed too much oxygen in the fields; maybe I was succumbing to a suggestion Herndon planted; or possibly it's the family masochism cropping out. But while I was observing the Eaters in the compound it seemed to me, for the first time, that they were behaving intelligently, that they were functioning in a ritualized way.

I followed them around for three hours. During that time they uncovered half a dozen outcroppings of oxygen-plants. In each case they went through a stylized pattern of action before starting to munch. They:

Formed a straggly circle around the plants.
Looked toward the sun.
Looked toward their neighbors on left and right around the circle.
Made fuzzy neighing sounds *only* after having done the foregoing.
Looked toward the sun again.
Moved in and ate.

If this wasn't a prayer of thanksgiving, a saying of grace, then what was it? And if they're advanced enough spiritually to say grace, are we not therefore committing genocide here? Do chimpanzees say grace? Christ, we wouldn't even wipe out chimps the way we're cleaning out the Eaters! Of course, chimps don't interfere with human crops, and some kind of coexistence would be possible, whereas Eaters and human agriculturalists simply can't function on the same planet. Nevertheless there's a moral issue here. The liquidation effort is predicated on the assumption that the intelligence level of the Eaters is about on a par with that of oysters, or, at best, sheep. Our consciences stay clear because our poison is quick and painless and because the Eaters thoughtfully dissolve upon dying, sparing us the mess of incinerating millions of corpses. But if they pray—

I won't say anything to the others just yet. I want more evidence, hard,

34.   VISION: Sundance

objective. Films, tapes, record cubes. Then we'll see. What if I can show that we're exterminating intelligent beings? My family knows a little about genocide, after all, having been on the receiving end just a few centuries back. I doubt that I could halt what's going on here. But at the very least I could withdraw from the operation. Head back to Earth and stir up public outcries.

I hope I'm imagining this.

I'm not imagining a thing. They gather in circles; they look to the sun; they neigh and pray. They're only balls of jelly on chicken-legs, but they give thanks for their food. Those big round eyes now seem to stare accusingly at me. Our tame herd here knows what's going on: that we have descended from the stars to eradicate their kind, and that they alone will be spared. They have no way of fighting back or even of communicating their displeasure, but they *know.* And hate us. Jesus, we have killed two million of them since we got here, and in a metaphorical way I'm stained with blood, and what will I do, what can I do?

I must move very carefully, or I'll end up drugged and edited.

I can't let myself seem like a crank, a quack, an agitator. I can't stand up and Denounce. I have to find allies. Herndon, first. He surely is on to the truth; he's the one who nudged *me* to it, that day we dropped pellets. And I thought he was merely being vicious in his usual way!

I'll talk to him tonight.

He says, "I've been thinking about that suggestion you made. About the Eaters. Perhaps we haven't made sufficiently close psychological studies. I mean, if they really *are* intelligent—"

Herndon blinks. He is a tall man with glossy dark hair, a heavy beard, sharp cheekbones. "Who says they are, Tom?"

"You did. On the far side of the Forked River, you said—"

"It was just a speculative hypothesis. To make conversation."

"No, I think it was more than that. You really believed it."

Herndon looks troubled. "Tom, I don't know what you're trying to start, but don't start it. If I for a moment believed we were killing intelligent creatures, I'd run for an editor so fast I'd start an implosion wave."

"Why did you ask me that thing, then?" Tom Two Ribbons says.

"Idle chatter."

"Amusing yourself by kindling guilts in somebody else? You're a bastard, Herndon. I mean it."

"Well, look, Tom, if I had any idea that you'd get so worked up about a hypothetical suggestion—" Herndon shakes his head. "The Eaters aren't intelligent beings. Obviously. Otherwise we wouldn't be under orders to liquidate them."

"Obviously," says Tom Two Ribbons.

IX. Increased Relevancy of Social Psychology

Ellen said, "No, I don't know what Tom's up to. But I'm pretty sure he needs a rest. It's only a year and a half since his personality reconstruct, and he had a pretty bad breakdown back then."

Michaelson consulted a chart. "He's refused three times in a row to make his pellet-dropping run. Claiming he can't take time away from his research. Hell, we can fill in for him, but it's the idea that he's ducking chores that bothers me."

"What kind of research is he doing?" Nichols wanted to know.

"Not biological," said Julia. "He's with the Eaters in the compound all the time, but I don't see him making any tests on them. He just watches them."

"And talks to them," Chang observed.

"And talks, yes," Julia said.

"About what?" Nichols asked.

"Who knows?"

Everyone looked at Ellen. "You're closest to him," Michaelson said. "Can't you bring him out of it?"

"I've got to know what he's in, first," Ellen said. "He isn't saying a thing."

You know that you must be very careful, for they outnumber you, and their concern for your mental welfare can be deadly. Already they realize you are disturbed, and Ellen has begun to probe for the source of the disturbance. Last night you lay in her arms and she questioned you, obliquely, skillfully, and you knew what she is trying to find out. When the moons appeared she suggested that you and she stroll in the compound, among the sleeping Eaters. You declined; but she sees that you have become involved with the creatures.

You have done probing of your own—subtly, you hope. And you are aware that you can do nothing to save the Eaters. An irrevocable commitment has been made. It is 1876 all over again; these are the bison, these are the Sioux, and they must be destroyed, for the railroad is on its way. If you speak out here, your friends will calm you and pacify you and edit you, for they do not see what you see. If you return to Earth to agitate, you will be mocked and recommended for another reconstruct. You can do nothing. You can do nothing.

You cannot save, but perhaps you can record.

Go out into the prairie. Live with the Eaters; make yourself their friend; learn their ways. Set it down, a full account of their culture, so that at least that much will not be lost. You know the techniques of field anthropology. As was done for your people in the old days, do now for the Eaters.

He finds Michaelson. "Can you spare me for a few weeks?" he asks. "Spare you, Tom? What do you mean?"

414

34.   VISION: Sundance

"I've got some field studies to do. I'd like to leave the base and work with Eaters in the wild."

"What's wrong with the ones in the compound?"

"It's the last chance with wild ones, Mike. I've got to go."

"Alone, or with Ellen?"

"Alone."

Michaelson nods slowly. "All right, Tom. Whatever you want. Go. I won't hold you here."

I dance in the prairie under the green-gold sun. About me the Eaters gather. I am stripped; sweat makes my skin glisten; my heart pounds. I talk to them with my feet, and they understand.

They understand.

They have a language of soft sounds. They have a god. They know love and awe and rapture. They have rites. They have names. They have a history. Of all this I am convinced.

I dance on thick grass.

How can I reach them? With my feet, with my hands, with my grunts, with my sweat. They gather by the hundreds, by the thousands, and I dance. I must not stop. They cluster about me and make their sounds. I am a conduit for strange forces. My great-grandfather should see me now! Sitting on his porch in Wyoming, the firewater in his hand, his brain rotting—see me now, old one! See the dance of Tom Two Ribbons! I talk to these strange ones with my feet under a sun that is the wrong color. I dance. I dance.

"Listen to me," I say. "I am your friend, I alone, the only one you can trust. Trust me, talk to me, teach me. Let me preserve your ways, for soon the destruction will come."

I dance, and the sun climbs, and the Eaters murmur.

There is the chief. I dance toward him, back, toward, I bow, I point to the sun, I imagine the being that lives in that ball of flame, I imitate the sounds of these people, I kneel, I rise, I dance. Tom Two Ribbons dances for you.

I summon skills my ancestors forgot. I feel the power flowing in me. As they danced in the days of the bison, I dance now, beyond the Forked River.

I dance, and now the Eaters dance, too. Slowly, uncertainly, they move toward me, they shift their weight, lift leg and leg, sway about. "Yes, like that!" I cry. "Dance!"

We dance together as the sun reaches noon height.

Now their eyes are no longer accusing. I see warmth and kinship. I am their brother, their redskinned tribesman, he who dances with them. No longer do they seem clumsy to me. There is a strange ponderous grace in their movements. They dance. They dance. They caper about me. Closer, Closer, Closer!

415

IX. Increased Relevancy of Social Psychology

We move in holy frenzy.

They sing, now, a blurred hymn of joy. They throw forth their arms, unclench their little claws. In unison they shift weight, left foot forward, right, left, right. Dance, brothers, dance, dance, dance! They press against me. Their flesh quivers; their smell is a sweet one. They gently thrust me across the field, to a part of the meadow where the grass is deep and untrampled. Still dancing, we seek for the oxygen-plants, and find clumps of them beneath the grass, and they make their prayer and seize them with their awkward arms, separating the respiratory bodies from the photosynthetic spikes. The plants, in anguish, release floods of oxygen. My mind reels. I laugh and sing. The Eaters are nibbling the lemon-colored perforated globes, nibbling the stalks as well. They thrust their plants at me. It is a religious ceremony, I see. Take from us, eat with us, join with us, this is the body, this is the blood, take, eat, join. I bend forward and put a lemon-colored globe to my lips. I do not bite; I nibble, as they do, my teeth slicing away the skin of the globe. Juice spurts into my mouth, while oxygen drenches my nostrils. The Eaters sing hosannahs. I should be in full paint for this, paint of my forefathers, feathers too, meeting their religion in the regalia of what should have been mine. Take, eat, join. The juice of the oxygen-plant flows in my veins. I embrace my brothers. I sing, and as my voice leaves my lips it becomes an arch that glistens like new steel, and I pitch my song lower, and the arch turns to tarnished silver. The Eaters crowd close. The scent of their bodies is fiery red to me. Their soft cries are puffs of steam. The sun is very warm; its rays are tiny jagged pings of puckered sound, close to the top of my range of hearing, plink! plink! plink! The thick grass hums to me, deep and rich, and the wind hurls points of flame along the prairie. I devour another oxygen-plant, and then a third. My brothers laugh and shout. They tell me of their gods, the god of warmth, the god of food, the god of pleasure, the god of death, the god of holiness, the god of wrongness, and the others. They recite for me the names of their kings, and I hear their voices as splashes of green mold on the clean sheet of the sky. They instruct me in their holy rites. I must remember this, I tell myself, for when it is gone it will never come again. I continue to dance. They continue to dance. The color of the hills becomes rough and coarse, like abrasive gas. Take, eat, join. Dance. They are so gentle!

I hear the drone of the copter, suddenly.

It hovers far overhead. I am unable to see who flies in it. "No," I scream. "Not here! Not these people! Listen to me! This is Tom Two Ribbons! Can't you hear me? I'm doing a field study here! You have no right—!"

My voice makes spirals of blue moss edged with red sparks. They drift upward and are scattered by the breeze.

I yell, I shout, I bellow. I dance and shake my fists. From the wings of the copter the jointed arms of the pellet-distributors unfold. The gleaming spigots extend and whirl. The neural pellets rain down into the meadow, each tracing a blazing track that lingers in the sky. The sound of the copter becomes a furry carpet stretching to the horizon, and my shrill voice is lost in it.

The Eaters drift away from me, seeking the pellets, scratching at the roots of the grass to find them. Still dancing, I leap into their midst, striking the pellets from their hands, hurling them into the stream, crushing them to powder. The Eaters growl black needles at me. They turn away and search for more pellets. The copter turns and flies off, leaving a trail of dense oily sound. My brothers are gobbling the pellets in terrible eagerness.

There is no way to prevent it.

Joy consumes them and they topple and lie still. Occasionally a limb twitches; then even this stops. They begin to dissolve. Thousands of them melt on the prairie, sinking into shapelessness, losing their spherical forms, flattening, ebbing into the ground. The bonds of the molecules will no longer hold. It is the twilight of protoplasm. They perish. They vanish. For hours I walk the prairie. Now I inhale oxygen; now I eat a lemon-colored globe. Sunset begins with the ringing of leaden chimes. Black clouds make brazen trumpet-calls in the east and the deepening wind is a swirl of coaly bristles. Silence comes. Night falls. I dance. I am alone.

The copter comes again, and they find you, and you do not resist as they gather you in. You are beyond bitterness. Quietly you explain what you have done and what you have learned, and why it is wrong to exterminate these people. You describe the plant you have eaten and the way it affects your senses, and as you talk of the blessed synesthesia, the texture of the wind and the sound of the clouds and the timbre of the sunlight, they nod and smile and tell you not to worry, that everything will be all right soon, and they touch something cold to your forearm, so cold that it is almost into the ultraviolet where you cannot see it, and there is a whir and a buzz and the deintoxicant sinks into your vein and soon the ecstasy drains away, leaving only the exhaustion and the grief.

He says, "We never learn a thing, do we? We export all our horrors to the stars. Wipe out the Armenians, wipe out the Jews, wipe out the Tasmanians, wipe out the Indians, wipe out everyone who's in the way, and then come out here and do the same damned murderous thing. You weren't with me out there. You didn't dance with them. You didn't see what a rich, complex culture the Eaters have. Let me tell you about their tribal structure. It's dense: seven levels of matrimonial relationships, to begin with, and an exogamy factor that requires—"

Softly Ellen says, "Tom, darling, nobody's going to harm the Eaters."

"And the religion," he goes on. "Nine gods, each one an aspect of *the* god. Holiness and wrongness both worshipped. They have hymns, prayers, a theology. And we, the emissaries of the god of wrongness—"

"We're not exterminating them," Michaelson says. "Won't you understand that, Tom? This is all a fantasy of yours. You've been under the influence of drugs, but now we're clearing you out. You'll be clean in a little while. You'll have perspective again."

"A fantasy?" he says bitterly. "A drug dream? I stood out in the prairie and saw you drop pellets. And I watched them die and melt away. I didn't dream that."

"How can we convince you?" Chang asks earnestly. "What will make you believe? Shall we fly over the Eater country with you and show you how many millions there are?"

"But how many millions have already been destroyed?" he demands.

They insist that he is wrong. Ellen tells him again that no one has ever desired to harm the Eaters. "This is a scientific expedition, Tom. We're here to *study* them. It's a violation of all we stand for to injure intelligent life-forms."

"You admit that they're intelligent?"

"Of course. That's never been in doubt."

"Then why drop the pellets?" he asks. "Why slaughter them?"

"None of that has happened, Tom," Ellen says. She takes his hand between her cool palms. "Believe us. Believe us."

He says bitterly, "If you want me to believe you, why don't you do the job properly? Get out the editing machine and go to work on me. You can't simply *talk* me into rejecting the evidence of my own eyes."

"You were under drugs all the time." Michaelson.

"I've never taken drugs! Except for what I ate in the meadow, when I danced—and that came after I had watched the massacre going on for weeks and weeks. Are you saying that it's a retroactive delusion?"

"No, Tom." Schwartz. "You've had this delusion all along. It's part of your therapy, your reconstruct. You came here programmed with it."

"Impossible," he says.

Ellen kisses his fevered forehead. "It was done to reconcile you to mankind, you see. You had this terrible resentment of the displacement of your people in the nineteenth century. You were unable to forgive the industrial society for scattering the Sioux, and you were terribly full of hate. Your therapist thought that if you could be made to participate in an imaginary modern extermination, if you could come to see it as a necessary operation, you'd be purged of your resentment and able to take your place in society as—"

He thrusts her away. "Don't talk idiocy! If you knew the first thing about reconstruct therapy you'd realize that no reputable therapist could be so shallow. There are no one-to-one correlations in reconstructs. No, don't touch me. Keep away. Keep away."

He will not let them persuade him that this is merely a drug-born dream. It is no fantasy, he tells himself, and it is no therapy. He rises. He goes out. They do not follow him. He takes a copter and seeks his brothers.

34. VISION: Sundance

Again I dance. The sun is much hotter today. The Eaters are more numerous. Today I wear paint, today I wear feathers. My body shines with my sweat. They dance with me, and they have a frenzy in them that I have never seen before. We pound the trampled meadow with our feet. We clutch for the sun with our hands. We sing, we shout, we cry. We will dance until we fall.

This is no fantasy. These people are real, and they are intelligent, and they are doomed. This I know.

We dance. Despite the doom, we dance.

My great-grandfather comes and dances with us. He too is real. His nose is like a hawk's, not blunt like mine, and he wears the big headdress, and his muscles are like cords under his brown skin. He sings, he shouts, he cries.

Others of my family join us.

We eat the oxygen-plants together. We embrace the Eaters. We know, all of us, what it is to be hunted.

The clouds make music and the wind takes on texture and the sun's warmth has color.

We dance. We dance. Our limbs know no weariness.

The sun grows and fills the whole sky, and I see no Eaters now, only my own people, my father's fathers across the centuries, thousands of gleaming skins, thousands of hawk's noses, and we eat the plants, and we find sharp sticks and thrust them into our flesh, and the sweet blood flows and dries in the blaze of the sun, and we dance, and we dance, and some of us fall from weariness, and we dance, and the prairie is a sea of bobbing headdresses, an ocean of feathers, and we dance, and my heart makes thunder, and my knees become water, and the sun's fire engulfs me, and I dance, and I fall, and I dance, and I fall, and I fall, and I fall.

Again they find you and bring you back. They give you the cool snout on your arm to take the oxygen-plant drug from your veins, and then they give you something else so you will rest. You rest and you are very calm. Ellen kisses you and you stroke her soft skin, and then the others come in and they talk to you, saying soothing things, but you do not listen, for you are searching for realities. It is not an easy search. It is like falling through many trap doors, looking for the one room whose floor is not hinged. Everything that has happened on this planet is your therapy, you tell yourself, designed to reconcile an embittered aborigine to the white man's conquest; nothing is really being exterminated here. You reject that and fall through and realize that this must be the therapy of your friends; they carry the weight of accumulated centuries of guilts and have come here to shed that load, and you are here to ease them of their burden, to draw their sins into yourself and give them forgiveness. Again you fall through, and see that the Eaters are mere animals who threaten the ecology and must be removed; the culture you imagined for them is your hallucination, kindled out of old churnings. You try to withdraw your objections to this necessary extermination, but you fall through again and discover that there is no extermination except in your mind, which is troubled and disordered by your obsession with the crime against your ancestors, and you sit up, for you wish to apologize to these friends of yours, these innocent scientists whom you have called murderers. And you fall through.

35.
VALENCE:
ARVN as Faggots:
Inverted Warfare in Vietnam

CHARLES J. LEVY

In the following article, the dynamics of interpersonal attitude formation have profound consequences in a contemporary setting.

The way in which civilians often view Vietnam from the United States suggests that too much perspective can be just as distorting as too little. For it seems to be popularly believed that the actions of American troops there have resulted from racism and depersonalization of the enemy. But racism would not explain why there has been a high regard for the Viet Cong and North Vietnamese Army (VC/NVA) who are racially indistinguishable from the Army of the Republic of (South) Vietnam (ARVNs) for whom there has been a low regard. Nor would depersonalization of the enemy explain why there was substantial hostility directed against the ARVNs with whom there was personal contact, and little or no hostility toward the more remote VC/NVA.

In the case of American marines, the beginning of an explanation could be found in boot camp. Homosexuality appeared in two contradictory themes of basic training. On the one hand, homosexuals were the enemy. Referring to navy corpsmen in general, and one in particular, a former marine explained:

> A lot of them were like prissy. I mean looked on the faggoty-type side. You could tell they were corpsmen. But I mean if that guy was in marine boot camp he'd of got bounced out. Or he'd have so many problems within the system that he fucking wouldn't be able to hack it. He'd go out of his mind. He'd be called "a faggot."

IX. Increased Relevancy of Social Psychology

On the other hand, marine recruits were called "faggots" by their drill instructors during boot camp. By compelling these men to accept such labels, the drill instructors achieved on a psychological level the same control that they had on a physical level when, for example, the men were not permitted a bowel movement for the first week of boot camp.

As defined by the boot camp experience, homosexuality was only incidentally a sexual condition. More important, it represented a lack of all the aggressive characteristics that were thought to comprise masculinity. The connection between passivity and homosexuality was made vivid to the marines in boot camp inasmuch as they were unable to combat either the label or the activities surrounding it. When a recruit mentioned that he and a friend had been separated in violation of the "buddy system" under which they joined, the drill instructor is reported to have asked, "Do you like Private R?" The next question was, "Do you want to fuck him?"

After sending six men into a small shower room, the drill instructor, in another account, shouted, "Everybody on your back."

> We're all nude. So you fall on top of each other. You get assholes in your face. And then they turn on cold water and they make you run out and stand there.

This ritual, like most others in boot camp, was coupled with violence. As the men left the showers, the drill instructors "beat your fucking head in."

The violence towards trainees was merged with their learning how to do violence, so that "We used to be disgusted with the other services because we considered them unaggressive." Aggression meant learning how to protect not only their lives, but also their masculinity. Accordingly, after boot camp they referred to the Marine Corps as "the crotch," while the other military branches were called "the sister services."

The overreaching lesson of boot camp had been that combat must be on the marines' terms. This point was made by the drill instructors in a way that led one veteran to recall: "You just get shit on all the time if you don't live by their rules. If you don't they'll screw you any way they can." One of these accepted rules involved the rationale for this training, "They have to do it to protect your lives if you're going in combat." Boot camp training was continually linked to Vietnam by such means as reminding the recruits of the date they would be arriving there and by indicating the number of casualties that would result "if you don't take the training seriously." It was made clear that submission to the drill instructors would provide the recruits with the training that was necessary to in turn make the VC/NVA submit.

Yet, in Vietnam, the marines discovered that the VC/NVA "fight on their fucking terms, not on ours," according to another veteran. Much effort was aimed at getting the VC/NVA to fight on the marine terms. "What we tried to do is fucking chase them around so they don't know what's going on. But it's never that way." The VC/NVA not only refused to fight on the marines' terms, by fighting on their own terms they made the marines' terms inoperable. The link that was established between boot camp and Vietnam reappeared to hinder rather than help morale. For instead of the promised discontinuity between the two settings, the marines vis-à-vis the VC/NVA bore an unexpected similarity to the recruits who were called "girl" by the drill instructors.

The ascendance of the VC/NVA's terms was possible in large part because these terms were unknown to the marines. Even after locating the VC/NVA, their intentions were unclear:

> It depends on where they want to fight. You never know if they want to fight there and get that one company and consider it a day. Or if they want to just really get out of there. You can't tell. Or if they're just sucking you into one big mob scene.

The last of these possibilities, that there were other VC/NVA waiting in ambush, was the governing one. It meant that the marines were never able to assume a correspondence between the VC/NVA they saw and the ones that saw them.

Because the marines were seen in their totality, their intentions were open. Their terms were correspondingly weakened. For the VC/NVA were given an opportunity to develop counter-terms: "They know every map square where they can hold a good defense. Where there's a lot of heavy brush that would be tough for us to move our heavy equipment in."

Some of the problems that arose from trying to prepare men who were still in the United States for Vietnam were inherent to using a low risk artificial setting to anticipate the high risk real one. Training in the United States did not pass for combat in Vietnam: "When they used to send us out we used to go make believe. We set up an ambush and make believe someone walked by. You knew when all this shit was over you got to get to bed. So I mean it's not good." Just as combat in Vietnam does not pass for training in the United States: "You're not sitting there in 'Nam saying to yourself: 'Let me think now, the instructor told me to do it this way.' What the hell!"

The deeper problems that arose had less to do with training for wars in general than with this war in particular. Booby traps caused a majority of deaths in Vietnam. But booby trap training was regarded as a contradiction in terms:

> They show you all the booby traps and stuff. What's good showing you the booby trap. I mean, if you find a booby trap, the odds are good you ain't going to see it 'til after it blows up.

Efforts to simulate a Vietnam in the United States suffered from a more general handicap: "How can you train a person to fight someone that they've been fighting for so long that they haven't done good enough a job to find out anything about them?" Training in the United States, then, was futile for the same principal reason that combat in Vietnam was to be futile for the marines. So the difficulty of anticipating the VC/NVA through training in the United States was at least one authentic reconstruction of the setting to be found in Vietnam. Also the apparent unreality of training in the United States may not have been entirely inappropriate preparation for Vietnam. The above example of marines setting ambushes for other marines was said to be "make believe." But it anticipated the internecine character of the war.

The military techniques of the VC/NVA compelled the marines to violate their own traditions. These traditions were not abstractions. They were reasons for being. They also provided a set of expectations for Vietnam. But after arriving there, it turned out they had no application when "You can't go in and kick ass like you could in other wars." Here is the process of discovery:

> When I first got there, two VC held down the whole platoon just by firing over our heads. Then word was passed out, 'Stay down. Don't waste rounds. They'll just do this for fifteen minutes and leave.' And being a new guy and thinking how the marines are supposed to be so tough, I said, 'Why don't we go get them?' But, of course, they [the experienced marines] knew what they were doing. We probably would've went and got them, there probably would've been booby traps all over the place and we would've probably lost another 20 guys getting two. So we just sit there and stay for 15 minutes, 20 minutes, until they got tired.

When they arrived in Vietnam, these men had belonged to the Marine Corps for about eight months. This is a short time to become deeply involved in traditions—even allowing for the intensity of the boot camp experience. The commitment to the traditions of the Marine Corps was largely a result of their coinciding with the traditions of the street corners to which these men had belonged before their enlistment. The interchangeability of the traditions could be seen when the same marine who was "thinking how the marines are supposed to be so tough" later described his Vietnam experience through a street corner analogy: "That's like some guy walking up to you and punching you in the face every night and then before you have time to turn around or put up your hands he's gone."

Oriental Smiles

The previously clear and central distinction between aggressiveness and passivity was lost for the marines when they arrived in Vietnam. They found themselves using aggressive means which had passive results. Meantime, the VC/NVA used passive means which had aggressive results.

35. VALENCE: ARVN as Faggots: Inverted Warfare in Vietnam

The passive aspects of the VC/NVA took a variety of forms. To begin with, the VC/NVA did not fit any of the traditional American notions of what a formidable adversary should look like. They were the wrong size. Sometimes they were the wrong sex. They wore the wrong clothes, since the VC and occasionally the NVA lacked uniforms. They even wore the wrong expression: "It's hard to look through an Oriental person. They could probably hate your guts and stab you in the back, but they'll always smile at you." As it turned out, the more passive they appeared, the more difficult it was to defend against their aggression.

The marines heard lectures about Vietnamese men expressing friendship among themselves and with other men through physical contact. But this behavior became all the more inexplicable as a result of the lectures. For if handholding between men was a custom, it meant—as far as the marines were concerned—that these gestures were not aberrations within the Vietnamese society: rather the whole society was an aberration. A marine recalled that

> we had classes before we went over: that's just their way of life. Like them holding their arm on another guy means they're friends. It don't mean—that's what we were told anyways.

Nevertheless, in Vietnam "most of us" believed it did mean they were homosexuals.

The marines needed an explanation that would enable them to relate these male gestures to their own culture, not that of the Vietnamese. This was possible by defining it as homosexuality, since it was a familiar category to marines. By placing the ARVN in it, his behavior ceased to be strange. Equally important, the marines understood what their own behavior ought to be in response:

> I had been in country a year by this time. We were going back to regiment in Danang. We pulled the truck over and the ARVN engineer stopped us at a roadblock. And they bore you to death. They make you sick. They're trying to be military. So they've got this roadblock up. And they stopped the truck. And the driver is saying, "Get out of our way, you little slopes." And they come out and they said, "We have a wounded veteran." We said, "So what?" They said, "He doesn't have one leg. Could you give him a ride up to the hospital?" So everybody's saying, "Let him hop." I was in charge of the detail so I said, "Let him on." I was in the back of the truck. It was a PC three-quarter. So he comes over on his crutches. I said, "Throw your crutches up." So he passed up the crutches. And I grabbed him under the arms and I pick him up and I set him in the seat. The little slope grabbed me by the leg. And I had been in the country long enough to know that most of them are queer. They hold hands and stuff. And this sort of irks most marines and soldiers. And we're told that it's a Vietnamese custom,

when you're really friendly you should hold hands. So they try to hold a lot of guys' hands. So they end up getting beat bloody. The guy grabbed my leg. So I got mad. I wasn't in a good mood that morning and I whacked him. And my buddies grabbed his crutches. And I said "Go!" So we took off. We threw his crutches in the rice paddy one time and went about another 150 yards and threw the other crutch and then out he went. He was screaming and crying and begging us. "Out you go." We all had a good laugh about that.

In more important ways, the classification of ARVNs as homosexuals was not based on their presumed sexual activity. The fact that ARVNs were living at bases with their wives contributed to the belief that they were homosexuals. For the presence of wives meant the ARVNs led a soft life. Hence they were not, to use a common marine term, "hard."

In the same way, the fact that ARVNs did not attempt to engage in homosexual activity with the marines was taken as proof that the ARVNs were homosexual. For it was thought that fear, a sign of homosexuality, kept them from making advances: "They wouldn't fool around with us anyway. They wouldn't even look at us the wrong way. 'Cause they knew how good we were, which I thought we were."

A literal interpretation of the war by the marines, among other results, would have made them allies of the ARVNs. But the ARVNs provided the model for a less literal approach that released the marines from whatever obligations remained to define them as allies. It was thought they interpreted the war out of existence: "They don't want nothing to do with the war, but yet it's their war."

The reluctance of ARVNs to engage in combat was treated as interchangeable with fighting on the side of the VC/NVA. A marine who regarded the ARVNs as homosexuals, "every one of them," cited as evidence: "They're just too scared where there is gooks. Where the gooks are, they go in the opposite direction. They don't want to go out and make contact with them at all." A related assumption was expressed by another marine who considered it just as likely they would go in the same direction as the VC/NVA: "I heard if you get a patrol of ARVNs with you, and if they're getting beat, they'll just go right on the opposite side. And they'll shoot at you instead of with you. They kind of get scared."

Unreliable Allies

The marines considered the ARVNs to be so far removed from the war that in the process of preventing their lives from being disrupted they were able to augment them. As one former marine observed "I think they got a good thing going for them because of the black market." Further, this remoteness from the war while in the midst of it often meant that the marines saw themselves being made more vulnerable to attacks from the VC/NVA:

> The ARVNs felt that being in the army was great. They used to wear starched utilities. Everything was so nice. And like the marines were all slobs, because we had our clothes washed in rice paddy water and everything else. Nothing starched. And they looked like they should be in recruiting posters all the time. We had ARVN security and it started to rain. They went in houses—into their buddy's house—until the rain stopped, so they wouldn't get their uniforms wet. And left us out there with no security.

Official ethnology was the response of the Marine Corps to a feeling among the marines that "We didn't like the idea of us fighting for an army of faggots." Specifically,

> You hear the propaganda report, you know, our bullshit, like public relations between us and the Vietnamese. Well our public relations give us propaganda material telling us how the Vietnamese are a proud, simple people and courageous. And give us history of the country and how they fought the Chinese and everybody. And the Vietnamese war heroes and all this other shit. To impress upon us the fact that they're really not fucking gutless bastards. But we all knew better and we used to just hate them all the more. The more they tried to justify the Vietnamese the more we didn't like them.

The troops were not in a situation that they thought lent itself to this or any other form of intellectualizing. What did matter was that where the marines were vulnerable to attack from the VC/NVA they became the passive party, and the ARVNs were seen contributing to this vulnerability. In at least one sense, moreover, the marines were more passive vis-à-vis the VC/NVA than the ARVN were. The marines had their passivity imposed upon them by the VC/NVA, while the ARVNs acted passively through their own volition.

At times, the marines worked almost as hard at making themselves the enemy of the ARVNs as they did at making the ARVN their enemy. The first process recreated the theme of boot camp that violence should be done *for* one group so that they might do violence *to* a second group. There was a consensus among marines that ARVNs had nothing to fight for: "They didn't give a shit." The marines tried to give them something to fight against by making themselves the foremost enemy of the ARVNs.

As the marines found it increasingly difficult to establish a direct link between means and intended ends, they resorted to these indirect links. The assumption was that a marine offense against the VC/NVA required an offense against the ARVN that would result in an ARVN defense against the marines that would take the form of an ARVN offense against the VC/NVA. The mechanics of this sequence appear in the following episode:

IX. Increased Relevancy of Social Psychology

The marines were in there putting out the fire but unbeknowingst to them, they were stomping to death a three-week-old baby. So this caused uncontrollable laughter among the marines when they found they had accidentally killed a baby. There's nothing else they could do. And they've got to keep up this pretense of being fucking raving maniacs in order to keep the respect of the Montagnards. The gooks think that we're fucking lunatics. And you've got to keep this. As long as they're afraid of us, they won't give you a hard time. If they're afraid you'll shoot them in any minute and you don't find anything wrong in killing. So the guys start laughing. First, it was sort of a nervous laugh and then they just had a fucking grand time.

However, it soon became clear to these marines that an indirect linkage of means and ends was at least as unattainable as a direct one. When they were ambushed soon afterwards, the marine squad leader

yelled to the commander of the Vietnamese to bring on line assaults. So the four marines get up and they're pumping away. And all the eight gooks just sat there and watched them. And then they withdrew in disorganized retreat. What they do is they ran like hell while the marines were on line shooting. What they [marines] had to do is pull some escape and evasion maneuvers to get away. They were pissed.

In other words, the sequence that materialized consisted of a VC offense that resulted in an ARVN defense that resulted in a marine defense.

In short, one reason the ARVNs became the enemy was that the marines were, after all, bound to them as allies. For the ineffectiveness of the ARVNs in combat meant the task of the marines was that much greater and more dangerous: "Most of the time when they did get into contact they always got their ass kicked. And we usually had to come in and help them out."

The marines were bound to the ARVNs in a more immediate way. They provided the marines with a means of trying to salvage a disrupted frame-of-reference. For the ARVNs were proof that there was, after all, a connection between passivity and homosexuality. The marines were not only able to focus on them as passive targets, they could act against them aggressively.

Locating homosexual ARVNs was a welcome relief from having to cope with an often unrecognizable and always evasive VC/NVA. There were no problems identifying the homosexuality of the readily available ARVNs. The identification was based on criteria that did not require interrogation or scrutiny. The proof was an impression:

We thought a lot of them were queer, because of the way they act. They were so, I don't know, prissy like, and awkward. And just the way they laughed and looked at you.

35. VALENCE: ARVN as Faggots: Inverted Warfare in Vietnam

This imprecise definition is appropriate considering that "prissy" owes its first two letters to precise.

However, the assaults against assumed homosexuals were in no sense a charade. They were more a form of warfare than an alternative to it. All that kept the beatings from escalating was a lack of resistance. The exceptions illuminated the usual case:

> They'll come up to you and they'll rub your leg and you sucker them. Because as far as we're concerned, they're queer. So the ARVN lieutenant told his men, "The next time a marine hits you, I want you to shoot him." So our lieutenant heard about it and he says, "As soon as you see an ARVN pick up a weapon, first I want you to kill the lieutenant, and then I want you to wipe out all his men." We continued to beat them up and nobody shot anybody.

Meantime, the VC/NVA imposed the ultimate passivity on marines by making them the instruments of their own death. For the VC/NVA were "good at skills that we didn't even know—like booby traps." Most booby traps are arranged to have the victim act as his own executioner. And there is a mockery involved which accounts for the term. It is a trap for the booby. The only aggression permitted the marine was against himself. The more aggressive the marine tried to be, the more susceptible he was to booby traps.

Marines continued to be their own victims when they tried to fight on the terms of the VC/NVA. The marines began using a highly sophisticated mine called the Claymore that they expected to be far more effective than the relatively crude booby traps of the VC/NVA. The Claymore has pellets in the front that are fired by an explosive in the back. However, the VC/NVA were able to carry the Claymore one step further:

> They can sneak right up and turn your Claymore around. And then you start moving around there so you'll hit the Claymore and it's turned around. You'll be the one that gets it.

Booby trapped by their own booby traps. As the marines sought a new means of becoming more aggressive, they were made still more passive.

The invisibility of the VC/NVA and the visibility of the marines were the underlying reasons for the success of one and the failure of the other with booby traps. For there are two conditions that must be met if a booby trap is to operate successfully. First, the hunter must know where his prey will be. Second, the prey must not know where the hunter has been.

There is an interval between planting and detonating a booby trap. The aggressor is removed in both time and space from his aggression. But the marines (and the corner boys before them) were unaccustomed to aggression that was not spontaneous. This was another reason they had both a problem setting booby traps and a propensity for tripping them.

IX. Increased Relevancy of Social Psychology

The ambush is closely related to the booby trap. It relies on one's own invisibility and the other's visibility. There are, in addition, elaborate preparations that require deferred aggression. For these reasons, the ambushes prepared by marines were subject to the same problems as the booby traps they set:

> Every night these NVA or VC used to come down and they used to screw up marine ambushes. And they always used to get away. They'd know where the ambush was set up and killer teams were set up. They'd sneak by them when they go into the village to get their rice and what they needed and leave. And then they'd screw them up on the way back. They'd fire on the ambush. And they'd take off up into the mountains. They did this every night. And they [marines] never got any of them.

Hiding entails actively seeking invisibility. It is ordinarily considered a passive act, because it is seen as the avoidance of action. More important, it is seen as the avoidance of being acted upon. But in the context of Vietnam, both these components were redefined when they became the means by which the VC/NVA were able to act aggressively. To speak of a means and end suggests a break that did not exist. Instead, the means and end were part of the same process. When the VC/NVA hid, it was not only a way to avoid disadvantageous encounters with the marines, it was preparation for engaging the marines on advantageous terms:

> A lot of times you don't see them. They suck you into some type of ambush situation where there's a lot of them and a lot of you's. And they've already preregistered the area. Like two weeks before that they'll lie in the same position and fire their weapons for effect.

Not only was the means not entirely passive because it was part of an aggressive end, but the end was not entirely aggressive because it was part of a passive means. That is, the VC/NVA strategy was all the more difficult for the marines to sort out because it was cyclical. The marines found that the VC/NVA "aren't staying and fighting." Instead, "they hit you and run." But the running could not be classified as passive, because in addition to being the last stage of an aggressive act, it was the first stage of the next aggressive act. The confusion that resulted from trying to classify the tactics of the VC/NVA is reflected in the following account where the VC are shuttled between categories of offense and defense:

> The VC was more or less on a defense all the time. Always hiding and coming out at night. But he still had to move around, unless he was in a large group. But he always had to be the aggressor. And he was always under cover and stuff. So when he did come out and you did get in contact with him, he was determined that either he was going to die or he was going to get one of us.

430

35. VALENCE: ARVN as Faggots: Inverted Warfare in Vietnam

When the VC/NVA hid, it was an aggressive act even if it did not lead to an engagement with the marines. For the marines had an aggressive mission in Vietnam. They were there to eliminate the VC/NVA. A status quo meant failure. The objective of the Marine Corps was summed up by the name given their "search and destroy missions." The VC/NVA could thwart these missions simply by hiding.

> You'd go in there for three days; you'd pull out. And if they were there anyways, they weren't there when we got there. I imagine they must have come back after we left. So those are the most useless operations I ever heard of. If they seen a hole they'd start saying, "Oh, I bet there's weapons down there. I bet there's rice down there." We'd dig it up and there'd be nothing there. We never found nothing. I went on three of those, never found nothing.

The only result of these operations would be "carrying a couple of dead guys back—our own," men who encountered booby traps.

Catching those who hide is a form of aggressiveness, except in Vietnam. The contradiction of being permitted by the enemy to take the initiative was described by a former marine: "You catch them when they want you to catch them. They have all their bunkers and everything all set for you."

Traditionally, setting the time and place of battle has been another aggressive characteristic. The marines found themselves helping to set these terms because the VC/NVA "just wait 'til I guess they think they have you at your weakest, then they hit you." Another veteran provides an illustration:

> Usually they'll hit the areas that are most secure. The lines are never checked. There won't be much bother about falling to sleep on watch. The platoon commander didn't care because we were never hit. Everyone gets to not caring.

Here too the apparent passivity of the VC/NVA was the means to an aggressive act. For they were able to make the camp vulnerable by not attacking it.

The marines had a sense of being objects that comes from being continually visible while those viewing them remain for the most part invisible. But they had not adapted to the dangers that follow from this condition. It was only in retrospect, that the marine veteran just quoted saw that the more secure they felt, the less secure they were in fact. In Vietnam, when the VC/NVA abstained from an attack it was regarded as security not as a forewarning. There was less stress for the marines in facing a disaster that would be observable than in admitting to themselves that they were living with an unseen threat.

Telescoped examples of this dilemma could occur several times a day to the same men. A former marine tells of walking at the head of a patrol along a trail:

IX. Increased Relevancy of Social Psychology

> You see a shell case. So you start to step over this way. But you think:
> "Maybe it was put there on purpose so I'd step over that way." So it
> really screws your head up. The hell with it. I'd step over this way. And
> if it blows, it'll blow.

The weakness of the marines was maximized by not only the behavior but
more particularly through the attitudes with which they were provided by
the VC/NVA. The invisibility of the VC/NVA provided them with a safe
view of marines as a prelude to safe action against them: "They could be
hiding under a rock or in a tunnel. We could walk right over them so they
could see everything you have. What the hell can you do? They're watching you all the time, you never see them."

All this means that the marines were less visible to themselves than they
were to the VC/NVA. Until the marines set off a mine or walked into an
ambush, they did not usually know where they were in relation to the
VC/NVA. In one way or another, "You wait to get hit; wait for them to
come to you." But there was more involved than the VC/NVA seeing
precisely what dangers the marines were exposed to. For the VC/NVA saw
into the operations of the marines as well as the context in which they were
held. It amounted to the marines having to rely on the VC/NVA in order
to view themselves. The VC made this reliance explicit:

> They talk to us all the time and shit—loud-speakers. In fact they told
> us one night, before anyone that was with us knew it, that we were
> going to move up to Phu Bai. Imagine that! They told us over a
> loud-speaker that they were pulling us out, because they knew if we
> stayed there that the VC were going to annihilate us. So the squad
> leader went to the CO and they checked on it and we *were* going to
> move out about three weeks later. So they knew it before we did. That
> kind of fucked up your mind a little, you know.

(The announcement by the VC was in English—which served to tell the
marines that their language, too, was visible.) Even a formal statement of
defeat by the VC/NVA could be made into an aggressive act by them:

> One day eight of them [NVA] turned themselves in. You could see
> their white flag. They had me walking up. I felt like an asshole. They're
> fucking clean. New uniforms. Spotless. Their boots were shined. Hair-
> cuts. And they're supposed to be living in the mud? They're doing
> better than we are. And they're walking up. They're clean as a whistle.
> They had tailored uniforms. So everyone's there wondering: What's
> going on out there?

In describing the episode, this former marine wonders if "they just sent
them out there to turn themselves in to make us look like they were doing
good out there." But he dismisses this possibility. It is a reassuring one

insofar as it indicates the prisoners were not typical. Yet, to accept this explanation would be an acknowledgement that the NVA were capable of deliberately redefining the terms of war by turning surrender on its head. Further, it would mean that the marines had accommodated the NVA.

Where the marines did succeed in killing, they often discovered that this could not be considered a form of domination, particularly when the victims were civilians. These deaths were both a cause and effect of the marines' passivity. For killing civilians usually meant the marines had lost control. The particular kind of control varied, but every case included a loss of control over the VC/NVA. When the marines were acting in rage, the civilians they killed served as surrogates for elusive VC/NVA. They were acting spontaneously at the time, but afterwards the marines saw their action as a loss of control over themselves:

> You see a guy you're really tight with for a period of months getting killed. We got really pissed off about it. You don't just say, "Well, fuck it." You go like kind of nutty. Anybody that even looked at you the wrong way you'd probably shoot. I think the American fighting man can be the most vicious ever. People don't realize this.

When civilians were killed through mistaken identity, it was a more direct reminder that the VC/NVA were beyond control, to the point of being unidentifiable. The misplaced aggressiveness of these acts sometimes resulted in ridicule, as when a marine shot a village elder one night and was afterwards nicknamed "killer" by his fellow marines. His death was the outcome of a curfew rule that required the shooting of any violators. The curfew was imposed as a means of assuring that the VC/NVA would be identifiable.

Whatever the circumstances, killing civilians weakened the position of the marines. For it meant the villagers became still more dedicated to the VC/NVA, as seen in the following episode about the death of another elder:

> There's a killer team out one night. They were outside this village. This old man, he was a villager, was going out to do a crap in the rice paddy. And he was killed. That was right at the edge of the village. He was mistaken for a VC. Immediately after that happened the villagers turned VC sympathizers. After that, there was always a build up of VC coming in. Along Highway 1, on the other side of the village, it was always mined. After this happened there was like a triple amount of mines planted in the road. And there was a road going up to the top of the hill. It was never really combed for any mines. Two days later a jeep went over a mine and blew up. That never happened before. But I imagine it was the villagers.

There were other ways in which the marines discovered that killing might not after all be the ultimate measurement of domination after all.

IX. Increased Relevancy of Social Psychology

For example, the VC/NVA were seen demonstrating a greater control of the situation when they abstained from killing. This realization by the marines made the control of the VC/NVA over them still greater:

> This [NVA soldier] goes "Good morning, marines." A lot of shit they did just to fuck up your head. I mean, they must have had a chance before that to really fucking zap someone. They did this shit just to fucking scare the fuck out of you. Just to let you know that they were on the ball and they weren't fucking around. Everyone fucking flies out of the trenches with their rifles. They're expecting attack. Fucking gook is probably laughing his ass off in the bushes. That's fucked up though.

The marines had finally recognized hiding as a means of killing. But here it was seen as a more subtle form of aggression—a means of killing morale. The VC/NVA directed the attention of marines to the importance of a psychological assault through their constant practice of it. However, the marines were as unable to cope with this sophisticated approach as they were with an apparently unsophisticated agrarian approach to combat.

The marines found that more than themselves was being relegated to passivity. The same thing was happening to the previously inviolate technology that had permitted the United States to maintain an aggressive stance in the world. Here, too, the victim brought on his own undoing, for the aggressiveness of this technology in Vietnam was often self-destructive. The following episode is typical of what could happen when technological superiority was invoked instead of dealing with the VC/NVA on equal terms:

> Say you had 30 gooks in the open. And you were too far away from them. Instead of losing men over them, artillery was the best bet. But we had too many restrictions on us. Like when we had to call an artillery mission. They had to get air clearance which is make sure there wasn't any helicopters flying around in the area or any jets, any Phantoms, flying over the area. So by the time we got that clearance then we'd have to get a ground clearance making sure that there wasn't any friendly troops around that area. So by the time the clearance came in, they were walking away. I mean they were just gone.

This failure had much to do with the characteristics of technology that were expedient or tolerated when they appeared in the United States. Its massiveness was inappropriate for the intimacy of combat in Vietnam where no one group was at a great distance from any other group. The bureaucracy attached to the technology was intended to make it manageable, but in the fluidity of this combat the bureaucracy made it all the more unmanageable.

Moreover, the futility of technology was carefully engineered by the VC/NVA. They were skilled at bringing out its limitations. Just as they made the visibility of marines a disadvantage by emphasizing the opposite characteristic among themselves, so they were able to turn technology into a disadvantage by not trying to fight it with technology. Again they stressed an opposite; this time, nature. It was a matter of building a strategy out of both their strength and the marines' weaknesses. Americans were unaccustomed to nature being used aggressively. When necessary, the land was used as a weapon:

> In valleys where you're pinned down—a lot of times we've had jets come in over the top of us, when it was hard to hit them any other way. They couldn't come across because of the mountains and stuff. They release the bombs right over our heads. And you can see the bombs. They'd be going towards us. And we're saying, "Ooh, fucking things just don't drop." But they like carried on the momentum of the speed they're going. They go in front of you. They blow up. That takes a lot of skill on an estimate. And a lot of fucking luck. The gooks choose this type of thing because they know that our jets can't come into a valley this way and make it, because there's a mountain there and they can't get up. So they set up their defenses so they can shoot down the planes as they're coming in.

The rationale for much of American technology had been the conquest of nature. But in Vietnam, the VC/NVA used nature for the conquest of technology.

Technological futility led to occasional attempts at de-emphasizing technology. But this only made way for problems that were more subtle and therefore less predictable. It brought out the other levels on which American culture was not transferable. These problems were subtle to the Americans, but they were obvious to everyone else. For example, a program was established to work with the villagers in a manner that minimized technology.

> We had an outfit that was called CAC—Combined Action Company. But cac in Vietnamese means prick. So they had to change it to Combined Action Platoons. They called it CAP. It was a laughing stock of the villages. And the VC played it to the hilt.

The extent to which the ethos of this war disoriented the marines was reflected in their way of trying to cope with it. For they engaged in a classification of the VC/NVA that was in itself disorienting. While the ARVNs represented what the marines feared they were becoming, the VC/NVA represented what the marines would like to have been. It was typically thought that in contrast to the ARVNs, the VC "have a lot of balls." Such metaphors of courage assisted in linking cowardice to a lack of masculinity, which is a short conceptual distance from homosexuality.

435

IX. Increased Relevancy of Social Psychology

Through relating to the VC/NVA, the marines were seeking a way to offset their inability to relate to the terms of the war. Their approval of the VC/NVA was reflected in the narrative of a former marine whose unit had suffered heavy casualties on several occasions, leading to its being known as "the walking dead." Eventually they found themselves at Khe Sanh. The NVA had them surrounded and were again inflicting substantial damage without being damaged. The siege was so thorough that the NVA were tunneling underneath the marine positions. During the excavation, a marine used a stethoscopic device to overhear the conversation of the NVA digging below:

> Scared as everybody was, you had to fucking laugh hearing them swearing and shit. 'Cause they were like us really. I figured the grunts [NVA] were there exactly like us. They didn't like the fucking shit more than we did. They're probably down there swearing about their fucking officers and fucking shit like that. It was funny. We were really laughing.

There was another way in which the marines benefited from thinking of the VC/NVA in personal terms. It made them visible—only to a slight degree—but it was that much of an improvement over invisibility. The contrasting visibility of the marines was indicated when "They'd shoot at you at midnight. You'd light up a smoke and he'd shoot at you." The unseen sniper was made visible insofar as he received a name from the marines: "Bed-Check Charley."

While the personalization of the VC/NVA operated in a way that introduced positive feelings, the impersonalization of the VC/NVA was invoked to prevent negative feelings. The fact that the NVA were trying to kill marines was explained away by one former marine who recalled that "you don't dislike them, because no one NVA ever did anything to you."

In other words, the marines did not suppose that the VC/NVA, on such occasions, were acting personally toward them. Clearly, the same could not be said about the ARVNs. The marines had no trouble relating specific grievances to specific ARVNs. Moreover, they had a sense that homosexuality was more personal than death.

36.
VISION:
Knots

R. D. LAING

The following selections from the book Knots *provide episodic and elliptical scenarios of interpersonal attitude formation.*

They are playing a game. They are playing at not
playing a game. If I show them I see they are, I
shall break the rules and they will punish me.
I must play their game, of not seeing I see the game.

There must be something the matter with him
    because he would not be acting as he does
        unless there was
    therefore he is acting as he is
    because there is something the matter with him

He does not think there is anything the matter with him
because
    one of the things that is
    the matter with him
    is that he does not think that there is anything
    the matter with him
therefore
    we have to help him realize that,
    the fact that he does not think there is anything
    the matter with him

is one of the things that is
the matter with him

It is the duty of children to respect their parents
And it is the duty of parents to teach their children
to respect them,
by setting them a good example.

Parents who do not set their children a good example
don't deserve respect.
If we do set them a good example
we believe they will grow up to be grateful to us
when they become parents themselves.

If he is cheeky
he doesn't respect you
for not punishing him
for not respecting you

You shouldn't spoil a child.
It's the easy way, to do what they want
but they won't respect you for letting them get away
with it when they grow up.

He won't respect you
    if you don't punish him
            for not respecting you.

JILL   I'm upset you are upset
JACK   I'm not upset
JILL   I'm upset that you're not upset that I'm
        upset you're upset
JACK   I'm upset that you're upset that I'm not
        upset that you're upset that I'm upset,
        when I'm not.

JILL   You put me in the wrong
JACK   I am not putting you in the wrong
JILL   You put me in the wrong for thinking you
        put me in the wrong.

JACK   Forgive me
JILL   No
JACK   I'll never forgive you for not forgiving me

36. VISION: Knots

It is boring that you are frightened
you are boring me by being interested in me.

In trying to be interesting,
you are *very* boring.

You are frightened of being boring, you
try to be interesting by not being interested,
but are interested only in not being boring.

You are not interested in me.
You are only interested that I be interested in you.

You pretend to be bored
because I am not interested
    that you are frightened
        that I am not frightened
that you are not interested in me.

Narcissus fell in love with his image, taking it to
be another.

Jack falls in love with Jill's image of Jack, taking
it to be himself.
She must not die, because then he would lose himself.
He is jealous in case any one else's image is reflected
in her mirror.

Jill is a distorting mirror to herself.
Jill has to distort herself to appear undistorted
to herself.

To undistort herself, she finds Jack to distort her
distorted image in his distorting mirror
She hopes that his distortion of her distortion may
undistort her image without her having to distort herself.

IX.   Increased Relevancy of Social Psychology

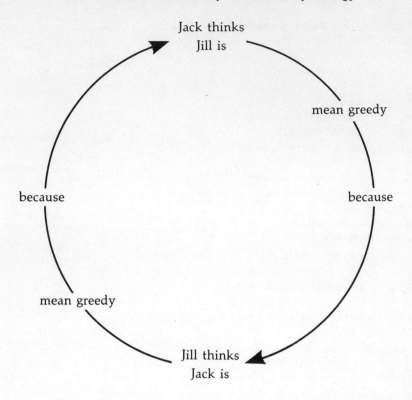

Jack thinks
Jill is

mean greedy

because   because

mean greedy

Jill thinks
Jack is

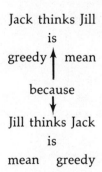

Jack thinks Jill
is
greedy ↑ mean

because
↓

Jill thinks Jack
is
mean   greedy

X.
On the Application of Psychology to Society

37.
VALENCE:
Selections
from *Beyond Freedom and Dignity*
B. F. SKINNER

Perhaps no psychologist has been as forthright as B. F. Skinner in his call for an application of behavioral psychology to the problems of society. In the following selection from his recent book Beyond Freedom and Dignity, *Skinner propounds some of the central aspects of his argument.*

A Technology of Behavior

Almost all of our major problems involve human behavior, and we cannot solve them by physical and biological technology alone. We need a technology of behavior, but we have been slow to develop the science from which we might draw such a technology. One difficulty is that almost all of what we call behavioral science continues to trace behavior to states of mind, feelings, traits of character, human nature, and so on. Physics and biology once followed similar practices and advanced only after discarding them. The behavioral sciences have been slow to change, partly because the explanatory entities often seem to be directly observed and partly because other kinds of explanations have been hard to find. The environment is obviously important but its role has remained obscure. It does not push or pull, it *selects,* and this function is difficult to discover and analyze. The role of natural selection in evolution was formulated only a little more than a hundred years ago, and we are only beginning to recognize and study the selective role of the environment in shaping and maintaining the behavior of the individual. As the interaction between organism and environment has come to be understood, however, functions once assigned to states of mind, feelings and traits are beginning to be traced to accessible conditions, and a technology of behavior may therefore become available. It will not solve our problems, however, until it replaces traditional prescientific views, and these are strongly entrenched. Freedom and dignity illustrate the difficulty. They are the possessions of the autonomous man of traditional theory, and they are essential to practices in which a person is held responsible for his conduct and given credit for his achievements. A scientific analysis shifts both the responsibility and the achievement to the environment. It also raises questions concerning "values." Who will use a technology and to what ends? Until we resolve these issues, a technology of behavior will continue to be rejected, and with it possibly the only way to solve our problems.

In trying to solve today's terrifying problems of war, over-population and pollution, we naturally play from strength, and our strength is science and technology. But while we have made many advances, things grow steadily worse, and it is disheartening to find that technology itself is increasingly at fault. War has acquired a new horror with the invention of nuclear weapons; sanitation and medicine have made the problems of population more acute, and the affluent pursuit of happiness is largely responsible for pollution.

Man must repair the damage or all is lost. And he can do so if he will recognize the nature of the difficulty. The application of the physical and biological sciences alone will not solve our problems because the solutions lie in another field.

What we need is a technology of behavior. We could solve our problems quickly enough if we could adjust the growth of the world's population as precisely as we adjust the course of a spaceship, or move toward a peaceful world with something like the steady progress with which physics has approached absolute zero (even though both presumably remain out of reach). But we do not have a behavioral technology comparable in power and precision to physical and biological technology, and those who do not find the very possibility ridiculous are more likely to be frightened by it than reassured.

Puzzle

Twenty-five hundred years ago man probably understood himself as well as he understood any other part of his world. Today he is the thing he understands least. Physics and biology have come a long way, but there has been no comparable development of anything like a science of human behavior. Greek physics and biology are now of historical interest only, but the dialogues of Plato are still assigned to students and cited as if they threw light on human behavior.

One can always argue that human behavior is a particularly difficult field. It is, and we are especially likely to think so just because we are so inept in dealing with it.

But modern physics and biology successfully treat subjects that are certainly no simpler than many aspects of human behavior. The difference is that the instruments and methods they use are of commensurate complexity. That equally powerful instruments and methods are not available in the field of human behavior is not an explanation; it is only part of the puzzle.

Gods

It is easy to conclude that there must be something about human behavior that makes a scientific analysis, and hence an effective technology, impossible. But we have by no means exhausted the possibilities. In a sense, we have scarcely applied the methods of science to human behavior. We have used the instruments of science: we have counted and measured and compared, but something essential to scientific practice is missing in practically all current discussions of human behavior. It has to do with our treatment of the causes of behavior.

Man's first experience with causes probably came from his own behavior: things moved because he moved them. If other things moved, it was because someone else was moving them: if the mover could not be seen, it was because he was invisible. Gods and demons served in this way as the causes of physical phenomena.

Physics and biology soon abandoned such explanations and turned to more useful kinds of causes, but the step has not been taken decisively in the field of human behavior. Intelligent people no longer believe that men are possessed by demons (although the daimonic has reappeared in the writings of psychotherapists), but they still commonly attribute human behavior to indwelling agents. They say, for example, that a juvenile delinquent suffers from a disturbed personality. There would be no point in saying it if the personality were not somehow distinct from the body that got itself into trouble. The distinction is clear when people say that one body contains several personalities that control it in different ways at different times. Psychoanalysts have identified three of these personalities —the ego, superego and id—and say that interactions among them are responsible for the behavior of the man in whom they dwell. And almost everyone still attributes human behavior to intentions, purposes, aims and goals.

Talk

Most persons concerned with human affairs—as political scientist, philosopher, man of letters, economist, psychologist, linguist, sociologist, theologian, anthropologist, educator, or psychotherapist—continue to talk about human behavior in this prescientific way. They tell us that to control the number of people in the world we need to change *attitudes* toward children, overcome *pride* in size of family or in sexual potency, and build some *sense of responsibility* toward offspring. To work for peace we must deal with the *will to power* or the *paranoid delusions* of leaders; we must remember that wars begin in the *minds* of men, that there is something suicidal in man—a *death instinct*, perhaps—that leads to war, and that man is aggressive by *nature*. This is staple fare. Almost no one questions it. Yet there is nothing like it in physics or most of biology, and that fact may well explain why a science and a technology of behavior have been so long delayed.

The important objection to mentalism is that the world of the mind steals the show. Behavior is not recognized as a subject in its own right. Psychotherapists, for example, almost always regard the disturbing things a person does or says as merely symptoms, and compared with the fascinating dramas staged in the depths of the mind, behavior itself seems superficial indeed. Linguists and literary critics almost always treat what a man says as the expression of ideas or feelings. Political scientists, theologians and economists usually regard behavior as the material from which one infers attitudes, intentions, needs and so on. For more than 2,500 years close attention has been paid to mental life, but only recently have we made any effort to study human behavior as something more than a mere by-product.

End

We also neglect the conditions of which behavior is a function. The mental explanation brings curiosity to an end. We see the effect in casual discourse. If we ask someone, "Why did you go to the theater?" and he says, "Because I felt like going," we are apt to take his reply as a kind of explanation. It would be much more to the point to know what happened when he went to the theater in the past, what he heard or read about the play he went to see, and what other things in his past or present environments might have induced him to go or to do something else.

The professional psychologist often stops at the same point. A long time ago William James corrected a prevailing view of the relation between feelings and action by asserting that we do not run away because we are afraid but are afraid because we run away. In other words, what we feel when we feel afraid is our behavior—the very behavior that in the traditional view expresses the feeling and is explained by it. But how many of those who have considered James's argument have noted that no antecedent event has in fact been pointed out? Neither "because" should be taken seriously. No explanation has been given as to why we run away *and* feel afraid.

Unable to understand how or why the person we see behaves as he does, we attribute his behavior to a person we cannot see, whose behavior we cannot explain either, but about whom we are not inclined to ask questions. We probably adopt this strategy not so much because of any lack of interest or power but because of a long-standing conviction that for much of human behavior there *are* no relevant antecedents. The function of the inner man is to provide an explanation that will not be explained in turn. Explanation stops with him. He is not a mediator between past

X. On the Application of Psychology to Society

history and current behavior; he is a *center* from which behavior emanates. He initiates, originates and creates, and in doing so, he remains, as he was for the Greeks, divine. We say that he is autonomous—and so far as a science of behavior is concerned, that means miraculous.

Task

The position is, of course, vulnerable. Autonomous man serves to explain only the things we are not yet able to explain in other ways. Autonomous man's existence depends upon our ignorance and he naturally loses status as we come to know more about behavior.

The task of a scientific analysis is to explain how the behavior of a person as a physical system relates to the conditions under which the human species evolved and the conditions under which the individual lives. Unless there is indeed some capricious or creative intervention, these events must be related, and no intervention is in fact needed. The contingencies of survival responsible for man's genetic endowment would produce tendencies to *act* aggressively, not feelings of aggression. The punishment of sexual behavior changes sexual *behavior*, and any feelings that may arise are at best by-products. Our age is not suffering from anxiety but from the accidents, crimes, wars and other dangerous and painful things to which people are so often exposed. The fact that young people drop out of school, refuse to get jobs and associate only with others of their own age is not due to feelings of alienation but to defective social environments in homes, schools, factories and elsewhere.

We can follow the path taken by physics and biology by turning directly to the relation between behavior and the environment and neglecting states of mind. We do not need to try to discover what personalities, states of mind, feelings, traits of character, plans, purposes, intentions or other perquisites of autonomous man really are in order to get on with a scientific analysis of behavior.

Inner

There are reasons why it has taken us so long to reach this point. The outer man whose behavior is to be explained could be very much like the inner man whose behavior is said to explain it. We have created the inner man in the image of the outer.

A more important reason is that we seem at times to observe the inner man directly. Indeed, we do feel things inside our own skin, but we do not feel the things we have invented to explain behavior. We feel certain states of our bodies associated with behavior, particularly with strong behavior, but as Freud pointed out, we behave in the same way when we do not feel them; they are by-products and not to be mistaken for causes.

A yet more important reason why we have been so slow in discarding mentalistic explanations: it has been hard to find alternatives. Presumably we must look for them in the external environment, but the role of the environment is by no means clear. The history of the theory of evolution illustrates the problem. Before the 19th Century, people thought of the environment as simply a passive setting in which many different kinds of organisms were born, reproduced themselves and died. No one saw that the environment was responsible for the fact that there *were* many different kinds (and that fact, significantly enough, was attributed to a creative mind). The trouble was that the environment acts in an inconspicuous way: it does not push or pull, it *selects*. For thousands of years in the history of human thought the process of natural selection went unseen in spite of its extraordinary importance. When it was eventually discovered, it became, of course, the key to evolutionary theory.

Unto

The effect of the environment on behavior remained obscure for an even longer time. We can see what organisms do to the world around them, as they take from it what they need and ward off its dangers, but it is much harder to see what the world does to *them*.

The triggering action of the environment came to be called a "stimulus" —the Latin for goad—and the effect on an organism a "response," and together they were said to compose a "reflex." Reflexes were first demonstrated in small decapitated animals, and it is significant that people challenged the principle throughout the 19th Century because it seemed to deny the existence of an autonomous agent to which they had attributed the movement of a decapitated body.

When Ivan Pavlov showed how to build up new reflexes through conditioning, he created a full-fledged stimulus–response psychology that regarded all behavior as reaction to stimuli. The stimulus–response model was never very convincing, however, and it did not solve the basic problem because something like an inner man had to be invented to convert a stimulus into a response.

After

It is now clear that we must take into account what the environment does to an organism not only before but *after* it responds. Behavior is shaped and maintained by its *consequences*. Once we recognize this fact we can formulate the interaction between organism and environment in a much more comprehensive way.

There are two important results. One concerns the basic analysis. We can study behavior that operates upon the environment to produce consequences ("operant behavior") by arranging environments in which specific consequences are contingent upon behavior. The contingencies have become steadily more complex, and one by one they are taking over the explanatory functions previously assigned to personalities, states of mind, feelings, traits of character, purposes and intentions.

The second result is practical: we can manipulate the environment.

X. On the Application of Psychology to Society

Though man's genetic endowment can be changed only very slowly, changes in the environment of the individual have quick and dramatic effects. A technology of operant behavior is already well advanced and it may prove to be commensurate with our problems. However, that possibility raises another problem that we must solve if we are to take advantage of our gains.

Stayer

We have dispossessed autonomous man, but he has not departed gracefully. He is conducting a sort of rear-guard action in which, unfortunately, he can marshal formidable support. He is still an important figure in political science, law, religion, economics, anthropology, sociology, psychotherapy, philosophy, ethics, history, education, child care, linguistics, architecture, city planning and family life. These fields have their specialists, every specialist has a theory, and almost every theory accepts the autonomy of the individual unquestioningly. Data obtained through casual observation or from studies of the structure of behavior do not seriously threaten the inner man, and many of these fields deal only with groups of people, where statistical or actuarial data impose few restraints upon the individual. The result is a tremendous weight of traditional "knowledge" that a scientific analysis must correct or displace.

Two features of autonomous man—his freedom and dignity— are particularly troublesome. In the traditional view, a person is free. He is autonomous in the sense that his behavior is uncaused. We therefore can hold him responsible for what he does and justly punish him if he offends. We must reexamine that view, together with its associated practices, when a scientific analysis reveals unsuspected controlling relations between behavior and the environment.

Of course, people can tolerate a certain amount of external control. Theologians have accepted the idea that man must be predestined to do what an omniscient God knows he will do, and the Greek dramatist took inexorable fate as his favorite theme. Folk wisdom and the insights of essayists like Michel de Montaigne and Francis Bacon imply some kind of predictability in human conduct, and the statistical and actuarial evidences of the social sciences point in the same direction.

Escape

Autonomous man survives in the face of all this because he is the happy exception. Theologians have reconciled predestination with free will, and the Greek audience, moved by the portrayal of an inescapable destiny, walked out of the theater free men. Very little behavioral science raises "the specter of predictable man." On the contrary, many anthropologists, sociologists and psychologists have used their expert knowledge to prove that man is free, purposeful and responsible. Freud was a determinist—on

450

faith, if not on the evidence—but many Freudians have no hesitation in assuring their patients that they are free to choose among different courses of action and are in the long run the architects of their own destinies.

This escape route slowly closes as we discover new evidences of the predictability of human behavior. Personal exemption from a complete determinism is revoked as a scientific analysis progresses, particularly in accounting for the behavior of the individual.

Shift

By questioning the control exercised by autonomous man and demonstrating the control exercised by the environment, a science of behavior also seems to question dignity or worth. A person is responsible for his behavior, not only in the sense that he may be justly blamed or punished when he behaves badly, but also in the sense that he is to be given credit and admired for his achievements. A scientific analysis shifts the credit as well as the blame to the environment, and traditional practices can then no longer be justified. These are sweeping changes and persons committed to traditional theories and practices naturally resist them.

There is a third source of trouble. As the emphasis shifts to the environment, the individual seems to face a new kind of danger. Who is to construct the controlling environment, and to what end? Autonomous man presumably controls himself in accordance with a built-in set of values; he works for what he finds good. But what will the putative controller find good and will it be good for those he controls? Answers to questions of this sort are said, of course, to call for value judgment.

Freedom, dignity and value are major issues and unfortunately become more crucial as the power of a technology of behavior becomes more nearly commensurate with the problems we must solve. The very change that has brought some hope of a solution is responsible for a growing opposition to the kind of solution proposed. This conflict is itself a problem in human behavior and we may approach it as such. A science of behavior is by no means as far advanced as physics or biology, but it has an advantage in that it may throw some light on its own difficulties. Science *is* human behavior, and so is the opposition to science. What has happened in man's struggle for freedom and dignity, and what problems arise when scientific knowledge begins to be relevant in that struggle? Answers to these questions may help to clear the way for the technology we so badly need.

The Design of a Culture

A culture is like the experimental space used in the study of behavior. It is a set of contingencies of reinforcement, a concept we have only recently begun to understand. The technology of behavior that emerges is esthetically neutral, but when it is applied to the design of a culture, the survival of the culture functions as a value. The designs found in the utopian literature appeal to certain simplifying principles. They have the merit of emphasizing survival value: Will the utopia work? The world at large is of course much more complex, but the processes are the same and practices work for the same reasons. Above all, there is the same advantage in stating objectives in behavioral terms. The use of science in designing a culture is commonly opposed. It is said that the science is inadequate, that its use may have disastrous consequences, that it will not produce a culture that members of other cultures will like, and in any case that men will somehow refuse to be controlled. The misuse of a technology of behavior is a serious matter, but we can guard against it best by looking not at putative controllers but at the contingencies under which they control. It is not the benevolence of a controller but the contingencies under which he controls benevolently that we must examine. All control is reciprocal, and an interchange between control and countercontrol is essential to the evolution of a culture. The interchange is disturbed by the literatures of freedom and dignity, which interpret countercontrol as the suppression rather than the correction of controlling practices. The effect could be lethal. In spite of remarkable advantages, our culture may prove to have a fatal flaw. Some other culture may then make a greater contribution to the future.

Many people design and redesign cultural practices. They make changes in the things they use and the way they use them. They invent better mousetraps and discover better ways of raising children. ("Better" is simply the comparative of "good," and goods are reinforcers.) It is, of course, much harder to call one culture better than another, in part because we need to take more consequences into account.

No one knows the *best* way of raising children, but it is possible to propose better ways than we now have and to support them by predicting and eventually demonstrating more reinforcing results. We have done this in the past with the help of personal experience and folk wisdom, but a scientific analysis of human behavior is obviously relevant. It helps in two ways: it defines what we are to do and suggests ways of doing it.

Ills

How badly we need it is indicated by a recent discussion in a news-weekly about what is wrong with America. It described the problem as "a disturbed psychic condition of the young," "a recession of the spirit," "a psychic down-turn" and "a spiritual crisis." It attributed the problem to "anxiety," "uncertainty," "malaise," "alienation," "generalized despair" and several other moods and states of mind, all interacting in the familiar intrapsychic pattern (lack of social assurance leading to alienation, for example, and frustration leading to aggression). Most readers probably knew what the writer was talking about and may have felt that he was saying something useful. But the passage—which is not exceptional—has two characteristic defects that explain our failure to deal adequately with cultural problems: it does not actually describe the troublesome behavior and it mentions nothing we can do to change it.

Consider a young man whose world has suddenly changed—he has graduated from college and is going to work, let us say, or has been inducted into the armed services. Most of the behavior he has acquired up to this point is useless in his new environment. We can describe the behavior he actually exhibits, and translate the description, as follows: he lacks assurance or feels insecure *(his behavior is weak and inappropriate);* he is discouraged *(he is seldom reinforced, and as a result his behavior undergoes extinction);* he is frustrated *(extinction is accompanied by emotional responses);* he feels anxious *(his behavior frequently has unavoidable aversive consequences that have emotional effects);* there is nothing he wants to do or enjoys doing well—he has no feeling of craftsmanship, no sense of accomplishment *(he is rarely reinforced for doing anything);* he feels guilty or ashamed *(he has previously been punished for idleness or failure, which now evoke emotional responses);* he is disgusted with himself *(he is no longer reinforced by the admiration of others, and the extinction that follows has emotional effects);* he becomes hypochondriacal *(he concludes that he is ill)* or neurotic *(he engages in a variety of ineffective modes of escape);* and he experiences an identity crisis *(he does not recognize the person he once called "I").*

The italicized paraphrases suggest the possibility of an alternative account, which alone suggests effective action. What the young man tells us about his feelings may permit us to make some informed guesses about what is wrong with the contingencies, but we must go directly to the contingencies if we want to be sure, *and it is the contingencies we must change if we are to change his behavior.*

See

Feelings and states of mind still dominate discussions of human behavior for many reasons. For one thing, they have long obscured the alternatives that might replace them; it is hard to see behavior as such without reading into it many of the things it is said to express. The selective action of the environment has remained obscure because of its nature. Nothing less than an experimental analysis was needed to discover the significance of contingencies of reinforcement, and contingencies remain almost out of reach of casual observation.

Until we had arranged contingencies and studied their effects in the laboratory, little effort was made to find them in daily life. This is the sense in which an experimental analysis makes possible an effective interpretation of human behavior. It permits us to neglect irrelevant details, no matter how dramatic, and to emphasize features which, without the help of the analysis, we would dismiss as trivial.

Access

Contingencies are accessible, and as we come to understand the relations between behavior and the environment, we discover new ways of changing behavior. The outlines of a technology are already clear. We identify behavior to be produced or modified and then we arrange relevant contingencies. We may need a programmed sequence of contingencies.

The technology has been most successful when we can specify behavior and can arrange appropriate contingencies fairly easily—for example, in child care, schools, and the management of retardates and institutionalized psychotics. The same principles are being applied, however, in the preparation of instructional materials at all educational levels, in psychotherapy beyond simple management, in rehabilitation, in industrial management, in urban design, and in many other fields of human behavior. There are many varieties of "behavior modification" and many different formulations, but they all agree on the essential point: that we can change behavior by changing the conditions of which it is a function.

Use

Such a technology is ethically neutral. Both villain and saint can use it. There is nothing in a methodology that determines the values governing its use. We are concerned here, however, not merely with practices but with the design of a whole culture, and the survival of a culture that emerges as a special kind of value.

Trio

We can describe three values that come into play when a person designs a better way of raising children. He may do it primarily to escape from children who do not behave well; he may solve his problem, for example, by being a martinet. Or his new method may promote the good of the children or parents in general; it may demand time and effort and the sacrifice of personal reinforcers, but he will propose and use it if he has been induced sufficiently to work for the good of others. Or, if his culture has induced in him an interest in its survival, he may study the contribution people make to their culture as a result of their early histories, and he may design a better method in order to increase that contribution.

The same three kinds of values may be detected in the design of a culture as a whole.

Purpose

A culture is very much like the experimental space we use in the analysis of behavior. Both are sets of contingencies of reinforcement. A child is born into a culture as an organism is placed in an experimental space. Designing a culture is like designing an experiment; we arrange contingencies and note effects. In an experiment we are interested in what happens; in designing a culture with whether it will work. This is the difference between science and technology.

We find a collection of cultural designs in utopian literature. Writers have described the good life and suggested ways of achieving it. Plato, in *The Republic*, chose a political solution; St. Augustine, in *The City of God*, a religious one. Thomas More and Francis Bacon, both lawyers, turned to law and order, the Rousseauan utopists of the 18th Century to a supposed natural goodness in man. The 19th Century looked for economic solutions, and the 20th Century saw the rise of what we may call behavioral utopias that began discussing a full range of social contingencies (often satirically).

A utopian community is usually composed of a relatively small number of persons living together in stable contact with each other. They can practice an informal ethical control and minimize the role of organized agencies. They can learn from each other rather than from the specialists called teachers. They can produce and exchange goods without specifying values in terms of money. They can avoid troublesome contacts with other cultures through geographical isolation, and they can facilitate the transition to a new culture by some formalized break with the past, such as a ritual of rebirth. A utopia is a total social environment and all its parts work together.

Perhaps the most important feature of the utopian design, however, is that it can make the survival of a community important to its members. The size, the isolation, the internal coherence—all these aspects give a community an identity that makes its success or failure conspicuous. The fundamental question in all utopias is "Would it really work?" The literature is worth considering just because it emphasizes experimentation. A traditional culture has been examined closely and found wanting, and a new version has been set up to be tested and redesigned as circumstances dictate.

Power

The simplification in utopian writing is nothing more than the simplification characteristic of all science, but it is not always available in the world at large. It is one thing to design a culture and quite another to put the design into effect. Controlling power rests in the hands of persons who are not likely to relinquish that power, persons who are probably already in conflict with each other and will almost certainly be in conflict with any new set of contingencies.

And the problem is much more difficult. We cannot bring a fluid population under informal social or ethical control because such social reinforcers as praise and blame are not exchangeable for the personal reinforcers on which they are based. Why should anyone be affected by the praise or blame of someone he will never see again? Ethical control survives in small groups, but we must delegate the control of the population as a whole to specialists—to police, priests, teachers, therapists and so on, with their specialized reinforcers and their codified contingencies.

Ways

It is easy to change informal instructions, for example, but nearly impossible to change an educational establishment. It is easy to change marriage, divorce and child-bearing practices as the significance for the culture changes, but it is nearly impossible to change the religious principles that dictate such practices.

It is not surprising that so far as the real world is concerned, the word utopian means unworkable. History seems to offer support; people have proposed various utopian designs for nearly 2,500 years, and most attempts to set them up have been ignominious failures. But historical evidence is always against the probability of anything new; that is what is meant by history. Scientific discoveries and inventions are improbable; that is what is meant by discovery and invention. And if planned economics, benevolent dictatorships, perfectionistic societies and other utopian ventures have failed, we must remember that unplanned, undictated and imperfect cultures have failed, too. A failure is not always a mistake; it may be simply the best one can do in the circumstances. The real mistake is to stop trying.

Perhaps we cannot now design a successful culture as a whole, but we can design better practices, piecemeal. The behavioral processes in the world at large are the same as those in a utopian community, and practices have the same effects for the same reasons.

Skeptics

The application of a science of behavior to the design of a culture is an ambitious proposal, often thought to be utopian in the pejorative sense. It is often asserted that there are fundamental differences between the real, natural world and the contrived world of the laboratory in which we analyze behavior. There are real differences, but they may not remain so as a science of behavior advances, and they are often not to be taken seriously even now.

Steps

Every experimental science simplifies the conditions under which it works, particularly in the early stages of an investigation. An analysis of behavior naturally begins with simple organisms behaving in simple ways in simple settings. When a reasonable degree of orderliness appears, we can make the arrangements more complex.

Behavior is a discouraging field because we are in such close contact with it. The behavioral scientist is all too aware that his own behavior is part of his subject matter. Subtle perceptions, tricks of memory, the vagaries of dreams, the apparently intuitive solutions of problems—these and many other things about human behavior insistently demand attention. It is difficult to find a starting point and to arrive at formulations that do not seem too simple.

Show

The interpretation of the complex world of human affairs in terms of an experimental analysis is no doubt often oversimplified. Claims have been exaggerated and limitations neglected. But the really great oversimplification is the traditional appeal to states of mind, feelings and other aspects of autonomous man that a behavioral analysis is replacing. And the same may be said for traditional practices. We should evaluate the technology that has emerged from an experimental analysis only in comparison with what is done in other ways. What, after all, have we to show for nonscientific or prescientific good judgment or common sense or the insights gained through personal experience? It is science or nothing, and the only solution to simplification is to learn how to deal with complexities.

A science of behavior is not yet ready to solve all our problems. But the analysis continues to develop and is in fact much more advanced than its critics usually realize. A proposal to design a culture with the help of a scientific analysis often leads to Cassandran prophecies of disaster. The culture will not work as planned, and unforeseen consequences may be catastrophic. The Cassandras seldom offer proof, possibly because history seems to be on the side of failure: many plans have gone wrong, and possibly just because they were planned. It is true that accidents have been responsible for almost everything men have achieved to this date and will no doubt continue to contribute to human accomplishments, but there is no virtue in an accident as such. The unplanned also goes wrong.

If a planned culture necessarily meant uniformity or regimentation, it might indeed work against further evolution. If men were very much alike, they would be less likely to hit upon or design new practices, and a culture that made people as much alike as possible might slip into a standard pattern from which there would be no escape. That would be bad design. But if we are looking for variety, we should not fall back upon accident. Many accidental cultures have been marked by uniformity and regimentation. The only hope is *planned* diversification, in which we recognize the importance of variety.

Planning does not prevent useful accidents. They still occur and indeed are furthered by those who investigate new possibilities. We might say that science maximizes accidents. The behavioral scientist does not confine himself to the schedules of reinforcement that just happen in nature; he constructs a great variety of schedules, some of which might never arise by accident. A culture evolves as new practices appear and undergo selection, and we cannot wait for them to turn up by chance.

Odor

Another reason why people oppose a new cultural design can be put this way: "I wouldn't like it," or in translation, "The culture would be aversive and would not reinforce me in the manner to which I am accustomed." The word reform is in bad odor, for we usually associate it with the destruction of reinforcers—"the Puritans have cut down the Maypoles and the hobbyhorse is forgot"—but the design of a new culture is necessarily a kind of re-form, and it almost necessarily means a change of reinforcers.

X. On the Application of Psychology to Society

The problem is not to design a world that will be liked by people as they now are but to design one that will be liked by those who live in it. "I wouldn't like it" is the complaint of the individualist who puts forth his own susceptibilities to reinforcement as established values. A world that would be liked by contemporary people would perpetuate the status quo. A better world will be liked by those who live in it because it has been designed with an eye to what is, or can be, most reinforcing.

Perverse

It is sometimes said that the scientific design of a culture is impossible because man simply will not accept the fact that he can be controlled. Even if it could be proved that human behavior is fully determined, said Dostoevsky, a man "would still do something out of sheer perversity—he would create destruction and chaos—just to gain his point . . . And if all this could in turn be analyzed and prevented by predicting that it would occur, then man would deliberately go mad to prove his point." The implication is that he would then be out of control, as if madness were a special kind of freedom or as if the behavior of a psychotic could not be predicted or controlled.

But there is a sense in which Dostoevsky may be right. A literature of freedom may inspire a sufficiently fanatical opposition to controlling practices to generate a neurotic response if not a psychotic one. There are signs of emotional instability in those who are deeply affected by the literature. We have no better indication of the plight of the traditional libertarian than the bitterness with which he discusses the possibility of a science and technology of behavior and their use in the intentional design of a culture. Name-calling is common. Arthur Koestler has referred to behaviorism as "a monumental triviality." It represents, he says, "question-begging on a heroic scale." It has spun psychology into "a modern version of the Dark Ages." Behaviorists use "pedantic jargon," and reinforcement is "an ugly word." The equipment in the operant laboratory is a "contraption." Peter Gay, whose scholarly work on the 18th-Century Enlightenment should have prepared him for a modern interest in cultural design, has spoken of the "innate naiveté, intellectual bankruptcy, and half-deliberate cruelty of behaviorism."

Strut

Another symptom is a kind of blindness to the current state of the science. Koestler has said that "the most impressive experiment in the 'prediction and control of behavior' is to train pigeons, by operant conditioning, to strut about with their heads held unnaturally high." He paraphrases "learning theory" in the following way: "According to the Behaviorist doctrine, all learning occurs by the hit-and-miss or trial-and-error method. The correct response to a given stimulus is hit upon by chance and has a rewarding or, as the jargon has it, reinforcing effect; if the reinforcement is strong or repeated often enough, the response will be 'stamped in' and an S–R bond, a stimulus and response link, is formed." The paraphrase is approximately 70 years out of date.

Among other common misrepresentations are the assertions that a scientific analysis treats all behavior as responses to stimuli or as "all a matter of conditioned reflexes"; that it acknowledges no contribution to behavior from genetic endowment; and that it ignores consciousness. Statements of this sort commonly appear in the humanities, a field once distinguished for its scholarship, but the historian of the future will find it difficult to reconstruct current behavioral science and technology from what its critics write.

Who?

There are, of course, good reasons for resisting the control of human behavior. The most common techniques are aversive, and some sort of countercontrol is to be expected. But as we have seen, the literatures of freedom and dignity have extended these countercontrolling measures in an effort to suppress all controlling practices even when they have no aversive consequences or have offsetting reinforcing consequences. The designer of a culture comes under fire because explicit design implies control (if only the control exerted by the designer). The issue is often formulated by asking: Who is to control? And the question is usually raised as if the answer were necessarily threatening. To prevent the misuse of controlling power, however, we must look not at the controller himself but at the contingencies under which he engages in control.

We are misled by differences in the conspicuousness of controlling measures. We are likely to single out the conspicuous examples of control because in their abruptness and clarity of effect they seem to start something, but it is a great mistake to ignore the inconspicuous forms.

The relation between controller and countercontroller is reciprocal. The scientist in the laboratory, studying the behavior of a pigeon, designs contingencies and observes their effects. His apparatus exerts a conspicuous control on the pigeon, but we must not overlook the control exerted by the pigeon. The behavior of the pigeon has determined the design of the apparatus and the procedures in which the apparatus is used. Some such reciprocal control is characteristic of all science. As Francis Bacon put it, nature to be commanded must be obeyed. In a very real sense, the slave controls the slave driver, the child the parent, the patient the therapist, the citizen the government.

Benevolence

The archetypal pattern of control for the good of the person controlled is the benevolent dictator. Feelings of benevolence or compassion may accompany his behavior, but they may also arise from irrelevant conditions. They are therefore no guarantee that a controller will necessarily control well with respect to either himself or others because he feels compassionate.

Although cultures are improved by people, whose wisdom and compassion may supply clues to what they do or will do, the ultimate improvement comes from the environment that makes them wise and compassionate.

Counter

The great problem is to arrange effective countercontrol and hence to bring some important consequences to bear on the behavior of the controller. Some classical examples of lack of balance between control and countercontrol arise when control is delegated and countercontrol then becomes ineffective. Hospitals for psychotics and homes for retardates, orphans and old people are noted for weak countercontrol because those most concerned for the welfare of such people often do not know what is happening. Control and countercontrol tend to become dislocated when organized agencies take over control.

Self-government often seems to solve the problem by identifying the controller with the controlled. The principle of making the controller a member of the group he controls should apply to the designer of a culture.

Lag

The design of a culture and the control it implies are sometimes called ethically or morally wrong. Ethics and morals have to do with the consequences of behavior, and particularly with the problem of bringing remote consequences into play. There is a morality of natural consequences (how is a person to avoid eating delicious food if it makes him ill?), but social contingencies are more likely to raise moral issues.

The practical question is how we can make remote consequences effective. Without help a person acquires very little moral or ethical behavior under either natural or social contingencies. The group supplies supporting contingencies when it describes its practices in codes or rules that tell the individual how to behave, and when it enforces those rules with supplementary contingencies. Maxims, proverbs and other forms of folk wisdom give a person reasons for obeying rules. Governments and religions somewhat more explicitly formulate the contingencies they maintain, and education imparts rules that make it possible to satisfy both natural and social contingencies without being directly exposed to them.

This is all part of the social environment called a culture, and the main effect is to bring the individual under the control of the remoter consequences of his behavior. The effect has had survival value in the process of cultural evolution, since practices evolve because those who practice them are as a result better off. There is a kind of natural morality in both biological and cultural evolution. Biological evolution has made the human species more sensitive to its environment and more skillful in dealing with

37.   VALENCE: Selections from *Beyond Freedom and Dignity*

the environment. Cultural evolution, which was made possible by biological evolution, has brought the human organism under a much more sweeping control of the environment.

Results

We say that there is something "morally wrong" about a totalitarian state, a gambling enterprise, or the sale of harmful drugs, not because of any absolute set of values but because all these things have aversive consequences. The consequences are deferred, and a science that clarifies their relation to behavior is in the best possible position to specify a better world in an ethical or moral sense.

Need

The intentional design of a culture and the control of human behavior it implies are essential if the human species is to continue to develop. Neither biological nor cultural evolution is any guarantee that we are inevitably moving toward a better world. Darwin concluded the *Origin of Species* with a famous sentence: "And as natural selection works solely by and for the good of each being, all corporeal and mental environments will tend to progress towards perfection." But extinct species and extinct cultures testify to the possibility of miscarriage.

What we need is more control, not less, and this is itself an engineering problem of the first importance. The good of a culture cannot function as the source of genuine reinforcers for the individual, and the reinforcers contrived by cultures to induce their members to work for their survival are often in conflict with personal reinforcers.

The automobile industry employs vastly more persons than are employed in improving ghetto life and the industry's technology is much further advanced than a technology of behavior. It is not that the automobile is more important than a way of life; it is, rather, that the economic contingencies that induce people to improve automobiles are very powerful. These facts underline the importance of the threat posed by the literatures of freedom and dignity.

Rights

The intentional design of a culture is often attacked as unwarranted meddling in the basic rights of man. It is true, of course, that life, liberty, and the pursuit of happiness are basic rights. But they are the rights of the individual and were listed as such at a time when the literatures of freedom and dignity were concerned with the aggrandizement of the individual. They have only a minor bearing on the survival of a culture.

The intentional designer is not an interloper or meddler. He does not step in to disturb a natural process; he is part of a natural process.

Those who have been induced by their culture to act to further its survival through intentional design must accept the fact that they are altering the conditions under which men live and hence are engaging in the control of human behavior. Good government is as much a matter of the control of human behavior as bad, good incentive conditions as much as exploitation, good teaching as much as punitive drill. We gain nothing by using a softer word. If we are content merely to "influence" people, we shall not get far from the original meaning of that word—"an ethereal fluid thought to flow from the stars and to affect the actions of men."

Disguise

An attack on controlling practices is, of course, a form of countercontrol. It may have immeasurable benefits if better controlling practices are thereby selected. But the literatures of freedom and dignity have made the mistake of supposing that they are suppressing control rather than correcting it. The reciprocal control through which a culture evolves is then disturbed. To refuse to exercise available control because in some sense all control is wrong is to withhold possibly important forms of countercontrol. We have seen some of the consequences. Punitive measures, which the literatures of freedom and dignity have otherwise helped to eliminate, are instead promoted. A preference for methods that make control inconspicuous or allow it to be disguised has forced those who are in a position to exert constructive countercontrol to use only weak measures.

This could be a lethal cultural mutation. Our culture has produced the science and technology it needs to save itself. It has the wealth it needs for effective action. It has, to a considerable extent, a concern for its own future. But if it continues to value freedom and dignity rather than its own survival as its principal value, then possibly some other culture will make a greater contribution to the future.

462

38.
VISION:

Skinner's position seems to many to be the prototype of a regimented and dehumanized society. Many would argue that Skinner assumes the position of the Ticktockman in the following story by Harlan Ellison. At the same time, Skinner has noted the dynamics of control and countercontrol of behavior —this is seen in the control exercised by the Ticktockman . . . and at last, the countercontrol of the Harlequin.

"Repent, Harlequin!"
Said the Ticktockman
HARLAN ELLISON

There are always those who ask, what is it all about? For those who need to ask, for those who need points sharply made, who need to know "where it's at," this:

The mass of men serve the state thus, not as men mainly, but as machines, with their bodies. They are the standing army, and the militia, jailors, constables, posse comitatus, etc. In most cases there is no free exercise whatever of the judgment or of the moral sense; but they put themselves on a level with wood and earth and stones; and wooden men can perhaps be manufactured that will serve the purpose as well. Such command no more respect than men of straw or a lump of dirt. They have the same sort of worth only as horses and dogs. Yet such as these even are commonly esteemed good citizens. Others—as most legislators, politicians, lawyers, ministers, and office-holders— serve the state chiefly with their heads; and, as they rarely make any moral distinctions, they are as likely to serve the Devil, without intending it, as God. A very few, as heroes, patriots, martyrs, reformers in the great sense, and *men,* serve the state with their consciences also, and so necessarily resist it for the most part; and they are commonly treated as enemies by it.

Henry David Thoreau,
CIVIL DISOBEDIENCE

X. On the Application of Psychology to Society

That is the heart of it. Now begin in the middle, and later learn the beginning; the end will take care of itself.

But because it was the very world it was, the very world they had allowed it to *become,* for months his activities did not come to the alarmed attention of The Ones Who Kept The Machine Functioning Smoothly, the ones who poured the very best butter over the cams and mainsprings of the culture. Not until it had become obvious that somehow, someway, he had become a notoriety, a celebrity, perhaps even a hero for (what Officialdom inescapably tagged) "an emotionally disturbed segment of the populace," did they turn it over to the Ticktockman and his legal machinery. But by then, because it was the very world it was, and they had no way to predict he would happen—possibly a strain of disease long-defunct, now, suddenly, reborn in a system where immunity had been forgotten, had lapsed—he had been allowed to become too real. Now he had form and substance.

He had become a *personality,* something they had filtered out of the system many decades before. But there it was, and there *he* was, a very definitely imposing personality. In certain circles—middle-class circles—it was thought disgusting. Vulgar ostentation. Anarchistic. Shameful. In others, there was only sniggering: those strata where thought is subjugated to form and ritual, niceties, proprieties. But down below, ah, down below, where the people always needed their saints and sinners, their bread and circuses, their heroes and villains, he was considered a Bolivar; a Napoleon; a Robin Hood; a Dick Bong (Ace of Aces); a Jesus; a Jomo Kenyatta.

And at the top—where, like socially-attuned Shipwreck Kellys, every tremor and vibration threatens to dislodge the wealthy, powerful, and titled from their flagpoles—he was considered a menace; a heretic; a rebel; a disgrace; a peril. He was known down the line, to the very heartmeat core, but the important reactions were high above and far below. At the very top, at the very bottom.

So his file was turned over, along with his time-card and his cardioplate, to the office of the Ticktockman.

The Ticktockman: very much over six feet tall, often silent, a soft purring man when things went timewise. The Ticktockman.

Even in the cubicles of the hierarchy, where fear was generated, seldom suffered, he was called the Ticktockman. But no one called him that to his mask.

You don't call a man a hated name, not when that man, behind his mask, is capable of revoking the minutes, the hours, the days and nights, the years of your life. He was called the Master Timekeeper to his mask. It was safer that way.

"This is *what* he is," said the Ticktockman with genuine softness, "but not *who* he is? This time-card I'm holding in my left hand has a name on it, but it is the name of *what* he is, not *who* he is. This cardioplate here in

38. VISION: "Repent, Harlequin!" Said the Ticktockman

my right hand is also named, but not whom named, merely what named. Before I can exercise proper revocation, I have to know who this what is."

To his staff, all the ferrets, all the loggers, all the finks, all the commex, even the mineez, he said, "Who is this Harlequin?"

He was not purring smoothly. Timewise, it was jangle.

However, it *was* the longest single speech they had ever heard him utter at one time, the staff, the ferrets, the loggers, the finks, the commex, but not the mineez, who usually weren't around to know, in any case. But even they scurried to find out.

Who is the Harlequin?

High above the third level of the city, he crouched on the humming aluminum-frame platform of the air-boat (foof! air-boat, indeed! swizzle-skid is what it was, with a tow-rack jerry-rigged) and stared down at the neat Mondrian arrangement of the buildings.

Somewhere nearby, he could hear the metronomic left-right-left of the 2:47 P.M. shift, entering the Timkin roller-bearing plant in their sneakers. A minute later, precisely, he heard the softer right-left-right of the 5:00 A.M. formation, going home.

An elfin grin spread across his tanned features, and his dimples appeared for a moment. Then, scratching at his thatch of auburn hair, he shrugged within his motley, as though girding himself for what came next, and threw the joystick forward, and bent into the wind as the air-boat dropped. He skimmed over a slidewalk, purposely dropping a few feet to crease the tassels of the ladies of fashion, and—inserting thumbs in large ears—he stuck out his tongue, rolled his eyes, and went wugga-wugga-wugga. It was a minor diversion. One pedestrian skittered and tumbled, sending parcels everywhichway, another wet herself, a third keeled slantwise and the walk was stopped automatically by the servitors till she could be resuscitated. It was a minor diversion.

Then he swirled away on a vagrant breeze, and was gone. Hi-ho.

As he rounded the cornice of the Time-Motion Study Building, he saw the shift, just boarding the slidewalk. With practiced motion and an absolute conservation of movement, they sidestepped up onto the slowstrip and (in a chorus line reminiscent of a Busby Berkeley film of the antediluvian 1930's) advanced across the strips ostrich-walking till they were lined up on the expresstrip.

Once more, in anticipation, the elfin grin spread, and there was a tooth missing back there on the left side. He dipped, skimmed, and swooped over them; and then, scrunching about on the air-boat, he released the holding pins that fastened shut the ends of the home-made pouring troughs that kept his cargo from dumping prematurely. And as he pulled the trough-pins, the air-boat slid over the factory workers and one hundred and fifty thousand dollars' worth of jelly beans cascaded down on the expresstrip.

Jelly beans! Millions and billions of purples and yellows and greens and licorice and grape and raspberry and mint and round and smooth and crunchy outside and soft-mealy inside and sugary and bouncing jouncing tumbling clittering clattering skittering fell on the heads and shoulders and hardhats and carapaces of the Timkin workers, tinkling on the slidewalk and bouncing away and rolling about underfoot and filling the sky on their way down with all the colors of joy and childhood and holidays, coming down in a steady rain, a solid wash, a torrent of color and sweetness out of the sky from above, and entering a universe of sanity and metronomic order with quite-mad coocoo newness. Jelly beans!

The shift workers howled and laughed and were pelted, and broke ranks, and the jelly beans managed to work their way into the mechanism of the slidewalks after which there was a hideous scraping as the sound of a million fingernails rasped down a quarter of a million blackboards, followed by a coughing and a sputtering, and then the slidewalks all stopped and everyone was dumped thisawayandthataway in a jackstraw tumble, still laughing and popping little jelly bean eggs of childish color into their mouths. It was a holiday, and a jollity, an absolute insanity, a giggle. But . . .

The shift was delayed seven minutes.

They did not get home for seven minutes.

The master schedule was thrown off by seven minutes.

Quotas were delayed by inoperative slidewalks for seven minutes.

He had tapped the first domino in the line, and one after another, like chik chik chik, the others had fallen.

The System had been seven minutes worth of disrupted. It was a tiny matter, one hardly worthy of note, but in a society where the single driving force was order and unity and promptness and clocklike precision and attention to the clock, reverence of the gods of the passage of time, it was a disaster of major importance.

So he was ordered to appear before the Ticktockman. It was broadcast across every channel of the communications web. He was ordered to be *there* at 7:00 dammit on time. And they waited, and they waited, but he didn't show up till almost ten-thirty, at which time he merely sang a little song about moonlight in a place no one had ever heard of, called Vermont, and vanished again. But they had all been waiting since seven, and it wrecked *hell* with their schedules. So the question remained: Who is the Harlequin?

But the *unasked* question (more important of the two) was: how did we get *into* this position, where a laughing, irresponsible japer of jabberwocky and jive could disrupt our entire economic and cultural life with a hundred and fifty thousand dollars' worth of jelly beans . . .

Jelly for God's sake beans! This is madness! Where did he get the money to buy a hundred and fifty thousand dollars' worth of jelly beans? (They knew it would have cost that much, because they had a team of Situation

38. VISION: "Repent, Harlequin!" Said the Ticktockman

Analysts pulled off another assignment, and rushed to the slidewalk scene to sweep up and count the candies, and produce findings, which disrupted *their* schedules and threw their entire branch at least a day behind.) Jelly beans! Jelly . . . *beans?* Now wait a second—a second accounted for—no one has manufactured jelly beans for over a hundred years. Where did he get jelly beans?

That's another good question. More than likely it will never be answered to your complete satisfaction. But then, how many questions ever are?

The middle you know. Here is the beginning. How it starts:

A desk pad. Day for day, and turn each day. 9:00—open the mail. 9:45 —appointment with planning commission board. 10:30—discuss installation progress charts with J. L. 11:45— pray for rain. 12:00—lunch. *And so it goes.*

"I'm sorry, Miss Grant, but the time for interviews was set at 2:30, and it's almost five now. I'm sorry you're late, but those are the rules. You'll have to wait till next year to submit application for this college again." *And so it goes.*

The 10:10 local stops at Cresthaven, Galesville, Tonawanda Junction, Selby, and Farnhurst, but not at Indiana City, Lucasville, and Colton, except on Sunday. The 10:35 express stops at Galesville, Selby, and Indiana City, except on Sunday & Holidays, at which time it stops at . . . *and so it goes.*

"I couldn't wait, Fred. I had to be at Pierre Cartain's by 3:00, and you said you'd meet me under the clock in the terminal at 2:45, and you weren't there, so I had to go on. You're always late, Fred. If you'd been there, we could have sewed it up together, but as it was, well, I took the order alone . . . " *And so it goes.*

Dear Mr. and Mrs. Atterley: in reference to your son Gerold's constant tardiness, I am afraid we will have to suspend him from school unless some more reliable method can be instituted guaranteeing he will arrive at his classes on time. Granted he is an exemplary student, and his marks are high, his constant flouting of the schedules of this school makes it impractical to maintain him in a system where the other children seem capable of getting where they are supposed to be on time *and so it goes.*

YOU CANNOT VOTE UNLESS YOU APPEAR ΛT 8:45 Λ.M.

"I don't care if the script is *good,* I need it Thursday!"

CHECK-OUT TIME IS 2:00 P.M.

"You got here late. The job's taken. Sorry."

YOUR SALARY HAS BEEN DOCKED FOR TWENTY MINUTES TIME LOST.

"God, what time is it, I've gotta run!"

And so it goes. And so it goes. And so it goes. And so it goes goes goes goes goes tick tock tick tock tick tock and one day we no longer let time serve us, we serve time and we are slaves of the schedule, worshippers of the sun's passing, bound into a life predicated on restrictions because the system will not function if we don't keep the schedule tight.

Until it becomes more than a minor inconvenience to be late. It becomes a sin. Then a crime. Then a crime punishable by this:

EFFECTIVE 15 JULY 2389, 12:00:00 midnight, the office of the Master Timekeeper will require all citizens to submit their time-cards and cardioplates for processing. In accordance with Statute 555-7-SGH-999 governing the revocation of time per capita, all cardioplates will be keyed to the individual holder and—

What they had done, was devise a method of curtailing the amount of life a person could have. If he was ten minutes late, he lost ten minutes of his life. An hour was proportionately worth more revocation. If someone was consistently tardy, he might find himself, on a Sunday night, receiving a communique from the Master Timekeeper that his time had run out, and he would be "turned off" at high noon on Monday, please straighten your affairs, sir, madame or bisex.

And so, by this simple scientific expedient (utilizing a scientific process held dearly secret by the Ticktockman's office) the System was maintained. It was the only expedient thing to do. It was, after all, patriotic. The schedules had to be met. After all, there *was* a war on!

But, wasn't there always?

"Now that is really disgusting," the Harlequin said, when Pretty Alice showed him the wanted poster. "Disgusting and *high*ly improbable. After all, this isn't the days of desperadoes. A *wanted* poster!"

"You know," Alice noted, "you speak with a great deal of inflection."

"I'm sorry," said the Harlequin, humbly.

"No need to be sorry. You're always saying 'I'm sorry.' You have such massive guilt, Everett, it's really very sad."

"I'm sorry," he repeated, then pursed his lips so the dimples appeared momentarily. He hadn't wanted to say that at all. "I have to go out again. I have to *do* something."

Alice slammed her coffee-bulb down on the counter. "Oh for God's *sake,* Everett, can't you stay home just *one* night! Must you always be out in that ghastly clown suit, running around an*noy*ing people?"

"I'm—" he stopped, and clapped the jester's hat onto his auburn thatch with a tiny tingling of bells. He rose, rinsed out his coffee-bulb at the spray, and put it into the drier for a moment. "I have to go."

She didn't answer. The faxbox was purring, and she pulled a sheet out, read it, threw it toward him on the counter. "It's about you. Of course. You're ridiculous."

He read it quickly. It said the Ticktockman was trying to locate him. He didn't care, he was going out to be late again. At the door, dredging for an exit line, he hurled back petulantly, "Well, *you* speak with inflection, *too!*"

Alice rolled her pretty eyes heavenward. "You're ridiculous." The Harlequin stalked out, slamming the door, which sighed shut softly, and locked itself.

There was a gentle knock, and Alice got up with an exhalation of exasperated breath, and opened the door. He stood there. "I'll be back about ten-thirty, okay?"

She pulled a rueful face. "Why do you tell me that? Why? You *know* you'll be late! You *know it!* You're *always* late, so why do you tell me these dumb things?" She closed the door.

On the other side, the Harlequin nodded to himself. *She's right. She's always right. I'll be late. I'm always late. Why do I tell her these dumb things?*

He shrugged again, and went off to be late once more.

He had fired off the firecracker rockets that said: I will attend the 115th annual International Medical Association Invocation at 8:00 P.M. precisely. I do hope you will all be able to join me.

The words had burned in the sky, and of course the authorities were there, lying in wait for him. They assumed, naturally, that he would be late. He arrived twenty minutes early, while they were setting up the spiderwebs to trap and hold him. Blowing a large bullhorn, he frightened and unnerved them so, their own moisturized encirclement webs sucked closed, and they were hauled up, kicking and shrieking, high above the amphitheater floor. The Harlequin laughed and laughed, and apologized profusely. The physicians, gathered in solemn conclave, roared with laughter, and accepted the Harlequin's apologies with exaggerated bowing and posturing, and a merry time was had by all, who thought the Harlequin was a regular foofaraw in fancy pants; all, that is, but the authorities, who had been sent out by the office of the Ticktockman; they hung there like so much dockside cargo, hauled up above the floor of the amphitheater in a most unseemly fashion.

(In another part of the same city where the Harlequin carried on his "activities," totally unrelated in every way to what concerns us here, save that it illustrates the Ticktockman's power and import, a man named Marshall Delahanty received his turn-off notice from the Ticktockman's office. His wife received the notification from the gray-suited minee who delivered it, with the traditional "look of sorrow" plastered hideously across his face. She knew what it was, even without unsealing it. It was a billet-doux of immediate recognition to everyone these days. She gasped, and held it as though it were a glass slide tinged with botulism, and prayed it was not for her. Let it be for Marsh, she thought, brutally, realistically, or one of the kids, but not for me, please dear God, not for me. And then she opened it, and it *was* for Marsh, and she was at one and the same time horrified and relieved. The next trooper in the line had caught the bullet. "Marshall! Termination, Marshall! OhmiGod, Marshall, whattl we do, whattl we do, Marshall omigodmarshall . . ." and in their home that night was the sound of tearing paper and fear, and the stink of madness went up the flue and there was nothing, absolutely nothing they could do about it.

(But Marshall Delahanty tried to run. And early the next day, when turn-off time came, he was deep in the Canadian forest two hundred miles away, and the office of the Ticktockman blanked his cardioplate, and Marshall Delahanty keeled over, running, and his heart stopped, and the blood dried up on its way to his brain, and he was dead that's all. One light went out on the sector map in the office of the Master Timekeeper, while notification was entered for fax reproduction, and Georgette Delahanty's name was entered on the dole roles till she could re-marry. Which is the end of the footnote, and all the point that need be made, except don't laugh, because that is what would happen to the Harlequin if ever the Ticktockman found out his real name. It isn't funny.)

The shopping level of the city was thronged with the Thursday-colors of the buyers. Women in canary yellow chitons and men in pseudo-Tyrolean outfits that were jade and leather and fit very tightly, save for the balloon pants.

When the Harlequin appeared on the still-being-constructed shell of the new Efficiency Shopping Center, his bullhorn to his elfishly-laughing lips, everyone pointed and stared, and he berated them:

"Why let them order you about? Why let them tell you to hurry and scurry like ants or maggots? Take your time! Saunter a while! Enjoy the sunshine, enjoy the breeze, let life carry you at your own pace! Don't be slaves of time, it's a helluva way to die, slowly, by degrees . . . down with the Ticktockman!"

Who's the nut? most of the shoppers wanted to know. Who's the nut oh wow I'm gonna be late I gotta run . . .

And the construction gang on the Shopping Center received an urgent order from the office of the Master Timekeeper that the dangerous criminal known as the Harlequin was atop their spire, and their aid was urgently needed in apprehending him. The work crew said no, they would lose time on their construction schedule, but the Ticktockman managed to pull the proper threads of governmental webbing, and they were told to cease work and catch that nitwit up there on the spire; up there with the bullhorn. So a dozen and more burly workers began climbing into their construction platforms, releasing the a-grav plates, and rising toward the Harlequin.

After the debacle (in which, through the Harlequin's attention to personal safety, no one was seriously injured), the workers tried to reassemble, and assault him again, but it was too late. He had vanished. It had attracted quite a crowd, however, and the shopping cycle was thrown off by hours, simply hours. The purchasing needs of the system were therefore falling behind, and so measures were taken to accelerate the cycle for the rest of the day, but it got bogged down and speeded up and they sold too many float-valves and not nearly enough wegglers, which meant that the popli ratio was off, which made it necessary to rush cases and cases of spoiling Smash-O to stores that usually needed a case only every three or four hours. The shipments were bollixed, the trans shipments were misrouted, and in the end, even the swizzleskid industries felt it.

"Don't come back till you have him!" the Ticktockman said, very quietly, very sincerely, extremely dangerously.

They used dogs. They used probes. They used cardioplate crossoffs. They used teepers. They used bribery. They used stiktytes. They used intimidation. They used torment. They used torture. They used finks. They used cops. They used search&seizure. They used fallaron. They used betterment incentive. They used fingerprints. They used *Bertillonage.* They used cunning. They used guile. They used treachery. They used Raoul Mitgong, but he didn't help much. They used applied physics. They used techniques of criminology.

And what the hell: they caught him.

After all, his name was Everett C. Marm, and he wasn't much to begin with, except a man who had no sense of time.

"Repent, Harlequin!" said the Ticktockman.

"Get stuffed!" the Harlequin replied, sneering.

"You've been late a total of sixty-three years, five months, three weeks, two days, twelve hours, forty-one minutes, fifty-nine seconds, point oh three six one one one microseconds. You've used up everything you can, and more. I'm going to turn you off."

"Scare someone else. I'd rather be dead than live in a dumb world with a bogeyman like you."

"It's my job."

"You're full of it. You're a tyrant. You have no right to order people around and kill them if they show up late."

"You can't adjust. You can't fit in."

"Unstrap me, and I'll fit my fist into your mouth."

"You're a non-conformist."

"That didn't used to be a felony."

"It is now. Live in the world around you."

"I hate it. It's a terrible world."

"Not everyone thinks so. Most people enjoy order."

"I don't, and most of the people I know don't."

"That's not true. How do you think we caught you?"

"I'm not interested."

"A girl named Pretty Alice told us who you were."

X. On the Application of Psychology to Society

"That's a lie."

"It's true. You unnerve her. She wants to belong, she wants to conform, I'm going to turn you off."

"Then do it already, and stop arguing with me."

"I'm not going to turn you off."

"You're an idiot!"

"Repent, Harlequin!" said the Ticktockman.

"Get stuffed."

So they sent him to Coventry. And in Coventry they worked him over. It was just like what they did to Winston Smith in "1984," which was a book none of them knew about, but the techniques are really quite ancient, and so they did it to Everett C. Marm, and one day quite a long time later, the Harlequin appeared on the communications web, appearing elfin and dimpled and bright-eyed, and not at all brainwashed, and he said he had been wrong, that it was a good, a very good thing indeed, to belong, to be right on time hip-ho and away we go, and everyone stared up at him on the public screens that covered an entire city block, and they said to themselves, well, you see, he was just a nut after all, and if that's the way the system is run, then let's do it that way, because it doesn't pay to fight city hall, or in this case, the Ticktockman. So Everett C. Marm was destroyed, which was a loss, because of what Thoreau said earlier, but you can't make an omelet without breaking a few eggs, and in every revolution a few die who shouldn't, but they have to, because that's the way it happens, and if you make only a little change, then it seems to be worthwhile. Or, to make the point lucidly:

"Uh, excuse me, sir, I, uh, don't know how to uh, to uh, tell you this, but you were three minutes late. The schedule is a little, uh, bit off."

He grinned sheepishly.

"That's ridiculous!" murmured the Ticktockman behind his mask. "Check your watch." And then he went into his office, going mrmee, mrmee, mrmee, mrmee.

39.
VALENCE:
The Pathos of Power
KENNETH CLARK

In the following selection from his "Presidential Address to the American Psychological Association," Kenneth Clark argues for the need of a psychotechnology exercised upon both the general population and the leaders of contemporary society.

The present generation of human beings is required to develop psychological and social sciences with that degree of precision, predictability, and moral control essential to the survival of man. The awesome advances in the physical and biological sciences have made psychotechnology imperative. Man can no longer afford the luxuries of a leisurely, trial-and-error, trivia-dominated approach to the behavioral sciences. The behavioral sciences are now the critical sciences; they will determine the answer to the ultimate moral question of human survival.

Given the urgency of this immediate survival problem, the psychological and social sciences must enable us to control the animalistic, barbaric, and primitive propensities in man and subordinate these negatives to the uniquely human moral and ethical characteristics of love, kindness, and empathy. The redirecting of power away from the absurd, the pathetic, and the self-defeating can be and now must be seen as a responsibility and goal of science and psychotechnology. We can no longer afford to rely solely on the traditional, prescientific attempts to contain human cruelty and destructiveness. The techniques and appeals of religion, moral philosophy, law, and education seemed appropriate and civilized approaches to the control of man's primitive and egocentric behavior in a prenuclear age. They are, in themselves, no longer appropriate because they permit too wide a margin of error and a degree of unpredictability that is rationally inconsistent with the present survival urgency. Furthermore, moral verbalizations of the past have been prostituted by the pathos of power; they have been perverted by the pretenses of rationality in the service of inhumanity if not barbarity.

The traditional perspective and training of psychologists, educators, and moral philosophers would lead them to continue to argue that moral controls of human primitive and egocentric impulses be sought by redoubling our efforts in developing more effective forms of moral education designed to produce individual human beings with ethical autonomy and integrity. They would argue that it is still possible to preserve human civilization by training human beings toward a higher quality of interpersonal relationships; by developing within individual human beings greater personal and social effectiveness through greater ego strengths. They would continue to assert that a variety of behavioral modification techniques, imposed particularly in childhood, could be expected to reinforce altruism, empathy, and group commitment and subordinate egocentricity in normal human beings.

An objective appraisal of the results of these approaches to a control of the negatives in man and the enhancement of his positives would seem to suggest that not only are they unpredictable in results but that they require continuous reinforcement and a prolonged period of time in order to demonstrate positive results. We do not now appear to have the amount of time which these techniques require for hoped-for success.

This present era of psychotechnology comes with the abrupt recognition of this fact of a very limited time within which the human brain can obtain and use that knowledge required to control, protect, and affirm humanity with precision and predictability. Already there are many provocative and suggestive findings from neurophysiological, biochemical, and psychopharmacological and psychological research. The work on the effects of direct stimulation of certain areas of the brain; the role of specific areas of the midbrain in controlling certain affects; the effects of certain drugs on exciting, tranquilizing, or depressing the emotional and motivational levels of the individual; and the effects of externally induced behavioral changes on internal biochemistry of the organism suggest that we might be on the threshold of that type of scientific biochemical intervention which could stabilize and make dominant the moral and ethical propensities of man and subordinate, if not eliminate, his negative and primitive behavioral tendencies.

On the basis of the presently available evidence, it is reasonable to believe that this type of precise, direct psychotechnological intervention geared toward strengthening man's moral and positive human characteristics could be obtained and implemented within a few years, and with a fraction of the cost required to produce the atom bomb; and much less than the present cost of our explorations in outer space.

474

39.   VALENCE: The Pathos of Power

It is here being suggested that with the mobilization of the necessary scientific personnel, financial resources, and research facilities, it is now possible—indeed, imperative—to reduce human anxieties, tensions, hostilities, violence, cruelty, and the destructive power irrationalities of man which are the basis of wars. This contemporary approach to assuring the survival of the human species offers a scientific basis for William James' philosophical wish for a moral equivalence or alternative to wars.

In reducing the negatives and enhancing the positive potentials in human beings, in addition to the political organizational and administrative problems to be resolved, there would be a number of important psychological barriers to be faced and solved with realism and due regard for that essential humanity which differentiates human beings from mere organisms or living machines. The process and techniques of direct biochemical intervention or any form of effective psychotechnology must take into account the totality, the interrelatedness, the complex gestalt of the human motivational, affective, and cognitive system. In seeking to enhance the positives of empathy and kindness and reduce the cruel and the barbaric in man, psychotechnology must not destroy the creative, evaluative, and selective capacities of human beings. Without the desire to explore, to reorganize things and ideas, to vary moods, and to produce, at least with the illusions of flexibility and volition, the human being would indeed be an empty organic vessel and it would be difficult to justify the mere fact of survival under these conditions. In addition to precision and predictability, this suggested psychotechnological intervention into human affairs must be affirmatively humane. An inviolable sense of moral responsibility is the essential new ingredient which this new era of the psychological sciences must bring to the contemporary requirements of science.

The implications of a precise and predictable psychotechnological intervention into the whole arena of human interaction are of such vast importance as to demand that the most careful and rigorous planning, research, and testing precede any attempts to apply these findings on a larger scale. Because these are uniquely human problems with which this program is concerned, the pretest subjects would have to be human beings. The implications of an effective psychotechnology for the control of criminal behavior and the amelioration of the moral insensitivities which produce reactive criminality in others are clear. It would seem, therefore, that there would be moral and rational justification for the use of compulsive criminals as pretest subjects in seeking precise forms of intervention and moral control of human behavior. This suggestion is based on the assumption that no human being who is not impelled by some forms of internal, biochemical or external, social forces—or some combination of both—would choose to be a criminal if he were provided with options.

It is a fact that a few men in the leadership positions in the industrialized nations of the world now have the power to determine among themselves, through collaboration or competition, the survival or extinction of human civilization. They can, in fact, exercise this power only within the present limitations of the pathos and contradictions of power for temporary good or unpredictable ultimate evil. There is no way of predicting the personal and emotional stability of these leaders with the life and death power over mankind. Nor do we now know the relationship between those personal characteristics which are related to success in obtaining positions of political and governmental power on the one hand and the degree of personal, emotional, and moral stability on the other hand. The masses of human beings are now required to live and continue to work on faith, hope, denial, and the acceptance of the chances that their powerful leaders will have the strength to use their power wisely and morally.

Given these contemporary facts, it would seem logical that a requirement imposed on all power-controlling leaders—and those who aspire to such leadership—would be that they accept and use the earliest perfected form of psychotechnological, biochemical intervention which would assure their positive use of power and reduce or block the possibility of their using power destructively. This form of psychotechnological medication would be a type of internally imposed disarmament. It would assure that there would be no absurd or barbaric use of power. It would provide the masses of human beings with the security that their leaders would not or could not sacrifice them on the altars of their personal ego pathos, vulnerability—and instability.

It is possible to object to the era of psychotechnology on "moral" grounds and to assert that these suggestions are repugnant because they are manipulative and will take away from man his natural right to make errors—even those errors which perpetrate cruelties and destruction upon other human beings. In the light of the realities of and possible consequences of nuclear weaponry, these allegedly moral arguments seem mockingly, pathetically immoral. It would seem that man could afford to indulge in this type of abstract, prescientific moralizing in the past when his most destructive weapons were clubs, bow and arrows, or even gunpowder. To continue this type of thinking in an age when nuclear weapons are capable of destroying millions of human beings in a single irrational man-made event would seem to be a form of self-defeating and immoral rigidity.

There could be the further objection that biochemical intervention into the inner psychological recesses of motivation, temperament, and behavior of human beings is an unacceptable, intolerable tampering with the natural or God-given characteristics of man. The negative connotations presently associated with discussions of drugs and the drug culture, particularly among young people, could be invoked to support this objection. One could also object on the ground that, in effect, what is here being suggested under the guise of an imperative psychotechnology is just another form of

39. VALENCE: The Pathos of Power

utopian mechanization of human beings through drugging the masses and their leaders.

These objections seem to be based on semantic grounds rather than on essential substance. In medicine, physical diseases are controlled through medication. Medicines are prescribed by doctors to help the body overcome the detrimental effects of bacteria or viruses—or to help the organism restore that balance of internal biochemical environment necessary for health and effectiveness. Medicines are not only used to treat the diseases of individuals, but are also used preventively in the form of vaccines. All medicines are drugs—and all drugs used therapeutically are forms of intervention to influence and control the natural processes of disease. Selective and appropriate medication to assure psychological health and moral integrity is now imperative for the survival of human society.

The era of psychotechnology, having been imposed upon man by the physical scientific advances of man, cannot now be avoided. It must be used affirmatively, wisely, and with compassion. To fulfill these requirements, it must have a sound scientific, factual base. It must also be firmly rooted in rational morality. It must respect and enhance that which is uniquely human in man—those positive qualities which promise a future of human grandeur. In meeting these and related requirements, a rigorous, tough-minded science and technology of psychology will save man from the more destructive consequences of his absurdities and propensities—the pathos of power—and will provide him with the time necessary to evolve and stabilize those centers of his brain which will make social morality and human survival no longer a matter of chance.

40.
VISION:
The Flying Machine
RAY BRADBURY

Despite the obvious sincerity of Kenneth Clark's demand for a psychology applied to society, there is the very reasonable objection that the knowledge of the discipline would only be applied in situations specified by the people or institutions who employ psychologists. A different, but related theme is seen by Ray Bradbury in "The Flying Machine," and it may be indicative of the reception given to psychologists when they appear with novel social innovations.

In the year A.D. 400, the Emperor Yuan held his throne by the Great Wall of China, and the land was green with rain, readying itself toward the harvest, at peace, the people in his dominion neither too happy nor too sad.

Early on the morning of the first day of the first week of the second month of the new year, the Emperor Yuan was sipping tea and fanning himself against a warm breeze when a servant ran across the scarlet and blue garden tiles, calling, "Oh, Emperor, Emperor, a miracle!"

"Yes," said the Emperor, "the air *is* sweet this morning."

"No, no, a miracle!" said the servant, bowing quickly.

"And this tea is good in my mouth, surely that is a miracle."

"No, no, Your Excellency."

"Let me guess then—the sun has risen and a new day is upon us. Or the sea is blue. *That* now is the finest of all miracles."

"Excellency, a man is flying!"

"What?" The Emperor stopped his fan.

"I saw him in the air, a man flying with wings. I heard a voice call out of the sky, and when I looked up, there he was, a dragon in the heavens with a man in its mouth, a dragon of paper and bamboo, colored like the sun and the grass."

"It is early," said the Emperor, "and you have just wakened from a dream."

40. VISION: The Flying Machine

"It is early, but I have seen what I have seen! Come, and you will see it too."

"Sit down with me here," said the Emperor. "Drink some tea. It must be a strange thing, if it is true, to see a man fly. You must have time to think of it, even as I must have time to prepare myself for the sight."

They drank tea.

"Please," said the servant at last, "or he will be gone."

The Emperor rose thoughtfully. "Now you may show me what you have seen."

They walked into a garden, across a meadow of grass, over a small bridge, through a grove of trees, and up a tiny hill.

"There!" said the servant.

The Emperor looked into the sky.

And in the sky, laughing so high that you could hardly hear him laugh, was a man; and the man was clothed in bright papers and reeds to make wings and a beautiful yellow tail, and he was soaring all about like the largest bird in a universe of birds, like a new dragon in a land of ancient dragons.

The man called down to them from high in the cool winds of morning. "I fly, I fly!"

The servant waved to him. "Yes, *yes!*"

The Emperor Yuan did not move. Instead he looked at the Great Wall of China now taking shape out of the farthest mist in the green hills, that splendid snake of stones which writhed with majesty across the entire land. That wonderful wall which had protected them for a timeless time from enemy hordes and preserved peace for years without number. He saw the town, nestled to itself by a river and a road and a hill, beginning to waken.

"Tell me," he said to his servant, "has anyone else seen this flying man?"

"I am the only one, Excellency," said the servant, smiling at the sky, waving.

The Emperor watched the heavens another minute and then said, "Call him down to me."

"Ho, come down, come down! The Emperor wishes to see you!" called the servant, hands cupped to his shouting mouth.

The Emperor glanced in all directions while the flying man soared down the morning wind. He saw a farmer, early in his fields, watching the sky, and he noted where the farmer stood.

The flying man alit with a rustle of paper and a creak of bamboo reeds. He came proudly to the Emperor, clumsy in his rig, at last bowing before the old man.

"What have you done?" demanded the Emperor.

"I have flown in the sky, Your Excellency," replied the man.

"What *have* you done?" said the Emperor again.

"I have just told you!" cried the flier.

X. On the Application of Psychology to Society

"You have told me nothing at all." The Emperor reached out a thin hand to touch the pretty paper and the birdlike keel of the apparatus. It smelled cool, of the wind.

"Is it not beautiful, Excellency?"

"Yes, too beautiful."

"It is the only one in the world!" smiled the man. "And I am the inventor."

"The *only* one in the world?"

"I swear it!"

"Who else knows of this?"

"No one. Not even my wife, who would think me mad with the sun. She thought I was making a kite. I rose in the night and walked to the cliffs far away. And when the morning breezes blew and the sun rose, I gathered my courage, Excellency, and leaped from the cliff. I flew! But my wife does not know of it."

"Well for her, then," said the Emperor. "Come along."

They walked back to the great house. The sun was full in the sky now, and the smell of the grass was refreshing. The Emperor, the servant, and the flier paused within the huge garden.

The Emperor clapped his hands. "Ho, guards!"

The guards came running.

"Hold this man."

"Call the executioner," said the Emperor.

"What's this!" cried the flier, bewildered. "What have I done?" He began to weep, so that the beautiful paper apparatus rustled.

"Here is the man who has made a certain machine," said the Emperor, "and yet asks us what he has created. He does not know himself. It is only necessary that he create, without knowing why he has done so, or what this thing will do."

The executioner came running with a sharp silver ax. He stood with his naked, large-muscled arms ready, his face covered with a serene white mask.

"One moment," said the Emperor. He turned to a near-by table upon which sat a machine that he himself had created. The Emperor took a tiny golden key from his own neck. He fitted his key to the tiny, delicate machine and wound it up. Then he set the machine going.

The machine was a garden of metal and jewels. Set in motion, the birds sang in tiny metal trees, wolves walked through miniature forests, and tiny people ran in and out of sun and shadow, fanning themselves with miniature fans, listening to tiny emerald birds, and standing by impossibly small but tinkling fountains.

"Is *it* not beautiful?" said the Emperor. "If you asked me what I have done here, I could answer you well. I have made birds sing, I have made forests murmur, I have set people to walking in this woodland, enjoying the leaves and shadows and songs. That is what I have done."

40. VISION: The Flying Machine

"But, oh, Emperor!" pleaded the flier, on his knees, the tears pouring down his face. "I have done a similar thing! I have found beauty. I have flown on the morning wind. I have looked down on all the sleeping houses and gardens. I have smelled the sea and even *seen* it, beyond the hills, from my high place. And I have soared like a bird; oh, I cannot say how beautiful it is up there, in the sky, with the wind above me, the wind blowing me here like a feather, there like a fan, the way the sky smells in the morning! And how free one feels! *That* is beautiful, Emperor, that is beautiful too!"

"Yes," said the Emperor sadly, "I know it must be true. For I felt my heart move with you in the air and I wondered: What is it like? How does it feel? How do the distant pools look from so high? And how my houses and servants? Like ants? And how the distant towns not yet awake?"

"Then spare me!"

"But there are times," said the Emperor, more sadly still, "when one must lose a little beauty if one is to keep what little beauty one already has. I do not fear you, yourself, but I fear another man."

"What man?"

"Some other man who, seeing you, will build a thing of bright papers and bamboo like this. But the other man will have an evil face and an evil heart, and the beauty will be gone. It is this man I fear."

"Why? Why?"

"Who is to say that someday just such a man, in just such an apparatus of paper and reed, might not fly in the sky and drop huge stones upon the Great Wall of China?" said the Emperor.

No one moved or said a word.

"Off with his head," said the Emperor.

The executioner whirled his silver ax.

"Burn the kite and the inventor's body and bury their ashes together," said the Emperor.

The servants retreated to obey.

The Emperor turned to his hand-servant, who had seen the man flying. "Hold your tongue. It was all a dream, a most sorrowful and beautiful dream. And that farmer in the distant field who also saw, tell him it would pay him to consider it only a vision. If ever the word passes around, you and the farmer die within the hour."

"You are merciful, Emperor."

"No, not merciful," said the old man. Beyond the garden wall he saw the guards burning the beautiful machine of paper and reeds that smelled of the morning wind. He saw the dark smoke climb into the sky. "No, only very much bewildered and afraid." He saw the guards digging a tiny pit wherein to bury the ashes. "What is the life of one man against those of a million others? I must take solace from that thought."

He took the key from its chain about his neck and once more wound up the beautiful miniature garden. He stood looking out across the land at the Great Wall, the peaceful town, the green fields, the rivers and streams. He sighed. The tiny garden whirred its hidden and delicate machinery and set itself in motion; tiny people walked in forests, tiny faces loped through sun-speckled glades in beautiful shining pelts, and among the tiny trees flew little bits of high song and bright blue and yellow color, flying, flying, flying in that small sky.

"Oh," said the Emperor, closing his eyes, "look at the birds, look at the birds!"